Series Editors:
Steven F. Warren, Ph.D.
Joe Reichle, Ph.D.

**Communication
and Language
Intervention
Series**

Volume 3

Communicative Alternatives
to Challenging Behavior

Also available in the Communication
and Language Intervention Series:

Volume 1
*Causes and Effects in Communication
and Language Intervention*
edited by Steven F. Warren, Ph.D.
and Joe Reichle, Ph.D.

Volume 2
*Enhancing Children's Communication:
Research Foundations for Intervention*
edited by Ann P. Kaiser, Ph.D.
and David B. Gray, Ph.D.

**Communication
and Language
Intervention
Series**

Volume 3

Communicative Alternatives to Challenging Behavior
Integrating Functional Assessment and Intervention Strategies

Edited by

Joe Reichle, Ph.D.
Professor
Department of Communication Disorders
University of Minnesota
Minneapolis, Minnesota

and

David P. Wacker, Ph.D.
Professor
Departments of Pediatrics
and Special Education
University Hospital School
The University of Iowa
Iowa City, Iowa

·P A U L·H·
BROOKES
PUBLISHING C°

Baltimore • London • Toronto • Sydney

Paul H. Brookes Publishing Co.
P.O. Box 10624
Baltimore, Maryland 21285-0624

Typeset by The Composing Room of Michigan, Inc., Grand Rapids, Michigan.
Manufactured in the United States of America by
The Maple Press Co., York, Pennsylvania.

This book is printed on recycled paper.

Library of Congress Cataloging-in-Publication Data
Communicative alternatives to challenging behavior : integrating
  functional assessment and intervention strategies / edited by Joe
  Reichle and David P. Wacker.
        p.   cm—(Communication and language intervention series: 3)
  Includes bibliographical references and index.
  ISBN 1-55766-082-4
  1. Behavior disorders in children—Treatment.   2. Problem
children—Behavior modification.   3. Behavioral assessment of
children.   I. Reichle, Joe, 1951–   .   II. Wacker, David P.,
  1953–   .
RJ506.B44C65   1993
618.92′89—dc20   93-14787
                                                                        CIP

(British Library Cataloguing-in-Publication data are available from the British
Library.)

Contents

Series Preface

THE PURPOSE OF THE *Communication and Language Intervention Series* is to provide meaningful foundations for the application of sound intervention designs to enhance the development of communication skills across the life span. We are endeavoring to achieve this purpose by providing readers with presentations of state-of-the-art theory, research, and practice.

In selecting topics, editors, and authors, we are not attempting to limit the contents of this series to those viewpoints with which we agree or which we find most promising. We are assisted in our efforts to develop the series by an editorial advisory board consisting of prominent scholars representative of the range of issues and perspectives to be incorporated in the series.

We trust that the careful reader will find much that is provocative and controversial in this and other volumes. This will be necessarily so to the extent that the work reported is truly on the so-called cutting edge, a mythical place where no sacred cows exist. This point is demonstrated time and again throughout this volume as the conventional wisdom is challenged (and occasionally confirmed) by various authors.

Readers of this and other volumes are encouraged to proceed with healthy skepticism. In order to achieve our purpose, we take on some difficult and controversial issues. Errors and misinterpretations are inevitably made. This is normal in the development of any field, and should be welcomed as evidence that the field is moving forward and tackling difficult and weighty issues.

Well-conceived theory and research on development of both children with and children without disabilities is vitally important for researchers, educators, and clinicians committed to the development of optimal approaches to communication and language intervention. For this reason, each volume in this series includes chapters pertaining to both development and intervention.

The content of each volume reflects our view of the symbiotic relationship between intervention and research: Demonstrations of what may work in intervention should lead to analyses of promising discoveries and insights from developmental work that may in turn fuel further refinement and development by intervention researchers.

An inherent goal of this series is to enhance the long-term development of the field by systematically furthering the dissemination of theoretically and empirically based scholarship and research. We promise the reader an opportunity to participate in the development of this field through the debates and discussions that occur throughout the pages of the *Communication and Language Intervention Series*.

Editorial Advisory Board

Foreword

A FOREWORD SHOULD PROVIDE the reader with a context or map by which to enjoy the content of a book. A foreword is not a review or description of the book. The foreword author presumes that the reader has already made the decision to read the book and can use the table of contents to obtain organizational information. The foreword then provides the integrating context in which to appreciate the different chapters—a map of the highlights. Joe Reichle and David Wacker have assembled a volume with many highlights, a volume with much to appreciate.

The context for this book is exciting. Since the early 1980s, important advances have occurred in our understanding and use of behavior analysis to change problem behaviors. This book provides a superb review and synthesis of the advances in functional assessment and the implications of these advances for our practical and theoretical understanding of behavior. In addition, the book provides information about the current struggle to use functional asessment information to build and implement behavior support programs. The book emphasizes the use of communication training as the foundation for effective behavioral programming, but this is a book about the broad future as much as about recent technical advances. It is a book about what we have just learned, and about what we need to learn. It is an exciting book because it describes theoretically elegant material in a manner that is both accessible and practical. The authors are not only brilliant scholars, but people who have direct contact with real people in real schools, homes, and work settings. Their descriptions of behavior are conceptually accurate and their descriptions of individual cases are practical and compelling. This is a book written by people who are actively involved in changing the way support is provided.

The book is organized into four parts. The first part presents a review of our knowledge related to functional assessment. The starting point for each of the four chapters is the greater clarity with which we now undertand what Skinner (1938), Bijou (Bijou, Peterson, & Ault, 1968), and others (Baer, Wolf, & Risley, 1968) proclaimed long ago: To change behavior we must understand not only the form of that behavior, but the context (setting events, controlling antecedents, consequences) in which it occurs. Human behavior is not random. To the extent we understand the physiological and contextual variables that influence behavior, we are positioned to undertand not just individual responses but patterns of behavior. To the extent that we understand patterns of behavior, we can change behavior. Functional assessment provides the lever with which to change *problem* behavior patterns to *positive* behavior patterns.

The reader is encouraged to note how the four chapters in Part I of the book operate from an assumption that: 1) functional assessment is necessary for good behavioral programming, and 2) an effective functional assessment will most often draw from several assessment procedures. Use of naturalistic observations, interviews, and systematic functional analyses all have their place in an assessment process. Note also how the authors lead us beyond a simplistic vision of functional assessment. The goal of a functional assessment is to define the variables that influence the occurrence of problem behaviors, and to use these variables to construct effective behavioral support plans. A functional assessment is successful if it results in behavioral support that is effective. The authors understand this, and emphasize with force the importance of conducting functional assessments that do much more than simply define a problem behavior as escape-motivated or attention-motivated. The assessment should provide information with sufficient precision to allow practical programming decisions. The assessment should indicate the effect of setting events, immediate antecedents, and consequences on the problem behavior. The assessment should also indicate the effect of child behavior on the environment (e.g., teacher behavior). Finally, the authors of Part I grapple with the growing need to define efficient (economical) procedures for conducting functional assessment. Throughout the chapters, the reader is provided with glimpses of directions for the future: glimpses of assessment protocols that can be implemented in regular contexts, by typical staff or family members, in short time periods; glimpses of assessment strategies that recognize the ongoing competition between and among members of response classes; glimpses of functional assessment that is at once more precise and more utilitarian. As we strive to balance speed, ease, utility, and precision in conducting functional assessment, the authors suggest that care should be taken to avoid oversimplifying our understanding of behavior. Through their clinical examples, the authors provide practical strategies for doing this, and a very encouraging vision for the future.

The second part of the book provides two chapters on the delicate art of moving from functional assessment to specific clinical programming. This is an area of intense activity, and the chapters in this section strive to provide a theoretical foundation for future development. The practical assumption behind this section is that if we use functional assessment information in the construction of behavioral support programs, those programs will be: 1) more likely to be effective, 2) less likely to be aversive, 3) more likely to fit the local context, and 4) more likely to be used over long periods of time by teachers, families, and support personnel. The key is to define the bridges that will link functional assessment output with programmatic input. For the authors of Part II, the key lies in understanding the theoretical variables that affect how different behaviors compete or covary. Carefully constructed reviews are provided to assist the reader in understanding how the matching law and research focused on response covariation can be used to organize behavioral support. These excellent chapters indicate that future behavioral support plans can be expected to contain multiple components. The era of single variable interventions is fast receding. Well-designed behavioral support plans will include consideration of a range of variables: 1) setting (contextual) variables, such as the physical features of a setting, the social interaction patterns, and the schedule of daily activity; 2) physiological variables, such as sleep and eating cycles, allergies, and medications (Bailey & Pyles, 1989); and 3) matching law variables, such as the comparative antecedents, response effort, and reinforcers associated with alternative response options. Our understanding of how best to integrate these variables will come in part through a much better understanding of how responses covary. The basic message is that we must move beyond an analysis of individual behaviors and toward an analysis of behavioral ecologies. We must extend our science toward a better understanding of how intervention procedures interact; how change in one response pattern affects changes in other response patterns; and how change in the behavior of one person affects change in the behavior of other people.

The third part of the book is of special interest to the editors, and includes six excellent chapters. These chapters are companions of those in Part II, but provide a more direct analysis of communication training as a behavioral support strategy. The six chapters are compelling in their application of behavioral theory to the development of effective communication systems. The authors provide practical and believable case histories that demonstrate the power of communication to control one's environment, and the important relationship between control via communication and control via problem behavior. While taking care to acknowledge that not all problem behaviors can be addressed through communication interventions, the authors offer impressive demonstrations of functional communication training being used to decrease problem behaviors, to build generalized communicative competence, and to alter unconventional verbal behavior.

In the six chapters in Part III, the reader should take time to appreciate the skillful manner in which the authors have stepped beyond the obvious, and often demonstrated message, that problem behaviors should be replaced by communication responses. This message is most eloquently present, but the power of Part III is that the authors offer the next phase in using communication technology. The reader will find recommendations about *when* communication training should be used, about *how* different communication options can and should be designed, and specific *strategies* for ensuring that communication skills become generalized, practical elements in a person's life. The authors use case examples to demonstrate both specific ideas and the integration of multiple recommendations in a single behavioral support program.

The final part of the book includes three chapters addressing the transfer of support/training technologies to school, work, and home settings. The issues raised in these chapters are not unique to the use of communication technology or problem behaviors. Together the three chapters pose a series of important challenges to the field and offer examples for addressing these challenges. At a fundamental level, the authors challenge us to examine the outcomes and standards that we use to determine the success of behavioral support (either in research reports or applied practice). The direction and manner in which behavioral support technology develops will depend on the way we define and measure outcomes. These outcomes will determine if the feedback we receive is positive or negative, and therefore maintains or does not maintain our behavior. The authors lead us to give careful consideration of the full range of issues in a person's life when we examine the clinical success of a procedure. As we strive to conduct research that both defines fundamental mechanisms of behavior and demonstrates clinically important effects, it is important to ensure that the outcome measures we adopt are those that we wish to guide the development of our technology. The clear warning is that if all we do is reduce a problem behavior and leave a person in an isolated, boring, controlling context, we have failed in the larger purpose of behavioral technology.

In addition to drawing attention to our need for inclusive outcomes, the authors of Part IV provide excellent examples of technology transfer procedures. Our field continues to suffer from the problem of incomplete implementation. Beyond the ubiquitous frustration with this implementation gap, we see a new area of legitimate scientific inquiry. We must better understand how effective procedures can be transferred to typical school, work, and home contexts. We must better understand the variables that contribute to the rejection or apathy that accompanies implementation of certain strategies. Two chapters in this part present systematic efforts to extend specific functional assessment and support plan procedures. Both report success in implementing the technology and in achieving change in the behavior (and lives) of people with severe disabilities. But both chapters join the authors of the third chapter in demonstrating just how little we know about the process of transferring technology, philosophy, theory, and practice to real world situations. The chapters in Part IV provide not only sound advice for how to proceed; they provide the challenge and direction for new ways of building a stronger bond between a functional science of human behavior and the practice of supporting people with challenging behavior.

Enjoy this book. Enjoy the precision with which the theory of behavior is described and transformed into practical procedures. Enjoy the many fine examples of how the procedures can be used. Enjoy the challenges that the authors offer for both research and practice. And most of all, enjoy the underlying message that we can, in fact, make a real difference in the lives of people who engage in dangerous and difficult behavior.

Rob Horner, Ph.D.
Division of Special Education
and Rehabilitation
University of Oregon

REFERENCES

Baer, D.M., Wolf, M.M., & Risley, R.R. (1968). Some current dimensions of applied behavior analysis. *Journal of Applied Behavior Analysis, 1,* 91–97.

Bailey, J.E., & Pyles, D.A.M. (1989). Behavioral diagnostics. In E. Cipani (Ed.), *The treatment of severe behavior disorders: Behavior analysis approaches* (pp. 85–107). Washington, DC: American Association on Mental Retardation.

Bijou, S.W., Peterson, R.F., & Ault, M.H. (1968). A method to integrate descriptive and experimental field studies at the level of data and empirical concepts. *Journal of Applied Behavior Analysis, 1,* 175–191.

Skinner, B.F. (1938). *The behavior of organisms.* New York: Appleton-Century-Crofts.

Contributors

The Editors

Joe Reichle, Ph.D., Professor of Communication Disorders and Educational Psychology, University of Minnesota, Minneapolis, MN 55455. Dr. Reichle has published extensively in the area of communication and language intervention and is actively involved in the training of speech-language pathologists and special educators. He currently serves as associate editor of the *Journal of The Association for Persons with Severe Handicaps*.

David P. Wacker, Ph.D., Professor of Pediatrics and Special Education, The University of Iowa, Iowa City, Iowa 52242. Dr. Wacker has conducted numerous studies on interventions for children who display problematic behavior and provides psychological services in two outpatient clinics in the Department of Pediatrics for children with behavior disorders. He recently completed a 4-year service as associate editor for the *Journal of Applied Behavior Analysis*.

The Chapter Authors

Richard W. Albin, Ph.D., Assistant Professor, Division of Special Education and Rehabilitation, College of Education, University of Oregon, Eugene, OR 97403-1235. Dr. Albin's areas of interest include positive behavioral support, generalization and maintenance of learned behaviors, and personnel training and preparation. One current focus of his research and demonstration activities is the development and implementation of effective inservice training systems and materials related to the topic area of positive behavioral support for persons with developmental disabilities and severe challenging behaviors.

Jacki L. Anderson, Ph.D., Professor, Department of Educational Psychology, California State University, Hayward, Hayward, CA 94542. Dr. Anderson is Coordinator of Credential and Master's Degree Programs in the area of Severe Disabilities at California State University, Hayward and Training Coordinator for the Rehabilitation Research and Training Center on Positive Behavioral Support. Her primary areas of research are inclusion of individuals with severe disabilities, positive behavioral support, and effective models of preservice and inservice training.

Wendy K. Berg, M.A., Division of Developmental Disabilities, The University of Iowa, Iowa City, IA 52242. Ms. Berg is currently co-investigator on two research grants evaluating the effects of induction as a method to improve parent/child social interactions and children's participation in prosocial activities. Her research interests include the effects of stimulus control and reinforcement schedules on displays of challenging behavior and their impact on the effects of intervention procedures.

Denise Berotti, M.A., Doctoral Student, Department of Psychology, State University of New York at Albany, Albany, NY 12222. Ms. Berotti's research has focused on communication interventions for challenging behavior, the use of augmentative communication with students with dual sensory impairments, and the relationship between ritualistic behavior and severe behavior problems. She is currently studying the effects of using augmentative communication to replace the severe behavior problems displayed by students with dual sensory impairments and assessing generalization of treatment effects to untrained staff and members of the community.

Edward G. Carr, Ph.D., Professor of Psychology, State University of New York at Stony Brook, Stony Brook, NY 11794-2500. Dr. Carr's work has focused on the analysis and remediation of severe problem behavior in people with developmental disabilities. He is particularly interested in the effects of communication training, multicomponent intervention, and stimulus control procedures in the treatment of problem behavior.

Linda J. Cooper, Ph.D., Department of Pediatrics, The University of Iowa Hospitals and Clinics, The University of Iowa, Iowa City, IA 52242-1083. Dr. Cooper is co-director of the Behavioral Feeding Disorders Service in Pediatric Psychology. Her research has focused on the application of functional analysis procedures in the assessment and treatment of children with mild disabilities and behavioral problems, feeding disorders, and biological–behavioral interactions.

Kristina Chambers DaVerne, B.A., Research Director, Carousel Preschool Program, Department of Child and Family Studies, Florida Mental Health Institute, University of South Florida, 13301 Bruce B. Downs Blvd., Tampa, FL 33612-3899. Ms. DaVerne has been conducting research on program systems and children's verbal regulation as part of the Carousel Preschool, an inclusion program serving children with behavior disorders and their peers who are developing typically.

Paris DePaepe, M.S., Department of Educational Psychology, University of Minnesota, 211 Pattee Hall, 150 Pillsbury Drive SE, Minneapolis, MN 55455. Ms. DePaepe is a doctoral candidate in the department of Educational Psychology at the University of Minnesota. Her research interests include positive interventions to address challenging behavior and augmentative and alternative communication systems.

Glen Dunlap, Ph.D., Director of Community Development Programs, Department of Child and Family Studies, Florida Mental Health Institute, University of South Florida, Tampa, FL 33612. Dr. Dunlap is interested in developing knowledge and programs that lead to life-style improvements for people with disabilities. He is also interested in issues surrounding family support.

V. Mark Durand, Ph.D., Associate Professor, Department of Psychology, State University of New York at Albany, Albany, NY 12222. Dr. Durand's research has centered around understanding and treating severe challenging behavior. In collaboration with Dr. Edward G. Carr, he developed functional communication training, a communication-based treatment for challenging behavior. He has also co-authored (with Daniel B. Crimmins) the *Motivation Assessment Scale*, an instrument for assessing the function of problem behaviors. Recent efforts include research on sleep disorders among persons with disabilities and an examination of the development of social relationships among students with and without severe disabilities.

Ian M. Evans, Ph.D., Professor of Psychology, State University of New York at Binghamton, P.O. Box 6000, Binghamton, NY 13902-6000. Dr. Evans is Director of Clinical Training and is Co-Director of the Center for Developmental Psychobiology (Institute for Children and Youth) at SUNY-Binghamton. His academic interests have been in the theory and empirical evaluation of behavior therapy and behavioral assessment. Working at the interface between clinical psychology and education, he has been interested in positive interventions for children with challenging behaviors and severe disabilities in inclusive social, community, and school settings. Currently he directs two externally funded projects concerned with evaluating partnerships between teachers, parents, and students as a strategy for the prevention of emotional disorders in children at risk for school failure.

James W. Halle, Ph.D., Professor, Department of Special Education, University of Illinois, Champaign, IL 61821. Dr. Halle's research has focused on communication intervention in natural settings and the contextual variables that influence communicative performances. His more recent interests include the general-case programming and the assessment of communicative function of prelinguistic behavior of learners with severe intellectual disabilities. He is currently the editor of the *Journal of The Association for Persons with Severe Handicaps*.

Han-Leong Goh, M.S., University of Florida, Gainesville, FL 32601. Han is currently a doctoral candidate (Experimental Analysis of Behavior) and graduate research assistant at the University of Florida under the advisement of Dr. Brian Iwata. Han was previously employed as a senior clinical specialist at the Biobehavioral Unit of the Children's Seashore House. Han was involved in the development and implementation of behavioral assessments and interventions for children with severe behavior disorders.

Jay Harding, Ed.S., University Hospital School, The University of Iowa Hospitals and Clinics, The University of Iowa, Iowa City, IA 52242-1011. Mr. Harding's research has focused on the application of functional analysis procedures in the assessment and treatment of young children with severe behavior problems. He is currently the project coordinator for a National Institute of Child Health and Human Development grant, "Inducing Reciprocal Parent and Child Interactions."

Lee Kern, Ph.D., School of Medicine, Children's Seashore House, University of Pennsylvania, Philadelphia, PA 19104. Dr. Kern is an instructor at the University of Pennsylvania School of Medicine. Her primary areas of interest are conduct/behavior disorders and emotional disturbance. Her research has focused on functional assessment and social skills.

Joseph S. Lalli, Ph.D., Assistant Professor, Behavioral Psychology, Department of Pediatrics, School of Medicine, University of Pennsylvania, Philadelphia, PA 19047. Dr. Lalli is Assistant Director of the Biobehavioral Unit at Children's Seashore House in Philadelphia. His research interests include the areas of stimulus control, stimulus equivalence, generalization, and induction, and the use of descriptive analysis methodologies. Dr. Lalli also serves on the Board of Editors for the *Journal of Applied Behavior Analysis*.

F. Charles Mace, Ph.D., Associate Professor, Department of Pediatrics, University of Pennsylvania School of Medicine, Philadelphia, PA 19104. Dr. Mace's research has focused on linking basic and applied research in behavioral psychology. He has published several studies on the functional analysis of problem behavior, behavioral momentum, and applications of the matching law to human behavior problems. He is currently Associate Editor of the *Journal of Applied Behavior Analysis* and on the Board of Editors for the *Journal of the Experimental Analysis of Behavior* and *Research in Developmental Disabilities*.

Luanna H. Meyer, Ph.D., Professor, School of Education, Syracuse University, 805 South Crouse Avenue, Syracuse, NY 13244-2280. Dr. Meyer is chair of Special Education Programs and Coordinator of the Inclusive Elementary and Special Education Program, as well as co-director of the New York Partnership for Statewide Systems Change and Director of the Consortium for Collaborative Research on Social Relationships. Her research and publications focus upon the validation of strategies to promote inclusion and address significant challenges to full participation by all, covering such topics as intervention research on severe behavior problems, curriculum and instruction to create inclusive schools for children with and without disabilities, and strategies for supporting positive social relationships among children with diverse abilities in their schools and communities.

Richard A. Mesaros, Ph.D., Associate Professor of Special Education, California State University, Northridge, Northridge, CA 91330. Dr. Mesaros was a National Trainer on contract no. GOO87CO234, Research and Training Center on Community-Referenced Nonaversive Behavior Management, from the National Institute on Disability and Rehabilitation Research (1987–1992), and provides consultation, training, and technical assistance to a variety of school districts, advocacy agencies, and agencies serving individuals with severe disabilities and severe behavior problems. He continues to be particularly interested in the relationship between learning characteristics, classroom ecology and behavior problems and has published in the areas of autism, qualitative research, alternatives to punishment, and behavioral assessment.

Marlene Morelli-Robbins, M.S., Hernando County Schools, 275 Oak Street, ESE Office, Brooksville, FL 34601. Ms. Morelli-Robbins is training coordinator for the University of South Florida collaboration site of the Research and Training Center and Community-Referenced Nonaversive Behavior Management. Her areas of interest include autism, integration of individuals with disabilities, preventive behavior management, and effective inservice training.

Rob O'Neill, Ph.D., Assistant Professor, Specialized Training Program, University of Oregon, Eugene, OR 97403. Dr. O'Neill's areas of interest include community-based functional assessment and support strategies for persons with severe disabilities and challenging behavior, strategies for teaching communication skills, and systems for training and supporting school personnel working with challenging students in integrated settings. In collaboration with Drs. Robert Horner and James Halle, he is conducting a research project in school environments on the application of general case training procedures to communication skills.

Pamela G. Osnes, M.A., Department of Child and Family Studies, Florida Mental Health Institute, University of South Florida, 13301 Bruce B. Downs Blvd., Tampa, FL 33612-3899. The research of Ms. Osnes has emphasized staff performances in integrated early childhood centers, the development of verbal control by young children, and the promotion of generalization across settings and maintenance of treatment effects across time. As the Project Director of the Carousel Preschool Program, she has been particularly interested in the effective integration of children classified as severely emotionally disturbed, at-risk children, and children who were exposed prenatally to chemical substances with typically developing children.

John M. Parrish, Ph.D., Associate Professor of Psychology in Pediatrics & Psychiatry, The University of Pennsylvania School of Medicine, Philadelphia, PA 19104. Dr. Parrish is Head of the Section of Pediatric Psychology, Division of Child Development & Rehabilitation, Department of Pediatrics at the University of Pennsylvania. His research has focused upon clinical applications of applied behavior analysis in the areas of behavioral pediatrics, clinical-child psychology, and developmental disabilities. He presently co-directs the two MCH-funded training curricula, one a university affiliated program for interdisciplinary education and the other a fellowship for pediatricians pursuing careers in behavioral pediatrics. He serves on three editorial boards and is a past associate editor for the *Journal of Applied Behavior Analysis*.

Barry M. Prizant, Ph.D., CCC-SLP, Division of Communication Disorders, Emerson College, 100 Beacon Street, Boston, MA 02116. Dr. Prizant is a professor in the Division of Communication Disorders at Emerson College. Previously, he was an Associate Professor of Child and Adolescent Psychiatry in the Brown University Program in Medicine, and the Director of the Communication Disorders Department at Bradley Hospital, Providence, Rhode Island. He is an editorial consultant for four professional journals in the areas of communication and language development, and autism and other social-communicative disorders in young children. He has published numerous articles and chapters, and has presented seminars nationally and internationally on these topics. Dr. Prizant's current research and clinical interests include relationships between communication and social and emotional development, and identification and treatment of infants, toddlers, and preschool children at risk for communication and emotional/behavioral problems. He is co-author of the *Communication and Symbolic Behavior Scales* (Wetherby & Prizant, 1992), a nationally standardized instrument that assesses communication, symbolic, and social-affective abilities in young children.

Maura L. Roberts, Ph.D., Assistant Professor, Department of Psychology, Illinois State University, Normal, IL 61761-6901. Dr. Roberts' research has focused on the momentum of human behavior, negative reinforcement schedules related to self-injurious behavior, and Curriculum-Based Assessment (CBA). She is particularly interested the use of CBA procedures to assess differential effects of fixed instructional ratios on students' academic progress.

Patrick J. Rydell, Ed.D., CCC-SLP, Autism Communication Services, 7125 West Jefferson Avenue, Suite 300, Lakewood, CO 80235. Dr. Rydell manages a private practice, Autism Communication Services in Lakewood, Colorado. His primary research focus has been on echolalia and the effects of adult interaction styles on verbal output in children with autism. His current research projects focus on the issue of validation of facilitated communication in persons with autism.

Gary M. Sasso, Ph.D., Associate Professor and Chair, Special Education, The University of Iowa, Iowa City, IA 52242. Dr. Sasso is co-director of the Self-Injurious and Aggressive Behavior Service in the Department of Pediatrics, where he holds a secondary appointment. His research has focused on social interactions/integration and the application of functional analysis procedures for individuals with severe disabilities.

Joseph E. Spradlin, Ph.D., Senior Scientist, Schiefelbusch Institute for Life Span Studies, and Professor, Department of Human Development and Family Life. Dr.

Spradlin is also the Director of the Parsons Research Center, Parsons, KS 67357. His research has focused primarily on stimulus control as it relates to the evaluation, education, and treatment of people with mental retardation. More recently he has become interested in the role of routines in the development and control of both challenging behaviors and adaptive verbal behaviors.

Trevor Stokes, Ph.D., Professor, Florida Mental Health Institute, University of South Florida, 13301 Bruce B. Downs Blvd., Tampa, FL 33612-3899. Dr. Stokes has a longstanding interest in the generalization functions of verbalization and language in behavior development and change. The relation of these processes to the enhancement of self-mediated generalization has been a focus of his research work with children. An additional emphasis of his current activity is the development of programs and research with families and children with traumatic brain injury.

Jill C. Taylor, Ph.D., Clinical Research Psychologist, The Devereux Foundation, Institute of Clinical Training and Research, 19 South Waterloo Road, Box 400, Devon, PA 19333-0400. Dr. Taylor's research focuses on three areas related to severe behavior problems: functional analysis and functionally derived treatment, reciprocal social influences, and parent and teacher training.

Jan S. Weiner, Ph.D., Assistant Professor, Department of Special Educaion, California State University, Fullerton, CA 92634-9920. As coordinator of the Severe Handicap credential program, Dr. Weiner is currently focused on general education teacher preparation in order to facilitate the integration of students with severe disabilities into the general education classroom. In addition, she is studying the effects of peer influence on the development of conversation skills in students with severe disabilities. Dr. Weiner served as Project Coordinator of the Albany Challenging Behavior Project, making use of functional communication and prescriptive techniques as nonaversive intervention for severe challenging behavior in students with developmental disabilities and emotional disturbance.

Acknowledgments

I AM GRATEFUL TO my colleagues William Keogh, Mary McEvoy, David Wacker, and Jim Halle, who have been a constant source of professional stimulation. I am also indebted to Rob Horner and his consortium of associates, who have expanded my knowledge as a communication interventionist. I also ackowledge my graduate students, who have taught me more than I could possibly ever teach them. Finally, to my family—Megan, Chris, and Patti—who have become experts in implementing proactive intervention strategies to address my challenging behavior.   —*Joe Reichle*

To MY MENTORS, Lee Meyerson and Nancy Kerr, who taught me not only how, but why, to analyze functional relations; to my parents, Jim and Lorraine Wacker, who showed me the value of both noncontingent and contingent reinforcement; and to my wife, Katie, who provides ongoing encouragement and support and who serves as my role model.   —*David P. Wacker*

1

Functional Communication Training as an Intervention for Problem Behavior

An Overview and Introduction to Our Edited Volume

David P. Wacker and Joe Reichle

Even a cursory review of the literature on challenging behavior makes it clear that the evolution of interventions for severe behavior disorders is still in a dynamic stage of development. Restricting the review to reinforcement-based interventions and beginning with Carr (1977), one is confronted by two trends. First, there is substantial agreement and replication of some assessment and intervention strategies by separate researchers. For example, there is apparent consistency of findings and widespread acceptance of techniques such as functional analysis. The amount of consistency, or degree of convergence, is both surprising and encouraging as we attempt to steadily advance intervention approaches. Second, there is substantial disagreement on even the most basic elements of these procedures, such as what constitutes a functional analysis.

OVERVIEW

Convergence and Divergence: A Rationale for the Organization of This Book

Both the convergence and the divergence in research are represented in the chapters of this book. Throughout the book, the use of functional analysis is a recurring theme, but it is described in different ways with different conceptual and methodological aspects emphasized. The labels and descriptions of behavior vary, but the need to reinforce socially appropriate behavior that can replace challenging behavior is consistently described. Although both molecular and molar evaluations of intervention are advocated, all authors agree that assessment and intervention activities should focus on functional behavior. Thus, in this book, as in the literature, both divergent and convergent themes are present, and the reader can choose the themes that he or she wishes to pursue.

Three themes of convergence guided us as we discussed the development of this book. First, effective intervention is based on our knowledge about the function of behavior. The extent to which we can identify the function of behavior is the single most important variable in establishing an effective intervention program. We simply cannot develop "generic" interventions that are compared to other interventions in a fruitless attempt to prove that one type of intervention is better than another. Instead, we must individualize the interventions. This individualization, in some instances, may result in using a package of several intervention techniques that once were the focus of debate as to which was better (e.g., functional communication training *and* differential reinforcement of other behavior).

Second, we view effective functional communication training as being based, as are other behavioral interventions, on underlying operant mechanisms. Functional communication intervention is based directly on extensions of an empirically derived set of operant techniques and is, therefore, subject to the same constraints as any other behavioral intervention. The appropriate communicative alternatives taught during intervention are behaviors that can, under specific conditions, suppress challenging behavior. We wanted, therefore, to place functional communication intervention solidly within an operant context.

Third, functional communication intervention, as are virtually all reinforcement-based interventions, is really a package of procedures that involve multiple, distinct components even at the most basic level of analysis. One does not just prompt an individual to communicate and then observe reductions in challenging behavior. At the very beginning of intervention, packages of separate but interacting components combine to affect the challenging behavior and, to a greater or lesser degree, a number of other responses within the individual's repertoire.

For maintenance to be achieved, an even more broad-based approach to intervention is required. The ongoing intervention plan must be maintained and modified, implemented in various situations, and incorporated into the ongoing habilitative programming for the individual. Other adaptive responses must be included in intervention and must be placed on compatible schedules of reinforcement.

On a procedural level, then, functional communication intervention is often a straightforward and surprisingly effective intervention when it includes two essential steps. First, the function of challenging behavior must be identified; we must identify the reinforcers maintaining behavior. Second, the identified reinforcers must be available only for one or more acceptable communicative responses and withheld for challenging behavior. If both the challenging behavior and alternative communicative response serve the same function but only the alternative communicative response is reinforced, relatively quick, positive, *initial* results should occur. This has been demonstrated repeatedly in the literature, and we refer to this phase of intervention as differential reinforcement of communication (DRC). DRC, therefore, is a specific form of differential reinforcement of alternative behavior (DRA). Desired behavior receives contingent reinforcement and undesired behavior is placed on extinction. The reasons for successful intervention, the underlying operant mechanisms, are identical for both DRA and DRC. However, what can make DRC distinct from DRA is the control over reinforcement governed by the individual. In DRC, the individual controls the presentation of reinforcement, whereas in DRA, caregivers control the schedule of reinforcement. This issue of control may be important, especially as we begin conducting better analyses of long-term maintenance. Otherwise, DRC and DRA are virtually identical. Given that DRC is a specific type of DRA, the more we know about differential reinforcement procedures, the more effective we can be in designing DRC programs. Of most importance initially is that the communicative replacement, the mand reinforced during intervention, serves the same function as the challenging behavior. To increase this probability, an assessment of the function of challenging behavior is the critical first step of intervention (see chaps. 2, 3, 4, and 5, this volume).

The next step is to ensure that the communicative replacement is more efficient in securing reinforcement for the individual than the existing repertoire of challenging behavior. This step can be accomplished in numerous ways; the critical point is if the communicative replacement and the challenging behavior both serve the same function *and* reinforcement is most easily or most often available by producing socially acceptable communication, increased displays of the communicative behavior should correspond to decreased displays of challenging behavior. Put another way, communicative behavior and challenging behavior should covary (see chaps. 6 and 7, this volume). Thus, covariation is the first step of intervention, and we refer to this first step as DRC.

To promote generalization and maintenance, intervention must quickly become more broad-based. The individual must learn, for example, to discriminate occasions for receiving reinforcement through newly taught communicative responses from occasions when the display of those responses is not appropriate (stimulus generalization). The individual's repertoire of appropriate communicative responses must be expanded to include different functions. We use the terms *functional communication training* (*FCT*) or *functional communication intervention* (*FCI*) as labels for this more broad-based approach to intervention. In most cases, FCI is initiated concurrently or shortly after DRC intervention, but it is then expanded quickly to include a variety of stimulus situations (settings) and communicative responses, which are incorporated into the individual's ongoing program (see Part III: Developing Effective Communication Interventions, this volume).

In summary, effective communication intervention usually consists of three phases: 1) an assessment phase, in which the function of behavior is identified; 2) an initial intervention or DRC phase, in which challenging behavior is replaced with one or more appropriate communicative responses; and 3) an applied FCI phase, in which the initial intervention is expanded to be more comprehensive. We believe that these phases are often points of convergence in the literature, and we organized this book around these perceived phases.

Possibilities and
Probabilities: Focus and Limitations

The possibilities of communication intervention for challenging behavior appear to us to be almost limitless. The number of successful communication interventions reported in the literature is growing, and the robustness of the procedures across diverse settings and subgroups is impressive. For this reason, the timing for books such as this volume (also see Durand, 1990) appears ideal. However, as replications are reported, a certain percentage of failures also occur, even when the interventions appear to have been conducted correctly. Thus, even as the possibilities for communication interventions seem most optimal, we must also closely examine the underlying reasons for success and failure to continue to improve the probability of success.

Communication interventions, as stated previously, are based on an empirically derived and conceptually driven set of operations. To maximize the probability of success, one must understand both the basis for the procedures and the rationale for variations of those procedures. Our intent in this book is to provide a firm empirical and conceptual basis for those who wish to conduct a communication intervention. Although some chapters rather explicitly operationalize assessment and intervention strategies, we attempted to emphasize the logic and empirical support for communication interventions rather than a detailed set of prescriptive procedures. Consequently, we have omitted an extensive data base on the programmatic methods most often utilized in communication intervention. For readers interested in a more comprehensive summary of specific procedures, we recommend the book by Durand (1990). We do not argue, or even attempt to be persuasive, that communication intervention is the "best" intervention for any given individual. Instead, we attempt to provide a better basis for implementing this type of intervention and for interpreting the effects of intervention. This is why we have no chapters that advocate strongly for this approach or that specifically contrast this approach to others.

Overall, our intent was to provide a conceptual basis for the reader to be able to develop and interpret communication intervention programs. We hope that the preceding discussion of our intent, and the subsequent discussion of the chapters, provides useful information on how to best utilize this book.

INTRODUCTION TO INDIVIDUAL CHAPTERS

Part I: Conducting Functional Assessments

There are a number of good reasons to conduct assessments of challenging behavior, but if the primary purpose of the assessment is to provide guidance for intervention, then the best assessment involves direct observation. There are two interrelated approaches to assessment that serve this purpose: 1) descriptive analysis of when and under what environmental conditions challenging behavior occurs, and 2) functional analysis of what maintains the problem behavior. The first two chapters in this section focus on these two types of assessment.

Lalli and Goh (Chapter 2) provide a comprehensive overview of the objectives of descriptive assessment. We elected to begin with this chapter because this is where most of us begin when working with individuals who display challenging behavior. Often, our initial impression is that challenging behavior is occurring randomly; we see little or no relationship between the behavior and the environment. Descriptive assessments permit us to better understand the behavior, and for that reason we believe that descriptive assessments are often the best way to begin the intervention process. Cooper and Harding (Chapter 3) argue for the need for a functional analysis, regardless of the completeness of a descriptive assessment. They also provide evidence that functional analysis methodologies are quite robust; they can be modified for use in outpatient and classroom settings and with typically developing children or with children with mild disabilities.

The final two chapters in this section suggest that we further extend functional analysis to be more inclusive of other variables. Taylor and Carr (Chapter 4) show that challenging behavior and intervention programs for challenging behavior affect caregivers as well as the individuals. By including caregivers in our assessment probes, we can begin to identify what variables are maintaining their behavior as well as how their behavior influences the individual's behavior. Halle and Spradlin (Chapter 5) suggest that we extend functional analysis methods to encompass sequences of behavior instead of single responses.

The four chapters in this section represent current applications and extensions of functional analysis methodologies described by Carr and Durand

(1985) and Iwata, Dorsey, Slifer, Bauman, and Richman (1982). Taken as a whole, they provide examples of how assessment can be conducted across diverse settings (inpatient unit, outpatient clinic, classrooms); groups of individuals (preschool children, young adults, and various diagnostic groups); behaviors (appropriate and inappropriate, multiple responses, and interactions between caregivers and individuals); and potential controlling variables (antecedents and consequences).

Part II: Developing Effective
Interventions: Empirical and Conceptual Considerations

Reinforcement-based interventions such as FCI are difficult to implement because they require at least some understanding of what maintains (reinforces) behavior and what sets the occasion for desired behavior. In the chapters previously discussed, the assessments all provide methods for analyzing behavior; they provide data that increase our knowledge about the environmental conditions that maintain behavior and its impact on other aspects of the environment. When intervention is initiated, we not only need to continue to monitor (understand) the interaction of behavior with the environment, but we also must know enough about potential interventions to select the most promising package of components. In addition, once selected, we need to know how to modify the intervention over time to maximize the effects of intervention.

In Chapter 6, Mace and Roberts provide a concise overview of the critical factors that affect behavioral interventions such as FCI. Knowledge of these factors permits us not only to construct optimal interventions, but also to "diagnose" problems with ongoing intervention. Knowing how to make needed adjustments in intervention requires knowledge about the factors influencing the effects of intervention; it requires a shift in our thinking from emphasizing the modification of behavior to understanding the underlying mechanisms for how to modify behavior.

When one considers FCI specifically, an essential requirement for effective intervention is that the communicative response serve as a replacement response—it must replace the challenging behavior. Parrish and Roberts (Chapter 7) comprehensively describe the conceptual and empirical basis for covariation via key study descriptions and then provide numerous examples of covariation in communication interventions. It is not sufficient, in our view, to know what constitutes an effective intervention. We must also understand why, or under what conditions, intervention is most likely to be effective.

Part III: Developing Effective
Communication Interventions: Programmatic Considerations

Given both a valid functional assessment of challenging behavior and the determination that FCI is an important component of an intervention package for an individual, a number of programmatic considerations confront us in developing and implementing the specific intervention procedures. These programmatic considerations are the focus for the third section of this book.

We begin this section with the chapter by Dunlap and Kern, who provide an example of how descriptive and functional analyses were used to develop and test hypotheses, and how communication was incorporated into an on-going educational program.

The chapters by O'Neill and Reichle (Chapter 9) and DePaepe, Reichle, and O'Neill (Chapter 10) offer specific guidance on how to train communicative alternatives that match the function of challenging behavior. In Chapter 10, the authors provide a conceptual basis for why general-case training should be incorporated into FCT interventions. In Chapter 10, the authors provide examples of how to apply general-case training procedures across the different social functions of challenging behavior. Thus, in Chapters 9 and 10, a specific instructional paradigm that emphasizes generalization is described, which is based on the assessed function of challenging behavior.

Prizant and Rydell (Chapter 11) describe repertoires of unconventional verbal behavior. They emphasize the applicability of functional assessment and identifying socially acceptable communicative alternatives to challenging behavior. They suggest a number of considerations in designing and implementing intervention strategies that address vocal and verbal unconventional behavior.

In Chapter 12, the correspondence between what is said and done is addressed by Stokes, Osnes, and DaVerne. They review intervention strategies that have been successfully implemented to increase the correspondence between an individual's actions and communicative behaviors. In functional communication programs, the assumption is made that each time the communicative response is given, it signals the desire for a specific reinforcer. As we begin to evaluate the long-term effects of intervention, we may find that the same appropriate communicative response may begin to serve more than one function. In this case, from the standpoint of an observer, there is a lack of correspondence between the communicative response and subsequent behavior.

Durand, Berotti, and Weiner (Chapter 13) discuss the factors associated with the successful implementation of functional communication training and focus specifically on the factors affecting generalization and maintenance of the communicative alternatives taught during intervention. This chapter incorporates the key points raised in many of the preceding chapters to provide both a conceptual and a programmatic basis for communication interventions.

Part IV: Facilitating the Application of Intervention Programs

Most of the intervention procedures described in the chapters preceding Part IV were developed in somewhat controlled situations. The applicability of the procedures has been demonstrated and use of the procedures in school settings is now more common. In this final section, the chapters provide descriptions of how this technology has been applied and offer guidance on future applications.

Berg and Sasso (Chapter 14) describe how the technologies of functional analysis and communication training have been implemented in four local school districts over a 2-year period. They provide additional evidence that these technologies were applicable with only minor technical assistance. Anderson, Albin, Mesaros, Dunlap, and Morelli-Robbins (Chapter 15) provide a detailed description of the issues surrounding training and ongoing support of the staff who implement behavioral interventions of challenging behavior. Ongoing support for staff is a frequently overlooked factor in maintenance. Finally, Meyer and Evans (Chapter 16) argue for a more molar evaluation of outcomes associated with intervention. In previous chapters, the benefit and need for molecular evaluations are discussed and center on our ability to identify functional relations. In this concluding chapter, Meyer and Evans suggest that the outcomes of intervention correlate with meaningful changes in lifestyle for the individuals receiving intervention.

CONCLUSION

Communication intervention for challenging behavior is a complex operant intervention that consists of multiple, interacting components. It begins with a valid assessment of the function of challenging behavior and facilitates, it is hoped, meaningful changes in the client's everyday life. The various components of the intervention package, including the communicative functions selected for intervention, the schedules of reinforcement, and the context for intervention interact to influence the success of intervention. Communication training, because it is built on solid empirical and conceptual bases, can be useful across a range of situations and individuals. Increased knowledge of the conceptual and empirical bases of communication training should facilitate the continued evolution of this intervention approach. This, at least, has been our goal in editing this book.

REFERENCES

Carr, E.G. (1977). The motivation of self-injurious behavior: A review of some hypotheses. *Psychological Bulletin, 84,* 800–816.

Carr, E.G., & Durand, V.M. (1985). Reducing behavior problems through functional communication training. *Journal of Applied Behavior Analysis, 18,* 111–126.

Durand, V.M. (1990). *Severe behavior problems: A functional communication training approach.* New York: Guilford Press.

Iwata, B.A., Dorsey, M.F., Slifer, K.J., Bauman, K.E., & Richman, G.S. (1982). Toward a functional analysis of self-injury. *Analysis and Intervention in Developmental Disabilities, 2,* 3–20.

PART I

Conducting
Functional Assessments

2

Naturalistic Observations in Community Settings

Joseph S. Lalli and Han-Leong Goh

THE GOALS OF THIS CHAPTER are to provide the reader with a conceptual basis regarding the use of naturalistic observation as a preintervention assessment procedure and suggestions for using this information to develop effective interventions. Case studies are presented through a consultation model and from actual cases at the Biobehavioral Unit of the Children's Seashore House. The unit is an inpatient facility that provides services (i.e., evaluation and intervention) to families and other service providers (e.g., residential programs, community-based group homes) with children who present with severe behavior disorders.

Increasing attention has been focused on the use of pretreatment assessment data to design interventions for the remediation of severe behavior problems. To date, most of the studies using pretreatment assessment procedures have used some form of analog functional analysis (Iwata, Dorsey, Slifer, Bauman, & Richman, 1982; Steege, Wacker, Berg, Cigrand, & Cooper, 1989). Briefly, these assessments consist of manipulating consequent environmental events to provide information regarding their functional relationships to problem behavior.

Another form of pretreatment assessment is naturalistic observation, frequently referred to as descriptive analysis. This assessment describes the interactions between behavior and environmental events via direct observations conducted in the individual's natural environment, but without manipulating the variables that are associated with problem behavior (Bijou, Peterson, & Ault, 1968). Descriptive data provide an empirical basis for the formulation of hypotheses regarding the function of the problem behavior. These hypotheses are then tested directly in a functional analysis (i.e., experimental analysis) or tested indirectly through an evaluation of the effects of an intervention on the problem behavior.

We are frequently asked to present a "cookbook" on naturalistic observations, that is, to address the questions of what the objectives are and how naturalistic observations are used. We cannot provide a "one size fits all" model, but we can provide a conceptual basis for their selection and a practical model for their use in community settings. As is the case with most direct assessments, the specific objectives and procedures are determined by the situation in each community setting (e.g., nature of the problem behavior, resources available).

In the following section, we provide a brief description of the basic objectives for using naturalistic observations (see Table 1). The objectives and benefits are discussed in regard to the identification of possible functional relations between a target behavior and environmental events (i.e., primary objective), and to the identification of relevant information for intervention development (i.e., secondary objectives).

OBJECTIVES AND BENEFITS OF NATURALISTIC OBSERVATIONS

Primary Objective: Data-Based Hypothesis Development

Identify Possible Functional Relations Between a Problem Behavior and Naturally Occurring Environmental Events

Naturalistic observations allow the consultant to observe the individual during a variety of situations in order to identify a reliable relationship between the problem behavior and naturally occurring environmental events. Environmental events that precede or occur concurrently with the target behavior are referred to as its antecedents and identify stimuli that may set the occasion for the target response to produce reinforcement (Mace, Lalli, & Pinter-Lalli, 1991). The environmental events that follow the target behavior are referred to as its subsequent events and are suggestive of a possible reinforcement relationship (Mace et al., 1991). Naturalistic observations have been used to

Table 1.   Objectives and benefits of naturalistic observations

Primary objective
  Data-based hypothesis development
    Identify possible functional relations between a problem behavior and naturally
    occurring environmental events.

Secondary objectives
  Use of descriptive data to design analog conditions for the functional analysis
    Identify the establishing conditions correlated with problem behavior.
    Identify discriminative stimuli that set the occasion for problem behavior.
  Provide information for intervention development.
    Identify the situations that set the occasion for problem behavior.
    Identify the schedule of reinforcement available for appropriate behavior.
    Identify skills required for successful functioning in community settings.
    Identify individual styles of interaction.
    Identify variables involved in response efficiency.

analyze the relationship between environmental events and a range of problem behaviors. (See Table 2 for a listing of behaviors and relevant citations.)

Basically, naturalistic observations attempt to answer the questions: Under which situation does the problem behavior occur most frequently, and what or which event(s) generally follow it? In one of the earliest studies using naturalistic observations, Ayllon and Michael (1959) observed the inappropriate behaviors of patients in a psychiatric hospital in order to identify the relationship between these behaviors and environmental events. The pretreatment assessment showed that the patients generally engaged in these behaviors during conditions of low adult attention (i.e., when nurses were attending to their ward duties) and that problem behavior frequently produced the nurses' attentive reactions. Based on these findings, the authors instructed the nurses to provide the patients with attention on a regularly scheduled basis and to withhold their attention after all problem behaviors. The authors reported substantial decreases in the problem behaviors within 6 weeks of implementing treatment.

Lalli, Browder, Mace, and Brown (in press) used a descriptive analysis (Bijou et al., 1968) to identify the relationship between three students' problem behaviors (i.e., self-injurious behavior, aggression) and classroom events. The observations showed that the students' problem behaviors occurred primarily during times when they were without one-to-one supervision or during times of transitions between classrooms. An analysis of the descriptive data indicated that problem behaviors typically produced attentive reactions from the teachers or permitted avoidance of nonpreferred instructional activities. Based on these observations, the teachers were then trained to provide the students with the reinforcers (i.e., attention, access to preferred activities) contingent on appropriate behavior rather than after the students' inappropriate self-injurious or aggressive behavior.

The pretreatment assessment data of Ayllon and Michael (1959) and Lalli et al. (in press) showed a clear relationship between individuals' problem behaviors and environmental events. These patterns of responding allowed the authors to implement interventions that quickly reduced the frequency of problem behavior and indirectly supported the hypotheses developed from the pretreatment assessment. However, cases in which there are no clear hypothe-

Table 2. Topographies of problem behaviors used as target behaviors in naturalistic observations and relevant citations

Aggression (Touchette, MacDonald, & Langer, 1985)
Alcohol consumption (Geller, Russ, & Altomari, 1986)
Bizarre speech (Mace & Lalli, 1991)
Disruptive behavior (Dunlap, Kern-Dunlap, Clarke, & Robbins, 1991)
Eating disorders (Epstein, Parker, McCoy, & McGee, 1976)
Pica (Mace & Knight, 1986)
Self-injury (Carr & McDowell, 1980; Lalli, Browder, Mace, & Brown, in press)
Stereotypy (Mace & Belfiore, 1990)

ses regarding the operant function of the problem behavior may require an experimental manipulation to verify possible functional relations. In these cases, a descriptive analysis may allow the consultant to narrow the range of hypotheses being tested by providing information on the influence of specific establishing conditions on problem behavior.

Secondary Objectives: Use of Descriptive Analysis Data To Design Analog Conditions for the Functional Analysis

Identify the Establishing Conditions Correlated with Problem Behavior

In the case of behaviors that have been resistant to intervention, previous assessments may have failed to identify the specific situations correlated with the problem behavior. For example, the data may show that the problem behavior occurred equally across all situations (i.e., an undifferentiated response pattern) and that there was no clear response–reinforcer relationship. These response patterns should indicate that a comprehensive functional analysis should be conducted to identify functional relationships.

A descriptive analysis may provide the consultant with information regarding the specific reinforcing events associated with the problem behavior and allow the consultant to limit the number of conditions tested during the functional analysis. Descriptive analyses, even when inconclusive, can still lead to a more precise and efficient assessment during the functional analysis. For example, descriptive analyses may often be useful for identifying establishing conditions (Michael, 1982). Establishing conditions are environmental stimuli that influence the value of a reinforcer to the individual. Their presence alters the probability of the appearance of any response that historically has been followed by the reinforcer. Establishing conditions are based on the operations of deprivation (e.g., hunger), satiation (e.g., fullness), and the presence of aversive stimuli that affect the relative value of potential reinforcers. Establishing conditions influence the individual to respond in a manner that allows him or her to change the conditions of deprivation or satiation or to remove the aversive stimuli. A simplistic example of establishing conditions is hunger. This establishing condition (i.e., deprivation) increases the probability that the individual will respond in a particular manner in the presence of food to alleviate any adverse physiological effects of hunger.

Mace and Lalli (1991) encountered a situation in which previous functional analyses failed to produce a differentiated response pattern. The individual's bizarre speech occurred equally across all assessment conditions. The authors linked descriptive and functional analyses to treat Mitch's bizarre vocalizations, which were classified as "delusional and hallucinatory" by his psychiatrist. Mitch was observed during a variety of naturally occurring situations at his home. Observations were 30–60 minutes in duration and were conducted across situations in which there was no adult interaction, during situations of one-to-one adult interaction, during task demands, and when Mitch was alone (e.g., in his bedroom). Data were collected concurrently on bizarre speech and its naturally occurring antecedent and subsequent events.

The initial results from the descriptive analysis showed that bizarre speech occurred equally across all situations. However, a closer examination of the data indicated that bizarre speech occurred most frequently during situations in which social interaction was unavailable (i.e., deprivation) and occurred less frequently during situations in which one-to-one adult interaction was supplied. Data also showed that Mitch's bizarre speech generally produced attentive reactions from staff and, that during task situations, Mitch voluntarily disengaged from work-related activities. Based on these data, two hypotheses were proposed and subsequently tested in a functional analysis. The first hypothesis proposed that Mitch's bizarre speech was positively reinforced through the staff's attentive reactions. The second hypothesis was that inappropriate speech was maintained by the termination of task-related activities. The results from the functional analysis supported the positive reinforcement hypothesis, but not the negative reinforcement hypothesis.

In this example, the descriptive analysis contributed to the functional analysis by identifying a common establishing condition across the situations associated with bizarre speech. No direct social interaction between Mitch and staff was occurring prior to bizarre speech, but adults were in close proximity to provide attention contingent on problem behavior. This information allowed the authors to narrow the scope of possible hypotheses and to design specific experimental conditions to evaluate Mitch's bizarre speech.

Naturalistic observations are useful, therefore, to identify establishing conditions that influence how an individual responds in the presence of a particular stimulus. Naturalistic observations also can be used to identify stimuli that are associated with the problem behavior itself. Data from descriptive analyses provide information regarding the specific person or object that is correlated with problem behavior in addition to the establishing conditions.

Identify Discriminative Stimuli that Set the Occasion for Problem Behavior

A discriminative stimulus is an environmental event that sets the occasion for a response to have a particular consequence (Catania, 1984). Discriminative stimuli may include the presence or absence of a specific person, a specific instructional technique (e.g., physical prompts), a particular form of instructional demand (e.g., "Finish your work"), repeated demands to perform individual components of a task (e.g., "You still have to clean over here," "Now pick up this toy"), time of day (e.g., immediately following lunch when the child is tired), activity (e.g., recess, transitions between instructional activities), instructional materials (e.g., math worksheets), or some combination of events. Discriminative stimuli differ from establishing conditions in that a discriminative stimulus (e.g., presence of food) "signals" to the individual that reinforcement is available for a particular response (e.g., consuming the food), and an establishing condition (e.g., deprivation or satiation) either increases or decreases the probability that the response will occur by affecting the value of the reinforcer.

We have found the information obtained from the descriptive analysis to be particularly useful for identifying the specific discriminative stimuli to be used during the functional analyses. By first identifying natural discriminative stimuli, the validity of the functional relations obtained in the functional analysis is strengthened because the differences between the natural and analog settings are minimized. Two case studies are reported below to illustrate the benefits of using the descriptive analysis findings to develop analog conditions within a subsequent functional analysis.

It is not unusual for a child to respond differentially in the presence of different adults because of the adults' history of responding to the child's inappropriate behavior. For example, Mark and James were both 6 years of age when referred for the evaluation and treatment of their aggressive and self-injurious behaviors. Both children lived with their biologic mothers in single-parent families and were referred to the unit because of their severe problem behaviors at home. Results from the descriptive analyses showed that the boys engaged in problem behaviors most frequently during situations in which their mothers' attention was divided between the child and another adult present in the room.

We designed our analog conditions to closely parallel those observed during the descriptive analyses by using the same situations, specific topographies of subsequent events, and the frequency in which the parent responded to the child's problem behaviors (i.e., schedule of reinforcement). However, we were unable to observe similar frequencies of problem behavior during the analog assessments when an interventionist delivered the consequences that were observed during the descriptive analyses with the mothers. These findings suggested that the child's problem behavior was maintained by a specific individual's attention (i.e., the mother's) and not by attentive reactions themselves. Based on these findings, the boys' mothers replaced the interventionists during the analog assessments, and this change resulted in a response pattern similar to that observed during the descriptive analyses. Immediately after the functional analyses, the mothers were successfully taught to use procedures for reducing the problem behaviors. Without the benefit of descriptive analyses, we may not have addressed the mothers' needs for assistance.

The preceding cases illustrate the benefit of a descriptive analysis for identifying a particular discriminative stimulus that sets the occasion for problem behavior. The children's mothers were a "signal" that problem behavior would produce reinforcement, because of their previous manner of responding. Using the mothers to implement the contingencies in our functional analysis phase allowed us to more closely parallel the situations found in the home setting, thus limiting the inferences required about the maintaining variables in the functional assessment. In addition to identifying specific persons who are associated with problem behavior, naturalistic observations can also provide information on specific situations that result in problem behavior.

Secondary Objectives: Provide Information for Intervention Development

Identify the Situations that Set the Occasion for Problem Behavior

There are some cases in which there is a clear response–reinforcer relationship, and the interventionist's objective is to identify the situations that reliably set the occasion for problem behavior. Problem behavior during these situations may result from an individual's lack of skills (e.g., in a particular academic area), insufficient reinforcement for appropriate behavior (e.g., the old adage of "let sleeping dogs lie" that tells parents to ignore the child when he or she is being good), or situations in which there are competing values of reinforcement (e.g., peer vs. teacher approval). Once the situations and the contributing factors are identified, (e.g., skill deficits), the intervention development phase can be proceeded to without directly testing functional relations via a functional analysis.

Lalli, Pinter-Lalli, Mace, and Murphy (1991) used a descriptive analysis in a group home to obtain information that allowed them to immediately proceed to treatment. They used an event-response-event observation procedure (Bijou et al., 1968) to record the antecedent social situation (e.g., an individual wearing another's clothing without permission), the response (e.g., the owner of the clothing approaching the individual with verbal threats), and the subsequent event (e.g., staff resolving the dispute). From these observations, the authors identified the situations that most frequently resulted in confrontations between individuals, selected appropriate skills that the individuals could use to resolve the problem, and taught those skills during role-play situations that were analogous to the naturally occurring confrontations.

The Lalli et al. (1991) study demonstrated the benefit of using a descriptive analysis to identify naturally occurring situations that result in problem behavior. Based on their observations, the authors conceptualized the inappropriate behavior of the individuals as a skill-deficit problem and were able to teach them a set of interactional skills that effectively prevented the social confrontations.

Identify the Schedule of
Reinforcement Available for Appropriate Behavior

In some cases, problem behavior may result from a lack of reinforcement (i.e., insufficient rate of reinforcement) available for appropriate behavior. During interviews at the biobehavioral unit, the authors asked parents to describe how they respond to their child when he or she is behaving appropriately. The typical response was, "We just leave him or her alone." This statement suggests that infrequent reinforcement is a typical response to appropriate behavior. In contrast, the parents stated that they respond with frequent reprimands for inappropriate behavior, which suggests that these behaviors produce a richer schedule of reinforcement than appropriate behavior.

The implications of these disparate schedules of reinforcement are described by Herrnstein's (1961) law of effect, or matching theory, which states that an individual will allocate his or her responses among concurrently available alternatives to produce the most favorable amount of reinforcement. For example, for Mark, we observed that during a homework activity, his mother provided him with infrequent praise for appropriate work behaviors but reprimanded him for each inappropriate response (e.g., looking away from his worksheet). Mark initially allocated his responding exclusively to on-task behavior, but eventually switched to inappropriate behavior when on-task behavior failed to produce his mother's attention, and inappropriate behavior produced reinforcement on an almost continuous basis. Based on these findings, we taught Mark's mother to provide him with descriptive praise for on-task behaviors on a regularly scheduled basis. This simple manipulation resulted in a substantial and immediate decrease in the frequency of Mark's problem behaviors during the instructional activity.

Martens and Houk (1989) used Herrnstein's (1961) law of effect to evaluate the manner in which an 18-year-old woman with mental retardation allocated her classroom responses from on-task behaviors to disruptive behavior. The authors used naturalistic observations to identify possible functional relations between student (i.e., on-task, disruptive) and teacher behavior (i.e., attention). Findings showed a positive relationship between the student's behavior and contingent teacher attention, and that the student distributed her responding (between on-task and disruptive behavior) to obtain the most reinforcement.

Identify Skills Required for
Successful Functioning in Community Settings

Most of the existing literature on naturalistic observations has focused on socially unacceptable responding as the target behavior. However, naturalistic observations also can be used to obtain information on an individual's socially acceptable behavioral repertoire that may be used for intervention development purposes. For example, naturalistic observations can help a consultant identify a variety of skills required for an individual to successfully function within his or her community. Teaching individuals these requisite skills provides them with a repertoire of socially acceptable behaviors with which to obtain naturally occurring reinforcement and decreases their motivation to engage in problem behavior. For example, Carta, Atwater, Schwartz, and Miller (1990) used the standardized observational codes ESCAPE (Ecobehavioral System for the Complex Assessment of Preschool Environments [Carta, Greenwood, & Atwater, 1985]) to identify structural differences between special preschool and regular kindergarten environments and ACCESS (Assessment Code/Checklist for the Evaluation of Survival Skills [Atwater, Carta, & Schwartz, 1989]) to observe students across three instructional formats to identify the skills critical for success in regular kindergarten settings. The observers recorded data on student activity engagement, teacher prompts, student compliance, teacher feedback to the target student and his or her instructional group, and student requests for assistance. The authors used these data to identify the relationship between teacher and student behaviors that were associated with the greatest levels of student engagement and to teach the students the behaviors that dependably produced reinforcement from others within their environment. These teaching programs facilitated the transitions for students with disabilities from early intervention programs to regular early educational environments.

Identify Individual Styles of Appropriate Behaviors

We have found naturalistic observations to be helpful for identifying a child's idiosyncratic interactional style. Naturalistic observations can provide useful information regarding the manner in which a child initiates interactions with others, requests assistance, requests access to an item or activity, or requests the termination of an activity. During the above situations, a child may give a response that previously has been correlated with reinforcement (e.g., in a different setting, with different individuals), but the individuals in his or her current environment may not be familiar with the child's interactional style and may not respond accordingly. Typically, the child will vary the topography of his or her responding until one form, or a variety of forms, results in the response–reinforcer contingency. Frequently, these "behavioral mutations" are members of a class of socially inappropriate behaviors. By "class," we are referring to different behaviors or different topographies of a behavior that produce the same reinforcer. We use the naturalistic observations to identify problematic situations and the unacceptable behavior and then to select an appropriate response that serves an equivalent function (Carr, 1988). The appropriate response serves as a "replacement" for the problem behavior because it produces the same reinforcer.

In a recent case at the biobehavioral unit, we evaluated and provided an intervention for a 10-year-old boy, Jake, for his severely aggressive behavior. Descriptive assessment data showed that aggression occurred frequently during situations in which Jake's access to a preferred item was restricted (e.g., at meals). During the observations with his parents, we noticed that Jake emitted vocalizations that his parents responded to with praise (e.g., "That's good talking "). Following these vocalizations, Jake frequently reached across the table and attempted to get a specific item. Generally, one of his parents used his or her hands to block Jake's access, which then resulted in Jake aggressing toward the parent and the parent providing Jake with the item. Based on these observations, we consulted with a speech therapist who indicated that Jake's vocalizations appeared to be a basic attempt at pronouncing the item (e.g., "milk").

We developed a procedure to address Jake's problem behaviors, which consisted of teaching him to present the adult with a photograph to request the item, a shaping program (i.e., reinforcing successive approximations of "milk") for his vocalizations, and discontinuing access to the preferred item contingent on problem behavior (i.e., an extinction schedule). Results showed a substantial decrease in the frequency of Jake's aggression with a concurrent increase in his appropriate requests.

In Jake's case, we taught him socially acceptable behaviors to request preferred items during problematic situations. This treatment was effective because: 1) we identified the maintaining variable of Jake's aggression (i.e., access to a preferred item), and 2) we taught Jake a "functionally equivalent" (i.e., produced the same reinforcer) response (i.e., requests).

Identify Variables Involved in Response Efficiency

The approach described above for Jake is referred to as functional equivalence training (Carr, 1988). The rationale for this approach is that the functionally equivalent, socially acceptable behavior will provide the individual with the same reinforcer as the problem behavior and, therefore, decrease the individual's motivation to respond with the unacceptable behavior. For this training approach to be most successful, the appropriate behavior must be as easily produced as the problem behavior (i.e., response effort), must produce reinforcement as frequently as the problem behavior (i.e., schedule of reinforcement), and must produce the reinforcer as quickly as the problem behavior (i.e., immediacy of reinforcement).

Although not based on naturalistic observations, Horner and Day (1991) provided a systematic evaluation of response efficiency in relation to functional equivalence training. The authors first conducted an interview (O'Neill, Horner, Albin, Storey, & Sprague, 1989) with direct-care staff to identify possible maintaining variables to the problem behaviors (i.e., escape from difficult tasks) of three individuals. After the interviews, Horner and Day (1991) examined the individual roles of: 1) physical effort, 2) schedule of reinforcement, and 3) the time delay between the discriminative stimulus and reinforcer delivery on the frequency of the problem behaviors. The results showed that the trained appropriate behaviors did not produce a decrease in the competing behaviors until the appropriate response matched the problem behavior's "efficiency." These findings highlight the importance of identifying not only the possible maintaining variables to problem behaviors, but also their efficiency, which includes the schedules of reinforcement, the immediacy in which they produce reinforcement, and the effort involved in producing these behaviors.

Concerns with Naturalistic Observations

As is clear from the preceding sections, we believe that there are multiple benefits to be derived from naturalistic observations. However, we also acknowledge that there are several important concerns, which can be classified under two broad categories: 1) the type of information obtained, and 2) the complexity of data collection.

Type of Information Obtained

Many of the endeavors using naturalistic observations have been based on the work of Bijou and his colleagues (Bijou et al., 1968; Bijou, Peterson, Harris, Allen, & Johnston, 1969). These authors developed a method for collecting, analyzing, and interpreting data on naturally occurring events in a regular education classroom (i.e., nursery school classroom). The authors collected data on a student's social contacts (appropriate and inappropriate) and sustained activities (i.e., appropriate use of instructional material) during a variety of classroom activities (e.g., art, reading, writing, arithmetic). These data showed the number of occurrences of social interactions during the different situations. Additionally, the authors proposed using these data for normative purposes to compare the student's performance across time (first quarter and last quarter of the school year) and across children (children within and across schools).

The objective of most of the previous studies that have used naturalistic observations has been on the identification of possible functional relations, basically limiting the assessment to one piece of the puzzle. By narrowing our focus in this manner, we fail to take advantage of the wealth of information available regarding the environmental variables that contribute to an individual's responding (either appropriate or inappropriate). In the preceding sections, we described the influence of variables such as schedules of reinforcement, immediacy of reinforcement, response effort, and idiosyncratic interactional styles in the maintenance of problem behavior. The exclusion of this information may adversely influence the effectiveness of our interventions.

An additional caution concerns the nature of the data. Data are typically presented as estimates of conditional probabilities, that is, the likelihood of observing a particular behavior during and after a specific antecedent event. This analysis shows the relative percentages of occurrences of a target behavior across the natural situations. Therefore, these data are not suggestive of functional relations between problem behavior and environmental events. They simply provide the consultant with information regarding the co-occurrence of problem behavior and given environmental events.

Complexity of Observations and Data Analysis

Although we have presented a number of examples concerning the use of naturalistic observations as a preintervention assessment, their widespread use has not been embraced by interventionists (Mace et al., 1991). The obvious reason for infrequent use of naturalistic observations is that they are often impractical. The observation systems are often complex and the results can be difficult to interpret. For this reason, we highlighted their use in the preceding sections within a consultation model; that is, a third party (the interventionist) conducted the observations, analyzed the data, and developed the intervention. If the use of naturalistic observations (or any preintervention assessment procedure) in community-based settings is to become more widespread, a systematic approach to training of caregivers must be undertaken or a method for obtaining trained consultants must be available to practitioners.

To address these concerns, the biobehavioral unit has recently entered into a reciprocal agreement with a service provider, which operates a number of community-based group homes, to provide their staff with training regarding the evaluation and treatment of severe problem behavior. Of specific interest to the service provider is our use of the preintervention assessment procedures (i.e., descriptive and functional analyses). The organization has agreed to send one staff member for training (during a 10-week period) to the biobehavioral unit. The staff member is provided with training on the conceptualization, development, implementation, and evaluation of the preintervention assessments and the intervention components. In return, the unit benefits directly by having a "volunteer" (the staff member is paid by the service provider) for 40 hours per week, and indirectly by disseminating the assessment and intervention methodologies to the community.

In the remaining sections, we provide a model for conducting descriptive analyses. We begin by providing a brief literature review on data-based hypotheses, because we believe that good descriptive analyses must begin with hypotheses and the best hypotheses are empirically derived. To develop hypotheses, the consultant must be familiar with the existing literature.

DATA-BASED HYPOTHESES

A number of investigators have used naturalistic observations to identify the role of environmental variables in the genesis and maintenance of problem behavior. Generally, these variables have been identified to influence an individual's behavior by: 1) positive reinforcement contingencies (i.e., the production of a stimulus), 2) negative reinforcement contingencies (i.e., the removal of a stimulus), or 3) automatic reinforcement contingencies (i.e., sensory stimulation produced by the behavior). In Table 3, examples of these environmental events are provided.

Table 3. Data-based hypotheses identified from naturalistic observations and environmental events typically produced or removed by emission of problem behavior

Hypothesis: Positive reinforcement
  Attention
    adult
    peer
  Tangible
    access to preferred item or activity
    decreased delay between requesting and accessing an item/activity
    regain possession of a previously removed item
  Events produced
    affectionate physical contact (hugs, pats on the back)
    aggression (slaps on the wrist)
    disapproving comments
    descriptive praise
    facial expressions (smiles, frowns, eye contact)
    instructional requests
    neutral comments
    peer interaction (either appropriate or inappropriate)
    access to a preferred activity (watching television)
    access to a preferred item (food, toys, money)

Hypothesis: Negative reinforcement
  Alleviate aversive conditions
  Avoid aversive stimulus altogether
  Prematurely terminate an aversive condition
  Events removed
    activity (academic, personal care, daily living activity)
    physical contact (manual guidance to complete a task)
    sensory stimulation (loud noises, bright lights, hot or cold temperatures)
    task-related materials (worksheets)

Hypothesis: Automatic reinforcement
  Auditory
  Kinesthetic
  Tactile
  Visual
  Events produced
    sounds
    sensation from muscle movement
    sensation produced from different textures
    moving images

Positive Reinforcement

Attention

The absence of adult attention (i.e., the establishing condition of deprivation) has frequently been found to maintain a variety of problem behaviors (see Mace et al., 1991, for a comprehensive review). The establishing condition of attention deprivation is generally assessed by one of two categories: 1) diverted attention—an adult diverts his or her attention from the individual to engage in another activity (e.g., reading a book, watching television, engaging in a household task); and 2) divided attention—the adult's attention is divided between the student and another individual (e.g., another student, sibling, peer). Attention-related situations are observed in order to evaluate a positive-reinforcement hypothesis regarding the problem behavior's operant function.

Carr and McDowell (1980) conducted observations of a 10-year-old child and his parents in their home. The child and his parents were observed across three situations (i.e., play, talk, and television), and data were recorded on the child's self-injurious behavior and the parents' responses to the problem behavior. The results of the observations showed that self-injurious behavior occurred most frequently during low adult, or diverted, attention situations (i.e., television), and that the problem behavior was correlated with some form of parental attention.

Hunt, Alwell, and Goetz (1988) used observation procedures similar to Carr and McDowell's (1980) to intervene in the disruptive behaviors in their classroom setting of three students with severe disabilities. Observations indicated that the students' problem behaviors resulted in some form of intermittent peer and staff attention during situations of divided attention. The students were taught to initiate conversation independently or to answer a question by pointing to a picture in a communication booklet. Results showed a covariation between the problem behavior and the acquired conversation skills; that is, the frequency of the problem behavior decreased as the students acquired conversational skills.

Tangible Reinforcement

The preceding cases described the relationship between the establishing condition of attention deprivation, problem behavior, and attentive reactions from the environment (i.e., vocalizations, physical contact). These relationships also are evident for tangible reinforcement; that is, an individual's problem behavior may be maintained by access to materials or activities that may not be as easily obtained through his or her socially appropriate repertoire. The situations may occur in a variety of ways, including: 1) denied access to a preferred or requested item or activity, 2) removal of an item from an individual that he or she had inappropriately manipulated, or 3) delays between the request and the actual presentation of the requested item.

Koegel, Dyer, and Bell (1987) conducted a series of observations to determine the conditions under which children with autism engaged in inappropriate social behavior. The children were observed during either a child-preferred or an adult-selected activity to evaluate the correlation between the type of activity and the frequency of the problem behaviors. The authors observed the problem behaviors to covary across the type of activity, and the adult-selected activities were correlated with the highest levels of inappropriate behavior. Based on these observations, the authors designed an intervention that consisted of prompting the children to independently initiate child-preferred activities across a variety of settings. Although the children's problem behaviors were conceptualized as avoidance related, the inappropriate behavior also functioned to obtain access to preferred activities because of the corresponding decreases in the levels of inappropriate behavior during the intervention conditions.

Regaining possession of previously removed items generally occurs when a child inappropriately manipulates an item and an adult removes the item from the child's possession. Typically, the child engages in problem behavior, which results in the child regaining possession of the item to "calm" him or her.

We recently observed Mick, a 6-year-old in the biobehavioral unit, engage in aggressive behavior during situations in which he was involved in a recreational activity with his mother. Observations indicated that Mick placed items in his mouth and his mother promptly removed them from his possession. Mick would typically begin to cry, and, if crying failed to produce the item, he would spit at and slap his mother until she provided the removed toy. Based on these observations, we instructed Mick's mother to: 1) provide a statement to Mick describing the inappropriate behavior (e.g., "No putting toys in your mouth") that resulted in toy removal; 2) provide a statement describing the expected appropriate behavior (e.g., "Now, I want you to play with these toys without placing them in your mouth"); and 3) provide a statement describing the consequences for appropriate and inappropriate behavior (e.g., "If you play without placing these toys in your mouth, I will give you the toys to play with. If you place any of these toys in your mouth, I will take them away from you"). Mick's mother then waited 60 seconds, and contingent on appropriate behavior (i.e., a differential reinforcement of other behavior [DRO] schedule), returned the previously removed item to Mick. These procedures effectively decreased Mick's crying and aggression as well as his inappropriate use of the toys.

Another example of problem behavior maintained by tangible reinforcement is of a child requesting an item and being told that there will be a brief period of time before the item can be obtained. Margo, a 10-year-old, was observed to engage in high frequencies (approximately 2,000 per hour) of self-injurious behavior (e.g., blows with her hand to the bridge of her nose) at mealtimes. Observations showed that Margo would sit at the table and request her food while her mother was still preparing the meal. When Margo's mother told her to wait a few minutes, Margo typically engaged in self-injury, which resulted in her mother providing her with crackers before the remaining family members were seated at the table.

Based on these findings, we instructed Margo's mother to discontinue providing the crackers after self-injurious behavior, and to teach Margo to appropriately request the crackers. Additionally, Margo's mother provided her with a preferred toy to manipulate during the delay period and access to the crackers was provided contingent on an appropriate request, appropriate use of the toy (i.e., a differential reinforcement of alternative [DRA] behavior schedule), and the absence of self-injury (DRO schedule). Results indicated a decrease in self-injury and a gradual increase in appropriate toy play and independent requests.

Negative Reinforcement

In addition to positive reinforcement contingencies, inappropriate behavior can be maintained by escape from or avoidance of an aversive stimulus (i.e., negative reinforcement). Demand situations, which usually involve task-related activities, are included in the assessment to evaluate an escape-related hypothesis regarding the problem behavior. Common examples of events removed are provided in Table 3.

Problem behavior may function to remove an already-present aversive stimulus. For example, during a personal care activity, a child may engage in aggressive behavior to terminate the task prematurely. Repp, Felce, and Barton (1988) used naturalistic observations of student–teacher interactions across two classrooms to identify possible functional relations between a student's self-injury and environmental events. During the descriptive assessments, the authors noted a consistent relationship between the student's head-banging and the removal of task-related stimuli. An intervention based on the hypothesis generated from the descriptive data (i.e., escape extinction and compliance training) was implemented in one classroom and compared to a different intervention in a second classroom. Results indicated that the intervention based on the descriptive data was the more effective intervention.

During aversive situations, problem behavior results in obtaining help to complete a task, thus reducing the performance requirements placed on the individual. Mace and Belfiore (1990) conducted naturalistic observations to assess and intervene in a 38-year-old woman's stereotypic responding. Observations were conducted during a variety of activities of daily living in the individual's home. The descriptive data showed that stereotypy was most probable during tasks and that these problem behaviors were intermittently followed by either the discontinuation of the activity or disapproving comments from staff. Based on these observations, the authors proposed two hypotheses regarding the operant function of the client's problem behavior: 1) stereotypy was negatively reinforced by escape from tasks, and 2) stereotypy was positively reinforced by staff's attentive reactions. A subsequent functional analysis supported the escape-from-demands hypothesis.

The researchers in the preceding examples evaluated the effects of staff behavior on the maintenance of individuals' problem behaviors. In contrast, Carr, Taylor, and Robinson (1991) evaluated the effects of students' inappropriate responding on the behavior of classroom teachers. The authors examined the relationship between a teacher's behavior and pairs of students, one of whom engaged in problem behavior and the other who typically did not. The children identified as the problem students generally engaged in aggression, disruption, and self-injury during tasks. Findings showed that the teacher directed instructional activities more frequently to the appropriately behaved children than to the children who engaged in problem behavior. Additionally, the researchers reported that when the teacher engaged in instructional activities with the children who engaged in problem behavior, the activities were those that were typically associated with low levels of problem behavior. The authors suggested that a conceptual analysis of problem behavior be viewed as a reciprocal interaction between the adult and the child.

Automatic Reinforcement

Some socially inappropriate behaviors may be maintained by the automatic sensory consequences produced by the behavior. Lovaas, Newsom, and Hickman (1987) proposed that stereotyped behaviors were a class of operant behaviors maintained by their automatically produced internal or external stimulation (Table 3). Internal stimulation may be in the form of kinesthetic feedback from the trunk and/or vestibular feedback from the ear produced by body-rocking (Lovaas et al., 1987). External stimulation may be in the form of visual feedback from a spinning object or the auditory feedback that results from banging objects against a hard surface (Rincover & Devany, 1982).

Repp, Felce, and Barton (1988) examined the relationship between stereotypy and classroom events for two children. During baseline, data were recorded on the students' stereotypy and on the subsequent environmental events correlated with that behavior for each child in order to develop hypotheses on the likely function of the problem behavior. Baseline data for both children revealed low levels of environmental engagement, and, accordingly, the authors selected a "self-stimulation" hypothesis for the function of these behaviors. The authors developed an intervention based on the self-stimulation hypothesis and compared it to an intervention based on a positive-reinforcement hypothesis (i.e., an extinction schedule for staff responses after problem behavior) for one student and to an intervention based on a negative-reinforcement hypothesis (i.e., never removing the task demand after problem behavior) for the other student. These interventions were implemented across classrooms (i.e., one intervention in each classroom). In both cases, the intervention based on the descriptive data (i.e., self-stimulation hypothesis) resulted in the lower levels of the problem behaviors.

NATURALISTIC OBSERVATION
AS AN ASSESSMENT INSTRUMENT

In the preceding section, we described the most common data-based hypotheses derived through the use of naturalistic observations. In the following section, we discuss what we consider to be the strengths and weaknesses of naturalistic observations as an assessment instrument for each functional category.

Positive Reinforcement

Based on the existing literature, it appears that the role of adult attention in the maintenance of problem behavior is well documented. However, the influence of peer or sibling attention has not been as well established. One factor to consider in studying peer or sibling attention may be the reactivity of the observation system. Peers and siblings may be very aware of unusual activities in their immediate environment and may behave in an "abnormal" manner. In these cases, the consultant must take steps to avoid the problem of reactivity by conducting the observations as unobtrusively as possible.

The contribution of tangible reinforcement to problem behavior also appears to have been neglected. Although there have been a number of studies that provided individuals access to preferred items to decrease the frequency of a problem behavior, few studies have identified the relationship between the establishing condition of deprivation (regarding the preferred item) and an individual's problem behavior. This neglect may result from the fact that the situations involved with tangible reinforcement typically co-occur in the presence of other establishing conditions.

Negative Reinforcement

More attention needs to be focused on the identification of discriminative stimuli that set the occasion for problem behavior. For example, we evaluated and designed an intervention for a 4-year-old's self-injurious behavior, which her mother reported appeared to be escape-motivated. During the observations, the data in the task situations were variable, ranging from 0 to 250 self-injurious behaviors per hour. A close examination of the specific tasks indicated that the higher rates of self-injury occurred during tasks in which the mother physically guided the girl to complete the activity. These observations allowed us to differentiate between the motivational and discriminative functions of environmental stimuli. It was *not* the task in itself that resulted in self-injurious behavior, but the presence of physical contact that signaled to the girl that reinforcement was available (i.e., termination of the task).

Automatic Reinforcement

Most of the work supporting the role of sensory consequences as maintaining variables for problem behavior has been conducted through experimental manipulations (see Lovaas et al., 1987, for a complete review). Based on our work in community settings, it appears to us that the difficulty in isolating the effects of individual establishing conditions (during naturalistic observations) contributes to the scarcity of evidence regarding the influence of automatic reinforcement in the maintenance of problem behavior. In such instances, naturalistic observations may assist the consultant in identifying the topographies of the problem behavior and the specific items used (if any) to test during experimental manipulations.

A PROPOSED MODEL FOR
CONDUCTING THE NATURALISTIC OBSERVATIONS

In this section, we describe the information and the specific procedures that are currently available to conduct direct observations in community settings. In Table 4, we provide a list of these procedures in the order that we use them. For each, we provide a reference supporting the validity of the procedure.

Functional Analysis Interview

Prior to data collection, we interview individuals significant to the student (i.e., parent, teacher, residential staff) following the format described by O'Neill et al. (1989). During the interview (see Table 5 for interview compo-

Table 4. Procedures involved in conducting naturalistic observations in community settings

Functional analysis interview (O'Neill, Horner, Albin, Storey, & Sprague, 1989)

Scatterplot analysis (Touchette, MacDonald, & Langer, 1985)

Training of data collectors

Data collection (Bijou, Peterson, & Ault, 1968)

Data analysis (Bijou, Peterson, & Ault, 1968; Mace, Lalli, & Pinter-Lalli, 1991)

Graphic display of data (Bijou, Peterson, & Ault, 1968; Iwata, Dorsey, Slifer, Bauman, & Richman, 1982; Mace, Lalli, & Pinter-Lalli, 1991)

Hypothesis development (Iwata, Dorsey, Slifer, Bauman, & Richman, 1982; Mace & Lalli, 1991)

Hypothesis testing (Iwata, Dorsey, Slifer, Bauman, & Richman, 1982; Lalli, Browder, Mace, & Brown, in press; Repp, Felce, & Barton, 1988)

Treatment development (Mace & Lalli, 1991)

Treatment implementation and evaluation (Dunlap, Kern-Dunlap, Clarke, & Robbins, 1991; Lalli, Browder, Mace, & Brown, in press; Mace & Lalli, 1991; Repp, Felce, & Barton, 1988; Touchette, MacDonald, & Langer, 1985)

Table 5. Functional analysis interview components

Operational definition of problem behavior
  topography
  frequency
  intensity
  duration

Context in which problem behavior occurs
  time of day
  persons present
  activity

Identify possible function of problem behavior
  antecedent events
  subsequent events

Define the efficiency of the problem behavior
  physical effort involved in producing problem behavior
  immediacy of consequences
  consistency of consequences

Define personalized reinforcers
  activities
  events
  objects

Define functional alternatives
  response modalities
  response topographies

Define the person's communication skills
  expressive
  receptive

Define the history of the problem behavior
  onset of behavior problem
  previous efforts to manage behavior
  current efforts to manage behavior

Adapted from O'Neill, Horner, Albin, Storey, and Sprague (1989).

nents), we ask these individuals to identify the problematic target behaviors and to prioritize these behaviors in order to address those that require immediate remediation. Information on the specific response topographies and on the environmental events that occur prior and subsequent to the problem behavior is also obtained. We also ask the adults to identify any possible establishing conditions and discriminative stimuli associated with the target behaviors. Additionally, we request information on the student's socially acceptable behaviors.

Horner and Day (1991) used this interview format to identify possible hypotheses regarding the operant function of the problem behaviors of three individuals in their community-based residence. The authors then tested these hypotheses in a functional analysis and used the supporting data as the basis for the selection of functionally equivalent behaviors for training.

Scatterplot Analysis

Data is collected using the data sheet in Figure 1 for scatterplot analysis (Touchette, MacDonald, & Langer, 1985) on the target behavior in order to

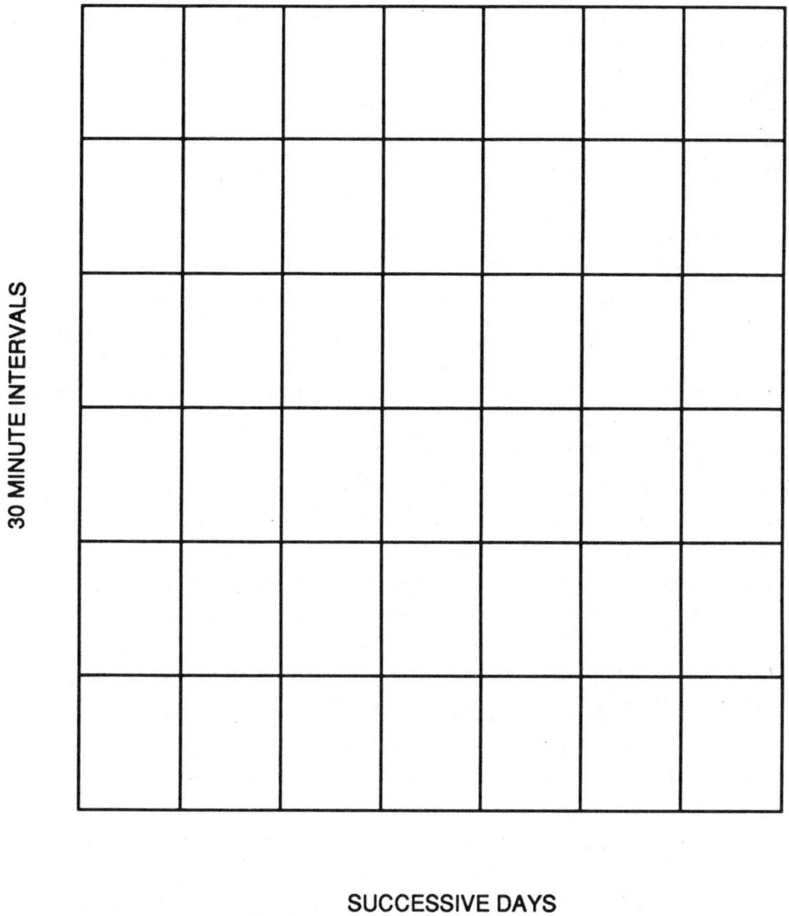

SUCCESSIVE DAYS

Figure 1. Scatterplot grid with each box corresponding to a 30-minute interval on successive days. (Adapted from Touchette, MacDonald, & Langer, 1985.)

identify patterns of responding throughout the day. These response patterns may identify environmental events (e.g., time of day, instructional activity) that are associated with high frequencies of undesirable behavior by a visual analysis of the data. The time periods associated with the highest rates of the problem behavior are selected for observational purposes. Scatterplot data collection generally lasts approximately 1 week, but the length can vary depending on the severity of the target behavior and the resources available in the community setting.

Touchette and colleagues (1985) used a scatterplot analysis to identify environmental variables associated with the aggressive behavior of a 14-year-old in a community-based residence. Data were collected throughout the day by program staff who recorded the number of aggressive behaviors within 30-

minute intervals. A pattern of responding was identified that indicated the most- and least-probable time segments during which aggression occurred. An intervention was designed that incorporated the instructional activities that were correlated with zero-levels of aggression into the time segments correlated with the problematic levels of responding. This intervention resulted in immediate decreases in the targeted behavior within the problematic time intervals. The instructional activities associated with high levels of aggression were gradually reintroduced into the previous time intervals with no increase in the aggressive behavior throughout a 12-month follow-up.

Primarily, a scatterplot analysis is used to identify environmental antecedent events that function as discriminative stimuli for problem behavior. These analyses are used when the problem behavior occurs in short bursts (i.e., constant frequency) and alternates with periods of no problem behavior.

Descriptive Analysis via Direct Observation

After the scatterplot data collection and analysis, we conduct a 1-hour observation of the individual in his or her particular environment to identify and define the specific topographies of the problem behavior. Data are recorded in a narrative manner (Bijou et al., 1968) on the individual's target behavior and on the antecedent and subsequent events of that behavior.

The topographies selected are as general or explicit as the individual analysis requires. For example, the establishing conditions may include general categories such as task-related demands, recreational activities, and low adult attention, or specific as physical guidance (during a task), proximity of others, and the type of attentive comments from others (e.g., instructional requests, disapproving comments, questions).

Data on the response class can be recorded collectively, for example, self-injury that includes hand-biting, head-banging, and face-slapping, or recorded individually across the respective topographies. We find it most beneficial to record data on the individual topographies in order to determine if each topography is a member of the same response class. However, recording the data this way is less practical than recording the data in a collective manner. Data on the individual's appropriate behaviors such as requests and social initiations are also collected with the respective topographies of appropriate behaviors, depending on the individual's method of interaction.

Graphic Display of Data and Hypothesis Formulation

The objective of a descriptive analysis is to identify the natural covariation between the problem behavior and environmental events occurring prior to and subsequent to the problem behavior. Therefore, we find it useful to graph the descriptive data in a multi-element fashion (Mace et al., 1991). In a multi-element design, the individual is exposed to multiple experimental manipulations (in this case, different contingencies for problem behavior) in rapid succession during a single experimental phase (Sidman, 1960). Support for hypotheses regarding functional relations are based on behavior stabilizing in the presence of the respective contingencies. Graphing the data in this manner shows the association of the target behavior with specific environmental establishing conditions and the variability of the target behavior over time. Two case studies (Lalli et al., in press) are presented in Figures 2 and 3, which provide a model for the graphic display of data. Figure 2 presents a positive reinforcement paradigm, and Figure 3 depicts a negative reinforcement paradigm.

Figure 2 shows the relationship between Mary's self-injurious behavior (i.e., scratching) and various environmental events. The top part of Figure 2 shows the probability of observing Mary's self-injury during different establishing conditions. This analysis indicates that Mary engaged in self-injurious behavior most frequently during situations of low adult attention. In contrast, Mary engaged in self-injurious behavior infrequently during conditions in which she had access to the staff's attention on an individual basis.

We also find it useful to analyze and graphically display the percent of target behaviors followed by each environmental event. This analysis may identify events that naturally follow the target behavior and that may be a possible consequence of that response. The middle and bottom segments of Figure 2 depict the probability of observing a specific environmental event contiguous to the occurrence of self-injurious behavior (i.e., within 20 seconds of the behavior) during a particular establishing condition. These two analyses were conducted to evaluate if Mary's target behavior was naturally followed by attentive reactions from the staff. This relationship would be expected if self-injurious behavior were positively reinforced by social interaction. Analyzed collectively, these relationships suggest an attention hypothesis for Mary's self-injurious behavior.

Figure 3 presents two analyses of Al's descriptive data. The upper portion shows the probability of observing Al's targeted behavior during various establishing conditions. These data indicate that Al's self-injurious behavior occurred exclusively during transitions between his regular and special education classrooms.

The bottom portion of Figure 3 reflects the percent of self-injurious responses that occurred during classroom transitions that were naturally followed by either attentive reactions from the teacher or interruptions in the transitional process. This analysis was conducted to examine whether transition interruption naturally followed self-injurious behavior, a relation that would be expected if self-injurious behavior were negatively reinforced by escape from task-related demands. The data show that transitional activities were frequently interrupted during and following Al's self-injurious episodes and that these self-injurious behaviors were also followed by attentive reactions from staff. Based on these analyses, two hypotheses were proposed for

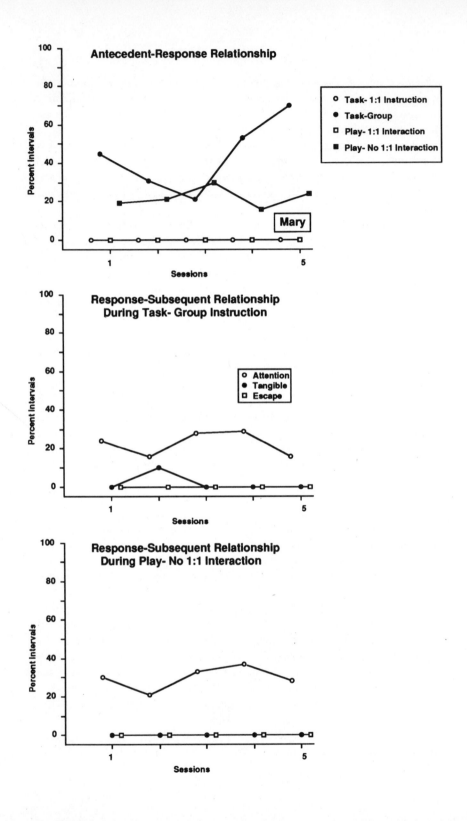

Al's targeted behavior: 1) self-injurious behavior was negatively reinforced by the delay in the presentation of aversive stimuli (i.e., the return to the special education classroom), and 2) self-injurious behavior was positively reinforced by the attentive reactions from others.

Hypotheses Testing and Treatment Development

The descriptive data presented in Figures 2 and 3 indicate the likelihood of observing a problem behavior during a specific establishing condition or during an environmental event contiguous to the problem behavior. These data are only suggestive of possible functional relations and, therefore, experimental methods are required to verify these relations. The experimental methods may be direct assessment through a functional analysis under analog conditions, or indirect assessment through the evaluation of the treatment effects on the problem behavior.

Data obtained in the descriptive analysis of Mary's self-injurious behavior suggested that the behavior was maintained by her teacher's attentive reactions during periods when Mary did not have individualized attention. Based on an attention hypothesis, the authors developed two interventions for Mary's problem behavior. The first intervention was designed to weaken the response–reinforcer relationship by providing response-independent reinforcement (i.e., attention) through a differential reinforcement of alternative behavior schedule (DRA) while concurrently discontinuing attention contingent on self-injurious behavior (i.e., an extinction schedule). The second intervention consisted of teaching Mary an adaptive verbal response that was functionally equivalent to her targeted behavior (i.e., produced the same reinforcer).

The results of the descriptive analysis for Al suggested that the operant function of his self-injurious behavior was either negative reinforcement through the delay in the presentation of aversive stimuli, or positive reinforcement by the attentive reactions from the teacher. Based on this information, the authors designed two interventions to decrease the frequency of Al's self-injurious behavior during the transitions between classrooms. The first intervention consisted of providing Al with attention through the use of a DRA procedure and an extinction schedule for the targeted behavior. The extinction schedule consisted of discontinuing attentive comments and using a guided compliance procedure to prevent transition interruptions contingent on self-injurious behavior. The second intervention focused on teaching Al an adaptive verbal response that was functionally related to his self-injurious behavior. Given that this behavior occurred at the conclusion of an activity in which

Figure 2. Positive reinforcement paradigm. Results of the descriptive analysis of Mary's self-injurious behavior. Percent intervals of self-injurious behavior during four antecedent situations (top). Percent intervals of subsequent events observed within 20 seconds of self-injurious behavior during task-group instruction situation (middle), and during play—no one-to-one interaction situation (bottom). Ordinate = percent intervals, abscissa = sessions. (Adapted from Lalli, Browder, Mace, & Brown, in press.)

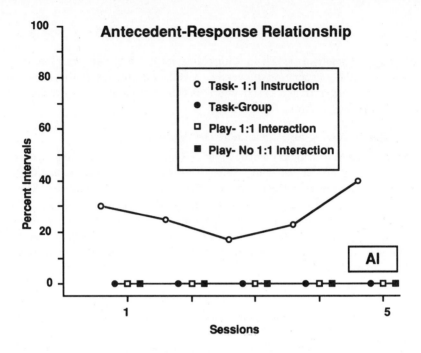

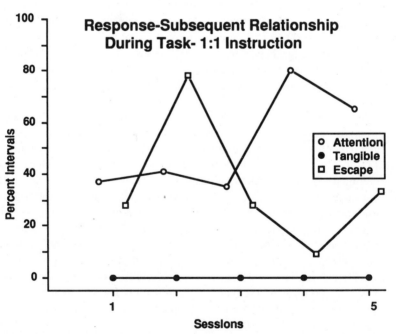

Figure 3. Negative reinforcement paradigm. Results of the descriptive analysis of Al's self-injurious behavior. Percent intervals of self-injurious behavior during four antecedent situations (top). Percent intervals of subsequent events observed with 20 seconds of self-injurious behavior during task—one-to-one instruction situations (bottom). Ordinate = percent intervals, abscissa = sessions. (Adapted from Lalli, Browder, Mace, & Brown, in press.)

Al participated (e.g., gym class, arts and crafts, recess, music), and during the return to his special education classroom, Al learned to select his next instructional activity in the special education class by pointing to a photograph in a picture booklet.

CONCLUSION

This chapter describes the conceptual basis of naturalistic observations, the types of information obtained from naturalistic observations, the hypotheses developed through their use, and a model for use in community settings. Descriptive analyses have been used to identify possible functional relations between socially appropriate and inappropriate behaviors and environmental events. Findings have implicated the role of attention, access to preferred items, escape from task-related activities, and automatic reinforcement in the maintenance of problem behavior. As shown in the final two individual cases, descriptive, naturalistic observations often can lead to testable hypotheses, making the subsequent functional analysis more efficient. However, a comprehensive descriptive analysis is very complex both conceptually and practically. We offer our specific version of the descriptive assessment to highlight both the complexity and the ability to obtain a variety of information.

REFERENCES

Atwater, J.B., Carta, J.J., & Schwartz, I.S. (1989). *Assessment code/checklist for the evaluation of survival skills: ACCESS.* Kansas City: Juniper Gardens Children's Project, Bureau of Child Research, University of Kansas.

Ayllon, T., & Michael, J. (1959). The psychiatric nurse as a behavioral engineer. *Journal of the Experimental Analysis of Behavior, 2,* 323–334.

Bijou, S.W., Peterson, R.F., & Ault, M.H. (1968). A method to integrate descriptive and experimental field studies at the level of data and empirical concepts. *Journal of Applied Behavior Analysis, 1,* 175–191.

Bijou, S.W., Peterson, R.F., Harris, F.R., Allen, E., & Johnston, M.S. (1969). Methodology for experimental studies of young children in natural settings. *Psychological Record, 19,* 177–210.

Carr, E.G. (1988). Functional equivalence as a mechanism of response generalization. In R.H. Horner, R.L. Koegel, & G. Dunlap (Eds.), *Generalization and maintenance: Life-style changes in applied settings* (pp. 221–241). Baltimore: Paul H. Brookes Publishing Co.

Carr, E.G., & McDowell, J.J. (1980). Social control of self-injurious behavior of organic etiology. *Behavior Therapy, 11,* 402–409.

Carr, E.G., Taylor, J.C., & Robinson, S. (1991). The effects of severe behavior problems in children on the teaching behavior of adults. *Journal of Applied Behavior Analysis, 24,* 523–535.

Carta, J.J., Atwater, J.B., Schwartz, I.S., & Miller, P.A. (1990). Applications of ecobehavioral analysis to the study of transitions across early education settings. *Education and Treatment of Children, 13,* 298–315.

Carta, J.J., Greenwood, C.R., & Atwater, J.B. (1985). *Ecobehavioral system for the complex assessment of preschool environments: ESCAPE.* Kansas City: Juniper Gardens Children's Project, Bureau of Child Research, University of Kansas.

Catania, A.C. (1984). *Learning* (2nd ed.). Englewood Cliffs, NJ: Prentice Hall.

Dunlap, G., Kern-Dunlap, L., Clarke, M., & Robbins, F.R. (1991). Functional assessment, curricular revision, and severe behavior problems. *Journal of Applied Behavior Analysis, 24,* 387–397.

Epstein, L.H., Parker, L., McCoy, J.F., & McGee, G. (1976). Descriptive analysis of eating regulation in obese and nonobese children. *Journal of Applied Behavior Analysis, 9,* 407–415.

Geller, E.S., Russ, N.W., & Altomari, M.G. (1986). Naturalistic observations of beer drinking among college students. *Journal of Applied Behavior Analysis, 19,* 391–396.

Herrnstein, R.J. (1961). Relative and absolute strength of response as a function of reinforcement. *Journal of the Experimental Analysis of Behavior, 4,* 267–272.

Horner, R.H., & Day, H.M. (1991). The effects of response efficiency on functionally equivalent competing behaviors. *Journal of Applied Behavior Analysis, 24,* 719–732.

Hunt, P., Alwell, M., & Goetz, L. (1988). Acquisition of conversation skills and the reduction of inappropriate social interaction behaviors. *Journal of The Association for Persons with Severe Handicaps, 13,* 20–27.

Iwata, B., Dorsey, M., Slifer, K., Bauman, K., & Richman, G. (1982). Toward a functional analysis of self-injury. *Analysis and Intervention in Developmental Disabilities, 2,* 3–20.

Koegel, R.L., Dyer, K., & Bell, L.K. (1987). The influence of child-preferred activities on autistic children's social behavior. *Journal of Applied Behavior Analysis, 20,* 243–252.

Lalli, J.S., Browder, D.M., Mace, F.C., & Brown, D.K. (in press). Teacher use of descriptive analysis data to implement interventions to decrease students' problem behaviors. *Journal of Applied Behavior Analysis.*

Lalli, J.S., Pinter-Lalli, E., Mace, F.C., & Murphy, D.M. (1991). Training interactional behaviors of adults with developmental disabilities: A systematic replication and extension. *Journal of Applied Behavior Analysis, 24,* 167–174.

Lovaas, I., Newsom, C., & Hickman, C. (1987). Self-stimulatory behavior and perceptual reinforcement. *Journal of Applied Behavior Analysis, 20,* 45–68.

Mace, F.C., & Belfiore, P. (1990). Behavioral momentum in the treatment of escape-motivated stereotypy. *Journal of Applied Behavior Analysis, 23,* 507–514.

Mace, F.C., & Knight, D. (1986). Functional analysis and treatment of severe pica. *Journal of Applied Behavior Analysis, 19,* 411–416.

Mace, F.C., & Lalli, J.S. (1991). Linking descriptive and experimental analysis in the treatment of bizarre speech. *Journal of Applied Behavior Analysis, 24,* 553–562.

Mace, F.C., Lalli, J.S., & Pinter-Lalli, E. (1991). Functional analysis and treatment of aberrant behavior. *Research in Developmental Disabilities, 12,* 155–180.

Martens, B.K., & Houk, J.L. (1989). The application of Herrnstein's law of effect to disruptive and on-task behavior of a retarded adolescent girl. *Journal of the Experimental Analysis of Behavior, 51,* 17–28.

Michael, J. (1982). Distinguishing between discriminative and motivational functions of stimuli. *Journal of the Experimental Analysis of Behavior, 37,* 149–155.

O'Neill, R.E., Horner, R.H., Albin, R.W., Storey, K., & Sprague, J.R. (1989). The functional analysis interview. In R.H. Horner, J.L. Anderson, E.G. Carr, G. Dunlap, R.L. Koegel, & W. Sailor (Eds.), *Functional analysis: A practical assessment guide* (pp. 10–23). Eugene: University of Oregon Press.

Repp, A.C., Felce, D., & Barton, L.E. (1988). Basing the treatment of stereotypic and self-injurious behaviors on hypotheses of their causes. *Journal of Applied Behavior Analysis, 21,* 281–289.

Rincover, A., & Devany, J. (1982). The application of sensory extinction procedures to self-injury. *Analysis and Intervention in Developmental Disabilities, 2,* 67–81.

Sidman, M. (1960). *Tactics of scientific research evaluating experimental data in psychology.* Boston: Authors Cooperative.

Steege, M.W., Wacker, D.P., Berg, D.P., Cigrand, K.K., & Cooper, L.J. (1989). The use of behavioral assessment to prescribe and evaluate treatments for severely handicapped children. *Journal of Applied Behavior Analysis, 22,* 23–33.

Touchette, P.E., MacDonald, R.F., & Langer, S.N. (1985). A scatter plot for identifying stimulus control of problem behavior. *Journal of Applied Behavior Analysis, 18,* 343–351.

3

Extending Functional Analysis Procedures to Outpatient and Classroom Settings for Children with Mild Disabilities

Linda J. Cooper and Jay Harding

A GREAT DEAL OF RESEARCH, some of which is summarized in the chapters of this book (i.e., see chap. 2, this volume) has demonstrated that the *function* of behavior is more important than its form in the intervention of behavior problems. Given this finding, effective intervention is, initially, an assessment problem. To develop an effective intervention, we must first identify what function the problem behavior serves for the individual. To identify the function, the best approach is to conduct a functional analysis (Iwata, Dorsey, Slifer, Bauman, & Richman, 1982), which involves the direct observation of target behavior under different environmental conditions. Only when the function has been identified can we develop an effective intervention. In this case, function refers to what reinforces the behavior (Berg & Wacker, 1991).

The next step of intervention is to use the results of the functional analysis to withhold the reinforcers for problem behavior and to make the delivery of reinforcers contingent upon more appropriate behavior. Iwata, Pace, Kalsher, Cowdery, and Cataldo (1990) referred to this approach as matching the intervention to the function of behavior.

A good example of this approach is described in a recent study by Iwata et al. (1990). In the functional analysis, each participant was exposed to a series of analog conditions (environmental situations that simulated or represented naturally occurring environmental events) to identify variables maintaining (reinforcing) problem behavior (hand-biting, face-slapping, head-banging). The results of the functional analysis procedures indicated that each participant engaged in the problem behavior to avoid or escape aversive events (e.g., educational tasks). Thus, the motivation for problem behavior was negative reinforcement. Treatment involved escape extinction (i.e., not allowing the individuals to avoid the tasks after displays of problem behavior) *and* permitting escape contingent upon appropriate behavior (i.e., compliance with the task demands). By identifying the motivation for problem behavior, the investigators developed an intervention to remove all motivation for problem behavior and maximize reinforcement for the desired response. Relatively quick and effective results were achieved.

Another example of matching intervention to the results of a functional analysis was provided by Wacker, Steege, Northup, Sasso, et al. (1990). The results of a functional analysis for one participant in this study suggested that hand-biting occurred to gain access to a preferred tangible item. Intervention consisted of providing access to the tangible item contingent upon use of a mand to request it, but time-out (removal of the item) occurred for hand-biting. As shown in these two examples, the investigators matched the intervention to the function of the problem behavior by withholding the identified reinforcers for the problem behavior and providing them contingently for alternative behavior.

Similar results have been achieved for a wide variety of behavior problems, including self-injury, aggression, destruction, reluctant speech, pica, and stereotypy (see Mace, Lalli, & Lalli, 1991, for a comprehensive review). The overall results strongly suggest that the function of problem behavior is more important than the form it takes. Given this supposition, functional analysis procedures should be applicable across virtually all forms of problem behavior and across all groups of children. The procedures should be as viable for children with mild disabilities (i.e., children with mild mental retardation, average abilities and emotional disabilities, or learning disorders) who tantrum or who are noncompliant, as with children who have severe disabilities. Furthermore, given that effective intervention begins with a functional analysis, it is critical that these procedures be used in settings other than inpatient units so that more children can receive this type of assessment. For children with mild disabilities, the most common settings for assessment and intervention are outpatient clinics and classrooms.

The purpose of this chapter is to discuss recent research with functional analysis procedures that has been conducted in outpatient and classroom settings with children with mild disabilities. We provide a brief overview of previous research involving functional analyses with persons who have severe disabilities to point out the conceptual basis of our current work in outpatient settings and with children with mild disabilities. We next discuss how functional analysis procedures can be blended with descriptive assessments when the intervention setting is the classroom. Finally, we provide an overview of our research that extends these procedures to classroom settings.

PREVIOUS RESEARCH ON FUNCTIONAL ANALYSES

Extended Functional Analysis

Iwata et al. (1982) developed the first systematic operant method to analyze environmental variables affecting self-injurious behavior (SIB). The study included nine individuals with developmental delays who ranged in chronological age from 3 to 17 years and who displayed moderate to high rates of SIB. The individuals were exposed to four analog conditions that consisted of the manipulation of antecedent and consequent events to determine which variables maintained SIB. In the "social disapproval" condition, individuals were allowed to play with toys, and attention was given to them contingent upon each episode of SIB (e.g., "Don't do that"); thus, positive reinforcement (i.e., social attention) was provided for each occurrence of SIB. In the "academic demand" condition, individuals were given difficult educational activities. Each time self-injurious behavior occurred, the trial was terminated and the individual was turned away from the task, thus providing negative reinforcement (i.e., escape) for the occurrence of problem behavior. The "unstructured play" condition consisted of praise and physical contact contingent on the display of appropriate play behavior by the individual, thus providing reinforcement only for the occurrence of the appropriate behavior. The play condition served as a control for the disapproval and escape conditions because no demands were placed on the individual and attention was differentially applied for playing. In the "alone" condition, which represented an impoverished environment, subjects had no access to toys, no demands were made, and SIB was ignored. Each of these four conditions was repeated until a stable pattern of problem behavior occurred. If SIB occurred primarily in the disapproval conditions, it was likely maintained by positive reinforcement, whereas if it occurred most often in the demand conditions, it was probably maintained by negative reinforcement. If it occurred only in the alone condition, or occurred in an undifferentiated manner across all assessment conditions, it probably served an automatic function. Different functions were reliably identified for six of the nine individuals, demonstrating that SIB was maintained by different sources of reinforcement for each; thus, knowledge of the diagnosis and type of problem behavior was irrelevant for identifying effective intervention.

Carr and Durand (1985) used a slightly different type of functional analysis with four children with developmental disabilities who displayed aggressive or destructive behavior. As with Iwata et al. (1982), results demonstrated that, although the children displayed similar behaviors, they occurred for different reasons (positive or negative reinforcement), showing, again, that function is more important than form with different topographies of problem behavior. Intervention was initiated that involved teaching the children mands to obtain the same reinforcement (i.e., to solicit praise or assistance with a task) that was identified as maintaining the problem behavior, and the problem behavior decreased substantially.

The studies by Carr and Durand (1985) and Iwata et al. (1982) are, perhaps, the two "classic" studies in functional analysis. They demonstrated that problem behavior displayed by persons with severe disabilities is often responsive to the environment and that these environmental influences can be assessed in a systematic and valid manner. Although there are several minor differences in how the functional analyses were conducted, both studies used extended periods of direct observation conducted within single-case experimental designs, focused on severe behavior problems with individuals with severe disabilities, and were conducted in highly controlled settings. These studies formed the basis on which virtually all subsequent studies were conducted, but left open questions about the generality of the procedures to other settings and children.

Applications to Outpatient Clinics and Classroom Settings for Persons with Severe Disabilities

Recently, researchers have demonstrated that functional analyses can be conducted successfully in alternative settings such as outpatient clinics and classrooms for persons with severe disabilities. The first of these extensions was reported by Northup et al. (1991), who modified the procedures to fit the time constraints of an outpatient clinic (see Wacker, Steege, Northup, Reimers, et al., 1990, for a description of the clinic). The focus of the clinic was the evaluation of self-injury and aggression displayed by individuals with severe disabilities. In the Northup et al. (1991) study, a "brief functional analysis" of aggression was completed within 90 minutes (instead of several days) using assessment conditions described by Carr and Durand (1985) and Iwata et al. (1982). Due to time limitations, single data points were obtained for each 10-minute assessment condition rather than obtaining multiple data points over several days. Control over target behavior was demonstrated by rapidly alternating the assessment conditions to produce differing frequencies of the aggression.

To partially replicate these findings, Northup and colleagues (1991) demonstrated the generality of the procedures across target behaviors to include appropriate as well as aggressive behavior. This was accomplished through the addition of a "contingency reversal" phase during assessment. When a maintaining condition was identified, a second phase was conducted for each individual assessed to see if this same condition could be used to increase an appropriate mand. For example, the results of the brief functional analysis suggested that one individual's aggression was maintained by social attention. After the functional analysis, attention was provided differentially for an appropriate mand ("Come here please"), and aggression was ignored. Aggression decreased as manding increased, thus demonstrating that the contingencies identified as maintaining aggressive behavior also served to reinforce a functionally equivalent mand. Similar results occurred for the other two participants who displayed aggression for different functions.

Derby et al. (1992) recently conducted a retrospective analysis of 79 individuals evaluated in an outpatient clinic using the brief functional analysis. The individuals ranged in age from 1 to 32 years, were diagnosed as having mild to profound disabilities, and exhibited virtually all forms of problem behaviors (i.e., self-injurious behavior, aggression, stereotypy). Results such as those achieved by Northup et al. (1991) occurred more than 50% of the time, with the major limiting factor being that a large percentage of the individuals (37%) did not display problem behavior in the clinic. For those who did display problem behavior, a maintaining condition was identified for 74%. These results suggest that even under the severe restrictions of an outpatient clinic, brief functional analysis procedures are often effective in identifying maintaining events and are thus useful for developing treatments.

A study by Northup, Wacker, Berg, Kelly, and Fus (1990) demonstrated that the brief functional analysis procedure can also be used by teachers in classroom settings with students with severe disabilities. Five teachers were trained to use the procedures and to develop interventions based on the results of the analyses for children who displayed severe self-injurious or aggressive behavior. Videotaped probes of the treatments were conducted weekly for over 1 year, with results showing that effective intervention occurred for four of five children. Of importance was that the teachers conducted most or all of the assessments and interventions, with only biweekly consultation from "experts."

Taken as a whole, the results by Derby et al. (1992) and Northup et al. (1990, 1991) show that the extended functional analyses developed by Carr and Durand (1985) and Iwata and colleagues (1982) can be modified for effective use in outpatient clinics and classrooms for persons with severe disabilities. These studies supported our belief that similar methods could be used in similar settings with children who have mild disabilities. In applying this technology, we also believed that the descriptive assessment models developed by other researchers would be beneficial, and, thus, we sought to blend descriptive assessments with functional analyses.

BLENDING FUNCTIONAL ANALYSIS AND
DESCRIPTIVE ASSESSMENT IN CLASSROOM SETTINGS

As described previously, one of the benefits of using a functional analysis approach is that it can greatly facilitate the identification of the maintaining contingencies of aberrant behavior because environmental variables are directly and systematically manipulated. However, the variables that might be selected for evaluation are numerous, and it is pragmatically impossible to include all potential antecedent and consequent events that might influence behavior. In the classroom, there are a number of continually changing variables (e.g., peers, tasks). Analog conditions allow an approximation of controlling variables but typically identify only classes of reinforcers that may serve to maintain the problem behavior. Some variables are extremely difficult to simulate (e.g., establishing operations such as fighting with a peer [Michael, 1982]), and others might never occur to us, such as "rules" of behavior taught at home. Thus, one difficulty is the identification of specific variables to be included in the assessment process.

In addition, a number of intervention variations are possible within each class of reinforcement. For example, if a problem behavior is maintained by negative reinforcement, intervention might include teaching the child how to produce a more appropriate escape response (e.g., Carr & Durand, 1985), extinction of inappropriate behavior (Iwata et al., 1990), or extinction plus access to preferred activities contingent on appropriate behavior (Steege, Wacker, Berg, Cigrand, & Cooper, 1989). Alternatively, if behavior problems are maintained by positive reinforcement, interventions might include time-out from reinforcement (Mace, Page, Ivancic, & O'Brien, 1986), extinction, or teaching mands to gain access to attention or desired activities (Carr & Durand, 1985). Therefore, a second difficulty is the identification of a very specific intervention strategy from the large number of available options.

One general assessment strategy that appears to be useful to specify variables is to use descriptive analyses to identify variables that appear to influence behavior (are correlated with behavior) and then to conduct a more precise, functional analysis of controlling variables (Bijou, Peterson, & Ault, 1968; Mace et al., 1991). Descriptive analyses provide observational data on the child's behavior in relation to naturally occurring events in the environment (Bijou et al., 1968). Preliminary observations and caregiver reports often serve to focus the subsequent functional analysis by providing information that *suggests* that the occurrence of behavior is *related* to particular environmental conditions. However, because descriptive assessments are correlational, they must be followed by an experimental (functional) analysis.

A variety of methodologies (e.g., scatterplot, antecedent-behavior-consequence assessment) have been suggested to establish hypothesized relations between problem behavior and naturally occurring environmental antecedents and consequences. In an antecedent-behavior-consequence assessment (A-B-C) (Bijou et al., 1968), descriptive accounts of observed behavior are recorded as well as temporally related environmental events. A scatterplot involves plotting occurrences of the target behavior against time of day across consecutive days (Touchette, MacDonald, & Langer, 1985). The resulting data may be expressed as correlational coefficients, as a proportion of responses that occur in relation to different environmental events, or, our preference, as a graphic display to illustrate the variability of behavior in relation to the environmental events (Mace & Shea, 1990).

Descriptive analyses may be useful in classrooms to the extent that they provide an empirical basis for hypothesized functional relations between behavior and the environment, but may in fact generate multiple hypotheses regarding the variables that appear to be controlling behavior (Mace & Lalli, 1991). For example, a descriptive analysis may show that problem behavior occurs most often during a teacher-led group activity. Although this information is helpful in directing examiner attention to a particular event, it remains unclear which components of the event are actually operating to prompt or maintain the problem behavior. Potential variables might include the student's preference for the activity, the presence of one or more peers, and the type and frequency of teacher responses to the child's behavior.

Dunlap, Dunlap, Clarke, and Robbins (1991) demonstrated the utility of combining descriptive and functional analysis procedures in a classroom setting for a student with mild disabilities by using a hypothesis-testing approach (Repp, Felce, & Barton, 1988). The student was evaluated in her special education classroom, and initial hypotheses about curriculum variables thought to influence the student's disruptive behavior were formulated based on descriptive data (interviews, rating scales, observations, and questionnaires). The hypothesized variables included the type of motor activity required, duration of the task, outcome of the task, and choice of the task. Each variable was evaluated using functional analysis procedures. An effective intervention was implemented based on the results of the functional analysis and included using tasks of short duration that led to concrete, preferred outcomes; interspersing fine and gross motor activities; and using a menu of activities and materials from which the student could choose. This example shows how specific the interventions can be when descriptive assessments are blended with functional analyses.

More general approaches, such as scatterplot assessments, provide a narrow range of information, thus limiting their utility as an assessment device. More complex forms of descriptive assessment, such as the A-B-C assessment (Bijou et al., 1968), might appear preferable in that they provide more extensive data on observed behavior and environmental correlates. However, an A-B-C assessment has certain practical limitations. First, continuous recording can be a tedious and time-consuming procedure. Second, it may be difficult to sort out the multiple variables that can, and do, occur simultaneously during an observation session. Finally, the results may not readily provide empirical data that can be used directly during the subsequent functional analysis. These limitations underscore the need for descriptive assessment procedures that have demonstrated utility but are reasonably simple to use and provide empirical data.

One potential solution is the preselection of environmental variables and activities to be recorded during the descriptive assessment. Prior selection of variables enables examiners to more efficiently collect empirical data regarding the influence of these variables on the occurrence of designated child behaviors. In our experience, when teachers refer children for classroom behavior problems, a common concern is the "amount of time" they spend in addressing the child's behavior. A second concern is that, despite their intervention efforts, "nothing seems to work." These may or may not be accurate assessments, but they do reflect the perceptions of the teachers. With students with mild disabilities, behavior is rarely problematic 100% of the time. A reasonable assumption, therefore, is that certain classroom conditions (i.e., teacher interventions) are effective in controlling and maintaining appropriate behavior, but they are used too infrequently to be so identified by the teacher. Thus, conceptualizing various teacher behaviors as "intervention components" and evaluating the relationship between these teacher variables and child behavior would appear to be a useful method of generating hypotheses regarding naturally occurring conditions that control and maintain appropriate child behavior. A modified version of the A-B-C assessment (Bijou et al., 1968) could be used to identify the correlation between these preselected teacher variables and student behavior, which would be followed by a brief functional analysis to better confirm these relations.

USE OF DESCRIPTIVE ASSESSMENT AND FUNCTIONAL ANALYSIS PROCEDURES FOR CHILDREN WITH MILD DISABILITIES

The previous research conducted with extended and brief functional analyses and descriptive assessments provided the empirical and conceptual basis we used to extend these procedures to children with mild disabilities. Our intent was to develop assessment procedures that are applicable to both outpatient and classroom situations and to children diagnosed with mental retardation, emotional disabilities, and learning disorders who displayed behavior problems at home or school. We provide examples of our approach with two groups of children: elementary-age children (Cooper, Wacker, Sasso, Reimers, & Donn, 1990; Cooper et al., 1992) and preschool/kindergarten-age children (Harding et al., 1991).

Outpatient Evaluations

Initially, we used functional analysis procedures with children of average intellectual abilities who were referred to the Behavior Management Clinic. The Behavior Management Clinic is a multidisciplinary clinic in the Department of Pediatrics at the University of Iowa Hospitals and Clinics, and services are provided for a number of behavior problems including noncompliance, tantrums, and hyperactivity. Following an evaluation by each discipline (medicine, psychology, speech and hearing), a staff meeting is held and recommendations are developed for families to carry out. In our first study, we evaluated children who displayed problem behaviors at home (Cooper et al., 1990). Similar to Northup et al. (1991), we conducted brief functional analyses in the outpatient clinic, but we included several differences. We conducted the study with eight children (ages 4–9) of average intellectual abilities. The children's parents conducted the assessments with our "coaching," and the focus of the assessment was the identification of the maintaining conditions for appropriate, rather than inappropriate, behavior. The assessment was completed within 2 hours. Assessment conditions lasted 5–10 minutes and consisted of having the parents vary the difficulty of task demands (easy or difficult) and the amount of attention given (attention or ignore) within a multielement design in order to identify which conditions resulted in the best behavior. Each child was exposed to all combinations of independent variables, with replication of the best and worst assessment conditions on a second task. Results showed unique patterns of responding for seven of the eight children relative to the best condition. Appropriate behavior varied as a function of both task demand and parental attention and was not predictable given the history, diagnosis, or other demographic characteristics of the children. A brief functional analysis was needed to identify how to best improve appropriate behavior.

In a second investigation (Cooper et al., 1992), we extended our previous findings by directly assessing the role of task preference, as well as task demand and parent attention, on appropriate behavior in the outpatient clinic. Given that the children in the study demonstrated good oral communication skills, task preference was assessed by presenting each child with eight groups of three academic tasks and asking the child which he or she would most/least like to do; this appeared to be an efficient way for the child to select a preferred task relative to other tasks. The study was conducted with 10 children (ages 6–14 years) who displayed behavior problems at home and/or school. As with our previous study, the assessment was conducted during a 90-minute outpatient evaluation, it focused on appropriate child behavior, and parents conducted the assessment; however, rather than exposing every child to all possible independent variables, we used a hierarchy of assessment conditions (each approximately 10 minutes) to facilitate the assessment and social validity (Kazdin, 1982) of the recommended interventions. Rather than asking parents to assess all possible conditions, we initially assessed variables that appeared easiest to implement at home. The effects of task preferences were assessed first because it was hypothesized that a change in this variable would be easier to implement in natural settings than either task demands (which require a change in instructional level) or adult attention (which requires more constant monitoring of child behavior). The effects of task demands were assessed next because, as with task preference, intervention involved a manipulation of the task itself rather than of adult behavior. Finally, manipulation of the level of adult attention was conducted. The three variables were sequentially "added into" the assessment until the child's behavior improved. Once improvement occurred, a less effective condition and a second assessment with the more effective condition were conducted as a "minireversal" to demonstrate adequate control over behavior.

The results, again, showed that different patterns of behavior occurred across assessment conditions for 8 of the 10 children, with the children's appropriate behavior varying as a function of unique combinations of treatment variables (preference, demands, or attention). This study showed that a larger number of independent variables could be assessed in addition to the variables typically assessed (demand, attention) in studies of functional analyses. This approach appeared desirable to us because we wanted the assessment results to generate specific recommendations.

Given that interventions with behavior problems are typically composed of multicomponent intervention packages, it makes intuitive sense that if assessments, even brief assessments, can incorporate as many variables as possible, the greater the specificity of our recommended interventions will be. However, as we expand the number of variables assessed, we have more problems with time restrictions in the clinic, and the assessment is more complex for parents to conduct. We continued to want the parents to conduct the assessments, because children often responded differently with their families than with us.

We decided that a partial solution to this problem involved conducting subsequent assessments in a hierarchical manner and conducting immediate reversals whenever an effective condition was identified. This current approach to assessment is exemplified in the recently completed study by Harding and colleagues (1991), in which we assessed an even greater number of variables than previously. Harding et al. (1991) assessed 12 children (ages 2–6 years) with mild mental retardation or average intellectual abilities who were noncompliant. The assessment conditions (5–10 minutes in duration) were constructed to form a hierarchical, cumulative arrangement of both antecedent and consequent conditions (see Table 1). The assessment hierarchy began with a series of antecedent conditions (general directions, specific directions, choice-making) to test the hypotheses that manipulating the way tasks are presented to the children may control behavior, for example, by making the tasks more clear (specificity of directions) or by giving the child some control (choices). Positive outcomes led to intervention recommendations that focused on antecedent manipulations (e.g., parents might be instructed to use specific directions, choice-making, or both as part of a management program). The second series of conditions assessed the effects of positive consequence manipulations (differential reinforcement of appropriate behavior, differential reinforcement of communication, preferred activities). These conditions assessed the effects of increased parental attention, in-

Table 1. Hierarchical model of assessment

Hypotheses	Antecedent components	Consequent components
(Control)	Free play	Constant attention
(Control)	General directions	Discussion (reprimand)
Improve behavior if directions to child more concrete	Specific directions	Discussion (reprimand)
Improve behavior if child allowed more control	Specific directions + choices	Discussion (reprimand)
Improve behavior if child given attention for appropriate behavior	Specific directions + choices	Differential reinforcement of appropriate behavior (DRA)
Improve behavior if child given mand to request desired reinforcer	Specific directions + choices	DRA + functional communication training (FCT)
Improve behavior if given access to preferred activity	Specific directions + choices	DRA + FCT + preferred activity
Decrease behavior by removing reinforcers for inappropriate behavior	Specific directions + choices	DRA + FCT + preferred activity + punishment (time-out or guided compliance)

creased child control over parental attention, and access to preferred activities, respectively. Taken as a whole, the antecedent and consequent conditions provided several representative examples of positive and negative reinforcement. If successful, a reinforcement-based intervention was available. The final assessment condition incorporated the use of mild punishment techniques to control behavior. Time-out was used if noncompliant behavior appeared to be maintained primarily by attention from the parent(s), and guided compliance was used if it appeared to function primarily as an escape response.

The functional analysis model evaluated by Harding et al. (1991) is conceptualized as a "least-to-most restrictive" assessment of intervention conditions based on what was required of the parent. Antecedent manipulations were tested first because changes in these variables were thought to be easier to implement than changes in consequences. For example, if increasing the specificity of a direction was sufficient to improve compliance, intervention focused simply on how to phrase directives. Subsequent assessment conditions analyzed the effects of differential reinforcement contingencies in addition to antecedent manipulations. These were viewed as "more" restrictive in that they typically required more time from the parent in monitoring and responding to child behavior. Finally, the "most" restrictive intervention package included the use of a mild punishment contingency to decrease inappropriate behavior. The use of punishment was viewed as a "default" option (Iwata, 1988) and, thus, was placed last in the hierarchy.

The inclusion of multiple intervention components within the assessment hierarchy is consistent with the clinical practice of providing caregivers with a comprehensive intervention package. Typically, this package includes a selection of potentially useful techniques; however, it may be unclear as to which specific technique, or combination of techniques, is most effective in improving the child's behavior. The assessment model used by Harding et al. (1991) empirically identified each intervention component recommended. Thus, every intervention package included those components that were shown to be effective. In addition, because the parents conducted the assessment, they were able to see the results, and we were able to teach them how to correctly implement each component.

Of the 12 children evaluated, improved behavior was obtained with all 11 children who displayed problematic behavior (1 child did not display any behavioral difficulties during the evaluation). Of the 11 children, 5 improved their behavior with manipulation of antecedent variables (specific directions, choice-making regarding the task) and 6 improved with a manipulation of consequent variables. Again, individual analyses were needed to identify effective interventions; the intervention selected was not predictable based on the demographic variables.

The results obtained in our initial studies have convinced us that direct assessment using single-case designs is needed in order to adequately identify interventions for common behavioral difficulties (Wacker, Northup, & Cooper, 1992). Checklists, rating forms, historical information, and interviews provide the descriptive information needed to formulate hypotheses; however, this information is correlational and must be confirmed via a functional analysis.

Classroom Evaluations

Concurrent with the development of our outpatient assessments, we applied the same versions of these assessment procedures to classroom situations. Given our belief that descriptive assessments could make the functional analyses more efficient, we preceded our functional analyses with such assessments. As in the previous section, we provide examples of our approach with two age groups of children with mild disabilities.

In a second experiment in the study by Cooper et al. (1992), we conducted an assessment using the same independent variables (task preference, task demands, and adult attention) in a special education classroom (multicategorical for children with mild mental disabilities and/or behavior disorders). We began with a descriptive assessment using a behavior-rating form completed by the teacher in order to identify academic periods for assessment. The form was used to identify the most problematic periods and to generate hypotheses about why behavior problems were evidenced by the two children considered to be most difficult to manage. For both children, the teacher conducted the descriptive assessment and generated the hypotheses, and we served as consultants.

One change that we made in the assessment used in the clinic was that we based the hierarchy of assessment on the teacher's preference regarding which variable was most convenient to manipulate, rather than by preselecting the hierarchical order. For both students, the hierarchy was task preference, teacher attention, and task demands. Demands were placed last because the students were already working far below grade level, and the teacher did not want to lower the demands even further. After the descriptive assessment, an alternating treatments design was used in the functional analysis to evaluate the effects of each variable (e.g., high vs. low preference tasks) on child behavior and academic performance. The succession of assessment conditions was based on child performance and teacher hypotheses regarding child behavior. An example is provided in Figure 1 for one of the children.

Kurt was 9 years old, was diagnosed with a mild mental disability, and was frequently noncompliant with teacher requests. Baseline and three assessment phases were conducted with Kurt on math tasks in his curriculum during independent seat work. In addition, to substantiate the criteria used to judge "successful behavior" on the math tasks, observation data were collected intermittently throughout the evaluation on his behavior during one of his "best" academic times (group math activities) as identified by the descriptive teacher ratings. Data were collected during 10-minute sessions on Kurt's appropriate (on-task) behavior and on the quantity and accuracy of work completed.

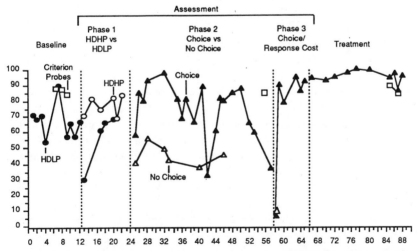

Figure 1.   Classroom assessment for Kurt. Ordinate = percent of appropriate behavior, abscissa = sessions. HD = high demand, LP = low preference, HP = high preference. (From Cooper, L.J., Wacker, D.P., Thursby, D., Plagmann, L.A., Harding, J., Millard, T., & Derby, M. [1992]. Analysis of the effects of task preferences, task demands, and adult attention on child behavior in outpatient and classroom settings. *Journal of Applied Behavior Analysis, 25*, 834; reprinted by permission of the Society for The Experimental Analysis of Behavior.)

As shown in Figure 1, we collected baseline data of Kurt's performance on a difficult (high demand [HD]), nonpreferred (low preference [LP]) task (math flash cards). Overall, his behavior was less appropriate than during the criterion probes. Assessment phase 1 was conducted using an alternating-treatments design to compare his performance on the HDLP task to his performance on a difficult (HD), more preferred (high preference [HP]) task (computer math program). Although improvement occurred in his behavior and work completion, his teacher believed that more improvement was needed. She also believed that preference was a critical component for Kurt; thus, the effect of "choice" on his behavior was assessed by giving him the option of completing either the preferred or nonpreferred task (as opposed to having one assigned to him). During assessment phase 2, we compared "choice" to teacher assignment ("no choice") of a preferred task. We continued to assess his performance on the assigned, preferred task to compare his behavior to the new choice condition. Thus, this assessment phase was conducted based on the hypothesis that Kurt would perform best when given choices of tasks and that the "choice" variable was at least as important as his relative preference for a task.

Based on variable and decreasing trends in his on-task performance and on anecdotal information (refusal to follow teacher directions), a third assessment phase was conducted. In this assessment phase, the "choice" condition, which was relatively more successful in the previous assessment phase than the no-choice condition, was augmented with a "preferred activity" intervention component. Kurt was still permitted to choose the math task, but he was now also given a choice of other preferred academic activities to perform after the successful (at criterion) completion of the math tasks. If he were unsuccessful, he was assigned a nonpreferred math task to complete. This assessment condition continued to be based on the hypothesis that preference was an important independent variable, but in this third assessment phase, choice of tasks was used as both an antecedent and a consequence, and loss of choice (response cost) was used as a mild punisher. As shown in the figure, Kurt's behavior, after a poor start, improved substantially and to a satisfactory level. For this reason, we initiated the "intervention," which was the same as assessment except that the successful components were extended throughout his school day.

By conducting the functional analysis in Kurt's classroom, we could assess very specific intervention components. Instead of assessing only a global variable labeled "preference," we could systematically assess distinctly different versions of this variable while Kurt continued to work on routinely assigned tasks in school. In addition, because the teacher conducted the assessment, she was able to easily implement the intervention. This approach led to consistent improvement in school and ultimately to an intervention that was effective for the remainder of the school year.

A second method for classroom-based assessment was proposed by Harding et al. (1992), who also extended their assessment from the clinic to school situations. Like Cooper et al. (1992), a descriptive assessment preceded the functional analysis, but rather than relying on teacher report, Harding and colleagues used a modified version of the A-B-C assessment (Bijou et al., 1968). This was done because they were working with multiple children in multiple school settings. In addition, the intent was to complete the assessment as quickly as possible. To improve the speed with which the assessment could be completed, the descriptive assessment was conducted to develop hypotheses of the maintaining variables for appropriate child behavior. In the descriptive assessment, potential intervention components were grouped into antecedent and consequent variables on an a priori basis, just as was done in the outpatient clinic evaluation (Harding et al., 1991). Because these components were used naturally by the teacher (e.g., specific directions, differential reinforcement of appropriate behavior) during regularly scheduled classroom activities (e.g., snacktime, teacher-led group activity), they were recorded along with their correlated effect on child behavior. At the completion of assessment conducted over several days, data on the child's appropriate behavior were used to separate the components into two general categories: 1) effective components, and 2) ineffective components.

As mentioned previously, children are rarely inappropriate all of the time. Ongoing fluctuations in behavior were simply noted, along with their corresponding antecedent and consequent variables associated with appropriate or inappropriate behavior. For all five children, an effective package of variables was identified; when these antecedent and consequent variables were implemented, appropriate behavior improved substantially. Behavior occurring with the "effective" components was plotted against behavior occurring with all other components in an alternating-treatment design.

A hypothetical case example (Ryan) is shown in Figure 2 for a 4-year-old child of average intellectual abilities observed in his preschool setting. In the first descriptive assessment condition (a teacher-led group activity), the teacher provided Ryan with specific directions (e.g., stating several behaviors needed to complete the task, modeling) and opportunities for choice-making related to the completion of a task (e.g., "You may use a pencil or you may use a crayon. You choose"). The second condition in Figure 2 displays Ryan's behavior in the same teacher-led activity, but the teacher was observed to reprimand Ryan for inappropriate behavior. The third condition displays Ryan's behaviors in a teacher-led group activity, but the teacher was observed to provide Ryan with general directions (e.g., ambiguous instructions for completion of the task, no modeling), reprimands for inappropriate behavior, and differential reinforcement for appropriate behavior (e.g., words of encouragement). The following day the same activities were observed, but different teacher behavior occurred, so Ryan's behavior was graphed under the new

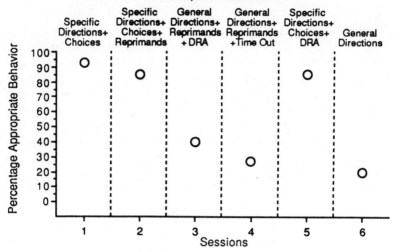

Descriptive Assessment

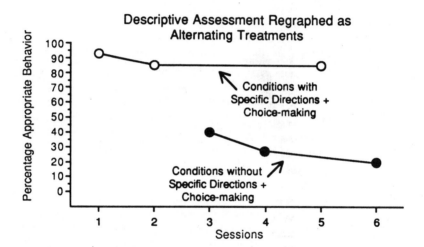

Descriptive Assessment Regraphed as Alternating Treatments

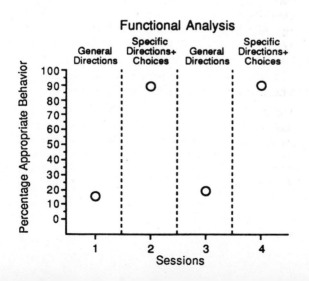

Functional Analysis

combinations of antecedents/consequences. During the fourth condition, the teacher provided Ryan with general directions, reprimands, and a brief time-out. During the fifth condition, the teacher used specific directions when giving Ryan a task, gave him choices within the activity, and praised him for remaining on-task. In the sixth condition, the teacher used only general directions with Ryan.

As shown in the top portion of Figure 2, data were initially graphed in the sequence in which events occurred. Session lines were drawn to indicate changes in observed independent variables as they occurred in conjunction with an identified activity. The data were then regraphed as alternating treatments based on the hypothesized functional effect an intervention package had on behavior (middle portion of Figure 2). That is, conditions with specific directions and choice-making were plotted against conditions without these variables. In this way, data graphed from the descriptive assessment suggested that providing Ryan with specific task directives and with opportunities to communicate preference (choice-making) about some aspect of a presented task increased the occurrence of his appropriate behavior.

The descriptive assessment generated three distinct hypotheses: 1) Ryan's inappropriate behavior was the result of not understanding how to complete a requested task (or teacher expectations of desired behavior were not made clear); providing specific directions may increase appropriate behavior; 2) inappropriate behavior was a function of Ryan's attempt to control some aspect of the environment; providing opportunities for him to communicate preference about some aspect of a presented activity may increase appropriate behavior; and 3) a combination of these hypotheses; appropriate behavior may increase the most when a combination of both specific directions and choice-making is provided.

To confirm these findings, a brief functional analysis was conducted by the teacher (see the bottom part of Figure 2). Rather than noting the natural occurrence of these variables, the teacher systematically implemented first the "ineffective" package and then an "effective" package within a reversal design. Based on the descriptive assessment, the two critical components appeared to be specific directions and choice-making. When compared with general directions/no choice in the brief functional analysis, a clear difference in compliance was evident.

Recent Applications in Regular Education Classroom Settings

Given our successful application of descriptive assessments and functional analysis procedures in classrooms with children who have mild disabilities, we have begun to use the procedures routinely for other children who have

---

Figure 2. Descriptive assessment and functional analysis for Ryan. Ordinate = percent of appropriate behavior, abscissa = sessions.

mild, but persistent, behavior problems in regular education classrooms. An example of this type of assessment is provided in Figure 3. This assessment was conducted by the school psychologist and the teacher in a regular education classroom. Laura was a second-grade student of at least average abilities and achievement who was referred for behavioral difficulties. Concerns included disruptive and off-task behavior (e.g., talking with peers, interrupting the teacher, playing with objects in her desk). A descriptive assessment was conducted by recording her behavior in relation to preselected variables (teacher or peer attention, challenging or easy tasks, group or independent activities). As in the study by Harding et al. (1992), child and teacher/peer behavior were recorded during naturally occurring classroom activities over the course of several days. Initially, as shown in the top panel of Figure 3, behavior was graphed as occurring in a group or during independent seat work and as involving difficult (new material, instructional level) or easy (repetition of previously learned material) tasks.

The initial display of behavior suggested variable, but somewhat better, behavior when given difficult independent seat work. However, when the data were reanalyzed and regraphed as alternating treatments based on the functional impact of variables (as shown in the middle section of Figure 3), it was hypothesized that: 1) Laura's inappropriate behavior was maintained by teacher/peer attention, 2) appropriate behavior might increase when Laura is provided with attention contingent upon the desired behavior or when opportunities for receiving attention are built into the task, and 3) appropriate behavior might increase when Laura is provided with more difficult activities.

The hypotheses were then evaluated via a functional analysis. On alternate days, Laura's teacher provided her with difficult or easy tasks, with and without teacher/peer attention. For example, allowing Laura to pass out papers to classmates was a high-attention task, as was permitting Laura to lead an academic group activity with peers. On other days, the intervention components were omitted (i.e., Laura was not given access to teacher/peer attention for appropriate behavior). As shown in the bottom section of Figure 3, the results of the functional analysis confirmed the hypotheses generated by the descriptive assessment. As with the study by Cooper et al. (1992), intervention included the same "successful" components found during assessment (teacher/peer attention, difficult tasks), except that the treatment was extended throughout the school day. Laura's behavior improved substantially when intervention was implemented.

CONCLUSION

Beginning with the functional analysis technology developed by Iwata et al. (1982), assessment of problem behavior has emphasized the systematic evaluation of the function of behavior and the functional relations between behavior and environmental events. Results of recent research suggest that a num-

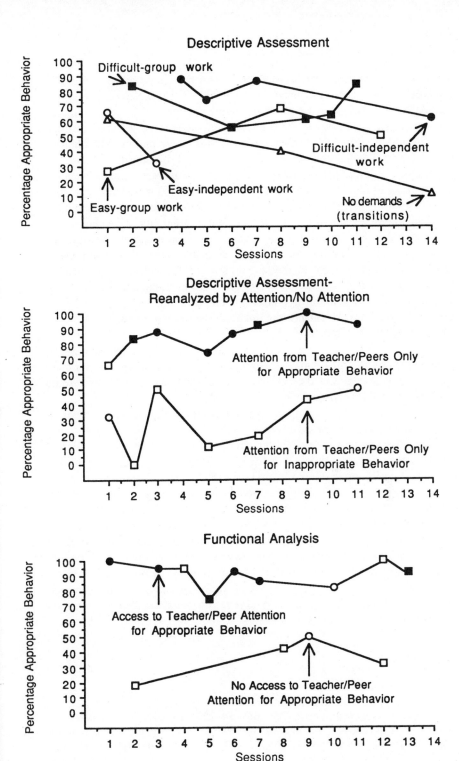

Figure 3. Descriptive assessment and functional analysis for Laura. Ordinate = percent of appropriate behavior, abscissa = sessions.

ber of assessment procedures based on this methodology are useful across diagnostic groups, settings, therapists, and behaviors in developing intervention plans. In this chapter, we provide examples of the use of both descriptive assessment and functional analysis techniques to guide the selection of interventions and to evaluate the effectiveness of those interventions with children of average intellectual abilities or with mild mental disabilities.

One direction for future research is the use of these methods on a more routine basis in regular education classrooms to maintain students with mild disabilities in regular education classrooms and to provide an empirical basis for inclusion of special education students into regular education. For example, if a student is successful in the special education program, the student's performance might first be observed in special education and the components hypothesized to contribute to the student's success identified (e.g., teacher attention, use of an instructional strategy) via a functional analysis. In other words, once identified, the hypothesized critical components might be removed and student performance measured. A decrease in performance would substantiate the importance of the variables, especially if performance improved if they were reinstated. Next, the identified critical variables might be implemented as part of a "mainstreaming intervention package" to maintain improved performance in the regular education classroom. Thus, for some students, an evaluation may involve identifying the variables that are effective in the special education setting and then generalizing the use of those variables in the regular education setting.

For other students who are in regular education but who display problem behavior, the evaluation might involve identifying why the student is having difficulty (via the procedures illustrated in Figure 3) and developing procedures to remediate those problems. In both cases, the assessment is driven by hypotheses about the variables that guide and motivate the student's performance followed by direct, ongoing assessments of those variables. The goal, therefore, is to provide a systematic set of procedures for identifying why a child is successful in special education (in order to assist with integration into regular education) or why a child is unsuccessful in regular education (in order to improve his or her performance). Based on our preliminary results, such an approach to inclusion of children with behavior disorders appears promising.

REFERENCES

Berg, W.K., & Wacker, D.W. (1991). The assessment and evaluation of reinforcers for individuals with severe mental handicaps. In B. Remington (Ed.), *The challenge of severe mental handicap* (pp. 25–45). West Sussex, England: John Wiley & Sons.
Bijou, S.W., Peterson, R.F., & Ault, M.H. (1968). A method to integrate descriptive and experimental field studies at the level of data and empirical concepts. *Journal of Applied Behavior Analysis, 1,* 175–191.

Carr, E.G., & Durand, V.M. (1985). Reducing behavior problems through functional communication training. *Journal of Applied Behavior Analysis, 18,* 111–126.

Cooper, L.J., Wacker, D.P., Sasso, G.M., Reimers, T.M., & Donn, L.K. (1990). Using parents as therapists to evaluate the appropriate behavior of their children: Application to a tertiary diagnostic clinic. *Journal of Applied Behavior Analysis, 23,* 285–296.

Cooper, L.J., Wacker, D.P., Thursby, D., Plagmann, L.A., Harding, J., & Derby, K.M. (1992). Analysis of the role of task preferences, task demands, and adult attention on child behavior in outpatient and classroom settings. *Journal of Applied Behavior Analysis, 25,* 823–840.

Derby, K.M., Wacker, D.P., Sasso, G., Steege, M., Northup, J., Cigrand, K., & Asmus, J. (1992). Brief functional assessment techniques to evaluate maladaptive behavior in an outpatient setting: A summary of 79 cases. *Journal of Applied Behavior Analysis, 18,* 713–721.

Dunlap, G., Dunlap, L.K., Clarke, S., & Robbins, F.R. (1991). Functional assessment, curricular revision, and severe behavior problems. *Journal of Applied Behavior Analysis, 24,* 387–397.

Harding, J., Wacker, D.P., Cooper, L.J., Millard, T., Jensen, P., Derby, K.M., & Rogers, L. (1991, May). *A hierarchical assessment of controlling variables of behavior problems in an outpatient setting with young children.* Paper presented at the Association for Behavior Analysis convention, Atlanta.

Harding, J., Wacker, D.P., Cooper, L.J., Millard, T.L., Jensen-Kovalan, P., Plagmann, L., & Asmus, J. (1992, May). Combining descriptive and functional analysis assessment procedures in classroom settings. In L.J. Cooper (Chair), *Use of functional assessments to promote curriculum changes.* Symposium conducted at the Association for Behavior Analysis convention, San Francisco.

Iwata, B.A. (1988, May). *The development and adoption of controversial default technologies.* Paper presented at the Association for Behavior Analysis convention, Philadelphia.

Iwata, B.A., Dorsey, M.F., Slifer, K.J., Bauman, K.E., & Richman, G.S. (1982). Toward a functional analysis of self-injury. *Analysis and Intervention in Developmental Disabilities, 2,* 3–20.

Iwata, B.A., Pace, G.M., Kalsher, M.J., Cowdery, G.E., & Cataldo, M.F. (1990). Experimental analysis and extinction of self-injurious escape behavior. *Journal of Applied Behavior Analysis, 23,*11–27.

Kazdin, A.E. (1982). *Single-case research designs.* New York: Oxford University Press.

Mace, F.C., & Lalli, J.S. (1991). Linking descriptive and experimental analyses in the treatment of bizarre speech. *Journal of Applied Behavior Analysis, 24,* 553–562.

Mace, F.C., Lalli, J.S., & Lalli, E.P. (1991). Functional analysis and treatment of aberrant behavior. *Research in Developmental Disabilities, 12,* 155–180.

Mace, F.C., Page, T.J., Ivancic, M.T., & O'Brien, S. (1986). Analysis of environmental determinants of aggression and disruption in mentally retarded children. *Applied Research in Mental Retardation, 7,* 203–221.

Mace, F.C., & Shea, M.C. (1990). New directions in behavior analysis for the treatment of severe behavior disorders. In S. Harris & J. Handleman (Eds.), *Aversive and nonaversive interventions: Controlling life threatening behavior by the developmentally disabled* (pp. 57–79). New York: Springer-Verlag.

Michael, J. (1982). Distinguishing between discriminative and motivational functions of stimuli. *Journal of the Experimental Analysis of Behavior, 37,* 149–155.

Northup, J., Wacker, D.P., Berg, W.K., Kelly, L., & Fus, L. (1990, May). Application of functional analysis and proactive treatment procedures to classroom settings serving severely handicapped students. In D.P. Wacker (Chair), *Applications of functional analysis across settings and procedures*. Symposium conducted at the Association for Behavior Analysis convention, Nashville.

Northup, J., Wacker, D., Sasso, G., Steege, M., Cigrand, K., Cook, J., & DeRaad, A. (1991). A brief functional analysis of aggressive and alternative behavior in an outclinic setting. *Journal of Applied Behavior Analysis, 24,* 509–522.

Repp, A.C., Felce, D., & Barton, L.E. (1988). Basing the treatment of stereotypic and self-injurious behavior on hypotheses of their causes. *Journal of Applied Behavior Analysis, 21,* 281–289.

Steege, M.W., Wacker, D.P., Berg, W.K., Cigrand, K.K., & Cooper, L.J. (1989). The use of behavioral assessment to prescribe and evaluate treatments for severely handicapped children. *Journal of Applied Behavior Analysis, 22,* 23–33.

Touchette, P.E., MacDonald, R.F., & Langer, S.N. (1985). A scatterplot for identifying stimulus control of problem behavior. *Journal of Applied Behavior Analysis, 18,* 343–351.

Wacker, D., Northup, J., & Cooper, L. (1992). Behavioral assessment. In D. Greydanus & M. Wolraich (Eds.), *Behavioral pediatrics* (pp. 57–68). New York: Springer-Verlag.

Wacker, D., Steege, M., Northup, J., Reimers, T., Berg, W., & Sasso, G. (1990). Use of functional analysis and acceptability measures to assess and treat severe behavior problems: An outpatient clinic model. In A.C. Repp & N.N. Singh (Eds.), *Perspectives on the use of nonaversive and aversive interventions for persons with developmental disabilities* (pp. 349–359). Sycamore, IL: Sycamore Publishing Co.

Wacker, D.P., Steege, M.W., Northup, J., Sasso, G., Berg, W., Reimers, T., Cooper, L., Cigrand, K., & Donn, L. (1990). A component analysis of functional communication training across three topographies of severe behavior problems. *Journal of Applied Behavior Analysis, 23,* 417–429.

4

Reciprocal Social Influences in the Analysis and Intervention of Severe Challenging Behavior

Jill C. Taylor and Edward G. Carr

THE TRADITIONAL FOCUS ON ADULT–CHILD interactions in applied behavior analysis has been on the impact of adult behavior on child behavior. Adult behavior has been emphasized as a variable that controls children's challenging behavior, both as an antecedent (as in the case of adult task demands) (Carr & Durand, 1985a) and as a consequence (as in the case of adult attention following problem behavior) (Iwata, Dorsey, Slifer, Bauman, & Richman, 1982). Similarly, child problem behavior is treated by teaching adults to implement procedures that are designed to change such behavior (Sulzer-Azaroff & Mayer, 1977). That is, adult behavior is changed, which in turn changes child behavior. In fact, adult-mediated interventions for child behavior problems have been a defining feature of applied behavior analysis for many years. Consequently, we believe that "adult effects" on child behavior have been emphasized. Within recent years, however, interventionists have been attending more closely to the reciprocal social influences that occur during socially unacceptable adult–child interactions. In particular, "child effects," or the impact of children upon adults (Bell, 1968), have increasingly become a focal point of investigations exploring challenging behavior.

Data from developmental psychology provide ample support for the significant influence that child behavior has on all subsequent adult behavior. Evidence suggests that global characteristics of infants, such as temperament,

Support for preparation of this chapter was provided in part by Cooperative Agreement No. G0087C0234 from the U.S. Department of Education, "A Rehabilitation Research and Training Center on Community-Reinforced Technologies for Nonaversive Behavior Management." Portions of this chapter were presented at the Association for Behavior Analysis annual meeting, Nashville, May 1990, and at the conference "Destructive Behavior in Developmental Disabilities" sponsored by the National Institute of Child Health and Human Development and the Institute for Disabilities Studies of the University of Minnesota, Minneapolis, April 1991.

exert powerful effects upon adults (Thomas, Chess, & Birch, 1968). Similarly, subtle, discrete infant social behaviors, such as vocalizations and head turns, influence adult behavior (Gewirtz & Boyd, 1976). Preschoolers' language capabilities reciprocally influence adult speech, as is exemplified by a plethora of studies demonstrating that adults simplify the speech they direct to younger, as compared to older, children (Snow, 1972). In addition, the type of transgressions children display exert considerable control over the disciplinary strategies used by their parents (Grusec & Kuczynski, 1980; Nucci & Turiel, 1978). Together, these studies suggest that child behavior directly affects adult behavior and the nature of adult–child interactions. Thus, children are active participants in the development and course of their relationships with adults.

Studies with child clinical populations also indicate that child behavior affects adult behavior. Studies suggest that child behavior problems influence adult behavior in a way that evokes and/or maintains additional behavior problems. For example, when children with hyperactivity receive acute treatment with stimulant medication (Barkley & Cunningham, 1979) and/or cognitive behavior therapy (Cohen, Sullivan, Minde, Novak, & Keens, 1983), they are less active and impulsive and more compliant. In response, their mothers have been described as being positive, reinforcing, and nondirective. Conversely, when children with hyperactivity are active and noncompliant, their mothers have been described as being critical, controlling, and negative (Barkley & Cunningham, 1979). Similarly, studies of children who display conduct problems confirm that adults respond to child behavior problems with negative, punitive, or even abusive control strategies (Anderson, Lytton, & Romney, 1986; Barkley & Cunningham, 1979; Mulhern & Passman, 1979). Punitive, controlling adult behavior, in turn, has been found to evoke and maintain child problem behavior (Forehand & McMahon, 1981; Patterson, 1982). Thus, through child effects, children can perpetuate their own problem behavior.

Only recently, researchers in the area of developmental disabilities have begun to study child effects and reciprocal influences. There is some indication that children with significant behavior problems can affect overall family functioning (Schopler & Mesibov, 1984). Discrete aspects of child behavior also influence adult responding. For example, the sophistication of children's communication skills influences the type and complexity of child-directed adult language (Hodapp, Evans, & Ward, 1989; Konstantareas, Zajdeman, Homatidis, & McCabe, 1988). Surprisingly, child effects associated with severe problem behavior have rarely been studied in individuals with developmental disabilities. This is surprising because research with other child populations indicates that child behavior problems influence adults negatively. Because children with developmental disabilities frequently exhibit severe problem behaviors, such as aggression and self-injury, the paucity of information on reciprocal influences represents a serious gap in the literature.

In this chapter, we argue that child effects play a significant role in the development and maintenance of child problem behavior and that knowledge of child effects is crucial for developing a comprehensive theory of behavior problems. That is, we describe the theoretical importance of studying child effects and reciprocal influences. Next, we review the literature on child effects in developmental disabilities. Finally, we conclude by discussing the applied implications of child effects for assessment, intervention implementation, and maintenance of intervention effects relevant to the treatment of severe challenging behaviors.

THEORETICAL IMPORTANCE OF CHILD EFFECTS AND RECIPROCAL INFLUENCES

There are two primary theoretical reasons why the investigation of child effects is important to the field of developmental disabilities. They concern operant theory and reciprocal influences in adult–child interaction (the give-and-take that exists in behavioral exchanges between child and adult).

Child effects play an implicit, but central, role in operant theory. More specifically, child effects purportedly contribute to the maintenance of child problem behavior. Escape behavior, for example, is problem behavior evoked by aversive task situations, purportedly maintained through negative reinforcement processes in which the termination of adult demands reinforces child problem behavior (Carr & Durand, 1985a; Iwata, 1987). For example, a father asks his son to make his bed. In response, his son bangs his head on the floor. Once head-banging occurs, the father stops asking his son to make his bed. In the absence of further demands, the son stops head-banging. In the scenario just described, both the adult and the child are negatively reinforced: The child is reinforced by the termination of demands, and the adult is reinforced by the termination of the child's self-injurious behavior (Carr & Durand, 1985a; Iwata, 1987). Thus, in operant theory, child effects (i.e., the adult terminating the demands) contribute to the maintenance of the child's problem behavior. Despite the importance of child effects to operant theory, adult responses to child problem behavior have rarely been measured directly.

Child effects also operate in the maintenance of attention-seeking problem behavior, or problem behavior exhibited under conditions of low adult attention. In this case, it is assumed that challenging child behavior is maintained through positive reinforcement in the form of contingent adult attention (e.g., Carr & Durand, 1985a). This is illustrated in the following example. A teacher is working with a small group of children in a far corner of the classroom. Consequently, he is not attending to the children doing independent tasks at their desks. One of these children leaves her desk and runs around the room screaming. In response, the teacher abandons his small group, walks over to the child, and assists her back to her seat. Upon receiving adult attention, the student stops screaming and running around the room, obediently returning to her seat. In the situation just described, the child's challenging behavior is positively reinforced by increased adult attention, and adult attention is negatively reinforced by the termination of the child's problem behavior. This sequence describes how child effects, adult behavior in response to the child's challenging behavior (i.e., contingent adult attention), purportedly maintained the child's problem behavior. Although such predictions of adult responses to child problem behavior are basic to an operant theory of problem behavior, they have not been tested systematically.

Child effects also contribute to the maintenance of socially avoidant problem behavior, problem behavior evoked by social interaction and/or physical contact. For example, a mother is playing cars with her son. She talks to him, moves a car near him, and ruffles his hair. In response, the child screams and hits his mother. As a result of screaming and aggressive behavior, the mother stops interacting with her son. Following the withdrawal of adult attention, the child stops screaming and aggressing. In this situation, both the adult and the child are negatively reinforced. The child is reinforced by the reduction in adult attention, and the adult is reinforced by the termination of child problem behavior. This sequence describes how child effects, adult behavior in response to challenging child behavior (i.e., the adult withdrawing attention), negatively reinforces the child's problem behavior. However, as in the examples of escape and attention-seeking problem behaviors, how adults respond to socially avoidant problem behavior has not been measured directly.

Studying child effects is also important for understanding reciprocal influences in adult–child interaction. Given that adult behavior affects child problem behavior in specific ways (Forehand & McMahon, 1981), does child problem behavior affect adult behavior in a reciprocal fashion? That is, does problem behavior that is *affected* by adult attention or demands also *affect* adult attention or demands? For example, if a child consistently responds to adult demands with aggression, does the adult, in turn, reduce the demands presented to the child? Or, if a child hits him- or herself when little or no attention is available, does the adult respond by increasing attention to him or her? Currently, we do not have empirically based answers to questions concerning reciprocal influences in adult–child interaction.

In summary, studying child effects and reciprocal influences has theoretical importance for the field of developmental disabilities. Such study could provide empirical information regarding clinical premises inherent in operant theory. It could also provide an understanding of the mutual basic reinforcement and punishment processes that occur during adult–child interaction.

CHILD EFFECTS AND RECIPROCAL
INFLUENCES RELEVANT TO CHALLENGING BEHAVIOR
IN INDIVIDUALS WITH DEVELOPMENTAL DISABILITIES

Initial Research

Research on the child effects of severe problem behavior has been conducted by Durand and colleagues (Durand, 1986; Durand & Kishi, 1987). Durand (1986) focused on the interaction between teachers in a residential care facility and two adolescents who exhibited self-injurious behavior. Prior to measuring these interactions, Durand assessed the variables controlling the adolescents' self-injury using the Motivation Assessment Scale (MAS) (Durand & Crimmins, 1992). Durand concluded that the self-injurious behavior of one adolescent was evoked and/or maintained by social attention, whereas the self-injurious behavior of the other adolescent was evoked and/or maintained by task stimuli (escape from task demands). Based on this information, Durand predicted that the teaching staff would interact more frequently with the first adolescent and less frequently with the second adolescent. Videotaped samples of teacher–student interactions taken during a 2-month period confirmed this prediction. That is, teaching staff remained in close proximity and provided many commands to the adolescent whose self-injurious behavior was evoked by low levels of attention. Conversely, staff infrequently remained close or presented commands to the student whose self-injurious behavior was maintained by escape from demands. This study suggested that challenging child behavior exerts control over adult behavior and that control may be consistent with the function of the problem behavior.

In a second study, Durand and Kishi (1987) assessed changes in staff (residential and teaching) interactions with five adolescents who exhibited severe problem behavior. Staff–adolescent interactions were assessed before and after the adolescents received a multifaceted intervention package for their problem behavior, including functional communication training, implementing functional tasks, and using preferred reinforcers. Prior to implementation, the authors used the MAS to determine the variables that controlled the adolescents' challenging behavior. Not surprisingly, measures of staff interaction taken prior to the intervention replicated the results of Durand (1986): Staff interacted more frequently with the adolescents whose problem behaviors were controlled by adult attention than with the adolescents whose problem behaviors were controlled by escape from task situations or by tangible stimuli. When the adolescents successfully completed the program, staff–adolescent interaction was reassessed. As the problem behaviors of the adolescents decreased, staff proximity and verbal interactions with the adolescents increased. These data suggest that child behavior has reliable effects upon adult behavior and as child behavior changes, so does its effect on adult behavior.

These studies represent important contributions to the literature on child effects, and they raise many questions. For example, several uncontrolled factors could potentially explain Durand's (1986) child effects data. As Durand noted, the two adolescents differed on several dimensions, perhaps accounting for variations in the amount of teacher attention provided to them. These dimensions could include gender, physical appearance, size, and differences in communication skills (gestures vs. no formal system). In Durand and Kishi (1987), the child effects data were not the primary focus of the study, and it is not clear which variable(s) accounted for changes in the amount of staff interaction with the adolescents. Changes in staff behavior could have been a result of improvements in the adolescents' problem behaviors, improvements in the adolescents' communication skills, or staff acquisitions of alternative methods of managing the adolescents' behavior (i.e., implementing functional communication training, functional activities, and preferred reinforcers). Nonetheless, the studies are heuristic and help provide a basis for additional investigations.

Subsequent Research

We conducted two studies specifically concerning child effects. The first of these studies (Carr, Taylor, & Robinson, 1991) examined the impact of severe problem behavior controlled by escape from demands on adults. The second study (Taylor & Carr, 1992b) documented the effects on adult behavior of children's problem behavior (i.e., attention-seeking and socially avoidant problem behavior) that is controlled by adult attention.

Study 1: Escape Behavior

Escape problem behavior is evoked by aversive task situations and is presumed to be maintained by negative reinforcement processes (Carr & Durand, 1985a; Iwata et al., 1982). In response to child problem behavior, adults purportedly stop presenting task demands to the child. Carr et al. (1991) analyzed the impact of child escape behavior on adult teaching practices. Specifically, Carr et al. (1991) attempted to determine whether adults respond to escape behavior by terminating task demands. In contrast to traditional research in which children are the subjects, the adults were the subjects of study.

Female undergraduates pursuing careers in special education or human services served as subjects. Before entering the study, all adult subjects received standardized, criterion-based training in discrete-trial teaching (Koegel, Russo, & Rincover, 1977) and basic child management strategies, such as differential attention and extinction (Lovaas, 1981). They were also required to pass a discrete-trial performance test.

Several pairs of preschool children participated in the study. Each pair included a child who exhibited significant challenging behavior in a task situation (escape behavior) and a child who exhibited relatively little or no challenging behavior in a task situation (no-problem behavior). The children had been diagnosed as having autism, developmental delay, mental retardation, and/or a speech impairment.

Each adult was assigned to a pair of children and conducted five teaching sessions with them. To ensure that the results of the study were not idiosyncratic to a particular adult, several adults taught each pair of children. During teaching sessions, adults presented the children with common table-top preschool tasks (e.g., matching objects). The behavior of the adult subject was not controlled so that child effects could be measured. That is, each adult was free to choose which child to work with, which task to present, task duration, and whether to provide a child with a play break.

The results of the study fell into two categories: 1) validation of the escape and nonproblem child behavior groups, and 2) child effects. The frequency, situational specificity, and severity of the problem behaviors exhibited by the children distinguished members of the escape group from the nonproblem group. Children from the escape group frequently exhibited severe challenging behavior contingent upon adult instructional behavior and task commands; these same children, however, engaged in less frequent challenging behavior following noninstructional behavior. In contrast, the children from the nonproblem group displayed few problem behaviors in either the instructional or noninstructional situation.

Regarding child effects, results indicated that adults responded differently to each of the two children in the pairs. Adult subjects distributed task commands unequally, presenting significantly more task commands to the children in the nonescape group than to the children in the escape group. In this way, child behavior problems influenced quantitative aspects of adult–child interaction. (i.e., how much the children were taught).

Problem behaviors also influenced qualitative aspects of adult–child interaction, that is, the variety and type of tasks presented to the children. For purposes of data analysis, the children's tasks were divided into two types: tasks that were followed by challenging behavior on less than 25% of the occasions in which they were presented (labeled tolerated tasks), and tasks that were followed by challenging behavior on more than 25% of the occasions in which they were presented (labeled nontolerated tasks). Recall that adults rarely presented task commands to the children from the escape group. However, when adults did present tasks, tolerated tasks were presented more often than nontolerated tasks. Thus, adults presented a restricted range of tasks to the escape group. In contrast, adult subjects presented a wider range of tasks to the nonproblem group.

In summary, when adults presented either general instructions or specific task commands, children in the escape group exhibited frequent, severe challenging behavior. In response to this challenging behavior, adult subjects presented few instructions and task commands to these children. In addition, on those occasions that adult subjects did present tasks to the children from the escape group, adults largely presented tolerated tasks. In contrast, children in the nonproblem group rarely displayed challenging behavior in either instructional or noninstructional situations. Consequently, adult subjects delivered many instructions and task demands to these children and presented a range of tasks. As can be seen, child behavior problems influenced both the amount of teaching that occurred and the curriculum (i.e., type of tasks) presented.

Study 2: Attention-Seeking and Socially Avoidant Behavior

The second study of child effects (Taylor & Carr, 1992b) concerned the impact on adults of severe challenging behaviors controlled by adult attention. Specifically, problem behavior associated with low levels of adult attention (attention-seeking), and problem behavior associated with high levels of adult attention (socially avoidant) were examined.

Attention-seeking problem behavior can occur under conditions of low adult attention (Carr & Durand, 1985a; Durand & Crimmins, 1988; Iwata et al., 1982). More specifically, children who exhibit the attention-seeking behavior pattern: 1) frequently initiate social interactions with adults, 2) display low levels of problem behavior under conditions of high adult attention, and 3) display high levels of problem behavior under conditions of low adult attention (Taylor & Carr, 1992a). Attention-seeking problem behavior is presumably maintained by positive reinforcement.

In contrast to attention-seeking problem behavior, socially avoidant problem behavior is evoked by high levels of adult attention and maintained through negative reinforcement processes. Children who exhibit the socially avoidant problem behavior pattern: 1) rarely initiate social interactions with adults, 2) exhibit higher levels of problem behavior under conditions of high adult attention, and 3) exhibit lower levels of problem behavior under conditions of low adult attention (Taylor & Carr, 1992a). Socially avoidant behavior is presumed to be maintained by negative reinforcement processes. In response to child problem behavior, adults purportedly decrease the amount of attention they give to the child.

Taylor and Carr (1992b) analyzed the impact of attention-seeking problem behavior and socially avoidant problem behavior on adult teaching practices. Specifically, they attempted to determine whether adults responding to attention-seeking problem behavior by increasing attention to the child and responding to socially avoidant problem behavior by decreasing attention to the child. In the study, undergraduates pursuing careers in special education or human services, who were blind to the purpose of the study and unfamiliar with the child participants, served as subjects. Adult subjects received discrete-trial training (Koegel et al., 1977), child behavior management training (e.g., Lovaas, 1981), and a performance test before entering the study.

Nine elementary-school–age children participated in this study: three exhibited attention-seeking problem behavior (AS), three exhibited socially avoidant problem behavior (SA), and three exhibited virtually no problem behavior (NP). The children had received diagnoses such as autism, pervasive developmental disorder, and multiple handicapped with autistic features. All had mental retardation and significant language delay. Some children also had sensory or motor impairments such as blindness or cerebral palsy. Three trios were formed, each consisting of a child from the AS, SA, and NP groups. Several adults were assigned to each trio. Next, three pairs of children were selected from each trio: one pair consisted of a child from the AS group and a child from NP group (AS–NP pair), the second pair consisted of a child from the SA group and a child from the NP group (the SA–NP pair), and the third pair consisted of a child from the AS group and a child from the SA group (AS–SA pair). Pairs, rather than trios, were used in the teaching situation to facilitate analysis of the child effects. Thus, there were a total of three AS–NP pairs, three SA–NP pairs, and three AS–SA pairs. The adult subjects conducted multiple teaching sessions with each pair of children in their assigned trio and had a variety of tasks available to present to each child. In order to observe child effects, the behavior of the adult subjects was not controlled.

The results of the study fell into two categories: 1) those validating that the children exhibited their purported behavior profile (i.e., AS, SA, NP) and 2) those pertaining to child effects. Data concerning the frequency, severity, and specificity of the children's challenging behaviors verified their group membership. The children in the AS group engaged in frequent, severe challenging behavior (i.e., self-injury, aggression, tantrums) under conditions of low adult attention. In contrast, children in the SA group displayed frequent, severe problem behavior under conditions of high adult attention. Children in the NP group, in comparison, engaged in infrequent, mild problem behavior such as whining or crying.

Regarding child effects, adults responded differently to children in the three behavior profile groups. In addition, they responded to each type of child pair (e.g., AS–NP, SA–NP, AS–SA) as if it were a unique social system. As in the first study described (Carr et al., 1991), child effects exerted powerful control over both quantitative aspects of adult behavior (i.e., how much attention adults distributed to children) as well as qualitative aspects of adult behavior (i.e., how adults attended to children).

Within the AS–NP child pairs, children from the AS group exhibited frequent and severe challenging behavior under low adult attention, whereas children from the NP group occasionally exhibited infrequent mild challenging behavior under those same conditions. If challenging behaviors are conceptualized as an aversive stimulus or punisher for any adult behavior that they follow, then children in the AS group provided high-intensity punishment to adults who did not attend to the AS group, whereas children in the NP group provided mild and intermittent punishment when the adults did not attend to their group. Adults responded to these punishment contingencies by providing high levels of attention, physical contact, and high-interaction tasks (i.e., those requiring ongoing adult–child interaction, such as an expressive language drill) to both groups of children, and by exhibiting proportionately greater involvement with the AS group than with the NP group.

Within the SA–NP child pairs, children from the SA group frequently displayed severe challenging behavior contingent on adult attention, whereas children from the NP group occasionally exhibited mild challenging behavior under conditions of no adult attention. That is, children in the SA group provided high-intensity punishment to adults when they attended to them, whereas children in the NP group provided mild, intermittent punishment when adults ignored them. Adults responded to these punishment contingencies by decreasing attention, physical contact, and high-interaction tasks (as well as increasing independent tasks, or those that the child could complete without adult–child interaction) given to the SA group and by increasing those given to the NP group. In addition, because the child effects of both the SA and NP groups caused adults to attend more to the NP group, it is plausible that child effects were additive.

The child effects generated by the AS–SA pairs were most striking and conformed to the AS and SA patterns described earlier. That is, adults received frequent, high-intensity punishment for ignoring the AS group, and responded by increasing attention, physical contact, and high-interaction tasks to these children. In contrast, adults received frequent, high-intensity punishment for attending to the SA group, and adults responded by decreasing attention, physical contact, and high interaction tasks to these children. Again, the magnitude of the child effects are possibly the result of an additive process.

THEORETICAL IMPLICATIONS

The results of the Carr et al. (1991) and Taylor and Carr (1992b) studies have several theoretical implications. These data demonstrate that child behavior problems do have consistent, reliable effects on quantitative and qualitative aspects of adult behavior. Furthermore, different child behavior profiles have different effects upon adults. More specifically: 1) escape behavior reduced task demands, presumably negatively reinforcing problem behavior and increasing the likelihood that such behavior would recur; 2) attention-seeking challenging behavior increased adult attention, thereby positively reinforcing this behavior; and 3) socially avoidant problem behavior decreased adult attention, thereby negatively reinforcing challenging behavior. These studies also tested and supported a central premise of the operant theory of problem behavior: that child-produced challenging behavior affects adult behavior in a way that contributes to the maintenance of child problem behavior.

The results of these studies also demonstrate reciprocal influences between adults and children that occur during episodes of challenging behavior. These investigations demonstrated that challenging behaviors, in addition to being affected by adult attention, also influence subsequent patterns of adult attention. Problem behaviors of the escape group, which occurred contingent on task commands, punished adults for presenting task commands. This process caused adults to stop presenting task commands. The challenging behavior of the AS group, which occurred primarily under conditions of low adult attention, punished adults for *not* attending to group members and caused the adults to provide high levels of attention. In contrast, the challenging behavior of the SA group, which occurred almost exclusively under conditions of high adult attention, punished adults for attending to group members, causing the adults to reduce attention. Thus, adults and children constituted reciprocal social systems wherein adult attention influenced, and was influenced by, child problem behavior.

The data from Taylor and Carr (1992b) also suggest that the three different types of child pairs (i.e., AS–NP, SA–NP, AS–SA pairs) constituted three unique social systems, each with different effects upon adults. This is illustrated most clearly by the NP behavior profile group. When paired with members of the AS group, members of the NP group received little adult attention. Conversely, when paired with the SA group, NP group members received much attention. Thus, the AS–NP and SA–NP pairs created different social systems with opposite child effects. Thus, adult behavior may be best understood as the product of the combined child effects of each child in the pair.

The data from these studies (Taylor & Carr, 1992a, 1992b) are consistent with the conceptualization that child problem behavior was an aversive stimulus or punisher for the adult behaviors that it followed (demands, high attention, or low attention). Results indicated that when presented with the opportunity to interact or to teach a child who provided high rates of contingent negative reinforcement (i.e., challenging behavior), or a child who provided low rates of contingent negative reinforcement, the adult interacted with or taught the latter child. These data are consistent with basic research on human choice, which suggests that when presented with a choice between a frequently punished response (e.g., ignoring the AS children) and a less frequently punished response (e.g., ignoring the NP children), individuals choose the less frequently punished response more often (Deluty, 1982).

APPLIED IMPLICATIONS

Systems Functional Analysis

Attention to reciprocal influences and child effects may enhance functional analysis. There has been a growing emphasis on basing intervention with severe problem behavior on functional analysis (Carr, Robinson, & Palumbo, 1990; Iwata et al., 1982; Repp, Felce, & Barton, 1988). Research derived from functional analysis has provided a heuristic and conceptual framework for understanding challenging behavior. For example, research has shown that socially oriented problem behaviors fall into two general categories (Carr & Durand, 1985b): problem behaviors maintained by negative reinforcement processes, and problem behaviors maintained by positive reinforcement processes. This framework has applied value for the field of developmental disabilities. Specifically, interventions based on a functional analysis tend to be more successful than those not based on such an analysis (Carr, Robinson, Taylor, & Carlson, 1990; Repp et al., 1988).

Attention to reciprocal influences and child effects may enhance functional analysis. By identifying the environmental events that control challenging behavior, functional analysis enhances intervention outcomes. Nonetheless, relevant controlling variables are sometimes overlooked in functional analysis procedures. That is, whereas such procedures identify the environmental events that affect child problem behavior, they do not determine the effects of problem behavior on the social environment (Emery, Binkoff, Houts, & Carr, 1983). For example, when a functional analysis indicates that adult behavior such as ineffective commands (e. g., Forehand & McMahon, 1981) evokes challenging behavior, the analysis is considered complete because the variable that controls challenging behavior has been identified. A parallel functional analysis to determine the variables that maintain the adult's ineffective commands is usually not conducted. Presumably, however, just as child behavior problems are a product of adult antecedents and/or consequences, adult behavior is controlled by child antecedents and/or consequences. Thus, analyzing the controlling variables for adult behavior would be an important addition to the functional analysis literature.

Delineation of the child effects and reciprocal influences that occur during episodes of challenging behavior can be viewed as extending functional analysis. Functional analysis must be broadened to include the role of child behavior in maintaining ineffective adult behavior. In short, a functional analysis must be performed on both adult and child behavior. Such an analysis has been called a systems functional analysis (Emery et al., 1983). It is plausible that if knowledge of the antecedent and consequent stimuli that maintain child problem behavior enhances intervention outcomes, then knowledge of the variables that control the adult behavior that evokes and/or maintains challenging child behavior could also enhance intervention outcome. This type of functional analysis would provide more information about the full range of variables that control challenging behavior. As such, it is likely to yield more effective and efficient interventions. The following examples illustrate this point.

A functional analysis may reveal that contingent adult attention is maintaining a child's head-banging. One goal of intervention would be to have the adult stop providing contingent attention for head-banging and instead provide attention contingent on more appropriate attention-seeking behavior. To accomplish this goal, knowledge of the variables that maintain adult attention for head-banging may be useful. Knowledge (and manipulation) of these variables could be used to increase the likelihood that the adult will stop attending to head-banging and start attending to an. appropriate alternative behavior. As another example, a child tantrums each time her mother asks her to brush her teeth. The mother repeats her request several times and struggles with her daughter for several minutes. Her daughter continues to tantrum. Eventually, the mother stops requesting that her daughter brush her teeth. If an interventionist wants the mother to continue to request that her daughter brush her teeth, it would be helpful to determine the variables that control that request. For example, a functional analysis may indicate that her daughter's tantrums punish the mother's request. Therefore, to maintain the mother's requests, the child's tantrums should be reduced. One method might be to have the mother make several requests that her daughter *does* comply with and then request that she brush her teeth (Harchik & Putzier, 1990; Mace & Belfiore, 1990). This "behavioral momentum" approach does not generate any challenging behavior; that is, the mother is not punished for making requests and is therefore likely to follow through on the toothbrushing request.

Separating Effective Interventions from Child Effects

The data from child effect studies also have another applied implication. These data indicate that children shape teacher behavior and curriculum content. Specifically, over time, children influence the number and type of tasks and the amount of interaction that teachers give to them. In this way, child effects may explain why children who engage in challenging behavior early in the school year are no longer problematic by the end of the year. In some cases, it may be that the child no longer engages in problem behavior, and the reduction in his or her challenging repertoire is due to the successful application of intervention procedures. However, in other cases, it may be that child effects create the appearance that the child's behavior is no longer problematic. The child may have shaped his or her teacher into adopting interactive and teaching strategies that do not evoke challenging behavior. For example, a child with attention-seeking problem behavior may teach his or her teacher to provide high rates of attention and physical contact, thus reducing the frequency of problem behavior. Conversely, the teacher of a child with the socially avoidant problem behavior may learn to present low-interaction tasks and to avoid physical contact with that child. Thus, reductions in child challenging behavior may be the result of child effects rather than programmatic behavior change.

The child effects on curricular content, teaching, and interactive behavior (described above) themselves have implications for functional assessment. These effects may render the direct observation and/or questionnaire methodologies for functional assessment inaccurate. Teachers (or other adults) may adopt interactive and educational strategies that minimize child problem behavior and avoid or discontinue presenting the stimuli that evoke such challenging repertoires. As a result, direct observation and questionnaires that focus on the child's and adults' current behavior and environment may not capture the variables that control the child's challenging behavior because many relevant factors (e.g., specific task demands) may have been eliminated from the environment.

In order to conduct valid functional assessments that avoid the potential problems created by child effects, two procedures, in addition to those used to determine the antecedents and consequences of problem behavior, are recommended. First, child effects should be measured by assessing any changes that have occurred over time in adult behavior toward the child. For example, this might include determining whether adults have adopted or discontinued any strategies in order to reduce or prevent child problem behavior. Anecdotal reports noted during Taylor and Carr (1992b) strongly suggest that adults can identify such strategies, as well as the reason they adopted them. For example, with a child demonstrating the socially avoidant problem behavior, an adult might state that low-interaction tasks were used because the child preferred to work alone. Thus, interviewing the adult about child effects should be considered. In addition, direct observation can be used to assess child effects. For example, observers would want to note which students the teacher spends most of his or her time with and which he or she retains close proximity to, compared with students with whom the teacher rarely interacts or approaches. Observations could be enhanced through interviews as well. For example, an observer could ask a teacher, "I noticed that you stand very close to Johnny when you are working with him. Why is that?"

The second strategy that would circumvent functional assessment problems associated with child effects is the systematic manipulation of potential antecedent and consequent events. Manipulation of environmental events permits hypothesis testing about the relationship between child behavior and a wider array of stimuli than might be available in the usual environment. For example, a classroom teacher who avoids high-interaction tasks with a child could be requested to engage the child in such a task, alternated with periods of engaging the child in independent tasks. Without this systematic manipulation, information concerning the relationship between high-interaction tasks and child problem behavior would be difficult to obtain. Thus, systematic manipulation of adult behavior (preferably in the child's natural environment) is also recommended.

In short, child effects may negatively affect certain functional assessment and/or analysis procedures. To avoid this, multimethod systems of functional analyses that assess current maintaining variables, as well as changes that have occurred within adult–child interactions over time, are required. Interviews and questionnaires may be best suited for hypothesis testing prior to intervention.

TREATMENT SELECTION AND MAINTENANCE

Child effects have implications for selecting intervention strategies to reduce or eliminate challenging behavior. As previously noted, there has been a growing trend to base treatment strategies for challenging behavior on functional analysis (Carr et al., 1990; Repp et al., 1988), that is, to use functionally derived intervention strategies. Depending on the function of the problem behavior, however, there are typically several appropriate intervention alternatives available but few guidelines as to how to choose among them. For example, escape extinction (Mace & West, 1986), behavior momentum (Mace & Belfiore, 1990), reducing the aversiveness of the task (Weeks & Gaylord-Ross, 1981), and functional equivalence training (Carr & Durand, 1985b) have all been used successfully in intervention with escape behavior. In the absence of guidelines, child effects can have implications for which functionally derived treatment to select.

Information about the child effects of challenging behavior can be used for intervention selection. Frequently, the effects of child problem behaviors upon adults are implicit. That is, they must be inferred or hypothesized and then measured. Once the effects of problem behavior on adults have been determined, it would be logical to choose treatments that are based directly on a consideration of the child effects, specifically, teaching the child socially appropriate behavior that produces the same effects. This strategy has been called functional equivalence training (e.g., Carr & Durand, 1985b) and has been used successfully to treat challenging behavior. The strategy is illustrated in the following example. A child bites her hand during periods of low adult attention. Direct observation indicates that the child effects of hand-biting are increased adult attention. An appropriate alternative behavior that recognizes these child effects involves teaching the child to elicit adult attention directly, for example, by saying, "Come here, please" to the adult.

A second child effects consideration for intervention selection concerns the maintenance of intervention effects. Research on intervention acceptability or social validity (e.g., Kazdin, 1981; Wolf, 1978) indicates that adults prefer interventions that pose little risk to the child, generate few undesirable side effects, and do not disrupt the child's environment (Kazdin, 1981). Therefore, if an intervention generates child problem behavior, adults may not use it. Obviously, if an intervention is not used, positive effects will not be achieved or maintained. This outcome is illustrated in the Carr et al. (1991) and Taylor and Carr (1992b) studies. Recall that when teaching strategies evoked child challenging behavior, adult teaching attempts were negatively reinforced and adults stopped teaching (Carr et al., 1991). If teaching is terminated, maintenance of academic skills is almost certain to be poor. Similarly, Taylor and Carr (1992b) found that when some types of tasks (e.g., high-interaction tasks) evoked child challenging behavior, adults stopped presenting those tasks. In these examples, it is the behavior of the interventionist that fails to maintain over time, and the result is poor maintenance of related academic and social skills.

Traditionally, maintenance failure has been attributed to procedural inadequacies (Sulzer-Azaroff & Mayer, 1977). While procedural inadequacies may account for many instances of maintenance failure, child effects may also contribute. The general implication is that, when possible, interventions that generate few negative child effects should be chosen over those that generate many negative child effects. For example, assume that an educational intervention is being implemented for a child with the attention-seeking behavior pattern and that the targeted skill can be taught equally well using either a high-interaction task or a low-interaction task. In the interest of maintaining the teacher's instructional behavior, it would seem effective, at least initially, to prescribe the high-interaction task as it will generate fewer problem behaviors. In contrast, given a choice between a high- versus low-interaction task for a child with the socially avoidant behavior pattern, it would seem effective to use the low-interaction task initially because this type of task generates fewer challenging behaviors for these children. In general, intervention strategies that produce few negative child effects (problem behaviors) are more likely to be implemented by adul   and maintained over time. When adults continue to implement effective intervention strategies, children are more likely to benefit from those interventions and show maintenance effects themselves.

Treatment Accountability

Children influence the amount of interaction they receive and the amount and content of what they are taught, suggesting the need for greater accountability for curricular decisions. This especially is true in cases of children for whom curricula are not balanced among skill and content areas, or when tasks or skill areas are removed from curricula. Increased accountability would ensure that curriculum decisions are based on the educational well-being of the child, rather than on the child effects created by the severe problem behaviors of the child. Consider the following example. Shoe-tying is removed from a child's instructional schedule and replaced with learning to use Velcro fasteners. Initially, it was assumed that this outcome occurred because the child was not acquiring shoe-tying. Further investigation, however, may indicate that shoe-tying evoked severe aggression, and the teacher was therefore unable to teach the skill. In this case, it is not that the shoe-tying program was implemented and, in spite of this program, the child could not learn to tie his shoes; he did not learn to tie his or her shoes because the teacher did not implement the program. These two situations have different implications. If a child does not learn a task in which teaching is implemented consistently and accurately, this outcome suggests that the teaching procedures should be modified, or that an alternative form of the task should be selected. However, if a child does not learn a task because teaching was not implemented, then this outcome would suggest that modifications be made in the way that the challenging behavior is managed.

CONCLUSION

Challenging behavior is best understood as involving a process of reciprocal social influences. Different functional patterns of problem behavior affect others in reliable and individual ways. The systematic analysis of child effects has direct implications for theory, assessment, and intervention applications, and therefore merits the attention of both researchers and clinicians.

REFERENCES

Anderson, K.E., Lytton, H., & Romney, D.M. (1986). Mother's interactions with normal and conduct disordered boys: Who affects whom? *Developmental Psychology, 22*, 604–609.

Barkley, R.A., & Cunningham, C.E. (1979). The effects of methylphenidate on the interactions of hyperactive children. *Archives of General Psychiatry, 36*, 201–208.

Bell, R.Q. (1968). A reinterpretation of the direction of effects in studies of socialization. *Psychological Review, 75*, 81–95.

Carr, E.G., & Durand, V.M. (1985a). Reducing behavior problems through functional communication training. *Journal of Applied Behavior Analysis, 18*, 111–126.

Carr, E.G., & Durand, V.M. (1985b). The social communicative basis of severe behavior problems in children. In S. Reiss & R. Bootzin (Eds.), *Theoretical issues in behavior therapy* (pp. 219–254). New York: Academic Press.

Carr, E.G., Robinson, S., & Palumbo, L.W. (1990). The wrong issue: Aversive versus nonaversive treatment. The right issue: Functional versus nonfunctional treatment. In A.C. Repp & N.N. Singh (Eds.), *Current perspectives on the use of nonaversive and aversive interventions for persons with developmental disabilities* (pp. 361–379). Sycamore, IL: Sycamore Publishing Co.

Carr, E.G., Robinson, S., Taylor, J.C., & Carlson, J.I. (1990). Positive approaches to the treatment of severe behavior problems in persons with developmental disabilities: A review and analysis of reinforcement and stimulus-based procedures. *Monographs of The Association for Persons with Severe Handicaps, 4*, 1–40.

Carr, E.G., Taylor, J.C., & Robinson, S. (1991). The effects of severe behavior problems in children on the teaching behavior of adults. *Journal of Applied Behavior Analysis, 24,* 523–535.

Cohen, N.J., Sullivan, J., Minde, K., Novak, C., & Keens, S. (1983). Mother–child interaction in hyperactive and normal kindergarten-aged children and the effect of treatment. *Child Psychiatry and Human Development, 13,* 213–224.

Deluty, M.Z. (1982). Maximizing, minimizing, and matching between reinforcing and punishing situations. In M.L. Commons, R.J. Herrnstein, & H. Rachlin (Eds.), *Quantitative analyses of behavior: Vol. 2. Matching and maximizing accounts* (pp. 305–325). Cambridge, MA: Ballinger.

Durand, V.M. (1986). Self-injurious behavior as intentional communication. In K.G. Gadow (Ed.), *Advances in learning and behavioral disabilities* (Vol. 5, pp. 141–155). Greenwich, CT: JAI Press.

Durand, V.M., & Crimmins, D.B. (1988). Identifying the variables maintaining self-injurious behavior. *Journal of Autism and Developmental Disorders, 18,* 99–117.

Durand, V.M., & Crimmins, D.B. (1992). *The Motivation Assessment Scale.* Topeka, KS: Monaco & Associates.

Durand, V.M., & Kishi, G. (1987). Reducing severe behavior problems among persons with dual-sensory impairments: An evaluation of a technical assistance model. *Journal of The Association for Persons with Severe Handicaps, 12,* 2–10.

Emery, R.E., Binkoff, J.A., Houts, A.C., & Carr, E.G. (1983). Children as independent variables: Some clinical implications of child-effects. *Behavior Therapy, 14,* 398–412.

Forehand, R., & McMahon, R. (1981). *Helping the noncompliant child: A clinician's guide to treatment.* New York: Guilford Press.

Gewirtz, J.L., & Boyd, E.F. (1976). Experiments on mother-child interaction underlying mutual attachment acquisition: The infant conditions the mother. In T. Alloway, P. Pilner, & L. Kranes (Eds.), *Attachment behavior: Advances in the study of communication and affect* (Vol. 3, pp. 109–143). New York: Plenum.

Grusec, J.E., & Kuczynski, L. (1980). Direction of effect in socialization: A comparison of the parent's versus the child's behavior as determinants of disciplinary techniques. *Developmental Psychology, 16,* 1–9.

Harchik, A.E., & Putzier, V.S. (1990). The use of high-probability requests to increase compliance with instructions to take medication. *Journal of The Association for Persons with Severe Handicaps, 15,* 40–43.

Hodapp, R.M., Evans, D.W., & Ward, B.A. (1989). Communicative interaction between teachers and children with severe handicaps. *Mental Retardation, 27,* 388–395.

Iwata, B.A. (1987). Negative reinforcement in applied behavior analysis: An emerging technology. *Journal of Applied Behavior Analysis, 20,* 361–378.

Iwata, B.A., Dorsey, M.F., Slifer, K.J., Bauman, K.E., & Richman, G.S. (1982). Toward a functional analysis of self-injury. *Analysis and Intervention in Developmental Disabilities, 2,* 3–20.

Kazdin, A. (1981). Acceptability of child treatment techniques: The influence of treatment efficacy and adverse side effects. *Behavior Therapy, 12,* 493–506.

Koegel, R.L., Russo, D., & Rincover, A. (1977). Assessing and training teachers in the generalized use of behavior modification with autistic children. *Journal of Applied Behavior Analysis, 10,* 197–205.

Konstantareas, M.M., Zajdeman, H., Homatidis, S., & McCabe, A. (1988). Maternal speech to verbal and higher functioning versus nonverbal and lower functioning autistic children. *Journal of Autism and Developmental Disorders, 18,* 547–565.

Lovaas, O.I. (1981). *Teaching developmentally disabled children: The ME book.* Baltimore: University Park Press.

Mace, F.C., & Belfiore, P.J. (1990). Behavioral momentum in the treatment of escape-motivated stereotypy. *Journal of Applied Behavior Analysis, 23,* 507–514.

Mace, F.C., & West, B.J. (1986). Analysis of demand conditions associated with reluctant speech. *Journal of Behavior Therapy and Experimental Psychiatry, 12*(4), 285–294.

Mulhern, R.K., & Passman, R.H. (1979). The child's behavioral pattern as a determinant of maternal punitiveness. *Child Development, 50,* 815–820.

Nucci, L.P., & Turiel, E. (1978). Social interactions and the development of social concepts in preschool children. *Child Development, 49,* 400–407.

Patterson, R.G. (1982). *Coercive family processes.* Eugene, OR: Castalia.

Repp, A.C., Felce, D., & Barton, L.E. (1988). Basing the treatment of stereotypic and self-injurious behaviors on hypotheses of their causes. *Journal of Applied Behavior Analysis, 21,* 281–289.

Schopler, E., & Mesibov, G.B. (Eds.). (1984). *The effects of autism on the family.* New York: Plenum.

Snow, C.E. (1972). Mothers' speech to children learning language. *Child Development, 43,* 549–565.

Sulzer-Azaroff, B., & Mayer, G.R. (1977). *Applying behavior analysis procedures with children and youth.* New York: Holt, Rinehart & Winston.

Taylor, J.C., & Carr, E.G. (1992a). Severe problem behaviors related to social interaction I: Attention-seeking and social avoidance. *Behavior Modification, 16,* 305–335.

Taylor, J.C., & Carr, E.G. (1992b). Severe problem behaviors related to social interaction II: A systems analysis. *Behavior Modification, 16,* 336–371.

Thomas, A., Chess, S., & Birch, H.G. (1968). *Temperament and behavior disorders in children.* New York: New York University Press.

Weeks, M., & Gaylord-Ross, R. (1981). Task difficulty and aberrant behavior in severely handicapped students. *Journal of Applied Behavior Analysis, 14,* 449–463.

Wolf, M.M. (1978). Social validity: The case for subjective measurement or how applied behavior analysis is finding its heart. *Journal of Applied Behavior Analysis, 11,* 203–214.

5

Identifying Stimulus Control of Challenging Behavior

Extending the Analysis

James W. Halle and Joseph E. Spradlin

Functional analysis of challenging behavior has produced a research literature that is as exciting and as sophisticated as any in the field of applied behavior analysis. It has combined disparate avenues of investigation (e.g., setting events, competing behavior, stimulus- and response-class notions, multiple or conditional control) into a coherent, logical, and pioneering program of research. In this chapter, we attempt to extend the assessment of challenging behavior by focusing on some limitations of functional analysis as currently practiced.

OVERVIEW

In the first section, we offer a brief review of assessment strategies with an emphasis on antecedent variables. Some limitations of this assessment process are delineated. A more refined and sophisticated analysis of antecedent events is presented with a specific illustration. Finally, we describe the potential contribution of setting events as an extension to the functional analysis of challenging behavior. The second and final section of the chapter concentrates on extending the analysis by viewing challenging behavior as embedded in routines, or as links in behavior chains. New phenomena must be considered and assessed when this perspective is assumed, such as remote contingencies

The writing of this chapter was completed while the first author received support from Leadership Training Grant No. H029D90107 awarded to the University of California at Santa Barbara by the U.S. Department of Education. Support also was provided by Grant No. H086P90024 awarded to the University of Illinois by the U.S. Department of Education, Anne Smith, Project Officer. Points of view or opinions expressed in this chapter do not necessarily represent official positions of the U.S. Department of Education and no official endorsement should be inferred.

(those occurring earlier and later in the routine), stimulus and response classes, and environmental responsiveness, to name only a few. Brief summaries follow each major section.

In their review of treatments for severe behavior problems, Carr, Taylor, Carlson, and Robinson (1989, p. 38) noted the "increasing centrality of functional analysis to the practice of positive intervention." They recommended examining general classes of variables that may be influential in the control of challenging behavior. Within their discussion, they distinguished between analyses of antecedents and of consequences and noted that the latter has received far more attention than the former. Although this seems true, a proliferation of literature pertaining to the assessment of antecedents has occurred since the 1980s. In the first section of this chapter, we characterize this literature by elaborating the methodologies used to assess antecedent control of severe problem behavior. (Throughout the chapter, we use the terms *antecedents* and *consequences* when controlling properties are unknown, and *stimuli* and *reinforcers* when control is demonstrated.)

An excellent model for the development of a conceptual scheme for categorizing antecedents is that used to classify motivational variables or functions (Carr, 1977; Iwata, Vollmer, & Zarcone, 1990; O'Neill, Horner, Albin, Storey, & Sprague, 1990). Carr et al. (1989) advocate such an approach because the two are so inextricably tied together. Stimulus variables derive their influence from their close association with reinforcers. Thus, if in the presence of a cookie and Mom, a child has a tantrum that produces access to the cookie, then the motivation for the tantrum is positive reinforcement and the stimulus complex "cookie-and-Mom" is discriminative for positive reinforcement. This means of classifying stimulus variables was further elaborated by Repp and Karsh (1990), who referred to a taxonomy of antecedent events. Such a conceptual scheme or taxonomy is important because it permits the identification of functional classes of antecedents with direct implications for intervention.

Although the development of a conceptual system is germane to a discussion of functional analyses of antecedent variables, our primary objective is to elaborate an array of procedures that researchers and practitioners might use to identify the stimuli controlling challenging behavior. To accomplish this objective, another organizing scheme may be helpful. O'Neill et al. (1990) described three strategies for gathering information relevant to a functional analysis: interview, direct observation, and systematic manipulations. Iwata et al. (1990) labeled these same three strategies *indirect assessment, descriptive analysis,* and *functional analysis.* We review these strategies briefly and cite examples of their application in the literature. Others have generated similar reviews that are more elaborate and comprehensive (e.g., Lennox & Miltenberger, 1989; O'Neill et al., 1990). The focus of our review is restricted to the assessment of antecedent variables. Therefore, for each application, the anal-

ysis of antecedent (vs. subsequent) events is emphasized. To strive for technical accuracy, we should note that some of these strategies do not meet the
criterion of *analysis* (i.e., demonstration of a functional relationship) and may
be referred to as functional *assessment*.

Strategies for Information-Gathering for Functional Analysis

Interview

Information can be obtained efficiently by talking to the learner directly or to
those who have direct contact with the learner and know him or her well. This
strategy narrows the range and facilitates the identification of variables that
may influence the target behavior (O'Neill et al., 1990). Two examples of this
strategy include O'Neill et al.'s (1990) Functional Analysis Interview (FAI)
and Durand and Crimmin's (1988) Motivational Assessment Scale (MAS). In
the FAI, a wide-ranging list of antecedent and consequent events are assessed.
In contrast, the MAS consists of 16 questions: four questions represent each
of four motivational functions (positive reinforcement by attention or by
access to materials, negative reinforcement, and sensory). *Interestingly, these
questions often describe explicitly only the stimulus conditions under which
the behavior occurs, not the function of the behavior.* The function of the
behavior is implied from the description of the stimulus conditions. For example, the following two questions are associated with *escape* and *obtain attention* functions respectively, yet they describe only stimulus conditions: "Does
this behavior occur following a command to perform a difficult task?" and
"Does this behavior occur when you are talking to other persons in the room?"
(Durand & Crimmins, 1988).

　　While interview techniques may narrow the range and facilitate the identification of variables that influence the target behavior, many investigators
question their utility. Unless careful attention is given to the way questions are
asked, the relationship between the informant and the learner with challenging
behavior, and the relationship between the interviewer and the informant, the
responses may be misleading. Recently, the utility of the MAS has been
questioned on the basis of these concerns (Zarcone, Rodgers, Iwata, Rourke,
& Dorsey, 1991).

Direct Observation

The second assessment strategy recommended by O'Neill et al. (1990) consists of observing the learner in ordinary everyday routines. Touchette, Mac-
Donald, and Langer (1985) pioneered the scatterplot assessment, consisting
of a grid using time along the ordinate. Learners are monitored throughout
their waking hours; the rate or frequency of the target behavior is gathered
during time intervals that coincide with changes in the learner's schedule. The
data produce a visual display of behavior over time. The goal is to assess the

correlation of behavior episodes with the local variables (i.e., settings, activities, events, and people) associated with them. There is a heavy emphasis on antecedents. For example, if it were determined that the 4:00 P.M.–5:00 P.M. period was associated with high rates of the target behavior, then additional assessment would focus on "ferreting out" the functional variables, such as time of day (hunger, fatigue), caregivers (Sds, discriminative stimuli for production of target behavior), activity (unpreferred or not competent), setting (too hot or too crowded), or any combination of these.

In their Functional Analysis Observational Form (FAOF), O'Neill and colleagues adopt the scatterplot notion, but require more explicit recording of the extant variables that are part of the learner's schedule at the moment an instance of challenging behavior occurs. This form provides space for the recording of a variety of antecedents (some are explicit on the grid and others can be written in). Antecedent events are emphasized, but data also are gathered on consequences and on "perceived" functions of the target behavior.

Gardner, Cole, Davidson, and Karan (1986), Mace, Lalli, and Shea (in press), and Repp and Karsh (1991) also have used direct observation in natural settings to assess antecedent factors associated with severe problem behavior. With the assistance of a computer-based data collection system, Repp and Karsh (1991) monitored events that were concurrent with and temporally proximate to occurrences of the target behavior. By determining conditional probabilities, they identified antecedent and concurrent events that were associated with instances of severe behavior at levels higher than those expected by chance. Using a different sequential-lag analysis, the researchers identified the probabilities with which particular events occurred subsequent to the target behavior. Both antecedent and subsequent events were monitored, but the authors emphasized the antecedent assessment.

Gardner et al. (1986) described a similar functional assessment of antecedents. They isolated stimulus events immediately preceding occurrences of aggression (potential Sds) and determined the conditional probability of an instance of aggression given the occurrence of each of the stimulus events. After arriving at probabilities that varied from .06 to .36 (e.g., given 100 occasions of a particular stimulus event, aggression followed 6–36 times, on average), Gardner and his colleagues determined that other variables also must be influencing occurrences. In another study they identified a number of potential *setting events,* added these to their analysis, and found dramatic increases in the conditional probabilities of the immediate stimulus events when the presence or absence of setting events was included. Gardner and his colleagues focused their investigations exclusively on antecedents.

Observational strategies lend a direct measure of challenging behavior to the assessment process. The strategies described above offer a more sophisticated approach to this process than their predecessors, but each has its drawbacks. For example, the Touchette et al. (1985) and O'Neill et al. (1990)

systems require the gathering of data for the entire day for a number of days to see the behavior-environment patterns emerge. They are more open-ended and discovery oriented. Such efforts are expensive and the fidelity of the system is difficult to maintain. The strategies recommended by Repp and Karsh (1991) and Gardner et al. (1986) are more limited in the scope of the observational time frame, but are more precise in recording the variables of interest. Although combinations of these strategies would address the weaknesses of any one, such combinations would be extremely expensive and impractical in most applied settings.

Systematic Manipulations

Having identified an association of antecedent variables with targeted behavior (using scatterplots, FAOFs, or conditional probability methods), questions remain about the resulting relationship. Correlations are not equivalent to causal relationships. Because we are searching for antecedents that *control* the occurrence (or nonoccurrence) of severe problem behavior, manipulation of these suspected variables is required to demonstrate functional relationships. O'Neill et al. (1990) suggested that this step may not be required in any particular application. (If provoking variables are identified based on interviews and systematic observation, logical interventions can be formulated and implemented.) Others (e.g., Iwata et al., 1990), however, would insist on this step for precise identification of functional relationships to ensure appropriate intervention selection. All would agree that for theoretical purposes such analyses are needed to support the conceptual basis of this approach to intervention.

Two investigations have been drawn from the research literature to exemplify *systematic manipulations*. Both are analog studies because they do not represent the natural environment for the learners involved. Carr and Durand (1985) explored the effects of low levels of adult attention and high levels of task difficulty on the disruptive behavior of four children with developmental disabilities. Two levels of adult attention (100% and 33% of the time intervals) and two levels of task difficulty (100% and 25% correct performance) were programmed. In a reversal design, three conditions were alternated to assess attention-motivated (Easy 100 vs. Easy 33) and escape-motivated (Easy 100 vs. Difficult 100) challenging behavior. These two motivational hypotheses were based on teacher reports and informal classroom observations by the experimenters.

The primary purpose of Carr and Durand's (1985) study was not to conduct a thorough analysis of the motivational functions of disruptive behavior; rather, it was to identify motivational functions of the disruptive behavior and to replace it with more socially acceptable behavior that fulfilled the same function. Note that the conditions established to assess the function of the problem behavior included manipulation of both antecedent and consequence features (e.g., contriving a difficult task [antecedent] and allowing escape from the task [consequence] contingent on instances of the target behavior).

In contrast to Carr and Durand's (1985) purpose, Iwata, Dorsey, Slifer, Bauman, and Richman (1982) pioneered an assessment methodology encompassing a broader range of motivational hypotheses to determine functional relationships between self-injurious behavior and environmental events. Iwata et al. (1990) distinguished between functional analyses focusing on one motivational function (singular) and those assessing several variables (general) that may be influencing the occurrence of a problem behavior. Eight participants were exposed to four analog conditions in a multi-element experimental design. Each of the four conditions was presented twice daily in randomly determined 15-minute sessions. The four conditions included: 1) *social disapproval* that assessed attention motivation, 2) *academic demand* that assessed escape motivation, 3) *unstructured play* in which each variable assessed was delivered at its optimal level with an expectation of producing low rates of self-injurious behavior (SIB), and 4) *self-play* that assessed sensory stimulation (i.e., automatic) motivation.

As in the Carr and Durand (1985) study, the conditions created to assess functional properties of self-injury comprised a mix of antecedent and consequent variables. For example, in the social-disapproval condition, attention in the form of verbal statements paired with nonpunitive brief physical contact was provided contingent on episodes of self-injury. Perhaps of equal importance, however, were the extant antecedent variables manipulated, such as the unavailability of the experimenter who sat in a chair across the room and appeared to be reading.

Although the objective of most functional analyses is to determine the function of the behavior (i.e., environmental effects), we would be remiss if we did not specify carefully the context in which the behavior occurs because the stimuli that comprise this context are the "triggers" that occasion the behavior of interest. Refer to Table 1 for a description and examples of contextual variables.

CURRENT LIMITATIONS OF ANALOG ANALYSIS

Analog analyses can produce at least two types of errors. A "false negative" error is one in which the variables assessed in the analog do not result in the target behavior because only part of the stimulus configuration that controls the behavior in the natural environment is included in the analog. For example, if a learner engages in escape-motivated behavior in the context of a toothbrushing routine, but does not display such behavior when a toothbrush is handed to him in an analog situation, it is possible that other parts of the brushing routine (e.g., the bathroom, a particular teacher) may have entered

Table 1. Potential contextual variables

Class	Definition of class	Examples
Current physiology	Emanate from within the learner; "state" variables	Drug effects, hunger, thirst, illness, pain, fatigue
Current social environment	Pertain to other people who co-exist in or share the environment	Others' presence or absence, smiles, eye contact, praise, demands, density, interactions
Current physical environment	Physical structure and arrangement of setting and its contents	Objects, materials, activities and their sequence, group size, space, pacing of instruction
Historical events	Learners' past interactions with their social and physical environments; their learning histories	A cancelled family visit the prior evening; history of consistent aversive interaction with a particular person; response to hospital due to past painful surgery

into a conditional relationship to occasion the behavior. A second type of error might be labeled a "false positive." In this case, a learner may demonstrate disruptive behavior under escape conditions contrived for the analog, yet the motivational function suggested by this result has no parallel in the natural environment (i.e., the disruptive behavior never functions to produce escape in everyday settings). Iwata et al. (1990) allude to this latter type of error as well as to limitations produced by analyses that assess only one (i.e., singular) motivational function. Because we know that a particular behavior may serve more than one function, any analysis assessing only one function is necessarily restrictive.

Whether the analog analysis is conducted to assess the influence of a single motivational function or multiple functions, concerns can arise about the way in which the antecedents are presented in the analog. Does the analog reflect naturally occurring conditions? That is, are the variables maintaining the behavior in the natural environment the same as those isolated in the analog conditions? Do the stimulus variables assessed have the same effect in the analog situation as they have in natural circumstances? The word analog connotes variation from the referent circumstance. Are there other relevant stimuli in the natural environment that have been omitted from the analog analysis—ones that when combined with the variable assessed (conditional or conjoint control) precipitate the problem behavior, but in whose absence the behavior does not occur? Is it possible that the *sequencing* and *pacing* of the analog manipulations may themselves inadvertently influence the probability of occasioning challenging behavior?

We have already described the differential results of the assessment of aggression with and without the influence of setting events (i.e., Gardner et al., 1986). Iwata et al. (1990) provide additional examples, including two learners exhibiting escape-motivated SIB, one in response to demands of a medical nature, not to academic demands, and another in response to academic demands requiring effort (e.g., adaptive tasks), not to academic demands requiring a pointing or sorting response. These responses were under conditional control in that demands alone did not necessarily provoke SIB; rather, particular types of demands (content or response requirement) had very difficult effects. Carr, Newsom, and Binkoff (1980) illustrated the potential for false positive errors by arranging (in analog) an escape contingency for aggression and finger-tapping. Both responses occurred at high levels when they produced escape from demands. With such a result, questions arise about the possibility of having established a new relationship unique to the analog that has no parallel in the natural environment (Iwata et al. 1990).

Mace, Lalli, and Shea (in press), Iwata et al. (1990), and Mace and Shea (1990) recommended careful assessment of the natural environment to inform or to aid in the selection of analog situations. Mace and Shea (1990) were critical of past applications of analog methodology because the design of the analog conditions lacked a clear relationship to naturally occurring events in the learner's everyday life. These authors identified a number of dimensions in which this correspondence may be lacking: persons present, instructions, materials and tasks, activity changes, activity interruptions, provocative statements, the topography and schedule of social consequences, and availability and history with alternative sources of reinforcement. Depending on the influence of these variables under natural conditions, the validity of the functional analysis depends on their accurate representation in the analog. Mace and Lalli (1991) advocated linking descriptive and functional analyses to enhance the accuracy of identifying functional relationships that exist under natural conditions.

In a similar vein, Iwata et al. (1990) suggested that a limitation of analog analysis can be overcome by observing directly in the natural environment. They cited a study by Tarpley and Schroeder (1979) demonstrating that, even when challenging behavior is found to be maintained by positive reinforcement (i.e., access to a ball), an analog may not illuminate all of the specific events serving as discriminative stimuli or as reinforcers (e.g., only a particular ball possessed reinforcing properties, thus only in its presence was the behavior emitted). When a generic analog assessment such as the one used by Iwata et al. (1982) is conducted, stimuli indigenous to the natural context may not be included. The analog situation is constructed to reflect a "pure" motivational function, one that may evoke behavior when lesser versions that mirror the natural environment may not. Influential contextual variables (conditional events), such as setting events or stimuli associated with prior steps in routines, may be lost in these analogs.

Future Directions

Interviews, direct observation, and systematic manipulations all have as a goal the determination of the antecedents and consequences that control challenging behavior in the natural environment. Each strategy may enable contributions to that goal under certain circumstances. However, as currently practiced, each method has limitations. Limitations relevant to interviews were described previously. The primary limitation of observational techniques is that they can detect only correlations between events operating in the natural environment. Such correlations do not imply causation. Analog analyses allow a determination of the functions of antecedents and consequences, but there is no assurance that those functions are relevant to the functions operating in a learner's natural environment.

To address these concerns about analog analysis, we need to move beyond an unspecified linking of descriptive and experimental analyses (based on interview and observational information) to refined and systematic linkages that reflect accurately the functional variables operating in natural settings. At least two strategies can be delineated to accomplish this outcome. The first would focus on an attempt to obtain sufficient control in the natural environment to manipulate the variable(s) thought to be relevant, while leaving irrelevant variables undisturbed. The major problem with this approach is that each manipulation of a variable may involve changing the entire social ecology of the natural environment. This may be costly if the wrong variable is chosen, and, even if the "correct" variable is selected, the ecology has to be "reversed" to ensure that the relevant variable has been isolated.

A second strategy entails "piecing together" aspects of the natural environment and transferring them to the contrived analog situation. At some point, these two strategies will meld together and become indistinguishable. Perhaps the major feature differentiating these two approaches is the physical setting in which the analogs are conducted. Regardless of the strategy, much greater care can be exercised to simulate the setting events and the influential antecedent and consequent variables operating in the natural environment. Otherwise, the validity of analog assessments will be compromised and the results may have limited generality when applied to criterion environments (i.e., the natural environment).

Reflecting natural conditions in the analogs we develop is one suggestion for future work; perhaps an equally crucial and related recommendation entails a systematic analysis of the stimulus controls operating in natural environments. It is not sufficient to know that Joey's challenging behavior is escape motivated. We need to identify the stimulus conditions associated with escape in natural contexts and when we identify these conditions, we need to determine which are functional (i.e., those that influence the probability of the response). Rather than conceptualizing a response as being occasioned by a *single* discriminative stimulus, we now consider the influence of multiple stimuli (including setting events or establishing operations) that may enter into conditional relationships with one another. Assuming that behavior in natural environments is governed by such complex or conditional stimulus control would appear to be a more accurate model for describing how antecedent and concurrent events control behavior.

An illustration may be instructive. The first author was consulted about a 10-year-old boy who engaged in high-rate disruptive behavior. Interviews and direct observation provided information on stimulus variables that were highly correlated with the disruptive behavior. Transitions were identified as a major precipitating event, but not all transitions produced disruption. We began manipulating variables to determine which entered into a functional relationship with disruptive behavior. Transitions terminating in a particular scheduled activity with particular educational staff were much more likely to evoke the behavior than other transitions. A logical conclusion derived from these findings is that this student's disruptive behavior was controlled conjointly by specific people and subsequent activities in the context of a transition.

To identify which stimuli, of all those available, entering into a controlling relationship with the problem behavior may be a nearly impossible endeavor. However, Halle and Holt (1991) have elaborated a methodology that constitutes a first approximation toward this goal by permitting identification of conjoint stimulus control. In a prior study by Halle (1989), two children with mental retardation were taught coin labels under a stable set of conditions: the same trainer, setting, time of day, verbal instruction and positioning of trainer, and task stimuli were used on each instructional trial. When the acquisition criterion was met, probes were conducted to assess the stimuli that acquired control during training. Probes consisted of trials in which only one stimulus condition (of the eight specified) was changed at a time; the other seven remained intact. If the response repeatedly failed to occur during particular probes but not during others, then the stimulus controlling the response would have been identified. Unfortunately, none of the single-stimulus condition changes produced errors. When two stimuli were changed simultaneously, however, responding was disrupted for one of the children.

Halle and Holt's (1991) approach was modified in accord with the previous findings. Changing one condition at a time did *not* disrupt coin-label responses, and hence it appeared that changing only one stimulus did not provide a discriminating test of stimulus control. Thus, the authors decided to use the inverse strategy: On probe trials, only one condition remained the same as in training, and the remaining conditions were varied. Intuitively, this would provide a rigorous test of each condition, uncontaminated by other conditions associated with training. Flawless responding on probe trials such as that observed in the previous study (Halle, 1989) would not be expected.

In an effort to demonstrate experimental control, replications were effected. On each occasion that a single-stimulus probe produced an error, we would introduce a training trial on the next occasion to ensure that the target response remained intact; then we would repeat the probe that previously had produced the error to assess the reliability of effect. The results revealed that only one of three participants responded in the presence of a single-stimulus condition. Two others failed to respond in the presence of any one stimulus associated with training; both did respond, however, in the presence of two stimuli (i.e., conjoint stimulus control).

Invoking the example cited above about the 10-year-old exhibiting disruptive behavior, we can illustrate potential manipulations of stimuli necessary to determine those that influence the probability of disruptive responses. The first step requires identification of potentially controlling stimuli. In this example, transitions (i.e., time between two scheduled activities) terminating in math, as well as supervising adults (Lola and Alex), and time of day (morning) were implicated in the interviews and direct observations. The second step includes the manipulations themselves. To approximate the Halle and Holt (1991) approach, at first, each of these manipulations might include only one of the implicated variables (e.g., one of the identified adults would interact with the learner in the afternoon during transitions other than those terminating in math). Such manipulations already may occur naturally as part of the everyday schedule. If they do, these occasions can be used to conduct the assessments. Refer to Table 2 for additional examples of manipulations.

After each of the implicated variables has been probed repeatedly in isolation, depending on the results, the investigator could begin to combine variables in the manipulations (see examples in Table 2). That is, if it were discovered that none of the variables in isolation occasioned disruptions, then combinations would be tested. However, if only one of the variables consistently provoked disruptive behavior, then the analysis could stop and the intervention would be developed taking this information into account. During the implementation of these manipulated probe trials, it is important to maintain a baseline against which the performance on these probes is compared. Such a baseline in the present example would constitute repeated exposure to the known provoking context (i.e., morning transitions terminating in math with either Lola or Alex supervising). If responding in the presence of these known provoking circumstances occurred inconsistently, the control exerted by any single stimulus or by any combination could *not* be assessed accurately.

Although this analysis facilitates specification of the precipitating conditions and their conditional nature, it remains quite crude when one considers

Table 2. Examples of manipulations

Implicated variables		
Transition terminating in	Supervising adult	Time of day
math	*Lola or Alex*	*morning*

Examples of single-variable probe assessments		
Transition terminating in	Supervising adult	Time of day
recess	*Lola or Alex*	afternoon
reading	*Lola or Alex*	afternoon
math	Ralph	afternoon
math	Susan	afternoon
recess	Ralph	*morning*
reading	Susan	*morning*

Examples of combined variables probe assessments		
Transitions terminating in	Supervising adult	Time of day
math	Susan	*morning*
math	*Lola or Alex*	afternoon
reading	*Lola or Alex*	*morning*

additional levels of analysis. For example, questions about setting events and establishing operations (Michael, 1982) are currently not addressed in this approach. Furthermore, if we discover that only two particular supervising adults (in conjunction with other stimuli) occasion the target behavior, we do not know on what basis the learner has established this discrimination. Is it historical experiences with these two people? Is it the manner in which they deliver instruction? Is it the schedule of reinforcement they mediate? Likewise, if particular activities are implicated, many additional questions arise about these activities (e.g., the learner's level of competence, group vs. individual format, schedule and strength of reinforcement) that require answers before we have a complete analysis of the stimulus factors involved.

Although many of the studies pertaining to functional analysis of challenging behavior implicate only *one* stimulus or *one* function for the problem behavior, it is widely recognized that *across instances* a single topography may serve a number of functions (e.g., hitting may produce a desired item on one occasion and escape from an unpleasant task on another), or one function may be expressed by a number of topographies (e.g., escape may be realized by hitting another person, by destroying property, or by engaging in stereotypy). *Within one instance* of behavior, however, the concept of multiple or conditional control is not well developed. If we are to understand the variables that influence challenging behavior, we will need to conduct more microanalyses that include the assessment of multiple and conditional stimuli that exert stable control of target responses. A critical part of this analysis was alluded to previously in the discussion of setting events. A more thorough elaboration of these potentially influential variables follows.

THE CONTRIBUTION OF SETTING EVENTS

Until recently, applied behavior analysts have advocated an approach to understanding human behavior that encompasses the influence of conditions present immediately preceding and subsequent to the behavior of interest. In this approach, we analyze how these conditions enter into a functional relationship with the behavior (i.e., influences its probability of occurrence). By examining such antecedents and consequences, many determinants of human behavior may be identified; however, it is naive to think that the only influences are those that occur immediately before, coincidental with, or immediately subsequent to the target behavior.

Numerous illustrations demonstrating that more temporally distant and complex events may influence behavior have been described. For example, Bijou and Baer (1961) related a hypothetical example of an infant who had a routine of napping in his crib followed by lively play in his playpen. On a particular occasion, noises outside his room prevented his napping, and he remained active during his naptime. When his mother placed him in his playpen, he cried and protested. The outside noises and the sleeplessness they produced functioned as a setting event for the infant's crying when placed in the playpen. Placement in the playpen could be considered the discriminative stimulus. The setting event is different from a discriminative stimulus in two ways: The outside noises and sleeplessness are stimuli occurring *earlier in time,* and together they constitute a *stimulus–response (S–R) relationship* (i.e., the outside noises produced sleeplessness) instead of a simple discrete event.

The first author of this chapter has three young children at home; the quality of his interaction with them is adversely affected by lack of sleep, illness, or having previously been in an argument with his spouse (as well as a multitude of other variables). These are all setting events that may have occurred at points in time much earlier than the interactions that defy description as discrete events. The discriminative stimuli for such negative interactions might be a loud scream or a push, an event that was discrete and immediately preceded the interaction. These stimuli may assume evocative properties only when preceded by a setting event such as fatigue, illness, or a "bad day at the office."

Bijou and Baer (1961), Gardner et al. (1986), Kantor (1959, 1970), Wahler and Fox (1981), and others have advocated extending the scope of our analysis to include events that may be more complex and temporally distant than those traditionally labeled discriminative stimuli. Different investigators have developed various methods of categorizing setting events. For current purposes, we divided them into two general classes: *durational* or *concurrent* events and *prior* or *historical* events.

Durational or concurrent events include physiologic conditions (e.g., deprivation, satiation, drug effects, infections, physical discomfort, pain) as well as discrete or complex events (e.g., presence or absence of people, materials, activities; attention from others; amount of space; ratio of adults to children; availability of competing activities; task difficulty) that occur concurrently with the behavior of interest. That is, these stimuli are present or operational prior to the target behavior (e.g., background stimuli that Goldiamond [1966] discussed) and remain available until the production of the behavior of interest. Prior or historical events refer to a class of behavior-environment interactions that are separate in time and space from the currently impinging stimulus conditions and corresponding behavior. Such interactions can be a single, intense negatively or positively reinforcing event or a number of less intense events that exert control by virtue of their density. Examples of this class of setting events might include the effects that a weekend visit with his or her family may have on an adolescent's aggressive behavior at work the following Monday, or the effects of a prior argument between spouses on their current interaction with their children. Such historical events are no longer available as stimuli, but they may generate a state, such as physiologic arousal, that is maintained over time and thus may exist concurrently (and enter into a conditional relationship) with later triggering events.

An elegant example of the influence of setting events is that of those operating in the determination of aggressive behavior. Gardner, Karan, and Cole (1984) identified six stimulus events (e.g., teasing by peers or being corrected for mistakes) that preceded occurrences of verbal aggression by John, a young adult with mental retardation. The researchers then gathered data on the frequency with which these stimulus events provoked aggression by John. Of the six events, teasing was most likely to produce aggression. During 1 month, teasing occurred 55 times and provoked aggression on 18 of the 55 occasions, or 32% of the time. None of the six events exerted consistent control over aggression; thus, other events or variables must also have influenced the probability of John's aggression. By adding setting events to the analysis (e.g., weekend family visits, difficulty arising in the morning, presence of a particular staff member), the predictability of aggression, given a particular setting event plus an identified precipitating stimulus, was vastly improved.

Horner, Dodson, Tuesday-Heathfield, and Ramsden (1991) conducted a preliminary analysis of the relationship between setting events and excess behavior. Three learners with severe disabilities who attended a middle school were monitored for 45 days. As soon as the participants arrived at school, the teacher assessed potential setting events by contacting the bus driver and their parents and interviewing them about the occurrence of previously established events (e.g., health, sleep, eating, seizures, social contacts). Targeted problem behaviors of each learner were assessed throughout the school day as well as during instructional sessions. Preliminary findings of the study indicate statistically significant relationships between particular setting events and target behaviors.

Perhaps an even greater contribution than their pilot study to a setting-event analysis of challenging behavior is the conceptual framework that Horner, O'Neill, and Albin (1991) offer. Citing an earlier work by Michael (1982), they define setting events as:

> Those events that occur any time prior to a response (seconds before or years before), are not discriminative stimuli, yet change the value of available reinforcers. . . . By changing the value of the available reinforcers, setting events increase the control exerted by stimuli associated with responses that lead to that reinforcer. (Horner, O'Neill, & Albin, 1991, p. 10)

One implication of including setting events within our framework for understanding severe problem behavior is *the recognition* that we must determine the continually shifting value of available reinforcers (Horner, O'Neill, et al., 1991) and the stimuli that signal their availability.

Setting events are an elegant example of multiple or conditional stimulus control in that temporally earlier or more complex events or interactions may enter into controlling relationships with concurrent (discriminative) stimuli to occasion challenging behavior. As a field, we (i.e., applied behavior analysts) need to move toward these extended and more complex analyses if we are to describe, explain, and control challenging behavior with precision.

In summary, we have made steady progress in the development of methods for assessing motivational functions of challenging behavior. The work has focused primarily on the effects that the behavior produces on the environment. A second, but crucial, part of the analysis has received much less attention: the identification of stimuli that influence the probability of occurrence. We have tried to characterize the relevant literature by reflecting on how different researchers have analyzed the variables that are present before or concurrent with the behavior of interest. Using a stimulus-control perspective, we have identified limitations of our current applications of functional analysis and have provided recommendations that begin to address these shortcomings.

EXTENDING THE ANALYSIS OF CHALLENGING BEHAVIOR OCCURRING IN THE CONTEXT OF ROUTINES

To adapt to infinite potential variation, human (and other animal) behavior is organized in stable patterns that produce efficiency in completing many routine tasks of daily living. By conceptualizing challenging behavior as links in such patterns or behavior chains, novel analyses of function are possible.

Routines or Behavioral Chains

The daily lives of people include a great number of recurrent sequences of behavior. For example, many people arise from sleep in the morning, get dressed, eat breakfast, eat lunch, eat dinner, undress, and return to bed at night. These recurrent sequences often seem to terminate with reinforcing events or, as in the case of eating meals, may constitute reinforcing events in themselves. Within each of these events are smaller units of recurrent behavior. In the case of eating a meal, motor responses that move food to one's mouth are immediately and continually reinforced. However, these small units that immediately precede food in the mouth are not the only behaviors that are being reinforced. The food and drink that function as immediate reinforcers for putting the fork or glass to the mouth also result in the reinforcement of behavior more remote from the terminal reinforcer. In the mid-1960s, the second author and colleagues (Spradlin, Girardeau, & Corte, 1965) conducted a series of operant laboratory studies with children with profound mental retardation, which provided an opportunity to observe the development of a chain of behavior. The experiments were simple: The children learned to pull a plunger to produce a bit of candy that they consumed immediately. In the first phases of training, we often had to take the candy from the food receptacle and place it on a child's tongue. Soon, the children reached out and retrieved the candy from the experimenter's hand; and, still later, the children took the candy from the receptacle. After shaping, manual guidance, and modeling, the children began pulling the plunger and retrieving the candy when it was delivered. The behavior in the laboratory, however, was not the only thing that the children learned. Initially, they had to be guided to the laboratory by another person, but after several visits, they could be taken to the door of the cottage and sent to the laboratory alone. The children's learning involved responses quite remote from the laboratory. In short, they had learned a rather lengthy routine of going from the cottage to the laboratory, operating the plunger for food, and then returning to the cottage. Theoretically, each event in this sequence came to serve as a conditioned reinforcer for preceding behavior and a discriminative stimulus for subsequent behavior.

Because the routines discussed above terminated in positive reinforcement, it is not difficult to see why events within the routine would serve as conditioned reinforcers for the behavior they follow and discriminative stimuli for the behavior they precede. However, some routines terminate in negative reinforcement. For example, the routine of going to a restroom is maintained by the elimination of the aversive stimuli produced by a full bladder or bowel. In the case of routines maintained by negative reinforcement, delays, no doubt, have the same effects as those produced by routines terminating in positive reinforcement.

Another set of routines may involve the presentation of averse stimuli. For example, trips to the dentist's or physician's office may involve unpleasant events. For young children and for learners with developmental disabilities, these routines may result in behaviors such as temper tantrums, physical attacks, and self-injury. Occasionally these behaviors may be sufficiently severe that the learner escapes or avoids the procedure. Dentists, physicians, caregivers, and parents have developed a number of techniques to maintain recalcitrant learners in such routines. One technique employed by physicians and dentists involves reducing or masking the aversive stimulus. Reduction can occur by introducing an anesthetic and masking may be achieved by playing music. Finally, parents, caregivers, physicians, and dentists may introduce positive reinforcers during the routine or after the aversive stimulus has been presented. For example, after the dentist completes his work, children may be given a small toy or a balloon. A parent may allow a child who has completed a dental visit to engage in a favorite activity. All of these procedures may function to encourage the recalcitrant learner to complete the routine without engaging in challenging behavior. Once a learner has completed such a routine on several occasions, the integrity of the routine may be quite similar to that of other routines, so that delays in moving through the routine may function in much the same way as those not involving the presentation of aversive stimuli.

If each component of a behavioral sequence serves both as a discriminative stimulus for the next component and as a conditioned reinforcer for the previous component, then within a well-established routine there are always reinforcers and punishers available for use in behavioral programs. Allowing advancement to the next component can function as a positive reinforcer and delaying access to the next component can serve as a punisher. Researchers repeatedly have demonstrated that when a delay is introduced into an ongoing routine, new responses that reduce or eliminate the delay can be acquired rapidly (Charlop, Schriebman, & Thibodeau, 1985; Charlop & Trasowech, 1991; Goetz, Gee, & Sailor, 1985; Halle, Baer, & Spradlin, 1981; Halle, Marshall, & Spradlin, 1979; Schussler & Spradlin, 1991; Sigafoos, Reichle, Doss, Hall, & Pettitt, 1990). The typical pattern for each of these studies involved establishing a new routine or using a routine that already had been established by the natural environment. For example, Halle et al. (1979) used a standard institutional dining routine in which individuals' names were called, they were handed a food tray, and then they went to their seats at a table. Their procedure involved having dining room personnel simply hold the tray for 15 seconds and then prompt the learner to request, "Tray, please." Six participants came to request the tray prior to receiving the prompt. Essentially, Halle et al. had introduced a new link into the chain, simply by allowing that link to reduce or eliminate the delay in moving to the next link in the chain. Each of the studies cited above involved teaching the learners a new response or to use an old response in a new chain to advance through the chain. The response introduced was a request, and the request allowed continuation or short-cutting of the routine and more rapid contact with the reinforcer.

Challenging behavior, such as tantrums, self-injury, and screaming, may be a component of a routine that reduces delay in reinforcement. For example, a child who is waiting in line at a wading pool may tantrum and then be allowed to proceed to the pool ahead of others who are waiting. Such a response may begin to occur earlier and earlier in the routine. In fact, it may occur so early that the caregiver may not realize that it is related to the routine. Although these comments are speculative, Schussler and Spradlin (1991) demonstrated this kind of phenomenon with verbal requests, and there is no reason that challenging behavior that has a request function should not function similarly. Not only may such challenging behaviors come earlier and earlier in a routine, but they may also come to occur in new routines so that eventually they occur almost any time a routine involves delays or aversive components.

Time-out from reinforcement may constitute a delay or an interruption in a routine. Time-out has long been recognized as a procedure for reducing rates of behavior (e.g., Baer, Rowbury, & Baer, 1973; Porterfield, Herbert-Jackson, & Risley, 1976). Spradlin (1962) reported on his efforts to teach a child with severe mental retardation to feed herself. When her hands were free, she patted the food. This behavior was eliminated simply by interrupting the child's feeding by holding her hands to her side for 20–30 seconds each time she patted the food. The procedure involved interrupting a very short chain: filling a spoon, moving it to her mouth, and consuming the contents of the spoon. It is likely that this procedure could be used to eliminate behavior occurring in the context of much longer routines.

Stimulus and Response Classes within a Routine

Rarely do the links in a behavioral chain involve single stimuli or single responses. The links usually involve stimulus and response classes. Let us consider stimulus classes first. Although there are many types of stimulus classes, the most important for understanding self-injurious behavior are classes of people and situations. People may be grouped in any number of ways. Classes may be established on the basis of physical features, such as size, sex, hair color, skin color, or facial features. Such classes are formed readily and may lead to unfortunate behavior patterns. Suppose a person with a specific set of physical features ignores a child unless the child engages in self-injurious behavior. The child may come to exhibit self-injurious behavior in the presence of people who share those physical features. In other words, in both avoidance and positive reinforcement learning, different people may become members of the same stimulus class if they share common physical features.

In addition to establishing stimulus classes based on personal physical characteristics, classes may be formed on the basis of dress. For example, a child who has been given a shot by a person wearing a white uniform may come to fear a restaurant worker who is wearing a white uniform. The stimulus classes described above are quite familiar and typically have been discussed under the rubric of primary stimulus generalization.

Shared physical features are not the only basis for the development of stimulus classes. For example, there are no defining physical features for distinguishing toys from tools or accountants from engineers, dentists, or teachers. These classes are based on functions within routines or contexts. Numerous laboratory studies have demonstrated that stimuli that do not share common physical features may become members of the same functional stimulus class if they can be substituted in some contexts without a change in the response-reinforcer contingencies (Devany, Hayes, & Nelson, 1986; Dixon & Spradlin, 1976; Saunders, Wachter, & Spradlin, 1988; Sidman, 1971; Sidman, Wynne, Maguire, & Barnes, 1989; Silverman, Anderson, Marshall, & Baer, 1986; Spradlin, Cotter, & Baxley, 1973). With the exception of the Silverman et al. study (1986), strong experimental demonstrations of such stimulus classes developing with people do not exist. However, there is no reason to believe that the same principles should not hold for classes of people as for other stimuli.

Haavik, Spradlin, and Altman (1984) conducted a study in which an interventionist taught children a number of discrete responses in a controlled situation. The children then were tested to determine whether they would perform the tasks for their mothers. As expected, the children's performances were unstable. Then the mothers were taught to teach and reinforce one or two of the responses in the same way that they were taught by the interventionist. When the children were retested, their performances on those responses that had not been taught by the mothers improved. In this limited context, mothers had become members of the same stimulus class as the interventionist. That is, mothers had become members of the class of people who controlled appropriate responding in a teaching context. We speculate that there are a number of conditions that will result in different individuals becoming members of the same stimulus class.

If different people exercise the same contingencies in a number of situations, it is likely that children will come to respond similarly to them, even in contexts in which they do not exercise the same contingencies. For example, suppose a caregiver has bathed a child in the morning, laid out her clothes, given her breakfast, and then left her alone until she engaged in self-injurious behavior, at which time the caregiver comforted her with caresses and soft words. Now suppose another caregiver bathes the child, dresses her, gives her breakfast, and then leaves her unengaged for some period of time. It would not be surprising if the child engaged in self-injurious behavior in the presence of this second caregiver who had never reinforced self-injurious behavior. Moreover, the self-injurious behavior may be very resistant to extinction with the second caregiver because it is not under extinction with the first.

The same principles also may hold for self-injurious behavior that has an avoidance function. Suppose two or more caregivers interact with a child in a number of common routines, and one or more of those caregivers frequently terminates tasks when the child engages in self-injurious behavior. It might be anticipated that the child would exhibit self-injurious behavior with caregivers who had never reinforced this behavior.

Response Classes

Generally, response classes have been defined as a set of responses so organized that an operation performed on a subset of the class will change not only the rates of the subset, but also the rates of other responses in the class not subject to that operation (Peterson, 1968). Just as certain stimuli may be substituted into a routine without changing the contingencies operating in that routine, responses may be substituted in a routine without changing contingencies. For example, any one of the following—kicking, biting, or hitting other people—is likely to lead to their retreat. Or, perhaps face-slapping, screaming, or head-banging may cause a teacher to stop a teaching session. If the teaching procedure is aversive, then any response that terminates the task will be strengthened.

Carr, Taylor, and Robinson (1991) demonstrated the potential influence of child effects. For example, a task that is likely to produce self-injury may become aversive for a teacher. By avoiding engagement in such tasks, the teacher is negatively reinforced.

To some degree, all responses are interchangeable. The member of a response class that occurs on a specific occasion may depend on a number of factors. For example, screaming may require less effort or pain than head-banging and, therefore, may occur first (Horner & Billingsley, 1988). If screaming is successful in obtaining positive reinforcement or avoiding aversive stimuli, then head-banging may not occur. However, if screaming fails, then another more severe response may occur. It is also possible that in certain contexts or with certain people, the most severe form occurs immediately, because in those contexts or with those people, mild forms of the behavior have never been successful.

Once response chains are reconceptualized in terms of a sequence of stimulus and response classes, it becomes apparent that the chain will involve variation from occurrence to occurrence. Perhaps one of the major characteristics of persons with mental retardation is that they have developed too few and too narrow a range of stimulus and response classes. Many learners with mental retardation have few, if any, conventional ways of requesting objects or assistance necessary to complete a routine, or of avoiding entrance into aversive routines. Such learners may instead engage in a variety of behaviors that are sufficiently aversive to caregivers, coercing them into making changes that will terminate the aversive routine. However, because the responses tend to occur under varying conditions in a variety of routines, they are not discriminative for caregivers to make the rapid adjustments demanded. In a sense, they provide the motivation for caregivers to act, but they do not inform them *how* to act. This may lead to a rather prolonged period of time prior to the caregiver making the appropriate or reinforcing change. If the intensity of the challenging behavior is maintained at a sufficiently high level to keep the caregiver responding, the reinforcing change will occur eventually. Note that the combination of primitive responses and making reinforcing changes after variable periods of high intensity behavior is the ideal consequence for developing and maintaining very intense and durable behavior. It may also be highly generalized (i.e., it may occur across a variety of settings and routines).

Researchers have demonstrated that some learners who exhibit challenging behavior do so to obtain attention or tangible reinforcers (Carr & Durand, 1985; Durand & Carr, 1987). Other learners, or the same learners under different conditions, exhibit challenging behavior primarily to escape from or to avoid aversive situations (Day, Rea, Schussler, Larsen, & Johnson, 1988; Iwata et al., 1982).

For a large percent of learners who exhibit self-injurious behavior, no specific environmental variables have been identified. It has been assumed that learners who injured themselves while alone did so because of consequences produced by the self-injurious behavior. Those consequences might function as either positive or negative reinforcement (Carr, 1977).

Most of the attempts to isolate the variables that control challenging behavior have focused on events occurring in close proximity to the challenging behavior. As mentioned previously, however, events somewhat remote from the setting in which the behavior occurs may in fact influence the probability or rate (Gardner et al., 1986). Gardner and his colleagues focused on events that occurred earlier in the chain or routine and demonstrated that such events may enter into controlling relationships with proximal events to occasion challenging behavior. Behavior chains or routines may be convenient mechanisms to invoke to describe the effects of setting events. Although not discussed by Gardner et al. (1986), it is important to note that consequences terminating the chain may affect the probability of environment-behavior interactions occurring at earlier points in the chain.

Considering challenging behavior in terms of routines or behavioral chains may suggest slight variations in the assessment procedures described earlier in the chapter, although the basic interview, observation, and manipulation approaches are still germane. The focus of all three assessment procedures is on events that occur within routines. The interviewer could begin the interview by asking the informant to provide an hour-by-hour account of the activities in which the learner engages. The interview would cover each day of the week, and an attempt would be made to determine those routines that occur several times a day, those that occur daily, and those that occur less frequently. Once a detailed description of the learner's routines is developed, the interviewer would begin to ask specific questions about whether challenging behavior occurred during specific routines. If the informant indicated specific routines in which challenging behavior was likely to occur and others in which it was unlikely, the interviewer would ask questions aimed at obtaining more detail about these routines. Who is present during the routines? Does the routine involve little or a great deal of engagement? What routine follows? Is the subsequent routine pleasant or unpleasant? Are there routines that begin very similarly but end in very different outcomes? For example, trips to the dentist or to the grocery store may begin with bathing and dressing, but the outcomes of such excursions are very different. Such confusion might cause learners to engage in challenging behavior at times quite remote from the event that is ultimately controlling it.

Within an hour or two, such an interview might lead to hypotheses concerning the routines in which challenging behavior was likely and unlikely to occur. Because observation is time-consuming, observational assessment would focus initially on those routines that were reported to involve the highest and lowest rates of challenging behavior. These observations would result in a more elaborate description of the routines in which challenging behavior co-occurred as well as those in which such behavior was unlikely. If the observations confirmed the information obtained in the interview, then having limited observations of these routines would result in a great saving of observational time. If not, then observations would need to be scheduled across additional routines and would require much more time. The basic observations (typical of behavior assessment) would focus on events that preceded challenging behavior as well as events that followed it. The time span involved, however, would be longer than in the typical assessment. Of special interest would be the identification of earlier links and terminal points of routines, not just those events occurring immediately before and after an instance of challenging behavior.

Changing Routines as a Way of Reducing Challenging Behavior

There are a number of ways of reducing rates of challenging behavior if the aspects of the routine that are evoking or maintaining it are known (i.e., the controlling conditions). Recently, a number of investigators have shown that persons who exhibited self-injurious or aggressive behavior under positive reinforcement conditions could be taught conventional communication responses to obtain the same reinforcers. When this strategy has been implemented, the rate of self-injury and aggression has decreased dramatically. This same procedure also has been used to reduce levels of challenging behavior that functioned to terminate task demands. Conventional communication responses can be effective substitutes (functionally equivalent, according to Carr, 1988) for challenging behavior when caregivers are sensitive to individuals and responsive to the message communicated. Teaching conventional communication responses, however, may not be a panacea for eliminating challenging behavior. The success in reducing levels of challenging behavior depends on the responsiveness of caregivers. If caregivers are not responsive to newly acquired communicative acts, the old challenging responses will return at full strength. Because caregivers are not always maximally responsive, the probability of communication training producing a total elimination of challenging behavior is something less than 100%.

If individuals are sensitive and consistently honor the requests of learners who exhibit challenging behavior under the control of reinforcers, then severe challenging behavior might never develop. When challenging behavior is maintained by its consequences, the development of severe forms of the behavior depends on the withholding of the consequence until more and more severe forms occur. If every problematic response is reinforced immediately, the learner gradually will come to produce less intense forms. In fact, if the challenging behavior is not demanded by the contingencies, it will cease to occur. Functionally equivalent communicative responses may reduce rates of self-injury because they require less effort and pain than do self-injurious responses (Horner & Billingsley, 1988); they also may enable a caregiver to provide a reinforcer more rapidly. Communicative responses by themselves do not eliminate the likelihood that self-injurious behavior will reoccur if they prove unsuccessful in producing efficient access to the same reinforcers.

Pyles and Bailey (1990) reported an anecdote involving a slight change in a routine that had a major impact on a young man's life. In the initial routine, the young man was placed in a wheelchair when he returned from school. After this routine was in effect for a while, he began to jump out of his wheelchair. This sometimes led to injury. The typical consequence for injury, and thus part of the routine, was attention. Traditional procedures might involve providing attention while he is in his wheelchair. Pyles and Bailey noted, however, that the young man spent many hours seated in the wheelchair. When he jumped out of it, he was placed on a mat or couch. They surmised that the reinforcer was being placed on the mat, not the attention received. Thus, they instituted a procedure in which the young man was placed on the mat or couch on arrival from school. Jumping and injury were eliminated. Apparently, the end point or reinforcement for jumping out of the chair was indeed placement on the mat; the behavior was eliminated simply by shortcutting the routine.

CONCLUSION

In summary, by conceptualizing challenging behavior as occurring in the context of routines or behavior chains, a number of novel avenues for investigation arise. To understand the function of challenging behavior, we need to consider more remote variables that are part of the chain. For example, routines that share similar early events, but terminate in very different outcomes (e.g., dressing for a trip to the dentist or to shop), may come to occasion challenging behavior. Such behavior may seem to defy all logic to a caregiver who knows that the learner enjoys shopping trips. Likewise, if learners discover they can gain more rapid access to favored activities (or delay nonpreferred events) by engaging in challenging behavior, they may do so at earlier and earlier points in a routine so that the timing of the behavior and its controlling contingency become quite remote.

From the perspective of challenging behavior that occurs in the context of routines, the phenomena of stimulus and response classes simultaneously complicate any effort at analysis of challenging behavior and provide potential explanatory power for understanding how such behavior functions. This same perspective has direct implications for the assessment practices described in the beginning of the chapter: A variety of questions must be asked in the interviews and more remote events must be considered and then assessed in the observations and manipulations. Finally, even state-of-the-art strategies such as functional communication training may be sabotaged if the environment remains unresponsive to newly acquired functionally equivalent responses. Interactive routines among learners and caregivers must be modified so that caregivers recognize and are responsive to less coercive communicative responses.

REFERENCES

Baer, A.M., Rowbury, T.G., & Baer, D.M. (1973). The development of instructional control over classroom activities of deviant preschool children. *Journal of Applied Behavior Analysis, 6,* 289–298.

Bijou, S.W., & Baer, D.M. (1961). *Child development I: A systematic and empirical theory.* Englewood Cliffs, NJ: Prentice Hall.

Carr, E.G. (1977). The motivation of self-injurious behavior: A review of some hypotheses. *Psychological Bulletin, 84,* 800–816.

Carr, E.G. (1988). Functional equivalence as a mechanism of response generalization. In R.H. Horner, G. Dunlap, & R.L. Koegel (Eds.), *Generalization and maintenance: Life-style changes in applied settings* (pp. 221–241). Baltimore: Paul H. Brookes Publishing Co.

Carr, E.G., & Durand, V.M. (1985). Reducing behavior problems through functional communication training. *Journal of Applied Behavior Analysis, 18,* 111–126.

Carr, E.G., & McDowell, J.J. (1980). Social control of self-injurous behavior of organic etiology. *Behavior Therapy, 11,* 402–409.

Carr, E.G., Newsom, C.D., & Binkoff, J.A. (1980). Escape as a factor in the aggressive behavior of two retarded children. *Journal of Applied Behavior Analysis, 13,* 101–117.

Carr, E.G., Taylor, J.C., Carlson, J.I., & Robinson, S. (1989). Reinforcement and stimulus-based treatments for severe behavior problems in developmental disabilities. *Proceedings of the Consensus Conference on the Treatment of Severe Behavior Problems in Developmental Disabilities* (pp. 173–229). Washington, DC: National Institutes of Health.

Carr, E.G., Taylor, J.C., & Robinson, S. (1991). The effects of severe behavior problems in children on the teaching behavior of adults. *Journal of Applied Behavior Analysis, 24,* 523–525.

Charlop, M.H., Schreibman, L., & Thibodeau, M.B. (1985). Increasing spontaneous verbal responding in autistic children using a time delay procedure. *Journal of Applied Behavior Analysis, 18,* 155–166.

Charlop, M.H., & Trasowech, J.E. (1991). Increasing autistic children's daily spontaneous speech. *Journal of Applied Behavior Analysis, 24,* 747–761.

Day, R.M., Rea, J.A., Schussler, N.G., Larsen, S.E., & Johnson, W.L. (1988). Functionally based approach to the treatment of self-injurious behavior. *Behavior Modification, 12,* 565–589.

Devany, J.M., Hayes, S.C., & Nelson, R.O. (1986). Equivalence class formation in language-able and language-disabled children. *Journal of Experimental Analysis of Behavior, 46,* 243–258.

Dixon, M.H., & Spradlin, J.E. (1976). Establishing stimulus equivalence among retarded adolescents. *Journal of Experimental Child Psychology, 21,* 144–164.

Durand, V.M., & Carr, E.G. (1987). Social influences on self-stimulatory behavior: Analysis and treatment application. *Journal of Applied Behavior Analysis, 20,* 119–132.

Durand, V.M., & Crimmins, D.B. (1988). Identifying the variables maintaining self-injurious behavior. *Journal of Autism and Developmental Disorder, 18,* 99–117.

Gardner, W.I., Cole, C.L., Davidson, D.P., & Karan, O.C. (1986). Reducing aggression in individuals with developmental disabilities: An expended stimulus control, assessment, and intervention model. *Education and Training of the Mentally Retarded, 21,* 3–12.

Gardner, W.I., Karan, O.C., & Cole, C.L. (1984). Assessment of setting events influencing functional capacities of mentally retarded adults with behavior difficulties. In A.S. Halpern & M.J. Fuhrer (Eds.), *Functional assessment in rehabilitation* (pp. 171–185). Baltimore: Paul H. Brookes Publishing Co.

Goetz, L., Gee, K., & Sailor, W. (1985). Using a behavior chain interruption strategy to teach communication skills to students with severe disabilities. *Journal of The Association for Persons with Severe Disabilities, 10,* 21–30.

Goldiamond, I. (1966). Perception, language, and conceptualization rules. In B. Kleinmetz (Ed.), *Problem solving: Research, method, and theory* (pp. 183–197). New York: John Wiley & Sons.

Haavik, S.F., Spradlin, J.E., & Altman, K.I. (1984). Generalization and maintenance of language responses: A study across trainers, school, and home settings. *Behavior Modification, 8,* 331–359.

Halle, J.W. (1989). Identifying stimuli in natural settings: An analysis of stimuli that acquire control during training. *Journal of Applied Behavior Analysis, 24,* 579–589.

Halle, J.W., Baer, D.M., & Spradlin, J.E. (1981). Teachers' generalized use of delay as a stimulus control procedure to increase language use in handicapped children. *Journal of Applied Behavior Analysis, 14,* 398–409.

Halle, J.W., & Holt, B. (1991). Assessing stimulus control in natural settings: An analysis of stimuli that acquire control during training. *Journal of Applied Behavior Analysis, 24,* 579–590.

Halle, J.W., Marshall, A.M., & Spradlin, J.E. (1979). Time delay: A technique to increase language use and facilitate generalization in retarded children. *Journal of Applied Behavior Analysis, 12,* 431–439.

Horner, R.H., & Billingsley, F.F. (1988). The effect of competing behavior on the generalization and maintenance of adaptive behavior in applied settings. In R.H. Horner, G. Dunlap, & R.L. Koegel (Eds.), *Generalization and maintenance: Lifestyle changes in applied settings* (pp. 197–220). Baltimore: Paul H. Brookes Publishing Co.

Horner, R.H., Dodson, S., Tuesday-Heathfield, L.T., & Ramsden, J.A. (1991). *Setting events and severe problem behavior for students with severe disabilities.* Proposal to the U.S. Department of Education from the Specialized Training Program at the University of Oregon, Eugene.

Horner, R.H., O'Neill, R.E., & Albin, R.W. (1991). *Supporting students with high intensity problem behavior.* Proposal to the U.S. Department of Education from the Specialized Training Program at the University of Oregon, Eugene.

Iwata, B.A., Dorsey, M.F., Slifer, K.J., Bauman, K.E., & Richman, G.S. (1982). Toward a functional analysis of self-injury. *Analysis and Interaction in Developmental Disabilities, 2,* 3–20.

Iwata, B.A., Vollmer, T.R., & Zarcone, J.R. (1990). The experimental (functional) analysis of behavior disorders: Methodology, applications, and limitations. In A.C. Repp & N.N. Singh (Eds.), *Perspectives on the use of nonaversive and aversive interventions for persons with developmental disabilities* (pp. 301–330). Sycamore, IL: Sycamore Publishing Co.

Kantor, J.R. (1959). *Interbehavioral psychology.* Granville, OH: Principia Press.

Kantor, J.R. (1970). An analysis of the experimental analysis of behavior (TEAB). *Journal of Mental Deficiency, 87,* 458–461.

Lennox, D.B., & Miltenberger, R.G. (1989). Conducting a functional assessment of problem behavior in applied settings. *Journal of The Association for Persons with Severe Handicaps, 14,* 304–311.

Mace, F.C., & Lalli, J.S. (1991). Linking descriptive and experimental analyses in the treatment of bizarre speech. *Journal of Applied Behavior Analysis, 24,* 553–562.

Mace, F.C., Lalli, J.S., & Lalli, E.P. (1991). Functional analysis and treatment of aberrant behavior. *Research in Developmental Disabilities, 12,* 155–180.

Mace, F.C., Lalli, J.S., & Shea, M.C. (in press). Functional analysis and treatment of self-injury. In S. Axelrod & R. Vanhouten (Eds.), *Effective behavioral treatment: Issues and implementation* (pp. 122–152). New York: Plenum.

Mace, F.C., & Shea, M.C. (1990). New directions in behavior analysis for the treatment of severe behavior disorders. In S. Harris & J. Handleman (Eds.), *Advances and the treatment of severe behavior disorders* (pp. 57–79). New York: Springer-Verlag.

Michael, J. (1982). Distinguishing between discriminative and motivational functions of stimuli. *Journal of the Experimental Analysis of Behavior, 37,* 149–155.

O'Neill, R.E., Horner, R.H., Albin, R.W., Storey, K., & Sprague, J.R. (1990). *Functional analysis: A practical assessment guide.* Sycamore, IL: Sycamore Publishing Co.

Peterson, R.F. (1968). Some experiments on the organization of a class of imitative behaviors. *Journal of Applied Behavior Analysis, 1,* 225–235.

Porterfield, J.K., Herbert-Jackson, E., & Risley, T.R. (1976). Contingent observation: An effective and acceptable procedure for reducing disruptive behavior of young children in a group setting. *Journal of Applied Behavior Analysis, 9,* 55–64.

Pyles, D.A.M., & Bailey, J.S. (1990). Diagnosing severe behavior problems. In A.C. Repp & N.N. Singh (Eds.), *Perspectives on the use of nonaversive and aversive interventions for persons with developmental disabilities* (pp. 381–402). Sycamore, IL: Sycamore Publishing Co.

Repp, A.C., & Karsh, K.G. (1990). A taxonomic approach to the nonaversive treatment of maladaptive behavior of persons with developmental disabilities. In A.C. Repp & N.N. Singh (Eds.), *Perspectives on the use of nonaversive and aversive interventions for persons with developmental disabilities* (pp. 331–349). Sycamore, IL: Sycamore Publishing Co.

Repp, A.C., & Karsh, K.G. (1991, May). *A taxonomy for managing behavior problems.* Paper presented at the annual convention of the Association for Behavior Analysis, Nashville.

Saunders, R.R., Wachter, J.A., & Spradlin, J.E. (1988). Establishing auditory control over an eight-member equivalence class via conditional discrimination procedures. *Journal of the Experimental Analysis of Behavior, 49,* 95–115.

Schussler, N.G., & Spradlin, J.E. (1991). Assessment of stimuli controlling the requests of students with severe mental retardation during a snack routine. *Journal of Applied Behavior Analysis, 24,* 791–797.

Sidman, M. (1971). Reading and auditory-visual equivalences. *Journal of Speech and Hearing Research, 14,* 5–13.

Sidman, M., Wynne, C.K., Maguire, R.W., & Barnes, T. (1989). Functional classes and equivalence relations. *Journal of the Experimental Analysis of Behavior, 52,* 261–274.

Sigafoos, J., Reichle, J., Doss, S., Hall, K., & Pettitt, L. (1990). "Spontaneous" transfer of stimulus control from tact to mand contingencies. *Research in Developmental Disabilities, 11,* 165–176.

Silverman, K., Anderson, S.A., Marshall, A.M., & Baer, D.M. (1986). Establishing and generalizing audience control of news language repertoires. *Analysis and Intervention in Developmental Disabilities, 6,* 21–40.

Spradlin, J.E. (1962). Effects of reinforcement schedules on extinction in severely retarded children. *American Journal of Mental Deficiency, 66,* 634–640.

Spradlin, J.E., Cotter, V.W., & Baxley, N. (1973). Establishing a conditional discrimination without direct training: A study of transfer with retarded adolescents. *American Journal of Mental Deficiency, 77,* 556–566.

Spradlin, J.E., Girardeau, F.L., & Corte, E. (1965). Fixed ratio and fixed interval behavior of severely and profoundly retarded subjects. *Journal of Experimental Child Psychology, 2,* 340–353.

Tarpley, H.D., & Schroeder, S.R. (1979). Comparison of DRO and DRI on rate suppression and self-injurious behavior. *American Journal of Mental Deficiency, 84,* 188–194.

Touchette, P.E., MacDonald, R.F., & Langer, S.N. (1985). A scatterplot for identifying stimulus control of problem behavior. *Journal of Applied Behavior Analysis, 18,* 343–351.

Wahler, R.G., & Fox, J.J. (1981). Setting events in social networks: Ally or enemy in child behavior therapy? *Behavior Therapy, 14,* 19–36.

Zarcone, J.R., Rodgers, T., Iwata, B.A., Rourke, D.A., & Dorsey, M.F. (1991). Reliability analysis of the Motivation Assessment Scale: A failure to replicate. *Research in Developmental Disabilities, 12,* 349–360.

PART II

Developing
Effective Interventions
Empirical and Conceptual Considerations

6

Factors Affecting Selection
of Behavioral Interventions

F. Charles Mace and Maura L. Roberts

APPLIED BEHAVIOR ANALYSIS UNDERWENT A quiet revolution in the 1980s. Prior to this period, behavioral treatments relied largely on potent reinforcers or punishers to override the reinforcement contingencies or biologic processes that maintained problem behavior. The treatments were effective, but they were often artificial, conspicuous, difficult to implement for long periods of time, and deemed unacceptable by some caregivers. Known collectively as "behavior modification," these treatments received a mixed review from the public, and they may have been a key factor contributing to the field's image problem. However, with no viable alternative, behavior modification was supported by some professional groups in developmental disabilities as superior to ineffective psychotherapies and intrusive pharmacologic therapies.

Approaches to behavioral intervention changed remarkably in the 1980s following a shift in thinking about the nature of behavior problems and the development of new assessment methodologies. The "new thinking" gave consideration to the environmental etiology of problem behaviors as a basis for the rational selection of treatment procedures. This meant, for example, that aggressive behavior maintained by positive reinforcement would be treated differently than aggressive behavior maintained by negative reinforcement. The focus of intervention became the disruption of the maintaining contingency and differential reinforcement of adaptive replacement behaviors, rather than the suppression of the target behavior with behavior modification procedures.

Adoption of this intervention model hinged on the development of practical and valid methodologies to identify the environmental etiology of an individual's problem behavior. A variety of descriptive methods (e.g., Bijou, Peterson, & Ault, 1968; Touchette, MacDonald, & Langer, 1985), experimental methods (e.g., Carr, Newsom, & Binkoff, 1976, 1980; Cooper, Wacker, Sasso, Reimers, & Donn, 1990; Iwata, Dorsey, Slifer, Bauman, &

Richman, 1982), and combined descriptive and experimental methodologies (e.g., Mace & Lalli, 1991) have emerged that are capable of isolating the environmental basis for problem behaviors (see Iwata, Vollmer, & Zarcone, 1990, and Mace, Lalli, & Pinter-Lalli, 1991, for reviews). These assessment methodologies are known collectively as *functional analysis* methods. Their emergence has allowed behavior analysts to classify behavior disorders according to their operant functions and to select intervention procedures suited specifically to these functions.

This chapter reviews important factors to consider when designing behavioral interventions based on the operant function of the behavior disorder. Considerations for intervention selection for the four major operant functions of behavior disorders (attention, tangibles, escape, and automatic reinforcement) are presented in the context of matching theory. We also propose a model for deciding when pharmacologic intervention and default behavioral intervention of behavior disorders are indicated.

MATCHING THEORY AND INTERVENTION SELECTION

A successful functional analysis identifies one or more reinforcement contingencies that maintain an individual's problem behavior. When intervention is based on the operant function of problem behavior, the general strategy is to both weaken the maintaining contingency and strengthen a concurrently available alternative response. Because aberrant behavior and adaptive behavior can be viewed as concurrent operants, matching theory provides a general conceptual framework for intervention selection that is applicable across operant functions (McDowell, 1988; Myerson & Hale, 1984).

Matching theory is a framework extrapolated from basic research on concurrent schedules of reinforcement and the matching law (de Villiers, 1977; Herrnstein, 1961, 1970). In concurrent schedules and matching research, subjects have two or more response options available to them at the same time. Each alternative is paired with a discriminative stimulus and is subject to an independent schedule of reinforcement. The primary focus is on how differences in the schedules of reinforcement affect the subject's allocation of behavior among the response alternatives. Basic research with animals and humans (Davison & McCarthy, 1988; Lowe & Horne, 1985; Pierce & Epling, 1983), as well as a handful of applied studies (Conger & Killeen, 1974; Mace, McCurdy, & Quigley, 1990; Martens, Lochner, & Kelly, in press; Neef, Mace, Shea, & Shade, 1992), have shown that response allocation is lawful and affected by four major factors: rate of reinforcement, quality of reinforcement, response effort, and immediacy of reinforcement. These factors appear to converge to affect the probability that an individual will choose one option over another (McDowell, 1989), and, in the case of behavior disorders, the important choice is whether the individual engages in problem behavior or adaptive behavior.

Rate of Reinforcement

Herrnstein (1961, 1970) described the lawful relationship between rate of reinforcement delivered according to concurrent variable-interval (VI) schedules and rate of responding on each alternative. Specifically, the rate of responding on each alternative tends to *match* (or be proportional to) the rate of reinforcement obtained from each response alternative. Thus, in a typical experiment with pigeons (Davison & McCarthy, 1988), arranging VI 60-second food reinforcement for red key pecks concurrently with VI 120-second food reinforcement for green key pecks would result in roughly twice as many pecks on the red key than the green key. Neef, Mace, Shea, and Shade (1992) demonstrated the generality of the matching relation with adolescents with learning and behavior problems. Token or money reinforcers were available concurrently for performing math problems according to VI 30-second and VI 120-second schedules. As predicted by the matching law, the students completed nearly four times more problems subject to the richer schedule of reinforcement. Similar results have been reported for the allocation of on- and off-task behavior (Martens & Houk, 1989), conversation between a subject and two experimenters (Conger & Killeen, 1974), and disruptive versus on-task behavior in a classroom (Martens et al., in press).

Matching response allocation to obtained reinforcement is expected only when the behaviors are subject to concurrent (and in some cases multiple) variable-interval schedules of reinforcement because response rate and reinforcement rate are independent (e.g., response rates on the keys do not necessarily lead to changes in rates of reinforcers). By alternating among response alternatives, individuals can obtain more overall reinforcement than would be available on either VI schedule alone. However, in ratio-schedule reinforcement, the rate of reinforcement is *dependent* on the rate of responding. Hence, with concurrent ratio schedules, subjects typically respond exclusively on the alternative yielding the highest rate of reinforcement (Herrnstein & Loveland, 1975). Exclusive responding to the richer of two concurrent ratio schedules also has been reported in the applied literature. Mace, Lalli et al. (1990) arranged concurrent fixed-ratio (FR1) and VR2 food reinforcement for two vocational tasks for a student with profound mental retardation. After several sessions, the student completed only the vocational task resulting in FR1 reinforcement.

Quality of Reinforcement

Consequent events vary greatly in their capacity to reinforce behavior. When one event is preferred over another, we say that the preferred event has the higher *quality of reinforcement,* and the choice between the two is asymmetrical (McDowell, 1989). In some cases, relative reinforcer qualities are stable and absolute (e.g., ice cream vs. green beans for the first author). However, it is more likely that relative reinforcer quality is a highly fluid phenomenon, varying as a function of deprivation and satiation, as well as the availability of other reinforcers.

The availability of different quality reinforcers for different concurrent operants can affect the allocation of behavior across these alternatives. This influence can occur independent of differing rates of reinforcement, or reinforcer quality may interact with the rate of reinforcement to jointly determine preference. Although most basic concurrent-schedule research has examined the effects of various schedule combinations (e.g., conc VI VR, conc VR FR, mult VI VI, etc., [Davison & McCarthy, 1988]), only a few studies have demonstrated the substantial impact reinforcer quality can have on choice behavior. For example, Hollard and Davison (1971) arranged 3-second access to wheat and 15 seconds of brain stimulation on concurrent VI VI schedules, and Miller (1976) varied grain types across concurrent VI schedules (buckwheat, hemp, and wheat). Subjects in these studies showed a preference, or bias, for one reinforcer that was independent of the rate at which the reinforcers were delivered. The Neef et al. (1992) study also showed that reinforcer quality can affect students' choices between academic tasks subject to different VI schedules of reinforcement. Three of the four students in this study allocated all of their behavior to the tasks yielding the preferred reinforcer (money), even when the rate of money reinforcement was four times lower than the rate of token reinforcement.

Response Effort

Another important dimension that differentiates one response alternative from another is the *effort* required to engage in the behavior. In basic research, the effect of response effort on choice behavior has been studied by varying the pressure required to depress a response key (Bauman, Shull, & Brownstein, 1975) or by varying fixed-ratio (FR) response requirements within VI schedules of reinforcement (Beautrais & Davison, 1977). Subjects in these studies generally showed a preference for the alternative with the lower response effort, which was independent of differences in rate of reinforcement.

We have found no published applied research directly investigating how varied response efforts affect choice behavior on concurrent schedules of reinforcement. However, numerous studies have shown that increases in task difficulty can result in increased maladaptive behavior in some individuals (e.g., Center, Deitz, & Kaufman, 1982; Durand & Carr, 1987; Gaylord-Ross, Weeks, & Lipner, 1980; Horner, Day, Sprague, O'Brien, & Heathfield, 1991; Mace, Browder, & Lin, 1987; Mace & West, 1986; Sailor, Guess, Rutherford, & Baer, 1968; Weeks & Gaylord-Ross, 1981). These studies generally showed that easier tasks produced more task engagement and less maladaptive behavior, whereas more difficult tasks resulted in less task engagement and more problem behavior. Viewed from a matching theory perspective, task difficulty (response effort) affected how subjects allocated their behavior between task engagement and maladaptive behavior.

Immediacy of Reinforcement

Given the choice between 2-second access to food or 4-second access to food, a pigeon will reliably make the response yielding the longer access duration. However, if a delay is imposed on the delivery of the longer duration reinforcement, the pigeon is likely to switch to the shorter access alternative, rather than incur the delay of reinforcement. In this scenario, the delay in reinforcement can be said to have *discounted* the quality of the 4-second food access to the point where its relative value was less than the 2-second access (see Logue, 1988, and Rachlin, 1989, for a discussion of delay of reinforcement and behavioral self-control paradigms).

Similar findings have been reported in a few applied studies. For example, with adolescents with behavior disorders as subjects, Neef, Mace, and Shade (in press) arranged concurrent VI 30-second and VI 120-second reinforcement (nickels) for performing math problems. Students were given the money they earned immediately after each session. Under these baseline conditions, the students closely matched their completion of problems to the rates of reinforcement derived from each alternative. Following baseline, problems completed on the VI 30-second schedule were reinforced with vouchers for the money earned, which could be redeemed 1 week later. Thus, the higher-rate reinforcement was delayed and the lower-rate reinforcement was immediate. The delay of reinforcement produced substantial departures from matching with a preference for low-rate immediate reinforcement.

Implications for Intervention Selection

If maladaptive behavior is aptly characterized as one response alternative among an array of concurrently available behaviors, then the allocation of behavior across these alternatives can presumably be altered by manipulating one or more of the four factors affecting choice discussed above. This conceptualization of maladaptive behavior has some important implications for both assessment and intervention of behavior disorders.

Intervention with behavior disorders can be viewed as a competition between maladaptive behaviors and adaptive behaviors selected to replace them. However, in order to incorporate rate of reinforcement, quality of reinforcement, response effort, and immediacy of reinforcement into the design of intervention protocols, specific information about the maladaptive behavior and its controlling variables is needed from the pretreatment assessment. Analog functional analysis methodologies alone have a limited capacity to provide this information. They have been used generally to identify the maintaining *reinforcement contingencies* for an individual's maladaptive behavior. Behavior disorders are globally classified as maintained by attention, access to tangible items, escape, or automatic reinforcement. However, analog assessments alone provide little information about the natural conditions that support maladaptive behavior vis-à-vis factors affecting choice.

We have proposed a functional analysis model that combines descriptive and experimental (analog) methodologies and is capable of yielding specific information about factors affecting choice (Mace & Belfiore, 1990; Mace et al., 1991; Mace & Lalli, 1991; Mace, Lalli, & Shea, 1992). In the descriptive phase, systematic observations of caregiver–client interactions under natural conditions are recorded via computer or with paper-and-pencil interval recording methods. The data can be analyzed to identify: 1) the naturally occurring antecedent events correlated with more and less maladaptive behavior; and 2) the timing, distribution, and form of events subsequent to maladaptive behavior that may function as reinforcers. A successful descriptive analysis results in one or more hypotheses concerning specific maintaining contingencies. These hypotheses are then tested in the experimental phase. However, the analog conditions are designed to simulate, as closely as possible, the circumstances observed to occur naturally. Special attention is given to provide instructions and respond to maladaptive behavior as the caregiver did and to schedule these consequences at the same ratio, or slightly richer, than the schedule observed in the descriptive analysis (e.g., VR 4).

Hypotheses that are confirmed in the experimental phase provide specific information for the selection of behavioral interventions. The aim of these interventions is to arrange reinforcement contingencies for adaptive replacement behaviors that can compete effectively with the contingencies maintaining maladaptive behavior. We illustrate the process with a recent case, an 11-year-old girl (Gail) with severe mental retardation, seen at The Children's Seashore House in Philadelphia. During the descriptive analysis, Gail's self-injurious behavior (SIB) was observed to occur primarily during periods of low adult attention (i.e., when her parents were interacting with each other or preoccupied with another activity). An SIB incident began with a tantrum that rarely attracted parental attention and escalated to head-hitting and face-slapping. After about 10 self-injurious responses, the parents scolded the child with stern voices, with intermittent reprimands following an average of 7 responses. It is noteworthy that following intense blows, Gail appeared to be startled and in pain. Occasionally, the incidents became so severe that the mother wrapped her arms around the child and tried to calm her. Replicating these interactions in the experimental analysis resulted in high rates of SIB and very low levels in other conditions. Thus, the combined descriptive and experimental analyses indicated that Gail's SIB was maintained by parental reprimands on a VR 7 (approximately 20/hour) schedule and physical contact on a VR 78 (approximately 2/hour) schedule.

Our intervention with Gail's SIB consisted of prompted differential reinforcement of mands for attention, noncontingent attention on a fixed-time (FT) schedule, and extinction (Mace & Lalli, 1991). However, the specific treatment procedures were designed to compete effectively with the contingencies found to maintain SIB under natural conditions. Gail was taught to use picture cards to initiate interaction or an activity with her parents. She was prompted to use the cards every 15 minutes during periods of low adult attention and at the onset of tantrums. In addition, her parents used a timer to prompt them to initiate pleasant interaction with Gail every 10 minutes during noninteractional periods. Finally, Gail's parents were asked to refrain from attending to Gail within 60 seconds of SIB.

The rationale for selecting this model of intervention can be seen by comparing these intervention procedures to the contingencies maintaining SIB along the four factors affecting choice:

1. Rate of reinforcement. SIB: 20/hour reduced to < 1/hour; Mands/FT attention: > 10/hour
2. Quality of reinforcement. SIB: reprimands; Mands: pleasant/affectionate interaction
3. Response effort. SIB: tantrums escalating to pain-producing responses; Mands: presenting a picture to a parent
4. Immediacy of reinforcement. SIB: immediate; Mands: immediate

On three of the four factors (rate and quality of reinforcement and response effort), the intervention contingencies favor a preference for mands over self-injurious behavior. Mands resulted in a higher quality reinforcer available at a comparatively higher rate and accessible by a response requiring less effort than self-injurious behavior.

To summarize, when viewing maladaptive responses as choice behavior, matching theory can guide the selection of behavioral interventions based on the operant function of the problem behavior. Altering the relative response effort and rate, quality, and immediacy of reinforcement for the maladaptive and adaptive target behaviors can promote a desirable change in the distribution of behavior among available alternatives. This approach to treatment selection is facilitated by using pretreatment functional analysis methodologies that specify the natural maintaining contingencies.

OPERANT FUNCTIONS AND TREATMENT OPTIONS

Behavioral movement inevitably changes some aspect of the environment (Skinner, 1938, 1953, 1969). Changes that benefit the individual are potential reinforcers capable of strengthening the behaviors that produce them. The changes produced by behavior have been functionally classified either as positive (i.e., they add something to the environment) or negative (i.e., they subtract something from the environment). Thus, any behavior, maladaptive or adaptive, may be maintained by positive or negative reinforcement. When a functional analysis indicates that an individual's maladaptive behavior is maintained by one or more reinforcement contingencies, various intervention options are available to *weaken the maintaining contingency* and *reinforce alternative replacement behaviors.* Recent research suggests that many individuals respond best when these strategies are used in combination (Wacker, Steege, Northrup, & Sasso, 1990).

Positive Reinforcement by Attention

Social reactions to maladaptive behavior are generically referred to as "attention." When attention occurs contingent on maladaptive responses, these behaviors can be positively reinforced. Attention directed to the individual can take a multitude of forms including vocalizations (e.g., reprimands, sympathy, redirection), physical contact (e.g., restraint, consolation), and facial expressions (e.g., eye contact, frowns, smiles, interest). During any given period of time, attention varies in its capacity to function as a reinforcer for maladaptive behavior. The circumstances that establish attention as a positive reinforcer are known as *establishing conditions* (Michael, 1982; Vollmer & Iwata, 1991). In general, the establishing conditions for attention-motivated behavior are periods of low adult attention and the presence of stimuli signaling the nonavailability of attention (e.g., preoccupation with an activity). These conditions constitute the environmental context in which behavioral intervention for attention-motivated behavior is implemented.

Procedures To Weaken the Maintaining Contingency

There are two general strategies available for weakening the response–reinforcer relationship maintaining attention-motivated maladapted behavior. First, *extinction* of the maladaptive behavior may be achieved by discontinuing attention to the target behaviors. We recommend a passive approach to extinction in most cases (i.e., planned ignoring) because it introduces nothing to the environment that may inadvertently reinforce problem behavior. However, some caregivers may find ignoring maladaptive behavior especially difficult. In these cases, an active extinction procedure may be used, such as exclusion time-out that deliberately withholds attention (and other sources of reinforcement) for a brief interval (e.g., Mace, Page, Ivancic, & O'Brien, 1986). Although extinction is important to include in any behavioral intervention, extinction alone can be accompanied by unwanted side effects (Lovaas & Simmons, 1969; Sajwaj, Twardosz, & Burke, 1972). These side effects include initial increases in the rate of maladaptive behavior; induction of new topographies of maladaptive behavior; and emotional reactions such as crying, screaming, and aggression. However, combining extinction with alternative reinforcement can attenuate or eliminate most adverse reactions to extinction.

A second means of weakening the response–reinforcer relationship is response-independent reinforcement (Mace, McCurdey et al., 1990). For attention-maintained behavior, providing attention at predictable intervals (i.e., on an FT schedule) and discontiguous to occurrences of maladaptive behavior can produce sharp reductions in the target behavior. For example, subsequent to a functional analysis showing that a 47-year-old man's bizarre speech was maintained by attention, Mace and Lalli (1991) provided noncontingent attention to him on a conjunctive FT, DRO schedule. A conjunctive, FT, DRO schedule provided response-independent attention at regular intervals, with the added contingency that no bizarre comments would occur contiguous to the scheduled attention. Bizarre speech decreased immediately to near-zero levels. In our view, scheduled noncontingent attention is a treatment strategy appropriate for most cases of this operant function. This component can enrich environments where availability of positive reinforcement is minimal in the absence of disruptive behavior.

Reinforcement of Alternative Replacement Behaviors

Differential reinforcement of alternative replacement behaviors becomes possible when the operant function of maladaptive behavior is known. This strategy is predicated on the assumption that the emergence and maintenance of maladaptive behavior indicates that the behavior has an important environmental function for the individual (Carr, 1988; Carr & Durand, 1985; Wacker et al., 1990). Therefore, the intervention protocol is designed to preserve this operant function for the individual, but also to supplant the maladaptive behavior with other more adaptive behaviors.

Reinforcement of replacement behaviors for attention-motivated maladaptive behavior can be achieved by differential reinforcement of other behavior (DRO) or differential reinforcement of alternative behavior (DRA). Using a DRO procedure, a caregiver supplies attention to the individual contingent on the elapse of a specified time interval with no occurrences of the target behavior. Although DRO does not strengthen a particular adaptive behavior, it can teach the individual an important contingency: Maladaptive behavior delays the availability of attention. When appropriate time intervals are selected, DRO has proven effective in intervention with a variety of behavior disorders, alone and in conjunction with the results of a functional analysis (see Vollmer & Iwata, in press, for a review).

DRO may be most effective when used in combination with a DRA procedure (Carr, McConnachie, Levin, & Kemp, in press). Two general strategies have been used in DRA treatment. First, one or more general classes of appropriate behavior are identified for reinforcement (e.g., play, social inter-action, activity engagement). Reinforcement is then provided on a VI or VR schedule contingent on occurrences of the targeted classes of appropriate behavior. The goal here is to strengthen a range of adaptive behaviors that caregivers will attend to naturally, thereby reinforcing a broad repertoire of adaptive behavior. The second strategy is to identify a specific target response that will directly replace the maladaptive behavior. One basis for selecting the replacement behavior is whether persons without disabilities will respond to it naturally by providing the functional reinforcer. Accordingly, many re-searchers have taught individuals to use one or more "communication" re-sponses to replace maladaptive behavior (Carr, 1988; Carr & Durand, 1985; Carr & Kemp, 1989; Horner & Budd, 1985; Mace & Lalli, 1991; Wacker, Wiggins, Fowler, & Berg, 1988). A distinct advantage of teaching individuals communication responses is that, to some extent, the individual can control the timing and rate of reinforcement, thereby avoiding periods of deprivation that may lead to a recurrence of maladaptive behavior.

Positive Reinforcement by Access to Tangibles

Several researchers have found that a variety of problem behaviors are pos-itively reinforced when they provide access to objects or activities that are otherwise restricted (Allen & Harris, 1966; Day, Rae, Schussler, Larsen, & Johnson, 1988; Durand & Kishi, 1987). Foods, toys, music, television, and specific articles of clothing are among the tangibles that can maintain mal-adaptive behavior.

Many of the considerations relevant to intervention with attention-maintained behavior problems are applicable to the selection of interventions for tangible-motivated aberrant behavior and are not reiterated in this section. However, some exceptions include the establishing conditions for behaviors with this function and the procedures for weakening of the response–reinforcer relationship with response-independent reinforcement.

For attention-maintained behavior problems, a period of deprivation may be necessary to momentarily establish attention as a reinforcer. However, in the absence of published studies examining this issue, we have observed that stimuli signaling the onset or pending onset of deprivation may be an impor-tant establishing operation for tangible-motivated maladaptive behavior. Spe-cifically, during our descriptive analyses, the withdrawal of a preferred item or activity, or statements indicating that a preferred item or activity is about to be withdrawn, are often followed by agitation leading to occurrences of aberrant behavior. When this pattern of behavior is observed, we suggest that consideration be given to altering the manner in which tangibles are restricted when designing treatment protocols. Presenting the onset of restricted access as a "do" request (e.g., "Give [bring] me ____," "sit down," "open [close] the door," and "come here") (Neef, Shaefer, Egel, Cataldo, & Parrish, 1983), and indicating the future availability of the tangible may be effective preventive measures.

In addition to frequent noncontingent presentations to an individual of specific preferred items or activities, general enrichment of the environment with a variety of stimulating objects may weaken the response–reinforcer relationship for a given maladaptive behavior and tangible item. Some evidence for this proposition comes from studies by Horner (1980) and Finney, Russo, and Cataldo (1982) showing that the availability of toys, attractive materials, and/or alternative activities reduced considerably occurrences of disruptive behavior and pica. This finding is also consistent with numerous animal studies reporting decreased response rates following both pre-feeding periods and response-independent food (Nevin, 1974).

Negative Reinforcement by Escape/Avoidance of Tasks

For reasons not yet explicated by research, the performance of basic self-care, academic, or vocational tasks acquires aversive properties for some individuals. Presentation of these tasks often elicits emotive responses that can include aberrant topographies that may terminate or postpone a caregiver's expectations for performance. When maladaptive behaviors serve to escape or avoid performance demands, the responses may be negatively reinforced. Some fundamental differences between maladaptive behavior maintained by positive reinforcement and that maintained by negative reinforcement have implications for the intervention options available for weakening response–reinforcer relationships and reinforcing alternative replacement behaviors that merit consideration.

Procedures To Weaken the Maintaining Contingency

Weakening the response–reinforcer relationship maintaining escape or avoidance of tasks involves one or more of the following operations: 1) preventing escape or avoidance of performance demands, 2) suspension of performance demands independent of maladaptive behavior, and/or 3) gradually increasing performance demands without concomitant occurrences of maladaptive behavior.

Preventing escape or avoidance of performance demands can be accomplished in two ways. The most common procedure reported in the literature is guided compliance (Iwata, Vollmer, et al., 1990). Guided compliance typically involves the caregiver using hand-on-hand physical guidance to prompt the individual's performance of a task (e.g., Repp, Felce & Barton, 1988), and can sometimes be combined with response-blocking (Iwata, Pace, Cowdery, Kalsher, & Cataldo, 1990). The procedure can result in extinction of maladaptive behavior, because these responses cease to terminate or avoid the performance requirements of the task. Although guided compliance can be very effective with some individuals, use should be restricted to young people of relatively small stature. The second means of preventing escape or avoidance is to continue task instruction and maintain expectations for performance until the task is completed (e.g., Mace et al., 1987; Mace & West, 1986; Repp et al., 1988). Although continued instruction permits delay in performing the task, the task is never completely avoided. This procedure is well-suited to tasks requiring vocal responses (which cannot be physically guided) and for larger and older individuals who do not become overly aggressive.

Some researchers have advocated suspension of performance requirements at regular intervals as a means of weakening the motivation to engage in escape-motivated behavior. For example, Gaylord-Ross, Weeks, and Lipner (1980) showed that scheduling frequent breaks from tasks substantially reduced rates of self-injurious behavior. In our view, the viability of scheduled breaks as an intervention option depends on the frequency of breaks required to prevent problem behavior. If the required frequency interferes with important habilitative programming, or differs substantially from practices accepted in community settings, the procedure is not a good long-term option for the individual (see Bannerman, Sheldon, Sherman, & Harchik, 1990, for another perspective).

A third means of weakening the response–reinforcer relationship for escape-motivated behavior is to introduce easy tasks that have been correlated with positive reinforcement and then gradually increase performance requirements until an acceptable criterion is met. This strategy, based on the principle of stimulus fading (Catania, 1984), systematically transfers the stimulus control evident in easy tasks to increasingly more difficult tasks. The intervention makes it difficult to discriminate easy tasks from difficult tasks and establishes a history of positive reinforcement for task performance. Although stimulus fading is an attractive option, its use is limited to individuals who will perform at least some tasks.

Reinforcement of Alternative Replacement Behaviors

Several researchers have demonstrated that differential negative reinforcement of mands that have a function similar to maladaptive escape behavior is an effective strategy for behavior disorders with this operant function (Iwata, 1987). For example, Day et al. (1988) and Durand and Kishi (1987) taught children with self-injurious behavior maintained by escape from demands to request a break from work after brief periods of task engagement and did not permit escape contingent on aberrant responses. As the rate of mands increased, self-injurious behavior decreased, presumably because mands replaced the operant function of self-injurious behavior. A similar strategy was used by Steege et al. (1990) in which microswitch activation of taped messages was negatively reinforced as a means of manding a break from grooming tasks. Carr and Durand (1985) and Durand and Carr (1987) reported an alternative manding strategy for children whose problem behaviors occurred in the presence of difficult tasks only. They taught these children to request teacher assistance when difficult tasks were presented as an alternative to maladaptive behavior. As with the scheduled-break intervention, both approaches to mand training seem to us to be appropriate interventions for escape-motivated behavior to the extent that the treatments do not abridge the individual's right to habilitative programming and the development of functional skills. To the extent that manding for breaks or assistance significantly reduces skill instruction, these options are best viewed as an initial step toward achieving the goal of full engagement in an individualized habilitative program. For example, the amount of work engagement prior to each break can slowly be increased over time. Eventually the goal of full engagement can be achieved as the individual's time on-task increases and the length of breaks decreases.

Automatic Reinforcement

For some persons who engage in self-injurious behavior or stereotypy, the results of a functional analysis can either be inconclusive or show high levels of the target behavior in a low stimulation condition. An inconclusive finding is one in which the targeted behavior is elevated in all conditions and undifferentiated by condition (Iwata et al., 1982). That is, the controlling variables for the maladaptive behavior have not been isolated. Although this assessment outcome is inherently ambiguous, there has been widespread speculation that the maintaining mechanism for these behaviors may still be operant in nature.

The unusual topographies associated with self-injurious behavior and stereotypy suggest that the responses may be maintained by sensory or perceptual consequences that automatically accompany the actions (Cataldo & Harris, 1982; Iwata, Vollmer, et al., 1990; Lovaas, Newsom, & Hickman, 1987). When these consequences are appetitive or stimulating, the behavior producing these effects may be positively reinforced. Alternatively, if the consequences alleviate or mask an aversive physiologic condition (e.g., pain), the response may be negatively reinforced. Evidence for the validity of the automatic-reinforcement hypothesis is necessarily indirect because the controlling antecedent and consequent variables are not readily observable or subject to direct manipulation (see Iwata, Vollmer, et al., 1990, and Lovaas et al., 1987, for excellent reviews of this issue). Although the evidence suggests that an operant mechanism is plausible in these cases, it is also possible that the mechanism is more biologic in nature (see Aman & Singh, 1988, and Farber, 1987). Until the weight of the evidence supports one of these viewpoints, or methodologies develop to distinguish operant from biologic mechanisms, we believe considerable caution is needed in interpreting the results from an exclusively operant perspective.

Procedures To Weaken the Maintaining Contingency

Two approaches have been used to weaken the response–reinforcer relationship for behavior maintained by automatic reinforcement. *Sensory extinction* has been attempted in the treatment of various stereotypic behaviors, such as hand-flapping and toy-spinning. Because sensory consequences cannot be completely discontinued given the occurrence of the behavior, efforts have centered around masking or attenuating the sensations produced by the behavior. For example, Rincover, Cook, Peoples, and Packer (1979) carpeted tabletops to reduce the auditory stimulation from plate-spinning and placed gloves on a child's hands to reduce the stimulation of hand-rubbing. Both procedures reduced stereotypy, perhaps because the sensory consequences were significantly altered. In a similar vein, blocking responses early in the response cycle has been used with the hopes that the full reinforcing effects of the behavior are prevented. Although response blocking has been used in effective intervention with stereotyped and self-injurious behavior, it is difficult to attribute the effects entirely to a reduction in sensory consequences (e.g., Favell, McGimsey, & Schell, 1982).

The second approach to weakening the response–reinforcer relationship has been to provide copious amounts of alternative sensory stimulation noncontingently to the individual. A number of studies have shown that simply increasing the level of stimulation in the environment, via social interaction (e.g., Mace & Knight, 1986), visual displays (Forehand & Baumeister, 1970), or music (Mace, Yankanich, & West, 1989), is correlated with lower levels of stereotyped or other maladaptive behaviors that may be maintained by automatic reinforcement. The presumption is that noncontingent stimulation diminishes the establishing conditions for behavior maintained by automatic positive reinforcement (e.g., punishment and increases in response effort [Iwata, Vollmer et al., 1990]).

Reinforcement of Alternative Replacement Behaviors

Increasing engagement in alternative behaviors that produce sensory stimulation can be a viable strategy for maladaptive behavior maintained by automatic reinforcement. Individuals who display less problem behavior during periods of interaction or play may benefit from instruction in skills aimed at initiating and maintaining social interaction (e.g., Day et al., 1988; Mace & Lalli, 1991; Odom, Hoyson, Jamieson, & Strain, 1985) or engagement in leisure activities (Mace, Browder, & Martin, 1988). A complementary strategy reported widely is to enrich the individual's environment with a variety of interesting materials and objects (e.g., Berkson & Mason, 1965; Davenport & Berkson, 1963; Parrish, Iwata, Dorsey, Bunck, & Slifer, 1985; Steege, Wacker, & McMahon, 1987). Increased availability of attractive items introduces numerous discriminative stimuli for alternative behaviors from which the individual may derive stimulation sufficient to compete with the problem behavior.

PHARMACOLOGIC TREATMENT
AND DEFAULT BEHAVIORAL TECHNOLOGIES

Behavioral treatment based on the operant function of aberrant behavior may not be possible or effective for some individuals. In such cases, pharmacologic treatment or default behavioral treatments may be needed to reduce maladaptive behavior to acceptable levels and facilitate the development of adaptive repertoires. The decision to use medication or default behavioral treatments rests on the interpretation of undifferentiated data series in the functional analysis.

Interpretation of Undifferentiated Data Series

When the results of the functional analysis fail to identify one or more environmental contingencies maintaining maladaptive behavior, interpretation of the findings is difficult. In general, three interpretations are plausible in such cases. First, the target behavior is operant in nature, but the functional analysis failed to isolate the controlling contingencies. Although this interpretation cannot be confirmed directly (without a subsequent successful functional analysis), tentative indirect support may be gathered by demonstrating that the maladaptive behavior is responsive to one type of intervention based on one operant function and not responsive to another type based on a different function (e.g., Lalli, Browder, Mace, & Brown, in press; Repp et al., 1988). A second possible interpretation of undifferentiated functional analysis results is that the aberrant behavior has multiple functions depending on the establishing conditions in effect at a given time. Thus, the problem behavior may produce attention when an adult is preoccupied, escape when task demands are presented, access to restricted items when they are unavailable, and sensory consequences in the absence of alternative stimulation. Support for this interpretation may be provided by introducing, for example, a treatment based on an attention function in all experimental conditions (e.g., VI/VT attention). If improvement is observed only in the attention condition, the plausibility of the multiple function hypothesis is strengthened.

    If support for these two interpretations cannot be obtained, it is reasonable in some cases to suspect that the behavior is maintained by a biologic variable operating across all environmental conditions. This interpretation is especially plausible when the target responses are self-injurious or stereotypic behaviors, which have been shown to have biologic correlates or causes (Cataldo & Harris, 1982; Farber, 1987).

Pharmacologic Treatment

When undifferentiated functional analysis results point to the presence of biologic factors maintaining aberrant behavior (e.g., endogenous opiate production and self-injury, excessive dopamine production and stereotypy), pharmacologic treatment is an option. Some recent advances in the treatment of behavior disorders in persons with developmental disabilities indicate that behaviors such as self-injury, stereotypy, aggression, and hyperactivity can be improved with certain medications (Aman & Singh, 1988; Cataldo & Harris, 1982; Farber, 1987; Singh & Millichamp, 1985). Perhaps the most promising development is pharmacologic treatment based on a match between presenting clinical features and selection of specific medications, especially when the medication is directed at alleviating an underlying biochemical abnormality. In the pharmacologic treatment of self-injury, for example, the presence of extreme tissue damage has been an indication for the use of an opioid antagonist, naltrexone hydrochloride; repetitive, stereotypic self-injurious behavior has been responsive to low-dose haloperidol treatment; high-rate self-injury with agitation when interrupted has been treated successfully with chlomipramine; and self-injurious behavior co-occurring with agitation has been responsive to lithium carbonate (Aman & Singh, 1988). Future developments in psychopharmacology promise to improve the rational selection of medications for the treatment of specific behavior disorders that are not maintained primarily by environmental variables.

Default Behavioral Treatments

If an operant function of aberrant behavior cannot be identified, and the disorder is unresponsive to pharmacologic therapy, alternative behavioral treatments shown to be effective in suppressing aberrant behavior may need to be considered if the behavior threatens the health or placement of the individual (Iwata, 1987). Default behavioral treatments are effective in one of three ways. First, a very potent (primary) positive reinforcer (e.g., favorite foods) may be arranged (under conditions of deprivation) contingent on an alternative adaptive behavior. The reinforcer needs to be sufficiently powerful to override the variables that are maintaining the problem behavior. Second, the maladaptive behavior can be prevented from occurring by physically blocking the response or applying brief mechanical restraint. Because an operant function for maladaptive behavior has been ruled out, the rate of the response is unlikely to change, and the intervention will need to remain in effect indefinitely. Finally, an aversive stimulus can be presented contingent on each occurrence of the targeted behavior. Again, the aversive stimulus must be sufficiently powerful to override the mechanism maintaining the target behavior.

These treatment options are default technologies because their use is based on the reductions produced in aberrant behavior rather than on an understanding of the environmental or biologic etiology of the disorder (Iwata, 1987). There is general agreement that these interventions are far less desirable than treatments based on operant function or biochemical abnormalities. However, in the absence of valid diagnostics, default treatments are the only effective alternatives available. We believe that the decision-making process outlined above maximizes the likelihood of detecting maintaining variables and, accordingly, minimizes the need for default treatments in emergency or life-threatening situations.

CONCLUSIONS

We have proposed a model for integrating contemporary developments in matching theory and research with the functional analysis of behavior disorders. Whereas the goal of functional analysis is to identify the operant function of aberrant behavior, matching theory suggests that specific information about the conditions maintaining problem behavior can be used to design interventions with greater specificity and, perhaps, greater effectiveness. Combining descriptive and experimental methods in a functional analysis can provide information about the rate, quality, and immediacy of reinforcement maintaining the aberrant behavior and the response effort required to produce reinforcement. Behavioral treatments can then be designed to effectively compete with the maintaining conditions, producing a preference for adaptive alternative behavior over maladaptive behavior. To the extent that this model results in more effective treatments, the need for default technologies to manage severe behavior disorders will be minimized.

REFERENCES

Allen, K.E., & Harris, F.R. (1966). Elimination of a child's scratching by training the mother in reinforcement procedures. *Behavior Research and Therapy, 4,* 79–84.

Aman, M.G., & Singh, N.N. (1988). *Psychopharmacology of the developmental disabilities.* New York: Springer-Verlag.

Bannerman, D.J., Sheldon, J.B., Sherman, J.A., & Harchik, A. (1990). Balancing the right to habilitation with the right to personal liberties: The rights of people with developmental disabilities to eat too many donuts and take a nap. *Journal of Applied Behavior Analysis, 23,* 79–89.

Bauman, R.A., Shull, R.L., & Brownstein, A.J. (1975). Time allocation on concurrent schedules with asymmetrical response requirements. *Journal of the Experimental Analysis of Behavior, 24,* 53–57.

Beatrais, P.G., & Davison, M.C. (1977). Response and time allocation in concurrent second-order schedules. *Journal of the Experimental Analysis of Behavior, 25,* 61–69.

Berkson, G., & Mason, W.A. (1965). Stereotyped movements of mental detectives. IV: The effects of toys and the character of the acts. *American Journal of Mental Deficiency, 68,* 511–524.

Bijou, S.W., Peterson, R.F., & Ault, M.H. (1968). A method to integrate descriptive and experimental field studies at the level of data and empirical concepts. *Journal of Applied Behavior Analysis, 1,* 175–191.

Carr, E.G. (1988). Functional equivalence as a mechanism of response generalization. In R. Horner, R.L. Koegel, & G. Dunlap (Eds.), *Generalization and maintenance: Life-style changes in applied settings* (pp. 221–241). Baltimore: Paul H. Brookes Publishing Co.

Carr, E.G., & Durand, M.V. (1985). Reducing behaviors problems through functional communication training. *Journal of Applied Behavior Analysis, 18,* 111–126.

Carr, E.G., & Kemp, D.C. (1989). Functional equivalence of autistic leading and communicative pointing: Analysis and treatment. *Journal of Autism and Developmental Disorders, 19,* 561–578.

Carr, E.G., McConnachie, G., Levin, L., & Kemp, D.C. (in press). Communication-based treatments of severe behavior problems. In R. Van Houten & S. Axelrod (Eds.), *Behavioral analysis and treatment.* New York: Plenum.

Carr, E.G., Newsom, C.D., & Binkoff, J.A. (1976). Stimulus control of self-destructive behavior in a psychotic child. *Journal of Abnormal Child Psychology, 4,* 139–153.

Carr, E.G., Newsom, C.D., & Binkoff, J.A. (1980). Escape as a factor in the aggressive behavior of two retarded children. *Journal of Applied Behavior Analysis, 13,* 101–118.

Catania, A.C. (1984). *Learning* (2nd ed.). Englewood Cliffs, NJ: Prentice Hall.

Center, D.B., Deitz, S.M., & Kaufman, M. (1982). Student ability, tasks difficulty and inappropriate classroom behavior. *Behavior Modification, 6,* 355–374.

Cooper, L.J., Wacker, D.P., Sasso, G.M., Reimers, T.M., & Donn, J. (1990). Using parents as therapists to evaluate appropriate behavior of their children: Application to a tertiary diagnostic clinic. *Journal of Applied Behavior Analysis, 23,* 285–296.

Conger, R., & Killeen, P. (1974). Use of concurrent operants in small group research. *Pacific Sociological Review, 17,* 339–416.

Davenport, R.K., & Berkson, G. (1963). Stereotyped movements of mental detectives. II: Effects of novel objects. *American Journal of Mental Deficiency, 67,* 879–882.

Davison, M., & McCarthy, D. (1988). *The matching law: A research review.* Hillsdale, NJ: Lawrence Earlbaum Associates.

Day, R.M., Rae, J.A., Schussler, N.G., Larsen, S.E., & Johnson, W.L. (1988). A functionally based approach to the treatment of self-injurious behavior. *Behavior Modification, 12,* 565–589.

de Villiers, P.A. (1977). Choice in concurrent schedules and a qualitative formulation of the law of effect. In W.K. Honig & J.E.R. Studdon (Eds.), *Handbook of operant behavior* (pp. 233–287). Englewood Cliffs, NJ: Prentice-Hall.

Durand, V.M., & Carr, E.G. (1987). Social influences on "self-stimulatory" behavior: Analysis and treatment application. *Journal of Applied Behavior Analysis, 20,* 119–132.

Durand, V.M., & Kishi, G. (1987). Reducing severe behavior problems among persons with dual sensory impairments: An evaluation of a technical assistance model. *Journal of The Association for Persons with Severe Handicaps, 12,* 2–10.

Farber, J.M. (1987). Psychopharmacology of self-injurious behavior in the mentally retarded. *Journal of American Academic Child Adolescent Psychiatry, 26,* 296–302.

Favell, J.E., McGimsey, J., & Schell, R. (1982). Treatment of self-injury by providing alternative sensory activities. *Analysis and Intervention in Developmental Disabilities, 2,* 83–104.

Finney, J., Russo, D., & Cataldo, M. (1982). Reduction of pica in young children with lead poisoning. *Journal of Pediatric Psychology, 7,* 197–207.

Forehand, R., & Baumeister, A.A. (1970). The effect of auditory and visual stimulation on stereotyped rocking behavior and general activity of severe retardates. *Journal of Clinical Psychology, 26,* 426–429.

Gaylord-Ross, R., Weeks, M., & Lipner, C. (1980). An analysis of antecedent, response, and consequence events in the treatment of self-injurious behavior. *Education and Training of the Mentally Retarded, 15,* 35–42.

Herrnstein, R.J. (1961). Relative and absolute strength of response as a function of frequency of reinforcement. *Journal of the Experimental Analysis of Behavior, 4,* 267–272.

Herrnstein, R.J. (1970). On the law of effect. *Journal of the Experimental Analysis of Behavior, 13,* 243–266.

Herrnstein, R.J., & Loveland, D.H. (1975). Maximizing and matching on concurrent ratio schedules. *Journal of the Experimental Analysis of Behavior, 24,* 107–116.

Hollard, V., & Davison, M.C. (1971). Preference for qualitatively different reinforcers. *Journal of the Experimental Analysis of Behavior, 16,* 375–380.

Horner, R.D. (1980). The effects of an environmental "enrichment" program on the behavior of institutionalized profoundly retarded children. *Journal of Applied Behavior Analysis, 13,* 473–491.

Horner, R.H., & Budd, C.M. (1985). Acquisition of manual sign use. Collateral reduction of maladaptive behavior and factors limiting generalization. *Education and Training of the Mentally Retarded, 20,* 39–47.

Horner, R.H., Day, H.M., Sprague, J.R., O'Brien, M., & Heathfield, L.T. (1991). Interspersed requests: A nonaversive procedure for decreasing aggression and self-injury during instruction. *Journal of Applied Behavior Analysis, 24,* 265–278.

Iwata, B.A. (1987). Negative reinforcement in applied behavior analysis: An emerging technology. *Journal of Applied Behavior Analysis, 20,* 361–378.

Iwata, B.A., Dorsey, M. Slifer, K., Bauman, K., & Richman, G. (1982). Toward a functional analysis of self-injury. *Analysis and Intervention in Developmental Disabilities, 2,* 3–20.

Iwata, B.A., Pace, G.M., Cowdery, G.E., Kalsher, M.J., & Cataldo, M.F. (1990). Experimental analysis and extinction of self-injurious escape behavior. *Journal of Applied Behavior Analysis, 23,* 11–27.

Iwata, B.A., Vollmer, T.R., & Zarcone, J.R. (1990). The experimental (functional) analysis of behavior disorders: Methodology, application, and limitations. In A.C. Repp and N.N. Singh (Eds.), *Current perspectives in the use of nonaversive and aversive intervention with developmentally disabled persons* (pp. 301–330). Sycamore, IL: Sycamore Publishing Company.

Lalli, J.S., Browder, D.M., Mace, F.C., & Brown, K. (in press). Teacher use of descriptive analysis data to implement interventions to decrease students' maladaptive behavior. *Journal of Applied Behavior Analysis.*

Logue, A.W. (1988). Research on self-control: An integrating framework. *Behavioral Brain Sciences, 11,* 665–709.

Lovaas, O.I., Newsom, C., & Hickman, C. (1987). Self-stimulatory behavior and perceptual reinforcement. *Journal of Applied Behavior Analysis, 20,* 45–68.

Lovaas, O.I., & Simmons, J.Q. (1969). Manipulation of self-destruction in three retarded children. *Journal of Applied Behavior Analysis, 2,* 143–157.

Lowe, C.F., & Horne, P.J. (1985). On the generality of behavioral principles: Human choice and the matching law. In C.F. Lowe (Ed.), *Behavior analysis and contemporary psychology* (pp. 97–115). London: Erlbaum.

Mace, F.C., & Belfiore, P. (1990). Behavioral momentum in the treatment of escape-motivated stereotypy. *Journal of Applied Behavior Analysis, 23,* 507–514.

Mace, F.C., Browder, D.M., & Lin, Y. (1987). Analysis of demand conditions associated with stereotypy. *Journal of Applied Behavior Analysis, 19,* 411–416.

Mace, F.C., Browder, D.M., & Martin, D.K. (1988). Reduction of stereotypy via instruction of alternative leisure behavior. *School Psychology Review, 17,* 156–165.

Mace, F.C., & Knight, D. (1986). Functional analysis and the treatment of severe pica. *Journal of Applied Behavior Analysis, 19,* 411–416.

Mace, F.C., & Lalli, J.S. (1991). Linking descriptive and experimental analyses in the treatment of bizarre speech. *Journal of Applied Behavior Analysis, 24,* 553–562.

Mace, F.C., Lalli, J.S., & Pinter-Lalli, E. (1991). Functional analysis and the treatment of aberrant behavior. *Research in Developmental Disabilities, 12,* 155–180.

Mace, F.C., Lalli, J.S., & Shea, M.C. (1992). Functional analysis of self-injury. In J. Luiselli, J. Matson, & N. Singh (Eds.), *Assessment, analysis, and treatment of self-injury* (pp. 122–152). New York: Springer-Verlag.

Mace, F.C., Lalli, J.S., Shea, M.C., Lalli, E., West, B., Roberts, M.L., & Nevin, J.A. (1990). The momentum of human behavior in a natural setting. *Journal of the Experimental Analysis of Behavior, 54,* 163–172.

Mace, F.C., McCurdy, B., & Quigley, E.A. (1990). A negative side-effect of reward predicted by the matching law. *Journal of Applied Behavior Analysis, 23,* 197–206.

Mace, F.C., Page, T.J., Ivancic, M.T., & O'Brien, S. (1986). Analysis of environmental determinants of aggression and disruption in mentally retarded children. *Applied Research in Mental Retardation, 7,* 203–221.

Mace, F.C., & West, B.J. (1986). Analysis of demand conditions associated with reluctant speech. *Journal of Behavior Therapy and Experimental Psychiatry, 17,* 285–294.

Mace, F.C., Yankanich, M.A., & West, B. (1989). Toward a methodology of experimental analysis and treatment of aberrant classroom behaviors. *Special Services in the School, 4,* 71–88.

Martens, B.K., & Houk, J.L. (1989). The application of Herrnstein's law of effect to disruptive and on-task behavior of a retarded adolescent girl. *Journal of the Experimental Analysis of Behavior, 51,* 17–28.

Martens, B.K., Lochner, D.G., & Kelly, S.Q. (in press). The effects of variable-interval reinforcement on academic engagement: An experimental demonstration of matching theory. *Journal of Applied Behavior Analysis.*

McDowell, J.J. (1988). Matching theory in natural human environments. *Behavior Analyst, 11,* 95–109.

McDowell, J.J. (1989). Two modern developments in matching theory. *Behavior Analyst, 12,* 153–166.

Michael, J. (1982). Distinguishing between discriminative and motivational functions of stimuli. *Journal of the Experimental Analysis of Behavior, 37,* 149–155.

Miller, J.T. (1976). Matching-based hedonic scaling in the pigeon. *Journal of the Experimental Analysis of Behavior, 26,* 335–347.

Myerson, J., & Hale, S. (1984). Practical implications of the matching law. *Journal of Applied Behavior Analysis, 17,* 367–380.

Neef, N.A., Mace, F.C., & Shade, D. (in press). Impulsivity in students with affective disorders: The interactive effects of reinforcer rate, delay and quality. *Journal of Applied Behavior Analysis.*

Neef, N.A., Mace, F.C., Shea, M.C., & Shade, D.B. (1992). Effects of reinforcer rates and reinforcer quality on time allocation: Extension of matching theory to educational settings. *Journal of Applied Behavior Analysis.*

Neef, N.A., Shaefer, M.S., Egel, S., Cataldo, M.A., & Parrish, J.M. (1983). The class specific effect of compliance training with "do" and "don't" requests: Analogue analysis and classroom application. *Journal of Applied Behavior Analysis, 16,* 81–100.

Nevin, J.A. (1974). Response strength in multiple schedules. *Journal of the Experimental Analysis of Behavior, 21,* 389–408.

Odom, S.L., Hoyson, M., Jamieson, B., & Strain, P.S. (1985). Increasing handicapped preschoolers' peer social interactions: Cross-setting and component analysis. *Journal of Applied Behavior Analysis, 18,* 3–17.

Parrish, J.M., Iwata, B.A., Dorsey, M., Bunck, T., & Slifer, C. (1985). Behavior analysis, program development, transfer of control in the treatment of self-injury. *Journal of Behavior Therapy and Experimental Psychiatry, 16,* 159–168.

Pierce, W.D., & Epling, W.F. (1983). Choice, matching and human behavior: A review of the literature. *Behavior Analyst,* 57–76.

Rachlin, H. (1989). *Judgment, decision and choice: A cognitive/behavioral synthesis.* New York: Freeman.

Repp, A.C., Felce, D., & Barton, L.E. (1988). Basing the treatment of stereotypic and self-injurious behaviors on hypotheses of their causes. *Journal of Applied Behavior Analysis, 21,* 281–290.

Rincover, A., Cook, R., Peoples, A., & Packer, D. (1979). Sensory extinction and sensory reinforcement principles for programming multiple adaptive behavior change. *Journal of Applied Behavior Analysis, 12,* 221–233.

Sailor, W., Guess, D., Rutherford, G., & Baer, D.M. (1968). Control of tantrum behavior by operant techniques during experimental verbal training. *Journal of Applied Behavior Analysis, 1,* 237–243.

Sajwaj, T., Twardosz, S., & Burke, M. (1972). Side effects of extinction procedures in a remedial preschool. *Journal of Applied Behavior Analysis, 5,* 163–175.

Singh, N.N., & Millichamp, C.J. (1985). Pharmacological treatment of self-injurious behavior in mentally retarded persons. *Journal of Autism and Developmental Disorders, 15,* 257–267.

Skinner, B.F. (1938). *The behavior of organisms.* New York: Appleton-Century.

Skinner, B.F. (1953). *Science and human behavior.* New York: MacMillan.

Skinner, B.F. (1969). *Contingencies of reinforcement: A theoretical analysis.* New York: Appleton-Century-Crofts.

Steege, G.M., Wacker, D.P., Cegrand, K.C., Berg, W.K., Nova, K.C., Reimers, T.M., Sasso, G.M., & DeRaad, A. (1990). Use of negative reinforcement in the treatment of self-injurious behavior. *Journal of Applied Behavior Analysis, 23,* 459–467.

Steege, M.W., Wacker, D., & McMahon, C. (1987). Evaluation of the effectiveness and efficiency of two stimulus prompt strategies with severely handicapped students. *Journal of Applied Behavior Analysis, 20,* 293–299.

Touchette, P.E., MacDonald, R.F., & Langer, S.N. (1985). A scatterplot for identifying stimulus control of problem behavior. *Journal of Applied Behavior Analysis, 18,* 343–351.

Vollmer, T.R., & Iwata, B.A. (1991). Establishing operations and reinforcement effects. *Journal of Applied Behavior Analysis, 23,* 417–429.

Vollmer, T.R., & Iwata, B.A. (in press). Differential reinforcement as treatment for behavior disorders: Procedural and functional variation. *Journal of Applied Behavior Analysis.*

Wacker, D.P., Steege, M.W., Northup, J., & Sasso, G.M. (1990). A component of analysis of functional communication training across three topographies of severe behavior problems. *Journal of Applied Behavior Analysis, 23,* 417–429.

Wacker, D.P., Wiggins, B., Fowler, M., & Berg, W.K. (1988). Training students with profound or multiple handicaps to make requests via microswitches. *Journal of Applied Behavior Analysis, 21,* 331–343.

Weeks, M., & Gaylord-Ross, R. (1981). Task difficulty and aberrant behavior in severely handicapped students. *Journal of Applied Behavior Analysis, 14,* 449–463.

7

Interventions Based on Covariation of Desired and Inappropriate Behavior

John M. Parrish and Maura L. Roberts

INTERVENTIONISTS OFTEN ENCOUNTER INDIVIDUALS WHO exhibit multiple problem behaviors (Kazdin, 1982). When an individual presents an extensive repertoire of challenging responses, the conscientious interventionist may be overwhelmed initially, especially if he or she assumes reflexively that for each chief complaint a separable etiology and corresponding assessment/intervention paradigm must be identified.

When confronted with complex arrays of problem behavior, even the most skillful tacticians often struggle to determine where best to intervene (Kazdin, 1985; Rincover, 1981). For instance, consider Brendan, a 5-year-old boy who defecates only when handed a diaper and allowed to stand, who insists upon sleeping in bed with his parents, and then proceeds to suck his dominant thumb to a point of dental malocclusion while wetting the parents' bed! His constellation of problem behaviors, and others similar to it, is neither fictitious nor infrequent!

In response to this actual case, would you intervene at all? If so, where would you begin? With one or more of these presenting problems? Or with an intervention that directly addresses none of the above, choosing instead to examine first a fundamental set of issues that contributes indirectly to each of them?

Upon encountering an individual who displays an array of behavioral excesses and deficits, the application of principles of behavior change to one

The development of this chapter was supported by the National Institute of Child Health and Human Development (NICHD) Mental Retardation Research Center Core Grant P30 DH26979 and by Maternal and Child Health Bureau Grants MCJ9164 and MCJ429308-01-0. The positions taken in this chapter have not been endorsed by these federal agencies nor should they be construed as having their endorsement.

problem behavior at a time often seems inadequate. Alternatively, the astute interventionist is often in search of tactics that are capable of yielding broad gains. This chapter examines some empirically based considerations for the interventionist who must meet such challenges every day.

BACKGROUND CONSIDERATIONS

Problem behaviors are often described as if they were independent phenomena with uniquely defining characteristics that arise from distinguishable etiologies. For example, nosological systems, such as the *Diagnostic and Statistical Manual of Mental Disorders* (DSM-III-R) (American Psychiatric Association, 1987), are chiefly predicated upon topographical descriptors that have been derived in an attempt to discriminate one diagnostic entity from each of the others (American Psychological Association, 1987; Kazdin, 1983). Within such paradigms, differential diagnosis centered upon the topography (or form) of the individual's behavior is frequently considered an important prerequisite to classification and to identification of an effective intervention.

Although such differential diagnoses may at times facilitate communication among scientist-practitioners, may occasionally dictate a specific intervention strategy, and may eventually further the detection of causative mechanisms of action, they may also perpetuate myths that contribute to inefficient, or even unethical, interventions (Russo, Cataldo, & Cushing, 1981). For example, within these frameworks, interventionists often assume that each symptom presented by the individual requires a specific assessment/intervention protocol. Based upon this assumption, interventionists typically proceed with a serial approach to behavior modification by which they apply interventions for one behavior at a time. Frequently, the order in which problems are addressed is determined by a set of presumptions, such as it is better to prioritize according to the individual's or his or her caregivers' preferences (Wacker et al., 1990) or to address more severe problems first (Kazdin, 1983). However, what if the former resulted in an inefficient sequence of problem-specific interventions? Alternatively, what if the latter led to aversive interventions that may not have been necessary had the initial intervention facilitated the acquisition of a prosocial replacement behavior that simultaneously decreased the probability of the more severe problem behavior (Axelrod, 1987; Horner et al., 1990)? This is, indeed, the premise of functional communication training; namely, that mands will replace challenging behavior.

Although it is unlikely that all individuals presenting with dangerous or destructive behavior can be managed by way of skill acquisition (e.g., mand training) alone, many interventionists may rely less upon intrusive interventions aimed principally at the suppression of problem behavior if and when their educative efforts produce such positive results. Or, what if treating more severe problems initially decreased the change agent's (e.g., parent, teacher) motivation to continue the intervention, especially when such problems are relatively intractable?

In many cases, it is preferable to first intervene either with those problems that are likely to resolve quickly with little effort, those problems that require the change agent to acquire generalizable problem-solving skills, or those problems that are "keystone" behaviors (i.e., their improvement results in generalized change in other targeted behaviors) (Rincover, 1981). Given the burgeoning concern with the cost-effectiveness of alternative interventions (Levin, 1983), it is imperative to identify intervention strategies that resolve several presenting problems as efficiently as possible.

In theory as well as in practice, it is difficult to fathom how any intervention would not affect multiple responses. Correspondingly, quality research into the efficacy of any intervention entails the evaluation of multiple effects. Increasingly, investigators are observing coincidental changes in selected, nonmanipulated behaviors when the rate of a target behavior is systematically altered. Changes in collateral behavior may be intended or not and may be beneficial or harmful. Research that elucidates the variables that influence concurrent changes in multiple behaviors continues to receive high priority. Indeed, generating pervasive effects is critical to the comprehensive care of persons with disabilities.

RESPONSE COVARIATION: WHAT IS IT?

For some time, behavior analysts have been intrigued by stimulus–response relationships. In the presence of a particular stimulus, how does a person respond? Recently, researchers have begun to explore more complex response–response relationships (Kazdin, 1982; Koegel, Firestone, Kramme, & Dunlap, 1974; Voeltz & Evans, 1982) through which they examine changes in one response coterminous with the assessment or manipulation of another response. Said differently, increased attention has been directed to studying the interrelationships among responses in an individual's repertoire.

Such interdependence among responses may occur where there are: 1) response chains in which each response cues the subsequent response, with the latter functioning as a conditioned reinforcer for the former; 2) response classes or clusters of functionally equivalent responses that may be topographically similar or dissimilar; or 3) response hierarchies in which the individual has learned to produce alternative responses whenever the function of another response is disrupted.

To a behavioral scientist, a key question is: What happens to behavior B when behavior A changes? For the practicing behavior analyst, analogous questions include: Is there an intervention that can be applied to a "keystone" behavior (Rincover, 1981) that will result in pervasive change? What are the side effects as well as main effects of my intervention? Another way to pose these questions is: Does one behavior vary as a function of another?

What is "response covariation"? Put in the most simple terms, response covariation is the observation that two or more behaviors vary directly or inversely (Kazdin, 1982). Others (Lovaas & Simmons, 1969; Reynolds, 1963) have proposed that response covariation occurs when change in a non-manipulated response is observed concurrently with the manipulation of another response.

In some instances, the term response covariation has been used interchangeably with the term *response generalization,* especially when two response classes both increase when only one is manipulated. In general terms, response generalization represents a spread of effects from the target response to other responses, just as stimulus generalization is said to occur when there is a spread of effects from one situation to others.

Direct or "positive" response covariation occurs when the probability of one behavior increases or decreases along with increases or decreases in the probability of another behavior. Indirect or "negative" response covariation occurs when increases or decreases in one behavior reliably result in collateral increases or decreases in another behavior. A response–response relationship may be uni- or bidirectional in nature, although the term *response covariation* itself typically implies that the relationship is bidirectional. For instance, if increases in smiling and shaking hands commonly co-occur, we say that these two behaviors directly (or positively) covary. If, however, increases in the work rate are typically associated with fewer incidents of negative vocalizations, we say that these two behaviors vary inversely (or negatively).

APPLIED IMPLICATIONS FOR INTERVENTIONISTS: AN OVERVIEW

One of the more important implications of an understanding of response covariation for intervention is that the occurrence of covariation may make it more feasible, as well as effective, to intervene with some problem behaviors indirectly (Wahler, 1975). As a case in point, consider the challenge of intervening with a covert behavior such as stealing, or an infrequent behavior such as rape. If such difficult-to-treat behaviors are functionally related to behaviors that are more overt and/or frequent, then contingencies that manage these latter behaviors may contribute, albeit indirectly, to the successful management of these challenging behaviors.

In the case of functional communication training, the hope is that a mand (or mands) will replace problem behavior. As manding increases via contingent reinforcement, problem behavior decreases. Elucidating the fundamental processes underlying response covariation has implications for intervention strategies other than functional communication training. For instance, this process may also yield useful tactics for the management of socially significant problem behaviors resulting in unhealthy lifestyles (e.g., cigarette smoking, overeating, excessive consumption of alcohol, drug use), poor response to medical treatment (as a consequence of nonadherence to the prescribed regimen), and sexual transmission of disease (e.g., HIV, syphilis, gonorrhea).

Another applied implication is that the interventionist who can capitalize upon response–response relationships has increased access to a multiplicity of options for management of a specific challenging behavior. In some situations, it may be that change in some behaviors will have a greater impact than change in other behaviors (including the particular behavior that is presented as the chief complaint). In such cases, a behavior other than the chief complaint may be profitably selected because its modification may have a more positive, pervasive influence. Likewise, as mentioned above, an understanding of interrelationships among behaviors may help practitioners to avoid implementing interventions that will produce unwanted side effects (Evans, Meyer, Kurkjian, & Kishi, 1988). With the increased focus upon inducing behavior change through exclusive reliance upon "positive practices," an appreciation of response covariation as a process contributing to constructive intervention gains has increased (Helmstetter & Durand, 1990; Horner et al., 1990).

The phenomenon of response covariation and the specific mechanisms responsible for it may also serve to explain partially why intervention effects do not always generalize. It may be that one or more responses within an individual's repertoire exert greater and more sustained control over the targeted problem behavior than does the intervention itself.

RESPONSE COVARIATION: CONCEPTUAL AND METHODOLOGICAL OVERVIEW

In this section, we present a chronological overview of the applied literature and provide detailed descriptions of some of the landmark studies. Our intent is to provide the conceptual and methodological basis for interventions predicated upon response covariation.

As a phenomenon, response covariation has been observed, if not systematically evaluated, within a variety of situations. The process of response covariation has been studied by applied behavior analysts less frequently, and the specific mechanisms responsible for its development and action have, to this point, received surprisingly little attention. Table 1 presents a descriptive profile of selected studies pertaining to response covariation, some of which are discussed in more detail below.

Much of the early literature regarding response covariation is constituted by intervention studies that attempted to increase a prosocial behavior and/or decrease a problem behavior, only to find, serendipitously, that unintended positive or negative collateral (side) effects also occurred. During these stud-

Table 1. Selected studies examining response covariation and related phenomena

Authors	Date	Number of subjects	Subject classification	Dependent variables	Independent variables	Experimental design	Outcomes
Ayllon and Roberts	1974	5	Elementary school children	Academic performance; disruption	Systematic token reinforcement	Reversal	As academic performance increased, disruption decreased and vice versa
Barton and Ascione	1979	16	Average-to-superior intelligence	Percentage of verbal and physical sharing	Training for verbal sharing (VS), physical sharing (PS), verbal and physical sharing (VPS)	ABA reversal with follow-up	Unidirectional response generalization from VS to PS, VS and PS distinct response classes
Budd, Green, and Baer	1976	1	Preschool special classroom	Noncompliance with parental requests, inappropriate behaviors	Parent training: Modified attention, instruction-giving	MBL across behaviors	Increases in compliance, collateral decreases in inappropriate behavior
Buell, Stoddard, Harris, and Baer	1968	1	Preschool	Teacher-initiated interaction with child, child-initiated interaction with teacher, student's cooperative or parallel play, baby-like behavior demonstrated by child	Social reinforcement contingent upon use of outdoor play equipment	ABCD	Equipment use increased, with desirable changes in other DVs
Carr and Durand	1985	4	Autism, brain damage, developmental disabilities	Disruptive behavior, academic behavior, adult attention	Manipulation of task difficulty (easy/hard), adult attention (high/low)	Reversal with altered sequences across children	Increased disruption, decreased task completion in high task difficulty and low adult at-

Author	Year	N	Subjects	Dependent variable	Independent variable	Design	Results
							tention conditions; increased task completion, decreased disruption in low task difficulty and high adult attention conditions
Cooper, Wacker, Sasso, Reimers, and Donn	1990	8	Low average to superior intelligence with conduct disorders	Percentage of intervals of (ir)relevant child verbal responses and disruption	Functional verbal communication training (relevant/irrelevant response phrases)	ABAC counterbalanced across subjects	Increased functional communication responses with collateral decreases in disruption
				Severe conduct problems	High-demand parent attention (HDA), high-demand parent ignore (HDI), low-demand parent attention (LDA), low-demand parent ignore (LDI)	Multi-element with replication assessment	Conduct problems decreased with reciprocal changes in appropriate behaviors
Day and Horner	1989	5	Mental retardation	Performance errors	General versus easy case training	MBL across subjects	General-case training promoted generalization (formation of response classes); easy case training resulted in predictable errors during generalization tasks

(continued)

141

Table 1. (continued)

Authors	Date	Number of subjects	Subject classification	Dependent variables	Independent variables	Experimental design	Outcomes
Doleys, Wells, Hobbs, Roberts, and Cartelli	1976	4	Mental retardation	Noncompliance, aggression	Social punishment (SP), positive practice (PP), time-out (TO)	ABAC (AD) counterbalanced across subjects	SP reduced noncompliance more than PP and TO with collateral increases in aggression with TO but not with SP
Durand and Carr	1987	4	Developmental disabilities	Body-rocking, hand-flapping	Decreased adult attention, increased task difficulty	ABAC counterbalanced across subjects	Self-stimulatory behavior increased with increased task difficulty, but not with decreased parental attention
					10-second time-out plus removal of task materials	Reversal	Self-stimulatory behavior maintained by escape
					Assistance-seeking training ("Help me")	MBL across subjects	Increases in assistance-seeking with collateral decreases in self-stimulatory behavior
Durand and Carr	1991	3	Mental retardation	Task performance, challenging behavior (e.g., head-hitting, face-slapping, head-banging, pinching and slapping others)	Escape, attention	ABAC counterbalanced across subjects	Challenging behavior increased with increased task difficulty for 2 of 3

142

Author	Year	N	Disability	Target behavior	Treatment	Design	Results
				Challenging behavior (e.g., head-hitting, face-slapping, head-banging, pinching and slapping others), use of functional communication skills	Functional communication training	MBL across students	Increased functional communication with collateral decreases in challenging behavior
Foxx, Faw, McMorrow, Kyle, and Bittle	1988	3	Mental retardation	Echolalia, use of correct verbal labels	Cues-pause-point-training (CPPT)	MBL across subjects	Decreased maladaptive speech with increased use of correct verbal labels
Friman and Hove	1987	2	Habit disorders	Hair-pulling, thumb-sucking	Aversive taste solution	MBL across subjects	Decreased thumb-sucking with collateral decreases in hair-pulling
Haring and Kennedy	1990	2	Mental retardation	Body-rocking, loud vocalizations, biting, hand-flapping, head-bobbing, task performance	DRO or time-out (TO) during task and leisure conditions	MBL across subjects	DRO reduced problem behavior in task context with TO ineffective; TO reduced problem behavior in leisure context with DRO ineffective; DRO more effective than TO in increasing correct task performance

(continued)

143

Table 1. (continued)

Authors	Date	Number of subjects	Subject classification	Dependent variables	Independent variables	Experimental design	Outcomes
Horner and Day	1991	1	Mental retardation	Aggression, word- and sentence-signing	Break after aggression or 1, 15 trial(s); sentence- and word-sign training	Functional analysis followed by analysis of response efficiency	Use of efficient mand accompanied by decreases in problem behavior
				Self-injury, signing for assistance, immediate assistance, assistance after SIB	ASL training for "Help"	Functional analysis followed by analysis of response efficiency	Use of efficient mand accompanied by decreases in problem behavior
				Aggression, card use	Break after 1, 20 trials or aggression; card use training; 1- or 20-second delay	Functional analysis followed by analysis of response efficiency	Use of efficient mand accompanied by decreases in problem behavior
Horner, Day, Sprague, O'Brien, and Heathfield	1991	3	Mental retardation	Aggression or self-injury, task completion	Tasks (easy/hard) plus interspersed requests	Reversal	Interspersed requests increased instruction-following with decreases in aggression and self-injury
				Aggression or self-injurious behavior (SIB), task completion	Tasks (easy/hard) plus interspersed requests	Reversal	Interspersed requests increased instruction-following with decreases in aggression and self-injury
Koegel, Firestone, Kramme, and	1974	2	Autism	Self-stimulatory behavior, develop-	Punishment	ABA	When self-stimula-tory behavior was

Author	Year	N	Population	Dependent variable	Independent variable	Design	Results
Dunlap				mentally appropriate play			suppressed spontaneous appropriate play increased
Kohler and Greenwood	1990	7	Elementary school children with spelling difficulties	Academic performance, achievement gains, instructional skills of peer tutors	Classwide peer tutoring	Multi-element	Peer tutors enhanced academic responding, with achievement gains in spelling
Mace, McCurdy, and Quigley	1990	1	Special education	Completion of multiplication and division problems	Changing concurrent schedules of reinforcement for math facts	Combined simultaneous treatments and reversal	Increased completion of multiplication facts with concurrent decreased completion of division facts and vice versa
				Rate of completion of alternative functional tasks	Changing concurrent schedules of reinforcement for completion of functional tasks	Combined simultaneous treatments and reversal	Increased rate of completion of one task with concurrent decrease in rate of completion of other tasks and vice versa
Neef, Shafer, Egel, Cataldo, and Parrish	1983	6	Autism, mental retardation	Compliance with do/don't requests	Reinforcement for compliance with targeted do requests, reinforcement for compliance with targeted don't requests	MBL across subjects	Increased compliance with targeted requests, increased compliance with other nontrained requests of same type, lack of generalized compliance with other types of requests

(continued)

Table 1. (continued)

Authors	Date	Number of subjects	Subject classification	Dependent variables	Independent variables	Experimental design	Outcomes
		5	Developmental disabilities	Compliance with do and don't requests	Reinforcement for compliance with each type of request, then for both	MBL across type of requests	Increases in compliance with targeted do and don't requests with little/no generalization to non-targeted requests
Nordquist	1971	1	Mild conduct disorder	Enuresis, oppositional behaviors/tantrums	Time-out (TO), differential attention	Reversal	Oppositional behavior/tantrums decreased with collateral decreases in enuresis
Parrish, Cataldo, Kolko, Neef, and Egel	1986	4	Mental retardation	Compliance, inappropriate behavior (e.g., aggression, disruption, property destruction, pica)	Social disapproval, reinforcement for compliance, DRO, contingent observation	Reversal plus MBL across settings with order of conditions varied across children and settings	As compliance increased, inappropriate behavior decreased and vice versa
Rincover, Cook, Peoples, and Packard	1979	4	Developmental disabilities	Self-stimulation, spontaneous play	Sensory extinction, instruction (e.g., physical prompting, prompt fading)	Reversal	As sensory reinforcement decreased, self-stimulation decreased with collateral increases in appropriate toy play
Rolider, Cummings, and Van Houten	1991	2	Dual diagnosis, Prader-Willi syndrome	Maladaptive behavior, academic performance	Functional teaching plus punishment	Alternating treatments counterbalanced across therapists	Decreases in inappropriate behavior with collateral improvements in academic performance

Russo, Cataldo, and Cushing	1981	3	Preschool	Compliance, inappropriate behavior	Reinforcement for compliance	MBL across therapists	Increased compliance accompanied by decreases in inappropriate behavior
Sajwaj, Twardosz, and Burke	1972	1	Mental retardation	Initiated speech to teacher/children, cooperative play, use of toys, appropriate and disruptive behavior	Prompting, alternative phases of attend and ignore	Reversal	In attend (vs. ignore) conditions, increased initiated speech to teacher, decreased initiated speech to children, increased cooperative play, increased use of cross-gender toys, increased appropriate behavior, decreased disruptive behaviors
					Alternating phases of attend and ignore	Reversal	In attend (vs. ignore) conditions, increased initiated speech to children, increased cooperative play, decreased use of cross-gender toys, increased appropriate behavior, decreased disruptive behavior

(continued)

147

Table 1. (Continued)

Authors	Date	Number of subjects	Subject classification	Dependent variables	Independent variables	Experimental design	Outcomes
Twardosz and Sajwaj	1972	1	Mental retardation	Sitting, posturing, walking, toy use, proximity to children	Prompting, differential reinforcement	Reversal	Increased sitting, decreased posturing, no change in walking, increased toy use and proximity to children
Wacker, Steege, Northup, Sasso, Berg, Reimers, Coopers Cigrand, and Donn	1990	3	Severe disabilities	Hand-biting, body-rocking, aggression	Time-out (TO), DRO, functional communication training (FCT), FCT plus prompting plus TO or extinction or graduated guidance	Alternating treatments and reversal	Increases in functional communication skills with collateral decreases in aberrant behavior
Wahler	1975	2	Conduct disorder	Multiple child behaviors across home and school settings	Time-out (TO) plus positive reinforcement plus point system, intensive special education	ABAC	Response covariation during baseline generally setting-specific, contingency man-

The first unnamed row (top of table) contains the following partial outcomes column: Differential attention, time-out | Modified MBL across behaviors | Decreased disruptions, increased appropriate circle time behavior, cooperative play remained constant agement procedures had planned effects in target setting accompanied by unplanned effects in other setting

Study	Year	N	Population	Target behavior	Procedure	Design	Results
Wahler and Fox	1980	4		Oppositional and aggressive behavior, social interaction	Social play contract (SPC) versus solitary toy play (STP) versus STP plus time-out (TO)	Reversal	Increased social behavior with collateral decreases in problem behavior
Wahler, Sperling, Thomas, Teeter, and Luper	1970	2		Stuttering, oppositional behavior	Contingency management (e.g., time-out plus other differential consequences)	Reversal	Decreases in oppositional behavior with collateral decreases in stuttering
Zawlocki, Wesolowski, and Thaler	1983	7	Mental retardation	Aggression, property destruction, self-injurious behavior	Modified physical restraint contingent upon occurrence of aggression or property destruction	MBL across subjects and behaviors	As aggression decreased, destruction and self-injurious behavior decreased; as property destruction decreased, aggression decreased

ies, the observed collateral effects were not monitored systematically as a central component of the experimental design, and there was no attempt to demonstrate or analyze response covariation. Nonetheless, these investigations reveal an evolution in the analysis and application of response covariation.

One of the first reports through which covariation was assessed appeared in a description of a study conducted by Risley (1968). Following the failure of time-out and differential attention to reduce problematic climbing behavior exhibited by a 6-year-old with multiple disabilities, Risley applied mild faradic shock to suppress this behavior. The observed suppressive effects were replicated. Subsequently, a contingent reprimand paired with shaking diminished nonpurposeful rocking. Of particular relevance, Risley assessed several dependent variables concurrently and, in so doing, demonstrated how to examine the side effects as well as main effects of an intervention. Many of the observed side effects were desirable, thereby suggesting that so-called "symptom substitution" could be adaptive as well as detrimental.

Buell, Stoddard, Harris, and Baer (1968) presented a somewhat similar paradigm during an examination of the effects of positive reinforcement. In this study, teachers provided social reinforcement contingent upon use of outdoor play equipment by a preschooler presenting with motor and social disabilities. This study also yielded repeated measures of multiple collateral behaviors. Dependent variables included percentage of intervals during which a teacher touched or spoke to the child, the child touched or spoke to a teacher, the child engaged in cooperative or parallel play, and/or the child exhibited "baby behavior." Although reinforcement-specific effects on use of play equipment were observed, clear patterns of response covariation did not emerge among the collateral measures as reinforcement was introduced or withdrawn. However, in general, desirable changes in the child's behavior were detected over time. This study was one of the first published in the applied behavior analytic literature that examined the collateral effects of a systematic intervention.

Other investigations that revealed response covariation were conducted at about the same time. For instance, Lovaas and Simmons (1969) examined the conditions under which the self-destructive behavior of three children could be ameliorated. In one case, avoidance of the therapist, whining, and self-destructive behavior, decreased. Lovaas and Simmons asserted that such collateral changes may indicate that, although distinctive in topography, problem behaviors may be members of the same "functional response class." Put simply, a functional response class is a set of responses that share a similar reinforcement history and current function, although the specific members of the response class may be either topographically similar or dissimilar.

Wahler, Sperling, Thomas, Teeter, and Luper (1970) reported two cases in which stuttering improved coterminous with the effective treatment of oppositional behavior or shifts in activity. With each child, it became unnecessary to target stuttering for direct intervention. The work of Wahler et al. represents one of the earliest descriptions of functional relationships between verbal and nonverbal behaviors. However, the experimental paradigm did not permit an analysis of the basis for the observed relationships.

Nordquist (1971) examined response–response relationships during the treatment of a preschool child who presented with both nocturnal enuresis and tantrums. Time-out and differential attention procedures contingent upon oppositional behavior resulted in both increases in child compliance with parental requests and decreases in tantrums. The number of enuretic episodes per week decreased from baseline levels when the intervention was in effect. Thus, Nordquist was one of the first investigators to report that typographically dissimilar behaviors (i.e., nocturnal enuresis, tantrums, child compliance) were functionally related. His findings suggested that changes in behaviors that are more readily amenable to direct contingency management (e.g., tantrums, noncompliance) may favorably affect behaviors that are more challenging (e.g., bed-wetting).

Sajwaj, Twardosz, and Burke (1972) described covariation among four topographically distinct behaviors: cooperative play, use of toys, other appropriate behavior, and disruptive behavior. Specifically, they studied the effects of a teacher-mediated intervention for excessive talking by a school-age child with mental retardation. When differential attention was implemented in one setting, it produced positive results in that setting, while it was associated with decrements in performance in another setting. Some of the behaviors covaried considerably, whereas others did so only a little or not at all. Importantly, some of the behaviors covaried directly and/or inversely with other behaviors. Thus, complex relationships among behaviors that differed under specific stimulus conditions were revealed.

Sajwaj and his colleagues speculated about the mechanisms responsible for the observed covariation and extended the previous literature by speaking to the possible role of physical (in)compatibility among the behaviors, the discriminability of the contingencies in effect, alteration in setting conditions and its influence upon changes across behaviors, and schedules of reinforcement. They asserted that at least four types of side effects to an intervention may occur: 1) desirable behaviors may increase, 2) undesirable behaviors may increase, 3) desirable behaviors may decrease, and 4) undesirable behaviors may decrease. Such effects may co-occur in varying combinations in the clinical context.

Ayllon and Roberts (1974) sought to demonstrate that children could learn effectively without having teachers first intervene to reduce their disruptive behavior in the classroom. Specifically, they evaluated the relationship between academic performance and disruptive behavior with five fifth-grade boys referred because of disciplinary concerns. Academic performance was measured in terms of percentage of correct answers to reading comprehension and vocabulary questions, whereas disruptive behavior was defined as being out of seat without permission, talking out of turn, and engaging in motor behavior that interfered with another student's work.

A point system designed to reinforce accurate completion of reading tasks was introduced. Subsequently, reading performance improved in each of the five individuals. Concomitantly, levels of disruptive behavior decreased (see Figure 1). When the point system in effect for reading was withdrawn, disruption increased. Upon the reintroduction of the point system, academic performance again improved, with associated reductions in disruptive behavior.

Ayllon and Roberts (1974) concluded that academic performance and disruptive behavior may be related reciprocally, so that if students were taught "better," they may be more likely to "sit still," in contrast to the dictum, "make them sit still so they will learn" (p. 75). In essence, Ayllon and Roberts provided further evidence that an indirect approach to alteration of problem behavior by way of augmenting prosocial behavior may be an effective strategy for the management of problem behavior.

Koegel et al. (1974) demonstrated the occurrence of behavioral covariation during intervention with two children with autism. During baseline, each child displayed high levels of self-stimulatory behavior and low levels of play during developmentally appropriate educational tasks. When self-stimulatory behavior was suppressed, spontaneous and appropriate play increased without any specific contingencies to promote such play. When sup-

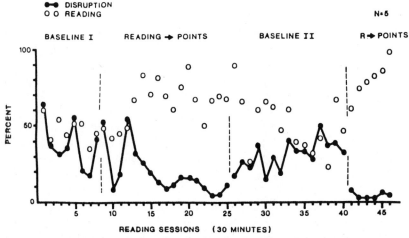

Figure 1. Mean percentage disruption and mean percentage correct on reading assignments for five target students. Each point represents 30 minutes of assignment. Ordinate = percentage, abscissa = reading sessions.

pression of self-stimulatory behavior was discontinued, levels of play as well as self-stimulatory behavior approximated baseline levels (see Figure 2).

Koegel et al. (1974) concluded that punishment per se was not responsible for the observed increases in play. Likewise, their data suggested that play did not appear to function, even superstitiously, as an avoidance response. Although self-stimulatory behavior and play were at times motorically incompatible, it is unlikely that the observed effects could be explained solely in terms of structural considerations, given that reductions in self-stimulatory behavior could have been (but were not) accompanied by increases in several behaviors alternative to play. Koegel et al. speculated that self-stimulatory behavior and play may be functionally (in contrast to physically) related, given that each may be reinforcing in and of itself. Hence, as reinforcement obtained by one set of responses (e.g., self-stimulatory behavior) is diminished, the reinforcement value of another set of responses (e.g., play) increases. This line of reasoning is evident in several more recent investigations.

In a seminal study, Wahler (1975) assessed naturally occurring covariations among 19 categories of child behavior across home and school settings for two boys. During experimental phases that extended over 2 years, Wahler

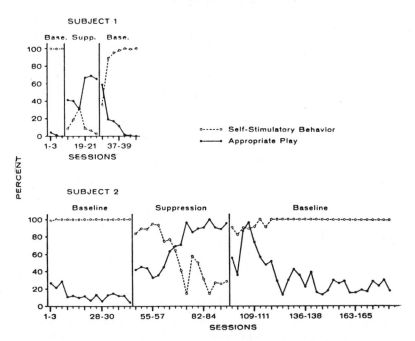

Figure 2. Percentage of time sample intervals of self-stimulatory and appropriate play behaviors during baseline, suppression, and reversal conditions. Ordinate = percentage, abscissa = sessions. Dotted line = self-stimulatory behavior, solid line = appropriate play.

identified stability in some functional clusters of behavior that were setting-specific. For instance, one such cluster consisted of schoolwork that was correlated positively with self-stimulatory behavior and inversely associated with "fiddling of objects" and "staring into space." However, the environmental determinants of these functional clusters could not be isolated. This study was one of the earliest applied investigations to demonstrate in a highly molecular fashion that an individual's repertoire is likely to include responses that predictably covary with one another. Observed covariations were often situation-specific.

Although this study did not reveal mechanisms responsible for response covariation, it did suggest that some problem behaviors were members of response classes (Bijou & Baer, 1961; Skinner, 1935) and thereby could perhaps be treated indirectly through the management of the behaviors with which they covary. Wahler (1975) addressed the prospective importance of identifying functional clusters. He suggested that covert or otherwise difficult-to-treat behaviors could possibly be ameliorated indirectly.

Wahler's (1975) study illustrates a conceptual, if not altogether practical, framework for an effective intervention based on observed behavioral covariation. Initially, covariation among behavior categories is assessed over a series of baseline sessions. Next, distributions of scores for each behavioral category are subjected to product-moment correlational analysis. This results in inter-correlations being computed for all distributions. These analyses yield correlational matrices that reflect response covariations within and across examined settings. Subsequently, groupings of correlated behavior categories are extracted from the matrices on the basis of a hierarchical clustering technique (e.g., Johnson, 1967), with the resultant clusters identified as response classes within the individual's repertoire.

Finally, intervention ensues, being predicated on the observed relationships among responses. As a result, either a behavior that covaries with problem behavior is weakened, or a prosocial behavior that covaries inversely with targeted inappropriate behavior is strengthened. Throughout intervention, computation of correlational analyses continues in order to evaluate effects of each intervention among specific functional clusters, as well as to assess stability of clusters over time. As noted by Wahler (1975), a major shortcoming of this approach (in regard to an understanding of mechanisms underlying response covariation) is that correlational analyses do not identify, in and of themselves, specific environmental determinants of response–response relationships.

Rincover, Cook, Peoples, and Packard (1979) provided an exemplar of how changes in collateral behavior can be effected without use of punishment contingencies for problem behavior or ongoing systematic administration of positive reinforcers. They assessed the impact of sensory reinforcement upon response covariation between self-stimulatory behavior and play in four children with developmental disabilities. Rincover et al. found that self-stimulatory behaviors extinguished subsequent to removal of sensory reinforcers, and contingent application of the same reinforcers promoted acquisition of new, appropriate toy play skills. In general, as adaptive play behavior increased, self-stimulatory behavior decreased.

Russo et al. (1981) reported the effects of a compliance-training procedure on problem behaviors. The participants were three children of preschool age who each exhibited crying, aggression, self-injurious behavior, hair-pulling, and/or thumb-sucking, in addition to noncompliance with adult requests. Baselines revealed low rates of compliance and high rates of problem behavior in each child. Subsequently, compliance was enhanced through a combination of social and tangible reinforcement, with or without guided compliance. In each case, as compliance improved, levels of targeted problem behaviors decreased, despite the absence of any programmed contingencies in effect for problem behaviors (see Figure 3 for an example). Problem behaviors typically increased when compliance-enhancement procedures were discontinued, only to decrease again as soon as reinforcement for compliance resumed.

Neef, Shafer, Egel, Cataldo, and Parrish (1983) conducted two experiments through which they examined class-specific effects of compliance training with "Do" and "Don't" requests. The first experiment was an analog investigation designed to reveal collateral effects of reinforcement for compliance with one type of request (Do) on another type of request (Don't). The second experiment was a systematic replication of the first in an applied (classroom) setting. Previous studies (e.g., Bucher, 1973; Whitman, Zakaras, & Chardos, 1971) had demonstrated that reinforcement contingent upon compliance with a subset of requests often produced generalized instruction-following in response to other requests. These investigations focused upon child compliance with Do requests that stipulated initiation, completion, or continuation of a prosocial behavior. Relatively few studies (e.g., Patterson, Ray, Shaw, & Cobb, 1969) had examined methods of promoting child compliance with Don't requests, which entail cessation or inhibition of a proscribed behavior.

The principal finding of experiment 1, which was replicated by experiment 2, was that generalized compliance occurred only among requests of the same type as the exemplar targeted for contingent reinforcement. When compliance with a target request was reinforced, increases in compliance with other requests of the same type were observed. Compliance with requests of the other type either remained essentially unchanged or decreased. High levels of compliance with both Do and Don't requests were noted only when compliance with both types was reinforced.

One of the important implications of these findings is that for an intervention predicated upon response covariation to be of maximal benefit, one

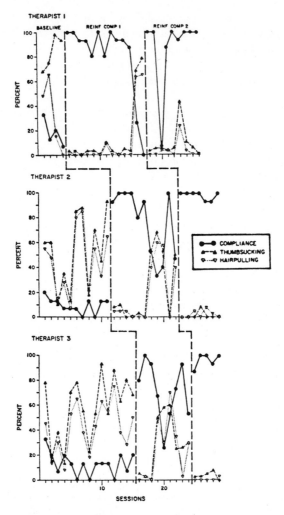

Figure 3. Percentage of occurrence of compliance and two untreated corollary behaviors (thumb-sucking and hair-pulling) across therapists and experimental conditions. Ordinate = percentage, abscissa = sessions. Solid line = compliance, broken line = thumb-sucking, dotted line = hair-pulling.

would need access to data that suggest the limits of response generalization within and across behaviors similar in function that may or may not be similar in topography. For instance, compliance with Do and Don't requests may constitute two functional responses classes, despite similarities in the process of issuing and acknowledging each type of request. Under the conditions tested, generalization across the two functional clusters is limited.

Parrish, Cataldo, Kolko, Neef, and Egel (1986) demonstrated experimentally that compliant and inappropriate behaviors form inverse response classes. Four children with developmental disabilities participated in the study on the basis of low levels of compliance with adult requests and high rates of problem behaviors, including aggression, disruption, property destruction, and pica. In order to observe collateral effects upon targeted inappropriate behavior, levels of compliance were increased through contingent reinforcement (e.g., praise, physical affection, edibles) or guided compliance. To examine collateral effects upon compliant behaviors, inappropriate behaviors were suppressed through use of differential reinforcement of other behavior (DRO) or contingent observation. The predicted inverse relationships between compliant and inappropriate behaviors were observed. As compliance increased, problem behaviors reliably decreased, and vice versa. The generality of these relationships was demonstrated across interventions, subjects, and settings.

RECENT APPLICATIONS BASED UPON RESPONSE COVARIATION

Steege, Wacker, Berg, Cigrand, and Cooper (1989) assessed stimulus preferences of two children with developmental disabilities and studied the generalizability of these preferences to management of the children's chronic self-injurious behavior. During the first experiment, Steege and his colleagues identified one child's reinforcers through a systematic assessment. Subsequent to intervention, which entailed the child gaining access to identified reinforcers (e.g., operation of a fan and radio) via activation of a microswitch, observed rates of self-injurious behavior plummeted and remained low across 6 months of follow-up.

In the second experiment, the maintaining conditions for the other child's self-injurious behavior were revealed through a functional analysis. A concurrent assessment of reinforcer preferences indicated that access to a drink of water and signing with a language book were reinforcers. As these preferred events were made available contingent upon satisfactory completion of tasks (e.g., sorting silverware and discs), on-task behavior rapidly increased and remained at high levels. Of particular interest, rates of self-injurious behavior decreased simultaneously to zero or near-zero levels.

Thus, in these two illustrative cases, Steege and his colleagues were able to effect reductions in targeted inappropriate behavior without applying any direct punishment contingencies. Importantly, they demonstrated the relevance of combining technologies of reinforcer assessment and functional analysis to the selection of an indirect intervention strategy that resulted in effective management of challenging behavior while it promoted acquisition of prosocial skills by way of differential reinforcement of appropriate behavior (DRA).

With increasing vigor, applied behavior analysts are integrating the findings of their basic-science counterparts into their analyses of response–

response relationships. A recent case in point is the work of Mace, McCurdy, and Quigley (1990). Mace and his colleagues provisionally examined the operation of the matching law in applied settings. Matching is an operant process whereby an individual allocates his or her behavior among two or more schedules of reinforcement dependent upon the rate of reinforcement available by each schedule (Herrnstein, 1961). In general, the relative frequency of one behavior closely approximates the relative frequency of reinforcement contingent upon occurrence of that behavior.

The allocation of an individual's behavior among alternative responses is of obvious relevance to interventionists. Consider the student who is confronted with the choice of remaining on-task or engaging in a disruptive behavior that may result in teacher—as well as peer-mediated—reinforcement. According to the matching law, the student will engage more often in those alternatives that have been associated with higher rates of reinforcement.

Mace et al. (1990) confirmed that an adolescent who was presented two academic alternatives (multiplication or division problems) on concurrent reinforcement schedules would distribute his responding in approximate proportion to the rate of reinforcement provided for each alternative. When edibles were dispensed on a continuous-reinforcement schedule contingent upon completion of multiplication problems, while they were provided on a VR2 schedule for completion of division problems, the rate at which the adolescent completed the former was approximately 50% greater. When these schedules were applied conversely, the rate at which the youth completed division problems more than doubled that of multiplication problems.

In a second experiment, Mace et al. (1990) again assessed the effects of changing concurrent schedules of reinforcement upon response allocation. The relative frequency of completion of two tasks (assembling a pen and sorting silverware) by a boy with profound mental retardation was evaluated. Generally, the boy's allocation of responses across the two tasks conformed to that predicted by the matching law. By the end of the experiment he was responding almost exclusively to the alternative that offered the greater rate of reinforcement, although some reinforcement remained available for the other alternative.

As a result of the preceding experiments, Mace et al. (1990) provided evidence that positive reinforcement for one adaptive response may have unplanned and undesirable collateral effects on other adaptive responses. When reinforcement contingencies are altered to favor prosocial behavior, thereby making reinforcement for problem behavior relatively unfavorable, one can expect response allocation by the individual among appropriate and inappropriate behavior to be affected. Hence, the matching law may serve to explain why use of differential reinforcement of appropriate behavior (DRA) may not only result in collateral decreases in inappropriate behavior, but also decreases in concurrent adaptive responses. Interventionists who aim to manage problem behaviors indirectly through reinforcement of adaptive behaviors should monitor effects of such interventions on other adaptive responses as well as on the targeted behavior. In this way, the phenomenon of response covariation can be more fully evaluated as the basis for the success of indirect intervention strategies.

Haring and Kennedy (1990) examined the influence of contextual variation on the differential effectiveness of DRO and time-out as methods of suppressing problem behavior. In so doing, they also demonstrated that response–response relationships as well as alternative interventions can be affected by contextual factors. Haring and Kennedy (1990) asserted that contextual variables may exert a form of complex stimulus control, in which they function as conditional (or higher order) events that alter the probability of occurrence of specific response classes within an individual's repertoire. As a result, an intervention that is effective in one context may be rendered ineffective by contextual factors in another setting.

For purposes of their demonstration, Haring and Kennedy (1990) conducted functional analyses of three problem behaviors exhibited by two adolescents with severe disabilities across two contexts (instructional periods and leisure time). Problem behaviors for one adolescent included body-rocking, loud vocalizations, and spitting; for the other, problem behaviors consisted of body-rocking, hand-flapping, and head-bobbing. Each problem behavior was observed in each context. Following a stable baseline, DRO and time-out conditions were alternately introduced in the two settings to determine the effects of each intervention on the problem behaviors. The order of experimental conditions was counterbalanced across subjects and contexts.

Results indicated that DRO reduced problem behavior in the task context, whereas time-out in this context was ineffectual. In contrast, time-out reduced problem behavior in the leisure context, whereas DRO was not effective. Interestingly, in the task context, the rate of correct task performance by both youths increased more when DRO was in effect than when baseline and time-out were in effect. Consequently, the intervention that most suppressed the problem behavior was associated with the greatest degree of improvement in appropriate behavior. Because the implementation of DRO was conjunctive with correct task performance, it is not possible to assess the extent of inverse covariation between appropriate and inappropriate behavior per se.

Nonetheless, this study documents that structural analyses of behavior based solely on the frequencies of specific behaviors during baseline are not sufficient to predict the differential effectiveness of alternative interventions across settings. An analysis of topographies across settings may not reveal differences in a class of responses across different contexts. A functional analysis based on the controlled alternation of specific interventions, similar to the imposition of different stimulus conditions, ascertained that the functional control of behaviors that appeared to be topographically similar across contexts was actually context-specific. Haring and Kennedy (1990) concluded that interventionists would be well-advised to assess contextual factors when attempting to gain functional control over problem behavior. They contended that study and manipulation of contextual factors would augment the efficiency, as well as the effectiveness, of alternative interventions.

APPLICATION OF COVARIATION TO FUNCTIONAL COMMUNICATION TRAINING (FCT)

Two exciting conceptual and methodological developments based on response covariation, with far-reaching technological implications for interventions, have recently emerged. These are functional analysis and functional equivalence training. These advances warrant particular emphasis because of their relevance to increasing our understanding and effective use of response–response relations specific to functional communication training (FCT).

Functional Analysis

Perhaps the most generative technology to be developed by applied behavior analysts in the 1980s is functional analysis (Axelrod, 1987; Mace, Lalli, & Pinter-Lalli, 1991; O'Neill, Horner, Albin, Storey, & Sprague, 1990). Predicated upon a conceptual analysis of motivational hypotheses set forth by Carr (1977), Iwata, Dorsey, Slifer, Bauman, and Richman (1982) validated a replicable paradigm through which the operation of specific environmental variables on problem behavior could be isolated for study and treatment. The practice of functional analysis has proliferated. As indicated in other chapters of this volume, behavior analysts have demonstrated the applicability of functional analysis methods with numerous problem behaviors.

Within-subject variability is often associated with specific maintaining variables, more so than with response topography or clinical diagnosis. Intervention protocols developed directly from implications of the functional analysis are often effective in managing problem behavior. When a "functional match" occurs between the problematic response and the ensuing intervention (Iwata, Pace, Kalsher, Cowdery, & Cataldo, 1990), positive clinical outcomes are often efficiently achieved. For example, Durand, Crimmins, Caulfield, and Taylor (1989) and Repp, Felce, and Barton (1988) evaluated the comparative efficacy of two interventions for the same target behavior, with one intervention based on a preceding functional analysis of maintaining contingencies and with the other not based on a functional analysis. In both experiments, the intervention that was matched functionally to the target behavior was documented to be more effective.

Inherent to functional analysis, or to its adaptation in the form of brief functional assessment (Cooper, Wacker, Sasso, Reimers, & Donn, 1990), is a concern with response–response relationships. Almost all functional analyses examine more than one dependent variable at a time under an array of carefully constructed stimulus conditions. Many of the variables are structurally compatible and can covary directly or inversely. The methodology of functional analysis will continue to be critical to the identification of specific conditions under which response covariation is observed. Additionally, through descriptive analyses followed by functional analyses (Mace & Lalli, 1991), it will become increasingly possible to reveal conditional probabilities for the direction and magnitude of this covariation. Of prospective clinical import, functional analyses are likely to identify functional response classes (Catania, 1984) or functional clusters (Wahler, 1975). Once these classes are identified, the member behaviors within such classes or clusters that are most amenable to intervention and are also likely to produce generalized change among other member behaviors can be pinpointed in order to promote efficient, as well as effective, clinical interventions.

Functional Equivalence Training

Carr and Durand (1985a) asserted that the key concept that explains the operation of communication skills training on problem behavior is functional equivalence. Described in its most basic terms, functional equivalence is the maintenance of two or more response classes by the same class of reinforcers. The response classes may be quite distinct topographically (e.g., verbal and motor classes of behavior), yet they function similarly (i.e., they elicit the same reinforcers).

Carr (1988) postulated that if a prosocial behavior is taught that serves a function equivalent to that of a maladaptive behavior, while contingencies maintaining challenging behavior are prevented or disrupted, then the individual will demonstrate the acquisition of desired behavior with a concurrent decrease in problem behavior. For example, among persons with developmental disabilities or speech disorders with or without language disorders, higher rates of problem behaviors are often associated with greater deficits in communication skills (Baker, Cantwell, & Mattison, 1980; Talkington, Hall, & Altman, 1971).

The acquisition of more appropriate communication responses that are functionally equivalent to problem behavior has been shown to be an effective intervention (Carr & Durand, 1985a, 1985b; Donnellan, Mirenda, Mesaros, & Fassbender, 1984; Durand, 1990; Wacker et al., 1990), especially if augmented with additional communication training via an individually tailored communication system (e.g., Wacker, Wiggins, Fowler, & Berg, 1988) and overall lifestyle planning (Meyer & Evans, 1989) that supports an individual's attempts to communicate in naturalistic settings on an incidental basis.

CHRONOLOGICAL OVERVIEW OF SPECIFIC
STUDIES OF FUNCTIONAL COMMUNICATION TRAINING

Carr and Durand (1985a) provided a compelling illustration that an analysis of function is more critical to behavior change than an assessment of form. They demonstrated that some problem behaviors can be suppressed as a result of reinforcement of prosocial replacement behaviors. In the first experiment, Carr and Durand evaluated the occurrence of disruptive behavior, academic behavior (e.g., correct responding to task), and adult attention (e.g., praise, mands, comments) under varying stimulus conditions (e.g., easy/difficult tasks, low/high adult attention). Observed patterns of responding revealed the operation of controlling variables in each case. Among the controlling variables were the processes of positive and negative reinforcement, in that challenging behavior was most likely to occur reliably under conditions of high task difficulty and low adult attention.

In their second experiment, Carr and Durand (1985a) used the information obtained through the preceding functional analysis to select functional replacement behaviors. In each of the four cases, the child was taught to emit either task-relevant or -irrelevant communicative phrases, while the level of task difficulty; overall level of adult attention; and adult use of praise, commands, and comments were held constant. The communicative phrases were designed to elicit either adult assistance (e.g., "I don't understand") or attention ("Am I doing good work?"). Subsequent to FCT, several interesting response–response relationships were observed. One of the most noteworthy relationships involved the impact of this training on the children's disruptive behavior. Following FCT, low levels of disruptive behavior were typically observed. In contrast, levels of disruptive behavior remained high following training to give task-irrelevant verbal phrases.

Carr and Durand (1985a) speculated that some problem behaviors can be diminished by teaching children communication skills that alter the establishing conditions controlling problem behavior. For instance, teaching a child to request assistance may result in simplification of a difficult task and avoidance of failure. Likewise, enabling a child to request attention may solicit social reinforcement more consistently than negative attention-seeking, resulting in a strengthening of the former at the expense of the latter. Thus, the acquisition of functional communication skills may result in reliable reductions in problem behavior, without any contingencies applied directly to the aberrant behavior. Carr and Durand hypothesized that many problem behaviors may function as communicative behaviors that elicit socially mediated reinforcers. As individuals acquire functional communication skills that enable them to procure reinforcement or to avoid or escape aversive situations, problem behaviors become less efficient than verbal communication as a means of achieving these ends and, therefore, are relied upon less frequently.

For example, in the cases presented by Carr and Durand (1985a), both the motor act of aggression and the verbal phrase "Am I doing good work?" elicited adult attention. If these response classes had not been functionally equivalent (i.e., they did not elicit the same reinforcers), it is likely that any attempt to replace one class with another would have failed. Identifying replacement behaviors that are functionally equivalent to the challenging behavior speaks to the importance of conducting a functional analysis of the problem behavior prior to effecting an intervention based upon response covariation or generalization.

Durand and Carr (1987) documented that some repetitive, nonpurposeful behavior is maintained by socially mediated consequences. In four cases involving children with developmental disabilities, they showed that stereotypy (e.g., hand-flapping and body-rocking) increased contingent on the presentation of difficult academic tasks. Removal of demands contingent on the occurrence of stereotypy resulted in increases in stereotypy. Based upon these findings, Durand and Carr taught the children to request assistance for difficult tasks and observed concomitant reductions in stereotypy without intervening directly with the repetitive movements. Again, a communication response that obtained reinforcement equivalent to that obtained as a consequence of problem behavior proved to be an effective intervention. Thus, as in their 1985a study, Carr and Durand (1987) demonstrated that problem behaviors can be remediated through acquisition and use of prosocial replacement behaviors (e.g., communication skills) without use of punishment contingencies.

Wacker et al. (1990) hypothesized that the effectiveness of FCT may be attributable to: 1) differential consequences for communicative responding, in that a dense schedule of reinforcement contingent upon requests for praise or assistance may itself result in decreased problem behavior; 2) the degree of control over delivery of reinforcement, in that children who produce functional communicative responses have greater control over obtaining their reinforcers than children who are more passive participants in an adult-generated contingency management procedure such as DRO; 3) the differential consequences directly applied to targeted inappropriate behavior; and 4) the efficiency of the communicative response in promoting the consistency and immediacy of reinforcement.

While maintaining the efficiency of the communicative response, Wacker et al. (1990) examined the following two facets of FCT: 1) the contribution of control over the schedule of reinforcement exerted by the communicative response, and 2) the contribution of differential consequences delivered directly for inappropriate behavior. Subsequent to functional analyses of the variables maintaining the challenging behavior (self-injury, stereotypy, and aggression) exhibited by three patients, Wacker et al. facilitated acquisition and use of functional communication skills until significant decreases in challenging behaviors were observed. Later, they implemented reversal designs to separate the contributions of control over reinforcement and differential consequences (time-out, graduated guidance) on inappropriate behavior.

In addition to replicating the findings of Carr and Durand (1985a), Wacker et al. (1990) found that both components were critical to suppression of challenging behavior (for an example, see Figure 4). In two of the three cases, when direct contingencies for inappropriate behavior were removed, the observed covariation between usage of communication skills and problem behavior weakened, being marked by increases in the latter. Wacker et al. (1990) concluded that control over reinforcement is a key variable contributing to the effectiveness of FCT as a means of managing problem behavior. Moreover, they speculated that the efficiency of the communicative response as a means of acquiring reinforcement is at least as important as the functional equivalence between the communicative response and the problem behavior.

Through three experiments, Horner and Day (1991) evaluated the contribution of response efficiency to the impact of functional equivalence training. Response efficiency was assessed in terms of: 1) response effort, 2) schedule of reinforcement, and 3) delay between presentation of the discriminative stimulus and the delivery of reinforcement. During each experiment, the problem behaviors of one individual were subjected to functional analysis. Based upon the results of this analysis, an adaptive, alternative response functionally equivalent to the problem behavior was taught. However, each of the adaptive alternative manding responses that was initially trained was arranged to be less efficient than the problem behavior in terms of effort, schedule, or time delay. Later, a second more efficient manding response was taught, and the relative efficacy of the less versus more efficient manding

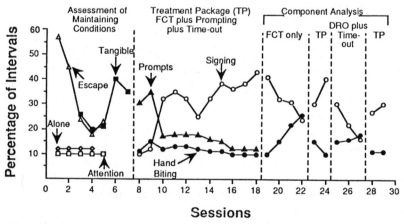

Figure 4.   Percentage of occurrence of hand-biting, independent signing, and prompts across conditions for one individual. Ordinate = percentage intervals, abscissa = sessions.

alternatives was determined. In each case, the first new mand did not compete effectively with the problem behavior. However, when replaced with the more efficient mand, significant reductions in the problem behavior were observed.

Horner and Day (1991) concluded that functional equivalence training is effective when the newly acquired alternative response is: 1) under the same stimulus control as the problem behavior, 2) produces the same outcome as the problem behavior, and 3) is more efficient than the problem behavior. On the basis of their findings, Horner and Day (1991) conclude that response efficiency plays a key role in the degree to which functional equivalence training is effective.

Durand and Carr (1991) demonstrated that the effects of FCT upon collateral inappropriate behaviors were transferable across new tasks, new settings, and new change agents. Furthermore, subsequent to training, effects were maintained for at least 18–24 months. In discussing their findings, Durand and Carr (1991) not only appealed to the relevance of functional equivalence as a mechanism for response generalization, but also cited the possible role of choice as a contributing factor to the efficacy of FCT. Put simply, the learner is taught the skills necessary to choose between obtaining reinforcement by way of appropriate or inappropriate behavior. As the efficiency of the appropriate behavior as a means of acquiring reinforcement increases, the learner's reliance upon inappropriate behavior diminishes with relatively few extinction bursts. Durand and Carr ruled out physical incompatibility between appropriate and inappropriate behavior and the influence of stimulus control as factors responsible for the observed response covariation.

MECHANISMS OF RESPONSE COVARIATION

The mechanisms responsible for response covariation are not yet fully understood. However, further advances in intervention strategies based on descriptive/functional analyses and subsequent functional equivalence training are likely to extend our understanding of the conditions under which, and the processes by which, response covariation occurs. With this understanding, change agents can better manipulate pivotal behaviors to the individual's advantage. Indeed, as stated previously, an assessment of response covariation is inherent to functional analysis and to the assessment of the effects of functional equivalence training.

As scientist-practitioners proceed to refine and employ curricula to promote the acquisition of functionally equivalent responses, they are likely to be increasingly guided by the following important assumptions: 1) any given aberrant behavior may serve multiple functions for a particular individual, 2) more than one inappropriate behavior may serve the same function, 3) the topographies and functions of the behavior exhibited by a particular individual may be highly inconsistent across time and settings, and 4) behaviors similar in topography may serve different functions for different individuals (Helmstetter & Durand, 1990).

Through refining the technology of functional analysis and functional equivalence training based upon findings from the literature on the experimental analysis of behavior, applied behavior analysts are likely to develop a better understanding of the mechanisms for response covariation. For instance, research on concurrent operants generally demonstrates that such operants are related not so much in terms of rates of occurrence as they are in terms of differential consequences (Catania, 1963, 1966, 1969, 1973); that is, changes in the rate of one response do not necessarily alter the rate of another response. However, given a concurrent schedule of reinforcement, an increase in the rate of reinforcement of one response often results in a decrease in the frequency of another response. Conversely, subsequent to the punishment of one response, an increase in some responses may occur.

The specific responses that change may be indicated by additional research into multiple-response repertoires (Dunham, 1971, 1972). For example, when one response is punished, only the most probable of the other responses in the organism's repertoire is likely to increase, while the response most likely to follow the punished response is also typically suppressed (Dunham & Grantmyre, 1982). Hence, when examining the relationships between appropriate and challenging behaviors, it is important to identify highly probable responses. In addition, it is essential to understand, as noted above, that what may be a highly probable response in one setting at one point in time may not be at another place or time.

How response–response relationships form, either direct or inverse, is also not well understood. Some investigators have speculated that imitative behaviors constitute a response class over time, based upon repeated trials during which similarity between the teacher's behavior and the student's behavior sets the occasion for reinforcement, thereby becoming both a discriminative stimulus for reinforcement and a conditioned reinforcer (e.g., Baer, Peterson, & Sherman, 1967; Baer & Sherman, 1964; Brigham & Sherman, 1968). A similar argument can be advanced in regard to prosocial and inappropriate behaviors that have been shown to be members of inverse response classes (Parrish et al., 1986). Such response classes may emerge simply because parents and teachers are more likely to reinforce desired behaviors when they are not accompanied by problem behaviors. Or, when interventionists extinguish or punish inappropriate behaviors, individuals may demonstrate highly probable alternative behaviors, such as compliance and/or prosocial communication skills.

FUTURE DIRECTIONS

What do we know? Simply put, we know that many interventions produce multiple effects. Some of these effects are intended, some not. Some are welcome, others are to be avoided. There is evidence that certain responses may be members of response classes or functional clusters in that they share similar reinforcement histories and serve common functions. These responses may be quite distinct topographically. When contingencies associated with one member of a class shift, resulting in a change in that member, generalized changes in other members may be observed. For instance, when compliance with selected tasks is reinforced, generalized compliance often occurs. Such response generalization is especially likely to occur when the responses are functionally equivalent; that is, when they obtain and are maintained by the same set of reinforcers.

Response covariation may be uni- or bidirectional in nature and may be direct or inverse. For example, it has been shown that, among some individuals, as compliance increases as a function of contingent (vs. noncontingent) reinforcement, collateral decreases in some inappropriate behaviors are noted without any systematic contingencies being in effect for the problem behavior. However, the specific problem behaviors that covary inversely with increases in compliance are idiosyncratic across clients, and within clients, across changes in settings and time. In the case of compliance and inappropriate behavior, covariation occurs under different contingencies designed to increase or decrease compliance or problem behavior. In contrast, functional communication training has been found to result in collateral decreases in some nontargeted problem behaviors. What is less clear is whether programmed suppression of problem behavior is associated with augmented communication skills.

What is yet to be examined? In actuality, there are far more unanswered questions than answers. For instance, what determines the generality of covariation or the observed individual differences in the degree of covariation across individuals and, within individuals, across settings? What explains the increases in the magnitude of covariation sometimes observed across time as one member or members of a response class are repeatedly manipulated?

Several parametric questions are still to be addressed. Such questions include: What are the specific conditions under which behaviors do or do not covary? What conditions facilitate or restrict covariation? Would covariation be observed if only one member of a response class, as opposed to more than one member, who systematically altered, or if the behavior targeted for intervention had not been shown to covary with other behaviors of concern? What degree of correlation between two behaviors is sufficient for covariation to occur?

Most studies of response covariation have been conducted in analog, or at least highly structured, environments. In such tight circumstances, the robustness of the phenomenon of response covariation has been demonstrated across behavior-change procedures, subjects, and settings. However, very little is known about the process of response covariation in the field. Under natural conditions outside of the well-controlled laboratory, what interventions result in the most pervasive covariation and are associated with the most significant clinical gains? Systematic replications in less structured, more applied settings, such as classrooms, homes, employment sites, or clinics are warranted. Such replications would not only provide additional evidence of the external validity of previous observations of response covariation, but they also may better demonstrate the functional utility of interventions formulated on the basis of predicted covariation.

In terms of ontogeny, under what conditions does a response class form? For example, what is the role of a discriminative stimulus in the formation of a response class? Consider the experiment in which a stimulus (e.g., a phrase that had not appeared previously in the individual's learning history) is presented just prior to a request that, if completed satisfactorily, results in reinforcement on a CRF schedule. As the schedule of reinforcement contingent upon reinforcement is thinned, would the phrase take on the properties of a discriminative stimulus so that, if and when the phrase is administered just prior to untrained requests, it would serve to promote generalized compliance in the absence of programmed reinforcement? Would such generalized effects of a discriminative stimulus be observed over time and across settings?

Related questions include: Is the function of a discriminative stimulus in the formation of a response class predicated upon the individual's ability to predict the probability of reinforcement? Under what schedule of reinforcement are the effects of a discriminative stimulus most likely to maintain and/or generalize? Can a neutral stimulus that acquires the characteristics of a discriminative stimulus be used to form response classes within and across topographically similar responses, such as Do and Don't requests? Likewise, can a neutral stimulus associated with the nonavailability of reinforcement be used similarly to alter response classes?

CONCLUSION

Applied implications derived from an understanding of response covariation are likely to continue to have a pervasive impact on the selection and relative efficacy of alternative interventions. Although traditional interventions based upon the topography of the targeted responses may serve to ameliorate some challenging behaviors, progressive procedures predicated upon observed response covariation will probably be equally or more effective, while being far more economical and efficient. Interventions that capitalize upon response covariation will result in desirable changes in multiple behaviors prior to the establishment of programmed contingencies designed to alter each target behavior.

Programming multiple changes requires careful consideration of functional equivalence as well as response topography and response–response relationships. As has been demonstrated by the vanguard line of inquiry into functional analysis and functional equivalence training, an appreciation of function serves to identify pivotal behaviors and their key contingencies for change, more so than does an analysis of structure or form. An analysis of functional relationships among behaviors that are members of a covarying response class offers information necessary to facilitate response generalization and may reveal new interventions that promote far-reaching skill acquisition, such as has been demonstrated through studies of functional communication training.

Significantly, interventions built upon the phenomenon of response covariation are likely to circumvent the ethical issues associated with the use of punishment or coercive procedures. Indirect interventions centered on the acquisition of prosocial skills that are functionally equivalent to problem behavior minimize both the ethical reservations associated with and the negative side effects of aversive procedures. Through such indirect, yet efficacious, covariant approaches, aversive procedures may be rendered unnecessary, except in the most intractable cases in which an individual's challenging behavior puts him or her and others at imminent risk for mortality or morbidity. Otherwise, highly restrictive or intrusive interventions are not indicated, especially as long as the training of prosocial behaviors that covary inversely with the problem behaviors results in nonprogrammed reductions in the latter.

Given the increasing focus upon community-referenced services, the importance of intervention paradigms that are cost-effective as well as ethical has increased. Strategies based upon response covariation and functional equivalence may lead to the simultaneous, desired modification of several behaviors by teaching individuals a prosocial response inversely related to aberrant behavior, without reliance on costly serial, aversive interventions for one target behavior at a time.

REFERENCES

American Psychiatric Association. (1987). *Diagnostic and statistical manual of mental disorders (3rd ed. rev.)*. Washington, DC: Author.

Axelrod, S. (1987). Functional and structural analyses of behavior: Approaches leading to reduced use of punishment procedures? *Research in Developmental Disabilities, 8*, 165–178.

Ayllon, T., & Roberts, M.D. (1974). Eliminating discipline problems by strengthening academic performance. *Journal of Applied Behavior Analysis, 7*, 71–76.

Baer, D.M., Peterson, R.F., & Sherman, J.A. (1967). The development of imitation by reinforcing behavioral similarity to a model. *Journal of the Experimental Analysis of Behavior, 10*, 405–416.

Baer, D.M., & Sherman, J.A. (1964). Reinforcement control of generalized imitation in young children. *Journal of Experimental Child Psychology, 1*, 37–49.

Baker, L., Cantwell, D.P., & Mattison, R.E. (1980). Behavior problems in children with pure speech disorders and in children with combined speech and language disorders. *Journal of Abnormal Child Psychology, 8*, 245–256.

Barton, E.J., & Ascione, F.R. (1979). Sharing in preschool children: Facilitation, stimulus generalization, response generalization, and maintenance. *Journal of Applied Behavior Analysis, 12*, 417–430.

Bijou, S.W., & Baer, D.M. (1961). *Child development: A systematic and empirical theory. Vol. 1.* New York: Appleton-Century-Crofts.

Brigham, T.A., & Sherman, J.A. (1968). An experimental analysis of verbal imitation in preschool children. *Journal of Applied Behavior Analysis, 1*, 151–158.

Bucher, B. (1973). Some variables affecting children's compliance with instructions. *Journal of Experimental Child Psychology, 15*, 10–21.

Budd, K.S., Green, D.R., & Baer, D.M. (1976). An analysis of multiple misplaced parental social contingencies. *Journal of Applied Behavior Analysis, 9*, 459–470.

Buell, J., Stoddard, P., Harris, F.R., & Baer, D.M. (1968). Collateral social development accompanying reinforcement of outdoor play in a preschool child. *Journal of Applied Behavior Analysis, 1*, 167–174.

Carr, E.G. (1977). The motivation of self-injurious behavior: A review of some hypotheses. *Psychological Bulletin, 84*, 800–816.

Carr, E.G. (1988). Functional equivalence as a mechanism of response generalization. In R. Horner, R. Koegel, & G. Dunlap (Eds.), *Generalization and maintenance: Life-style changes in applied settings* (pp. 221–241). Baltimore: Paul H. Brookes Publishing Co.

Carr, E.G., & Durand, V.M. (1985a). Reducing behavior problems through functional communication training. *Journal of Applied Behavior Analysis, 18*, 111–126.

Carr, E.G., & Durand, V.M. (1985b). The social-communicative basis of severe behavior problems in children. In J. Reiss & R.R. Bootzin (Eds.), *Theoretical issues in behavior therapy* (pp. 219–254). New York: Academic Press.

Catania, A.C. (1963). Concurrent performances: Reinforcement interaction and response independence. *Journal of the Experimental Analysis of Behavior, 6*, 253–263.

Catania, A.C. (1966). Concurrent operants. In W.K. Honig (Ed.), *Operant behavior: Areas of research and application* (pp. 213–270). New York: Appleton-Century-Crofts.

Catania, A.C. (1969). Concurrent performances: Inhibition of one response by reinforcement of another. *Journal of the Experimental Analysis of Behavior, 12*, 731–744.

Catania, A.C. (1973). Self-inhibiting effects of reinforcement. *Journal of the Experimental Analysis of Behavior, 19*, 517–526.

Catania, A.C. (1984). *Learning* (2nd ed.). Englewood Cliffs, NJ: Prentice Hall.

Cooper, L., Wacker, D., Sasso, G., Reimers, T., & Donn, L. (1990). Using parents as therapists to assess the appropriate behavior of their children: Application to a tertiary diagnostic clinic. *Journal of Applied Behavior Analysis, 23*, 285–296.

Day, H.M., & Horner, R.H. (1989). Building response classes: A comparison of two procedurres for teaching generalized pouring to learners with severe disabilities. *Journal of Applied Behavior Analysis, 22*, 223–229.

Doleys, D.M., Wells, K.C., Hobbs, S.A., Roberts, M.W., & Cartelli, L.M. (1976). The effects of social punishment on noncompliance: A comparison with time out and positive practice. *Journal of Applied Behavior Analysis, 9*, 471–482.

Donnellan, A.M., Mirenda, P.L., Mesaros, R.A., & Fassbender, L.L. (1984). Analyzing the communicative functions of aberrant behavior. *Journal of The Association for Persons with Severe Handicaps, 9*, 201–212.

Dunham, P.J. (1971). Punishment: Method and theory. *Psychological Review, 78*, 58–70.

Dunham, P.J. (1972). Some effects of punishment upon unpunished responding. *Journal of the Experimental Analysis of Behavior, 17*, 443–450.

Dunham, P.J., & Grantmyre, J. (1982). Changes in a multiple-response repertoire during response-contingent punishment and response restriction: Sequential relationships. *Journal of the Experimental Analysis of Behavior, 37*, 123–133.

Durand, V.M. (1990). *Severe behavior problems: A functional communication training approach.* New York: Guilford Press.

Durand, V.M., & Carr, E.G. (1987). Social influences on "self-stimulatory" behavior: Analysis and treatment application. *Journal of Applied Behavior Analysis, 20*, 119–132.

Durand, V.M., & Carr, E.G. (1991). Functional communication training to reduce challenging behavior: Maintenance and application in new settings. *Journal of Applied Behavior Analysis, 24*, 251–264.

Durand, V.M., Crimmins, D.B., Caulfield, M., & Taylor, J. (1989). Reinforcer assessment I: Using problem behaviors to select reinforcers. *Journal of The Association for Persons with Severe Handicaps, 14*, 113–126.

Evans, I.M., Meyer, L.H., Kurkjian, J.A., & Kishi, G.S. (1988). An evaluation of behavioral interrelationships in child behavior therapy. In J.C. Witt, S.N. Elliot, & F.M. Gresham (Eds.), *Handbook of behavior therapy in education* (pp. 189–215). New York: Plenum.

Foxx, R.M., Faw, G.D., McMorrow, M.J., Kyle, M.S., & Bittle, R.G. (1988). Replacing maladaptive speech with verbal labeling responses: An analysis of generalized responding. *Journal of Applied Behavior Analysis, 21*, 411–417.

Friman, P.C., & Hove, G. (1987). Apparent covariation between child habit disorders: Effects of successful treatment of thumb sucking on untargeted chronic hair pulling. *Journal of Applied Behavior Analysis, 20*, 421–425.

Haring, T.G., & Kennedy, C.H. (1990). Contextual control of problem behavior in students with severe disabilities. *Journal of Applied Behavior Analysis, 23*, 235–243.

Helmstetter, E., & Durand, V.M. (1990). Nonaversive interventions for severe behavior problems. In L.H. Meyer, C.A. Peck, & L. Brown (Eds.), *Critical issues in the lives of people with severe disabilities* (pp. 559–600). Baltimore: Paul H. Brookes Publishing Co.

Herrnstein, R.J. (1961). On the law of effect. *Journal of the Experimental Analysis of Behavior, 13*, 243–266.

Horner, R.H., & Day, H.M. (1991). The effects of response efficiency on functionally equivalent competing behaviors. *Journal of Applied Behavior Analysis, 24*, 719–732.

Horner, R.H., Day, H.M., Sprague, J.R., O'Brien, M., & Heathfield, L.T. (1991). Interspersed requests: A non-aversive procedure for reducing aggression and self-injury during instruction. *Journal of Applied Behavior Analysis, 24*, 265–278.

Horner, R.H., Dunlap, G., Koegel, R.L., Carr, E.G., Sailor, W., Anderson, J., Albin, R.W., & O'Neill, R.E. (1990). Toward a technology of "nonaversive" behavioral support. *Journal of The Association for Persons with Severe Handicaps, 15*, 125–132.

Iwata, B.A., Dorsey, M.F., Slifer, K.J., Bauman, K.E., & Richman, G.S. (1982). Toward a functional analysis of self-injury. *Analysis and Intervention in Developmental Disabilities, 2*, 3–20.

Iwata, B.A., Pace, G.M., Kalsher, M.J., Cowdery, G.E., & Cataldo, M.F. (1990). Experimental analysis and extinction of self-injurious escape behavior. *Journal of Applied Behavior Analysis, 23*, 11–27.

Johnson, S.C. (1967). Hierarchical clustering schemes. *Psychometrica, 32*, 241–254.

Kazdin, A.E. (1982). Symptom substitution, generalization, and response covariation: Implications for psychotherapy outcomes. *Psychological Bulletin, 91*, 349–365.

Kazdin, A.E. (1983). Psychiatric diagnosis, dimensions of dysfunction, and child behavior therapy. *Behavior Therapy, 14*, 73–99.

Kazdin, A.E. (1985). Selection of target behaviors: The relationship of the treatment focus to clinical dysfunction. *Behavioral Assessment, 7*, 33–47.

Koegel, R.L., Firestone, P.B., Kramme, K.W., & Dunlap, G. (1974). Increasing spontaneous play by suppressing self-stimulation in autistic children. *Journal of Applied Behavior Analysis, 7*, 521–528.

Kohler, F.W., & Greenwood, C.R. (1990). Effects of collateral peer supportive behaviors within the classwide peer tutoring program. *Journal of Applied Behavior Analysis, 23*, 307–322.

Levin, H.M. (1983). *Cost-effectiveness: A primer*. Beverly Hills: Sage Publications.

Lovaas, O.I., & Simmons, J.Q. (1969). Manipulation of self-destruction in three retarded children. *Journal of Applied Behavior Analysis, 2*, 143–157.

Mace, F.C., & Lalli, J.S. (1991). Linking descriptive and experimental analyses in the treatment of bizarre speech. *Journal of Applied Behavior Analysis, 24*, 553–562.

Mace, F.C., Lalli, J.S., & Pinter-Lalli, E. (1991). Functional analysis and treatment of aberrant behavior. *Research in Developmental Disabilities, 12*, 155–180.

Mace, F.C., McCurdy, B., & Quigley, E.A. (1990). A collateral effect of reward predicted by matching theory. *Journal of Applied Behavior Analysis, 23*, 197–205.

Meyer, L.H., & Evans, I.M. (1989). *Nonaversive intervention for behavior problems: A manual for home and community*. Baltimore: Paul H. Brookes Publishing Co.

Neef, N.A., Shafer, M.S., Egel, A.L., Cataldo, M.F., & Parrish, J.M. (1983). The class specific effects of compliance training with "do" and "don't" requests: Analogue analysis and classroom application. *Journal of Applied Behavior Analysis, 16*, 81–89.

Nordquist, V.M. (1971). The modification of a child's enuresis: Some response-response relationships. *Journal of Applied Behavior Analysis, 4*, 241–248.

Northup, J., Wacker, D., Sasso, G., Steege, M., Cigrand, K., Cook, J., & DeRaad, A. (1991). A brief functional analysis of aggressive and alternative behavior in an outpatient clinic. *Journal of Applied Behavior Analysis, 24*, 509–522.

O'Neill, R.E., Horner, R.H., Albin, R.W., Storey, K., & Sprague, J.R. (Eds.). (1990). *Functional analysis of problem behavior: A practical assessment guide*. Sycamore: IL: Sycamore Publishing Co.

Parrish, J.M., Cataldo, M.F., Kolko, D.J., Neef, N.A., & Egel, A.L. (1986). Experimental analysis of response covariation among compliant and inappropriate behaviors. *Journal of Applied Behavior Analysis, 19*, 241–254.

Patterson, G.R., Ray, R.S., Shaw, D.A., & Cobb, J.A. (1969). *Manual for coding of family interactions*. New York: Microfiche.

Repp, A.C., Felce, D., & Barton, L.E. (1988). Basing the treatment of stereotypic and self-injurious behaviors on hypotheses of their causes. *Journal of Applied Behavior Analysis, 21*, 281–289.

Reynolds, G.S. (1963). Potency of conditioned reinforcers based on food and on food and punishment. *Science, 139*, 838–839.

Rincover, A. (1981). Some directions for analysis and intervention in developmental disabilities: An editorial. *Analysis and Intervention in Developmental Disabilities, 1*, 109–115.

Rincover, A., Cook, R., Peoples, A., & Packard, D. (1979). Sensory extinction and sensory reinforcement principles for programming multiple adaptive behavior change. *Journal of Applied Behavior Analysis, 12*, 221–233.

Risley, T.R. (1968). The effects and side effects of punishing the autistic behaviors of a deviant child. *Journal of Applied Behavior Analysis, 1*, 21–34.

Rolider, A., Cummings, A., & Van Houten, R. (1991). Side effects of therapeutic punishment on academic performance and eye contact. *Journal of Applied Behavior Analysis, 24*, 763–773.

Russo, D.C., Cataldo, M.F., & Cushing, P.J. (1981). Compliance training and behavioral covariation in the treatment of multiple behavior problems. *Journal of Applied Behavior Analysis, 14*, 209–222.

Sajwaj, T., Twardosz, S., & Burke, M. (1972). Side effects of extinction procedures in a remedial playschool. *Journal of Applied Behavior Analysis, 5*, 163–175.

Skinner, B.F. (1935). The generic nature of the concepts of stimulus and response. *Journal of General Psychology, 12*, 40–65.

Steege, M.W., Wacker, D.P., Berg, W.K., Cigrand, K.K., & Cooper, L.J. (1989). The use of behavioral assessment to prescribe and evaluate treatments for severely handicapped children. *Journal of Applied Behavior Analysis, 22*, 23–33.

Talkington, L.W., Hall, S., & Altman, R. (1971). Communication deficits and aggression in the mentally retarded. *American Journal of Mental Deficiency, 76*, 235–237.

Twardosz, S., & Sajwaj, T. (1972). Multiple effects of a procedure to increase sitting in a hyperactive retarded boy. *Journal of Applied Behavior Analysis, 5*, 73–78.

Voeltz, L.M., & Evans, I.M. (1982). The assessment of behavioral interrelationships in child behavior therapy. *Behavioral Assessment, 4*, 131–165.

Wacker, D., Steege, M., Northup, J., Sasso, G., Berg, W., Reimers, T., Cooper, L., Cigrand, K., & Donn, L. (1990). A component analysis of functional communication training across three topographies of severe behavior problems. *Journal of Applied Behavior Analysis, 23*, 417–429.

Wacker, D., Wiggins, B., Fowler, M., & Berg, W. (1988). Training students with profound or multiple handicaps to make requests via microswitches. *Journal of Applied Behavior Analysis, 21*, 331–343.

Wahler, R.G. (1975). Some structural aspects of deviant child behavior. *Journal of Applied Behavior Analysis, 8*, 27–42.

Wahler, R.G., & Fox, J.J. (1980). Solitary toy play and time out: A family treatment package for children with aggressive and oppositional behavior. *Journal of Applied Behavior Analysis, 13*, 23–39.

Wahler, R.G., Sperling, K.A., Thomas, M.R., Teeter, N.C., & Luper, H.L. (1970). The modification of childhood stuttering: Some response-response relationships. *Journal of Experimental Child Psychology, 9*, 411–428.

Whitman, T.L., Zakaras, M., & Chardos, S. (1971). Effects of reinforcement and guidance procedures on instruction-following behavior of severely retarded children. *Journal of Applied Behavior Analysis, 4*, 283–290.

Zawlocki, R.J., Wesolowski, M.D., & Thaler, G.A. (1983, May). *Behavioral covariation of multiple behavior problems of severely retarded children using a modified restraint procedure.* Paper presented at the Association for Behavior Analysis annual proceedings.

PART III

Developing Effective Communication Interventions
Programmatic Considerations

8

Assessment and Intervention for Children within the Instructional Curriculum

Glen Dunlap and Lee Kern

T HIS CHAPTER INTRODUCES A MODEL of behavior management in which a process of functional assessment leads to individualized modifications in students' curricula and instructional procedures. The model is designed to prevent behavior problems in educational settings by removing those curricular and instructional characteristics that have been associated with the problems and by presenting alternatives that lead to desirable responding. The model is based on considerable recent research and is intended for use as one important component in a comprehensive program of behavioral support.

INTRODUCTION

Some children enrolled in public schools exhibit challenging behaviors that teachers find extremely difficult to manage within the ongoing framework of their instructional programs. These children may be described with any number of labels, may be functioning at various academic and intellectual levels, and may be found at any point on the continuum from special to regular educational placements. What they share are patterns of behavior that teachers find uncontrollable. The children's problem behaviors range from dangerous and violent acts, such as aggression and property destruction, to behaviors that are incompatible with a preferred classroom decorum and that are distracting to other students, such as crying, tantrumming, vocal outbursts, and

Preparation of this manuscript was supported by U.S. Department of Education Cooperative Agreement No. G0087C0234 (National Institute on Disability and Rehabilitation Research) and Field-Initiated Research Grant No. H023C10102 (Office of Special Education Programs). However, opinions expressed in this chapter are those of the authors and no endorsement by supporting agencies should be inferred.

conspicuous stereotypy. Associated problem characteristics are often identified as an absence of desirable behavior, such as failure to perform assignments or follow classroom rules. When children become known as intransigent "behavior problems," several consequences may follow: 1) they may be transferred to more restrictive and secluded educational placements, 2) they may be suspended or expelled from school, or 3) they may be prescribed intrusive discipline regimes and/or restrictive medications. None of these alternatives is consistently desirable because they all have the potential to limit the student's opportunities for optimal achievement, a satisfying learning experience, and the development of positive interactions with teachers and peers in typical educational contexts.

The students to whom we are referring are those whose behavior problems are not managed successfully with standard, classroom-wide programs designed to motivate desirable performance and discipline. Such programs often rely on scheduled rewards (e.g., points or privileges) for compliance and productivity, and on punishment (e.g., loss of points or loss of privileges) for violations of classroom rules. That is, these standard programs use procedures of contingency management to promote desirable behavior. When classroom-wide systems are insufficient for a particular student, the common next step is to strengthen the contingencies with denser schedules of rewards and, often, with more powerful punishers, including time-out in a corner or, in extreme cases, in an isolation room. In some instances, however, even these enhanced procedures fail to produce the expected outcomes.

Since the 1980s, the practice of contingency management has been improved substantially with the advent of functional assessment and functional analysis. As Iwata, Carr, Durand, Wacker, Mace, and many other authors have demonstrated, the general process of functional assessment can identify specific classes of reinforcers that are maintaining an individual's problem behaviors. This knowledge can be used to develop effective programs of instruction (i.e., teaching the student preferred ways to obtain the reinforcers) and contingency management (i.e., scheduling the reinforcers to follow desirable rather than undesirable behaviors). A great deal of research has now shown that interventions that focus on operant functions and that are based on the results of functional assessments can be effective when other efforts involving contingency management have failed. Other chapters in this volume consider the concepts and operations of functional assessment in some detail; therefore, we will not repeat this information except to describe the process as it applies to the current model's identification of curricular and instructional variables.

Although reinforcers and punishers are central determinants of problem (and nonproblem) behavior, it is important to recognize that their functions are determined by the context in which they occur. Attention will serve as a reinforcer only if it has been established as such by a student's learning history and if the student is relatively deprived of attention at the time that it is delivered. Similarly, the opportunity to escape will serve as a reinforcer only if the student is in a circumstance that is relatively unpleasant and if the escape leads to a relatively preferred situation. The point is that the context (the stimuli that impinge upon a student prior to the target behavior) has a great deal to do with the reinforcing or punishing value of the stimuli (consequences) that follow the behavior. Similarly, the context may be said to evoke (or occasion) the behavior because much of a student's responding is intended to change the context to a more preferred status.

The context in which a student interacts at school is made up of many events and stimuli, but chief among them are the curricular requirements and the instructional procedures that determine the student's educational program. These features have a great influence on student behavior. An expanding literature is demonstrating that curricular and instructional variables are powerful determinants of behavior problems. It is becoming increasingly clear that manipulation of these variables can be a crucial component of positive behavior management.

The remainder of this chapter is devoted to a presentation of curricular and instructional influences on problem behavior. For simplicity, we will use the term *curriculum* in a very broad sense to refer to the entire context of educational programming, including the content that is to be taught, the setting and materials, the manner in which lessons and instructions are scheduled and presented, and all other physical and instructional arrangements that may be considered to be antecedent or contextual variables that may impinge upon a student's behavior. In this chapter, we review some of the pertinent literature, but the principal purpose is to describe a process, or model, for assessing these influences and designing appropriate revisions. As we present the model, we provide examples from our experiences in working with challenging behaviors in public school settings. The first and most detailed example was an especially intransigent case that required great efforts in both the assessment and intervention phases. However, we urge the reader to recognize that most cases are relatively straightforward and do not demand the time or personnel that were needed in this instance.

AN OVERVIEW OF CURRICULAR
INFLUENCES ON PROBLEM BEHAVIOR

A child's curriculum defines both the content and mode of instructional delivery. A number of recent studies (e.g., Dunlap, Kern-Dunlap, Clarke, & Robbins, 1991) have demonstrated that specific curricular variables can influence the occurrence or nonoccurrence of problem behavior. By identifying these variables through functional assessment, features of a child's curriculum can be modified to reduce or eliminate problem behaviors. The host of instructional and curricular variables can be broadly grouped as setting or ecological factors, instructional and curricular content, instructional delivery, and social variables.

Setting or ecological variables include both temporally distant and temporally contiguous phenomena that influence students' behavior during the school day. Temporally distant phenomena may include events such as skipping breakfast, experiencing allergies, having a poor bus ride, or engaging in negative social exchanges at an earlier time. For example, Wahler and Graves (1983) found that problematic social exchanges earlier in the day influenced the later occurrence of problem behaviors. Temporally contiguous phenomena include immediate circumstances that influence problem behavior. Such circumstances may be noise level, crowding, and schedule predictability. McAfee (1987) found that a crowded classroom led to the occurrence of problem behavior in some individuals. Disruptive and aggressive behaviors in adolescents with moderate and severe disabilities were reduced by increasing the amount of floor space per child.

The role of instructional or curricular content has been well documented in the literature, with the findings being that problem behavior may be a manifestation of skill deficiencies. If skill deficiencies are identified, curriculum content can be adjusted so that the difficulty level is modified and/or replacement skills are taught. Weeks and Gaylord-Ross (1981) showed that difficult tasks evoked problem behaviors in three children with severe disabilities. Self-injury, aggression, and crying were reduced substantially by decreasing task difficulty or providing opportunities for errorless learning. Carr and Durand (1985) demonstrated that problem behaviors may serve a communicative function. Teaching appropriate communicative alternatives reduced problem behaviors. A variety of communicative alternatives have been taught (e.g., Horner & Budd, 1985; Wacker, Wiggins, Fowler, & Berg, 1988) including hand-raising, gesturing, pressing a microswitch, holding a sign, and other simple topographies.

In addition, studies have demonstrated that when the content of a student's curriculum consists of activities identified as being of high interest to that student, problem behaviors are less likely to occur. For example, Kern-Dunlap, Clarke, and Dunlap (1990) were able to reduce the problem behaviors of a 13-year-old girl with multiple disabilities by incorporating a favorite hobby into her daily assignments. During baseline observations, her daily handwriting assignment of copying pages from a workbook was associated with high levels of aggressive behavior. Disruptive behavior was reduced when her handwriting assignment was changed so that it consisted of writing captions for photographs she had taken at an earlier time, which were later pasted in a photograph album.

Choice-making strategies can be useful in ensuring that curricular content is responsive to students' individual preferences (see chap. 3, this volume). Several authors have demonstrated that allowing opportunities for choice-making can result in reduced levels of problem behavior. Dyer, Dunlap, and Winterling (1990) compared teacher-selected versus student-selected tasks and rewards on the problem behavior of students with autism and mental retardation. In one condition, the students were asked to complete tasks selected by the teacher. When successful, the students earned rewards that were also selected by the teacher. In the choice-making condition, the students were presented with the same tasks and rewards; however, they were allowed to select what task they would work on and what reward they would earn. The choice-making condition consistently resulted in reduced levels of problem behavior. In addition, the frequency of correct responding indicated that the students were equally productive in both conditions.

Instructional delivery, or the manner in which instructions are delivered to a student, has also been shown to influence problem behavior. For example, a procedure described as "task variation" has been demonstrated to be effective in reducing problem behavior. This procedure consists of interspersing previously acquired tasks with target tasks historically associated with high frequencies of problem behavior. Using this strategy, Winterling, Dunlap, and O'Neill (1987) were able to reduce problem behaviors in three individuals described as having autism. Singer, Singer, and Horner (1987) used a related strategy to assist elementary school students with disabilities who were experiencing difficulties transitioning from play periods to instructional periods. Before requests to transition, the students were presented with brief instructions associated with high levels of compliance (e.g., "Give me five"). Following the rapid presentation of these "pre-task requests," transition performance was greatly improved. This approach is related to the phenomenon of behavioral momentum as described by Mace and his colleagues (Mace et al., 1988).

A range of social variables form an important component of curricular design. The social context of curriculum is increasingly being viewed as an essential element of meaningful and responsive instruction. Curriculum content that is socially responsive produces an outcome that is valued by society (Horner, Sprague, & Flannery, in press). Such a curriculum is embedded in the values, opportunities, and demands of the local community in which an individual lives. The content of an individual's curriculum should focus on skills that will result in independent competence in his or her local community. A curriculum composed of activities with meaning or functional value to an individual has been shown to decrease the frequency of problem behaviors. In a study by Dunlap et al. (1991), the influence of traditional academic activities was compared with the influence of activities identified as having meaningful or functional outcomes within that individual's environment. Disruptive classroom behavior was completely eliminated in a 13-year-old girl with multiple disabilities when traditional tasks were modified so that the content became socially relevant. For example, one set of manipulations consisted of arithmetic tasks. In the traditional activity condition, the task consisted of completing worksheets or textbook exercises containing subtraction problems. This was compared with a condition in which similar skills were required; however, rather than completing practice problems, her task consisted of reading a local school bus schedule and completing subtraction problems to determine the arrival time of various buses. She was then permitted to walk to the corner bus stop to see whether the bus arrived on time.

There are a great number of curricular and instructional variables that may influence a student's performance in the classroom. These variables may affect different students in different ways. Often, severe problem behavior is maintained by multiple variables. In these instances, successful interventions will require multiple concurrent modifications. For example, a student's behavior problems may result from a short attention span, low interest in the required task, and difficulty performing the task. A successful intervention might involve shortening task sessions, embedding the task in areas of interest to the student, and interspersing the difficult task with previously acquired tasks. Thus, the importance of first conducting an assessment to determine the role of specific variables and subsequently linking the information obtained from that assessment to an intervention must be emphasized. In addition to providing an identification of variables influencing problem behavior, a comprehensive functional assessment generally yields information on the relative influence those variables have on problem behavior. Such information can then be translated into a comprehensive and thorough intervention plan. In the following section, a model of curriculum-based behavior management is presented. This model describes assessment methods to identify potentially influential curricular variables, empirically test those variables, and develop a curriculum responsive to the information obtained through the assessment process.

FUNCTIONAL ASSESSMENT
AND CURRICULUM-BASED INTERVENTION

The purpose of a functional assessment is to develop an understanding of a student's behavior. More specifically, a functional assessment of a student's problem behavior is designed to articulate functional relationships between the behavior and events or conditions that may be present in the student's environment. The identified functional relationships are described as hypotheses or statements regarding the environmental variables that govern the occurrence and nonoccurrence of the problem behavior. When a functional assessment has been completed, it should be possible to predict with a high degree of certainty the conditions under which the behavior will occur. With this level of understanding, the hypotheses should be readily converted into logical and effective strategies of individualized intervention.

Functional relationships may be sorted into two general categories that are governed by the operation of reinforcement. The first category has to do with operant functions. Hypotheses that fit this category refer to the motivation or purpose of the behavior and are stated in terms of contingencies of reinforcement. Although the variations are infinite, operant motivations are either "to get something" (e.g., attention, sensory stimulation, a tangible commodity) or "to escape or avoid something" (e.g., a difficult lesson, a boring activity, a disliked peer). Examples of this kind of hypothesis are: "Johnny cries to obtain the teacher's attention," "Fred repeatedly waves sticks in front of his eyes because he enjoys the visual stimulation," and "Sheila bangs her head because when she does so, she is removed from schoolwork, which she detests." This first category of functional relationships focuses on the operant consequences that are associated with, and presumably maintain, the problem behavior. This is the category that is most frequently represented in the literature.

The second category focuses on the antecedent and contextual stimuli that are associated with behavior. Hypotheses that fit this category do not identify operant contingencies explicitly, although they may be inferred, but instead address the contextual associations between environmental circumstances and the presence and absence of the target behavior. This category focuses on the stimuli and events that occur or are present prior to the problem behavior. Examples of such hypothesis statements are: "Belinda is apt to tantrum when she is engaged in her math assignment, but she never tantrums when she works on other lessons;" "Homer often punches his neighbor when he is standing in line during transitions, although he rarely hits anybody at other times;" and "Helen destroys her papers and tips over her desk only when she has been working on academic tasks for more than 10 minutes." As is illustrated in these examples, hypothesis statements in this category seek to describe those stimulus situations in which the problem behavior is likely to occur as well as those circumstances in which the behavior is *not* likely to occur.

This latter type of functional relationship is the category that we will emphasize in this chapter. This is not to imply that we believe that it is sufficient or preferred. Rather, we believe that both kinds of hypotheses are valuable and that it is desirable if the second category (antecedent and contextual stimuli) leads to clear inferences about the operant functions, which are the subject matter of the first category. Frequently, hypotheses about antecedent variables are indicative of student motivation. For example, the statements above pertaining to Belinda and Helen may be followed reasonably by hypotheses that these students were motivated by a desire to escape their respective assignments. It might be very sensible to base interventions on this assumption. However, in many situations in the natural classroom environment, the consequences (i.e., the maintaining contingencies) for problem behaviors are not very consistent or clear. In these situations, it can be very difficult to formulate statements about operant functions, whereas it may be more feasible to identify the antecedent variables. This is one advantage that may be associated with the second category (see chap. 5, this volume).

Another advantage of interventions based on antecedent manipulations is that they can be relatively simple to implement. In addition, the change in behavior is often very rapid as a result of antecedent manipulations. In contrast, there are many instances in which logical interventions based solely on hypotheses of operant functions can be difficult to administer and slow to be effective in typical educational settings. These interventions typically involve changing the reinforcement contingencies (e.g., delivering the identified reinforcers only after desirable performances, and never after problem behavior), and/or teaching the student more desirable responses for procuring the desired outcomes, such as by functional communication training (Durand, 1990). Although generally and ultimately effective, implementing these strategies can be arduous, especially if the consequences are difficult to control and if the student has experienced a long and complex learning history.

Initiating the Functional Assessment Process

The first step in providing individualized behavioral support is to utilize the process of functional assessment to identify relationships that involve both antecedent and operant functions. These functional relationships should identify variables that can be manipulated within the educational setting and that are measurable and testable. When such relationships are identified, intervention strategies can be developed that are based on the behavioral understanding produced by the assessment process. In the following paragraphs, we describe the steps of the assessment process and illustrate these steps with a case drawn from our experience (Dunlap et al., 1991).

> "Jill" was a 12-year-old student in an elementary school program for students described as having "severe emotional disturbance." She was referred for our consultation and assistance because she engaged frequently in intense disruptions and destructive behaviors that were described as relentless, unpredictable, and uncontrollable. Several times each day she would scream, cry, swear, spit, destroy property, aggress toward others, remove her clothes, and generally act in a manner that made instruction for herself or her classmates an impossible endeavor. As a result, she spent an average of fifty percent of her school day in an isolation "time out" room. Jill's problem behaviors were not new. They had been part of her repertoire since she entered the school system in kindergarten. However, they were now much more salient because Jill was growing rapidly into a young woman of size and power. When her disruptions occurred, at least two

adults were required to subdue her and escort her to the time out room. Although Jill had received the attention of expert interdisciplinary teams of professionals for several years, no approach had been successful at managing her behavior for more than a brief period of time. The inability to change these serious problem behaviors had led to thoughtful considerations of hospitalization.

In addition to her label of "severely emotionally disturbed," Jill's test results indicated mild mental retardation. She had also been described as having schizophrenia and attention deficit disorder. Her academic performance in reading and math was at least three years below grade level and in social competence she was judged to be functioning at about the level of a five or six-year-old. Jill's speech was communicative at times, but on other occasions it was described as perseverative and delusional. For about six years, Jill had been on and off various medications. When our consultation began, she was taking 15 mg of Mellaril per day.

Although Jill's severe problem behaviors were her most salient characteristic, she was also noted to have an engaging personality, a sense of humor, and many interests that were typical of her age group. She enjoyed popular music and, despite social immaturity, she displayed budding sensitivity to boys and to other concerns of the teenage years.

Jill lived at home with her mother and grandparents. Although her family was further challenged by the disability of another family member, her caregivers were devoted to her and participated with the school and with the consultants to the greatest possible extent. Jill's school classroom included seven other children, a teacher, and two aides. In addition, two instructors, working alternate days, had been hired specifically to work with Jill and to contain her disruptions as much as possible.

Previous behavior management programs for Jill had focused primarily on the manipulation of rewards and punishers. These included dense schedules of differential reinforcement for desirable behavior and various response cost (e.g., loss of points) and time out contingencies for inappropriate and disruptive episodes. Jill's current program included a point system, isolation time out for serious infractions, and opportunities to leave the classroom whenever she made such a request.

The plan that was initiated with the consultation, and discussed with Jill's teachers, administrators, and family, included a three-step process of assessment and intervention. The first step was to conduct a thorough functional assessment of Jill's problem behaviors ending with the development of clearly-stated and agreed-upon hypotheses. It was expected that this step would be relatively lengthy because her behaviors were reported to be so inconsistent and unpredictable and because the pattern of disruptive behavior had proven to be very resistant to even very meticulous and intensive interventions. It was also expected that the functional assessment would need to focus heavily on the antecedent conditions because previous, unsuccessful emphases had involved mainly consequences and because reports suggested that relatively little attention had been paid to the role of curriculum and context. The second step of Jill's program was a test of the hypotheses by conducting systematic manipulations within her school program. This second step was anticipated because of the consultant's desire to be extremely confident of the functional relationships before prescribing another in a long line of intervention strategies. The third step of the program was to use the results of the assessment and testing to derive a logical intervention.

Methods of Functional Assessment

The process of functional assessment consists of two steps. The first step involves the collection of information in order to develop hypotheses about functional relationships. The second step involves testing or confirming the hypotheses through direct manipulations. In ordinary practice, information gathering and hypothesis development are considered to be sufficient and, thus, are followed directly by the formation and implementation of a program of intervention. However, the second step, hypothesis testing, is used when there is some reason to firmly establish the validity of the hypotheses, as in research, or when it is considered important to obtain further information that can be produced only through direct testing. This second step, in which a student's behavior is observed during direct and systematic manipulation of hypothesized variables, is referred to in the literature as a functional analysis (Iwata, Vollmer, & Zarcone, 1990; O'Neill, Dunlap, & Horner, 1991). In the ensuing section, we discuss some of the methods used to develop hypotheses, and, subsequently, we discuss hypothesis testing. The functional assessment process is depicted in Figure 1.

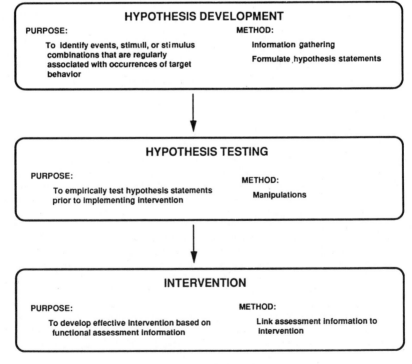

Figure 1.   The process of functional assessment.

Hypothesis Development

The process of developing hypotheses regarding the relationships between a behavior and the environment has not been articulated very clearly, especially if antecedent variables, including curriculum, are considered. Strategies for identifying operant motivations (e.g., Durand & Crimmins, 1988) or communicative functions (e.g., Donnellan, Mirenda, Mesaros, & Fassbender, 1984) are somewhat more developed. The process of generating hypotheses about antecedent relationships is an exercise in careful observation and deductive reasoning. The demand is to identify those events, stimuli, or stimulus combinations that are regularly associated with occurrences of the target behavior. The number of potential influences can be great, and, thus, the task is to narrow the field of possibilities until eventually the governing variables are identified.

The methods that are used to obtain the information necessary for hypothesis development are interviews, direct observations, and archival data (see Lalli & Goh, chap. 2, this volume). *Interviews* obtain information from people who know the student well and have observed the student over time and in a variety of circumstances. Interviews should be conducted with more than one informant in order to evaluate the reliability of information, to obtain a broader sample of reporting, and to allow for the consideration of differing perspectives and interpretations. In general, it is recommended that interviews be conducted with at least two members of the school staff and with at least one member of the student's family. Interviews may be brief and simple, or they may be very detailed and structured, depending upon the complexity and severity of the behavior and observation and reporting skills of the informant. In most cases, interviews need to be detailed enough to focus in on specific details of the environment that are rarely identified in initial descriptions of the behavior and its context.

The literature contains several interview forms and guidelines that are useful for conducting structured interviews. For example, Bailey and Pyles (1989) described a process of behavioral diagnostics in which they include a "behavioral diagnosis and treatment information form" (p. 92) that offers pertinent questions regarding situational variables and setting events, physiological variables, operant variables, and other considerations. O'Neill, Horner, Albin, Storey, and Sprague (1990) developed a "functional analysis interview" form that is designed to yield detailed and comprehensive information regarding the topography of the behavior and the environmental circumstances that might be influencing the behavior's occurrence. These materials can be very useful in conducting interviews with school personnel in order to determine the circumstances that are associated with the behavior.

In our experience, it is usually most efficient to tailor interviews so that they address the student and classroom circumstances that were identified in the referral; however, there are two pervasive questions that should always be included because they represent the fundamental objectives of the interview process. These questions are: 1) What are the specific environmental circumstances that are associated with the greatest likelihood that the behavior problem will occur? and 2) What are the specific environmental circumstances that are never associated with an occurrence of the behavior problem? Depending upon the status of the informant, the words used in these questions may need to be changed, but the purpose of the questions is integral to hypothesis development. When presenting these questions, it is important to explain that "circumstances" refer to all aspects of the context including the physical location, the time of day, the characteristics of the activity that the student is engaged in, the presence or absence of particular peers and adults, the student's physiologic condition, and any other variables that might be associated. In order to obtain sufficiently detailed responses to these two questions, it is virtually always necessary to follow the questions with a series of focused inquiries designed to solicit increasingly detailed observations.

Some form of *direct observation* is also required. At a minimum, observations are needed to confirm relationships described during the interviews. More typically, a period of formal data collection is recommended. Formal data collection serves at least two purposes: It provides an empirical baseline to be used as a comparison with data collected during intervention, and it offers a quantifiable index of relationships between environmental events and occurrences of the target behavior. There are many ways to record behavioral events in a systematic manner. A common approach is the A-B-C recording (Bijou, Peterson, & Ault, 1968), in which each occurrence of the problem behavior (B) is detailed with regards to its antecedent (A) events and its immediate consequences (C). Another useful approach has been described as the scatterplot (Touchette, MacDonald, & Langer, 1985). When used in a school situation, this technique requires that the school day is divided into intervals and that frequency counts of the behavior are obtained within each interval. The intervals can be defined as time periods (e.g., half-hour blocks) or as activities (e.g., math, vocational training, lunch). The data are then plotted with the intervals represented on the ordinate and days represented on the abscissa, and the cells are filled in, usually with symbols or different shading, to represent the frequency of occurrence. The result is a scatterplot that depicts patterns in the occurrence of the behavior. It is usually possible to attribute observed differences in the cells to activities or other environmental variables that are associated differentially with the behavior. Such associations contribute importantly to the development of hypotheses. O'Neill et al. (1990) presented a "functional analysis observation form" that uses the framework of a scatterplot approach and adds additional information that can contribute to a more precise assessment.

Archival records often provide additional useful information. Medical and school records can provide information on physiologic and other variables that may interfere with successful school adaptation. In addition, many times the school records include detailed programs of behavior management, which may have been more or less effective. This information may help to identify variables in the stage of hypothesis development.

When adequate information has been gathered through interviews and direct observations, it should be possible to form hypothesis statements. These statements represent one's best guess about the relationship of environmental events to occurrences of the challenging behavior. The statements should be phrased in terms that are observable and testable and that identify variables that can be manipulated or modified to create an intervention. The development of these hypotheses is the culmination of the initial information gathering phase of functional assessment (see Dunlap et al., 1991).

The demonstrated intransigence of Jill's serious challenging behaviors indicated that the information gathering process was apt to be more demanding than is typically the case. Therefore, multiple interview and direct observation methods were included in the functional assessment process.

Because a large number of individuals had worked with Jill and had strong opinions regarding her challenges and her treatment, it was decided to conduct structured interviews with 28 of the people who had the most recent and close contact with her. These 28 people included teachers, aides, psychologists, family members, administrators, and other school staff, such as her bus driver and the school secretary. An 11-item questionnaire was developed [see Figure 2]. Respondents were given the option of being interviewed or providing their responses in writing. In addition, 3 people were administered the functional analysis interview form (O'Neill et al., 1990).

Direct observations were conducted by the consultants during all hours of the school day. Records were kept of all disruptive episodes in the form of A-B-C reports. During four hours each day, detailed recordings were obtained of Jill's on-task behavior, positive and negative social interactions, and instances of psychotic and delusional speech.

The results of the direct observations and the interviews were analyzed by the consultants as the data were received, and weekly team meetings with the school staff were used to discuss the findings and attempt to formulate hypotheses. Consensus was difficult to achieve because Jill's serious disruptions seemed to occur at any time during the day, with the single exception of the brief periods during lunch when she was actively engaged in swallowing and chewing her food. However, the data analysis and discussion among the staff gradually led to four hypotheses that the team could agree were reasonable predictors of Jill's positive and challenging behaviors. The four hypotheses were:

(1) *Jill is better behaved when she is engaged in large motor as opposed to small motor activities.* This statement emerged from direct observation data that indicated, on the average, that Jill's disruptions were less frequent in large motor activities and that severe problems often accompanied activities that required care with handwriting, cutting with scissors, and similar fine motor skills.

(2) *Jill is better behaved when her fine motor and academic requirements are brief as opposed to lengthy.* This hypothesis was developed from many reports that Jill's attention span and tolerance were limited and that extended periods of frustration would lead typically to severe disruptions. Some of the direct observa-

---

Respondent_____   Date of interview_____

Interviewer_____

How long has respondent known Jill?_____

Approximate hours spent with Jill per week_____

1. What do you see as Jill's major problems? Prioritize them from most to least severe.

2. In what situations do these behaviors occur?

3. In what situations are her behaviors most appropriate?

4. What do you see as Jill's greatest strengths?

5. What do you see as Jill's greatest weaknesses?

6. Why do you think that Jill is the way she is?

7. What do you think needs to be done to help Jill? How?

8. What does Jill like the most?

9. What does Jill like the least?

10. What things seem to trigger an outburst during
    a teaching session?

    unstructured time?

    lunch?

11. What things can be done to improve the likelihood of compliance during
    a teaching session?

    unstructured time?

    lunch?

Figure 2. Interview questions administered as part of the functional assessment of Jill's challenging behaviors.

tion data also indicated that demanding sessions began with acceptable behavior, but would produce serious challenging behaviors after five or 10 min[utes].

(3) *Jill is better behaved when she is engaged in functional activities resulting in concrete and preferred outcomes.* The interviews and observations identified some activities that were associated with desirable behavior and enthusiastic performance. The common features of these activities appeared related to the fact that they were meaningful to Jill in the sense that they had a functional purpose, and they involved stimuli or events that were among Jill's interests.

(4) *Jill is better behaved when she has some choice regarding her activities.* This hypothesis was developed from many interview responses indicating that Jill liked to control her surroundings and that her problem behaviors might be produced because they represented one means through which she could control others.

Hypothesis Testing

On some occasions, it is desirable to empirically test the veracity of the hypothesis statements before implementing an intervention. Hypotheses are tested by conducting direct manipulations (i.e., functional analysis) of an implicated variable and observing whether the manipulations produce any alterations in the rate of the target behavior. The manipulations are conducted in an experimental fashion, using a reversal, withdrawal, or alternating treatments single-case design. If the behavior changes systematically in the expected direction, the hypothesis can be said to have received some support or confirmation. If the behavior does not change according to expectations, then it is possible that the hypothesis was faulty or that the functional relationships were not understood adequately.

There are several reasons that an educator or interventionist might wish to test hypotheses prior to intervention. First, if direct manipulations are conducted and they tend to confirm a hypothesis, then the practitioner can have greater confidence that the manipulated variable will produce desired results during intervention. This can be quite important, especially when the projected intervention requires considerable time or expense. However, if the manipulations fail to produce expected changes, then the hypothesis may require reworking or refinement. This is also valuable because interventions that are based on faulty hypotheses are not likely to be effective. The experience obtained from conducting tests of hypotheses can also be beneficial for selecting curricular parameters and for determining the logistical feasibility of many curricular modifications. In addition, hypothesis testing can be useful for evaluating the strength of a variable's influence. The magnitude of change in the frequency and intensity of a behavior can be an important consideration in designing interventions.

Despite these advantages, it should be pointed out that this form of experimental hypothesis testing, although preferred, is not essential. In a classroom context, it may be difficult for teachers to carry out manipulations with adequate control and to collect data in a systematic manner needed to empirically validate the hypotheses statements. In such cases, the intervention itself must serve as a test of the hypotheses. If the hypotheses are not completely accurate, the hypotheses will need to be modified and the intervention revised.

> Jill's case presented such degrees of uncertainty and urgency that the consultants opted to test the hypotheses systematically prior to designing and implementing the intervention. The hypotheses were tested over the course of four school days, with one hypothesis being tested per day. Jill's regular instructors conducted the sessions and data were collected on severe disruptive behavior and on-task responding by the consulting personnel. Between six and nine sessions were conducted each day. Each session lasted 15 min[utes] except for those sessions that were conducted to assess the influence of brief session durations as indicated by the second hypothesis. The number of sessions conducted per day made it possible to test each hypothesis with several reversals of conditions. This was useful because it was expected that her most serious challenging behaviors would not be displayed during each of the conditions.
>
> Hypothesis 1 was tested on the first day. In these manipulations, sessions with large motor activities (e.g., tossing a frisbee) were alternated with sessions

comprised of fine motor activities (e.g., cutting and coloring). The activities were selected from those commonly presented in Jill's regular school routine. The top two graphs in Figure 3 show the results from these sessions. These data show that the only serious disruptions occurred during the fine motor activities and, in general, levels of on-task behavior were higher during the large motor sessions.

The second hypothesis, having to do with long (about 15 min.) versus short (about 5 min. or less) sessions of difficult work, was tested on the second day. The actual length of the sessions was determined by the amount of work that was assigned. The second row of graphs shows that the short sessions were associated with superior behavior, with the exception of the fifth session (marked by the asterisk). This session differed from the other short-task sessions in that verbal instructions were the only cues that signalled that the session would be short in duration. In the other short task sessions, Jill was also provided with visual cues by presenting her a worksheet containing only the problems she was required to complete. Thus, this unanticipated finding helped to refine the hypothesis by adding the caveat that Jill would need to clearly comprehend (e.g., with the assistance of visual as well as verbal cues) that the session would be relatively brief in duration.

Hypothesis number 3 was evaluated by alternating sessions that were comprised of functional tasks with sessions that included analog tasks. Functional tasks were defined as activities that involved content or materials that Jill had expressed an interest in and/or that led to clear outcomes related to her interests or to daily living activities. For example, one functional task session required that she write a letter to a teacher in another classroom requesting the opportunity to read a story to her class. In contrast, an analog task was to copy a letter from her handwriting book. The analog and functional task requirements were closely matched in response to topography and difficulty; the differences were in the materials, the content, and Jill's interest in the outcomes. Figure [3] shows that the functional tasks were consistently associated with more desirable behavior than the analog tasks.

The final hypothesis to be tested had to do with choice-making options. In one set of sessions, Jill was offered a choice from a menu of four academic tasks. In the "no choice" sessions, she was assigned the same work but her instructor made the task selections. These data show that the choice-making opportunities consistently led to more desirable behavior.

After the four days of hypothesis testing, it was apparent that the careful work involved in developing hypotheses had yielded important information about curricular influences on Jill's challenging behaviors. Each of the hypotheses received support during the testing, and one of the hypotheses was refined. It was encouraging to note that virtually no disruptive behavior had occurred during those sessions that were expected to produce desirable responding (with the informative exception of the single short-task condition as described above), although substantial problems were associated with the comparison conditions. This consistency and apparent predictability led to hopes that Jill's serious disruptions could be functionally prevented through a comprehensive process of curricular revision.

Linking Assessment to Curriculum-Based Intervention

Indeed, the ultimate value of the functional assessment process is achieved only when the information is translated into an effective and positive interven-

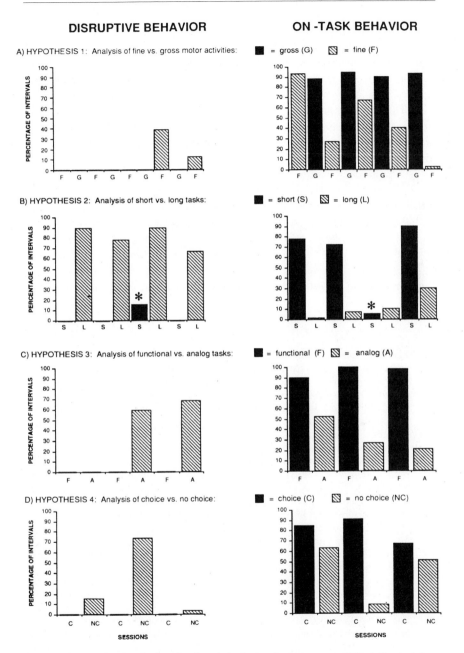

Figure 3. Results of the hypothesis-testing phase during the functional assessment of Jill's challenging behaviors. Levels of disruptive behavior (left) and on-task responding (right) are shown for each of the four hypotheses. Ordinate = percent intervals, abscissa = sessions. (From Dunlap, G., Kern-Dunlap, L., Clarke, S. & Robbins F. R. [1991]. Functional assessment, curricular revision, and severe behavior problems. *Journal of Applied Behavior Analysis, 24,* 387–397. Copyright © 1991 by The Society for The Experimental Analysis of Behavior; reprinted by permission.)

tion approach. In this chapter we are concentrating on those functional relationships that pertain to antecedent variables, especially in the form of curricular and instructional influences on student behavior in the educational setting. As we have discussed and illustrated, it is logical and common that such factors assume a major role in governing students' challenging behaviors. The question now has to do with using the functional assessment information to design appropriate intervention strategies. The solution is logical and straightforward, although the specific means through which the strategies are implemented are limitless.

Hypothesis statements that pertain to curricular and instructional variables should specify conditions under which a student is likely to exhibit the target behavior, as well as those conditions that are unlikely to be associated with the target behavior. Therefore, the logical intervention approach is: 1) to increase the prevalence of those stimuli or circumstances that produce desirable behavior, and 2) to remove or ameliorate those stimuli or circumstances that produce the undesirable target behavior. If these conditions can be achieved, the result should be a clear and immediate deceleration of the student's challenging behaviors.

This process of linking functional assessment outcomes to intervention programs may be depicted best with examples, so let us return to Jill.

> The functional assessment of Jill's challenging behaviors required 5 weeks of data collection, analysis, and team meetings. Although this process was particularly lengthy with Jill, her behavior problems had persisted for years and occurred with extremely high frequency across multiple settings and contexts. Thus, the process was intentionally comprehensive and thorough. Throughout this period, Jill's ongoing educational program remained in place. This curriculum consisted of standard academic tasks interspersed with periods of art, music, physical education and recreation, lunch, and group activities designed to develop positive peer interactions. Her behavior management program consisted of a point system which provided rewards for desirable behavior and academic productivity and a loss of points for disobeying class rules. Serious behavior problems, including aggression and prolonged property destruction, resulted in Jill being placed in a seclusion time-out room where she was required to stay until she was quiet for three consecutive minutes.
>
> As described previously, the functional assessment produced four hypotheses that related Jill's challenging behaviors to features of her curriculum. Therefore, the intervention that was developed involved a revision of her curriculum. Circumstances and activities that were associated with desirable behavior were increased and those that were associated with serious disruptions were removed as far as possible. This was accomplished by implementing the following guidelines. First, sessions that involved difficult academic or fine motor activities were scheduled to occur only for brief durations (e.g., 5 mins. or less), unless Jill asked to work for a longer time period. Second, the amount of work that was required was made very clear with visual as well as verbal cues. Third, large motor activities were scheduled frequently throughout the school day and interspersed among her other school work. Fourth, functional activities that led to concrete outcomes, and activities that reflected Jill's preferences were added in

dense proportions. These activities replaced the majority of workbook and practice tasks that had dominated her curriculum previously. Fifth, whenever possible, Jill was given a menu of options from which she could select her assignments. The choices that were made available were all of educationally appropriate activities from her IEP [Individualized Education Program].

These revisions in Jill's curriculum were extensive and, therefore, they were implemented first during the after-lunch hours only. After approximately one month, the revised curriculum was introduced to the morning hours as well. At that time, the intervention covered Jill's entire day. The principal outcomes associated with the curriculum revision are shown in Figure 4.

This figure presents the data for seriously disruptive behavior as well as for intervals with on-task responding. These results show that Jill exhibited no serious behavior challenges with the revised curriculum and that her desirable responding became stable at high levels. These changes occurred very rapidly and without any modification to the existing schedule of contingency management. Also, the changes maintained over 7 months of implementation. Because novel classroom activities often result in temporary reductions of undesirable behavior, it is important that maintenance of behavioral changes be monitored. Curricular modifications which address the variables maintaining the undesirable behavior generally result in long-term behavioral improvements. Thus, it is important to assess the effects of the intervention over time.

The changes in Jill's behavior were a function of the individualized curricular revisions that were implemented following the functional assessment process. A key point that demands emphasis is that the particular modifications that were made in Jill's curriculum could not have been identified without the functional assessment. If the same curricular modifications had been provided for another student, they might well have been ineffective.

A useful feature of Jill's case is that it raises a number of questions and considerations that are pertinent to this approach. One issue, for example, has to do with the amount of learning that Jill might have achieved (or missed) as a result of the extensive reworking of her curriculum. This is a legitimate concern because the new curriculum provided very little time for the workbooks or other lesson plans that the school system ordinarily scheduled for students in her educational program. However, the available data indicated that Jill demonstrated much greater progress in academic subjects than she had during the previous 3 years and that her age-equivalent composite score on the Vineland Adaptive Behavior Scales (Sparrow, Balla, & Cichetti, 1984) showed a gain of 21 months over the 7-month period. These gains are probably related to her improved behavior and motivation. Because she stopped displaying tantrums and other disruptive responses, she had much more time for active engagement with learning activities.

Another question has to do with the feasibility of such a high level of individualization. Jill's program was different from that of her peers and thus required an amount of one-to-one supervision that is beyond typical expectations even in most special education programs. The amount of personnel and resources that can be devoted to individualization in educational programs is

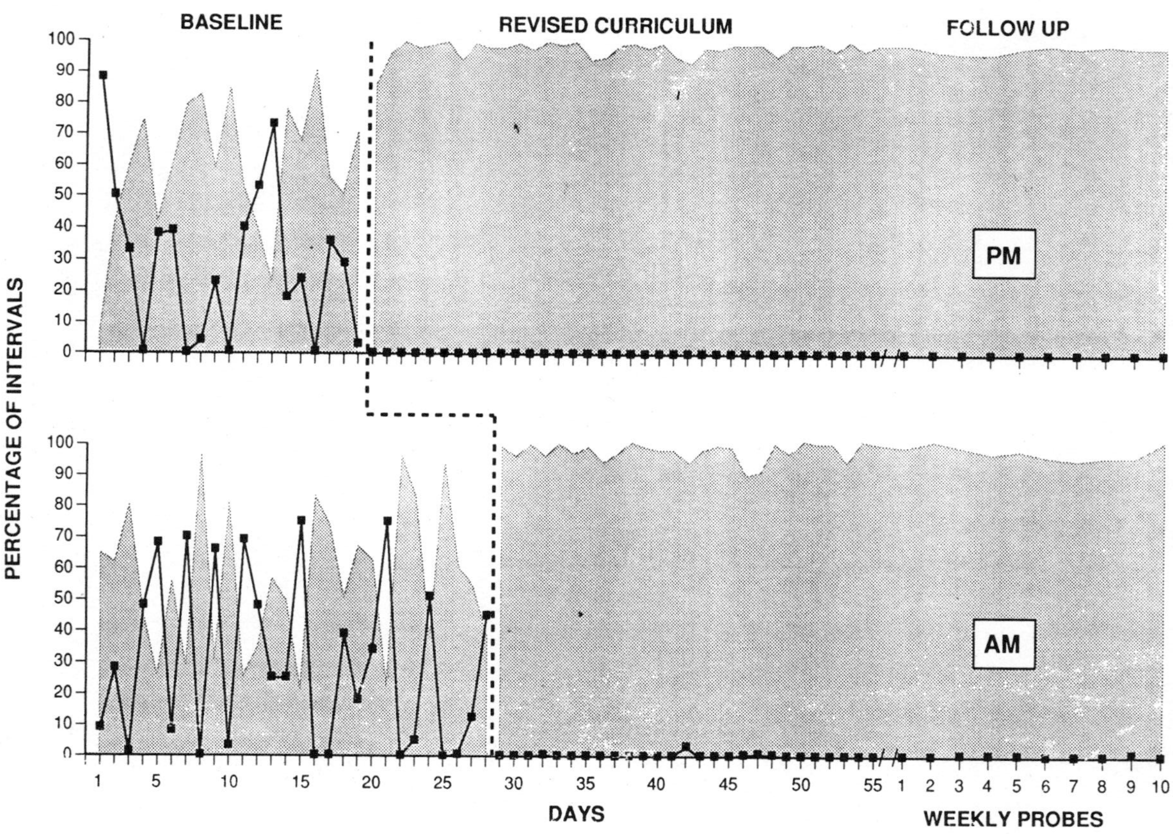

Figure 4.   Results of the multiple baseline analysis for on-task responding (shaded) and disruptive behavior (lines) across baseline, revised curriculum, and follow-up phases. Ordinate = percent intervals, abscissa = days (1–55), weekly probes (1–10). (From Dunlap, Kern-Dunlap, Clarke, & Robbins [1991]. Functional assessment, curricular revision, and severe behavior problems. *Journal of Applied Behavior Analysis, 24*, 387–397. Copyright © 1991 by The Society for The Experimental Analysis of Behavior; reprinted by permission.)

an unending source of debate and fiscal concern. In most cases, curricula that contain individualized components can be developed and implemented without adding resources to the classroom setting. In Jill's case, the severity and intransigence of the problem behaviors were so great that the curricular revisions were pervasive and demanded a commitment of one-to-one supervision during much of the school day. However, this did not require the addition of resources because the one-to-one instruction was already in place prior to the assessment and intervention process.

Another issue that relates to individualized curricula has to do with the student's ability to adjust and adapt to "the real world." Some educators may question the wisdom of highly individualized curricula because such individualization can be viewed, in some instances, as avoiding the demands and rigors that are expected in typical settings and in life in general. It may be argued that individualization may cater excessively to the student's idiosyncrasies and thereby limit the student's chances to learn to adapt to real-life circumstances. A counterargument is that the purpose of special education is to offer individualized curricula, that many students need and deserve individualized support, and that this need is particularly apparent when students fail to respond successfully in their classrooms. If learning does not occur and if challenging behaviors persist, then it should be clear that the curriculum, the instructional procedures, or some other factors are not appropriate. Altering key aspects of the program make it possible to redirect the student's experience so that it becomes positive and educational. When the problem behaviors are reduced to normative levels, then more typical expectations can be gradually introduced so that the student learns to cope with more standard circumstances. This may be desirable for many students, but other students, especially those with very severe disabilities, should always be provided with curricula that are highly individualized.

The support provided for Jill was intensive, and the revised curriculum deviated considerably from the school programs provided for her peers. Although the curriculum revisions resolved the problem of Jill's disruptive behavior, and although Jill displayed a positive effect and improved performance, it was nevertheless desirable to normalize some of the more individualized features of her program. Therefore, over the course of intervention, some changes were implemented. For example, after a few months, instead of offering her a choice of activities at the beginning of a session, she was asked to work on a teacher-assigned task for a brief period and then was given the choice menu. The teacher assignments were gradually extended so that choices were offered less frequently throughout the day. Similarly, the duration of difficult task sessions was gradually extended so that these sessions more closely approximated those of her peers. These modifications were introduced cautiously, with careful attention paid to the data and to Jill's effect. The primary objectives of preventing problem behaviors and promoting a positive and productive learning experience continued as overriding issues.

Although Jill's case provides one illustration of functional assessment and curricular revision, it is not a typical example. Jill's challenges were very severe and the procedures that were followed were time-consuming and exhaustive. The following two examples also depict the process that we have been describing, but they may be more representative.

Ryan was 6 years old and enrolled in a special education classroom for students with mild intellectual disabilities. He spent the latter part of every morning in a regular first grade classroom where he participated in art, music, and language activities. In the early morning and in the afternoons, his special education teacher provided instruction in academics, self-care, and other topics. Recently, the proportion and difficulty of academics had been increased because the school wanted to enroll Ryan for additional time in the regular classroom. His teacher was becoming concerned because over the past 2 months Ryan had developed a tendency to cry, yell, and rip his materials.

Fortunately, there had been no complaints from the regular education teachers, but Ryan's special educators were nevertheless planning to withdraw him temporarily from first grade participation in fear that his problem behaviors would jeopardize their school-wide mainstreaming program.

The school psychologist was consulted, and she initiated a functional assessment protocol. She interviewed the teacher, aide, and the regular education teacher, and she talked with Ryan's parents. She discovered that there had been no increase in problems in the mainstreamed environment and, in fact, Ryan was described as doing very well in that setting. The detailed questions that she asked of Ryan's special educators made it clear that the problems almost always occurred in the afternoon and typically during lessons on academics. Ryan's parents mentioned that although Ryan had been having difficulty falling asleep, they had not noticed any particular deterioration in his behavior. The school psychologist observed in the classroom for most of 2 days and saw no problems in the mornings, but did see fussing and restlessness in the afternoon, especially during the most intensive instruction. From the interviews and the direct observations, she developed an hypothesis that Ryan was tired and frustrated by the difficult academic lessons and that his disruptions served a protest function leading to escape.

A change in schedule was engineered in which Ryan's academic lessons were presented in the morning hours only, and self-care and other social activities consumed the afternoon. This change produced an immediate elimination of the disruptions. Ryan performed much more successfully on the academic lessons, and his teacher saw no more reason for concern regarding his deportment.

The final example that we present raises issues of designing curricula for children who are placed in specialized settings, but whose cognitive and social abilities indicate that special educational supports may not necessarily be needed in the future. For these children, in order to prepare for integration, it may be best to offer an educational program that does not deviate substantially from programs provided for children in regular classroom settings. The student in the following example demonstrated emotional and behavioral challenges that appeared to relate specifically to academic activities. The goal was to determine the particular characteristics of his curriculum that caused him the greatest difficulty and then to redesign his curriculum in a manner that would require little additional effort on the part of his teachers and little or no outside support. The following paragraphs describe how this was accomplished (Kern, Childs, Dunlap, Clarke, & Falk, 1993).

Eddie was an 11-year-old boy receiving special education services in a self-contained classroom for students described as having "severe emotional disturbance." He interacted well with adults and his peers, consistently scored in the high average range of intelligence, and was functioning at or above grade level in all academic subjects. In spite of his large repertoire of adaptive skills, he was referred for assessment and consultation services because he was unable to attend to and complete his classroom assignments, resulting in a great deal of stress, frustration, and episodes of uncontrollable crying and self-injury.

A functional assessment process was initiated by reviewing archival information, interviewing each of his teachers and his father, and conducting direct observations during his academic subjects. In addition, an interview was conducted with Eddie to solicit specific information regarding the features of academic tasks that he found difficult and the changes he thought could be made to help him be more productive in the classroom. This student interview proved to be extremely beneficial in developing hypotheses. Eddie was very verbal and was able to provide detailed information about the types of assignments he found difficult and the classroom conditions that were both distracting and helpful. With Eddie's assistance, the following five hypotheses were developed: 1) Eddie is more likely to be engaged in his work when activities do not require excessive amounts of writing. Eddie very clearly expressed that writing was difficult for him. This was also suggested in his school records. 2) Eddie is more likely to be engaged in academic tasks that require problem solving skills rather than drill and practice. This hypothesis reflected Eddie's report that he preferred to do "new" activities and learn "new" things, which was supported by direct observations. 3) Eddie is more likely to be engaged academically when provided with multiple brief tasks during an academic session rather than a single long task. Eddie reported that he likes his school work when he can finish his assignments. 4) Eddie is more likely to be engaged in academics when he is reminded to attend to his work instead of being left alone for the class session. During the student interview Eddie stated that he sometimes likes the activities he is presented, but that his mind often wanders to other topics. Eddie's records revealed that the use of a kitchen timer reminding him to stay on task had been a helpful intervention in the past. This strategy was currently being implemented, and teacher reports as well as direct observations suggested that it did result in increased engagement, at least for brief periods of time following the timer's bell. 5) Eddie is more likely to be academically engaged when he is given the option of working in a study carrel rather than being required to work in the presence of visual distractions. This hypothesis resulted from Eddie's suggestion alone.

Eddie's daily schedule required changing classes so that he had three different instructors for his academic subjects. In Eddie's case, we decided to test the hypotheses through experimental manipulations for several reasons. First, the hypotheses were based largely on Eddie's reports. Although supplementary information confirmed most of his reports, student interviews are not a traditional method of collecting functional assessment information. In addition, he had several different teachers for his academic subjects, and each had his or her own style of teaching and individual preferences. By conducting manipulations, it was possible to evaluate the relative strength of each of the identified variables as they related to engaged versus problem behavior. The information obtained was then used to develop individually tailored curriculum-based interventions, involving various combinations of the identified influential variables, to meet each teacher's individual style and needs.

After the hypotheses were formulated, each of Eddie's teachers selected one or two to manipulate in her or his class. Each of the five hypotheses was tested by his teachers across five or six school days. During the manipulations, direct observation data were collected. In addition, following each session Eddie was asked to rate, on a Likert-type scale, how much he liked the session, and to describe what he liked or disliked about the session. The manipulations as well as Eddie's evaluations supported all of the hypotheses. Although some variables were more distinct than others, each of the manipulated variables resulted in differences in the rates of engaged behavior, self-injury, and crying. The information from the experimental manipulations resulted in a hierarchical list of variables that could be modified to develop a revised curricular program.

When the list of variables associated with the presence or absence of desirable behavior was created, the teachers were again convened to develop an intervention. Each teacher was more or less comfortable with making specific modifications suggested by the five manipulations. For example, Eddie's math teacher showed interest in modifying the content of his lessons so that only a short period of time would be spent completing drill or practice problems. His spelling teacher, however, was less comfortable manipulating the content of Eddie's lessons, but was interested in making other modifications such as requiring less of his work to be completed in a written fashion. The teachers and consultants worked together to design an individualized intervention package for each of the three academic subjects in which Eddie was having difficulty. Each intervention differed slightly depending on the teacher's preferences. For example, in spelling his typical weekly schedule prior to intervention was to spend Monday and Tuesday writing his twenty spelling words three times each. Wednesday and Thursday were spent completing workbook pages. Following the manipulations, several curricular modifications were made. First, rather than completing only one activity in his 40-minute spelling period, his weekly work was divided so that he completed three separate activities each day. Also, instead of writing his words, he was given the option of spelling them orally into a language master or tape recorder. When exercises required a large amount of writing, such as completing a story, he was allowed to use a computer. During work requiring writing, to encourage him to develop an awareness of his engaged behavior, he was taught to self-monitor. In math, modifications were made so that practice exercises were required only to provide evidence of material mastery. This generally took only 10 or 15 min[utes] at the beginning of the period. The remainder of the period was spent completing problem solving or application types of activities. He also self-monitored his engaged behavior throughout the math period.

The interventions designed for Eddie resulted in significantly increased rates of engaged behaviors and reduced rates of self-injury and crying. The menu of options identified through the several manipulations allowed an effective intervention to be created that accommodated each teacher's specific teaching style and that each teacher thought could be easily implemented within the ongoing structure of his or her own classroom. The curricular modifications that were made required very little additional preparation time on the part of his teachers. In addition, the modifications did not result in a curriculum that deviated much from that of typical classrooms. Some of the procedures, such as the self-monitoring, were selected because they placed little burden on teachers and could be faded easily prior to integrating him into a typical classroom.

Eddie's academic progress is being carefully monitored to make sure that gains continue. Thus far, his rate of daily work completion has increased five times, and his test grades still reflect high levels of achievement. He continues to complete daily activity ratings, which indicate that he is satisfied with his current curriculum.

CONCLUSION

In this chapter, we have described a model for reducing, and preventing, challenging behaviors in the classroom through functional assessment and curricular modification. The critical outcomes are that specific variables associated with problem and nonproblem behavior are identified through the functional assessment process, and curricular modifications are derived logically from the assessment information. One of the case studies demonstrated a lengthy process that required major curricular modifications. The other individuals required only a brief assessment phase, minor classroom modifications, and little to no additional support. The latter examples are representative of the majority of cases to which this approach might be applied.

Several issues related to curricular redesign should be emphasized at this point. First, it is important to note that assessment and modification of curricular variables must be viewed as only one component of a comprehensive plan of behavioral support (Dunlap, Ferro, & dePerczel, in press; Horner et al., 1990). Many challenging behaviors are multidimensional and complex, and, thus, must be addressed from a variety of lifestyle and educational perspectives. Although some children's behavioral challenges may be specific to a single setting or circumstance, and although curricular manipulations may fully resolve certain problems, these circumstances should be viewed as the exception rather than the rule. Second, the causes and correlates of an individual's behavioral challenges are likely to change over time in association with physiological and environmental changes. Thus, curricular changes, like all other program components, may be effective at one point in time and ineffective at some later point. For this reason, it is important to view functional assessment and the individualization of curricula as an ongoing endeavor.

REFERENCES

Bailey, J.S., & Pyles, D.A.M. (1989). Behavioral diagnostics. In E. Cipani (Ed.), *The treatment of severe behavior problems* (pp. 85–106). Washington, DC: American Association on Mental Retardation.

Bijou, S.W., Peterson, R.F., & Ault, M.H. (1968). A method to integrate descriptive and experimental field studies at the level of data and empirical concepts. *Journal of Applied Behavior Analysis, 1*, 175–191.

Carr, E.G., & Durand, V.M. (1985). Reducing behavior problems through functional communication training. *Journal of Applied Behavior Analysis, 18*, 111–126.

Donnellan, A.M., Mirenda, P.L., Mesaros, R.A., & Fassbender, L.L. (1984). Analyzing the communicative functions of aberrant behavior. *Journal of The Association for Persons with Severe Handicaps, 9*, 201–212.

Dunlap, G., Ferro, J., & dePerczel, M. (in press). Nonaversive behavioral intervention in the community. In E. Cipani & F. Spooner (Eds.), *Curricular and instructional approaches for persons with severe handicaps*. New York: Allyn & Bacon.

Dunlap, G., Kern-Dunlap, L., Clarke, S., & Robbins, F.R. (1991). Functional assessment, curricular revision, and severe behavior problems. *Journal of Applied Behavior Analysis, 24*, 387–397.

Durand, V.M. (1990). *Functional communication training: An intervention program for severe behavior problems*. New York: Guilford Press.

Durand, V.M., & Crimmins, D.B. (1988). Identifying the variables maintaining self-injurious behavior. *Journal of Autism and Developmental Disorders, 8*, 607–626.

Dyer, K., Dunlap, G., & Winterling, V. (1990). The effects of choice making on the serious problem behaviors of students with developmental disabilities. *Journal of Applied Behavior Analysis, 23*, 515–524.

Horner, R.H., & Budd, C.M. (1985). Teaching manual sign language to a nonverbal student: Generalization of sign use and collateral reduction of maladaptive behavior. *Education and Training of the Mentally Retarded, 20*, 39–47.

Horner, R.H., Dunlap, G., Koegel, R.L., Carr, E.G., Sailor, W., Anderson, J., Albin, R.W., & O'Neill, R.E. (1990). Toward a technology of "nonaversive" behavioral support. *Journal of The Association for Persons with Severe Handicaps, 15*, 125–132.

Horner, R.H., Sprague, J.R., & Flannery, K.B. (in press). Building functional curricula for students with severe intellectual disabilities and severe problem behaviors. In R. Van Houten & S. Axelrod (Eds.), *Behavioral analysis and treatment*. New York: Plenum.

Iwata, B.A., Vollmer, T.R., & Zarcone, J.H. (1990). The experimental (functional) analysis of behavior disorders: Methodology, applications, and limitations. In A.C. Repp & N.N. Singh (Eds.), *Perspectives on the use of nonaversive and aversive interventions for persons with developmental disabilities* (pp. 301–330). Sycamore, IL: Sycamore Publishing Co.

Kern, L., Childs, K.E., Dunlap, G., Clarke, S., & Falk, G.D. (1993). *Using assessment-based curricular intervention to improve the classroom behavior of a student with emotional and behavioral challenges*. Manuscript submitted for publication.

Kern-Dunlap, L., Clarke, S., & Dunlap, G. (1990). *Increasing the "meaningfulness" in curriculum content to reduce problem behaviors in a severely emotionally disturbed student.* Paper presented at the tenth annual convention of the Florida Association for Behavior Analysis (FABA), Orlando.

Mace, F.C., Hock, M.L., Lalli, J.S., West, B.J., Belfiore, P., Pinter, E., & Brown, D.K. (1988). Behavioral momentum in the treatment of noncompliance. *Journal of Applied Behavior Analysis, 21,* 123–141.

McAfee, J.K. (1987). Classroom density and the aggressive behavior of handicapped children. *Education and Treatment of Children, 10,* 134–145.

O'Neill, R.E., Dunlap, G., & Horner, R.H. (1991). *Functional analysis and functional assessment: The need for standardized terminology and criteria for application.* Unpublished manuscript.

O'Neill, R.E., Horner, R.H., Albin, R.W., Storey, K., & Sprague, J.R. (1990). *Functional analysis of problem behavior: A practical assessment guide.* Sycamore, IL: Sycamore Publishing Co.

Singer, G.H.S., Singer, J., & Horner, R.H. (1987). Using pretask requests to increase the probability of compliance for students with severe disabilities. *Journal of The Association for Persons with Severe Handicaps, 12*(40), 287–291.

Sparrow, S.S, Balla, D.A., & Cichetti, D.V. (1984). *Vineland Adaptive Behavior Scales.* Circle Pines, MN: American Guidance Service.

Touchette, P.E., MacDonald, R.F., & Langer, S.N. (1985). A scatterplot for identifying stimulus control of problem behavior. *Journal of Applied Behavior Analysis, 18,* 343–351.

Wacker, D.P., Wiggins, B., Fowler, M., & Berg, W.K. (1988). Training students with profound or multiple handicaps to make requests via microswitches. *Journal of Applied Behavior Analysis, 21,* 331–343.

Wahler, R.G., & Graves, M.G. (1983). Setting events in social networks: Ally or enemy in child behavior therapy. *Behavior Therapy, 14,* 449–463.

Weeks, M., & Gaylord-Ross, R. (1981). Task difficulty and aberrant behavior in severely handicapped students. *Journal of Applied Behavior Analysis, 14,* 19–36.

Winterling, V., Dunlap, G., & O'Neill, R.E. (1987). The influence of task variation on the aberrant behavior of autistic students. *Education and Treatment of Children, 10,* 105–119.

9

Addressing Socially Motivated Challenging Behaviors by Establishing Communicative Alternatives
Basics of a General-Case Approach

Rob O'Neill and Joe Reichle

ONE IMPORTANT PROACTIVE INTERVENTION STRATEGY in the management of challenging behavior involves replacing a socially unacceptable behavior with a socially acceptable alternative. Establishing communicative forms that are functionally equivalent to challenging behavior has represented a valid intervention option since the mid-1970s, but recently has gained increasing attention from researchers and practitioners. In this chapter, we provide an overview of a variety of issues and factors in interventions that focus on establishing communicative alternatives that are functionally equivalent to repertoires of challenging behavior.

STIMULUS CONTROL
OF COMMUNICATIVE BEHAVIOR

One consistent theme of communication intervention research with individuals who experience severe developmental disabilities has been a concern with establishing a communicative repertoire that can be used effectively across a range of stimulus variables. Traditionally, investigations of generalized

Preparation of this chapter was supported in part by Cooperative Agreement No. G0087C0234 from The National Institute on Disability and Rehabilitation Research, U.S. Department of Education (Research and Training Center on Community-Referenced Behavior Management). Points of view or opinions expressed in this chapter do not necessarily represent official positions of the U.S. Department of Education or the National Institute on Disability and Rehabilitation Research.

communicative behavior compare usage across a variety of objects, persons, and settings that were not directly addressed during acquisition opportunities. In each of these aspects of generalization, the learner must first recognize particular stimulus events as constituting opportunities for a particular behavior; stimulus generalization is the dimension being measured. Second, he or she must decide if the use of communication, of all possible actions that can be taken, is the most efficient option. Finally, if a communicative behavior is selected, he or she must determine which particular member(s) from his or her communicative repertoire best matches the stimulus situation. For example, if a learner wants a window opened and is physically capable of opening it, it may be more efficient for him to open it himself than to request that someone else open it. In this example, both opening the window oneself and requesting that someone else open the window constitute members of the same response class because both result in the same outcome. When an individual has several different behaviors within the same response class, subtleties across a range of discriminative stimuli and reinforcement characteristics provide the basis for determining which behavior will be most efficient, and the dimension being measured is response generalization.

The efficiency with which any given behavior achieves a social function appears to be especially important for persons who engage in challenging behaviors (Carr, 1988; Doss & Reichle, 1989, 1991; Horner & Day, 1991; Horner, Sprague, O'Brien & Heathfield, 1990; Mace & Roberts, chap. 6, this volume; Sundberg, 1987). Mace and Roberts (chap. 6, this volume) have operationalized efficiency in terms of: 1) quality of reinforcement, 2) immediacy of reinforcement, 3) physical effort required, and 4) schedule of reinforcement. Determining the efficiency of a given behavior becomes particularly difficult when one considers that relatively modest changes in environmental or speaking partner characteristics may significantly alter the efficiency of a particular communicative response. For example, touching a graphic symbol signifying a request may be very efficient when an individual already has the attention of a listener, but it is very inefficient when an individual does not have the listener's attention. Alternatively, the loudness with which a speaking partner's utterance is produced may significantly influence a learner's propensity to tantrum.

With individuals who engage in challenging behavior, interventionists have demonstrated that a socially acceptable communicative form can replace socially motivated challenging behavior (e.g., Carr & Durand, 1985). To date, interventionists have not focused on teaching learners the conditional use of each of several different socially appropriate actions that will achieve the same social function. However, most agree that doing so would maximize the efficiency of the learner's communicative repertoire. For example, when a learner desires an item that is nearby, reaching for it without using a person as a mediator may be more efficient than requesting the listener obtain the object for him or her. In other situations, such as when items are not immediately accessible, directing a request to another individual may be most efficient. On other occasions, previous learning history may suggest to the learner that neither requests nor reaching and obtaining an item constitutes an acceptable response. In these instances, the individual must postpone attempting to obtain the item.

Establishing, maintaining, and generalizing a set of conditionally used communication skills that are functionally equivalent and equally or more efficient than existing repertoires of challenging behavior have become very important components in maximizing community integration opportunities for those who engage in challenging behaviors (Bellamy, Newton, LeBaron, & Horner, 1990). It has been only recently that interventionists have begun to grapple with the development of an explicit instructional technology to establish repertoires of communicative behavior and other socially acceptable alternatives that are functionally equivalent to repertoires of challenging behavior (Carr, 1988). The purposes of this chapter are to describe a framework for developing repertoires of functional communicative responses that are functionally equivalent and more efficient than existing repertoires of challenging behavior. We briefly summarize some of the major factors that influence effective instruction, such as the motivation of the challenging behavior and the saliency of the training stimuli. We advocate the use of instructional strategies that treat the issue of stimulus and response generalization as an important aspect of designing acquisition procedures. An inherent thread woven throughout this chapter is the applicability of a technology of general-case instruction to the intervention process.

Our discussion begins with describing samples from the range of stimulus characteristics that may influence an individual's propensity to use communicative utterances. Next, we address characteristics of a variety of responses that an individual may use to achieve the same social function. Subsequently, we discuss the interrelationship of stimulus and response classes. Finally, we describe general case instructional strategies that we believe can be applied to the challenge of establishing a communicative repertoire that competes with problem behavior.

Some Characteristics of Stimuli
that Occasion Communicative Behaviors

A great deal of clinical and research attention has been focused on the occurrence of communication responses across persons not involved in training (e.g., Matson, Sevin, Fridley, & Love, 1990). Such environmental characteristics have often been the focus of strategies employing multiple exemplars to achieve generalization (Handelman, 1979, 1981). Whereas this approach has the basic goal of making certain stimulus characteristics irrelevant (e.g., gender, height, weight, ethnicity, wall color, furniture) while emphasizing others, this work has not always involved careful consideration in choosing and arranging the persons and setting conditions involved in training. That is, such research has often involved the use of a few persons and/or settings in probing for the occurrence of responding in untrained situations. These situations often appear to be chosen somewhat arbitrarily rather than through consideration of the range of relevant and irrelevant stimulus characteristics that need to be addressed. These include more concrete and discrete stimulus dimensions (e.g., height, gender), as well as less accessible setting factors such as physical or emotional state, thirst, and fatigue.

Kaczmarek (1990) described a number of listener variables that might influence a learner's propensity to emit a communicative utterance. These variables are important if the interventionist is to establish maximally discriminable opportunities to produce communicative behavior during the early phases of communicative intervention. Furthermore, if it is important that the learner emit his or her new communicative repertoire under less discriminable circumstances, it may be important that the interventionist purposely address aspects of listener state that may be less apt to recruit learner communicative behavior. Listener variables that are often cited as important to consider in establishing an initial communicative repertoire include listener proximity, listener attention, listener familiarity, and prior listener actions with respect to the speaker.

Listener Proximity and Attention

The proximity of a listener clearly influences a learner's propensity to engage in communicative behavior. For example, if a salesperson is standing nearby, a consumer may be far more likely to make an informational request. One is increasingly apt to greet an individual as he or she approaches closer. Similarly, learners are more apt to engage in requests when a listener is nearby than when a listener is proximally more distant (Reichle, 1985).

Visual regard of the listener interacts significantly with physical proximity of the listener in occasioning a learner's communicative behavior. Reichle (1985) examined the role that proximity and eye gaze had on a learner's propensity to engage in a communicative request. The greatest proportion of requests were made when the learner was in close physical proximity and the listner was visually attending to the learner. The fewest communicative requests were produced when the listener was across the room (far away) and not attending to the learner. Considering the status of the listener may be particularly important in thinking about augmentative or alternative communication systems. For example, if a learner is being taught to utilize a nonelectronic communication aid, it is important that the learner have a strategy to recruit the listener's attention. Otherwise the probability decreases that a learner's communicative attempt will be acted upon. In many instances, the learner may need a separate response to obtain the listener's attention as a first step in emitting a more explicit communicative utterance.

Listener Familiarity and Prior Relationship with Speaker

The familiarity and status of the listener clearly influence communicative interactions. Children are far more apt to engage in communicative acts with familiar individuals for a number of reasons. Among these is the fact that individuals who are familiar are apt to have a far greater number of shared topics about which to communicate. However, even though a learner may be extremely familiar with an individual, this does not ensure that communicative exchanges will occur.

Several years ago, we observed an individual who engaged in tangible-obtaining motivated tantruming only in the presence of his mother. Upon closer observation, it became obvious that his mother would oblige a high proportion of his requests for snacks. During instances in which snacks were refused, the learner usually tantrumed. A high proportion of these tantrums ultimately culminated in the mother providing a snack. Alternatively, the child's father did not believe in providing snacks between meals. Consequently, the child's requests did not get reinforced. If the child tantrumed, the father removed himself from the environment. Over time, a history developed in which the child interacted more frequently with his mother and less frequently with his father.

Number of Prospective Listeners

Some learners do less well in communicating their wants and needs using socially acceptable strategies when they are in large groups of listeners. Although there may be a variety of reasons for this, we have found that large groups tend to produce more noise and general confusion. Some learners find noise or "environmental business" a setting event for challenging behavior. In other instances, large groups of individuals provide the learner with greater competition for attention.

However, increasingly, interventionists and researchers are attending to the influence that speaking partners' immediate actions and history of actions may have on a learner's propensity to engage in socially motivated challenging behavior. Scrutinizing the influence that a listener's actions may have on challenging behavior is critical if intervention targets are broadened to include not only learner behavior, but communicative partner behavior as well.

The Relationship Between Symbols and Their Referents

Many responses are influenced significantly by objects or properties of objects (Skinner, 1957). Learners need to be able to respond appropriately (e.g., producing the vocabulary item "apple") to the range of examples that may be part of a stimulus class. Apples may be large or small, green or red or yellow, have stems or not; yet, they are all apples. Such variation in identifying examples is important to consider in teaching appropriate responses. We know that among individuals who are developing normally, there is a propensity to engage in several distinctively different types of generalization errors. For the most part, these errors result from a range of teaching examples that are either too narrow or too diverse to allow the learner to discriminate relevant perceptual dimensions of referents.

Overextension (overgeneralization) can be defined as applying a new vocabulary to a larger class of items or events than the adult-accepted definition would include (e.g., calling a large dog a horse). Alternatively, underextension occurs when children fail to extend the use of a new vocabulary item to the full range of its definition (i.e., calling a collie a dog but not referring to a small terrier as a dog). Interestingly, with the same referent, the learner may engage in both overgeneralization and undergeneralization. Generalization errors may represent the learner's failure to sample a sufficiently large array of examples that include perceptual features that both should and should not be considered relevant to a particular referent class. Among persons with severe disabilities, generalization errors may be fueled by stimulus overselectivity (Lovaas, Koegel, & Schreibman, 1979; Mullins & Rincover, 1985). Learners engaging in overselectivity appear to direct their attention to only a subset of features that should control responding. Unless the learner can match objects and events with their corresponding vocabulary items, it will be extremely difficult to establish a communicative repertoire as an efficient strategy to mediate social events.

The Specificity of Symbols

Traditionally, vocabulary selection criteria adhere to those suggested as a result of studying typical communicative development. For example, Bloom and Lahey (1974) suggested teaching vocabulary that represent an intermediate level of specificity. For example, in the hierarchy collie/dog/animal, dog would be taught first. It could be argued that this level allows the learner sufficient specific vocabulary to communicate in a large range of social contexts while at the same time being sufficiently explicit to minimize the communicative burden on the listener.

Keogh and Reichle (1985) proposed that vocabulary should be as explicit as necessary to maximize communicative efficiency. For example, learning the vocabulary item "coffee" may be sufficiently explicit for most individuals regardless of context. However, learning "soda" would not be sufficient to order food at a fast-food restaurant. In this environment, it is necessary to know the type (and size) of the item requested. Table 1 outlines relative advantages and disadvantages of highly general, compared to highly explicit, vocabulary as initial communicative forms.

Table 1. Advantages and disadvantages of general and explicit vocabulary applied to teaching communicative requests

General vocabulary	Explicit vocabulary
Advantages	
• Addresses the possibility that an individual might become satiated on an item represented by a single explicit vocabulary item	• Places minimal communicative burden on listener
• Increases number of situations in which intervention can occur	• Increases learners' accuracy in producing messages
• Addresses the possibility that specific items identified as highly preferred at program onset have lost their appeal	
Disadvantages	
• Places a greater communicative burden on the listener	• Satiation on a particular item may limit intervention opportunities
• Requires that multiple referents for a vocabulary item be identified from the outset of intervention to insure generalization	• Settings that support intervention opportunities may be more limited

Explicit vocabulary best serves the learner in community settings, and lessens the communicative burden placed on the listener. However, sometimes conditions may mitigate against using highly explicit vocabulary. Often, these conditions involve the status of reinforcers during the establishment of an initial requesting repertoire. Among learners who require large numbers of teaching opportunities to establish discrimination skills, satiation and reinforcer shifts may necessitate the initial use of a more general symbol. For example, consider an individual who likes a particular diet soda but after several sips desires no more. For this individual, there may be a small window of opportunity for the interventionist to implement meaningful instructional opportunities. In other instances, a shift in reinforcer preferences may render a previously explicit symbol relatively useless. A learner who found a particular brand of soda to be a preferred beverage may sample a new soft drink. Having done so, the learner establishes a preference for the new beverage over the formerly preferred brand. Individuals who are candidates for a gestural mode communication system may receive more general vocabulary introduction from the outset of instruction. For example, it is difficult to contemplate in the gestural mode how an interventionist would represent the particular diet soda. In the graphic mode, the particular soda could be represented by using a product logo. Establishing an initial repertoire of vocabulary among learners with severe developmental disabilities may require a substantial period of time. If a very explicit symbol is selected that cannot sustain the learner's interest over that period of time, the intervention program may be placed in jeopardy.

Decisions regarding the characteristics of the spoken vocabulary, gesture, or graphic symbol that is used to represent a given referent will directly influence the learner's acquisition of vocabulary. To date, there has been relatively little effort focused on examining the specificity with which to introduce an initial repertoire of vocabulary. Furthermore, the majority of discussion of this topic has focused on teaching an initial requesting repertoire (Reichle & Sigafoos, 1991b). There is a critical need to empirically scrutinize the role that vocabulary specificity may play in the acquisition and maintenance of an initial communication repertoire.

The Relationship Between Symbols and Communicative Functions

Communicative behavior may be produced for a variety of reasons (e.g., to request, to provide information, to protest). One major characteristic of communicative behavior is that individual words may serve different communicative functions. For example, an individual who has referential grasp of the word "apple" may produce the word to request one. Alternatively, he or she may produce the word "apple" simply to comment to a listener about an ongoing or previous event with no intent of requesting one. There is a growing body of literature suggesting that individuals with developmental disabilities may not necessarily generalize the use of a vocabulary item taught exclusively in the context of a single communicative function (Cipani, 1988; Sundberg, 1980). This functional independence between pragmatic functions has been demonstrated with typical preschool children (LaMarre & Holland, 1985), as well as with individuals with severe developmental disabilities (Hall & Sundberg, 1987; Sigafoos, Reichle, Doss, Hall, & Pettitt, 1990; Romski, Sevcik, & Pate, 1988; Sigafoos, Doss, & Reichle, 1989).

The difficulty that some learners have in generalizing the use of a vocabulary item across several different pragmatic functions may have significant implications for the establishment of an initial communication repertoire. If it is important that a learner be able to use a given word to express several distinctly different pragmatic functions, we believe that the interventionist must consider using this contextual range in the teaching examples that are chosen for instruction.

The Relationship Between Social Function and Communicative Function

Generally, basic pragmatic classes such as requesting, rejecting, and providing information are thought of as an explanation of why the individual produced a communicative utterance. However, in the case of replacing challenging behavior with communicative alternatives, it may be necessary to be more explicit in describing the social motivation behind a substantial portion of the learner's communicative utterances.

On any given occasion, a single communicative behavior may be produced to obtain either positive or negative reinforcement. For example, an individual who is learning to become a building custodian may request assistance in order to escape a particular unpleasant component of a job that is otherwise quite acceptable. Alternatively, the same individual may request assistance in opening a package of gum that is difficult to unwrap in order to chew a stick (positive reinforcement).

Unless both of the instances just described are addressed by the interventionist, some learners may not perceive both stimulus events as discriminative stimuli for the production of a communicatively acceptable response of requesting assistance. For example, among children with moderate intellectual disabilities, Reichle (1985) reported that learners who were taught to request assistance to obtain desired items readily generalized their newly acquired requesting assistance skills to new objects, settings, and listeners, representing desirable outcomes. However, generalization was not observed in situations in which requesting assistance could have been used to escape, avoid, or postpone an undesired event. Learners who were taught to request assistance to escape less desired events readily generalized to events that previously had not involved escape responses. In the preceding example, it seems clear that requests for assistance can occur to address very different social motivations. Consequently, addressing only communicative function categories such as requesting may not adequately address the range of social functions that a communicative utterance needs to address.

One possible solution to the generalization difficulties just described involves establishing a single pragmatic function to serve two discretely different social functions. Wacker (1992) suggested teaching escape-motivated learners to request access to tangibles as a strategy to gain respite from work, instead of engaging in aggression to achieve the same social function. Additionally, the same requests for tangibles could be taught at times when the learner was not seeking escape but was acutely interested in obtaining an available desired object. By targeting a single pragmatic function, a single communicative form may be taught as both escape and tangible motivated. Golonka, Wacker, Derby, Plagmann, and Sasso (1992) have further suggested that, even if the learner is primarily escape motivated, establishing a requesting response as an escape mechanism can serve to increase the range and frequency of opportunities that can be used to establish the topography of new communicative utterances, while at the same time lessening the discriminative demands on the learner.

The rationale for the suggestion of Golonka et al. (1992) appears increasingly practical when the potentially overlapping nature of positive and negative reinforcement paradigms is considered (see Iwata, 1987; Michael, 1975). Depending on the perspective, the delivery of a raincoat during a cloudburst contingent on the learner's request can be viewed either as an example of positive or negative reinforcement. Initially, by selecting at least some teaching examples of escape-motivated behavior that can be satisfied by a socially acceptable utterance to obtain a positive reinforcer, it may be possible to increase the probability of generalized use of a pragmatic function across two different social functions.

The available evidence suggests that an analysis of communicative functions may not always sufficiently address the underlying social motivation for a particular communicative behavior. Consequently, interventionists may identify a range of teaching examples that are far too narrowly focused to result in functional use of the new communicative behavior. In our opinion, addressing the communicative function requires careful consideration of the social functions of utterances. At a practical level, we believe that it is quite possible to teach a communicative function that concurrently addresses both an escape-motivation and a reinforcer-obtaining (item or attention) function.

The Status of the Referent in the Environment

Even if learners have acquired the ability to accurately respond to stimulus classes based on perceptual features of referents and are able to match relevant vocabulary and pragmatic functions to these referents, there are a variety of other variables that may limit the generalized use of the newly acquired communicative repertoire. As mentioned earlier, some of these variables involve the learner's relationship with a listener, while other variables involve the specific relationship between the learner and the referent that is the focus of a communicative behavior.

Referent Visibility and Proximity

The position of a perceived item in the environment may influence the learner's propensity to engage in a communicative utterance. For example, young, typically developing children have a propensity to talk about events that are present and visible from the time of their first words through their second birthday. Interestingly, few investigators have examined the influence that referent visibility may have on a learner's likelihood of emitting a particular utterance. Carr and Kologinsky (1983) demonstrated that for some learners to initiate an object request, the item had to be visible. Although personal experience suggests that much the same is true in addressing other communicative functions, such as commenting or rejecting, there are few empirical data that bear directly on this issue.

In some instances, the referent itself need not be visible as long as some item associated with the referent is visible. For example, while walking down the street, a learner may observe a candy bar wrapper lying on the ground. Upon seeing it, the learner immediately requests the item. In these instances, it is likely that the wrapper has been paired a number of times with the delivery of the desired item, candy, and, as a result, has come to be closely associated with it. Thus, stimulus generalization occurs when stimuli associated with the desired item, or reinforcer, are perceived (Halle & Holt, 1991).

To prevent over generalization, it is critical that learning opportunities be provided for both irrelevant and relevant stimulus conditions. Otherwise, the learner may display the communicative response at incorrect times following training.

Many learners with severe developmental disabilities appear to have significant deficiencies in their ability to visually explore the environment around them. For these individuals, the proximity of salient referents may represent an important aspect of the environment in promoting a communicative emission. Karlan (personal communication, May 1991) observed that among persons with severe physical disabilities, the influence of referent positioning may be particularly important. When individuals spend a significant portion of their day lying supine or on their sides, exploring their environment may be significantly more difficult.

Although we suspect that the closer proximity of referents to learners increases the likelihood of a communicative behavior, we also know that close proximity presents a discriminative challenge to the learner. When desired referents are very close, it may become more efficient to reach and take the item rather than requesting it. Similarly, with nearby referents, the learner may be more apt to pick up and show an item to another rather than engage in a communicative behavior.

These examples demonstrate just how difficult the training of functional request-motivated responses can be. Enough clear examples of the item must be intermixed with irrelevant aspects of those items to promote desired generalization. To be functional, the position of the items should be distanced to provide a proper context for using the communicative response. Finally, as discussed by Stokes, Osnes, and DaVerne (chap. 12, this volume), the correspondence between the requesting response and the item must be established. The point of note here is that the initial training received by an individual may substantially influence subsequent generalization and maintenance. Thus, determining just how to set up a training program is no simple task.

The Influence of a Predictable Routine on the Stimulus Control of Referents

As Halle and Spradlin (chap. 5, this volume) discuss, predictable chains of events can serve as natural salient cues for challenging behavior and socially acceptable communicative responses. In many activities, there may be few permanent products that can serve as natural instructional prompts. Consequently, establishing chains of predictable temporal events may represent an important component of comprehensive communication intervention strategy. For example, at the conclusion of a meal, young children often request a dessert, although none is present. Alternatively, when going in the direction of the dentist's office, a learner may begin protesting although neither the dentist, the drill, nor office are visible. Undoubtedly, children learn to respond to chains of antecedents that, in the past, have led to a visible stimulus that occasions a response.

The influence that predictable chains of antecedents have on the acquisition of an initial communication repertoire has been studied in the context of developing strategies for teaching communicative responses, particularly requests (mands). The procedures have received different labels, including "interrupted chain strategies" (Hunt & Goetz, 1988) and "conditioned establishing operations" (Michael, 1989; Sigafoos et al., 1989; Sigafoos et al., 1990; Sundberg, 1987). The basic strategy involves initially working with a learner and going through an activity routine that results in a reinforcing outcome (e.g., going through the steps of making soup, using an opener to open a bottle of soda). Then, certain steps or items of the activity are blocked or removed in order to provide a motivating opportunity for the learner to produce a communicative response. For example, a learner may be given a dish of pudding without a spoon to provide an opportunity to request that item.

As mentioned, these procedures exemplify a process involving what are known as establishing operations or setting events (Leigland, 1984; Michael, 1988; Wahler & Fox, 1981). While there is some continuing conceptual and methodological confusion around these terms, Michael (1989) has discussed establishing operations as events that function to change the value of particular reinforcers at a given point in time. These value changes influence the stimulus control over responses that typically produce different relevant reinforcers. If a learner has just consumed a 12-ounce soda, its immediate reinforcing value may be significantly reduced, along with the probability that the learner will request more.

There are a variety of examples of such relations. As described above, interrupted chains are presumed to be effective, in part, because they manipulate the reinforcing value of certain steps or items, thereby increasing the probability that a learner will produce a communicative response. Establishing operations may play a significant role in determining whether or not challenging behaviors or socially acceptable behaviors will occur in particular situations (Horner, O'Neill, & Flannery, 1993). A learner may typically respond in a positive and cooperative manner when asked to assist in a domestic chore such as mowing the lawn. However, if earlier during the day the learner has experienced a high rate of similar demands (i.e., doing laundry, sweeping, washing dishes), the value of a break or rest may be very high, while the value of staff praise for completing a task may be very low. This would lead to an increased probability of behaviors that result in avoiding or escaping the task (e.g., aggressive or self-injurious behavior). Of course, what we would prefer to happen in such situations is for the learner to use a more appropriate communicative response (e.g., signing "break"). Whether or not this occurs will depend on the relative effectiveness and efficiency of the problem and appropriate responses, and the learner's history of training and experience (see sections below on relations between stimulus and response classes). Teaching alternative responses is one strategy for reducing the impact of establishing operations or setting events on a learner's behavior. Others include preventing or reducing the occurrence of particular problematic establishing operations or events (e.g., monitoring and reducing demands, avoiding states of great fatigue/hunger/thirst, preventing negative interactions with classmates).

These preceding examples illustrate how important it may be to track sequences of stimuli, responses, and consequences across a learner's day. This is important with regard to assessing the motivational properties of particular situations that provide opportunities for the occasion of challenging behaviors or appropriate communicative responses. Additionally, identifying sequences of stimuli may provide important information useful in identifying natural instructional prompts that can be used in teaching alternatives to challenging behavior. That may mean establishing several different forms of social responses that are functionally equivalent, although their efficiency is specific to a particular constellation of stimulus events.

SOME CHARACTERISTICS OF RESPONSE CLASSES

Carr (1988) defined a response class as "a group of two or more topographically different behaviors, all of which have the same effect on the environment" (p. 222). Identifying response classes among individuals who engage in challenging behavior has a significant impact on the communicative repertoire selected. If several different challenging behaviors express the same social motivation, a single communicative function may be able to replace all of the challenging topographies. Conversely, if each of several different behavioral forms serve different social functions, it makes intuitive sense that more than a single communicative form will need to be established.

For example, suppose that a functional assessment demonstrates that an individual screams to obtain attention and hits and bites to escape task demands. Instructional logic might suggest teaching a socially acceptable attention-getting strategy (to compete with screaming) and a socially acceptable protesting response (to compete with biting and hitting). However, in some instances, the social function of a behavior may be under the control of a range of different stimuli that make establishing a single communicative alternative difficult.

A subtle variety of different stimulus conditions may lead to the same social function being served by different utterances. For example, when someone stubs his or her toe, he or she might say, "ouch," "owie," or some expletive. Although each of these utterances serves the same function, each may have been occasioned by somewhat different stimuli. An expletive may have been produced only in the presence of a very familiar peer. "Owie" may have been emitted only in the presence of one's immediate family. "Ouch" may serve as the utterance used with anyone not fitting the former two groups of communicative partners. On a general level, they all serve the same function. On another level, they are not totally interchangeable because of the different stimuli that control their production.

Discovering Subtleties in Stimulus and Response Class Relationships

Interactions between learners and their environments may involve complex stimulus–response relationships. Consequently, it is somewhat problematic to consider stimulus and response classes as having independent effects on communicative repertoires. Knowing that two behaviors are part of the same response class is of limited usefulness unless the interventionist knows whether the same stimulus characteristics evoke each of the topographies comprising the response class. Often, an individual who engages in challenging behavior will produce a number of different forms of socially unacceptable behavior that appear to be focused on the same social function. Consider, for example, the social function of avoiding undesired objects. One individual that we observed engaged in hitting, pinching, biting, grabbing and throwing objects, and darting. Each of these behaviors occurred exclusively in the presence of an offer of an undesired object or event. However, individual members of this response class did not appear to be selected randomly. Instead, they appeared to be selected to maximize the efficiency of an escape- or avoidance-motivated response. For example, when an item or event was offered and there was a clear avenue of escape, the learner might run. If there was no avenue of escape, the learner might accept the offered item or utensil and throw it. If no utensil or object was involved, the learner interchangeably hit or pinched. Biting occurred when hitting or pinching did not achieve the desired effect.

In each of these examples, the stimulus events associated with each of the topographically distinct responses were slightly different. Although the function served by each of the topographies was the same, we can be fairly certain that differential histories of reinforcement and reinforcement delay served to teach the learner that the greatest efficiency in achieving the desired social outcome occurs when certain forms of behavior are used in the presence of certain stimulus situations.

Because of the unique interaction between stimulus and response events that may result in a particular social motivation, two different socially acceptable communicative forms that address the same response motivation may be needed. For example, Durand and Carr (1985) taught two learners with escape-motivated behavior to engage in requests for assistance. Presumably, these requests resulted in a more rapid conclusion of the task, which, in turn, speeded the learner's escape. However, an important aspect of this situation was that the learner first had to be willing to work at the task in order for the request-assistance program to be implemented. In other tasks, the learner may have vehemently reacted to the presentation of the task, making it impossible to implement the request-assistance program. Instead, in this situation, the interventionist may have chosen to implement a reject-motivated program to provide the learner with immediate escape contingent on a socially acceptable response. Over time, the interventionist could have shaped a chain in which the learner's rejection was acknowledged but with increasing amounts of participation prior to release. For a more detailed discussion of the array of different communicative functions that may as part of the same response class, see DePaepe, Reichle, and O'Neill, Chapter 10, this volume.

The Role of Prior Intervention History and Conditional Efficiency in the Production of a Response Class Member

In some instances, communicative efficiency may be heavily skewed as a function of past experiences. In these instances, what might appear to a naive observer to be a more efficient communicative strategy may not be. For example, one learner with whom we became acquainted had a history of banging his head on a surface in order to obtain a soft drink from the refrigerator. Interestingly, the learner had been observed to travel independently to the refrigerator to retrieve a number of different food and snack items. After mentioning that it seemed strange that Brian did not independently retrieve soda from the refrigerator, his parents said that they did not allow him free access to cola because of the sugar that it contained. At a later point in the interview, when querying them about the actions contingent on Brian's head-banging, his parents reported that giving Brian cola was often the only way to calm him down. In Brian's case, the family began purchasing sugar-free cola. An intervention strategy was established to teach Brian to go to the refrigerator and help himself. The result was a substantial decrease in head-banging. In this example, an efficient and socially appropriate response had been rendered inefficient. The result was Brian's use of a more effective and efficient procurement of strategy (head-banging) for which his parents were unable to discover an acceptable intervention procedure. In this example, his parents had very consistently (although quite unsuccessfully) intervened with his behavior. As a result of their intervention, Brian had expanded his response class to include a new, socially unacceptable tangible-motivated strategy. The consistency of the parents' intervention in this example made identification of the problem and its solution relatively straightforward. However, in other instances, the inconsistency with which consequences have been delivered may result in a learner having difficulty in discriminating among the members of a response class that should be used. In these instances, the learner may be producing a chain of different topographies to achieve a desired social outcome.

Reichle (1991) observed learners with socially acceptable communicative repertoires engage in what he referred to as "sign frenzy." That is, each evening the pleasant smell of cooking food wafted into the living room. This appeared to serve as a discriminative stimulus for the learner to get up and go to the kitchen. Upon arriving and securing the attention of the cook, the learner would randomly emit a chain of signs representing cookie, hamburger, candy, apple, and each of several other signs corresponding to desired food items. A series of probes was implemented outside of a mealtime context. When shown one of the food items, the learner was asked to produce the corresponding sign. The learner's performance was nearly errorless. In this example, it is possible that the learner could not associate smells with actual food items and proceeded to randomly produce his repertoire until his communicative partner acknowledged an item that was to be served. Of course it is possible that if the desired consequence is not forthcoming, the learner may begin to chain more socially unacceptable members into his or her chain of responses.

Sometimes, clusters of socially unacceptable responses are produced in a reasonably systematic hierarchy. For example, a learner that we knew, Sam, sometimes attempted to escape domestic chores (e.g., sweeping the floor, dusting the furniture) before the task was completed. Usually his escape repertoire began by a marked decrease in his engagement. If this did not gain release, he began pacing. Subsequently, his pacing would turn into body-rocking. Eventually, he would head-slap, which almost always resulted in the group-home staff releasing him from the task. In Sam's case, there appeared to be some unidentified setting events or establishing operations that influenced his escape-motivated behavior. That is, on some occasions he appeared to enjoy his domestic chores, while on other days he attempted to escape them after relatively little engagement.

Two challenges confronted interventionists. First, how to eliminate head-slaps and, second, how to determine those instances in which Sam was most apt to engage in challenging behavior. In Sam's case, staff decided that they would utilize the initial behavior in Sam's chain of escape-motivated behavior as their cue to implement a proactive instructional procedure. That is, once Sam ceased working, staff approached him and prompted him to communicate, "I want a break." Immediately, respite from the task was granted. By using the initial behavior in Sam's chain as a cue to the interventionist, it was possible to teach a socially acceptable response that made it unnecessary for Sam to produce the remainder of the chain that culminated in head-slapping. As Sam became increasingly proficient, he began using his communicative utterance at the same time he disengaged.

In our preceding example, each behavior in the chain shared the same social function (escape), thereby making it part of the same response class. The only aspect of the situation that resulted in Sam's use of another topography was when the prior behavior did not match the learner's expectation. In this example, if a history developed in which the learner was reinforced near the completion of the chain, it is likely that the learner's behavior would appear to become more and more severe over time. That is, less overt members of the chain never receive reinforcement, but the most severe member of the response class is reinforced. Over time, the learner may become increasingly likely to produce the more severe member of the response class in isolation. Alternatively, if all forms are intermittently reinforced, the learner may be likely to continue working his or her way through all members of the response class (from those that require the least effort to those that require the most effort). In the case of sequential response chains, the primary decision for the interventionist is whether the "lowest level/least challenging behavior" is sufficiently normalized that it can be permitted to remain in the learner's repertoire (and perhaps even be strengthened). If the answer to this question is an unqualified yes, the objective of an intervention procedure may well be to interrupt the chain of challenging behavior that has been established.

Conditionally Using Communicative Alternatives to Challenging Behavior

If interventionists are to establish functional and socially acceptable alternatives to challenging behavior, it is necessary to carefully establish the conditional use of a socially acceptable repertoire. That is, a range of functional responses must be selected to maximize the efficiency with which a learner can achieve an outcome without resorting to challenging behavior.

Sulzer-Azaroff and Mayer (1977) defined discrimination as "the restriction of responding to certain stimulus situations and not others . . ." (p. 515). They went on to point out that "Discrimination may be established by differential reinforcement in one stimulus situation and extinction . . . of that response in other situations. . . ." In other words, first the learner must be taught both when and when *not* to respond. Furthermore, he or she must be taught to produce the most appropriate response from among several plausible alternative behaviors. A child learns (sometimes!) not to yell loud greetings to friends in church as he or she might on the playground, or not to ask for help when he or she encounters a knotted shoelace or jar lid that he or she can successfully manipulate. Similarly, a child may learn to request a trip to the bathroom in a whisper while in church, as opposed to loudly proclaiming it from the back seat of the car while driving down the highway. Table 2 displays a variety of communicative situations that may require the learner to engage in the conditional use of communicative behavior. The remainder of this chapter focuses on an instructional technology that, when implemented rigorously, results in the establishment of well generalized and conditionally used repertoires of socially acceptable communicative alternatives to challenging behavior.

Table 2. Examples of the conditional production of communicative behavior

Condition	Example
Setting specific	• Does not request food and beverage during church
	• Requests food and beverage at a restaurant
Listener familiarity	• Produces semi-intelligible speech when communicating with familiar individuals
	• Uses a communication board with unfamiliar individuals who are less skilled in deciphering semi-intelligible speech
Task specific	• Requests assistance with difficult tasks
	• Completes easy tasks independently
Item satiation	• Requests initial cup of coffee
	• Refuses subsequent offers

Identifying a Framework for Developing Repertoires of Social-Communicative Behavior

Since the landmark article authored by Stokes and Baer (1977), researchers and interventionists have become increasingly aware that stimulus and response generalization are concurrent aspects of acquisition. Generalization strategies such as utilizing common stimuli, training sufficient exemplars, and using natural maintaining contingencies alluded to an inherent interrelationship between aspects of acquisition and generalization. Recently, an instructional package referred to as general-case instruction (Horner, McDonnell, & Bellamy, 1986; Horner, Sprague, & Wilcox, 1982) has received significant discussion in the intervention literature.

At the heart of the general-case approach is the concept of stimulus control; that is, intervention should result in an outcome in which all members of particular stimulus classes control appropriate members of corresponding response classes (Reichle & Sigafoos, 1991a). The general-case model is based on principles and procedures first developed as part of Direct Instruction (Becker, Engelmann, & Thomas, 1975). Direct Instruction was primarily developed for, and has been applied to, teaching pre-academic and academic skills to disadvantaged preschool and young elementary-school children (Becker, 1977). This approach to teaching has placed great emphasis on a careful analysis of the stimulus features of particular tasks and how they are presented in an instructional sequence. Such analysis is aimed at facilitating appropriate discriminations and responding to stimuli that share common features, and at not responding to irrelevant features that may vary across stimuli and settings (Engelmann & Carnine, 1982). Direct Instruction focuses on teaching the general case. That is, Direct Instruction focuses on bringing appropriate classes of responses under the control of appropriate classes of stimuli. in order to increase the probability that skills will be successfully performed with target stimuli or in settings that may differ from those used in training, but that are still part of the relevant stimulus class (Becker & Engelmann, 1978).

General-case strategies have been shown to be effective in achieving generalized performance of a variety of adaptive community-based skills by adolescents and adults with severe disabilities (Horner & Albin, 1988; Horner et al., 1986). These skills have included grocery purchasing (McDonnell, Horner, & Williams, 1984), dressing skills (Day & Horner, 1986), telephone use (Horner, Williams, & Stevely, 1987), fast-food restaurant skills (Steere, Strauch, Powell, & Butterworth, 1990), street crossing (Horner, Jones, & Williams, 1985), vending machine use (Sprague & Horner, 1984), and electronic assembly tasks (Horner & McDonald, 1982). In a comprehensive review and quantitative analysis of the generalization literature, White et al. (1988) concluded that, "It would appear, on the basis of admittedly limited evidence, that general case programming is the strategy of choice for facilitating generalization from instructional to applied situations" (p. 39). In all of the investigations cited, persons were taught to respond effectively over a range of stimulus contexts (e.g., different streets, different vending machines, different shirts), including those that had not originally been the focus of direct instruction.

In spite of the extensive application of the general-case approach across a variety of vocational, domestic, and community skills, there are virtually no empirical investigations describing its application in the establishment of an initial communicative repertoire, although a number of authors (Halle, Chadsey-Rusch, & Collett-Klingenberg, in press; O'Neill, 1990; Reichle & Sigafoos, 1991c) have suggested that establishing communicative behavior represents an important application of general-case instruction.

One common concern of interventionists has been whether general-case instruction can be applied only in didactic training formats. While it is true that the bulk of empirical demonstrations of general-case instruction have focused on discrete trial intervention formats, this instructional strategy can accommodate a variety of instructional techniques. For example, milieu language instruction (Hart, 1985; Hart & Rogers-Warren, 1978) has gained increasing popularity as a package of intervention techniques to teach learners with moderate developmental disabilities an initial communicative repertoire. The component procedures of incidental teaching, mand-model instruction, and time delay fading techniques emphasize distributed teaching opportunities that, to the extent possible, are learner initiated. We believe that general-case logic can accommodate less structured, less didactic intervention approaches such as these. First, general-case instruction is applied to assist the interventionist in selecting types of trials or teaching opportunities. Second, it ensures that the interventionist has ordered teaching opportunities that emphasize the most relevant features and discriminations. When teaching opportunities are learner-generated (as in milieu teaching), it may be impossible to control the discriminability of all teaching opportunities. That is, some opportunities that are highly motivating to the learner may involve sophisticated discriminations, while other teaching opportunities that represent relatively easy discriminations may not be sufficiently motivating to the learner to be utilized. Applying general-case instructional strategies in these situations may require that the interventionist take advantage of all learner-generated teaching opportunities while attempting to ensure that a substantial portion (or greatest proportion possible) focus on maximally discriminable opportunities at the outset of instruction. The remainder of this chapter focuses on describing the components of general-case instructional procedures and the issues that are important for efficient implementation.

OPERATIONALIZING GENERAL-CASE INSTRUCTION

Detailed descriptions of the general-case approach can be found in Horner and Albin (1988), Horner et al. (1986), and Horner et al. (1982). The six components of general case instruction are: 1) defining the instructional universe, 2) defining the range of relevant stimulus and response variation within that universe, 3) selecting examples to teach, 4) sequencing the teaching examples, 5) teaching the examples, and 6) testing with previously untaught probe stimuli to ensure that desired generalization has occurred. Each of these components is described briefly.

Defining the Instructional Universe

The major defining feature of general-case instruction, compared with more typical instruction, is the careful emphasis on analysis of the appropriate range of stimulus and response variation that is systematically included in selecting and sequencing teaching opportunities. The instructional universe consists of all the stimulus situations in which a student would be expected to perform a given response to achieve a particular outcome and the behaviors necessary to produce that outcome. Unless the instructional universe is identified carefully, it will be impossible to identify teaching examples that sufficiently represent the conditions under which the behavior being taught should be used.

In recent years, careful sampling of the environment in which a learner has opportunities and obligations to communicate has become standard practice for deriving an initial communicative repertoire to teach. Often the procedures used to systematically scrutinize the learner's environments to derive instructional targets have been referred to as an ecological analysis or inventory (Rainforth, York, & MacDonald, 1992; Sigafoos & York, 1991). Ecological inventories typically identify those stimulus events that call for a particular behavior. A general-case analysis, however, extends to stimulus conditions that should occasion either no response or an action that achieves the same function as the target communicative response. For example, assume that a learner wants a hamburger. At home (eating family style), he or she may simply reach to the center of the dining table and serve him- or herself. At a fast-food restaurant, he or she must communicate an order. At a movie theater where there are no hamburgers, he or she must refrain from requesting one.

Including a range of exemplars that sample a range of contexts in which the communicative alternative should and should not occur may seem fairly straightforward when teaching specific vocabulary items (e.g., balls, cups, cars) (see Halle, 1989). However, defining and incorporating the needed range of controlling stimuli for specific communicative functions for more complex forms of verbal behavior appears to be a much more difficult task (Halle & Holt, 1991).

Defining the Range of Relevant Stimulus and Response Variation

When the instructional universe has been defined, the interventionist must determine how much stimulus and response variability exists within that universe. This involves determining the responses that need to be performed and the variability in the stimuli and settings that will occasion the responses.

Escape- and avoidance-motivated challenging behaviors provide a good example of the stimulus and response variation that an interventionist is apt to encounter. Some learners may vehemently avoid engaging in certain activities. Their initial protests may occur upon seeing the interventionist move to the setting where the task occurs or when the interventionist verbally directs them to the activity. In some instances in which a standard daily routine operates, the learner may anticipate the undesired activity at the completion of the task that precedes it. In other instances, the learner may engage in an activity for significant periods of time before he or she attempts to escape. In these instances, the strength of the reinforcer may diminish as the task progresses. Alternatively, the cumulative duration of the task may make it increasingly aversive. This extensive range of stimulus conditions has been the focus of a substantial number of potential replacement responses. For example, as mentioned earlier, Durand and Carr (1985) taught learners who had a history of limited engagement in activities (without significant prompting) prior to an escape attempt to use a request for assistance. Requesting assistance increased the speed with which release from the activity occurred.

In instances in which learners can independently perform all components of a job, but for whom duration of performance is a problem, it might prove productive to establish increasingly sustained performance. Reichle (1991) described implementing a "safety signal." That is, initially, the interventionist chose the length of time that the learner typically engaged in an activity prior to an escape attempt. Several seconds prior to the completion of that interval, the interventionist said, "Just a second—almost break time." After the passage of several seconds of no challenging behavior, the learner was released to break. Across opportunities, the latency between the delivery of a safety signal and task release was systematically increased.

In some instances, a task is sufficiently aversive that the learner attempts to escape prior to task engagement. Horner (personal communication) described a strategy in which prior to vehement challenging behavior, the learner is prompted to make a socially acceptable rejecting response. The response is honored immediately. However, from the earliest point of instruction, the interventionist controls the learner's release from the activity. That is, the learner makes the request to leave, but does not go until the interventionist says, "Okay, we're done." Across teaching opportunities, the interventionist's goal is to gradually increase the length of time between the learner's rejection and the interventionist's release. Eventually, the interventionist may begin to include a relatively palatable task demand to which the learner is apt to respond, with the learner's release contingent on modest participation. Eventually, quality or duration of learner participation in the job is increased. Powerful reinforcers are made available contingent on learner participation. We have just described several different communicative forms for responding to particular stimulus conditions, each of which results in the same social outcome. A learner's escape from an undesired activity may occur from attending to a safety signal, requesting assistance, or producing a generalized rejecting response, depending on the specific escape or avoidance situation.

Selecting, Sequencing, and Teaching Examples

Having defined the range of stimulus and response variations to be addressed, the interventionist must select teaching examples from this universe to use for training and probe testing. General-case instruction suggests that multiple *critical* examples should be the focus of initial intervention efforts. For example, for an individual who was being taught to request assistance, opportunities to request assistance included opening desert pudding cups, opening plastic silverware wrappers, opening candy bar wrappers, and unfastening twist ties on bread wrappers. When each of these instances is addressed concurrently, a significant number and variety of teaching opportunities can be generated. Examples should include the range of variation that is present in the instructional universe. For example, if it were the interventionist's expectation that the learner use a request-assistance utterance to speed the completion of undesirable activities, it would be important to include teaching examples that are escape motivated.

Traditionally, interventionists have selected a single response form to replace an entire class of socially motivated challenging behavior. However, the stimulus conditions associated with this class may permit a fairly broad range of response forms. Each of these forms might individually be better suited to a specific cluster of provoking stimulus conditions. For example, for an individual who engages in escape-motivated challenging behavior, a request for assistance, a request for a break and/or safety signal instruction may represent viable options. As mentioned in the preceding section, choosing between these options may involve a careful consideration of the conditions surrounding escape- and avoidance-motivated behavior.

For example, teaching requests for assistance might best be considered as an option with tasks for which there are discrete points at which the learner tends to get "hung up" or frustrated. Similarly, requesting assistance may be a desirable option with a learner who evidences both escape- and attention-motivated challenging behavior. Teaching requests for assistance may ensure that during less-preferred tasks, the learner gets ample attention. However, if a learner attempted to escape activities that he or she had clearly mastered, but his or her behavior was attention motivated, the interventionist might choose to teach the learner to request the work checks, "How am I doing?" Doing so would provide the learner with a socially appropriate attention-getting strategy that would prolong his or her engagement in an otherwise nonpreferred activity.

In still other instances, an individual's task-avoidance behavior may be so intense that the most efficient strategy is to empower the learner by teaching a rejecting utterance that can be used to gain total escape. Subsequently, efforts are made to shape participation prior to task release.

Thus far, our selection of teaching examples has focused on teaching examples in which the learner should emit a targeted communicative utterance. However, equally important in general-case instruction is teaching the learner when it is appropriate to refrain from engaging in the communicative utterance that is being taught. In the examples that we have discussed, requesting assistance provides a good example. With learners who are both escape and attention motivated, there is an inherent possibility that the learner might begin to use a request-assistance utterance to obtain attention rather than assistance with a task. In this instance, if the assistance provided does not involve giving the learner significant attention, the learner may return to his or her former repertoire of challenging behavior, which had a prior history of efficiently gaining attention. Durand and Carr (1985) have elegantly demonstrated the importance of being precise in matching the social motivation for challenging behavior with specific replacement skills.

Another vitually important component in identifying teaching examples is the inclusion of "exceptions" or negative examples. These involve situations in which the learner might readily generalize the use of his or her new replacement communicative behavior but should refrain from doing so. Initially, the interventionist should strive to make teaching opportunities maximally discriminable. That is, it should be very obvious to the learner when it is to his or her advantage to use the new behavior being taught. Alternatively, it should be made clear when it is to his or her advantage to refrain from engaging in the new behavior being taught or to use a different socially acceptable behavior that already is in his or her repertoire. As the learner becomes increasingly more proficient in using the new skill, the discriminability of the situation calling for each of the different socially acceptable behaviors that may now be in the learner's repertoire is made increasingly more challenging. An example of the importance of emphasizing the learner's ability to discriminate among stimulus situations and response options is highlighted in the following example.

Reichle, Anderson, and Schermer (1986) described a procedure that was implemented to teach a learner with severe developmental disabilities to make a peanut butter sandwich. The learner had difficulty getting the lid off the peanut butter jar. Two sets of teaching procedures were implemented. One set of teaching examples taught the learner to open peanut butter jars under conditions in which he had the strength to loosen the jar lid. The other condition taught the learner to request assistance when the jar lid was too tightly affixed to allow him to loosen it himself.

Initially, to maximize the discriminability of these two conditions, the "loose lid" condition involved the jar lid simply set on the jar without being screwed on. In the "tight lid" condition, the jar lid was so tightly affixed that the interventionist had difficulty removing it. Across successful opportunities, the discriminability of each of these two conditions was altered systematically to make them increasingly less discriminable. In this example, discriminative responding was critical if the learner's independence was to be maximized while at the same time frustration from being unable to successfully complete an activity was to be minimized.

Although best practice clearly requires the introduction of both positive and negative teaching examples, it has not yet been clearly determined at what point negative examples are most efficiently introduced. The sequence in which teaching examples are presented can have a significant effect on the efficiency of instruction. For example, some research has demonstrated that it is more efficient to present different examples (concurrent instruction) during an instructional period rather than focus on a single example (Panyan & Hall, 1978; Schroeder & Baer, 1972). In implementing a general-case instructional strategy, Reichle et al. (1986) found that concurrent implementation of positive and negative teaching examples was most efficient. When the researchers first employed only positive teaching examples, learners failed to generalize to negative teaching examples. For example, one learner who had been taught to request assistance to remove a peanut butter jar lid under conditions that required assistance continued to produce a request-assistance response even when the jar lid had been removed prior to a sandwich-making activity. However, other investigators (Halle et al., 1992) reported first introducing positive teaching examples. Subsequently when negative probes were introduced, learners appropriately refrained from producing the communicative behavior being taught. For example, when a water fountain had a constant water flow, the learner drank without requesting assistance. However, when there was no water flow, the learner appropriately requested assistance.

There are several plausible explanations for differences across studies by Halle et al. (1992) and Reichle et al. (1986). First, it is possible that subjects participating in Halle's investigation had previously acquired a socially acceptable response in the negative exemplar condition prior to implementing positive teaching examples, while subjects in Reichle's study had not. Second, it is possible that the positive and negative exemplars used by Halle were more discriminable than those used by Reichle. That is, it may be easier to discriminate a water fountain as on or off than it is to distriminate a peanut butter jar lid that is affixed tightly or loosely.

In establishing a program to teach requests for assistance, interventionists often complain that for any one activity, there are only a limited number of times to engage in that activity. For example, in considering our preceding example involving requesting assistance, there are only so many times that one can make a sandwich in a day. Consequently, interventionists may feel that they have a dilemma in which they either alter the environment to create more teaching opportunities or they have relatively few teaching opportunities, which may jeopardize skill acquisition. This potential dilemma is magnified when one considers that teaching opportunities may be distributed between those in which the learner need not emit the communicative utterance and other opportunities in which the learner must emit the communicative utterance.

Although the discussion of sequencing the teaching examples seems relatively straightforward, it can actually be quite complex. Some teaching examples may permit both a positive and a negative stimulus condition. For example, peanut butter jar lids may be tightly affixed or loosely affixed to the jar. Other teaching examples call exclusively for the use of the communicative behavior or call exclusively for not using the communicative behavior. For example, a learner with severe physical disabilities may always require assistance pushing a straw in a drink box. Similarly, if an individual has learned to be independent in tying his or her shoes, it is unlikely that he or she will need to request assistance.

The preceding examples, then, suggest there are at least three general classes of stimuli that can be selected in sequencing instructional opportunities: 1) those that require conditional use of the behavior being taught, 2) those that require always using the communicative behavior being taught, and 3) those that require refraining from using the communicative behavior being taught. This latter group of negative teaching examples may be further broken down into those situations in which the learner should refrain from acting at all to those situations in which an alternative, more efficient and/or more socially acceptable strategy should be used. The actual teaching (e.g., prompting, shaping) follows the same guidelines and procedures that have been developed for effective teaching of learners with disabilities in general (Bellamy, Horner, & Inman, 1979; Sailor, Wilcox, & Brown, 1980; Snell, 1987).

In a general-case analysis, the interventionist's objective is to gradually and systematically decrease the discriminability between positive teaching examples (those that require the behavior being taught) and negative teaching examples (those that require the learner to refrain from the target behavior). At the same time, the interventionist must take care to ensure that all stimuli that are irrelevant in making a discrimination are varied sufficiently so that the learner does not become dependent on them. These issues, as well as the other steps in the general-case process (testing with untrained examples), will be discussed further in the next chapter (DePaepe, Reichle, & O'Neill, chap. 10, this volume).

CONCLUSION

Establishing socially acceptable alternatives to socially unacceptable behavior represents a tremendous challenge to families and professionals. As elegantly stated in Taylor and Carr (chap. 4, this volume), there is a tendency for those who are familiar with individuals who engage in challenging behavior to acquiesce and accommodate the behavior. With persons who engage in attention-motivated challenging behavior, there is a tendency to provide tremendous positive attention to minimize challenging behavior. With individuals whose challenging repertoires are escape motivated, social partners have a tendency to avoid giving task demands. Although these strategies may appear to lessen the propensity for challenging behavior, they simply defer challenging behavior.

This chapter is predicated on the belief that both the learner who engages in challenging behavior and his or her social community must establish a socially viable repertoire that allows the learner to exert a level of control over his or her environment that is commonly afforded to all citizens. We believe that general-case instructional technology provides the learner and those around him or her with an instructional logic that can maximize the probability that socially acceptable alternatives to challenging behavior are established across the range of situations necessary in order to significantly improve the quality of life for everyone in the learner's social ecology.

At the heart of the general-case approach is the recognition that stimulus and response classes are interactive. Consequently, examining one in the absence of the other is fruitless. In addition, as Mace and Roberts (chap. 6, this volume) have explained, the socially acceptable alternatives being taught must be maximally efficient if the learner is to use them fluently. To be maximally efficient, the interventionist may find it necessary to implement several different communicative forms to replace socially unacceptable forms used to express a single social motivation. Consequently, the acquisition process may require teaching the learner relatively sophisticated discriminations. Currently, the field of education struggles with how to best maintain instructional rigor while using the most naturalistic intervention strategies. Although we expect this struggle to continue, general-case instructional technology offers the interventionist a logic that can be mapped on to a variety of teaching styles.

In spite of the challenges that interventionists face, tremendous progress has been made since the 1970s and 1980s in our efforts to provide increasingly proactive intervention for individuals who evidence socially motivated challenging behavior. Interventionists now recognize that reactive strategies are not only inefficient, but socially nonprogressive. Perhaps most importantly, we have learned that communicative approaches to managing challenging behavior allow the intervention to occur prior to the challenging behavior. Consequently, learners are more apt to be receptive to instructional procedures when their anxiety, frustration, and anger has not yet reached a peak.

Most recently, we have learned that to be maximally efficient, several different communicative alternatives may be necessary to address the same social motivation. That is, depending on the circumstances, learners may attempt to escape situations in which they simply need assistance, while in other situations the entirety of the event is repugnant and can be resolved only with a communicative rejecting response.

To more fully illustrate the application of general-case procedures, the next chapter provides detailed examples of the instructional steps used in establishing functional communicative alternatives for challenging behavior that is motivated by the desire to obtain attention or tangibles, or to escape and avoid task demands.

If we are to continue to advance our ability to proactively manage challenging behavior, we must focus on strategies to ensure instructional rigor while using the most natural intervention styles. This focus will be particularly important with an increasing shift to home-based instruction to serve young toddlers in preschool programs and others where the primary interventionist is apt to be the learner's family. In spite of the increasing challenges facing interventionists, the opportunity for increased emphasis on the social validity of intervention strategies that address challenging behavior offers tremendous opportunities for those who have chosen to serve a very difficult population.

REFERENCES

Becker, W.C. (1977). Teaching reading and language to the disadvantaged: What we have learned from field research. *Harvard Educational Review, 47,* 518–543.

Becker, W.C., & Engelmann, S. (1978). Systems for basic instruction: Theory and applications. In A.C. Catania & T.A. Brigham (Eds.), *Handbook of applied behavior analysis* (pp. 325–377). New York: Irvington Publishers.

Becker, W.C., Engelmann, S., & Thomas, D.R. (1975). *Teaching 2: Cognitive learning and instruction.* Chicago: Science Research Associates.

Bellamy, G.T., Horner, R.H., & Inman, D.P. (1979). *Vocational rehabilitation of severely retarded adults.* Baltimore: University Park Press.

Bellamy, G.T., Newton, J.S., LeBaron, N.M., & Horner, R.H. (1990). Quality of life and lifestyle outcomes: A challenge for residential programs. In R.L. Schalock (Ed.), *Quality of life: Perspectives and issues* (pp. 127–137). Washington, DC: American Association on Mental Retardation.

Bloom, L., & Lahey, M. (1974). *Language development and language disorders.* New York: John Wiley & Sons.

Carr, E.G. (1988). Functional equivalence as a mechanism of response generalization. In R.H. Horner, G. Dunlap, & R.L. Koegel (Eds.), *Generalization and maintenance: Life-style changes in applied settings* (pp. 221–241). Baltimore: Paul H. Brookes Publishing Co.

Carr, E.G., & Durand, V.M. (1985). Reducing behavior problems through functional communication training. *Journal of Applied Behavior Analysis, 18,* 111–126.

Carr, E.G., & Kologinsky, E. (1983). Acquisition of sign language by autistic children II: Spontaneity and generalization effects. *Journal of Applied Behavior Analysis, 16,* 297–314.

Cipani, E. (1989). *The treatment of severe behavior disorders.* Washington, DC: American Association on Mental Retardation.

Day, H.M., & Horner, R.H. (1986). Response variation and the generalization of a dressing skill: Comparison of single instance and general case instruction. *Applied Research in Mental Retardation, 7,* 189–202.

Doss, S., & Reichle, J. (1989). Establishing communicative alternatives to the emission of socially motivated excess behavior. *Journal of The Association for Persons with Severe Handicaps, 14,* 101–112.

Doss, S., & Reichle, J. (1991). Replacing excess behavior with an initial communicative repertoire. In J. Reichle, J. York, & J. Sigafoos, *Implementing augmentative and alternative communication: Strategies for learners with severe disabilities* (pp. 215–237). Baltimore: Paul H. Brookes Publishing Co.

Durand, M.V., & Carr, E.G. (1985). Self-injurious behavior: Motivating conditions and guidelines for treatment. *School Psychology Review, 14,* 171–176.

Engelmann, S., & Carnine, D. (1982). *Theory of instruction.* New York: Irvington Publishers.

Golonka, Z., Wacker, D., Derby, K.M., Plagmann, L., & Sasso, G. (1992, May). *The use of choice making and positive reinforcement in the treatment of stereotypic behavior in an outpatient clinic.* Paper presented at the Association for Behavior Analysis annual conference, San Francisco.

Hall, G., & Sundberg, M.L. (1987). Teaching mands by manipulating conditioned establishing operations. *The Analysis of Verbal Behavior, 5,* 41–53.

Halle, J.W. (1989). Identifying stimuli in the natural environment that control verbal responses. *Journal of Speech and Hearing Disorders, 54,* 500–504.

Halle, J.W., Chadsey-Rusch, J., & Collet-Klingenberg, L. (in press). Applying stimulus control features of general-case instruction and interactive routines to enhance communication skills. In R.A. Gable & S.F. Warren (Eds.), *Advances in mental retardation and developmental disabilities: Vol. 5. Research bases of instruction.*

London: Kingsley Publishers.

Halle, J.W., & Holt, B. (1991). Assessing stimulus control in natural settings: An analysis of stimuli that acquire control during training. *Journal of Applied Behavior Analysis, 24,* 579–589.

Handelman, J.S. (1979). Generalization by autistic-type children of verbal responses across settings. *Journal of Applied Behavior Analysis, 12,* 273–282.

Handelman, J.S. (1981). Transfer of verbal responses across instructional settings by autistic-type children. *Journal of Speech and Hearing Disorders, 46,* 69–76.

Hart, B. (1985). Naturalistic language training techniques. In S.F. Warren & A.K. Rogers-Warren (Eds.), *Teaching functional language* (pp. 63–88). Austin, TX: PRO-ED.

Hart, B., & Rogers-Warren, A. (1978). Milieu language training. In R.L. Schiefelbusch (Ed.), *Language intervention strategies* (Vol. 2., pp. 193–235). Baltimore: University Park Press.

Horner, R.H., & Albin, R.W. (1988). Research on general-case procedures for learners with severe disabilities. *Education and Treatment of Children, 11,* 375–388.

Horner, R., & Day, H.M. (1991). The effects of response efficiency on functionally equivalent competing behaviors. *Journal of Applied Behavior Analysis, 24,* 719–732.

Horner, R.H., Jones, D., & Williams, J.A. (1985). A functional approach to teaching generalized street crossing. *Journal of The Association for Persons with Severe Handicaps, 10,* 71–78.

Horner, R.H., & McDonald, R.S. (1982). A comparison of single instance and general case instruction in teaching a generalized vocational skill. *Journal of The Association for Persons with Severe Handicaps, 7,* 7–20.

Horner, R.H., McDonnell, J.J., & Bellamy, G.T. (1986). Teaching generalized skills: General case instruction in simulation and community settings. In R.H. Horner, L.H. Meyer, & H.D.B. Fredericks (Eds.), *Education of learners with severe handicaps: Exemplary service strategies* (pp. 289–314). Baltimore: Paul H. Brookes Publishing Co.

Horner, R.H., O'Neill, R.E., & Flannery, K.B. (1993). Effective behavior support plans. In M. Snell (Ed.), *Instruction of students with severe disabilities* (pp. 184–214). New York: Merrill.

Horner, R., Sprague, J., O'Brien, M., & Heathfield, L. (1990). The role of response efficiency in the reduction of problem behaviors through functional equivalence training: A case study. *Journal of The Association for Persons with Severe Handicaps, 15*(2), 91–97.

Horner, R.H., Sprague, J.R., & Wilcox, B. (1982). General case programming for community activities. In B. Wilcox & G.T. Bellamy (Eds.), *Design of high school programs for severely handicapped students* (pp. 61–98). Baltimore: Paul H. Brookes Publishing Co.

Horner, R.H., Williams, J.A., & Stevely, J.D. (1987). Acquisition of generalized telephone use by students with moderate and severe disabilities. *Research in Developmental Disabilities, 8,* 229–247.

Hunt, P., & Goetz, L. (1988). Teaching spontaneous communication in natural settings through interrupted behavior chains. *Topics in Language Disorders, 9,* 58–71.

Iwata, B. (1987). Negative reinforcement in applied behavior analysis: An emerging technology. *Journal of Applied Behavior Analysis, 20,* 361–378.

Kaczmarek, L.A. (1990). Teaching spontaneous language to individuals with severe handicaps: A matrix model. *Journal of The Association for Persons with Severe*

Handicaps, 15, 160–169.

Keogh, W., & Reichle, J. (1985). Communication intervention for the difficult-to-teach severely handicapped. In S. Warren and A. Rogers-Warren (Eds.), *Teaching functional language* (pp. 157–194). Austin, TX: PRO-ED.

LaMarre, J., & Holland, J.G. (1985). The functional independence of mands and tacts. *Journal of the Experimental Analysis of Behavior, 43,* 5–19.

Leigland, S. (1984). On "setting events" and related concepts. *Behavior Analyst, 1*(1), 41–46.

Lovaas, O.I., Koegel, R., & Schriebman, L. (1979). Stimulus overselectivity in autism: A review of research. *Psychological Bulletin, 86,* 1236–1254.

Matson, J.L., Sevin, J.A., Fridley, D., & Love, S.R. (1990). Increasing spontaneous language in three autistic children. *Journal of Applied Behavior Analysis, 23,* 227–233.

McDonnell, J.J., Horner, R.H., & Williams, J.A. (1984). A comparison of three strategies for teaching generalized grocery purchasing to high school students with severe handicaps. *Journal of The Association for Persons with Severe Handicaps, 9,* 123–134.

Michael, J. (1975). Positive and negative reinforcement: A distinction that is no longer necessary, or a better way to talk about bad things. *Behaviorism, 3,* 33–44.

Michael, J. (1988). Establishing operations and the mand. *The Analysis of Verbal Behavior, 6,* 3–9.

Michael, J. (1989). Motivative relations and establishing operations. In J. Michael (Ed.), *Verbal and nonverbal behavior: Concepts and principles* (pp. 40–53). Kalamazoo: Western Michigan University.

Mullins, M., & Rincover, A. (1985). Comparing autistic and normal children along the dimensions of reinforcer maximization, stimulus sampling, and responsiveness to extinction. *Journal of Experimental Child Psychology, 40,* 350–374.

O'Neill, R.E. (1990). Establishing verbal repertoires: Toward the application of general case analysis and programming. *The Analysis of Verbal Behavior,* 113–126.

Panyan, M., & Hall, R.V. (1978). Effects of serial versus concurrent task sequencing on acquisition, maintenance, and generalization. *Journal of Applied Behavior Analysis, 11,* 67–74.

Rainforth, B., York, J., & Macdonald, C. (1992). *Collaborative teams for students with severe disabilities: Integrating therapy and educational services.* Baltimore: Paul H. Brookes Publishing Co.

Reichle, J., Anderson, H., & Schermer, G. (1986). *Establishing the discrimination between requesting objects, requesting assistance and "helping yourself."* Unpublished manuscript, University of Minnesota, Minneapolis.

Reichle, J., & Sigafoos, J. (1991a). Bringing communicative behavior under the control of the appropriate stimuli. In J. Reichle, J. York, & J. Sigafoos, *Implementing augmentative and alternative communication: Strategies for learners with severe disabilities* (pp. 193–213). Baltimore: Paul H. Brookes Publishing Co.

Reichle, J., & Sigafoos, J. (1991b). Establishing an initial repertoire of requesting. In J. Reichle, J. York, & J. Sigafoos, *Implementing augmentative and alternative communication: Strategies for learners with severe disabilities* (pp. 89–114). Baltimore: Paul H. Brookes Publishing Co.

Reichle, J., & Sigafoos, J. (1991c). Establishing spontaneity and generalization. In J. Reichle, J. York, & J. Sigafoos, *Implementing augmentative and alternative communication: Strategies for learners with severe disabilities* (pp. 157–171).

Baltimore: Paul H. Brookes Publishing Co.

Romski, M.A., Sevcik, R., & Pate, J. (1988). Establishment of symbolic communication in persons with severe mental retardation. *Journal of Speech and Hearing Disorders, 53,* 94–107.

Sailor, W., Wilcox, B., & Brown, L. (Eds.). (1980). *Methods of instruction for severely handicapped students.* Baltimore: Paul H. Brookes Publishing Co.

Schroeder, G.L., & Baer, D.M. (1972). Effects of concurrent and serial training on generalized vocal imitation in children. *Developmental Psychology, 6,* 293–301.

Sigafoos, J., Doss, S., & Reichle, J. (1989). Developing mand and tact repertoires in persons with severe developmental disabilities using graphic symbols. *Research in Developmental Disabilities, 10,* 183–200.

Sigafoos, J., Reichle, J., Doss, S., Hall, K., & Pettitt, L. (1990). "Spontaneous" transfer of stimulus control from tact to mand contingencies. *Research in Developmental Disabilities, 11,* 165–176.

Sigafoos, J., & York, J. (1991). Using ecological inventories to promote functional communication. In J. Reichle, J. York, & J. Sigafoos, *Implementing augmentative and alternative communication: Strategies for learners with severe disabilities* (pp. 61–70). Baltimore: Paul H. Brookes Publishing Co.

Skinner, B.F. (1957). *Verbal behavior.* Englewood Cliffs, NJ: Prentice Hall.

Snell, M. (1987). *Systematic instruction of persons with severe handicaps.* Columbus, OH: Merrill.

Sprague, J.R., & Horner, R.H. (1984). The effects of single instance, multiple instance, and general case training on generalized vending machine use by moderately and severely handicapped students. *Journal of Applied Behavior Analysis, 17,* 273–278.

Steere, D.E., Strauch, J.D., Powell, T.H., & Butterworth, J. (1990). Promoting generalization from a teaching setting to a community-based setting among persons with severe disabilities: A general case programming approach. *Education and Treatment of Children, 13,* 5–20.

Stokes, T., & Baer, D. (1977). An implicit technology of generalization. *Journal of Applied Behavior Analysis, 10,* 349–367.

Sulzer-Azaroff, B., & Mayer, G.R. (1977). *Applying behavior analysis procedures with children and youth.* New York: Holt, Rinehart & Winston.

Sundberg, M.L. (1980). *Developing a verbal repertoire using sign language and Skinner's analysis of verbal behavior.* Unpublished doctoral dissertation, Western Michigan University, Kalamazoo.

Sundberg, M.L. (1987). *Teaching language to the developmentally disabled: A course manual.* Prince George, BC: College of New Caledonia Press.

Wahler, R., & Fox, J. (1981). Setting events in applied behavior analysis: Towards a conceptual and methodological expansion. *Journal of Applied Behavior Analysis. 14*(3), 327–338.

White, O.R., Liberty, K.A., Haring, N.G., Billingsley, F.F., Boer, M., Burrange, A., Connors, R., Farman, R., Fedorchak, G., Leber, B.D., Liberty-Laylin, S., Miller, S., Opalski, C., Phifer, C., & Sessoms, I. (1988). Review and analysis of strategies for generalization. In N.G. Haring (Ed.), *Generalization for students with severe handicaps* (pp. 15–51). Seattle: University of Washington Press.

10

Applying General-Case Instructional Strategies When Teaching Communicative Alternatives to Challenging Behavior

Paris DePaepe, Joe Reichle, and Rob O'Neill

As THE PREVIOUS CHAPTER DISCUSSES, the stimulus relationships involved in communicative repertoires can be subtle and complex, involving variables that may be difficult to manage. The goal of general-case instruction is to ensure that the full range of exemplars that comprise a stimulus class come to control members of a corresponding response class. This chapter discusses examples of how general-case instructional strategies can be applied to assist in teaching communicative responses to request desired items or activities and attention, as well as to reject undesired objects and activities.

We have constructed four examples that we believe are representative of typical situations in which interventionists may attempt to replace challenging behavior with communicative alternatives. Related intervention programs that might have been developed for each situation are presented, with an emphasis on including general-case instructional strategies within the interventions. The first example describes a communication program designed to teach a learner who exhibited challenging behavior to request preferred objects and activities. Next, a program to teach requesting as a more socially acceptable strategy of obtaining attention is detailed. In the third example, a procedure to teach a conversation initiation response to assist in the replacement of perserverative vocal utterances is described. Finally, two programs designed to

This work was supported in part by Contract No. H133B80048 to the Research and Training Center on Community Living from the National Institute on Disability and Rehabilitation Research, U.S. Department of Education. The points of view or opinions expressed in this chapter do not necessarily represent the official positions of the U.S. Department of Education National Institute on Disability and Rehabilitation Research.

237

teach a generalized rejecting response and a leavetake response to replace avoidance- and escape-motivated challenging behavior are presented.

ESTABLISHING AN INITIAL REQUESTING RESPONSE TO REPLACE TANGIBLE-MOTIVATED CHALLENGING BEHAVIOR

Jessie was a 9-year-old girl with a diagnosis of severe mental retardation. She exhibited no functional verbalizations, but had a repertoire of three or four gestures. Her parents and teacher reported that Jessie infrequently used these gestures to request desired items. Results from a functional assessment that included a functional analysis indicated that often Jessie exhibited head-slapping and aggressive pinching and scratching when she was unable to obtain desired foods and activities. These behaviors occurred in different environments, including Jessie's home, school, and a number of community locations (e.g., grocery store, park). After conducting the assessment, the interventionist and parents agreed that teaching Jessie an alternative for requesting desired items and activities was a high priority.

Identifying the Instructional Universe for Jessie

For Jessie, the primary instructional focus was to teach an appropriate communicative response to request desired items and activities. Minimally, the instructional universe for her would have included the specific settings, activities, and objects that had been identified as related to her challenging behavior, as well as future situations in which challenging behavior might be anticipated. The instructional universe traditionally discussed in the literature refers to a positive class of stimuli, all of which share a set of relevant characteristics that *should* set the occasion for a specific response to be produced. Conversely, one could also identify a negative stimulus class-stimulus conditions that do not share these relevant stimulus features and consequently *should not be* discriminative for the targeted communicative utterance. This negative stimulus-class is used to identify negative examples for use in teaching an individual when to *refrain* from responding with the target response. Defining an entire instructional universe of negative examples would be impractical, as too many negative examples can be identified, many of which would be highly unrelated to the target response. Instead, negative examples that are more closely related to the positive stimulus-class examples presented in the instructional opportunities should be identified. (See Lalli & Goh, chap. 2, this volume, for methods to facilitate identification of the stimulus conditions that typically set the occasion for challenging behavior in natural environments.)

For Jessie, consistent relevant stimuli that should occasion a request included the presence of a listener, an item or activity to be requested, and the capability of the listener to fulfill the request. The socially appropriate requesting utterance *should be* produced by Jessie under general stimulus conditions (i.e., positive stimulus-class) when she would like a specific item or activity but could not obtain the item or materials herself and could be allowed to participate in or be given the activity or item (e.g., a bowl of ice cream that she could not independently obtain, additional paper for a drawing activity). Conversely, Jessie was to *avoid* requesting specific items and activities under other general negative stimulus conditions. For example, Jessie *should not* produce the requesting response when a desired item was nearby and free access to the item had been given, when a request for a specific item or activity had just been denied, during specific times or situations when a desired item or activity could not physically be delivered, or when an undesired item or activity (that she would not be required to take) was presented. Table 1 displays the initial instructional universe that should occasion Jessie's requesting responses. Additionally, the negative stimulus-class, or the general conditions under which Jessie should refrain from producing the requesting response, is also presented.

Identifying Teaching Examples

After defining the instructional universe, the range of relevant stimulus and response variations within that instructional universe would have then been defined to facilitate the identification of teaching examples. This would have involved determining the responses that needed to be performed and the variability of the stimuli and settings that should occasion the new communicative response. The mode of the communicative response would also have been selected and could include vocal, gestural, or graphic representations. Additionally, the interventionist should have determined whether different modes were to be trained in different contexts. For example, an individual might have been taught to use a gesture that was already in his or her repertoire (e.g., a finger point) to request specific times from familiar listeners at home. However, this same individual might have been taught to use a graphic system to request desired items in a fast-food restaurant because of the variety of items that could be requested and the unfamiliarity of the listeners (i.e., the restaurant employee who takes the orders). To a great extent, these decisions would be based on the efficiency of the behaviors relative to the identified challenging behaviors (Durand, Berotti, & Weiner, chap. 13, this volume; Mace & Roberts, chap. 6, this volume; Reichle, York, & Sigafoos, 1991).

As mentioned previously, consistent relevant stimuli that should occasion Jessie's requesting response included the presence of a listener, as well as a desired item or activity to be requested. Aspects such as age and gender of the listener were found via a functional analysis to be irrelevant stimulus features. These irrelevant stimuli would be varied during intervention so they did not come to control the requesting utterance. After the instructional universe was identified and the range of relevant stimulus and response variation within that universe defined, the interventionist would have selected positive examples

Table 1. General-case instructional framework for the intervention with Jessie of requesting tangibles

Instructional universe	Specific examples
Positive stimulus class	
1. Preferred items or activity materials are not accessible during times when they could be consumed or used.	During snacktime, crackers and cheese are out of reach on a tall bookcase [a]
	Catsup is at the far end of the table during dinner [a]
	A teacher is holding a kickball during free-time [a]
	A bowl of ice cream has been consumed and additional ice cream is desired and available [b]
2. Additional or different items or activity materials are required or desired when they could be consumed or used.	Additional paper is required while drawing pictures during freetime at school [a]
	A book is desired after listening to several music tapes during unstructured time [b]
3. Unstructured time at home or at school with a peer, sibling, or adult present who is unoccupied.	Going outside for a walk with a parent is desired during playtime at home [a]
Negative stimulus class	
1. Free access is given to preferred items or activity materials when they could be consumed or used.	During snack, free access is given to a plate of graham crackers or pitcher of juice [a]
	Ketchup bottle is on the table next to the learner's place setting [b]
2. Preferred items or activities are desired at a time when they cannot be delivered.	Playing a video game is desired but a parent says it is time for bed [a]
	After eating a small dish of ice cream, more ice cream is desired but the ice cream container is empty [a]
	Learner is on the playground and desires a kickball but has been directed to line up to go into the school [b]
3. Nonpreferred item or activity is available.	A nonpreferred food item has been offered to the learner [a]
	A nonpreferred activity has been offered to the learner [a]

[a] Teaching example
[b] Probe example

(i.e., specific positive stimulus conditions, such as person/setting combinations, materials that were presented during instruction) from the defined universe for use in instruction and later probe testing. For example, positive examples for Jessie included requesting paper to complete a preferred drawing activity, requesting a desired ball from a teacher, and requesting a walk with a parent. The specific items and activities initially targeted for inclusion in this requesting program could be identified using naturalistic observations, as discussed by Lalli and Goh (chap. 2, this volume) and by more systematic preference testing (Green, Reid, Canipe, & Gardner, 1991; Parsons & Reid, 1990).

Additionally, it would have been equally important to identify and include negative examples to assist Jessie in discriminating when to *refrain* from producing the alternative communicative utterance (e.g., Jessie should request ice cream, a preferred item, but refrain from requesting green beans, a nonpreferred item). This step is necessary initially to teach an individual that responding is not always appropriate and, later, to assist the learner in making more difficult discriminations (Albin & Horner, 1988). Selected negative teaching examples could be placed on a continuum with some examples maximally different from the positive examples, as well as to the other extreme where a negative example was only minimally different from a positive example. A negative example that would have been maximally different from the positive example of ice cream might have involved presenting Jessie with a household chore (e.g., sweeping the floor), a nonpreferred activity that she should refrain from requesting. In contrast, Jessie could have also been presented with a bowl of yogurt, another nonpreferred item, which looked very similar to the preferred bowl of ice cream. This was a negative example that was only minimally different from the positive example. The positive and negative teaching examples that could have been selected for use in Jessie's communication intervention are shown in Table 1.

Sequencing and Teaching the Selected Examples

The intervention focused on teaching Jessie to explicitly request preferred items and activities using a more socially acceptable requesting response of pointing to line drawings or product logos. An explicit requesting repertoire using graphics was selected for Jessie because her preferences for specific items and activities were stable (i.e., the specific items and activities that she highly preferred did not change substantially across time) and typically requires less interpretation by listeners in her school, home, and community.

The intervention involved establishing an explicit requesting repertoire that allowed Jessie to request specific items or activities in different environments (e.g., school, home, and community). Initially, the interventionist could have offered Jessie a choice of two items, one that was demonstrated to be highly preferred and the other that was neither particularly preferred or nonpreferred. After a history was established where Jessie had consistently reached for the preferred item, a graphic symbol or product logo corresponding to the item would have placed on the table in front of the item. As Jessie reached for the item, the interventionist would have physically guided Jessie's hand until it touched the symbol or product logo. After Jessie touched the symbol or logo, she would have been given access to the corresponding item (e.g., bowl of ice cream, video game). To better ensure that this communicative alternative would have eventually replaced the challenging behavior, it would have been critical that the desired items and activities were made available only after Jessie produced the requesting utterance and were not made available contingent on any challenging behavior.

The physical prompt provided by the interventionist could have been faded across instructional opportunities until Jessie touched the symbol or logo when she wanted a desired item that she could not obtain independently. At that point a distractor symbol with fairly similar stimulus features (e.g., size of symbol, colors of product logo) would have been introduced simultaneously with the original item symbol or logo. A distractor symbol should be introduced early in the intervention to allow Jessie to discriminate between the responses needed to establish explicit requesting skills. Jessie should point to the symbol or logo that represented the desired item but refrain from touching the distractor symbol. As the intervention progressed, Jessie could have been taught to request additional preferred items through a similar instructional sequence. Additionally, Jessie could have been taught to request specific activities by first being offered an item needed to participate in a preferred activity. For example, Jessie initially could have been offered some markers that were needed for drawing and gradually was taught to touch a line drawing representing the markers to indicate her request to draw. Eventually, a communication wallet or board with a menu of several activities or items could have been developed for use both at school and home.

The intervention procedure just described would require Jessie to respond with a behavior chain of touching the symbol and subsequently reaching for the item. An alternative procedure could have been implemented in which a package of desired cookies with a distinct product logo could have been systematically transformed across teaching opportunities into a symbol for that item. Initially, a small package of cookies would have been placed within Jessie's reach. The rule would be established that she could reach into the package and take a cookie. Across successful opportunities, the contents of the package could have been removed and Jessie presented with the empty package. Contingent upon her touching the package, a cookie would be offered or placed within her reach. Gradually, the package would have been trimmed away until only the product logo remained. This remaining logo could have then been placed on a communication board or in a wallet for Jessie to use to request cookies.

The selected positive and negative teaching exemplars (i.e., situations that called for Jessie's requesting utterance and conditions under which the request should *not* be produced) could have been implemented concurrently. This strategy would have been necessary to assist her in learning the needed discrimination skills from the beginning of the instructional opportunities. For example, an instructional opportunity might have been arranged so that when Jessie was sitting at a table with peers during snacktime, she would have an opportunity to request cheese and crackers that were placed out of reach on a shelf. Later, she could have been offered a nonpreferred item (e.g., a food item or activity assumed to be nonpreferred) that she should refrain from requesting. Albin and Horner (1988) recommend that, initially, the positive and negative examples used be maximally different from each other in order to teach the differential responding that is required by the learner. Subsequently, negative exemplars that were less discriminable from the positive exemplars (i.e., they share some, but not all, of the relevant stimulus features) should also be included to teach more subtle conditional discriminations. For example, after Jessie learned to request preferred cheese and crackers that were out of reach, teaching opportunities could have provided Jessie with free access to a preferred food item. In these later teaching opportunities, Jessie should refrain from requesting the food item and instead independently take the item. Negative examples that were maximally discriminable from the positive examples could have been introduced first in Jessie's requesting intervention, and the less discriminable negative examples were introduced later.

Providing sufficient positive and negative teaching examples would have ensured that the examples covered the range of variation present in the instructional universe. In addition, irrelevant stimulus features (e.g., location of the intervention opportunity, specific person serving as the interventionist, time of day) of both the selected positive and negative teaching examples would have been systematically varied from the beginning of the intervention to better ensure that Jessie's requests did not come under the control of irrelevant stimulus features. Additionally, during some instructional opportunities it may have been natural to provide several consecutive requesting opportunities. For example, during a drawing activity, Jessie might have been initially provided with two sheets of drawing paper. After she had drawn on these, she would have been able to request more paper. In addition, a most-to-least prompting system would have been used during the requesting skill acquisition unless Jessie was not resistive to physical prompting by the interventionists (Sigafoos, Mustonen, DePaepe, Reichle, & York, 1991). If she had been, an alternative procedure might have been implemented instead. Finally, error-correction strategies would have been identified and implemented in the communication intervention to assist in the establishment of the desired communicative replacement behavior.

Several positive and negative teaching examples could have been selected and implemented across different settings in Jessie's natural daily routine. Initially, instructional opportunities could be conducted so Jessie could request items or activities at school, at home, and in specific community locations. For example, intervention opportunities could have been arranged across the day to allow Jessie to request food during snacktime at school, desired activities and materials during free time, and to go on a walk outside with a parent during the evening. Further variation in Jessie's communication program could have been arranged by implementing the requesting program across the variety of settings by a variety of interventionists.

Testing for Generalization with Probe Examples

As discussed by O'Neill and Reichle (chap. 9, this volume), probe testing must be conducted using untaught or minimally utilized examples to assist the interventionist in determining whether generalized responding was the result of intervention. Both untaught positive and negative probe examples would have been implemented periodically during initial acquisition to test whether an adequate range of positive and negative teaching examples had been sampled in intervention opportunities. Probe testing should indicate whether the intervention procedures had been successful for Jessie to establish a fully generalized functional requesting repertoire. That is, Jessie should produce the requesting response during positive untaught probe examples and refrained from producing the requesting response during the untaught negative probe examples. The probe testing that could have been conducted might have indicated, however, that Jessie emitted the requesting utterance to obtain preferred items in the presence of one specific teacher only and continued to exhibit challenging behavior to obtain preferred items when other instructors were present. Alternatively, Jessie might have also demonstrated an error pattern, in which she produced requests in situations where she should have independently obtained a desired item. Identifying error patterns such as these would have required the interventionist to identify additional teaching examples to be included in the instruction to better establish the desired range of discriminative performance of the requesting utterance. Positive and negative probe examples that might have been selected for testing whether Jessie displayed an appropriate discriminative requesting response are indicated in Table 1.

Summary

We briefly delineated the steps that might have been followed to apply general-case instructional strategies in an intervention designed to teach an individual a more socially acceptable means of requesting desired items and activities. Of course, teaching a learner a communicative utterance to request desired items and activities will have limited utility unless the learner can gain the attention of a listener prior to making a request. This is a particularly important consideration in establishing a graphic mode (communication board or wallet) repertoire in which the learner may not be able to produce sounds that will recruit a listener's attention prior to or concurrent with the actual request. The following example outlines an intervention program implemented to teach a socially acceptable attention-recruiting response.

ESTABLISHING AN INITIAL ATTENTION-REQUESTING RESPONSE TO REPLACE ATTENTION-MOTIVATED CHALLENGING BEHAVIOR

Michael was 40 years old with diagnoses of mental retardation and cerebral palsy. He was ambulatory but had limited use of his left arm. He lived with two other men with developmental disabilities and worked as a janitor each weekday from 9:00 A.M. to 2:30 P.M. Staff from both home and work reported that Michael frequently screamed and threw objects throughout the day. Results of a functional assessment indicated that Michael often began to scream and throw objects if he had not received any attention for approximately 30 minutes. Direct observations of Michael indicated that his challenging behavior frequently occurred in a chain of behavior. This chain began with Michael tapping his right hand on the table, wall, or other nearby surface. On some occasions, staff provided brief attention contingent upon Michael's tapping. Unfortunately, the efficiency of Michael's tapping was not great, because in the majority of instances, staff failed to attend when he tapped. Observation indicated that if tapping did not result in immediate attention from staff, Michael usually threw nearby objects onto the floor and screamed. On occasions when there were no objects nearby, he directed his behavior to repeated and increasingly more intense screaming contingent upon no attention as a result of his tapping. A requesting program could have been developed to allow Michael to utilize a more socially appropriate attention-requesting response (i.e., touching a graphic symbol) during stimulus conditions similar to those identified during the assessment process as functionally related to his attention-motivated behavior.

Identifying the Instructional Universe for Michael

A functional assessment identified several types of situations in which Michael was most likely to exhibit challenging behavior to recruit attention. Relevant stimulus features of the instructional universe (positive stimulus class) included the presence of a listener who was not interacting with Michael, as well as the ability of the listener to provide attention contingent upon a socially acceptable requesting utterance. Conversely, Michael should not request attention when no listeners were present, when an available listener was occupied or already attending to him, or when he was involved in an activity that required him to be independently engaged. Table 2 displays the positive and negative stimulus classes in which Michael was to produce and not produce the requesting-attention response.

Identifying Teaching Examples

Subsequent to identifying the instructional universe, positive and negative teaching examples should have been identified for Michael that included

Table 2. General-case instructional framework for the intervention with Michael for requesting attention

Instructional universe	Specific examples
Positive stimulus class	
1. Unstructured time in the presence of one or more peers and one or more other listeners who are not directly interacting with him but could deliver attention contingent on a socially acceptable requesting response.	During unstructured time after work while in the living room with a staff member nearby and unoccupied [a]
	After arrival at work, prior to work starting with a staff member nearby and unoccupied [a]
	Morning break at work in the lounge area with a staff member nearby and unoccupied [b]
2. During work or household chores when in the presence of one or more familiar listeners who are not directly attending to him, but could deliver attention to him.	Filling the clothes washer at his parents' home while a parent is nearby folding clothes [a]
	When waiting for his turn for one-to-one instruction at work [a]
	Vacuuming his bedroom while a staff member is nearby [b]
Negative stimulus class	
1. Unstructured time when in the presence of a listener who is occupied or who is already providing attention to the learner.	During breaktime a staff member is nearby helping a peer who fell down [a]
	During lunch a family member is talking to the learner [a]
	While at a park a familiar adult is standing next to the learner talking to him [b]

[a] Teaching example
[b] Probe example

situations in which it was socially acceptable to request attention and situations in which Michael should refrain from requesting attention. For example, Michael could produce the requesting response during free time at home when a listener was nearby and unoccupied (positive teaching example). However, Michael should not produce the requesting-attention utterance when a listener was already talking to him, when a listener was talking on the phone or working, or when Michael was independently engaged in an activity at work or at home (negative teaching examples). Examples of positive and negative teaching examples that could have been identified for Michael's program are presented in Table 2.

Sequencing and Teaching the Selected Examples

An intervention designed to teach Michael a more socially appropriate requesting response might involve shaping his tapping behavior (that typically appeared at the beginning of his chain of challenging behavior) into a pointing response. To achieve this objective, any time that Michael was observed or heard to begin tapping his hands on a table or surface when a listener was not attending to him, the listener could immediately approach and speak to him for a brief time. When listeners were consistently approaching and attending to Michael when he initiated tapping, a card stating "I would like some attention" could have been placed within Michael's reach. One individual would then approach Michael at these times and provide a prompt to direct him to touch the card. When Michael had touched the card, a second listener would then approach and provide attention. Because the first interventionist would have served as the prompter and Michael would consequently already have his or her attention, the need to request attention from that individual would be unnecessary. Thus, the second person would have been the target listener (i.e., the person who provided immediate attention to Michael after he produced the requesting response). Across instructional opportunities, the interventionist would have then faded the prompts used to direct Michael to touch the card. Additionally, after the initial requesting response had been established, Michael could have been taught to pick up, go to, and hand the card to different listeners who were not in the immediate area. One strategy that could have been used to accomplish this was to systematically increase the distance of the target listener from Michael after he had been prompted to produce the communicative response.

An alternative attention-requesting response option could be used in situations when an individual is unable to independently move to a listener to obtain desired attention. In situations such as this, requesting attention might involve pressing a button to activate a microcassette tape with the message "Could you please come here?" Subsequently, an interventionist would have then physically prompted the learner to press the button on the microcassette recorder, which had been placed on the learner's belt. After the tape was activated, a second individual would immediately approach the learner and provide attention. Gradually, the physical prompt to press the button would have been faded.

For Michael, several positive and negative teaching examples might have been selected. For example, Michael could have been taught to request attention from an unoccupied job supervisor before work or at home from a parent who was folding clothes. Initially, maximally discriminable negative teaching examples should have been implemented. A maximally discriminable teaching example might have consisted of a situation in which an adult was alone with Michael and was already providing attention to him. A situation in which Michael was alone with an adult who had just answered the telephone would be a less discriminable negative example to teach Michael to *refrain* from requesting attention. Teaching examples could have been selected so that irrelevant stimuli (e.g., interventionists, settings) were varied. A sufficient number of positive and negative teaching examples that adequately sampled the range of stimulus variations that Michael was likely to encounter in his daily activities should have been included within the instructional opportunities.

Testing for Generalization with Probe Examples

As discussed in the preceding example, probe testing could have been conducted using untaught stimulus conditions and situations to examine Michael's generalized use of requests for attention. For example, probe testing in this case might have indicated that Michael produced attention-seeking requests only during breaks or lunchtime at work, while he continued to display the throwing and screaming behavior in other situations (e.g., at home or in locations other than his workplace). After identifying the problem, the interventionist could have then identified additional teaching examples for inclusion in the communication instruction to better ensure the generalized acquisition of requests for attention. Probes that might have been selected for use in Michael's communication program are also indicated in Table 2.

Summary

A beginning attention-requesting program such as the one just described could be beneficial in providing a more socially acceptable method of recruiting attention that replaces an existing repertoire of attention-motivated challenging behavior. However, although some individuals do exhibit socially acceptable attention-getting responses, they may continue to produce challenging behavior after the listener has provided attention to him or her in order to maintain the social contact or interaction. A program could be implemented to replace attention-maintaining perseverative vocal utterances with socially acceptable conversational initiations once attention has been gained.

ESTABLISHING AN INITIAL CONVERSATION INITIATION RESPONSE TO REPLACE CHALLENGING BEHAVIOR ASSOCIATED WITH PERSEVERATIVE UTTERANCES

Ann was a 26-year-old woman with mental retardation. She lived with another woman with developmental disabilities and with a couple who assisted Ann and her housemate. Ann produced many vocalizations that the staff and her parents believe to be referants to specific people or activities (e.g., going to visit her family, recent vacation, favorite TV show, bowling). However, many of these vocalizations were unintelligible and not readily understood by most listeners.

Observational data indicated that frequently Ann approached a listener and obtained his or her attention by tapping his or her arm. Subsequently, Ann produced a vocalization such as "Ta" or "Ho." The couple who lived with Ann reports that she frequently utters "Ho" immediately prior to going to visit her family. Listeners often state that they are unaware that she is referring to visiting her family. At this point in the social exchange, Ann often begins to repeat the vocalization over and over (vocally perseverate) in a loud voice and at times starts to wave her arms and gesture. Interventionists hypothesized that, although Ann exhibits a socially acceptable attention-getting response, her challenging behavior appeared to be associated with situations in which she is unable to convey the topic of her conversational initiation. A program using a communication board with photographs to allow Ann to initiate conversation, which might recruit topic-maintaining utterances from her listener, represents a viable intervention option.

Identifying the Instructional Universe for Ann

For Ann, the relevant stimulus features that should serve as discriminative stimuli for her to initiate a conversation included the presence of one or more familiar listeners at times when a conversation could be initiated. Conversely, Ann should refrain from producing the commenting utterance under conditions in which a potential listener could not participate in a conversation (e.g., the listener was talking with a salesperson at the door or had just received a phone call) or when she was in situations in which conversations *should not* be initiated (e.g., during a religious service or concert). Table 3 displays the instructional universe or conditions that should occasion the commenting

Table 3. General-case instructional framework for the intervention with Ann of conversation initiation

Instructional universe	Specific examples
Positive stimulus class	
1. Unstructured time in the presence of one or more listeners who are not directly talking with her, but who could engage in a conversation on a given topic contingent on a socially acceptable commenting response.	During unstructured time after work while in the living room with a listener nearby and unoccupied [a]
	While on the bus home while in the presence of a familiar listener who is nearby and unoccupied [a]
	After arrival at work prior to starting work with a familiar listener nearby and unoccupied [b]
Negative stimulus class	
1. Unstructured time in the presence of a listener who is occupied.	During break, a familiar listener is nearby helping someone [a]
	A family member is talking on the phone [a]
	Staff member has stated that she has to work on a report [b]
2. When in the presence of totally unfamiliar listeners.	While in a coffeeshop sitting next to a stranger [a]
3. With a familiar listener in a location where extended conversations should not be conducted.	Attending a religious service [a]
	Watching a movie at a local movie theater [a]
	Attending a play or concert [b]

[a] Teaching example
[b] Probe example

utterance as well as the negative stimulus class under which the commenting response should not be emitted.

Identifying Teaching Examples

After the instructional universe had been identified and the negative stimulus class had been defined, positive and negative teaching examples could be identified. The examples must sample the range of the stimulus conditions that should be discriminative for a socially acceptable conversational initiation utterance. For Ann, critical discriminative stimuli for conversational initiations include the presence of a listener who was available to engage in a communicative interaction when neither Ann nor her listener were engaged in an activity that did *not* permit social exchanges. For example, Ann could initiate a conversation with a familiar person who was sitting next to her on the bus home. Conversely, Ann should not initiate a conversation during a concert. Positive and negative teaching examples that could have been selected for use in Ann's communication intervention are shown in Table 3.

Sequencing and Teaching the Selected Examples

After identifying the teaching examples, the interventionist might have then developed a portable bifold communication board that contained photographs of persons, activities, and places Ann would be likely to want to talk about (e.g., her family, a recent vacation, her job, a favorite baseball team). Related topics that a listener could use to maintain a conversation once it had been initiated could have been written next to each photograph. The listener could have then conversed with Ann about preferred topics contingent upon her touching a photograph on the board. For example, topics listed next to a photo from a recent vacation might have included where she went on the vacation, who went along on the trip, what she did on the trip, and plans for future vacations. When Ann or the listener had to end the conversation, a response prompt could have been used to direct Ann to close the communication board.

To teach Ann to use the communication book to initiate and sustain social interactions with others, any time Ann approached a listener at a time when a conversation was appropriate, the interventionist would have prompted Ann to obtain and open her communication book. At that point, the interventionist could have then prompted Ann to touch a picture that corresponded to a topic that she might like to talk about at that time. For example, when Ann approached a familiar listener after returning home from a baseball game, the listener could have prompted Ann to touch the photo of the baseball team and then talked with her about related topics (e.g., who won the game, who her favorite players were, the team's place in the standings). Later, another listener could approach Ann and asked her what she had done earlier in the evening, in order to provide an additional opportunity for her to use her communication book. Gradually the initial rehearsals provided by the different interventionists could have been faded. The interventionists could maintain a menu of different topics in the communication book from which Ann could select. When Ann attempted to repeat the same conversation with a listener within a brief time, the interventionist could tell Ann that they had already talked about that topic. Subsequently, attention could be briefly withdrawn, and at a later time her communicative partner could make a new conversational overture to Ann. Additional instructional opportunities could have also been arranged by interventionists at times when a conversation could take place, but when Ann did not independently approach a listener. To do this, the interventionists could approach Ann periodically throughout the day and prompt her to get her communication book and then follow the instructional sequence just described.

Selected teaching examples, both positive and negative, could have been arranged to occur systematically within all critical environments during the natural routine of Ann's day. For example, the communication board could have been routinely accessible during breaks at work, while on the bus to and from work, while visiting her family, at home during free time, and when she was in community situations. Teaching opportunities provided during instruction should have included positive teaching examples in which Ann should produce the conversation initiation response in addition to negative teaching examples or occasions where she should refrain from producing the response. For example, Ann could produce the conversation initiation response at work during breaks with a familiar listener who was nearby and unoccupied, but should not produce the response to a complete stranger. Again, maximally different teaching examples should be employed first during instruction, with less discriminable negative teaching examples utilized later. A maximally discriminable negative teaching situation in which Ann should not initiate a conversation might occurr when Ann was sitting in a coffee shop next to a stranger. Less discriminable stimulus conditions might be arranged to occur while at a movie theater with a familiar listener. That is, although Ann could have initiated a conversation with a listener prior to the movie starting (i.e., positive teaching example), she could have had an opportunity to *refrain* from initiating a conversation during the movie (i.e., negative teaching example). Providing multiple teaching opportunities in different locations with different listeners could have also aided Ann in establishing the discriminative conversation initiation utterance. For example, instructional sessions could have been arranged to provide Ann with opportunities to initiate conversations with staff in her vocational setting and at her home, with her parents and other family members, as well as with neighbors and friends.

Testing for Generalization with Probe Examples

Probe testing should also have been conducted during intervention to confirm whether the instructional procedures were effective in establishing socially acceptable conversational initiations. For example, the interventionist might have determined through the probe testing that Ann made conversational initiations in a limited range of opportunities while she continued the perseverative behavior (i.e., repeatedly stating "Ta") in other situations (e.g., during breaks and lunchtime at work). Again, identifying patterns of use would provide the interventionist with critical information needed to guide the modification in the instructional procedures. Probe examples that might have been selected for use in this intervention are listed in Table 3.

Summary

The preceding intervention and the two earlier examples each discussed situations in which a selected communicative response was targeted to allow individuals to either obtain or maintain access to items or events that served as reinforcers. However, other individuals who exhibit challenging behavior may do so to avoid or escape specific items or situations. The following section describes several interventions designed to teach communicative alternatives to replace challenging behavior that is escape or avoidance motivated.

TEACHING REJECTING AND LEAVETAKING RESPONSES TO REPLACE AVOIDANCE- AND ESCAPE-MOTIVATED CHALLENGING BEHAVIOR

Angelo was 22 years old with mental retardation. His communicative repertoire consisted of a few verbal utterances (e.g., "juice") and some gestures, a few of which appeared to be used to indicate desires. Results from a functional assessment (including a functional analysis) indicated that his screaming, attempts to bite others, and throwing objects appeared to be maintained by escape from undesired objects or activities. Typically, Angelo exhibited challenging behaviors under two general stimulus conditions: 1) when he was approached or presented with undesired items or activities, and 2) after he had been actively engaged in work tasks or chores for some time.

Two different interventions, a generalized rejecting program and a leave-take program that includes the use of a "safety signal" (i.e., a stimulus that signals release from a task is eminent contingent on little to no challenging behavior), could have been implemented to assist in replacing Angelo's range of avoidance- and escape-motivated challenging behavior. A generalized rejecting utterance could be selected so that Angelo could avoid nonobligatory items or events (i.e., items or events that were not mandatory that he could reject). For example, Angelo could have taught to communicate that he did not want an activity or item by producing a reject gesture (i.e., a push-away hand gesture). For Angelo, a gestural mode was selected for the rejecting utterance because the gesture could be produced quickly with minimal effort, could be easily seen at a distance, and was readily "guessable" by listeners in his daily environments. As discussed by Durand, Berotti, and Weiner (chap. 13, this volume), establishing a communicative alternative escape (rejecting) response that was functionally equivalent to Angelo's existing challenging behavior should successfully address the need to decelerate his avoidance- and escape-motivated challenging repertoire. For Angelo, the socially acceptable rejecting utterance could have been honored in all instances in which Angelo was presented with nonpreferred, nonobligatory activities or items that he tried to avoid.

However, escape (after a brief period of participation) from other obligatory items or events might require a different intervention program. In situations that *required* Angelo's participation (e.g., taking seizure control medicine, having his fingernails trimmed, cleaning his bedroom), his rejecting response could not be honored. For these obligatory activities, Angelo's participation must be made more palatable. In these instances, a series of programmatic steps could lead to the establishment of an alternative leavetake response to allow Angelo to request a break from ongoing activities after a specific minimum period of participation in the activity. This could be accomplished by the conditioning of a safety signal or verbal cue that informed Angelo that release from a task or activity was eminent. For example, when presented with a nonpreferred activity in which Angelo was required to participate, a safety signal ("You're almost done") would be delivered by the interventionist after the minimum period of participation and then Angelo would be immediately prompted to produce a leavetake response (i.e., push-away hand gesture). Angelo would then be released from the activity if he refrained from any challenging behavior after producing the leavetake response. Gradually, Angelo could have been required to participate in the activity for increasingly longer periods of time before the safety signal was delivered, and alternatively, the period between the safety signal and Angelo's release from the task could also be lengthened.

REJECTING PROGRAM

Identifying the Instructional Universe for Angelo's Rejecting Program

Minimally, the instructional universe for generalized rejecting would have included specific tasks, activities, and objects that were regularly avoided and that Angelo's instructional team were willing to allow him to avoid. Angelo *should* produce the rejecting utterance when presented with nonobligatory items or activities (e.g., offer of broccoli, wiping tables), but he *should not* produce the rejecting response when presented with obligatory items or activities that he cannot be permitted to escape (e.g., taking seizure control medication, completing physical therapy exercises). Relevant stimuli for the generalized rejecting program include the presence of a listener as well as a nonpreferred item, activity, or task to be rejected. The obligatory or nonobligatory nature of the nonpreferred items or activities was also identified as a relevant stimulus feature. However, aspects such as the age and gender of the listener or the specific materials used to perform a given work task or chore were found to be irrelevant stimulus features. Table 4 displays the instructional universe that was identified for Angelo, with the individual positive stimulus class listed that should eventually occasion the rejecting response. In addition, the negative stimulus class, or the general conditions under which Angelo should refrain from producing the rejecting response, is presented.

Identifying Teaching Examples for the Rejecting Program

Both positive and negative examples should have been identified for use within the instructional opportunities to assist Angelo in discriminating when to produce and when to *refrain* from producing the communicative rejecting utterance. The generalized rejecting response should be produced by Angelo when he is presented with nonobligatory, nonpreferred items or activities that he could be allowed to escape (e.g., offer of yogurt, wiping tables). These examples would constitute positive teaching examples. Alternatively, Angelo should refrain from giving his generalized rejecting response when presented with obligatory items or activities that require his acceptance or participation or when presented with preferred items or activities that he actually desires (e.g., offer of ice cream or a video game). These stimulus conditions would constitute negative teaching examples in this program to teach generalized rejecting. Negative teaching examples that are both maximally different as well as minimally different from the positive examples should be included. Positive and negative teaching examples that might have been selected from

Table 4. General-case instructional framework for the intervention with Angelo for rejecting

Instructional universe	Specific examples
Positive stimulus class	
1. Offer of items or events that the learner could be allowed to avoid or escape contingent on production of a socially acceptable rejecting response.	Offer of yogurt [a]
	Offer of tomato juice [b]
	Offer of broccoli [a]
	Wiping tables [a]
	Loading soda machines [b]
Negative stimulus class	
1. Activities and objects that the learner attempts to escape after limited participation.	Trimming his fingernails [a]
	Taking seizure control medication [a]
	Physical therapy exercises [b]
2. Offer of desired item or activity.	Offer of ice cream when not satiated [a]
	Offer to play preferred video games [a]
	Offer of coffee when not satiated [b]

[a] Teaching example
[b] Probe example

the instructional universe for Angelo's rejecting program are indicated in Table 4.

Sequencing and Teaching the Rejecting Program Examples

After determining the range of possible positive and negative teaching examples and the mode of the communicative rejecting response to be taught, the interventionist would have selected several of these nonpreferred items or activities to present to Angelo in the beginning phases of intervention. During the beginning of instruction, it would have been important that the interventionist establish teaching opportunities in which Angelo could be prompted to give the rejecting response prior to demonstrating challenging behavior. This would be important to prevent the establishment of a chain of behavior where Angelo first engaged in a challenging behavior and only then produce the targeted rejecting response. In Angelo's case, it might have been difficult to approach him with a highly nonpreferred item and deliver a prompt to him before he engaged in challenging behavior. Consequently, if the interventionist was unable to deliver a prompt without the challenging behavior occurring, one option would be to begin instruction by first introducing activities or items that were nonpreferred but least likely to provoke challenging behavior. More provoking events or items from which Angelo was allowed to escape, contingent on a socially acceptable rejecting response, could have been systematically introduced as the instruction progressed.

Once these teaching examples had been identified, the interventionist would have approached Angelo with one item or activity. The interventionist could have then used selected response prompts to assist Angelo in producing the rejecting response. As soon as the rejecting response was produced, the offered item or event would have been withdrawn immediately. Gradually, as Angelo began to more independently produce the rejecting response when presented with these less provoking items or activities, the interventionist might have presented items and activities determined to be more provoking. At this point, response prompts by the interventionist might have been unnecessary, as Angelo begins to independently produce the rejecting response when presented with more provoking nonpreferred items or events.

Establishing a rejecting response was prioritized as a goal for Angelo to assist in the immediate reduction of his challenging behavior associated with the presentation of nonpreferred activities and items. However, once a rejecting response was established, efforts could proceed to increase Angelo's participation in activities after rejecting them. For example, although Angelo might attempt to escape wiping tables, it is viewed as an activity that he could be allowed to escape by producing a rejecting response (although eventually learning to wipe tables to increase his repertoire of functional domestic skills was important). Subsequently, a second intervention phase could have been implemented. In this phase, after producing a rejecting response, a latency period of several seconds would be imposed prior to release. Eventually, small task demands could replace the pause. For example, the interventionist could have required Angelo to perform a brief part of the task (e.g., place a wet rag on the table) prior to releasing Angelo from the activity. Over successive opportunities, Angelo would have been required to perform more and more of the task (after producing the rejecting response) before he was released. This progression would have allowed Angelo to gradually approximate a schedule more typical of work and breaks. However, he would have been able to produce his rejecting utterance at any time and it would have at least been acknowledged.

Adequate positive and negative teaching examples should be included during initial instruction and should be systematically arranged by the interventionist to occur throughout the natural routine of Angelo's day. For example, a positive teaching example for the rejecting program could have been arranged by ensuring that at least one nonpreferred food item would be served during a given meal at Angelo's home. (Care must be taken when determining the frequency with which a nonpreferred item or activity, which a learner is allowed to reject, is presented during individual instructional opportunities.) Clearly, nonpreferred items and activities would have been offered to Angelo to provide the instructional opportunities needed for him to acquire the rejecting response. For example, the nonpreferred item broccoli might have been presented to Angelo at the beginning of a meal as he selected foods he wanted to eat. After Angelo was prompted to produce the rejecting response to this initial offer, a second offer of the broccoli should not have been presented until Angelo consumed most of the food on his plate. However, the more frequent a nonpreferred item or activity is presented in a brief time interval, the greater the likelihood that challenging behavior will be exhibited.

Negative teaching examples that were very different from the positive examples should be included in the initial instruction, and negative teaching examples that are more similar to the positive examples should be included during later instructional opportunities. For example, a positive teaching example could have first be used where Angelo was presented with a small bowl of yogurt that he could communicatively reject. A negative example that was maximally different might have involved presenting Angelo with a videogame, a highly preferred item. In contrast, presenting Angelo with a bowl of ice cream, another highly preferred item that looked very similar to the bowl of yogurt would be a more similar negative teaching example. This negative example might have subsequently been presented during a later instructional opportunity. Finally, variation within the rejecting communication program could have been arranged by implementing the programs across different settings (e.g., at work, home, in the community) by a variety of interventionists (e.g., supervisor at work, parent, staff member at his home, family members) to best ensure that the rejecting utterance did not come under the control of irrelevant stimuli such as a specific location or interventionist.

Testing for Generalization with Rejecting Probe Examples

Again, untaught probe examples should have been used to test the range of responding that Angelo will produce when presented with untrained stimulus conditions (both positive and negative) in order to ensure that he is producing the rejecting response under the appropriate stimulus conditions, as well as refraining from producing the responses when inappropriate. For example, the probe testing might have indicated that Angelo will only produce the rejecting response when a specific person presents him with nonpreferred items and that he continues to demonstrate challenging behaviors when other individuals present him with the same nonpreferred items. Consequently, additional teaching examples using multiple interventionists would have been needed to be included to establish use of the rejecting response in the presence of the greater range of individuals with whom Angelo interacts.

Summary

A generalized rejecting program such as the one just described could assist in reducing Angelo's challenging behavior when he is presented with nonpreferred items and activities that he could be allowed to reject. In contrast, a leavetake program that could be implemented to reduce challenging behavior associated with nonpreferred activities and items that Angelo cannot be allowed to simply reject is described in the following section. The manner in which general-case instructional procedures could be embedded within this intervention is emphasized.

LEAVETAKE PROGRAM

Identifying the Instructional Universe for Angelo's Leavetake Program

A socially acceptable leavetake response (after a safety signal or verbal cue that release from the task is eminent had been delivered) could be taught to allow Angelo to escape obligatory, ongoing tasks or activities after an acceptable level of participation. At a minimum, the instructional universe would include the specific tasks and activities that involve his challenging behaviors (i.e., obligatory tasks or activities that he tried to escape).

Identifying the stimulus conditions that were related to Angelo's challenging behaviors, as well as determining other frequently encountered situations that typically do not occasion his challenging behavior, would be necessary to define the instructional universe for this leavetake program. Angelo should produce the leavetake utterance only after engaging in an *obligatory* activity for a brief time and after the safety signal had been delivered. However, Angelo should not produce the leavetake response when he is participating in a desired activity that he wishes to continue or when he is presented with an activity that he *could* be permitted to simply reject (e.g., eating broccoli is a nonobligatory activity). Table 5 displays the instructional universe that should eventually occasion the leavetake response as well as the negative stimulus class under which Angelo should refrain from producing the leavetake response.

Identifying Teaching Examples for the Leavetake Program

Both positive and negative examples would have been identified to assist Angelo in discriminating when to produce and when to *refrain* from producing the communicative leavetake utterance. Positive examples for the leavetake program would consist of situations in which Angelo is presented with items or activities that he must take or participate in (e.g., taking seizure control medication, cleaning his bedroom, completing physical therapy exercises). Negative examples would have included situations in which undesired items or activities are presented that are not obligatory and that could be avoided by producing the communicative rejecting response (e.g., offer of yogurt, offer of broccoli). In addition, situations where desired items or activities were presented to Angelo would also constitute negative examples for the leavetake program (e.g., offer of ice cream when not satiated, playing video games). As previously discussed, negative teaching examples that were both maximally different as well as minimally different from the postive examples should have been identified and used in the instructional opportunities. Positive and negative teaching examples that could have been identified for this intervention are seen in Table 5.

Table 5. General-case instructional framework for the intervention with Angelo of leavetaking

Instructional universe	Specific examples
Positive stimulus class	
1. Events that the learner could be allowed to escape after a brief period of participation contingent on production of a socially acceptable leavetake response.	Cleaning bedroom [a] Completing physical therapy exercises [a] Packaging and labeling task [a] Taking seizure control medication [a] Trimming fingernails [b]
Negative stimulus class	
1. Items or events that the learner could be allowed to *avoid* contingent on production of a socially acceptable rejecting response.	Offer of yogurt [a] Wiping tables [a] Offer of broccoli [a]
2. Offer of desired item or activity.	Offer of ice cream when not satiated [a] Playing video games [a] Playing basketball outside [b]

[a] Teaching example
[b] Probe example

Sequencing and Teaching the Selected Leavetake Program Examples

A leavetake program could have been implemented to set the occasion for Angelo to increase his participation in activities prior to requesting to escape. In this program, a safety signal that let Angelo know that the task will be terminated shortly (e.g., "You're almost done") would have been conditioned while the leavetake response was concurrently taught to him. To implement the leavetake program for Angelo, the interventionist would first need to develop a list of routine obligatory activities or events that Angelo tried to escape from after participating for at least a brief time. Data could have then been obtained to determine the length of time that he would work on each separate task prior to exhibiting any of his challenging behaviors. For example, the shortest length of time that Angelo worked on the packaging and labeling task before giving a challenging behavior might have been 5 minutes. Alternatively, Angelo could have been observed to participate in his physical therapy exercises for only 30 seconds before attempting to escape the activity. Determining the shortest time that Angelo will participate in each obligatory task without challenging behavior will ensure that an initial criterion of performance can be established in which Angelo can be released contingent on desirable behavior.

To start, Angelo might have been required to participate in a specified activity for the criterion period of time before the interventionist presented the safety signal or verbal cue that release from the task was imminent. Subsequently, a verbal warning of upcoming task completion could have been delivered ("You're almost done"). As soon as the safety signal was delivered, Angelo would have been prompted to produce the leavetake utterance (i.e., push-away hand gesture) and would have been immediately released from the activity if no challenging behavior had been produced subsequent to the delivery of the safety signal. When Angelo had engaged in challenging behavior after he had produced the communicative leavetake response, but before release from the task, he would have been required to remain at the task for a brief additional period of time during which no challenging behavior could be produced, after which he would have been released.

Gradually, Angelo would have been required to participate in the activity for increasing amounts of time between producing the leavetake utterance and before being released. This could have been accomplished by the interventionist using a time delay procedure where a brief stalling period was inserted after Angelo produced the leavetake utterance (e.g., "Okay, just finish a few more and then you'll be done") prior to releasing him from the activity. Gradually, the delay between the leavetake utterance and Angelo's release from the task could have been increased systematically from the initial immediate response (i.e., 0 seconds) to longer periods of time (e.g., 15 seconds, 30 seconds, 1 minute).

Adequate positive and negative teaching examples should have been included during initial instruction and systematically arranged by the interventionist to occur throughout the natural routine of Angelo's day. During the instructional opportunities, Angelo could have been allowed to request a leave or break from several different obligatory work tasks during a single day. Angelo could also request breaks from grooming routines in the morning, chores at home in the afternoon, and physical therapy exercises in the evening. Multiple instructional opportunities could have been provided to Angelo across different activities using different interventionists to better ensure that the leavetake utterance did not come under the control of irrelevant stimuli such as a specific location or interventionist. In addition, as mentioned earlier, maximally different negative teaching examples should be included in the initial instruction, with negative teaching examples that are only minimally different from the positive examples presented in the later instructional opportunities.

Testing for Generalization with Leavetake Probe Examples

As in the other communication interventions detailed previously, nontrained probe examples would have been used to test the range of Angelo's responding with the leavetake utterance. If the probe testing had indicated that Angelo was exhibiting either a restricted or overgeneralized responding pattern, additional teaching examples would need to be identified and implemented to address the problem.

Summary

For Angelo, procedures could be applied in two separate communication interventions designed to teach socially appropriate behaviors to replace avoidance- and escape-motivated challenging behavior that is displayed under different stimulus conditions. The rejecting program would have been designed to teach Angelo a generalized rejecting response to avoid nonobligatory activities or items. In addition, a leavetake program could have been implemented concurrently to teach Angelo a leavetake response to allow him to escape activities, which were or would be obligatory, contingent on a minimally acceptable level of engagement.

These rejecting and leavetake programs could be implemented to teach Angelo communicative alternatives to replace his escape and avoidance behavior. However, an alternative intervention approach that could also be used to address this challenging behavior would have been to teach him an alternative *requesting* response. This intervention approach would require establishing an alternative *requesting* response that Angelo could have produced to avoid or escape nonpreferred items and activities. For example, when Angelo was approached with a bowl of yogurt, a nonpreferred item, this intervention approach would focus on teaching him to request a different preferred item (e.g., ice cream) instead of teaching him to reject the yogurt. A potential difficulty with this approach of establishing a replacement response for escape- or avoidance-motivated challenging behavior is the possibility that a learner may avoid all nonpreferred items or activities, some of which may be obligatory, by requesting alternative items or activities.

Another alternative procedure, a high-probability command sequence or interspersed requests, is designed to increase the probability that an individual will follow a given request that he or she generally attempts to avoid. This procedure could also have been used to increase Angelo's participation in tasks or activities he attempted to escape or avoid (Horner, Day, Sprague, O'Brien, & Heathfield, 1991; Singer, Singer, & Horner, 1987). In this procedure, the interventionist would present a series of short, high-probability requests that Angelo would be likely to perform immediately prior to the target low-probability request that he usually attempted to avoid by displaying challenging behavior. For example, Angelo might be asked to perform three to five high-probability requests (e.g., "Give me five," "Hand me that paper") in close succession immediately prior to delivery of the target request (e.g., "Wipe the table," "Take your medication"). Reinforcement would be provided immediately following the completion of each high-probability request. After the last high-probability request was made, the target low-probability request would be presented. This antecedent procedure has been reported to increase the probability that individuals with severe disabilities will respond to target requests without exhibiting challenging behavior (e.g., Singer et al., 1987).

CONCLUSION

The major defining feature of general-case instruction is the emphasis on analyzing the universe in which the learner will be expected to perform and in ensuring that an appropriate range of stimulus and response variation is systematically included and appropriately sequenced in intervention. Careful attention to these steps should greatly enhance the probability that desired generalized performance on the part of a learner will result. Combining the general-case approach with other critical instructional aspects, such as choosing maximally efficient alternative responses and using appropriate prompting procedures, should enhance our ability to establish repertoires of communicative behaviors that effectively compete with socially motivated challenging behaviors.

The inherent emphasis in the general-case instructional strategy on the careful selection of stimuli and settings to use in teaching examples is especially critical given the range of relevant and irrelevant stimulus conditions that may surround any given communicative opportunity. This chapter provides illustrations of how the general-case approach can be applied in intervention programs designed to establish functional communicative repertoires targeted to compete with socially motivated challenging behaviors. The challenge in applying these concepts and technology to the subtle and complex stimulus control relationships involved in communicative interactions and in documenting their effectiveness continues.

REFERENCES

Albin, R., & Horner, R. (1988). Generalization with precision. In R. Horner, G. Dunlap, & R. Koegel (Eds.), *Generalization and maintenance: Life-style changes in applied settings* (pp. 99–120). Baltimore: Paul H. Brookes Publishing Co.

Green, C.W., Reid, D.H., Canipe, V.S., & Gardner, S.M. (1991). A comprehensive evaluation of reinforcer identification processes for persons with profound multiple handicaps. *Journal of Applied Behavior Analysis, 24,* 537–552.

Horner, R., Day, H.M., Sprague, J., O'Brien, M., & Heathfield, L. (1991). Interspersed requests: A nonaversive procedure for reducing aggression and self-injury during instruction. *Journal of Applied Behavior Analysis, 24,* 265–278.

Parsons, M.B., & Reid, D.H. (1990). Assessing food preferences among persons with profound mental retardation: Providing opportunities to make choices. *Journal of Applied Behavior Analysis, 23,* 183–195.

Reichle, J., York. J., & Sigafoos, J. (1991). *Implementing augmentative and alternative communication: Strategies for learners with severe disabilities.* Baltimore: Paul H. Brookes Publishing Co.

Sigafoos, J., Mustonen, T., DePaepe, P., Reichle, J., & York, J. (1991). Defining the array of instructional prompts for teaching communication skills. In J. Reichle, J. York, & J. Sigafoos, *Implementing augmentative and alternative communication: Strategies for learners with severe disabilities* (pp. 173–192). Baltimore: Paul H. Brookes Publishing Co.

Singer, G., Singer, J., & Horner, R. (1987). Using pre-task requests to increase the probability of compliance for students with severe disabilities. *Journal of The Association for Persons with Severe Handicaps, 12*(4), 287–291.

11

Assessment and Intervention Considerations for Unconventional Verbal Behavior

Barry M. Prizant and Patrick J. Rydell

T HE USE OF UNCONVENTIONAL VERBAL behavior (UVB) is a characteristic of the communication patterns of many persons with social-communicative problems. We use the term *UVB* to refer to vocal production that is composed of recognizable speech, but violates to some degree, socially acceptable conventions of linguistic communication. Unconventional verbal behavior includes immediate echolalia, delayed echolalia, perseverative speech, and incessant (repetitive) questioning. Table 1 provides definitions of each class of verbal behavior. Other descriptors used for UVB have included bizarre speech, psychotic speech, and metaphorical and irrelevant language. We refrain from using such terminology due to its subjective and often stigmatizing nature.

Within the category of UVB, there is a continuum of behavior ranging from highly unconventional, incomprehensible, and noninteractive speech patterns, which may be extremely challenging to most communicative partners, to forms with varying degrees of conventionality that violate some conventions of communication and may be challenging to some, but not all, communicative partners. Within the continuum of UVB, some forms clearly qualify as symbolic behavior. That is, an arbitrary form (e.g., speech) is being used intentionally to represent concepts, feelings, desires, and needs. In contrast, other forms of UVB are clearly presymbolic or quasisymbolic and may be produced with limited evidence of comprehension or intentionality (Schuler & Prizant, 1985). Although the term *verbal* most often is used to refer to truly symbolic, language-based behavior, we use it in reference to the continuum of UVB noted above, for lack of a better term.

UVB is most prevalent, and has been discussed and studied to the greatest extent, in children and adolescents with autism. In his first descriptions of

Table 1. Forms, definitions, and examples of unconventional verbal behavior

Form of UVB	Definition
Immediate echolalia	Repetition of speech that: 1. is produced either following immediately or within two turns of original production, 2. involves exact repetition (pure echolalia) or minimal structural change (mitigated immediate echolalia), and 3. may serve a variety of communicative and cognitive functions.

Example
Child repeats, "Want some juice?" immediately following an adult's question. The child's nonverbal behavior (i.e., reaching toward juice bottle) indicates child was repeating the utterance in order to acquire juice, serving the function of affirmation (Kanner, 1943) or "yes-answer" (Prizant & Duchan, 1981).

Delayed echolalia	Repetition of speech that: 1. is repeated at a significantly later time (i.e., at least three turns following original utterance), but more typically hours, days; or even weeks later, 2. involves exact repetition (pure echolalia) or minimal structural change (mitigated delayed echolalia); and 3. may serve a variety of communicative and cognitive functions.

Example
Child states, "Time to go for a walk" as a request to get a drink of water. The utterance is a repetition of what his teacher said to him 2 weeks earlier, prior to leaving the room for a drink.

Perseverative speech	Persistent repetition of a speech pattern that: 1. consists of a word, phrase, or combination of utterances that are imitated (echolalia) or self-generated; 2. is produced in a cyclical, recurring manner; and 3. is produced with no evidence of communicative intent or expectation of a response from the partner.

Example
Child states repeatedly, "We must clean up the mess" while pacing in a corner of the classroom away from the other students and teacher. His teacher said this to him 1 month before in the same location after he spilled some juice. In this example, the perseverative utterance is also a delayed echo.

Incessant (repetitive) Questioning	Repeated verbal inquiries that: 1. are directed toward the communicative partner; 2. are produced with communicative intent, with an expectation for a response; and 3. persist either immediately following a response or after a short respite even though a response was provided.

Example
Over a 2-hour period, a child asks his mother repeatedly, "Going swimming after lunch?" after his mother indicated they would go to the beach that afternoon. Questioning continues despite affirmative responses from his mother.

autism, Kanner (1943, 1946) described in great detail immediate and delayed echolalia, and "metaphorical and irrelevant language" used by his clients. UVB also has been documented in persons with other disabilities such as fragile X syndrome (Paul et al., 1987) and visual impairment (Prizant, 1987b). However, this discussion primarily addresses UVB of persons with autism and related social-communicative disorders, because most available literature addressing UVB concerns this population.

In this chapter, we discuss issues related to assessment and intervention from both a more traditional research as well as an educational (more practitioner-oriented) perspective. The diversity of opinions regarding the definition, the nature, and significance of UVB, and approaches to intervention is highlighted. This diversity of opinions is due to the varying definitions of UVB, the varying criteria for defining UVB as challenging, and different theoretical orientations underlying research, assessment, and intervention approaches. We hope that from our discussion researchers, educators, and clinicians can develop an appreciation for the complexity of the issues involved. From the careful scrutiny of unconventional verbal behavior, we believe that additional research strategies can be derived, leading to more efficient assessment and intervention strategies.

DEFINING THE RANGE OF UNCONVENTIONAL VERBAL BEHAVIOR

The term *unconventional* verbal behavior is not isomorphic with *challenging* verbal behavior. Forms of UVB may or may not be challenging. First, we consider the criteria qualifying verbal behavior as unconventional. Subsequently, the degree to which UVB may be challenging is considered.

As noted, UVB can be conceived along a continuum. The continuum of conventionality specifies the extent to which verbal behavior is comprehended or understood by members of a language community, allowing for successful communication (Prizant & Rydell, 1984). Determinants of whether UVB can be comprehended include whether: 1) words are used with similar underlying meanings shared by other members of a community, 2) utterances produced are seen as relevant to the communicative context, 3) utterances are produced with communicative intent, 4) the communicative partner is familiar with an individual's patterns of UVB, and 5) the communicative partner is responsive to such patterns. Research on the most common forms of UVB, including immediate echolalia (Prizant & Duchan, 1981), delayed echolalia (Prizant & Rydell, 1984), and incessant, perseverative questioning, (Hurting, Ensrud, & Tomblin, 1982) has found that UVB occurs along a continuum of conventionality (with and without evidence of communicative intent).

Verbal behavior may be considered challenging for a number of reasons: 1) it does not provide necessary information or contribute new information to a conversational interaction (e.g., some forms of immediate echolalia, repetitive and perseverative speech); 2) the content of an utterance is deemed irrelevant or of limited relevance to the situational or conversational context (e.g., some forms of delayed echolalia); 3) speech production interferes with a person's ability to attend to, and participate productively in, either communicative interactions or educational/vocational learning tasks; and 4) speech production brings negative attention or otherwise stigmatizes an individual. That is, the degree to which UVB is challenging covaries with the degree to which its use violates culturally accepted norms of linguistic social communication. Such norms are defined at both a societal and an individual level. Consequently, UVB produced with communicative intent may be challenging to partners in some contexts (e.g., with strangers in a store), but not so in others (e.g., with family at home). Furthermore, a developmental dimension must be considered. For a nonspeaking child, the emerging use of UVB in any context may be viewed in a positive light, for it may represent communicative progress. In order to clarify how the dimensions of conventionality and challenge may vary, the communicative patterns of two persons displaying UVB are described.

Mary and Kevin

Mary is a 9-year-old girl who communicates through the use of two- to four-word creative and spontaneous phrases, as well as through immediate and delayed repetition (i.e., immediate and delayed echolalia) of others' utterances. She also engages in verbal perseveration when upset by changes in her routine or in response to other anxiety-arousing circumstances. These circumstances include interacting with unfamiliar persons or being asked to do challenging tasks. In general, Mary is very motivated to communicate with others. However, her delayed echolalic phrases often have idiosyncratic meanings. For example, on one occasion, while working with her teacher, Mary observed an unfamiliar visitor to her classroom. After noticing the stranger, Mary turned toward the teacher and exclaimed in a distressed voice, "You got a splinter, got a splinter!" Mary's teacher responded, "Don't be afraid, that's Barry. He's come to spend some time with us today." Mary repeated, "That's Barry," shook his hand, and was able to continue working. Mary's teacher later explained that ever since Mary had a painful splinter the year before, she repeats this phrase, which was said to her at the time, whenever she is upset or is experiencing pain. The use of this utterance is obviously unconventional. That is, the meaning and intention of Mary's utterance can not be determined by a literal interpretation of her spoken words. The phrase also would be challenging to a naive listener who was either unfamiliar with Mary's original experience or with her history of using the phrase. However, as the example illustrates, Mary's speech production was not challenging to her teacher who was familiar with the relationship between Mary's utterance and the communicative intent that it expressed. Such idiosyncratic use of language is problematic when communicative partners are unable to interpret Mary's intentions, and thus such idiosyncratic use contributes to breakdowns in communication.

Kevin is a 16-year-old who has limited spoken language. He communicates most clearly by using concrete gestures (e.g., physically manipulating or leading others) and by using his communication wallet (when verbally prompted) containing photos and line drawings. He infrequently uses single spoken words, but often repeats memorized utterances. Kevin produces speech most consistently when he is asked questions or is asked to follow directions. At these times, he tends to repeat the last few words of the other person's utterance in a rapid, automatic fashion without demonstrating any comprehension of his partner's spoken words. On other occasions, when there is much movement or noise in a room, he isolates himself in a corner and repeats longer utterances from TV game shows in a chanting-like manner. These productions often are accompanied by repetitive rocking movements with his hands held over his ears. Finally, he sometimes requests objects when calm and relaxed by producing single spoken words, often accompanied by a point to a corresponding picture. To his teacher and family, Kevin's verbal behavior is most often unconventional. Kevin's family finds it is difficult to understand why he is able to repeat up to five words of another's speech (immediately or delayed) with little apparent meaning or communicative intent, yet he often does not use even a single word with clear meaning and intent. Additionally, his parents are concerned that Kevin attracts attention in public when he noninteractively verbally perseverates in uncomfortable situations. However, they also report that "chanting" (as they refer to it) appears to have a calming effect on Kevin. Consequently, they are reluctant to discourage such behavior.

In these two examples, both Mary and Kevin produce utterances that vary in their degree of conventionality and the degree to which they may be considered challenging. The variability across and within individuals described in the preceding examples strongly suggests that intervention approaches need to be highly individualized and based on patterns of UVB deciphered from functional assessment and functional analysis.

Informed decisions regarding intervention approaches must address factors such as the individual's communicative intentions underlying the unconventional behavior and the communicative functions served by UVB. The analysis of communicative intent and communicative function of behavioral acts involves similar, but not identical, processes. Analysis of intent focuses on what an individual intends to accomplish, or the purposes or goals underlying behavioral acts. An intentional communicative act may not always serve its intended purpose or function. For example, a child may intend to request assistance with a difficult task, but may not succeed if his or her speech is unintelligible. The use of an augmentative mode of communication may help such a child to express his or her intentions more successfully. The development of communicative intent involves emerging social-cognitive and communicative capacities (Wetherby & Prizant, 1989). Intentions are not directly observable, but can be inferred by documenting specific criteria used as evidence of intentionality (Wetherby & Prizant, 1989).

In contrast, an analysis of communicative function takes into account the actual effects that behavioral acts have on others. Behavioral acts may have specific effects (i.e., serve specific functions) although they may not be intended to have those effects (Prizant & Wetherby, 1985). For example, an adult may offer a drink to a child who is looking at a water fountain, even though the child does not direct communicative signals to the adult. Researchers have hypothesized that when caregivers assign intent and respond consistently to young children's behavioral acts, children come to associate their acts with specific outcomes, providing the foundation for the development of communicative intentionality (Wetherby & Prizant, 1989). When analyzing UVB, both intention and function need to be considered. Furthermore, it is important to understand how UVB may relate to different levels of emotional arousal associated with different states that an individual may experience. Emotional states may be negative (e.g., fear, anxiety, anger) or positive (e.g., content, happy, excited). Level of arousal for any one emotional state may range from minimal to extreme. In documenting the production of UVB, both emotional state and level of arousal displayed by an individual should be noted.

Additional considerations include how the production of UVB varies relative to situational and communicative contexts and whether it reflects individual learning styles such as a reliance on a rote-memory strategy in processing and producing verbal utterances (i.e., a gestalt learning style [Prizant, 1983]). (See O'Neill et al., 1990, for a comprehensive description of antecedents and consequences that may influence the production of UVB.) Finally, a longitudinal picture of the transitional role UVB may play toward the acquisition of more conventional and communicative language needs to be considered. Prior to a discussion of assessment and intervention approaches, the research on different forms of UVB is reviewed.

Forms of Unconventional Verbal Behavior

Incessant Questioning and Perseverative Speech

Incessant questioning, or frequent and repetitive use of questions, and perseverative speech, or stereotypic repetitive speech patterns, have been documented in numerous studies as characteristics of the speech and language of persons with autism (Prizant, 1988), and, to a lesser extent, of persons with fragile X syndrome and cognitive impairment who do not have autism (Paul et al., 1987). Hurtig et al. (1982) demonstrated that, in greater than one half of observed occurrences, the repetitive questioning by six children with autism was found to be a strategy for initiating conversation. Coggins and Frederickson (1988) studied the production of a frequently repeated utterance (i.e., "Can I talk?") of a 9-year-old boy with autism. Following a functional pragmatic analysis of the behavior in different interactive contexts, they concluded that the phrase was used as an "interactive bid." Both Coggins and Frederickson (1988) and Hurtig et al. (1982) argued that their subjects' use of a repetitive phrase and incessant questioning most often represented attempts to participate in social exchange despite language formulation and comprehension difficulties. Other than these studies, research on these forms of UVB is virtually absent. Although perseveration of language form (i.e., repeating the same words or phrases) as well as perseveration of topic (i.e., persistent repetition of content related to the same topic) is commonly observed in persons with autism (Prizant, 1988), only perseveration of form has been studied.

Incessant questioning and perseverative speech may or may not be forms of echolalia. Unfortunately, there is a paucity of research to help differentiate among these forms of UVB. Our experience suggests that some forms of incessant questioning and perseverative speech may be echolalic in that they involve repetition "triggered" by a communicative partner's immediately preceding utterance (i.e., immediate echolalia), or by recollection and repetitive production of an utterance associated with a particular context (i.e., delayed echolalia). In other instances, incessant questioning and perseverative speech are more generative in nature, with no evidence of having their origins in the repetition of the utterances of communicative partners. Thus, it is not uncommon to observe patterns of perseverative speech and incessant questioning in persons who are echolalic or who went through periods of echolalia in their development (Prizant, 1988).

Echolalia

Echolalia is clearly the most intensively studied form of UVB. Schuler (1979) emphasized that the lack of operationally defined criteria have precluded lucid discussions of echolalic behavior. She indicated that:

> The term echolalia appears to be used loosely, to refer to some not well specified type of repetition of words and phrases. Distinctions as to degree of repetition and comprehension are usually lacking as well as considerations about the intentionality and context sensitivity of the behavior. (p. 411)

Since Schuler's (1979) observation, little progress has been made in reaching a consensus in defining echolalic behavior.

Immediate echolalia has been defined as "the meaningless repetition of a word or word group just spoken by another person" (Fay, 1969, p. 39). Fay noted that the use of the term *meaningless* is a necessary qualifier, although this judgment is most often based on inference. Roberts (1989) defined immediate echolalia as "recognizable imitation occurring within two utterances of the model" (p. 276). Delayed echolalia has been defined as the "echoing of a phrase after some delay or lapse of time" (Simon, 1975, p. 1440). Similar to Roberts (1989) and Simon (1975), Prizant and Duchan (1981), Prizant and Rydell (1984), and Rydell and Mirenda (1991) used primarily structural criteria in their definitions of immediate and delayed echolalia (i.e., criteria specifying the degree of similarity between the model and repeated utterances). In contrast, Laski, Charlop, and Schreibman (1988) defined immediate echolalia as "inappropriate repetitions of word or phrases" (p. 394), and delayed echolalia as "non-functional repetitions (produced) out of context" (p. 394). Laski et al. (1988) termed appropriate repetitions *imitations*, yet criteria for determining appropriateness were not presented. In contrast to Laski et al. (1988), Zyl, Alant, and Uys (1985) and Prizant and Duchan (1981) viewed "relevance" as one dimension that varies *within* the category of echolalia, not as a criterion for defining echolalia.

The clearest distinction that has been made differentiates two general categories of echolalic behavior based on the temporal latency between the original production of an utterance and the subsequent repetition. Stated simply, *immediate echolalia* refers to utterances that are produced either immediately following or a brief time after the production of the model utterance. *Delayed echolalia* refers to utterances repeated at a significantly later time. The process involved with the production of delayed echolalia involves retrieval of information from some type of long-term memory, whereas short-term memory is most often implicated for immediate echolalia (Hermelin & O'Connor, 1970).

Many researchers argue against viewing echolalia solely as meaningless or inappropriate repetition. Researchers who have been interested in the structural linguistic aspects of echolalic behavior have provided evidence that echolalia is not always just rote repetition, but is at times produced with evidence of intervening rule-governed linguistic processes (Fay, 1967; Shapiro, Roberts, & Fish, 1970; Voeltz, 1977), as well as comprehension (Prizant & Duchan, 1981; Prizant & Rydell, 1984; Roberts, 1989). Telegraphic echoing and appropriate grammatical substitutions are forms of "mitigated echolalia," or echolalia with change, and such forms are interpreted as denoting some degree of linguistic processing. These studies have helped to extend our understanding of echolalia from reflex-like parroting behavior to a continuum of behavior that, while clearly repetitive, does not involve only exact repetitions. Shapiro et al. (1970), Prizant (1978), and Rydell (1989) observed that children who produced "rigidly congruent" echolalia frequently produced mitigated utterances as well, suggesting that, even within a child, various degrees of cognitive-linguistic processing may underlie the production of echolalia.

Due, in part, to definitional differences, research on echolalia clearly reflects conflicting points of view. These conflicting points of view range from descriptions of echolalia as pathological behavior, to considerations of echolalia as a socially motivated compensatory strategy serving the general function of maintaining social contact, to descriptions of echolalia as serving specific communicative functions. Inherent in this diversity of viewpoints are issues of the presence or absence of comprehension and communicative intent underlying echolalic productions. Echolalic behaviors, both immediate and delayed, are best described as a continuum of behaviors in regard to exactness of repetition, degree of comprehension, and underlying communicative intent (Fay & Schuler, 1980; Prizant, 1987; Schuler & Prizant, 1985). Unfortunately, until there is a greater consensus in defining echolalia, views of it will be clouded.

Echolalia as Pathologic Behavior

From this point of view, echolalia most typically has been discussed as a unitary phenomenon, rather than a continuum of behavior, determined on an a priori basis to be pathologic (and presumably challenging). Typically, few or no distinctions are made regarding exactness of repetition or functional usage. In this literature, it is common to find echolalia described as "maladaptive speech" (Foxx, Faw, McMorrow, Davis, & Bittle, 1988, p. 93), "psychotic speech" (Durand & Crimmins, 1987, p. 17), "a common language disorder in psychotic children" (Carr, Schreibman, & Lovaas, 1975, p. 331), or as undesirable and socially nonfunctional behavior (Lovaas, 1977). Thus, echolalia is considered to be at the extreme unconventional end of the continuum of conventional behavior.

Due to echolalia's abnormal appearance (especially in older persons) and a belief that it signals an individual's inability to respond appropriately, researchers have applied a variety of approaches to the "remediation" of echolalia. Such procedures range from the use of the command, "Don't echo" (Lovaas, 1977), to replacement of echolalia with utterances such as "I don't know" (Schreibman & Carr, 1978), or other trained verbal responses (Durand & Crimmins, 1988; Foxx et al., 1988).

With few exceptions (e.g., Durand & Crimmins, 1987), this literature does not consider individual differences that are apparent in the production of echolalia (e.g., situational and interpersonal determinants), in its functional usage in natural interactions, or in its possible relationship to language and communicative growth. In fact, echolalia has been studied most frequently in highly controlled, laboratory contexts, which do not allow for any consideration of its role in more natural social interactions. From this orientation, echolalia is rarely considered in reference to the expression of communicative intent or in reference to cognitive, communicative, and linguistic growth.

Social Motivation and Echolalia

While some researchers have advocated the extinction or replacement of echolalic behaviors, others have questioned the assumptions underlying this position. For example, Fay stated:

> If a doubt remains as to whether echolalia reflects the last failure of human connections or a struggle to maintain them, the child deserves the benefit of that doubt. A return to mutism, either by choice or by well-meaning clinical intervention intent only upon echo abatement, marks the last failure. (Fay, 1973, p. 487)

Fay (1969, 1973), Shapiro (1977), and Caparulo and Cohen (1977) discussed the social value of immediate echolalia, noting that it may allow for social closure and represent a primitive attempt to maintain social contact with others. While asserting that echolalia serves a general function of maintaining social contact, these researchers did not attempt to delineate specific social functions.

Functional Pragmatic Approaches to Echolalia

The first systematic studies that attempted to explore specific functions of immediate and delayed echolalia were conducted by Prizant and Duchan (1981) and Prizant and Rydell (1984). Prizant and Duchan (1981) derived seven functional categories of immediate echolalia based on videotape analyses of 1,009 echolalic utterances of four children with autism. Segmental features, suprasegmental features (i.e., stress, intonation), nonverbal behavior, situational features, and response latency were taken into account in deriving the seven categories. Children with autism were videotaped in naturalistic interactions over an 8-month period and were found to produce echo-

Table 2.   Functional categories of immediate echolalia

Category	Description
Interactive functions	
Turn-taking	Utterances used as turn fillers in an alternating verbal exchange
Declarative	Utterances labeling objects, actions, or location (accompanied by demonstrative gestures)
Yes-answer	Utterances used to indicate affirmation of prior utterance
Request	Utterances used to request objects or others' actions. Usually involves mitigated echolalia
Noninteractive functions	
Nonfocused	Utterances produced with no apparent intent and often in states of high arousal (such as fear, pain)
Rehearsal	Utterances used as a processing aid, followed by utterance or action indicating comprehension of echoed utterance
Self-regulatory	Utterances that serve to regulate one's own actions. Produced in synchrony with motor activity

From Prizant and Duchan (1981).

lalic utterances that were interactive as well as noninteractive. The specific functional categories included: turn-taking, declarative, yes-answer, request, nonfocused, rehearsal, and self-regulatory (see Table 2). McEvoy, Loveland, and Landry (1988) and Zyl et al. (1985) later replicated, in part, the findings of Prizant and Duchan (1981).

Prizant and Rydell (1984) also delineated functional categories of delayed echolalia based on systematic analyses. Three hundred and seventy-eight delayed echolalic utterances were identified from language samples of three individuals with autism, and 14 functional categories were derived with significant individual differences identified across subjects (see Table 3). These studies provided evidence for Schuler's (1979) contentions that echolalia encompasses a range of intentionality, functionality, and communicativeness.

Table 3. Functional categories of delayed echolalia

Category	Description
Interactive functions	
Turn-taking	Utterances used as turn fillers in alternating verbal exchange
Verbal completion	Utterances that complete familiar verbal routines initiated by others
Providing information	Utterances offering new information not apparent from situational context (may be initiated or respondent)
Labeling (interactive)	Utterances labeling objects or actions in environment
Protest	Utterances protesting actions of others. May be used to prohibit others' actions
Request	Utterances used to request objects
Calling	Utterances used to call attention to oneself or to establish/maintain interaction
Affirmation	Utterances used to indicate affirmation of previous utterance
Directive	Utterances (often imperatives) used to direct others' actions
Noninteractive functions	
Nonfocused	Utterances with no apparent communicative intent or relevance to the situational context. May be self-stimulatory
Situation association	Utterances with no apparent communicative intent, that appear to be triggered by an object, person, situation, or activity
Self-directive	Utterances used to regulate one's own actions. Produced in synchrony with motor activity
Rehearsal	Utterances produced with low volume followed by louder interactive production. Appears to be practice for subsequent production
Label (noninteractive)	Utterances labeling objects or actions in environment with no apparent communicative intent. May be a form of practice for learning language

From Prizant and Rydell (1984).

COGNITIVE AND SOCIAL FACTORS INFLUENCING UVB

There currently are a variety of perspectives on echolalia and its relationship to other cognitive, social, and linguistic factors. As noted, a number of investigations (McEvoy et al., 1988; Prizant & Duchan, 1981; Prizant & Rydell, 1984; Zyl et al., 1985) explored echolalia from a functional perspective in which some forms of echolalia were found to be communicative strategies used for a variety of instrumental, social, and cognitive purposes. The primary focus of much of this research was to identify and describe the many ways in which children with autism used echolalia for communicative purposes in naturally occurring interactions. Another body of research has attempted to determine the conditions under which echolalia is likely to occur. These investigations sought to determine the possible internal and external influencing factors associated with increased frequency of echolalic productions.

Task Demand/Unfamiliar Environments

Cantwell, Baker, and Rutter (1978) found UVB to occur more frequently in highly demanding and unfamiliar social interaction settings. Similarly, Charlop (1986) found that children with autism were more likely to use echolalia in interactions with unfamiliar persons, settings, and tasks. Thus, it appears that one of the primary factors associated with an increase in UVB is more socially and cognitively demanding situations.

Comprehension

Several investigators have also suggested that the retrograde shift from use of generative language to echolalic patterns may indicate the difficulties that individuals have in comprehending the communicative behavior of their partners (Carr et al., 1975; Schreibman & Carr, 1978). For example, individuals are more likely to produce echolalia when they cannot comprehend the vocabulary and/or the linguistic structures directed to them. Roberts (1989) found that children with autism who had more advanced receptive language abilities exhibited fewer echolalic utterances. Viewed from an information-processing perspective, Curcio and Paccia (1987) and Paccia and Curcio (1982) studied the relationship between the incidence of immediate echolalia and the syntactic-semantic complexity of adult utterances. These studies demonstrated that children with autism produced echolalia more frequently following adult utterances that were higher in abstractness and were not semantically contingent on the child's previous turn in discourse. Baltaxe and Simmons (1975) also noted recurrent patterns of echolalia during instances of child fatigue, confusion, or distraction in children who were primarily generative language users.

Transitions

Individuals with autism often experience difficulties with changes in established routines. In educational settings, transitions between classes or activities pose particular difficulties. Transitions may thus be marked by increased agitation and UVB. Such behavior may also be the result of confusion (Doss & Reichle, 1991) caused by changes in an individual's routine.

The investigations cited suggest that echolalia may vary systematically in relation to a variety of social, cognitive, and linguistic factors. In particular, they suggest that higher incidences of echolalia and UVB are associated with highly demanding interactive contexts; more complex language input (i.e., higher order syntactic-semantic structures) resulting in potential problems in comprehension of language; and factors such as fatigue and distraction, contributed to by confusion around transition. Unfortunately, the existing investigations have not considered interactions among variables associated with more frequent production of UVB.

In studying the interrelationships among social, linguistic, and cognitive variables that influence the production of UVB, some researchers (Mirenda & Donnellan, 1986; Peck, 1985; Rydell & Mirenda, 1991; Violette & Swisher, 1992) used a interactionist approach in exploring the relationships of internal and external influences on UVB. The focus of the interactionist approach is to explore the dynamic relationship among the variables inherent in social-communicative interactions and the potential influence of these variables on an individual's communicative performance. The interactionist approach suggests that the style or quality of interaction between communicative partners is a significant variable in communicative performance and that communication difficulties are often the result of interactional mismatches rather than a function of an individual's disability (Duchan, 1983). The interactionist approach considers two primary factors in describing communicative performance of an individual: 1) the cognitive, social, socioemotional, and linguistic strengths or weaknesses of the individual that potentially affect the nature of the interaction; and 2) the potential influence of a partner's interactive style (i.e., facilitative vs. directive) on the individual's verbal output.

Rydell (1989) suggested that production of echolalia at more advanced stages in language development may be the result of multidimensional influences of the communicator's social-cognitive and linguistic abilities and of the interaction styles of communicative partners. Studies by Mirenda and Donnellan (1986), Peck (1985), Rydell (1989), and Rydell and Mirenda (1991) have highlighted the importance of interaction styles and their potential effects on the communicative performance of persons with unconventional communicative behavior. These studies suggest that social-communicative performances were influenced by whether the partner used a facilitative or directive style of interaction (see Table 4). Adult interaction styles differed

Table 4.   Directive and facilitative styles of interaction

Adult directive style of interaction
1. Adult controls the focus and direction of the verbal interaction the majority of the time.
2. Adult assumes the lead in conversation the majority of the time.
3. Adult structures the nature of the child's contributions to the ongoing topic.
4. Majority of adult utterances are high constraint.
5. Adult uses verbal statements, gestures, or physical prompts that serve to specify either the specific form or content of the child's response.
6. Adult uses verbal statements, gestures, or direct guidance to identify two or more response options a child may take.

Adult facilitative style of interaction
1. Child controls the focus and direction of the verbal interaction the majority of the time.
2. Adult follows the child's lead in conversation the majority of the time.
3. Adult encourages the child to contribute to the conversation in a variety of ways.
4. Adult allows periods of silence before initiating a new utterance.
5. Majority of adult utterances are low constraint.
6. Adult responses are similar in topography (imitations) or represent a suitable expansion (elaboration) of a previous child utterance.
7. Adult responses serve to deliver some object, activity, assistance, or attention for which the child has initiated (unprompted) a request.
8. Adult uses motor/gestural or vocal/verbal behaviors that prompt a social-communicative response without specifying either the form (syntax) or content (semantics) of the response.

Adapted from Peck (1985) and Rydell (1989).

primarily on: 1) adult responsiveness or adherence to the children's social-communicative agenda, 2) demands and obligations placed upon the children to participate in the social-communicative exchange in a particular manner, and 3) the degree of opportunity for child initiation and social control of the interaction. This interactionist perspective has its foundations in work emphasizing that communicative performance is dependent upon the social contexts in which a child participates (Bruner, 1975; Snow & Ferguson, 1977).

Rydell (1989) proposed that adult interaction styles can be differentiated based on social-communicative control and linguistic constraint factors. Within each of these dimensions, the partner's interaction style can place a high or low degree of demand, constraint, or obligation on the child to produce communicative behavior. The use of echolalia may be the child's attempt at processing information and producing intentional communicative acts in an efficient manner during highly demanding social-communicative interactions. Directive interaction styles place a high degree of social-cognitive demand on the child by controlling the social agenda and learning context, controlling the conversational topic, and obligating the child to respond in a particular manner through the use of high-constraint utterances (see Table 5 for examples). As a result of the child's attempt to participate in social exchange, the child's social-cognitive workload substantially increases in order to adhere to the adult's topic. Thus, instead of applying a more complex

Table 5.　High- and low-constraint utterance forms

High constraint forms
1. Directives
2. Commands
3. *Wh*-questions used to elicit specific responses
4. Yes-no question
5. Prompts eliciting specific verbal responses
6. Attention-eliciting devices
7. Negative corrective responses

Low constraint forms
1. Reflective questions that repeat, reduce, represent, or paraphrase the hearer's previous utterance without adding new information; or acknowledge or signal comprehension of the previous utterance; or describe or acknowledge the activity of the hearer, while at the same time passing the speaking turn to the hearer (e.g., "You are eating, aren't you?")
2. Report questions that comment on and inform the child of an event or fact of which he or she may or may not be aware, provide new information (e.g., "That car doesn't fit, does it?")
3. Positive responses or acknowledgments to previous child utterances
4. Comments

Adapted from Rydell (1989) and Rydell and Mirenda (1991).

linguistic strategy, the child uses a more ritualized production strategy. The trade-off becomes one of using a less labor-intensive communicative utterance, which may place a significantly greater communicative burden on the listener. Conversely, when the individual interacts in settings that involve fewer cognitive, social, and communicative constraints (e.g., using adult facilitative styles and low-constraint utterances), more cognitive resources are likely to be allocated for generative rule induction and higher-order linguistic processes. More conventional, generative, and flexible utterances might be expected under these circumstances.

To test the interactionist perspective, Rydell (1989) and Rydell and Mirenda (1991) investigated the influence of adult verbal interaction styles on echolalia and generative language for three children with autism who had a repertoire of both conventional spoken language and echolalia. Of primary interest were the types of adult verbal behaviors that tended to be associated with more and less frequent occurrences of echolalic and conventional language behaviors. The results of these investigations suggested that the level of social-communicative control exerted on the children during naturalistic play sessions affected their communicative output. The use of adult directive interaction styles (see Table 4) and adult high-constraint utterances (Table 5) elicited the majority of each child's echolalia. Children were more likely to resort to repetition strategies during situations of high social-communicative demands and constraints in order to fulfill their obligation in the verbal exchange. That is, a more directive and linguistically constraining interactive style (see Tables 4 and 5) elicited the highest incidences of both conventional (generative) and unconventional (echolalic) responses. Thus, it appears the children were responding to the obligatory nature of the adults' interactive style. A similar use of repetition strategies has been observed in the interactions of young children without disabilities (Keenan & Ochs, 1977). Results of this investigation support earlier work by Mirenda and Donnellan (1986) and Peck (1985) who found increased child social and communicative initiations under adult facilitative styles of interaction, in which adults followed the children's leads and placed few demands or constraints on the children to act or respond in a particular manner. Violette and Swisher (1992) examined interactional effects of linguistic input and adult directiveness on a child with echolalia and autism. They systematically varied linguistic input with familiar and unfamiliar lexical items and a more and less directive interactive style. Results indicated that the combination of a directive style and unfamiliar lexical items elicited the highest frequency of echolalia.

Thus, the available literature suggests that UVB is most likely to occur in highly demanding social-cognitive interactions, especially when linguistic input is complex or unfamiliar, than in less demanding and controlled interactions that have been associated with greater use of conventional language strategies.

Longitudinal Characteristics of Unconventional Verbal Behavior

As previously mentioned, two positions can be identified regarding the role of echolalia in the process of communicative growth. One position holds that echolalia is pathological behavior and stands outside the realm of cognitive and linguistic growth and may even interfere with such growth (Coleman & Stedman, 1974; Schreibman & Carr, 1978). This position assumes that processes underlying the production of echolalia, as opposed to processes underlying the production of creative, spontaneous language, are mutually exclusive and even competitive; thus, echolalia must be decelerated to allow for the acquisition and use of more functional communication. More recently, Carr and Durand (1985) have advocated that a functional analysis of any unconventional behavior be followed by intervention in which communicative functions being taught are closely matched to the functions of the challenging behavior. Interestingly, there is no evidence that deceleration of echolalic behavior (in the absence of procedures to establish replacement communicative behavior) has resulted in the acquisition of a more functional communicative repertoire.

A complementary approach attempts to understand echolalic behavior within the context of a child's cognitive and linguistic growth. This approach recognizes that movement from less conventional to more conventional communicative forms can be thought of as a developmental progression observed in persons with and without disabilities (Prizant & Wetherby, 1987). Kanner (1973) first alluded to echolalia as part of a progression in language acquisition. Discussing language acquisition in the follow-up of individuals with good "social adaptation," he noted a "steady succession of stages—no initiative or response—immediate parroting—delayed echolalia with pronominal reversals—utterances related to obsessive preoccupations—communicative dialogue" (p. 209).

Baltaxe and Simmons (1975) were the first to consider echolalia as a possible factor contributing to language acquisition. Phillips and Dyer (1977) hypothesized that echolalia is a necessary stage of language acquisition for persons with autism. In regard to receptive language, Charlop (1983) found that children's use of echolalia facilitated acquisition and generalization of receptive objective labeling.

The most specific position concerning the role that echolalia may play in language acquisition was first posited by Baltaxe and Simmons (1977) and has since been expanded upon in greater detail (Prizant, 1982, 1983, 1987a). Based on their research, Baltaxe and Simmons (1977) suggested that children with autism may acquire language by using a rote memory strategy, with subsequent segmentation of memorized linguistic forms. More specifically, they analyzed the echolalic "bedtime soliloquies" of an adolescent girl with autism and found that memorized or unanalyzed linguistic utterances (i.e., delayed echolalia) were initially produced as linguistic "chunks" and were subsequently segmented resulting in more generative linguistic productions. For example, the delayed echolalic utterance, "Do you wanna go out?" may initially be used as a general request to depart from or terminate an activity because the individual, based on past experience, has come to associate this utterance with shifting from one activity to another. Through exposure to appropriate language modeling, the individual may come to segment this utterance into two "chunks," a general request segment, "Do you wanna. . . " and a slot for a desired activity such as "go for a drink", or "time to eat lunch." Prizant and Rydell (1984) found that their subjects frequently recombined and conjoined language chunks, a process analogous to young children's early movement from single to multiword utterances. Baltaxe and Simmons (1977) hypothesized that such segmentation of unanalyzed forms provided the basis for the acquisition of a rule-governed and generative linguistic system.

Prizant (1983) further hypothesized that echolalic behavior may play a role in the acquisition of linguistic function, as well as structure, in persons with autism, and he emphasized that it is important to consider echolalic behavior within the larger context of the cognitive processing style of individuals with autism. That is, language acquisition in individuals with autism closely resembles what has been described as a gestalt style of language acquisition observed in typically developing children (Peters, 1977, 1983). This literature suggests that language learners fall along a continuum ranging from analytic processors to gestalt processors (Peters, 1983). Analytic processors acquire language with an appreciation of basic constituent structure and meaning and move through stages of increasing linguistic complexity (i.e., from single words to two- and three-word utterances and beyond). Gestalt processors acquire language by memorizing and repeating multiword units, initially with limited linguistic comprehension. As noted, these "chunks" are eventually analyzed into constituent components. Typically developing children demonstrate patterns reflecting each processing style, with different children falling at different points along the continuum (Peters, 1977).

It appears that individuals with autism who acquire spoken language may use an extreme form of a gestalt processing style. An extreme gestalt processing strategy may help to explain other commonly cited problems in autism, such as limitations in understanding and coping with unpredictable change, in inducing rules of hierarchical systems, and in understanding and developing social-rule systems, as well as in acquiring a flexible and generative language system (Prizant, 1983). Communicative and linguistic skills are especially likely to be influenced by an extreme gestalt processing style because of the rapidly changing and contextually sensitive adjustments and repairs that successful ongoing interactions require. Additionally, because communication occurs in a social context, the relationship between social variables and a gestalt processing style must be considered.

Relationship of Gestalt and Interactionist Theories to Unconventional Verbal Behavior in Autism

From a developmental perspective, gestalt and interactionist theories are similar in their attempt to explain the occurrence of echolalia in language development. Both suggest that the major compensatory strategy in communication is the use of repetition strategies on occasions where the cognitive demands exceed an individual's linguistic and/or information-processing capacities. Prizant (1983) suggested that, in many instances, greater social-cognitive and linguistic abilities allow for the (primarily) gestalt processor to move toward a more analytic processing style, allowing for the possibility of creative language production. That is, echolalic productions increasingly become replaced by more flexible, rule-governed linguistic patterns over time. Even as an individual becomes more analytic in his or her processing capabilities, interactional demands and situational factors (e.g., partner's directive style, emotionally arousing contexts) may, at times, require the use of "information-handling" techniques (e.g., echolalia) as a compensatory language strategy. Thus, even those children who have reached a more analytic stage and have become primarily generative language users may still resort to repetition strategies to meet the demands of complex interactional environments. Clearly, further research is needed to test these hypotheses. However, it is our contention that approaches to UVB that address cognitive differences and social-interactive variables represent a significant departure from deficit models that define such behavior as pathological on an a priori basis (Prizant,

1983). Such approaches represent attempts to understand UVB in reference to patterns of cognitive and communicative development, as well as in reference to each individual's strategies for coping with his or her inherent social-cognitive processing constraints. This shift away from deficit models of UVB has been paralleled in considerations of nonverbal challenging behaviors (Carr & Durand, 1985; Doss & Reichle, 1991). Such approaches have profound educational and clinical implications and have provided new insights regarding communication assessment and intervention for persons with UVB.

ASSESSMENT CONSIDERATIONS
IN ANALYZING UNCONVENTIONAL VERBAL BEHAVIOR

If UVB is to be viewed as a dynamic and integral part of an individual's communicative, cognitive, and social functioning, rather than dismissed as isolated and nonfunctional behavior, assessment and intervention approaches should reflect this orientation. Following this line of reasoning, UVB should be viewed from two perspectives. First, UVB should be considered as one possible aspect of an individual's total system for communicating intentions, which may include other verbal, vocal, and nonverbal means. Second, UVB should be considered in reference to an individual's communication and language development history, including evidence of progressive change with respect to functional usage. Both perspectives require that UVB be viewed on a continuum of intentionality and conventionality (Schuler & Prizant, 1985). The individual differences that are inherently an aspect of UVB preclude using "cookbook" or predetermined approaches to assessment and intervention, which by definition, ignore such differences. Therefore, the following discussion of assessment and intervention issues provides guidelines and directions rather than overly prescriptive procedures. Intervention approaches should be derived from systematic assessment and functional analyses of UVB (e.g., Durand & Crimmins, 1987; Evans & Meyer, 1985; Prizant & Wetherby, 1985). To reflect the multiple factors that underlie the occurrence of UVB, assessment must address: 1) situational determinants and antecedent conditions associated with the occurrence of UVB, 2) the range of communicative functions served by UVB, 3) the range of verbal and communicative behavior other than UVB, 4) the match between specific situations and type of communicative behavior produced, 5) the degree to which UVB is challenging to both the individual and to others, and 6) the relationship between UVB and other communicative behavior over time (i.e., is UVB a transitional phenomenon reflecting an individual's growing communicative competence).

Some of the preceding assessment dimensions have been discussed in the literature on the analysis of communicative functions (Burke, 1990; Donnellan, Mirenda, Mesaros, & Fassbender, 1984; Evans & Meyer, 1985; Prizant & Wetherby, 1985, 1987; Wetherby & Prizant, 1989). Although each dimension is considered individually, assessment practice must account for co-occurrence and dynamic interaction among these factors.

Clear agreement among clinicians and educators about the definition of the behavior to be evaluated is essential for both assessment and intervention. Operational definitions for the forms of UVB under scrutiny need to be derived by gathering information from persons familiar with the individual whose communicative behavior is being assessed. Obtaining a language sample, including UVB and more conventional language forms and functions along with contextual information, is critical.

Assessing Situational Determinants and Antecedent Conditions of Unconventional Verbal Behavior

Research has indicated that UVB is more likely to occur in some situational and communicative contexts than others (Charlop, 1983; Rydell & Mirenda, 1991). Specific contextual features that correspond to the production of UVB should be documented. As discussed earlier, an individual may be more likely to produce UVB when faced with unfamiliar situations, challenging tasks, relatively unstructured time, transitions, or unmotivating and boring activities.

Specific interpersonal interactive styles or social and linguistic demands also are factors associated with UVB. These include an individual's use of complex language (Curcio & Paccia, 1987), high-constraint utterances (Rydell & Mirenda, 1991), or excessive task demands (Durand & Crimmins, 1987). Table 6 lists possible variables associated with the occurrence of UVB. Documenting these variables are important because for some individuals, reducing challenging UVB can be accomplished by modifying learning situations, by increasing predictability and structure, or by calibrating a partner's language use and interactive style to a more appropriate level.

Table 6.   Possible variables associated with the occurrence of UVB

I.   Situational factors
  A.   Unstructured, unpredictable, or transitional periods
  B.   Unfamiliar tasks or situations
  C.   Difficult or challenging tasks
  D.   Emotionally arousing contexts or activities that cause:
    1.   anxiety or fear
    2.   distress
    3.   elation
II.   Interactional factors
  A.   Complex linguistic input
  B.   High constraint linguistic input
  C.   Partner's directive interaction style
III.   Person-specific factors
  A.   Gestalt style of language acquisition and use
  B.   Language comprehension difficulties

Range of Intentionality and Communicative
Functions Served by Unconventional Verbal Behavior

Schuler (1979) stated that:

> No conclusions about . . . echolalic-like behaviors can be drawn without systematic and detailed descriptions of these behaviors across various conditions. . . . Careful functional analyses of individual cases have to be performed before any decisions are made as to intervention techniques to be applied. (pp. 429–430)

Prizant and Wetherby (1987) summarized behavioral evidence used to infer intent. In UVB, behavioral evidence should be observable just prior to, during, or subsequent to its production, and may include: 1) alternating eye gaze between a goal and the listener; 2) persistence in the production of UVB until a goal has been met; 3) changes in the quality of UVB until the goal has been met; 4) awaiting a response from the listener; 5) termination of UVB when the goal has been met; and 6) displaying satisfaction or reduction of arousal or distress when the goal has been attained, or dissatisfaction or increased negative emotional arousal when it has not. Intentionality is not an all-or-none phenomenon. Differing degrees of intent may underlie the production of UVB depending upon an individual's awareness of a specific goal and the effectiveness of the behavioral act in achieving that goal. Therefore, it is not uncommon for some forms of UVB to be produced initially with limited intentionality followed by usage with increased intentionality. Increased intentional usage may result from an individual's experiencing and learning the consistent effect of the UVB on the behavior of others. For example, an individual may repeat an utterance such as "Do you want a drink?" immediately following an adult query (immediate echolalia) with little evidence of comprehension or intent. If the repetition is followed by obtaining a drink, the child may use the same utterance in future situations as a request for a drink, having associated the form with the outcome.

As noted, some forms of UVB may be less intentional than other forms. UVB may be produced noninteractively serving intrapersonal functions such as anxiety reduction (i.e., emotional regulation) or rehearsal (Donnellan et al., 1984; Prizant, 1987a). Some forms also may be highly automatic with little evidence of comprehension or purposefulness. Determining whether occurrences of UVB serve intra- or interpersonal functions and whether occurrences are produced with intentionality may require scrutiny of the following variables.

Interactiveness

A determination must be made whether UVB is produced with the awareness of a communicative partner and whether it is directed to that partner. The interactiveness of UVB can be determined on the basis of the following behavioral evidence: 1) body posture or orientation; 2) gaze behavior, including eye contact and gaze checks; 3) accompanying gestures, including pointing or showing; and 4) qualities of the utterance, such as loudness. For example, an utterance would be considered interactive if it is produced with audible volume and directed gaze to a partner prior to, during, or following its production. Use of gestures accompanying an utterance directed to a partner provides further evidence of interactiveness.

Degree of Comprehension

A determination must be made whether the learner understands the utterance that he or she is producing by examining the individual's nonverbal interactions with objects and people during or following the production of UVB. Determination of comprehension is important as it will influence the choice of intervention strategies. For example, clear evidence of comprehension implies that teaching a more conventional verbal response (i.e., a replacement strategy) should be effective. Teaching a more conventional verbal response is especially appropriate for individuals whose communication is primarily symbolic. However, evidence of lack of comprehension, as is sometimes observed with highly automatic and perseverative forms, implies that teaching a nonverbal or augmentative means as a replacement strategy may be the most effective, especially if the individual's repertoire of UVB and communicative means is primarily presymbolic. Additionally, the use of more conventional forms of verbal or nonverbal communication prior to or following the production of UVB may yield information regarding the existence of more socially acceptable forms of communicative behavior that serve the same communicative function. This finding could prove very important in selecting a more socially acceptable communicative form to subsequently replace UVB. Examples of nonverbal communicative forms that may help to determine comprehension of UVB are described in Table 7.

Other factors such as rigidity of repetition also provide important information relative to intentionality and inter- and intrapersonal functions served by UVB.

Rigidity of Repetition

A determination must be made whether the UVB involves rigid reproduction of others' utterances or whether some structural linguistic change is imposed. Evidence of structural change may be indicative of some linguistic processing and may signal emerging linguistic competence (Schuler, 1979). That is, when an individual's utterance is composed largely of an immediate or delayed repetition (i.e., immediate or delayed echolalia), but modifications are introduced, this pattern may signal movement from echolalia to more creative and generative language (Prizant, 1983). Types of modifications may include

Table 7. Communicative forms that may help to determine comprehension of UVB

1. Gestures including reaching, pointing, showing, open-hand requests, movement to an object, or action performed on an object produced immediately prior to, during, or following production of UVB
2. Utterances produced semantically contingent to prior discourse (produced subsequent to UVB)
3. Behaviors indicating the expectation of further action by the communicative partner (e.g., gaze check or subsequent verbal or nonverbal requests)

pronominal adjustments (e.g., utterance: "You are doing a fine job"; response: "I doing a fine job"), telegraphic echoing (e.g., utterance: "Let's go get a drink"; response: "Go get drink"), and intonational changes (e.g., utterance: "Want a sandwich?"; response: "Want a sandwich.") In general, utterances produced with evidence of comprehension and clear communicative intent are often produced with structural changes that suggest intervening linguistic processing. Obviously, structural change is determined more easily for immediate echolalia; however, if one is familiar with an individual's linguistic behavior and repertoire of frequently repeated phrases, determining structural change for delayed echolalia also is possible. In addition to documenting aspects of linguistic structure, it is also important to document how utterances are used in communicative interactions.

Patterns of Initiation and Response

In contrast to immediate echolalia, which by definition is produced in response to another's utterance, delayed echolalia may be produced to initiate or continue a communicative exchange. Prizant and Rydell (1984) found that some forms of delayed echolalia involved self-initiated utterances. Pragmatically, these initiations served functions that included calling, protesting, and directives. Other forms of delayed echolalia were produced primarily in response to the speech of a communicative partner. Echolalia that continues communicative exchanges includes the communicative functions of turn-taking, verbal completion, and labeling (see Table 3 for definitions). Clinical experience suggests that individuals who initiate communicative acts using delayed echolalia often appear to demonstrate a greater appreciation of the instrumental value of language and may have a better prognosis for further functional linguistic growth than individuals who produce UVB primarily to continue social exchanges. Furthermore, in our experience, the extent to which an individual initiates communicative acts through UVB appears to be highly correlated with general social motivation (i.e., the desire to be and communicate with others) and negatively correlated with social isolation. There is a great need for further research into the relationships among these variables.

In contrast to analyzing evidence of intentionality underlying UVB and the specific functions served by UVB, functional analysis also refers to the "manipulable environmental variables the behavior was a function of" (Evans & Meyer, 1985, p. 27). Within this framework, Donnellan et al. (1984) presented a checklist and discussed the use of antecedent and consequent strategies for testing hypotheses about the functions of behavior. Use of observational checklists across contexts (e.g., Donnellan et al., 1984; Schuler, Peck, Willard, & Theimer, 1989) is a minimally intrusive strategy for developing hypotheses about functions of behavior. Input from family members and other familiar persons is essential to validate observations. Questionnaires and scales for determining functions of behavior are available and can be used in interviewing significant others (see Schuler et al., 1989; Durand & Crimmins, 1988).

Following the use of interviews and observational checklists, more direct and intrusive procedures for validating hypotheses can be implemented. Such procedures involve manipulating antecedent and consequential events (Donnellan et al., 1984) and documenting the effect of these manipulations on UVB and communicative behavior. Antecedent strategies include manipulating situational features hypothesized to precipitate unconventional behavior. For example, if an individual produces UVB when served a particular food at lunch and the UVB is hypothesized to serve a protest function, this hypothesis may be tested by systematically offering a different food at the next lunch (presumably more desirable) and noting whether UVB is subsequently produced. Consequential strategies include responding to the hypothesized intention (i.e., providing positive reinforcement) followed by teaching a more conventional form to accomplish the same goal with subsequent reinforcement of the more conventional form and by noting whether UVB terminates or persists contingent upon this response. In assessment, it is also important to document verbal and nonverbal communicative forms in addition to UVB in order to obtain a complete picture of a learner's communicative repertoire because decision-making in intervention should be based on a comprehensive profile of an individual's communicative abilities.

How Unconventional Verbal Behavior
Fits into an Individual's Communicative Profile

A focus only on production of UVB does not consider the full range of communicative abilities and strategies that may be part of an individual's communicative repertoire. It is essential to consider UVB as one aspect of an individual's communicative system, which often includes conventional as well as unconventional means of communicating intentions (Donnellan et al., 1984; Prizant and Wetherby, 1985; Wetherby, 1986). By profiling communicative abilities as well as needs, informed decisions can be made regarding direct and indirect intervention strategies addressing the production of UVB. Prizant & Schuler (1987) provided more specific information for deriving a comprehensive communication profile for individuals with UVB. Such a profile includes documentation of an individual's verbal and nonverbal expressive communication means that addresses form and function, receptive communication and language abilities, language-related cognitive abilities, and social-interactive behavior and social relatedness. Variability of communicative and social abilities across persons and contexts needs to be accounted for as well.

Document Developmental Change
in Unconventional Verbal Behavior Over Time

As discussed earlier, UVB is observed frequently in individuals demonstrating a gestalt style of language acquisition. Therefore, some patterns of UVB, especially those observed in young children, may represent a transitional phenomenon and be a positive prognostic indicator for communicative growth and change (Howlin, 1981; Prizant, 1983). Communicative change may include increased functional use of UVB, an increase of emerging creative language forms in proportion to UVB, and an increase in conventionality, and thus, understandability, of UVB. When patterns of UVB are documented over time, a determination of shifts away from overreliance on UVB to express communicative intentions can be made. However, older individuals may demonstrate patterns of UVB that remain static and are considered to be challenging. Intervention strategies must take these factors into account. For example, more indirect and naturalistic strategies, such as modifying the interactive style of partners, may be appropriate for the young child, whereas more direct strategies, such as training specific forms to replace UVB, may be more appropriate for an older individual (direct and indirect strategies are discussed in detail in the section on intervention).

Document the Degree to Which
Unconventional Verbal Behavior Is Challenging

Determining intervention strategies to address UVB are based, to a great extent, on the frequency of UVB and the degree to which it is challenging. As discussed earlier, factors to consider include whether UVB adds new and relevant information to a conversational interaction, whether UVB interferes with an individual's ability to attend to or participate in communicative interactions or learning experiences, and whether UVB is stigmatizing to an individual in different contexts. The decision to focus on UVB, when it is determined to be challenging, also depends on whether it is a perceived priority in an individual's educational or functional living program. For example, indirect intervention approaches that focus on communication and life-skills enhancement may result in a reduction of challenging UVB. As noted earlier, the decision as to whether UVB is deemed challenging is value-laden, and this determination is based upon the partners' perspectives and orientations. It is common for professionals to have less tolerance for unconventional behavioral characteristics than peers or family members (Evans & Meyer, 1985). Thus, it is imperative that decision-making be based on a team approach with family members and caregivers serving as team members.

In summary, some basic questions regarding UVB should be addressed as part of assessment. First, what can patterns of UVB tell us about an individual's communicative abilities at a particular point in time? Second, what functions are served by UVB? Third, under what circumstances is UVB more likely to occur? Fourth, do such patterns appear to play any role in communicative progress and linguistic growth? Finally, are particular forms of UVB considered challenging (to educators, clinicians, and/or the family) to the extent that direct intervention is warranted? Intervention approaches must consider these factors.

INTERVENTION DECISION-MAKING

It is beyond the scope of this chapter to provide a detailed discussion of intervention issues. Intervention approaches exemplifying "best practices" in communication enhancement and in strategies for dealing with challenging behavior are relevant for UVB. Due to the great variability in UVB across individuals, intervention approaches should be designed based on individual patterns derived from assessment (Durand & Crimmins, 1987; Prizant, 1987a). Approaches addressing UVB should always be only one dimension of a coordinated approach to communication enhancement (Prizant & Schuler, 1987; Wetherby & Prizant, 1992); this is a basic tenet that often has not been followed in more fragmented approaches to unconventional communicative behavior (Burke, 1990). Interventionists must consider the interrelationships among social-cognitive, socioemotional, and linguistic factors and their interactions on the communicative performance of individuals with UVB. Thus, when considered as part of a more encompassing approach to enhancement of social-communicative competence, strategies for addressing UVB may involve not only direct interventions, but may also involve indirect strategies.

Antecedent Strategies

Antecedent strategies include approaches that do not necessarily involve direct interventions with an individual. These strategies are analogous to what has been referred to as antecedent manipulations (Horner et al., 1990). Such strategies address interactive and situational determinants of UVB (antecedent conditions) and, if necessary, they alter those conditions to promote the use of more conventional forms of communication (Prizant & Wetherby, 1988). Ongoing monitoring of changes in UVB should follow the implementation of indirect strategies. The following are examples of indirect strategies.

Modify the Situation

Modify the situation if it is known to result in challenging UVB. When challenging UVB is associated with emotionally arousing (i.e., confused or disorganized) situations, modification of such situations may be an effective first-line strategy to reduce the occurrence of UVB. For example, reduction or dampening of aversive sensory stimulation (e.g., loud noises), or simplifying new and difficult tasks or routines may serve to reduce UVB. As an individual becomes familiar and more competent with a new task or routine, complexity can be increased gradually. Often, challenging UVB may be used to procure attention from others or to obtain desired objects. In these cases, providing opportunities for socially acceptable means to gain attention or obtain objects, and consistent responses to such attempts, may preclude the use of UVB.

Prepare the Individual

Prepare the individual for potential emotionally arousing situations. When patterns of UVB are precipitated by specific situational determinants or events that cannot be changed (e.g., unplanned disruptions of regular routines) or other "must do" events that may be negatively emotionally arousing, an individual can be prepared to anticipate such events. Strategies to achieve this end may include the use of picture or written schedules with some discussion about the events or the use of relaxation procedures (Cautela & Groden, 1981). The primary goal is to help an individual self-regulate emotionally. Achieving emotional self-regulation is supported by the predictability of events and a learner's ability to anticipate and plan cognitively for events (Prizant & Meyers, in press; Prizant & Wetherby, 1990). Anticipation and planning may be fostered by using supports such as calendars and daily schedules and should result in fewer negatively arousing incidents precipitated by the unpredictability of, or change in, scheduled activities or events.

Simplify Language Input

Simplify language input and vary the adult interaction style. Simplifying language input is a cardinal rule for interacting with individuals with a communication impairment. However, because of the apparent complexity of some forms of UVB, especially echolalia, an individual's comprehension and production abilities may be overestimated, thus resulting in a partner's use of language that is too complex for an individual to comprehend. For example, an individual who produces delayed echoic utterances of up to eight words may actually be at a one- to three-word utterance level of generative language (Prizant & Rydell, 1984), yet the production of these longer utterances may lead others to overestimate language competence. As mentioned earlier, a factor empirically demonstrated to result in greater occurrence of UVB is comprehension difficulty. Thus, complexity of language input is a major intervention consideration.

When UVB is indicative of limited comprehension and results from interpersonal communicative demands, appropriate modifications in the interactive style of communicative partners is warranted. For instance, facilitative styles of verbal interaction have been found to promote increased occurrences of communicative initiations, topic initiations, and unprompted requesting and providing of information. Although these social-communicative acts may include both conventional and unconventional verbal behaviors produced with evidence of communicative intent (Rydell, 1989; Rydell & Mirenda, 1991), conventional verbal behavior occurs with greater frequency in less demanding, adult-facilitative interaction contexts.

With individuals who are extremely passive and show little or no evidence of social-communicative initiation, a more directive adult style may be warranted. A higher level of adult social-communicative control and structure may be needed to elicit verbal interaction. More directive and demanding environments have been shown to increase the occurrence of unconventional verbal behaviors (e.g., echolalia). As stated previously, for many individuals, UVB may serve a useful purpose in reducing the information-processing load associated with high-demand interaction contexts while allowing a passive individual to experience some degree of reciprocity in social exchange. Furthermore, UVB may eventually come to serve a variety of cognitive and social-communicative functions, as well as serve as the vehicle by which an individual comes to acquire more conventional forms.

Provide Relevant Language

Provide relevant language during activities that allow for decision-making and choice-making. A major challenge faced by persons with UVB is to acquire language forms that relate appropriately to objects and events. Given that UVB often is "borrowed" language, based on the repetition of others' speech, it is essential that the language environment includes models that are relevant and meaningful in context. Opportunities for decision-making and choice-making in daily activities provide motivating context for individuals to learn to use conventional forms of verbal behavior with clear consequences. Due to the tendency of persons with UVB to repeat utterances when highly motivated, developmentally appropriate language models provided in contexts of requesting or rejecting items is an intervention strategy that can promote a conventional verbal repertoire. Choices of foods for lunch and leisure activities, for example, can be offered. Relevant and clear language should be modeled, along with visual supports (e.g., pictures), if necessary, when presenting possible choices to an individual.

Consequential Strategies

Consequential strategies often are more direct than antecedent strategies and are implemented as specific responses to the production of UVB in naturalistic contexts. Consequential strategies may also include teaching activities that attempt to replace UVB with more conventional and appropriate communicative forms.

Respond to Communicative Intent

Respond to communicative intent and relate UVB to objects and events in the environment. If UVB is produced with apparent communicative intent, we recommend that the interventionist respond with contingent simplification of the individual's utterance, approximating his or her true language level. If possible, communicative partners should attempt to emphasize the relationships between UVB and environmental referents (objects, actions, and people). While providing a simplified or recast model of UVB, demonstrative gestures (e.g., pointing, touching) and actions can be used to relate utterances to the immediate context. Modeling language in a context of active involvement and in synchrony with relevant action patterns is a powerful teaching strategy for children who produce UVB (Fay & Schuler, 1980). In reference to immediate echolalia, Charlop (1983) stated that, "Echolalia should not be eliminated, but taken advantage of as it may facilitate acquisition and generalization for autistic children" (p. 125).

If UVB is noninteractive and not relevant to the situational context and its production interferes with an individual's ability to participate in educational and social activities, it may be necessary to redirect the individual's attention and provide language models more relevant to ongoing activities. Physical guidance may be necessary to achieve this goal. Such forms of UVB may be highly perseverative and self-directed, with no apparent communicative intent (i.e., not attention-motivated), and may occur with repetitive motor activity. In extreme cases of negative emotional arousal, agitation, or distress, action should be taken to ensure the individual's safety and the safety of others.

Replace UVB with Conventional Language

A basic theme underlying approaches to challenging behavior is helping an individual to acquire more conventional forms that serve the same communicative function (Burke, 1990; Donnellan et al., 1984; Durand & Crimmins, 1987; Evans & Meyer, 1985; Prizant & Wetherby, 1985). Several studies have examined the efficacy of intervention strategies designed to eliminate and/or replace UVB with more conventional forms of language (e.g., Durand & Crimmins, 1987; Foxx et al., 1988; Schreibman & Carr, 1978). For the most part, these interventions have occurred in experimental contexts rather than in natural interactions; however, generalization to, and maintenance in, more natural contexts has been demonstrated to varying degrees. Unfortunately, clear definitions of UVB often are vague, as are descriptions of individuals' full communication systems prior to and following intervention. Nevertheless, current approaches to challenging and unconventional behavior that help individuals acquire more conventional communicative forms are most relevant to UVB.

Augment Verbal Communicative Behavior

Augment verbal communicative behavior with conventional nonspeech communicative means. When a systemic view is taken regarding UVB, introduction of nonspeech augmentative communicative means may be an important strategy to help individuals with UVB to communicate in more conventional ways. Unfortunately, because an individual may be producing some recognizable speech, interventions sometimes focus too narrowly on oral language development. We are not aware of any published research that directly addresses the effect of augmentative system use on UVB. However, in our experience, two general benefits are apparent: First, individuals with highly unconventional and challenging UVB are able to communicate intentions more efficiently and conventionally through augmentative means with a concomitant reduction in challenging UVB; and second, for individuals whose UVB is clearly functional and transitional and co-occurs with functional language, augmentative means may provide a backup or safety-net function in difficult or stressful circumstances. Augmentative means may also help an individual to participate more actively in communicative exchanges while transitioning to primarily oral language over time. This latter pattern appears more typical for younger individuals. (For a comprehensive consideration of these and other issues in augmentative communication, see Reichle, Sigafoos, and York [1991].)

Provide Positive Interventions for UVB

Interventions for UVB should be positive and supportive. As noted, research has demonstrated that UVB often is socially motivated and functional and, in some cases, may represent a transitional phase to more conventional communication. Therefore, an individual should never be punished for producing UVB. Regardless of whether UVB is intentional and interactive or a primary strategy for communication, the use of punishment amounts to admonishing a person for his or her limitations in acquiring conventional means to communicate. Direct intervention and physical redirection may be necessary for production of highly stereotypic repetitive UVB; however, this type of UVB usually comprises a small portion of an individual's verbal production and most typically occurs during unstructured or transitional periods or periods of high arousal. Use of positive interventions, including the direct and indirect strategies discussed above, should be sufficient to address even the most challenging forms of UVB.

CONCLUSION

In summary, communicative intervention strategies and goals addressing UVB should include use of indirect and/or direct strategies. Indirect strategies are less intrusive and include modifying environmental and situational determinants of UVB, including the partners' interactive styles, to preclude the production of UVB when it is a function of limited comprehension or when it becomes challenging. Direct strategies include helping an individual acquire more conventional language forms and, when appropriate, augmentative communication options. At the same time, interventions also must take into account that many forms of UVB (e.g., echolalia) may be important compensatory strategies, and they may be part of an individual's natural transition to more conventional communication.

Clearly, more research is needed on different forms of UVB, its dynamic relationship to an individual's communication system, its relationship to emotional arousal, and the functions it may serve (socioemotional, cognitive, and communicative). Such research should point to validation of intervention strategies that enable individuals with UVB to be more successful in communicative interactions.

REFERENCES

Baltaxe, C., & Simmons, J. (1975). Language in childhood psychosis: A review. *Journal of Speech and Hearing Disorders, 40,* 439–458.
Baltaxe, C., & Simmons, J. (1977). Bedtime soliloquies and linguistic competence in autism. *Journal of Speech and Hearing Disorders, 42,* 376–393.
Bruner, J. (1975). From communication to language. *Cognition, 3,* 255–287.
Burke, G. (1990). Unconventional behavior: A communicative interpretation in individuals with severe disabilities. *Topics in Language Disorders, 10,* 75–85.
Cantwell, D., Baker, L., & Rutter, M. (1978). A comparative study of infantile autism and specific developmental receptive language disorder. *Journal of Child Psychology and Psychiatry, 19,* 351–362.
Caparulo, B., & Cohen, D. (1977). Cognitive structures, language and emerging social competence in autistic and aphasic children. *Journal of the American Academy of Child Psychiatry, 15,* 620–644.
Carr, E., & Durand, V.M. (1985). The social-communicative basis of severe behavior problems in children. In S. Reiss & R. Bootzin (Eds.), *Theoretical issues in behavior therapy.* New York: Academic Press.
Carr, E., Schreibman, L., & Lovaas, O. (1975). Control of echolalic speech in psychotic children. *Journal of Abnormal Child Psychology, 3,* 331–351.
Cautela, J., & Groden, J. (1981). *Relaxation procedures for persons with developmental disabilities.* Champaign, IL: Research Press.

Charlop, M. (1983). The effects of echolalia on acquisition and generalization of receptive labeling in autistic children. *Journal of Applied Behavior Analysis, 16,* 111–126.

Charlop, M. (1986). Setting effects on the occurrence of autistic children's immediate echolalia. *Journal of Autism and Developmental Disorders, 16,* 473–483.

Coggins, T., & Frederickson, F. (1988). The communicative role of a highly frequent repeated utterance in the conversations of an autistic boy. *Journal of Autism and Developmental Disorders, 18,* 687–694.

Coleman, S., & Stedman, J. (1974). Use of a peer model in language training in an echolalic child. *Journal of Behavior Therapy and Experimental Psychiatry, 5,* 275–279.

Curcio, F., & Paccia, J. (1987). Conversations with autistic children: Contingent relationships between features of adult input and children's response adequacy. *Journal of Autism and Developmental Disorders, 17,* 81–93.

Donnellan, A., Mirenda, P., Mesaros, R., & Fassbender, L. (1984). Analyzing the communicative functions of aberrant behavior. *Journal of The Association for Persons with Severe Handicaps, 9,* 201–212.

Doss, L.S., & Reichle, J. (1991). Replacing excess behavior with an initial communicative repertoire. In J. Reichle, J. York, & J. Sigafoos, *Implementing augmentative and alternative communication: Strategies for learners with severe disabilities* (pp. 215–237). Baltimore: Paul H. Brookes Publishing Co.

Duchan, J. (1983). Autistic children are non-interactive: Or so we say. *Seminars in Speech and Language, 4,* 53–61.

Durand, V., & Crimmins, D. (1987). Assessment and treatment of psychotic speech in an autistic child. *Journal of Autism and Developmental Disorders, 17,* 17–28.

Durand, V., & Crimmins, D. (1988). Identifying the variables maintaining self-injurious behavior. *Journal of Autism and Developmental Disorders, 18,* 99–117.

Evans, I., & Meyer, L. (1985). *An educative approach to behavior problems: A practical decision model for interventions with severely handicapped learners.* Baltimore: Paul H. Brookes Publishing Co.

Fay, W. (1967). Mitigated echolalia of children. *Journal of Speech and Hearing Research, 10,* 305–310.

Fay, W. (1969). On the basis of autistic echolalia. *Journal of Communication Disorders, 2,* 38–47.

Fay, W. (1973). On the echolalia of the blind and the autistic child. *Journal of Speech and Hearing Disorders, 38,* 478–489.

Fay, W., & Schuler, A.L. (1980). *Emerging language in autistic children.* Baltimore: University Park Press.

Foxx, R., Faw, G., McMorrow, M., Davis, L., & Bittle R. (1988). Replacing maladaptive speech with verbal labeling responses: A case study promoting generalized responding. *Journal of the Multihandicapped Person, 1,* 93–103.

Hermelin, B., & O'Connor, N. (1970). *Psychological experiments with autistic children.* London: Pergamon.

Horner, R., Dunlap, G., Koegel, R., Carr, E., Sailor, W., Anderson, J., Albin, R., & O'Neill, R. (1990). Toward a technology of "nonaversive" behavioral support. *Journal of The Association of Persons with Severe Handicaps, 15,* 125–132.

Howlin, P. (1981). The effectiveness of operant language training with autistic children. *Journal of Autism and Developmental Disorders, 11,* 89–106.

Hurtig, R., Ensrud, S., & Tomblin, B. (1982). The communicative function of question production in autistic children. *Journal of Autism and Developmental Disorders, 12,* 57–69.

Kanner, L. (1943). Autistic disturbances of affective contact. *Nervous Child, 2,* 217–250.

Kanner, L. (1946). Irrelevant and metaphorical language in early infantile autism. *American Journal of Psychiatry, 103,* 242–246.

Kanner, L. (1973). How far can autistic children go in matters of social adaptation? In L. Kanner (Ed.), *Childhood psychosis: Initial studies and new insights* (pp. 189–213). Washington, DC: Winston.

Keenan, E., & Ochs, E. (1977). Making it last: The use of repetition in children's discourse. In S. Ervin-Tripp & C. Mitchell-Kernan (Eds.), *Child discourse.* New York: Academic Press.

Laski, K., Charlop, M., & Schreibman, L. (1988). Training parents to use the natural language paradigm to increase their autistic children's speech. *Journal of Applied Behavior Analysis, 21,* 391–400.

Lovaas, O.I. (1977). *The autistic child: Language development through behavior modification.* New York: Irvington Press.

McEvoy, R., Loveland, K., & Landry, S. (1988). The functions of immediate echolalia in autistic children: A developmental perspective. *Journal of Autism and Developmental Disorders, 18,* 657–668.

Mirenda, P., & Donnellan, A. (1986). Effects of adult interaction style on conversational behavior in students with severe communication problems. *Language, Speech, and Hearing Services in Schools, 17,* 126–141.

Paccia, J., & Curcio, F. (1982). Language processing and forms of immediate echolalia in autistic children. *Journal of Speech and Hearing Research, 25,* 42–47.

Paul, R., Dykens, E., Leckman, J., Watson, M., Breg, W., & Cohen, D. (1987). A comparison of language characteristics of mentally retarded adults with fragile X syndrome and those with nonspecific mental retardation and autism. *Journal of Autism and Developmental Disorders, 17,* 457–468.

Peck, C. (1985). Increasing opportunities for social control by children with autism and severe handicaps: Effects on student behavior and perceived classroom climate. *Journal of The Association for Persons with Severe Handicaps, 10,* 183–193.

Peters, A. (1977). Language learning strategies: Does the whole equal the sum of the parts? *Language, 53,* 560–573.

Peters, A. (1983). *The units of language acquisition.* Cambridge: Cambridge University Press.

Philips, G., & Dyer, C. (1977). Late onset echolalia in autism and allied disorders. *British Journal of Disorders of Communication, 12,* 47–59.

Prizant, B.M. (1978). *The functions of immediate echolalia in autistic children.* Unpublished doctoral dissertation, State University of New York at Buffalo.

Prizant, B.M. (1982). Gestalt processing and gestalt language in autism. *Topics in Language Disorders, 3,* 16–23.

Prizant, B.M. (1983). Language and communication in autism: Toward an understanding of the "whole" of it. *Journal of Speech and Hearing Disorders, 48,* 296–307.

Prizant, B.M. (1987a). Clinical implications of echolalic behavior in autism. In T. Layton (Ed.), *Language and treatment of autistic and developmentally disordered children* (pp. 65–88). Springfield, IL: Charles C Thomas.

Prizant, B.M. (1987b). Toward an understanding of verbal repetition in the language of visually-impaired children. *Australian Journal of Human Communication Disorders, 15,* 79–90.

Prizant, B.M. (1988). Communication problems in the autistic client. In N. Lass, J. Northern, L. McReynolds, & D. Yoder (Eds.) *Handbook of speech-language pathology and audiology* (pp. 1014–1039). Toronto: B.C. Decker, Inc.

Prizant, B.M., & Duchan, J. (1981). The functions of immediate echolalia in autistic children. *Journal of Speech and Hearing Disorders, 46,* 241–249.

Prizant, B.M., & Meyer, E.C. (in press). Socioemotional aspects of communication disorders in young children and their families. *American Journal of Speech–Language Pathology.*

Prizant, B.M., & Rydell, P.J. (1984). An analysis of the functions of delayed echolalia in autistic children. *Journal of Speech and Hearing Research, 27,* 183–192.

Prizant, B.M., & Schuler, A.L. (1987). Facilitating communication: Language approaches. In D. Cohen & A. Donnellan (Eds.), *Handbook of autism and pervasive developmental disorders.* New York: John Wiley & Sons.

Prizant, B.M., & Wetherby, A.M. (1985). Intentional communicative behavior of children with autism: Theoretical and applied issues. *Australian Journal of Human Communication Disorders, 13,* 21–58.

Prizant, B.M., & Wetherby, A.M. (1987) Communicative intent: A framework for understanding social-communicative behavior in autism. *Journal of the American Academy of Child Psychiatry, 26,* 472–479.

Prizant, B.M., & Wetherby, A.M. (1988). Providing services to children with autism (ages 0 to 2 years) and their families. *Topics in Language Disorders, 9,* 1–23.

Prizant, B.M., & Wetherby, A.M. (1989). Enhancing communication: From theory to practice. In G. Dawson (Ed.), *Autism: New perspectives on diagnosis, nature and treatment* (pp. 282–309). New York: Guilford Press.

Prizant, B.M., & Wetherby, A.M. (1990). Toward an integrated view of early communication language and socioemotional development. *Topics in Language Disorders, 10,* 1–16.

Reichle, J., York, J., & Sigafoos, J. (1991). *Implementing augmentative and alternative communication: Strategies for learners with severe disabilities.* Baltimore: Paul H. Brookes Publishing Co.

Roberts, J. (1989). Echolalia and comprehension in autistic children. *Journal of Autism and Developmental Disorders, 19,* 271–281.

Rydell, P.J. (1989). *Social-communicative control and its effect on echolalia in children with autism.* Unpublished doctoral dissertation, University of Nebraska–Lincoln.

Rydell, P., & Mirenda, P. (1991). The effects of two levels of linguistic constraint on echolalia and generative language production in children with autism. *Journal of Autism and Developmental Disorders, 21,* 131–157.

Schreibman, L., & Carr, E. (1978). Elimination of echolalic responding to questions through the training of a generalized verbal response. *Journal of Applied Behavior Analysis, 11,* 453–464.

Schuler, A.L. (1979). Echolalia: Issues and clinical applications. *Journal of Speech and Hearing Disorders, 44,* 411–434.

Schuler, A.L., Peck, C.A., Willard, C., & Theimer, K. (1989). Assessment of communicative means and functions through interview: Assessing the communicative capabilities of individuals with limited language. *Seminars in Speech and Language, 10,* 51–62.

Schuler, A.L., & Prizant, B.M. (1985). Echolalia. In E. Schopler & G. Mesibov (Eds.), *Communication problems in autism.* New York: Plenum.

Shapiro, T. (1977). The quest for a linguistic model to study the speech of autistic children. *Journal of the American Academy of Child Psychiatry, 16,* 548–565.

Shapiro, T., Roberts, A., & Fish, B. (1970). Imitation and echoing in young schizophrenic children. *Journal of the American Academy of Child Psychiatry, 16,* 608–619.

Simon, N. (1975). Echolalic speech in childhood autism. *Archives of General Psychiatry, 32,* 1439–1446.

Snow, C., & Ferguson, C. (Eds.). (1977). *Talking to children: Language input and acquisition.* Cambridge: Cambridge University Press.

Violette, J., & Swisher, L. (1992). Echolalic responses by a child with autism to four experimental conditions of sociolinguistic input. *Journal of Speech and Hearing Research, 35,* 139–147.

Voeltz, L.M. (1977, November). *Rule mediation and echolalia in autistic children: Phonological evidence.* Paper presented at the American Speech and Hearing Association annual meeting, Chicago.

Wetherby, A.M. (1986). Ontogeny of communicative functions in autism. *Journal of Autism and Developmental Disorders, 16,* 295–316.

Wetherby, A.M., & Prizant, B.M. (1989). The expression of communicative intent: Assessment guidelines. *Seminars in Speech and Language, 10,* 77–91.

Wetherby, A.M., & Prizant, B.M. (1992). Facilitating language and communication development in autism: Assessment and intervention guidelines. In D. Berkell (Ed.) *Autism: Identification, education, and treatment* (pp. 106–134). Hillsdale, NJ: Lawrence Erlbaum.

Zyl, I., Alant, E., & Uys, I. (1985). Immediate echolalia in the interactive behavior of autistic children. *Journal of the South African Speech and Hearing Association, 32,* 25–31.

12

Communicative Correspondence and Mediated Generalization

Trevor Stokes, Pamela G. Osnes, and Kristina Chambers DaVerne

IN ORDER TO SUCCESSFULLY PARTICIPATE in a conversation, a listener must be confident that the speaker's utterances are relevant and truthful regarding the topic being discussed. For example, if a speaker requests a pepperoni pizza but actually desires a sausage pizza, he or she will undoubtedly be disappointed at the arrival of a pepperoni rather than a sausage pizza. Even when speaker and listener agree on the relationship between referents and the language used to represent those referents, there are occasions in which a speaker's communicative utterance may fail to correspond to the context in which it is produced. For example, upon arriving home from school, a child is eagerly asked by his or her parent, "What did you do at school today?", to which the child responds, "Played outside." At first hearing, this would seem to be a plausible response, unless the parent knew that it had rained hard all day long. This chapter focuses on investigations that explore the functional relationship of correspondence between an individual's communicative productions and his or her actions. Unless a listener can depend on the relevancy and accuracy of utterances to represent environmental events, functional communicative behavior is not possible.

A second purpose in exploring the degree to which a speaker's utterances correspond with his or her actions rests in the possibility that learners can be taught to self-regulate their actions as a function of verbal prompts that they themselves deliver. Although verbalizations themselves do not have automatic effects on a speaker (or on other persons), they may come to function as discriminative stimuli for a speaker's actions. With carefully designed and implemented intervention procedures, a speaker's utterances alone may become reliable predictors of subsequent actions, even though there are no consequences directly applied for the performance of that behavior.

DESCRIBING COMMUNICATIVE CORRESPONDENCE

Lovaas (1964) showed that when utterances produced by nursery school children about a certain food were reinforced, an increased consumption of that food resulted. Similarly, Sherman (1964) increased children's rates of play with particular toys by reinforcing utterances about those toys. Others, however, failed to observe a controlling relationship between utterances and actions. For example, Brodsky (1967) reinforced an adolescent's statements about social behavior, but failed to observe a concomitant increase in social behavior matching the social behaviors described in the adolescent's spoken language. He concluded that the development of verbal discriminative control is not automatically achieved.

Risley and Hart (1968) provided an early example of a more systematic analysis of existing verbal control, correspondence, and its training. They focused on the play of 4- and 5-year-old children from low income families enrolled in preschool. During a morning play period, the children's use of play materials, blocks, and paints was noted. Ninety minutes later during a noon snack, the children were asked to report concerning their activity, that is, "What did you do that was good today?" Initially, the children were reinforced with access to snacks and social approval for increasing their frequency of utterances regarding the use of blocks and paints, independent of whether they actually played with those materials. The children displayed an increase in the targeted verbalizations, but no corresponding increase in the actual use of those materials. Risley and Hart then provided the reinforcers only when children played with materials with which they said that they were going to play. Under this condition, the children increased their play to correspond to the report, or decreased the frequency of their report to correspond accurately with the frequency of their utterances about play with the materials. In both examples, correspondence between utterances and actual play was demonstrated. Replication of these procedures with different toys occurred in a second experiment, with reinforcement of utterances preceding a condition in which reinforcement was provided only when children's utterances corresponded to their actions. After experiencing correspondence training with two different toys, investigators found that reinforcement of utterances alone resulted in an increase in the corresponding toy play. The reinforcement of an utterance corresponding to play with a material that was not previously the focus of training was sufficient to control the performance of that behavior.

Many investigators have assumed that a history of correspondence teaching that imparts a controlling function to utterances occurs naturally at an early age. Unfortunately, research suggests that assumptions cannot be made. Especially with young children, intervention may be necessary in order to reliably bring a child's behavior under the influence of the child's utterances.

DOES COMMUNICATIVE CORRESPONDENCE OCCUR NATURALLY?

If verbal regulatory function develops naturally in children through interactions with parents and teachers, some children can be expected to show correspondence without special intervention. It is probable that when children are given the unconstrained opportunity to speak about the performance of behaviors occurring at a high frequency in their repertoire, correspondence between utterances and performance may be high. For example, Osnes, Guevremont, and Stokes (unpublished) studied the naturally occurring correspondence with 12 preschoolers ages 2–5 years who attended an integrated preschool program. Observers made a narrative record of the children's correspondence statements for 30 minutes daily for 36 days, averaging almost 10 hours of observation for each child. This assessment yielded a mean frequency of nine statements per child. All children made statements allowing for assessment of correspondence; for example, "I'm going to play with the blocks," "I'm not going to play with the kitchen set." The overwhelming majority (96%) of the correspondence verbalizations were positive, in the form, "I'm going to _____." In this normative assessment, the level of naturally occurring correspondence was very high, approaching 100%. The investigators concluded that when children produced unprompted statements about their actions, it was very likely that they would actually perform the action as specified. The clinical issue, though, is what happens when an interventionist identifies actions that are not those with a high probability of a natural occurrence; that is, behaviors that may require a more intrusive prompting of the utterances.

Some intervention studies have incorporated an initial control condition in which utterances alone are reinforced in order to assess whether the child displays any extant verbal regulation skills. Williams and Stokes (1982) examined the performance of 3- and 4-year-old children under a condition in which appropriate content of utterances with regard to toy play was reinforced prior to any correspondence training (i.e., the children were reinforced for saying what they were going to do independent of their performance). The children displayed variable and transitory control over the performance of the targeted behavior. Initial increases in the occurrence of the behaviors decreased across days, showing that the antecedent verbal control of those behaviors was inconsistent without further training. Appropriate toy play was then facilitated by systematic intervention in which correspondence was reinforced.

A similar assessment was conducted by Baer, Williams, Osnes, and Stokes (1985). They assessed preexisting verbal regulatory control in a 4-year-old girl during toy play and interaction with peers. After baseline assessment of the occurrence of six target actions, utterances regarding the performance of the first behavior (e.g., use of crayons) were reinforced as in a "do-say" correspondence training paradigm. There was an increase in drawing with crayons as long as the child said she would play with them. The generality of this finding across behaviors was then assessed. A reinforced verbalization condition involving play with the kitchen set led to an initial increase in that play, but the effects were not maintained. Additional replication involving play with beads showed a similar effect. Verbal control did not result in a generalized and durable effect with this class of behaviors. A 14-day program of correspondence intervention with crayon play was then completed, followed by further examination of verbal control across the other behaviors. This brief contact with correspondence intervention with one behavior was sufficient to facilitate recovery of durable verbal control where previously it had been shown to be transitory. The reinforcement of utterances alone was sufficient as an intervention with behaviors that had not been previously targeted, whether the goal was to increase or to decrease their frequency. Although this study showed some preexisting, although transitory, correspondence between actions and communicative behavior, effective verbal control was reestablished with a brief refresher course of correspondence training.

Describing Procedures To Establish Communicative Correspondence

Correspondence intervention represents a strategy to develop a consistent relationship between a person's utterances and the performance of the behavior specified by those utterances. In training, when there is congruence between an individual's utterances and his or her actions, a positive consequence (presumably a reinforcer) results. When optimally effective, this intervention leads to the development of generalized verbal control of an individual's own behavior, in which previously untrained behaviors may be controlled by the reinforcement of relevant utterances.

Israel and O'Leary (1973) examined correspondence training with two typical teaching sequences, a do-say match between a report prior to (say-do) and after (do-say) the opportunity to play the play itself was reinforced using praise and edibles. Reinforcement of utterances about play without an additional correspondence contingency did not result in substantial increases in the related actions. Both correspondence training sequences were effective in improving play, with the say-do correspondence training showing some superiority. The say-do sequence was recommended as the optimal training strategy, although both may be used effectively.

In an assessment of children's sharing and use of praise during interactions, Rogers-Warren and Baer (1976) employed correspondence training that reinforced accurate reports of prior behavior by 3- and 4-year-old children in small groups. They found that, compared to a condition in which the children were reinforced for any true or false report, when reinforcers were delivered only for accurate reports of sharing and praising, children increased both reports as well as sharing and praising during subsequent opportunities. Guevremont, Osnes, and Stokes (1986a) found that, when optimally effective, this training leads to the development of generalized verbal control of an individual's own behavior, in which previously untrained behaviors may be controlled by the reinforcement alone of relevant verbalizations in the training or clinic setting. They examined the development of generalized verbal control (i.e., training to establish a controlling function of children's verbalizations for subsequent child-produced actions). Most notably, academic homework performance, as a result of training and intervention procedures implemented at school, was analyzed. Four-year-old children were assessed initially to determine whether they demonstrated any existing verbal regulatory control (i.e., whether their behaviors came under the control of verbalizations without any additional training). This was examined by reinforcing a verbalization about the performance of various play, interaction, group participation, and clean-up behaviors in the preschool, and about the completion of homework in the evening at home. Although the children reliably produced the utterances describing their proposed actions, this procedure had no effect on their subsequent actions. The children's utterances did not reliably correspond with their actions. Systematic intervention procedures were then implemented. Reinforcement was provided only on those occasions when children's utterances matched their subsequent actions when given the opportunity to engage in the corresponding action. The intervals between the child's utterance and subsequent action were systematically increased so that the latency between utterance and subsequent action became greater. At the conclusion of this investigation, performance at home after the preschool day was reliably controlled by the production of the child's descriptions of actions to be performed that evening at home, in the absence of any formal intervention occurring in the home.

Friedman, Greene, and Stokes (1990) examined the effects of correspondence training on the selection of appropriate nutritious snacks by 6- and 7-year-old children in elementary school. Following a baseline in which the children stated which snack they would choose, the implementation of an information program focusing on daily nutrition requirements and the nutritional value of the four food groups showed no effect on the choice of highly nutritious foods for snack. Within the multiple baseline design across the eight children studied, a correspondence training condition in which the children were reinforced for both saying they would eat a nutritious snack and actually selecting that food (fruits) demonstrated reliable correspondence.

Paniagua, Stella, Holt, Baer, and Etzel (1982) applied a variation of correspondence training that examined the effect of reinforcing behaviors occurring in the chain of behavior between the utterance and the final behavior that was the subject of the utterance. For example, if a child said that he or she would paint, the researchers used descriptive praise to reinforce behaviors such as the child's approaching the painting area and picking up the paint brushes. This procedure focused on behaviors produced subsequent to the verbalization, yet still antecedent to the final targeted action. This process of correspondence training probably increased the discriminative function of the utterance as well as the actions occurring prior to the final behavior. When intermediate behaviors were reinforced, in addition to the initial utterance, performance of the final behavior in the chain increased. In this study as well as others (e.g., Paniagua & Baer, 1982), correspondence between speech and actions was enhanced when the specific contingency for correspondence was made obvious at the time of verbalization and when the performance of the intermediate behaviors was reinforced.

Correspondence intervention procedures apply positive reinforcement when a learner's actions match a learner's utterance. Positive consequence procedures alone may not always work effectively. In some instances, a negative consequence for not corresponding may be the consequence applied along with positive procedures; for example, a mild cost applied for noncorrespondence, for not doing what the learner said he or she would do. For example, Osnes, Guevremont, and Stokes (1987) implemented only typical positive procedures with a 4-year-old child with developmental delays. This child's peer-directed talk during play did not improve under these conditions. Therefore, a more intrusive procedure was implemented. This involved the provision of positive consequences for correspondence (praise, affection, and a brief activity consequence such as a ride) as well as negative consequences for not corresponding (a time-out at the side of the play area for 3 minutes). With these procedures, the child's performance in talking to peers and in her proximity to peers improved substantially. Additionally, generalized improvements were documented in hand-raising and participation during the two large group activities at the beginning and end of the school day. This combination of contingencies to teach correspondence probably more resembles the procedures that would be used by parents and teachers in natural teaching interactions.

Further research has shown a need to incorporate consequences for noncorrespondence, especially with individuals with more severe disabilities. For example, Osnes, DaVerne, and Stokes (1989) employed correspondence training procedures with two 5-year-old children described as having severe emotional disturbances. Positive-consequence correspondence training incorporating social approval, brief activity consequences, and inexpensive trinkets as rewards was not effective in improving in-seat and hand-raising during two large group activities. These consequences did not act as reinforcers of the behavior for these children. When an additional consequence—the requirement that the children engage in a number of writing tasks for 4 minutes for not corresponding—was added to the procedures, performance consistently improved during both group activities.

The role of the intrusiveness and timing of consequences in correspondence training also was examined by DaVerne, Osnes, and Stokes (1992). A 5-year-old child with multiple behavior problems received correspondence intervention to improve nondisruptive and active participation in group activities at his preschool. During a period of regular say-do correspondence intervention, he received typical positive consequences for correspondence. These were delivered at the end of the group activity. No effects of these procedures were noted. Therefore, an additional consequence for noncorrespondence was added, a 3-minute time-out at the end of the group activity. These procedures were marginally effective and not well maintained. Therefore, a more intrusive immediate consequence was implemented. During this condition, immediate consequences were applied following 30 seconds of inappropriate behavior, rather than applying delayed consequences at the end of the activity. On-task behaviors increased substantially only when the correspondence training with delayed positive consequences and immediate consequences for noncorrespondence were implemented. These more restrictive and intrusive consequences allowed for the development of the discriminative stimulus properties of the antecedent verbalization.

Summarizing Procedural Guidelines for Correspondence Training

Given the diversity of procedures and outcomes for correspondence training described in the literature, it seems appropriate to outline some of the procedural recommendations that we would make to an interventionist who wishes to incorporate these techniques into ongoing practice.

Correspondence intervention refers to a process by which an individual's behavior changes in a desired direction after antecedent speech has received "coaching" by an interventionist. This coaching typically takes the form of: 1) the interventionist asking the individual a leading question (i.e., "What are you going to do in your group today?"), 2) the individual answering the question in a specific way (i.e., "I'm going to raise my hand to answer a lot of questions."), 3) the individual entering the setting in which the trained behavior is to be displayed, and 4) the interventionist providing feedback to the individual regarding the exhibition of the desired behavior in the targeted setting consistent with the antecedent verbalization. This format outlines a procedure that can be used in diverse settings with diverse individuals. Despite its straightforward nature, effective correspondence training requires attention to intervention details.

Identifying Individuals

Correspondence training can be used with virtually any individual regardless of verbal abilities. Highly developed cognitive abilities are not a prerequisite to effective intervention, although training may be accomplished more quickly with less variable results when an individual possesses more sophisticated cognitive abilities. For example, children who have more severe intellectual deficits appear to require greater persistence and procedural modifications by the interventionist throughout the course of training. Feedback contingent on the child's failure to exhibit the desired response in the targeted setting, in addition to the interventionist's typical provision of positive feedback contingent on the child's performance of the desired response, may be required. Precise application of training steps may be required consistently throughout correspondence intervention.

Asking the Question

The correspondence intervention question typically is very general, specifying only the setting in which the corresponding behavior is to occur. It usually focuses on a positive response (e.g., "What are you going to do in your group today?") rather than a negative response (e.g., "What are you *not* going to do in your group today?"). However, it is not limited to this positive-only focus. For example, after asking a general question, an interventionist can become more specific with further questions to address particular needs of the individual. In a case where a multiplicity of challenging social behaviors are apparent, an interventionist may continue questioning beyond the general question by asking, "Are you going to keep your hands and feet to yourself?" or "Are you going to be quiet and not speak out?", thus requiring an appropriate response to each question. In this way, each relevant clinical need is addressed through the question-asking process.

The interventionist should be aware of and facilitate normal social expectations throughout the question-asking and response-giving process. Particularly in the case of individuals who engage in challenging behavior, social skills may generally be lacking or limited. Because correspondence intervention requires an interaction between two people, at least in its early stages, it is a socially oriented process. Looking directly at the individual when asking the question sets up an expectation that eye contact will occur, a normal component of adaptive social interaction. Failure of the recipient to establish and/or maintain attention during question-asking should result in prompting an approximation of attending. Overlooking this step in the training process may inadvertently result in less precise responses by the individual.

Responding to the Question

Several behaviors typically occur simultaneously in social interactions. These behaviors include eye contact, articulation adequate to convey the message, appropriate use of language, adequate response duration to complete the message, and appropriate physical orientation to the person with whom the interaction is occurring. Because correspondence intervention occurs within the context of a social interaction, at least minimal attention to the varied components of well-formulated social interactions should guide the interventionist during the training of the response. Therefore, an interventionist can maximize intervention to achieve optimal results in several ways. As stated, the establishment and maintenance of eye contact throughout an interaction is important in normal social interactions. Articulating the response to the best of the individual's abilities and using appropriate language in the response reflects normal social expectations as well. The use of an appropriate amount of words (symbols) by the individual to convey a complete response to the question, while not persevering on the response, is another variable to which an astute interventionist must attend. Additionally, the physical orientation of the client should be monitored carefully by the interventionist. An individual who is turned away from the interventionist, moving away while responding, placing his or her hands on objects or people extraneous to the training situation, and/or putting his or her fingers in his or her mouth or nose is not demonstrating undivided attention. Establishing socially acceptable patterns of interaction are important components of correspondence intervention.

Providing Feedback

A critical part of the sequence of correspondence intervention is the provision of feedback to the individual. When an individual exhibits correspondence between what he or she said would be done and what actually was done, it is essential that reinforcement is provided. Careless administration of this link in the correspondence training sequence undermines any diligence the interventionist has provided to preceding links. With some individuals, the provision of reinforcement to correspondence is all that is necessary to result in steadfast effects. However, with more involved cases, often the most durable intervention effects result from the combined use of reinforcement for correspondence and some form of feedback for lack of correspondence. It is the responsibility of the interventionist to assess thoroughly what may function as reinforcers and punishers for individuals and then implement the most unobtrusive form of each, as indicated by the individual case.

After successful correspondence training, intervention can proceed on simple reinforcement of spoken utterances. In reinforcement of spoken utterances, positive feedback is provided immediately after the individual answers the question, or before the individual returns to the targeted setting. The advantage of this component of correspondence intervention is its cost efficiency in terms of intervention effort. The initial stages of correspondence intervention require an observer to note whether correspondence occurred and to deliver the appropriate consequence. Effective reinforcement of communication now produces the same result, without requiring an external agent to observe the target setting. Therefore, the time necessary to observe the presence or absence of correspondence is no longer required.

When correspondence intervention has proceeded to the stage of reinforcement of utterances, the bulk of the intervention has occurred and the interventionist has begun to target maintenance of training effects. It is at this point that the interventionist's diligence and careful attention to details in earlier intervention sequences prove fruitful. When procedures that promote the reinforcement of utterances produce adaptive responses over several consecutive opportunities, they can be implemented less and less frequently until they have been faded completely.

Maintenance of Effects of Communicative Correspondence Training

Although there is an impressive literature describing procedures to successfully establish communicative correspondence, the social validity of these procedures rests in their capabilities to establish maintenance of communicative correspondence. There are three issues discussed in the literature regarding the maintenance of correspondence intervention. First, does performance maintain for the child while correspondence procedures remain in effect? Second, does performance maintain following the discontinuation of successful correspondence training? Third, if performance does not maintain after correspondence training, can additional, less intrusive procedures effectively maintain performance of the target behaviors?

An examination of procedures to facilitate maintenance to follow the successful employment of correspondence training was conducted by Baer, Blount, Detrich, and Stokes (1987). They employed correspondence procedures to facilitate the choice of healthy snacks by 4- and 5-year-old children attending a day-care center. The children chose snacks from an array that included nutritious (fruits and vegetables) and less nutritious foods (cookies and crackers). In this study, correspondence training led to the children's consistent choice of "mostly healthy foods." More importantly, Baer et al. (1987) evaluated maintenance under conditions in which the child verbalized snack choice prior to snacktime, but there were no consequences programmed for these spoken utterances. Thus, the children's correspondence was examined under the conditions of an extinction schedule for spoken choices. Durability of performance was demonstrated over periods of up to 26 days. Following correspondence intervention, special transitional procedures were implemented to accomplish this maintenance. That is, following a condition of effective correspondence intervention, the schedule of consequences for correspondence was gradually reduced over 15–20 days from a reinforcer every day to a reinforcer, on average, every third day and then cessation of the reinforcer.

Osnes, Guevremont, and Stokes (1986) examined correspondence maintenance between saying and doing. Two children with poor interaction and play skills were reinforced for talking to peers. One child had developmental delays and the other child was bilingual. The report, "I'm going to play with the kids a lot," when followed by talk to preschool peers during play was reinforced by positive consequences such as attention and brief activity consequences including rides and blowing bubbles. Within the multiple baseline design, the level of talk increased to within the normative range displayed by other children in the preschool. Maintenance following the correspondence training was evaluated with both children; one child was evaluated under conditions of a reinforcement of the verbalization alone, and the other child was evaluated under baseline conditions. In both cases, appropriate talk to peers maintained across time after the withdrawal of more intrusive procedures.

Guevremont, Osnes, and Stokes (1986b) examined maintenance after correspondence training was established. Talk with peers, clean-up, on-task activity, and participation in groups were selected for intervention across group and play settings at a preschool. Correspondence intervention led to substantial increases in designated behaviors. Prior to a return to final baseline conditions, a maintenance strategy of indiscriminable contingencies was implemented. This involved a mixed presentation of procedures of reinforced verbalization, delayed reinforcement of verbalization, reinforcement of correspondence, no reinforcement of verbalization or correspondence, and no prompted verbalization. Maintenance occurred with this condition of indiscriminable contingencies and maintained also in the subsequent baseline up to 67 days. Reinforcement of utterances alone also was successful as a maintenance strategy following correspondence training, although the results were variable in a baseline following the reinforcement of utterances.

Although there is a limited literature examining the maintenance of effects resulting from correspondence intervention, there appear to be sufficient data to suggest that in many contexts there may be sufficient natural maintaining contingencies to make it an attractive intervention strategy.

Describing Generalized Effects Following Correspondence Training

With the development of a repertoire of generalized communicative correspondence, changes beyond those in the original intervention may occur (Stokes, Osnes, & Guevremont, 1987). There is general agreement that when correspondence intervention procedures are applied to some behaviors that match antecedent utterances, the extent of control can be maximized because utterances about performance become reliable discriminative stimuli occasioning the occurrence of behaviors previously untrained. Thus, behaviors may be changed by teaching the production of the utterance alone because a generalized widespread repertoire of verbal control has been reliably established.

An example of this productive outcome was provided by Williams and Stokes (1982). Working with 3- and 4-year-old children, they sought to increase toy play, invitations to peers to join play, and the predictability of clean-up after play. Prior to correspondence intervention, reinforcement of spoken utterances showed variable and transitory effects on the children's related performance. Subsequent to experience with correspondence intervention, the reinforcement of speech about previously untrained behaviors showed strong and stable control of behavior. Baseline data on these behaviors after the successful reinforcement of verbalization condition revealed typically transitory effects.

Baer, Osnes, and Stokes (1983) examined the role of correspondence intervention on a child's speech in a preschool during the afternoon and the relevant behaviors that occurred later that evening at home or the following morning. The home behaviors for the 4-year-old boy were picking up clothes and choosing healthy desserts in the evening. Baseline data showed low rates of intermittent performance of the behaviors. An initial assessment of correspondence showed that when delayed positive consequences were provided contingent on the utterances on the day after the utterance condition alone, there was no change in behavior at home. Correspondence between the utterances and the performance of the behavior was then reinforced with brief activity consequences or inexpensive trinkets. That is, at the end of the school day, the child would state that he was going to perform a particular action at home (e.g., pick up clothes and put them in the hamper after his bath). Positive consequences were provided at the beginning of school the next day, based upon the mother's reliable record of whether the child performed the behavior. Within a multiple baseline design, behavior improved on the two events for which correspondence intervention was applied. Furthermore, after this intervention, a condition in which the appropriate utterance was reinforced on a delayed basis was also effective. That is, the utterance was provided at the end of the day and the reinforcer was not delivered until the beginning of the next school day, irrespective of the child's behavior at home the previous evening. This less discriminable contingency of delayed reinforcement of utterances was also effective alone as an intervention with the behavior (e.g., choice of fruit for dessert), although there had not previously been any intervention focusing on that behavior. This is a demonstration that generalized verbal control can be effective across remote settings and time. The utterance being reinforced on a delayed basis acquired discriminative control over performance during correspondence intervention.

A replication of the delayed reinforcement of utterance procedures was described by Baer, Williams, Osnes, and Stokes (1984). Four children between 4 and 5 years old evidenced little or no correspondence with various play and interaction behaviors. The provision of positive consequences for verbalizations had no effect on performance of the relevant behaviors prior to any correspondence intervention directed at those behaviors. After correspondence intervention, delayed reinforcement of speech was effective in facilitating targeted performance. If the behavior did not maintain well under those conditions, a brief reinstatement of correspondence intervention was sufficient to recover generalized verbal control.

In order to examine the controlling effects of utterances, Deacon and Konarski (1987) employed different intervention procedures for children with mental retardation. Initial assessment showed that the children did not come under the control of antecedent verbalizations about the performance of manipulatory responses in a research setting. The children then received either correspondence intervention or direct reinforcement of particular actions. Similar improvements were seen with both interventions, and these effects maintained and generalized verbal control. The authors noted that generalization results could be interpreted both as an outcome of the correspondence intervention or as the result of the development of rule-governed behavior.

In a related study, Baer, Detrich, and Weninger (1988) found a similar level of performance under either of two conditions, correspondence intervention or direct reinforcement of toy play in an applied setting. Although generalized verbal control was not established, play occurred more frequently if either the child or an adult provided an antecedent utterance. This outcome suggested a guiding role for such verbalizations. A study by Ward and Stare (1990) found similar results but also showed facilitating generalization and maintenance effects.

Early research focused on making utterances salient and functional as controlling stimuli for subsequent actions. With replication of procedures across children and with the intensive nature of the repeated measures within subject analysis, we have sampled a diversity of children's reactions to these procedures. Many children respond to these procedures while other children do not. It may be a complex task to establish the discriminative stimulus control of behavior by relevant utterances. Establishment of verbal control with most children may be relatively straightforward, but the need for more sophisticated intervention is likely for some.

THE ROLE OF CORRESPONDENCE IN
ESTABLISHING SELF-REGULATION SKILLS

When the utterance precedes an individual's actions, the utterance may mediate subsequent actions. The process of self-mediated generalization describes the establishment of initial antecedent control in which utterances and the use of previously established relations between utterances and relevant behaviors enhance generalization over setting behaviors and time. Consequently, communicative correspondence may be highly relevant in teaching goal-setting and self-instructional techniques.

Guevremont, Osnes, and Stokes (1988b) examined the effects of goal-setting on pre-academic performance by 4-year-old preschoolers. Using a comparison/discrimination task, they employed both contracting procedures and goal-setting procedures to determine which were optimally effective for intervention effects and for maintenance of performance following the intervention condition. During the more intrusive contracting condition, the children negotiated goals with their teacher, selecting from an array of possible performance standards that were at least 20% above the level displayed during baseline. During goal-setting, the children were allowed to freely determine the number of problems they would complete that day. Compared to baseline, the data showed that the children's performance improved consistently when they worked under either the goal-setting or the contracting condition. The more intrusive negotiation and contracting condition was more effective than goal-setting as an intervention. Furthermore, maintenance of performance was superior after each child had experienced the contracting condition. In fact, after a period of contracting, maintenance occurred within 7–21 days when assessment occurred following both contracting and goal-setting conditions. Apparently, it was during the contracting condition that the children learned to set appropriately higher goals, and their performance was better maintained following these conditions. Additional data showed that during the interventions, on-task behavior and performance on related comparison tasks improved as well.

Results of this investigation have significant implications for investigations regarding choice-making. There is a significant and growing literature suggesting that choice-making represents an important aspect of empowerment (Guess, Benson, & Siegel-Causey, 1985; Houghton, Bronicki, & Guess, 1987; Shevin & Klein, 1984). Results of the preceding study suggest that structured choice-making may be very useful as a stepping stone to increased levels of responsibility in making decisions.

The use of *self-instructions* allows guiding utterances to be produced regarding the dimensions of appropriate performance occurring in the present or in the future. For example, Guevremont, Osnes, and Stokes (1988a) studied the mediating effect of children's use of self-instructions. Intervention included teaching the children to make self-statements regarding problem orientation, to make a task statement, to use guiding self-statements (e.g., "This one, so I will circle it"), and to conclude a task item with a statement of self-acknowledgment. Initially, children were taught to verbalize the self-instructions aloud so that the researchers could study their characteristics and the relation between the use of self-instructions and performance on the tasks. Later in the sequence and after spoken utterances had been demonstrated to serve a controlling function, the children were taught to read the instructions silently to themselves. The data on the pre-academic phonics discrimination tasks under the baseline conditions operating in the classroom throughout the study showed a strong relationship between use of self-instructions in the classroom and improved performance by the children.

The relationship between correspondence intervention and subsequent self-regulatory skills has significant implications for individuals who regularly interact with persons who evidence challenging behavior. If more subtle antecedent-based intervention strategies can be implemented to establish correspondence between an individual's communicative behavior and subsequent actions, the necessity for instructor-delivered prompts subsequent to an initial request should be minimized. Furthermore, if the learner has a history of communicative correspondence, the intrusiveness of the interventionist's prompt to move the learner to engage in a particular activity may be lessened. For example, the only prompt required to achieve participation in doing laundry may be approaching an individual at a time when laundry is normally done and ask, "What do you think we should do now?" As soon as the individual responds by communicating "laundry," no further prompting is required. In addition, rather than directly manding the individual into compliance, the social interaction takes on a far less coercive tone.

CONCLUSION

This chapter addresses the importance of the correspondence between an individual's communicative behavior and his or her actions. In a communicative exchange, a listener must be able to assume that the speaking partner's utterances are relevant and truthful with respect to the topic being discussed. The literature reviewed in this chapter suggests that interventionists should not make the assumption that having taught communicative functions, correspondence will necessarily occur. Correspondingly, the interventionist should not assume that if a learner's utterances correspond to his or her actions, there will be temporal reciprocity.

Fortunately, for individuals who do not display a correspondence between their actions and communicative behavior, there are practical and reasonably well-validated intervention strategies. These strategies are based on reinforcing both members that comprise the correspondence chain, the learner's action and spoken behavior. Although the effectiveness of intervention strategies has been well documented, there is a significant need to consider a host of variables. For example, among some learners it is possible that memory deficits could significantly contribute to a lack of communicative correspondence. For other learners, failure to correspond may represent an intentional attempt to award negative feedback. For example, a parent might ask a child who did not do his homework, "Did you do your homework?" Realizing that he might get in trouble if he answered, "No," the child might produce a noncorresponding utterance. There is a significant need for research that more precisely matches the conditions under which learners may fail to engage in communicative correspondence. A more careful examination of the reasons for a correspondence failure will enable interventionists to continue to improve their capability to create more efficient intervention strategies to improve communicative correspondence.

REFERENCES

Baer, R.A., Blount, R.L., Detrich, R., & Stokes, T.F. (1987). Using intermittent reinforcement to program maintenance of verbal/nonverbal correspondence. *Journal of Applied Behavior Analysis, 20,* 179–184.

Baer, R., Detrich, R., & Weninger, J. (1988). On the functional role of the verbalization in correspondence training procedures. *Journal of Applied Behavior Analysis, 21,* 345–356.

Baer, R.A., Osnes, P.G., & Stokes, T.F. (1983). Training generalized correspondence between verbal behavior at school and nonverbal behavior at home. *Education and Treatment of Children, 6,* 379–388.

Baer, R.A., Williams, J.A., Osnes, P.G., & Stokes, T.F. (1984). Delayed reinforcement as an indiscriminable contingency in verbal/nonverbal correspondence training. *Journal of Applied Behavior Analysis, 17,* 429–440.

Baer, R.A., Williams, J.A., Osnes, P.G., & Stokes, T.F. (1985). Generalized verbal control and correspondence training. *Behavior Modification, 9,* 477–489.

Brodsky, G. (1967). The relation between verbal and non-verbal behavior change. *Behaviour Research and Therapy, 5,* 183–191.

DaVerne, K.C., Osnes, P.G., & Stokes, T.F. (1992, May). *The role of the timing of consequences in correspondence training with a behaviorally disordered preschooler.* Presented at the Association for Behavior Analysis annual conference, San Francisco.

Deacon, J., & Konarski, E., Jr. (1987). Correspondence training: An example of rule-governed behavior. *Journal of Applied Behavior Analysis, 20,* 391–400.

Friedman, A.G., Greene, P., & Stokes, T. (1990). Improving dietary habits of children: Effects of nutrition education and correspondence training. *Journal of Behavior Therapy and Experimental Psychiatry, 21,* 263–268.

Guess, D., Benson, H.A., & Seigel-Causey, E. (1985). Concepts and issues related to choice-making and autonomy among persons with severe disabilities. *Journal of The Association for Persons with Severe Handicaps, 10,* 79–86.

Guevremont, D.C., Osnes, P.G., & Stokes, T.F. (1986a). Preparation for effective self-regulation: The development of generalized verbal control. *Journal of Applied Behavior Analysis, 19,* 215–219.

Guevremont, D.C., Osnes, P.G., & Stokes, T.F. (1986b). Programming maintenance after correspondence training interventions with children. *Journal of Applied Behavior Analysis, 19,* 215–219.

Guevremont, D.C., Osnes, P.G., & Stokes, T.F. (1988a). The functional role of preschoolers' verbalizations in the generalization of self-instructional training. *Journal of Applied Behavior Analysis, 21,* 45–55.

Guevremont, D.C., Osnes, P.G., & Stokes, T.F. (1988b). Preschoolers' goal setting with contracting to facilitate maintenance. *Behavior Modification, 12,* 404–423.

Houghton, J., Bronicki, G.J.B., & Guess, D. (1987). Opportunities to express preferences and make choices among students with severe disabilities in classroom settings. *Journal of The Association for Persons with Severe Handicaps, 12,* 18–27.

Israel, A., & O'Leary, K.D. (1973). Developing correspondence between children's words and deeds. *Child Development, 44,* 575–581.

Lovaas, O.I. (1964). Control of food intake in children by reinforcement of relevant verbal behavior. *Journal of Abnormal and Social Psychology, 68,* 672–678.

Osnes, P.G., DaVerne, S.R., & Stokes, T.F. (1989, May). *The use of positive/negative correspondence training with preschoolers.* Presented at the Association for Behavior Analysis annual conference, Milwaukee.

Osnes, P.G., Guevremont, D.C., & Stokes, T.F. (1986). "If I say I'll talk more, then I will": Correspondence training to increase peer directed talk by socially withdrawn children. *Behavior Modification, 10,* 287–299.

Osnes, P.G., Guevremont, D.C., & Stokes, T.F. (1987). Increasing a child's prosocial behaviors: Positive and negative consequences in correspondence behaviors: Positive and negative consequences in correspondence training. *Journal of Behavior Therapy and Experimental Psychiatry, 18,* 71–76.

Osnes, P.G., Guevremont, D.C., & Stokes, T.F. (unpublished). *Assessment of preschoolers' naturally occurring correspondence behaviors in play.*

Paniagua, F., & Baer, D. (1982). The analysis of correspondence training as a chain reinforceable at any point. *Child Development, 53,* 786–798.

Paniagua, F., Stella, M.E., Holt, W., Baer, D., & Etzel, B. (1982). Training correspondence by reinforcing intermediate and verbal behavior. *Child and Family Behavior Therapy, 4,* 127–139.

Risley, T.R., & Hart, B.M. (1968). Developing correspondence between the nonverbal and verbal behavior of preschool children. *Journal of Applied Behavior Analysis, 1,* 267–281.

Rogers-Warren, A., & Baer, D.M. (1976). Correspondence between saying and doing: Teaching children to share and praise. *Journal of Applied Behavior Analysis, 9,* 336–354.

Sherman, J.A. (1964). Modification of nonverbal behavior through reinforcement of related verbal behavior. *Child Development, 35,* 717–723.

Shevin, M., & Klein, N.K. (1984). The importance of choice-making skills for students with severe disabilities. *Journal of The Association for Persons with Severe Handicaps, 9,* 159–166.

Stokes, T. (1992). Discrimination and generalization. *Journal of Applied Behavior Analysis, 25,* 429–432.

Stokes, T.F., & Baer, D.M. (1977). An implicit technology of generalization. *Journal of Applied Behavior Analysis, 10,* 349–367.

Stokes, T.F., & Osnes, P.G. (1989). An operant pursuit of generalization. *Behavior Therapy, 20,* 337–355.

Stokes, T.F., Osnes, P.G., & Guevremont, D.C. (1987). Saying and doing: A commentary on a contingency-space analysis. *Journal of Applied Behavior Analysis, 20,* 161–164.

Ward, W., & Stare, S. (1990). The role of subject verbalization in generalized correspondence. *Journal of Applied Behavior Analysis, 23,* 129–136.

Williams, J.A., & Stokes, T.F. (1982). Some parameters of correspondence training and generalized verbal control. *Child and Family Behavior Therapy, 4,* 11–32.

13

Functional Communication Training
Factors Affecting Effectiveness, Generalization, and Maintenance

V. Mark Durand, Denise Berotti, and Jan Weiner

A COLLEAGUE ONCE RELAYED AN amusing anecdote at a conference about the possible limitations of using functional communication training as an intervention for challenging behavior. This person was working with a man who engaged in severe aggressive behavior. It was recounted that when the man was asked why he hit other people, he said that it was because he liked to see them bleed. The presenter at the conference noted that it would be difficult to use a communication-based approach with this man because they could not allow him to go around asking people, "Can I watch you bleed?"

This wryly humorous account highlighted for us a limitation of this approach to intervention. The limitation was not that functional communication training was inappropriate for the man described in the story above (we thought it could have been very appropriate). Instead, we believe that the apparent simplicity of the concept (i.e., replacing challenging behavior with communication) can lead to any number of different, and potentially unproductive, interpretations. It is not uncommon to hear the phrase, "We've done that already" when functional communication training is proposed as an intervention. And, just as we have often heard the phrase "We've done behavior modification already" when no behavioral interventions have been used appropriately, typically what was attempted in the name of functional communication training bore little resemblance to the procedures we have employed.

This chapter focuses on several factors that appear to be important to the successful use of functional communication training for reducing challenging behavior. As this method of intervention with challenging behavior receives greater acceptance, it can be expected that multiple variations will be designed. And while this diversity should be encouraged, there are several elements that appear to be necessary for initial reductions in challenging behavior, generalization across stimuli and responses, and maintenance across time. Following a description of functional communication training, we discuss several of these components, using case examples to highlight important points.

FUNCTIONAL COMMUNICATION TRAINING

The idea of replacing behavior problems with communication is deceptively simple. The process begins by assessing the function of the behavior(s) of interest, then teaching the person to use appropriate communicative responses to request those things previously obtained by the challenging behavior. In addition, attempts are made to make the behavior problem nonfunctional or at least less successful in obtaining reinforcers. Empirical support for this approach to reducing challenging behavior is growing (see reviews by Doss & Reichle, 1989; Durand, 1990; Durand & Crimmins, 1991; and this volume). These efforts have focused on severe challenging behaviors such as aggression and self-injurious behavior (e.g., Bird, Dores, Moniz, & Robinson, 1989; Durand & Kishi, 1987), stereotyped behavior (e.g., Durand & Carr, 1987; Wacker et al., 1990), and a variety of communication disorders (e.g., Carr & Kemp, 1989; Durand & Crimmins, 1987; Mace & Lalli, 1991). Intervention has been conducted in group homes (e.g., Durand & Kishi, 1987), schools (e.g., Hunt, Alwell, Goetz, & Sailor, 1990), and vocational settings (e.g., Bird et al., 1989). Table 1 lists published studies of functional communication training as an intervention.

Researchers are just beginning to explore the boundaries of this intervention approach through the study of maintenance (e.g., Bird et al., 1989; Durand & Carr, 1991; Durand & Carr, 1992) and the role of response efficiency (Horner, Sprague, O'Brien, & Heathfield, 1990). Recently, we have identified several assumptions in our own research that have guided work in this area. A few of the more important assumptions made about functional communication training are outlined below.

Conceptualizing Challenging Behavior

The first step in the process of replacing challenging behavior involves assessing the function of the behavior. This assessment process assumes one very important consideration—that we know what we are looking for. Although this may seem obvious to the point of being trivial, the way we view this behavior serves as the foundation for all later intervention efforts. Yet, the model of behavior being used has rarely been made explicit in published studies. As an example, Take the anecdote described in the beginning of the chapter to illustrate the point. In that case, an assumption was made that what the individual reported as maintaining his aggression (i.e., he liked to see people bleed) really was serving to continue his challenging behavior. This

Table 1. Published studies of functional communication training

Study	N	Behavior	Functional assessment method	Mode of communication
Bird, Dores, Moniz, and Robinson (1989)	2	Self-injury, aggression	Motivation assessment scale	Signs, symbols
Carr and Durand (1985)	4	Self-injury, aggression	Functional analysis	Verbal
Carr and Kemp (1989)	4	Autistic leading	Not reported	Verbal, gestures
Durand (in press)	3	Self-injury, aggression	Motivation assessment scale	Assistive devices
Durand and Carr (1987)	4	Body rocking, hand-flapping	Functional analysis	Verbal
Durand and Carr (1991)	3	Self-injury, aggression, tantrums	Functional analysis, motivation assessment scale	Verbal
Durand and Carr (1992)	12	Aggression, opposition, tantrums	Functional analysis, motivation assessment scale	Verbal
Durand and Crimmins (1987)	1	Unusual speech	Functional analysis	Verbal
Durand and Kishi (1987)	5	Self-injury, aggression	Motivation assessment scale	Signs, symbols
Horner and Budd (1985)	1	Tantrums	Observation of antecedents and consequences	Signs
Horner and Day (1991)	3	Self-injury, aggression	Functional analysis, interview	Signs, symbols
Horner, Sprague, O'Brien, and Heathfield (1990)	1	Aggression	Functional analysis, interview	Assistive device
Hunt, Alwell, and Goetz (1988)	3	Disruption	Observation of consequences	Verbal, symbols
Hunt, Alwell, Goetz, and Sailor (1990)	3	Aggression, disruption	Observation of consequences	Verbal, symbols
Mace and Lalli (1991)	1	Unusual speech	Descriptive analysis, functional analysis	Verbal
Northup, Wacker, Sasso, Steege, Cigrand, Cook, and DeRaad (1991)	3	Aggression	Motivation assessment scale, functional analysis	Signs, verbal
Smith (1985)	1	Self-injury, aggression	Observation of antecedents and consequences	Verbal
Smith and Coleman (1986)	1	Tantrums	Observation of antecedents and consequences	Verbal

(continued)

Table 1. (continued)

Study	N	Behavior	Functional assessment method	Mode of communication
Steege, Wacker, Cigrand, Berg, Novak, Reimers, Sasso, and DeRaad (1990)	2	Self-injury	Functional analysis, interview	Assistive device
Wacker, Steege, Northup, Sasso, Berg, Reimers, Cooper, Cigrand, and Donn (1990)	3	Self-injury, stereotypy, aggression	Functional analysis	Signs, assistive device

example, and the whole issue of adopting a conceptualization of behavior problems, raises several questions.

One concern can be expressed this way: Can people accurately report on the function of their own behavior? It is important to note here that persons *without* severe disabilities often have difficulty identifying why they behave the way they do. Therapists frequently refer to this phenomenon as "lacking insight" (e.g., Barrett, Hampe, & Miller, 1978; Casey & Berman, 1985; Hartmann, Roper, & Gelfand, 1977). Researchers in cognitive psychology have pointed out that adult subjects in studies of cognitive awareness are often unaware of the existence of a stimulus that importantly influences their behavior, and may even be unaware that a stimulus has affected their behavior (Nisbett & Wilson, 1977). Just as the interpretations of behavior made by persons without severe disabilities should be questioned, we should be equally cautious to uncritically accept interpretations made by people with severe disabilities.

A second step involves ascertaining the range of stimuli that maintain challenging behavior. For example, can we assume that "watching people bleed" could be maintaining someone's challenging behavior? What is at issue here is the nature of the search for the functions of behavior. At one extreme, one could assume that there are an unlimited number of maintaining variables that can differ in endless combinations from person to person. At the other extreme, the conceptualization of behavior could be limited to a very circumscribed categorization system (e.g., positive and negative reinforcement). Which approach should be taken in order to adequately assess a person's behavior?

In our work, we have adopted a pragmatic approach to assessing the variables maintaining challenging behavior. Guiding this choice has been both the extant research literature as well as a concern over how to translate the role of these influences into interventions (Durand, 1990). This strategy mirrors a recent approach to conceptualizing the scientist-practitioner model (see Hoshmand & Polkinghorne, 1992); in other words, letting pragmatic decisions guide research and applied work.

Once again, the anecdote described above may serve to illustrate our strategy for conceptualizing challenging behavior. Let us assume, for argument's sake, that the individual in question did indeed hit people to watch them bleed. Clearly, teaching him to ask for this would not be recommended. Instead, we would further assess *why* he would want to watch people bleed. For example, suppose he liked to watch people bleed because this was associated with a good deal of activity (e.g., people rushing around to assist the bleeding person), and social attention directed toward the aggressor (e.g., people saying things such as, "Why did you do that?"). In this case, we would look for ways in which he could request more appropriate ways to increase the amount of activity around him (e.g., teaching him to ask, "Can we go out for a ride?"), as well as to request more and appropriate social attention. In each case, we try to isolate the basic reinforcement processes underlying the maintenance of the challenging behavior and then attempt to teach appropriate and adaptive alternatives.

Functional Assessment

Once we have decided *what* we are looking for (i.e., we have a preliminary conceptualization of behavior), the next step involves deciding *how* to assess the role of influences on challenging behavior. Because of its importance to the eventual outcome of the intervention, this step, too, should be considered seriously. This topic is handled in more detail in other parts of this book (see Halle & Spradlin, chap. 5, this volume). However, there are several points that seem important to reemphasize. For example, when should you perform a functional analysis, when should you use other functional assessment methods, and when should you combine them?

There are a number of factors that will determine how you will assess the function of behaviors. One issue is *accessibility to manipulation*. There are certain influences that you cannot or would not manipulate or change in order to perform a functional analysis. Things such as some illnesses, disrupted family life, and chromosomal aberrations can certainly affect behavior problems, but they can not or should not be turned on and off in order to assess their influence. It is here that other functional assessment techniques would be useful.

Another concern involves the *ethics* of conducting a functional analysis. There are other influences that you could manipulate, but you may not want to change if they will result in an increase in challenging behavior. In many instances, deliberately increasing a severe behavior problem in order to assess it (e.g., reinforcing challenging behavior) can be questioned on ethical grounds. In these cases, assessment that does not involve manipulation (and subsequent increases in challenging behavior) would be recommended.(For a more detailed discussion of these issues, see Durand, 1993.)

PREDICTING SUCCESSFUL OUTCOMES

We have identified four factors that seem to influence the success or failure of functional communication training: response match, response mastery, response milieu, and the consequences for challenging behavior. These elements of training appear to be necessary conditions for initial reductions in behavior, generalization across people and stimulus conditions, and maintenance across time. Specific predictions can be derived from these components, and, where available, data on their relationship to intervention outcomes will be described.

Response Match

An important consideration for the initial success of functional communication training seems to be matching the communicative behavior to the function of the challenging behavior. In other words, the newly trained response should evoke the same consequences (or be a member of the same response class) as the targeted challenging behavior (Carr, 1988; Johnston & Pennypacker, 1980; Meyer & Evans, 1989). As we discussed previously, the conceptualization and assessment process will guide this aspect of training. This component of functional communication training introduces a testable hypothesis: *Challenging behavior will only be reduced following this training if the alternative response serves the same function as the challenging behavior.* Conversely, teaching communicative responses that do not serve the same function as the challenging behavior will not lead to behavioral reductions.

Our first study of functional communication training directly addressed the issue of response match (Carr & Durand, 1985). Following a functional analysis of the challenging behaviors of four students, we taught them responses that matched the assessed function of their behaviors ("relevant responses") as well as responses that did not match the function of their challenging behavior ("irrelevant responses"). In each case, the student's challenging behavior was reduced only when they used the communicative response that matched the function of that behavior. The student's behavior problem was not reduced when they were taught a response that did not match the function of their challenging behavior.

To further assess this issue, a second study was conducted. This study focused on the unusual speech of a young boy with autism (Durand & Crimmins, 1987). Two separate analyses of the function of this boy's unusual speech were conducted. It was found that the unusual speech tended to increase when he was faced with difficult tasks. Our interpretation was that his unusual speech served to allow him to escape from situations that he found aversive (i.e., difficult tasks).

The intervention phase of this study involved teaching him to say, "Help me" when presented with difficult tasks. In one condition, the phrase "Help me" was followed by assistance from an experimenter. Under this condition, unusual speech decreased as expected. It was assumed that the assistance provided to the student in effect made the task easier. In a second condition, the phrase was instead followed by praise from the experimenter (e.g., "That's good talking!") but not with assistance. Under these conditions, unusual speech *increased* when compared with the previous condition and baseline. Therefore, although the student was taught the same communicative phrase in each condition, his unusual speech decreased only when the phrase served the same function as the behavior. In both studies, reductions in challenging behavior occurred only when alternative behaviors were taught that matched the function of the problem behaviors. Alternative explanations such as stimulus control or physical incompatibility could be ruled out.

Case Example: Carl

The following case illustrates how improper matching of responses can lead to less than successful intervention outcomes. We recently worked with a 21-year-old man, Carl, who engaged in episodic instances of severe aggressive and self-injurious behaviors. Carl had dual sensory impairments, with limited vision and hearing. He was well-liked by the people with whom he worked, but had no formal communication skills. Staff had conducted a preliminary functional assessment of his challenging behavior using A-B-C charts (Bijou, Peterson & Ault, 1968). These records seemed to point to tangible influences as maintaining these behaviors.

Staff interpreted the assessment to indicate that Carl engaged in aggressive and self-injurious behaviors to gain access to favorite things. Specifically, Carl had a favorite piece of cloth that he liked to hold, and staff believed he would become disruptive to get this cloth when he did not have it. Following this logic, the staff taught Carl to raise his hand to indicate that he wanted the cloth. For example, if he was working on a task and raised his hand, staff would bring him his cloth. Although staff were initially successful in teaching Carl to raise his hand, there was no immediate reduction in his challenging behavior. In fact, Carl began to throw the cloth away when they brought it to him.

After some discussion and additional assessments, an alternate explanation for Carl's behavior was proposed. It was suggested that his challenging behavior was maintained by escape from demands. The additional assessments revealed that although he seemed to want his cloth during most tantrums, having the cloth may have also signaled a period of time without work. Prior to the intervention, if Carl was becoming upset, the staff would give him the cloth and let him sit by himself for a while. However, after they tried to reduce his challenging behavior by teaching him to raise his hand, they would give him the cloth but not provide a break from work. This explanation seemed to fit with the recent observation that he no longer seemed to want his cloth.

Based on this new hypothesis about his challenging behavior, it was decided to teach him to raise his hand so that he could signal his need for a break from work. While on the break, Carl would have access to various activities and objects, including his cloth. This change in the intervention resulted in a significant drop in the rate of Carl's aggression and self-injurious behavior.

As this case and the previous review of research suggests, response match appears to be an essential component for initial reductions in challenging behavior. Teaching a communicative response that does not match the function of the challenging behavior should not result in significant reductions in behavior. Although response match may be a necessary component of the success of functional communication training, it does not appear to be a sufficient condition for success. What follows are additional components that are necessary for initial reductions as well as generalization and maintenance.

Response Mastery

Response mastery refers to the ability of the trained communicative response or responses to successfully and efficiently produce the desired outcomes. It is almost too obvious to say that in order for this approach to be effective, the trained communicative response must successfully evoke the desired outcome. *If the individual is making a request appropriately (e.g., saying, "Help me"), but no one responds in the preferred manner (e.g., provides assistance), then you should not expect to see a reduction in challenging behavior.* We have identified several aspects of response mastery that seem to affect initial success, generalization, and maintenance. The following is a description of four components of response mastery: response success, response efficiency, response acceptability, and response recognizability.

Response Success

As has been previously mentioned, response success refers to whether or not significant others respond to the trained communicative responses. Durand and Kishi (1987) examined this issue as it relates to service delivery systems. In addition to assessing the behavior of the five adults who were participants in the study, the behavior of the staff was also assessed. It was found that success or failure of functional communication training was attributable to specific efforts on the part of staff. In other words, despite the fact that each participant was taught to successfully use a new communicative response that matched the function of his or her challenging behavior, the problem behavior was only reduced when staff changed their interaction patterns as a result. As discussed later in this chapter, whether or not people respond to communicative attempts depends on factors such as response recognizability, acceptability, and the responsiveness of these environments. At this point it is clear, however, that simply *engaging in these communicative acts (i.e., making responses that match the function of challenging behavior) without a subsequent response by others will not result in reductions in challenging behavior.*

Response Efficiency

As mentioned previously, the form of communication being taught must not only match the function of the student's challenging behavior, it must also be more effective and efficient in getting the student the reinforcers he or she obtained with his or her problem behavior. In an elegant series of studies, Horner and his colleagues have begun to examine this aspect of functional communication training (Horner & Day, 1991; Horner et al., 1990). These researchers have found that three components of efficiency seem to be involved in the success of functional communication training.

The first component of response efficiency, *physical effort,* refers to the energy expended for both the challenging behavior and the communication. If it is physically easier to get what you want with the new communicative response, then that behavior will replace the challenging behavior. For example, Horner and Day (1991) describe how a 12-year-old boy's aggression was not reduced significantly when he was required to sign a full sentence to leave work ("I want to go, please "). However, when he was required to make only the simple sign for "break," his aggressive behavior decreased. The short sign was viewed as more efficient than the sentence, and thus was more successful in reducing his challenging behavior.

The second component, *schedule of reinforcement,* refers to how effective each response is in obtaining the reinforcers. If the communicative response is successful each time it occurs, but the challenging behavior is reinforced only occasionally, then the communication will replace it. Finally, the *delay* in receiving the reinforcers also affects whether or not functional communication training will be effective. If individuals delay too long in responding to the communication, it will not successfully compete with the challenging behavior.

The research on response match and response mastery points out that it is not enough just to teach communicative responses. In order for communication training to reduce challenging behavior, the new behaviors being taught must match the function of the challenging behavior and must be more effective in obtaining those things previously obtained through the problem behaviors.

Case Example: Sarah

Sarah is an 11-year-old student with severe disabilities. Her fine motor responses are limited, but she is able to independently care for herself. Sarah says a few words clearly, but most of the time she engages in protoconversational behavior—verbalizations that have no clear articulation or meaning but mimic the tone of conversation. On occasion, during a difficult task, Sarah will throw herself to the floor, pound her legs and feet, and will not get back up when requested. In fact, when requested to get back to work her challenging behavior accelerates. It was determined that Sarah was exhibiting these behaviors to escape difficult tasks, and in fact was very successful in doing so. The time Sarah spent on the floor consisted usually of long periods of between 20 minutes and 2 hours.

It was decided that Sarah would be taught to ask for a different assignment when the task was too difficult by saying, "I don't want to do this, can I do something else?" The speech therapist worked for several months attempting to train Sarah to say this long phrase. In the meantime, Sarah's challenging behavior was increasing in frequency, duration, and intensity. She was now resorting to kicking teachers while on the floor. On some days, Sarah would enter the classroom and simply lie down for the entire day.

Because of this lack of success, an alternative solution was chosen. It was decided to teach Sarah to say, "Done" (a word she frequently used at mealtime when she wanted to be excused from the table) after completing a few seconds of work. This training was ongoing throughout the day. Although this training was time-consuming, it was a great deal less disruptive than Sarah's target challenging behavior. In fact, teachers were very willing to allow Sarah to do other things when she spoke, and they reported that they enjoyed hearing her use words. Teachers also did not allow Sarah to do other things unless she said the word "Done." As a result, because it was easier for Sarah to escape tasks by speaking, her use of this word increased while the disruptive behavior decreased.

It can be predicted that even if you teach a student a response that matches the function of the challenging behavior, and others respond appropriately to the person when the response is made, unless the person can get what he or she wants more easily with the new response, he or she will not use it, and the challenging behavior will not be reduced. What follows is a description of several factors that seem to influence not only the initial effectiveness of functional communication training, but also whether or not generalization and maintenance are observed.

Response Acceptability

One aspect of response mastery involves the acceptability of the new response to significant others. If the new communicative response is seen as unacceptable in community settings, then others will not respond appropriately and the desired consequences will not be obtained. A number of anecdotes have attested to this aspect of generalization and maintenance. For example, one group relayed their dismay that, although functional communication training had been successful with one man they were working with, it had not been equally successful in the community. When questioned, it was revealed that they taught this man (31 years old) to ask for a hug each time he wanted attention. Although this was acceptable in their program, it was pointed out that this would probably not be acceptable in most communities (i.e., an adult man asking strangers for a hug). It made sense that his disruptive behavior did not decrease in his community (i.e., it would not generalize to others outside of the program) because community members would probably not respond to his requests for attention.

There is to date little empirical evidence for this aspect of functional communication training, although one study addressed this factor indirectly. Durand and Kishi (1987) used functional communication training to reduce the severe challenging behavior exhibited by five individuals with mental retardation and dual sensory impairments (deaf/blind). They observed that one individual would scream and remove her clothes, apparently to obtain staff attention. Their first attempt at intervention involved teaching her to raise her hand to signal the staff to attend to her. Despite the fact that she learned to raise her hand, over time some staff refused to participate consistently. They argued that they were very busy and did not have time to respond each time she raised her hand.

Instead of trying to coerce staff into responding, they decided to change the meaning of her raised hand. Thus, instead of meaning "Come spend some time with me," they now taught the staff that her raised hand was to mean "Can I help you?" Each time she raised her hand, it meant they were to take her along on the chores with which they were so busy. The staff accepted this form of attention as appropriate (she received their attention as well as learned new skills) and responded to these new requests. This experience suggested that *unless the response they teach is acceptable to others in the prevailing environment, it will not be consistently responded to by some people (no generalization) and may not be effective over time (no maintenance).*

Case Example: Jeff

Jeff is an 18-year-old student at a state community college and a part-time employee at a hardware store. Jeff is 6'3", weighs 250 pounds and has been described as being intimidating. On occasion, Jeff has pushed a classmate or co-worker. At times, he is very forceful and pushes people to the floor. This behavior has jeopardized his education, job, and social relationships. Assessment revealed that Jeff exhibits this problem behavior to get attention. As a result, it was decided that Jeff would be trained to use an alternative communicative response to get the desired reaction from teachers, co-workers, and friends.

The communicative response chosen was to have Jeff pat people on the shoulder when he wanted their attention. This seemed to be an appropriate behavior for Jeff to acquire because Jeff's verbal skills are severely limited.

The problem arose, however, that Jeff did not seem to know his own strength, and, once trained, he was too forceful in his patting, resulting in the same problematic consequences. A more acceptable response was chosen, which was to teach Jeff to reach his hand out to people as if initiating a handshake. This behavior was much more acceptable to significant others and in community settings, as evidenced by the willingness of people to respond in kind.

Case Example: Ann

Ann is a 28-year-old woman with autism and mental retardation who attends a day program along with several other adults who have developmental disabilities. Her verbalizations primarily consist of simple sentences and delayed echolalia. Staff were concerned about Ann because she frequently displayed intense tantrums, characterized by screaming and head-banging. These tantrums typically lasted anywhere from 10 minutes to several hours. Before our involvement, staff responded to Ann's tantrums by directing her to a padded time-out room in hopes of preventing severe injury.

Functional assessment suggested that these behaviors were maintained by access to tangibles. This was consistent with observations and staff interviews, which suggested that Ann most frequently banged her head and screamed when she was blocked from taking a walk through the hallway and when she was prevented from ripping used paper cups. Because Ann, on occasion, was known to request walks and cups, intervention began by encouraging staff to respond to all such requests. It was hoped that this would teach Ann to rely on her appropriate communication, rather than on her challenging behavior, as a means to acquiring the desired activities. However, the response by staff to this recommendation for Ann's intervention also highlights the importance of response acceptability. Staff reported an unwillingness to follow the program because they felt that ripping paper cups was not a behavior they wanted to allow.

Rather than give up this approach to intervention, an attempt was made to help staff consider these requests as more acceptable. This was done by encouraging staff to think about unique, but harmless, behavior they may occasionally engage in, such as collecting various objects (e.g., collecting coffee mugs from different cities). They were then encouraged to consider how frustrating it would be if they lived in an environment where other people evaluated all of their behaviors and if decisions about whether they could engage in them were based on the beliefs of other persons. This helped staff appreciate the diversity of interests all persons have and how much they valued the freedom to make decisions for themselves. Following this effort at "consciousness raising," staff were more willing to respond when Ann asked to do things such as ripping paper cups. This, in turn, resulted in a corresponding decrease in her severe challenging behavior.

There is sometimes a fine line between what is considered eccentric and what is unacceptable. In discussing these issues with the above-mentioned staff, most began to realize that they too had some unusual but harmless ritualistic habits such as Ann had. One person described how he bathed each morning and the exact order that had to be followed. He conceded that he would probably get upset if someone interfered with this order.

In Ann's case, we chose to try to influence the way the staff viewed Ann's requests rather than try to get Ann to request something else. It should be clear to readers that issues such as these go beyond our science and enter the realm of values and beliefs. Obviously, an adequate discussion of this topic is not possible here (see, for example, Bannerman, Sheldon, Sherman, & Harchik, 1990). Yet, it is important to point out that in our work, we frequently encounter situations such as this. We are often confronted with a clash of values among our students, their teachers, their parents, and ourselves. If Ann wants to rip up three or four paper cups each day, should we stop her?

The previous discussion highlights how important it is that the response being taught be acceptable to those in the prevailing environment. *If the communicative response is viewed as unacceptable (whether because of what is being requested or how it is being requested), then others will not respond to it over time and new persons also may not respond. If others do not respond to the communicative behavior, then challenging behavior will not be reduced.*

Response Recognizability

An important consideration for persons with severe disabilities is that of teaching them a response that can be recognized, especially by others who may not be highly trained. Once again, a prediction can be made from this observation. *If the trained response is not easily recognizable by significant others in the environment, then these other people will not respond and challenging behavior will not be reduced.*

To date, much of the research on functional communication training has used verbal and signed speech as the means of communication. Unfortunately, spoken speech can often be misunderstood and signed speech can be so idiosyncratic that few can understand the message being relayed. Several studies have addressed the issue of the recognizability of the communicative response as it relates to functional communication training. In a study of maintenance, we found that after initial success with functional communication training, one young boy had resumed engaging in his serious self-injurious behavior (Durand & Carr, 1991). Examining the situation further by using sequential observation analyses, we found that his new teacher could not understand what he was saying when he was trying to get her assistance. Because she did not provide assistance when he asked for it, he began to hit himself again, which tended to result in fewer demands being placed on him. In this study we found that by improving his articulation skills, the teacher responded appropriately. Following the improvement in the student–teacher interaction, the boy's challenging behavior was again reduced, the reduction generalized to a new teacher, and was maintained 1 year later (Durand & Carr, 1991).

This issue is of particular importance for students with the most severe disabilities. If these students cannot communicate with others in a way that can be recognized, important people in their environments will not respond appropriately, and the students will go back to what does work—their challenging behavior. In research with students with severe communicative disabilities, vocal output assistive devices have been used as the means of communication (Durand, in press; Durand & Berotti, 1991). Similarly, Wacker et al. (1990) used a taperecorder for one of their participants so that she could communicate, "I'm tired of rocking; somebody give me something to do." They observed a dramatic reduction in her rocking with this intervention.

We have found that not only can students with the most severe disabilities use these devices to communicate (Durand, in press), but untrained individuals in the community can also understand the requests made by these students and can respond appropriately (Durand & Berotti, 1991). In addition, such devices have been programmed to speak in both English and Spanish when a student's parents speak only Spanish at home and the teacher speaks only English at school. In essence, students having mental retardation and dual sensory impairments have been taught to be bilingual. These devices have permitted us to teach students to make relatively simple responses (pressing a pad on the machine) that result in sophisticated output (full sentences) in clear spoken English. Again, because the output can be recognized by anyone, the success of the communication training has been extended into the community.

Case Example: Cheryl

Cheryl is a 17-year-old student with mental retardation and visual impairments. Before intervention began, Cheryl's communication skills were severely limited. In fact, it appeared that crying and hand-biting were her only means of communicating with her teachers. Assessment suggested that her problem behaviors were maintained by escape from demands. Therefore, treatment began by teaching her to request a break from work while in the classroom. Because Cheryl was never observed to use verbal responses to communicate, she was taught to request the break by activating a vocal output device that was programmed to say, "I'd like to take a break."

Once Cheryl began requesting breaks and her problem behavior decreased, staff became interested in having her take the communication board to work, where Cheryl frequently dropped to the floor in response to demands. Because activating the communication device resulted in clear spoken English that could easily be understood by anyone, no attempt was made to train those at Cheryl's work site. It was hoped that the staff at work would recognize and respond to her requests without having to specifically teach them what to do. Several weeks later, Cheryl's teachers received reports from her job that she was dropping to the floor less frequently and that she was able to tolerate working for longer periods of time. This improvement was attributed to her success in communicating her wants and needs to others at the job site.

Further attempts to incorporate Cheryl's communication board into community life have also been successful. For example, Cheryl and several of her schoolmates, who have also been trained to use vocal output devices, have begun ordering their own lunches at restaurants and purchasing items at stores for the first time. Although workers in these stores have no formal training in augmentative communication, they can recognize and respond to the students' needs by means of the vocal output devices.

Once again, a prediction can be made about the nature of the trained communicative response and the success of functional communication training. *Unless the new communicative response can be recognized by significant others in the prevailing environment, these people will not be able to respond to requests and challenging behavior will not be reduced.* Response recognizability is particularly important for generalization and maintenance of intervention gains. As we have seen, if the response can be communicated clearly, even untrained persons can provide these students with the reinforcers they desire (Durand & Carr, 1992). The technology developing in augmentative and assistive communication should complement efforts to reduce challenging behavior among persons with the most severe disabilities (Baumgart, Johnson, & Helmstetter, 1990; Reichle, York, & Sigafoos, 1991).

Response Milieu

Up to this point, we have discussed aspects of functional communication training that primarily involve the specific communicative responses being taught to persons exhibiting challenging behavior. However, we have also alluded to the context in which these responses are taught and used and its importance for successful outcomes. Clearly, for communication to be successful, it has to occur within a context that is responsive and supportive. Unfortunately, however, research on interventions for severe challenging behavior (including our own work) often deals with the context of treatment as a variable to be controlled or as an incidental element unworthy of note. Despite this lack of empirical attention, the success of interventions such as functional communication training appears to rely heavily on the nature of the environment in which it is used.

What are the characteristics of the optimal environment in which such training should take place? Can we describe, and therefore design, settings that will facilitate the success, generalization, and maintenance of reductions in challenging behavior using functional communication training? Unfortunately, as we have said, our own research has not specifically focused on environmental and contextual influences as they relate to this intervention approach. To our knowledge, no research has yet systematically explored the types of environmental variables that would positively or negatively affect these outcomes. Therefore, it is not yet possible to provide a data-based answer to these questions.

Although there is a lack of data on the role of particular intervention settings, we do have extensive experience using functional communication training in a variety of environments. During the past several years, we have intervened in over 100 cases with individuals experiencing severe challenging behavior using functional communication training (Durand, 1990). This work has been conducted in a broad range of residential, educational, vocational, and community settings. This experience has led us to collect a number of hypotheses regarding this issue. What follows are some of our observations on the role of the environment in the success of functional communication training.

The Role of Control

One factor that appears to influence the outcome of efforts to implement functional communication training is the degree of control or choice that is generally available to the individuals involved. The availability of choice-making opportunities has received recent attention and has been implicated in the success of various educational activities (e.g., Datillo & Rusch, 1985; Guess, Benson, & Siegel-Causey, 1985; Parsons, Reid, Reynolds, & Bumgarner, 1990). The type of communication training described here relies heavily on allowing individuals to make choices in their daily activities (e.g., choosing when to take a break, when to have a drink, when to get social attention). If these types of opportunities are routinely discouraged in the individuals' present environments, significant others may not respond appropriately to their requests (see previous section on response acceptability).

A recent study may support this hypothesis regarding the role of choice availability in the success of functional communication training. Kearney, Durand, and Mindell (1991) examined the effects of relocating 57 former residents of a large developmental center to various residential settings. A variety of measures were used to assess both the new settings as well as their effects on the individuals. It was found that these new residences differed significantly in the extent to which they provided residents with choice-making opportunities (e.g., choices about morning waking time, clothes, roommate, bath or shower time). It was also found that the opportunity to make choices was correlated with scores on the American Association on Mental Retardation Adaptive Behavior Scale (Nihira, Foster, Shellhaas, & Leland, 1974). In other words, people improved in their adaptive behavior in those settings where choice-making opportunities were readily available.

The previous study is just one in a long line of studies that suggest that the expectations of significant others will affect the outcomes observed in persons with severe disabilities (Evans & Scotti, 1989). In the present context, we have observed that *in those settings where choice-making is encouraged, functional communication training is more likely to succeed.* Conversely, where choice-making is discouraged, functional communication training often has limited success. Functional communication training in these settings has sometimes been described as "giving in," and has been received with some reluctance. Again, this observation will require further empirical attention. However, this aspect of the intervention environment appears to be a fruitful avenue for study.

Homogeneous versus Heterogeneous Grouping

A second environmental factor that seems to be implicated in the success or failure of functional communication training involves the type of grouping of the participants. Despite initiatives to include all students in regular classrooms and community settings, settings still exist where students are grouped together because they engage in challenging behavior. Historically, the logic behind such groupings has been that, if placed together, these students would have access to staff who are specially trained to deal with challenging behavior. Additionally, these students should benefit from group-wide programs and contingencies and, finally, would not disrupt other students.

Space does not permit a full discussion of the anticipated, as opposed to the actual, results of such homogeneous groupings. However, we have had the opportunity to directly compare and contrast the ability of these different settings to support efforts at functional communication training. Our observation has been that staff who work in such "behavior classes" are at particular risk of being overtaxed by the demands of the classroom and may find it especially difficult to be responsive to all of their students. Staff in settings that are more heterogeneous appear to have more flexibility. They are able to shift priorities toward activities that may require more intensive, yet temporary, effort (e.g., functional communication training). This flexibility may be attributable to the other students in these classrooms. The children who benefit from functional communication training are in classrooms with students who benefit from working independently between lessons. In such a setting, the teacher is more available to be responsive to the children receiving communication training than a teacher in a "behavior class."

This can be illustrated by comparing the recent application of functional communication training in two classrooms. Students in the first classroom were grouped together because of their high rates of challenging behavior, and students in the second classroom were grouped according to age. Several critical differences were observed in these two groupings. From the beginning, staff in the first classroom appeared to be more overwhelmed by their

334 / DURAND, BEROTTI, AND WEINER

jobs. Finding time for onsite training was difficult because a great deal of staff time was spent attending to students' severe behavior problems. This history of crisis management seemed to make staff more reluctant to try an alternative educational approach to treatment. Furthermore, much effort was necessary to emphasize the importance of creating a responsive environment.

Alternatively, because staff in the second classroom worked with children who had a diversity of educational needs, and because fewer students displayed severe behavior problems, staff were more experienced with and better able to concentrate on a skill-building approach to learning. Thus, staff found functional communication training to fit in naturally with the current educational goals of their classroom, and a minimal amount of time was required to enhance their motivation. Once again, data do not exist to support or negate this hypothesis. Yet, our experience suggests that *intervention in homogeneous settings can be extremely difficult, and it is recommended that students not be placed in settings solely on the basis of their challenging behavior.*

Level of Support

One of the elements contributing to the success of functional communication training involves the systems in place to support such efforts. In order for any intervention for severe challenging behavior to be successful, factors including the addition of resources, staff training, consultant services, and organizational restructuring must be in place (Helmstetter & Durand, 1991). Only a handful of studies have addressed systems change as an important component of intervention success (e.g., Donnellan, LaVigna, Zambito, & Thvedt, 1985; Durand & Kishi, 1987; Janney & Meyer, 1990; Singer, Close, Irvin, Gersten, & Sailor, 1984).

In our most recent work, we have attempted to address this issue through the type of training we conduct. Critical to the success of this approach is *home-school collaboration*. Without a cooperative relationship between the school and home, any improvements observed following an intervention are likely to be short-lived and restricted to certain people, places, and times. Home-school collaboration, as used here, means more than just consultation by a teacher with a parent (Meyer, 1989). Rather, it involves the ongoing relationship of the family and the school working together as a team.

Specifically, we have targeted students with severe challenging behavior throughout the state of New York. Our training efforts began by developing a team of individuals who work and live with the student. These teams have included parents, other family members, teachers, school psychologists, speech therapists, and administrators. The initial training has been focused on the *team*. In addition to providing training to the team on how to assess the function of challenging behavior and how to design effective interventions, we have specifically focused on promoting the team process. Teams are encouraged to accept and adopt input from each member. No one approach is seen as correct; rather, the process of collaboration is seen as the most important first outcome. The "expert role" is downplayed, and trainees are encouraged to see the trainers as resources rather than the "givers of truth." Through this approach to training, it is hoped that the team members can provide mutual support for the often difficult job of intervening with challenging behavior.

To reiterate: *Without proper supports, functional communication training with people having severe challenging behavior will probably not be successful, nor will it generalize to new persons and settings or maintain over time.* Intervention in isolation, whether it be by a parent at home or by a teacher at school, will prove to be difficult.

Consequences for Challenging Behavior

A final and somewhat controversial concern involves the issue of how to respond to the challenging behavior itself. We have placed this section last because we hope to emphasize the importance of teaching alternatives over descriptions about how to respond to these behaviors. However, it is important to discuss consequences for both theoretical as well as clinical reasons. On a conceptual level, it is important for us to understand the role of consequences within the context of the organization of the person's responses, both the challenging as well as the more appropriate behaviors. It is anticipated that this knowledge will, in turn, assist us in designing better strategies for reacting to behavior problems while functional communication training is being implemented.

In our work with functional communication training, we have used *response-independent consequences* as the primary reactive strategy (Durand, 1990). In other words, we try (as much as possible) to continue to behave with the person as if the challenging behavior did not occur. The goal here is to try to make the challenging behavior "nonfunctional" in the environment. For example, if we are working with an individual, and he or she screams, we try to continue working. If he or she is alone and starts to tantrum, we try not to intervene. We also attempt to avoid negative consequences such as reprimands or withdrawing reinforcers. At the same time we are teaching an alternative behavior that serves the same function, we try to make the challenging behavior less efficient at obtaining reinforcers.

A caveat is in order when using response-independent consequences. *We have always regarded the safety of the student and those around him or her as the most important priority.* There are times when students are engaging in behaviors that are dangerous to themselves or others; in those circumstances we intervene to protect all involved. This intervention is always conducted in as neutral a manner as possible in order to limit the changes in the environment. To date, this type of consequence has been sufficient to reduce challenging behavior in the vast majority of students receiving functional communication training.

Recently, Wacker et al. (1990) described the use of functional communication training with three individuals and the use of specific consequences with two of these individuals. It was observed that hand-biting and aggression in these two were significantly reduced with a package of procedures including functional communication training and negative consequences (time-out from positive reinforcement for one person and graduated guidance for the second). The authors observed that, when they attempted to remove the negative consequences as part of the package, the challenging behaviors increased. It was concluded that some individuals may require mild forms of negative consequences, at least initially.

It is difficult to interpret why the individuals studied in previous research and the third participant in the Wacker et al. study (1990) did not require negative consequences to reduce their challenging behavior. One interpretation mentioned by the authors is that, because these negative consequences were introduced from the beginning of their treatment, these may have affected their later behavior. It is possible that if the negative consequences were never introduced concurrent with functional communication training, these consequences may not have been required to reduce their challenging behavior. These data suggest that "behavioral contrast" may have been at work in this study—with the effectiveness of functional communication training alone influenced by the removal of the contingencies for challenging behavior (i.e., time-out and graduated guidance).

At the very least, Wacker et al. (1990) point out the need to be cautious in implementing and interpreting such intervention packages. *One goal in functional communication training is to make the new communicative response more efficient in obtaining reinforcers than the challenging behavior.* As we discussed previously, one way to accomplish this goal is to teach a response that is, from the start, more efficient than the challenging behavior. However, as this last section suggests, another avenue to pursue is to make the challenging behavior *less* efficient than the communicative response. Our work has been aimed at removing the contingency between the challenging behavior and our behavior by using response-independent consequences (Durand, 1990). This should assist us in making the challenging behavior less efficient than the communicative response. However, the specific role of response-independent consequences (or any other consequences) in the success of functional communication training awaits further empirical study.

CONCLUSION

We have identified four factors that appear to account for the success or failure of functional communication training to initially reduce challenging behavior and to generalize and maintain over time. To date, the research has focused on only a few of these factors. We need to further explore the variables outlined in this chapter in order to provide people in the field with a more comprehensive plan for implementing functional communication training. Replacing challenging behavior with communication involves a closer attention to the types of responses taught, the consequences for the challenging behavior, as well as the context in which this training takes place. The results to date have been encouraging. It is expected that with further refinement, many more cases of challenging behavior will be positively affected by this approach to intervention.

REFERENCES

Bannerman, D.J., Sheldon, J.B., Sherman, J.A., & Harchik, A.E. (1990). Balancing the right to habilitation with the right to personal liberties: The rights of people with developmental disabilities to eat too many doughnuts and take a nap. *Journal of Applied Behavior Analysis, 23,* 79–89.

Barrett, C., Hampe, T.E., & Miller, L. (1978). Research on child psychotherapy. In S. Garfield & A. Bergin (Eds.), *Handbook of psychotherapy and behavior change* (pp. 411–436). New York: John Wiley & Sons.

Baumgart, D., Johnson, J., & Helmstetter, E. (1990). *Augmentative and alternative communication systems for persons with moderate and severe disabilities.* Baltimore: Paul H. Brookes Publishing Co.

Bijou, S.W., Peterson, R.F., & Ault, M.H. (1968). A method to integrate description and experimental field studies at the level of data and empirical concepts. *Journal of Applied Behavior Analysis, 1,* 175–191.

Bird, F., Dores, P.A., Moniz, D., & Robinson, J. (1989). Reducing severe aggressive and self-injurious behaviors with functional communication training: Direct, collateral and generalized results. *American Journal of Mental Retardation, 94,* 37–48.

Carr, E.G. (1988). Functional equivalence as a means of response generalization. In R.H. Horner, G. Dunlap, & R.L. Koegel (Eds.), *Generalization and maintenance: Life-style changes in applied settings* (pp. 221–241). Baltimore: Paul H. Brookes Publishing Co.

Carr, E.G., & Durand, V.M. (1985). Reducing behavior problems through functional communication training. *Journal of Applied Behavior Analysis, 18,* 111–126.

Carr, E.G., & Kemp, D.C. (1989). Functional equivalence of autistic leading and communicative pointing: Analysis and treatment. *Journal of Autism and Developmental Disorders, 19,* 561–578.

Casey, R.J., & Berman, J.S. (1985). The outcome of psychotherapy with children. *Psychological Bulletin, 98,* 388–400.

Datillo, J., & Rusch, F.R. (1985). Effects of choice on leisure participation for persons with severe handicaps. *Journal of The Association for Persons with Severe Handicaps, 10,* 194–199.

Donnellan, A.M., LaVigna, G.W., Zambito, J., & Thvedt, J. (1985). A time-limited intensive intervention program model to support community placement for persons with severe behavior problems. *Journal of The Association for Persons with Severe Handicaps, 10,* 123–131.

Doss, S., & Reichle, J. (1989). Establishing communicative alternatives to the emission of socially motivated excess behavior: A review. *Journal of The Association for Persons with Severe Handicaps, 14,* 101–112.

Durand, V.M. (1990). *Severe behavior problems: A functional communication training approach.* New York: Guilford Press.

Durand, V.M. (1993). Causes of behavior: Functional assessment and functional analysis. In M.D. Smith (Ed.), *Behavior modification for exceptional children and youth* (pp. 38–60). Stoneham, MA: Andover Medical Press.

Durand, V.M. (in press). Functional communication training using assistive devices: Effects on challenging behavior and affect. *Augmentative and Alternative Communication.*

Durand, V.M., & Berotti, D. (1991). Treating behavior problems with communication. *Asha, 33,* 37–39.

Durand, V.M., & Carr, E.G. (1987). Social influences on "self-stimulatory" behavior: Analysis and treatment application. *Journal of Applied Behavior Analysis, 20,* 119–132.

Durand, V.M., & Carr, E.G. (1991). Functional communication training to reduce challenging behavior: Maintenance and application in new settings. *Journal of Applied Behavior Analysis, 24,* 251–264.

Durand, V.M., & Carr, E.G. (1992). An analysis of maintenance following functional communication training. *Journal of Applied Behavior Analysis 25,* 777–794.

Durand, V.M., & Crimmins, D.B. (1987). Assessment and treatment of psychotic speech in an autistic child. *Journal of Autism and Developmental Disorders, 17,* 17–28.

Durand, V.M., & Crimmins, D.B. (1991). Teaching functionally equivalent responses as an intervention for challenging behavior. In R. Remington (Ed.), *The challenge of severe mental handicap: A behaviour analytic approach* (pp. 71–95). West Sussex, England: John Wiley & Sons, Ltd.

Durand, V.M., & Kishi, G. (1987). Reducing severe behavior problems among persons with dual sensory impairments: An evaluation of a technical assistance model. *Journal of The Association for Persons with Severe Handicaps, 12,* 2–10.

Evans, I.M., & Scotti, J.R. (1989). Defining meaningful outcomes for persons with profound disabilities. In F. Brown & D.H. Lehr (Eds.), *Persons with profound disabilities: Issues and practices* (pp. 83–107). Baltimore: Paul H. Brookes Publishing Co.

Guess, D., Benson, H.A., & Siegel-Causey, E. (1985). Concepts and issues related to choice-making and autonomy among persons with severe disabilities. *Journal of The Association for Persons with Severe Handicaps, 10,* 79–86.

Hartmann, D.P., Roper, B.L., & Gelfand, D.M. (1977). An evaluation of alternative modes of child psychotherapy. In B. Lahey & A.E. Kazdin (Eds.), *Advances in clinical child psychology* (Vol. 1, pp. 1–46). New York: Plenum Press.

Helmstetter, E., & Durand, V.M. (1991). Nonaversive interventions for severe behavior problems. In L.H. Meyer, C.A. Peck, & L. Brown (Eds.), *Critical issues in the lives of people with severe disabilities* (pp. 559–600). Baltimore: Paul H. Brookes Publishing Co.

Horner, R.H., & Budd, C.M. (1985). Acquisition of manual sign use: Collateral reduction of maladaptive behavior, and factors limiting generalization. *Education and Training of the Mentally Retarded, 20,* 39–47.

Horner, R.H., & Day, H.M. (1991). The effects of response efficiency on functionally equivalent competing behaviors. *Journal of Applied Behavior Analysis, 24,* 719–732.

Horner, R.H., Sprague, J.R., O'Brien, M., & Heathfield, L.T. (1990). The role of response efficiency in the reduction of problem behaviors through functional equivalence training: A case study. *Journal of The Association for Persons with Severe Handicaps, 15,* 91–97.

Hoshmand, L.T., & Polkinghorne, D.E. (1992). Redefining the science-practice relationship and professional training. *American Psychologist, 47,* 55–66.

Hunt, P., Alwell, M., & Goetz, L. (1988). Acquisition of conversational skills and the reduction of inappropriate social interaction behaviors. *Journal of The Association for Persons with Severe Handicaps, 13,* 20–27.

Hunt, P., Alwell, M., Goetz, L., & Sailor, W. (1990). Generalized effects of conversation skill training. *Journal of The Association for Persons with Severe Handicaps, 15,* 250–260.

Janney, R.E., & Meyer, L.H. (1990). A consultation model to support integrated educational services for students with severe disabilities and challenging behaviors. *Journal of The Association for Persons with Severe Handicaps, 15,* 186–199.

Johnston, J.M., & Pennypacker, H.S. (1980). *Strategies and tactics of human behavioral research.* Hillsdale, NJ: Lawrence Erlbaum Associates.

Kearney, C.A., Durand, V.M., & Mindell, J.A. (1991). *The relationship between choice and adaptive/maladaptive behavior in persons with severe handicaps: A longitudinal study.* Unpublished manuscript.

Mace, F.C., & Lalli, J.S. (1991). Linking descriptive and experimental analyses in the treatment of bizarre speech. *Journal of Applied Behavior Analysis, 24,* 553–562.

Meyer, L.H. (1989). Home-school collaboration. In A. Ford, R. Schnorr, L. Meyer, L. Davern, J. Black, & P. Dempsey (Eds.), *The Syracuse community-referenced curriculum guide for students with moderate and severe disabilities* (pp. 17–24). Baltimore: Paul H. Brookes Publishing Co.

Meyer, L.H., & Evans, I.M. (1989). *Nonaversive intervention for behavior problems: A manual for home and community.* Baltimore: Paul H. Brookes Publishing Co.

Nihira, K., Foster, R., Shellhaas, M., & Leland, H. (1974). *AAMR Adaptive Behavior Scale, 1974 revision.* Washington, DC: American Association on Mental Deficiency.

Nisbett, R.E., & Wilson, T.D. (1977). Telling more than we can know: Verbal reports on mental processes. *Psychological Review, 84,* 231–259.

Northup, J., Wacker, D., Sasso, G., Steege, M., Cigrand, K., Cook, J., & DeRaad, A. (1991). A brief functional analysis of aggressive and alternative behavior in an outclinic setting. *Journal of Applied Behavior Analysis, 24,* 509–522.

Parsons, M.B., Reid, D.H., Reynolds, J., & Bumgarner, M. (1990). Effects of chosen versus assigned jobs on the work performance of persons with severe handicaps. *Journal of Applied Behavior Analysis, 23,* 253–258.

Reichle, J., York, J., & Sigafoos, J. (1991). *Implementing augmentative and alternative communication: Strategies for learners with severe disabilities.* Baltimore: Paul H. Brookes Publishing Co.

Singer, G.H.S., Close, D., Irvin, L.K., Gersten, R., & Sailor, W. (1984). An alternative to the institution for young people with severely handicapping conditions in a rural community. *Journal of The Association for Persons with Severe Handicaps, 9,* 251–261.

Smith, M.D. (1985). Managing the aggressive and self-injurious behavior of adults disabled by autism. *Journal of The Association for Persons with Severe Handicaps, 10,* 228–232.

Smith, M.D., & Coleman, D. (1986). Managing the behavior of adults with autism in the job setting. *Journal of Autism and Developmental Disorders, 16,* 145–154.

Steege, M.W., Wacker, D.P., Cigrand, K.C., Berg, W.K., Novak, C.G., Reimers, T.M., Sasso, G.M., & DeRaad, A. (1990). Use of negative reinforcement in the treatment of self-injurious behavior. *Journal of Applied Behavior Analysis, 23,* 459–467.

Wacker, D.P., Steege, M.W., Northup, J., Sasso, G., Berg, W., Reimers, T., Cooper, L., Cigrand, K., & Donn, L. (1990). A component analysis of functional communication training across three topographies of severe behavior problems. *Journal of Applied Behavior Analysis, 23,* 417–429.

PART IV

Facilitating the Application
of Intervention Programs

14

Transferring Implementation of Functional Assessment Procedures from the Clinic to Natural Settings

Wendy K. Berg and Gary M. Sasso

A̶N EFFECTIVE BEHAVIORAL ASSESSMENT IS one that leads to effective treatment by accurately identifying the antecedent stimuli that trigger the display of challenging behavior and the subsequent stimuli that maintain that behavior. As discussed in other chapters in this volume, the robustness of functional analysis as an effective behavioral assessment has been well-documented (Carr & Durand, 1985; Derby et al., 1992; Durand & Carr, 1985, 1991; Iwata, Dorsey, Slifer, Bauman, & Richman, 1982; Mace & Lalli, 1991; Steege et al., 1990). By systematically manipulating the presence and absence of different antecedent and consequent stimuli and documenting the effects of these manipulations on the subsequent display of appropriate or challenging behaviors, we can interpret apparently random displays of behavior as comprising predictable patterns of responding.

Although the results obtained to date with functional analysis procedures across both outpatient and inpatient clinic settings are impressive, several recurring issues continue to hinder the progress we believe is possible in the treatment of challenging behavior. The success of an evaluation is dependent on two factors: 1) the relevance of the assessment results to the criterion setting, and 2) the integrity with which the subsequent intervention recommendations are implemented and continued over time. In our case, the fact that assessment is occurring in a location separate from the ultimate intervention setting may limit the degree to which our clinic-based assessment results meet these two criteria for success.

In this chapter, we discuss the transfer of functional analysis procedures from clinical to criterion settings. Specifically, this discussion centers on the application of descriptive and experimental analyses to classroom settings as implemented within four school districts in Iowa and the possible impact of setting on treatment implementation.

There are several benefits associated with conducting assessments of challenging behavior within the natural setting (Sasso et al., 1992). First, the relationship between maintaining variables within controlled (clinic) settings and those operating in classroom settings is unclear. Clinic-based functional analyses, characterized by the systematic manipulation of consequences within a tightly controlled set of analog conditions, have proven to be an effective means of identifying general classes of maintaining contingencies (i.e., positive and negative reinforcement) (Iwata, Pace, Kalsher, Cowdery, & Cataldo, 1990). Although experimental analyses conducted within controlled analog conditions can identify contingencies capable of maintaining challenging behavior, they may not be the contingencies operating in other settings, such as the classroom (Carr, Newsom, & Binkoff, 1980; Iwata, Vollmer, & Zarcone, 1990; Mace & Lalli, 1991).

Furthermore, establishing the effectiveness of an intervention in a setting other than the criterion setting, the setting in which treatment will ultimately be implemented, may not be the most effective means for ensuring intervention integrity. A lack of follow-through by caregivers in implementing and maintaining intervention recommendations has been an ongoing problem for both our inpatient and outpatient clinics. Problems with intervention integrity have continued even after attempts have been made to include the direct care staff in the development of the intervention procedures and after successful demonstrations of the intervention's effectiveness in the clinic setting.

A failure to implement the intervention plan as recommended may occur for two reasons. First, in some cases, the caregiver may not accept the recommendations because of the complexity of the intervention plan, the time commitment required, or conflicting philosophies regarding the appropriateness of different interventions. These problems revolve around the issues of intervention acceptability (Reimers, Wacker, & Koeppl, 1987) and are discussed later in this chapter.

In other cases, caregivers may be willing to implement the plan but do so incorrectly. Errors in intervention implementation are most likely due to a lack of generalization across settings (clinic to home or school) or activities (assessment tasks to daily routine) on the part of the caregiver. Some of the errors we have observed in implementing interventions across different settings have involved providing the prescribed consequences under the wrong antecedent stimulus conditions (e.g., teaching a child to sign for a "break" in the absence of any demands). In other cases, the prescribed consequence has been modified in a manner that makes it ineffective as a reinforcer.

For example, we were called to provide technical assistance to residential care staff for a young man whose self-injurious behavior was maintained by escape from demands (based on the results of a previous functional analysis). Although the direct care staff had followed the recommendation of teaching the man to manually sign for a break during mealtimes, self-injurious behavior continued to occur at high frequencies during meals. Our observation of the mealtime situation revealed that the prescribed consequence for signing break (removing the food tray from his laptray and stepping away from the wheelchair for approximately 1 minute) was preceded by 30–40 seconds of verbal praise for signing break. Verbal praise had been incorporated into the consequence routine to comply with the residential program's guidelines of consequating all instances of compliance with training goals with verbal praise. Unfortunately, in this situation, the addition of verbal praise resulted in a delay in the delivery of the prescribed reinforcer, and the occurrence of self-injurious behavior escalated. Conducting the evaluation within the individual's criterion setting has the potential of minimizing these problems, because the activities, people, materials, and circumstances common to the criterion environment are incorporated into the evaluation and can be addressed specifically as intervention recommendations are developed.

A final concern is the need to provide more immediate intervention to an increasing number of children. Each child evaluated within our outpatient clinic has engaged in the challenging behavior for an average duration of 10 years before the referral was made for a clinical evaluation (Derby et al., 1992). Within this 10-year period, a variety of interventions have been implemented and abandoned, increasing the resistance of the behavior to intervention and decreasing the confidence of parents and educational personnel that the behavior can be brought under environmental control.

Given these concerns, it appears that the application of functional assessment procedures needs to expand to serve more individuals earlier in the history of the behavior and with greater participation of the people who provide direct care to the individual on a routine basis. Given that functional analysis represents a best practice for identifying effective intervention, it is imperative that we make every attempt to transfer this powerful technology to other professionals. Furthermore, functional analysis services need to be delivered in such a manner that the likelihood of obtaining a display of the target behavior is increased. To accomplish these goals, a 2-year project, the Proactive Treatment Teams Project (Wacker & Berg, 1989), was implemented. In this project, the experimental analyses used in the clinic settings were modified and transferred to the classroom and, in some cases, the residential settings of the children needing services. The classroom was selected as the setting of choice because of its stability and the availability of highly skilled teachers and support staff who were familiar with the students' behavior and history.

OVERVIEW OF PROACTIVE TREATMENT TEAMS PROJECT

In the fall of 1989, the Iowa Department of Education, Bureau of Special Education, funded the Proactive Treatment Teams Project (Wacker & Berg,

1989) to implement assessment and proactive intervention procedures in classroom settings across four school districts in Iowa. The purpose of the project was to develop local teams of experts in each school district to address the needs of children who engaged in severe challenging behavior, such as self-injury and aggression. Volunteers from each district met on their own time to learn about functional analysis, functional communication training, and other approaches to the assessment and treatment of severe behavior disorders.

The volunteers from each district formed the local "proactive treatment teams," which included administrators, special education teachers, regular education teachers, special education consultants, school psychologists, speech therapists, and parents. The professionals on these teams had 1–10 years of experience in working with children with severe developmental disabilities who engaged in challenging behavior. None had previous experience in conducting functional analyses of behavior.

Following a brief (1-day) inservice training on functional assessment and proactive intervention procedures, each team received biweekly consultation on the implementation of descriptive assessments and experimental analyses. The behavioral consultant, a graduate student in school psychology, assisted the team members as they developed a referral system for assistance by the team, observation procedures, and assessment and intervention procedures.

The assessments were conducted in two phases: a descriptive assessment and an in-class experimental analysis of the variables maintaining the challenging behavior. During the descriptive assessment, the child was observed across several typical classroom activities that varied in the level of demands and social attention provided to the child. Based on this assessment, hypotheses were developed regarding the role of different antecedent and consequent stimuli in maintaining the behavior, and an in-class experimental analysis was conducted by the teacher, team members, and consultant to test these hypotheses.

During the 2-year period, the teams collectively evaluated 31 students who ranged in age from 4 to 18 years old. The levels of disability for these students ranged from profound mental retardation with multiple handicaps to moderate mental retardation. The majority of the students had no formal communication, and only six had a repertoire of more than four manual signs or verbalizations. The only requirements for participation in this project were the consent of the student's parents, willingness of the classroom teacher to participate in the Proactive Treatment Team, and a history of at least 1 year of engagement in severe challenging behavior.

The behaviors listed as the primary reason for referral to the local teams included self-injurious behavior ($N = 16$), aggression ($N = 9$), tantrumming ($N = 2$), noncompliance ($N = 1$), rumination ($N = 1$), pica ($N = 1$), and screaming ($N = 1$). Self-injurious behavior included head-banging, hitting or slapping the head or groin area, banging the head with a prosthesis, hand-biting, scratching or digging at the skin, and eye-gouging. Aggression included hitting and slapping others, pulling others' hair, and grabbing and pinching others. The frequency of these behaviors ranged from more than 600 instances within a 10-minute interval (head-banging) to a few times each week (aggression). All of the self-injurious and aggressive behaviors occurred with sufficient intensity that tissue damage was occurring. Many of the students engaged in multiple behaviors and most also engaged in some form of stereotypic behavior. The history of these behaviors ranged from 1 to 16 years.

In transferring the use of functional assessment technology from the clinic to the classroom setting, two sets of issues needed to be addressed. The first set of issues dealt with questions regarding the integrity with which the functional assessment procedures could be conducted in a classroom setting by educational personnel and the validity of the results of such an assessment. The second set of issues dealt with the acceptability of the resultant intervention recommendations to the educational personnel. The remainder of this chapter is devoted to a discussion of these issues.

CONDUCTING AN EFFECTIVE
FUNCTIONAL ASSESSMENT IN THE CLASSROOM SETTING

The initial concerns encountered in transferring the functional assessment procedures from the clinic to the classroom setting dealt with the integrity of a classroom-based assessment. An evaluation of the integrity of any functional assessment includes: 1) the ability to identify and present the antecedent stimuli that trigger the display of the challenging behavior, 2) the ability to identify and deliver consistently the consequences that maintain the challenging behavior, and 3) the ability of the examiner to interpret the results of the assessment accurately.

Moving the assessment into the child's routine setting provides an opportunity to identify the specific antecedents and consequences associated with occurrences of the challenging behavior. The impact of specific stimuli on the occurrence of the target behavior in some children is evidenced by the difficulties encountered in triggering a display of the target behavior in the clinic setting.

As noted by Derby et al. (1992), obtaining a display of the targeted behavior in the clinic evaluation can be problematic. In other words, the individual's behavior is often neither stable nor occurs at sufficiently high frequencies to permit an adequate probe of the maintaining conditions during the brief clinical evaluation. In summarizing the activities of the first 3 years of an outpatient clinic for self-injurious and aggressive behavior, Derby et al. (1992) reported that 37% of the individuals seen at the clinic did not display the target behavior during any of the assessment conditions conducted during the evaluation. In the absence of direct observation, the evaluator's ability to identify the antecedent and consequent stimuli associated with the target behavior is obviously compromised, thereby jeopardizing the validity of the assessment.

A failure to achieve occurrences of the target behavior may be due to several reasons. First, the occurrence of the target behavior may be associated with a narrow set of antecedent stimuli that are not present within the assessment setting. For example, the challenging behavior may occur only under certain circumstances, such as when the teacher or caregiver is in view but is not responsive to other behaviors produced by the student. Such an instance might be when the classroom teacher is providing direct instruction to other students and the targeted student is left to work independently.

Second, the consequences to the behavior may not be delivered in the manner typically experienced by the child and thus may not be sufficient to maintain a display of the target behavior throughout the assessment session. For example, the tone of voice used by the teacher may be more highly correlated with rates of challenging behavior than the specific verbal message provided. From our observations, the tone of voice used in providing verbal reprimands for self-injurious behavior in classroom settings ranged from harsh to coaxing. Furthermore, these messages may be accompanied by physical gestures, such as backrubs or holding and caressing the student's hands. Finally, it is possible that the specific antecedent and consequent stimuli associated with the occurrence of challenging behavior in the child's routine setting are present within the analog condition, but the novelty or presence of other stimuli obscure those that typically trigger and maintain the behavior.

Thus, the first goal for this project was to conduct a procedurally sound functional assessment in which functional control over the occurrence of challenging behavior was demonstrated, while the integrity of the naturally occurring package of antecedents and consequences affecting the display of behavior was maintained. To achieve this goal, the classroom-based functional assessment was conducted in two stages: 1) a descriptive analysis of the antecedent and consequence variables associated with high and low frequencies of the challenging behavior (*A-B-C analysis*) (Bijou, Peterson, & Ault, 1968) and 2) an experimental analysis in which the hypothesized controlling variables were systematically manipulated to determine their effects on the occurrence of the targeted behavior (Northup et al., 1991). An overview of the two assessment procedures is provided in Table 1.

Descriptive Analysis of the Occurrence of the Target Behavior

The purpose of the descriptive analysis was to provide an opportunity to observe the behavior within the context of the child's routine setting, under the stimulus configurations typically present within that setting and associated

Table 1. Elements of descriptive analysis and experimental analysis

Phase of assessment	Assessment activities	Purpose	Instructions to teacher	Type of analysis
Descriptive analysis	A sample of class activities that differ in the level of attention, demands, and structure provided to the student	Develop hypotheses regarding the role of different stimuli in eliciting or maintaining the target behavior	Conduct activities and provide consequences in typical manner	Correlational
Experimental analysis	Selected class activities that vary in the presence or absence of the hypothesized controlling variable	Confirm or disconfirm the hypotheses developed during the descriptive analysis	Consistently deliver or withhold the hypothesized variable while conducting the activities	Single-case experimental designs

with high frequencies of the challenging behavior. In clinic-based assessments, hypotheses regarding the effects of different stimuli on the occurrence of challenging behavior are generated from interviews conducted with parents or other caregivers (Derby et al., 1992; Northup et al., 1991), by direct observation of parent–child interactions, or through established clinic protocols. These hypotheses are used to structure the analog conditions that constitute the clinical assessment.

In transferring the functional assessment procedures to the classroom setting, the interviews, parent–child observations, and established protocols were replaced with direct observation of the child across a variety of activities throughout the school day. This method of assessment was based on two previously established procedures for field-based descriptive analyses: 1) a hypothesis testing approach (Repp, Felce, & Barton, 1988), and 2) descriptive analysis (Mace & Lalli, 1991).

Prior to the initiation of the assessments, specific activities were selected for observation. Two guidelines were used in selecting these activities: 1) the activity was associated with either very high or very low frequencies of the targeted behavior, and 2) the activity represented variations in the presence or absence of stimuli frequently associated with displays of the targeted behavior. Several types of activities were observed for each child in order to develop hypotheses regarding the effects of different antecedent and consequent conditions on the occurrence of the challenging behavior. The activities selected for observation varied in terms of the degree of structure, the level of social attention provided to the child, and the level of demands placed on the child. These variables were selected for observation because they represented the types of situations the child encountered throughout the school day, as well as the assessment conditions described by Northup et al. (1991).

For each child, at least one activity that represented a demand situation was selected by the classroom teacher for observation. A demand situation was identified as one in which the child was engaged in an activity that was considered to be either difficult or nonpreferred and that required frequent verbal or physical prompting by the teacher to ensure task participation. Examples of demand situations varied for each child. In most cases, however, they were activities that were conducted on a one-to-one basis with the teacher, and they included such tasks as grooming, eating, and academic or vocational activities. For some children, the demand activity occurred in a group situation, but the need for frequent verbal or physical prompts to maintain participation in the activity was constant across all children.

Additional activities that were fairly structured but not considered to be demanding for the child were also observed. These activities were characterized by high levels of social interactions and engagement in activities that the child performed with very little verbal or physical assistance. For most children, this was a group activity.

A third type of activity used for observation was an unstructured activity characterized by high levels of social interactions. These activities included one-on-one toy play with the teacher and one-on-one or small-group social interactions with the teacher.

The final type of unstructured activity used for observation was a situation characterized by low levels of social interactions and no demands. Such activities included transitions between activities, waiting for the school bus, and sitting in the classroom while the teacher attended to other students. These activities were selected to observe the child during times in which he or she was essentially alone or ignored with nothing to do.

The activities used for the descriptive observation of the child were all part of the child's typical school day, and the observations were conducted during the regularly scheduled time for each activity. For the purposes of the descriptive observations, we asked teachers to interact with the child in a "typical" manner during the observations. The consequences delivered to the child for engagement in both challenging and appropriate behavior were recorded across activities. By recording the antecedents and consequences typically associated with different frequencies of challenging behavior, it was possible to observe the covarying relationship between these stimuli and occurrences of aberrant behavior.

On-site observations of the child across different activities provided an opportunity to observe both the relationship between the presence or absence of different classes of stimuli on behavior (positive and negative reinforcement) and the impact of specific environmental stimuli, such as the presence or absence of peers, noise levels, and general activity level of the immediate surroundings. The importance of specific stimuli in triggering challenging behavior is illustrated through the case of Michael.

Case Study: Michael

Michael, a 6-year-old boy with mental retardation, appeared to engage in head-hitting on a random basis. Although head-hitting almost always occurred during demanding activities that appeared to be nonpreferred, it also occurred occasionally during what appeared to be preferred, nondemanding activities such as playtime. Thus, head-hitting occurred consistently during some activities and inconsistently during others.

A closer analysis of the occurrence of self-injurious behavior during "preferred" activities suggested that head-hitting occurred almost exclusively when these activities were accompanied by loud noises. For example, Michael often requested and appeared to enjoy riding his tricycle in the classroom, the hallway, and in the gymnasium. However, when another preschool class joined Michael's class for tricycle riding and ball-play in the gymnasium, he began to engage in self-injurious behavior and continued to do so until the other preschool students left the gymnasium. Similar instances were observed when Michael was riding his tricycle in the hallway and other classes entered the hallway to or from recess.

Michael also appeared to enjoy sitting on his mother's lap and playing with stuffed toys and engaging in finger play. However, when his mother switched to toys that made noise, he often engaged in self-injurious behavior. Observing Michael in both his classroom and home settings provided specific information that helped to explain the variability in his self-injurious behavior across activities that otherwise might not have been predicted based solely on the results of a functional analysis.

Although the presence of the naturally occurring stimulus configurations can provide additional information regarding the antecedent and consequent variables associated with challenging behavior, these benefits must be weighed against the difficulty of interpreting these data. We have often found it to be a very difficult task to sort out the role of specific antecedent and consequent variables in classroom settings. Determining the roles of these variables solely on the basis of a descriptive assessment can be problematic because, although all stimuli occur in the context of other stimuli, confounding stimuli are likely to be more prevalent and more variable in the classroom than in analog situations, making interpretation of the assessment results difficult. Furthermore, a descriptive analysis provides only correlational data, which is suggestive, not conclusive, of the function of challenging behavior. Therefore, an experimental (functional) analysis is needed to systematically evaluate the effects of the variables hypothesized to control the display of the targeted behavior. We use descriptive analyses, as suggested by Mace and Lalli (1991), to generate hypotheses about the function of challenging behavior. We then attempt to verify these hypotheses through experimental analyses conducted in the classroom.

Conducting an Experimental Analysis in the Classroom Setting

The information gathered from the descriptive analysis is used to generate hypotheses regarding the antecedent and consequent stimuli associated with high frequencies of challenging behavior. The effects of the hypothesized controlling stimuli on challenging behavior are then evaluated through the systematic manipulation of those stimuli in a series of analog sessions conducted in the classroom setting. This classroom analysis constitutes a functional analysis of the controlling stimuli for challenging behavior and is conducted using the people, materials, tasks, and settings typically present in the classroom setting. The specific people, tasks, and settings used in the experimental analysis are based directly on the descriptive analysis.

Analog sessions are conducted within the routine activities that were previously assessed during the descriptive assessment of the targeted behavior. The primary difference between the descriptive and experimental analyses is that during the experimental analysis, educational personnel are given specific instructions by the behavioral consultant regarding how to approach the student, what directions to provide, and what consequences to deliver. Thus, the teachers systematically control the delivery of both antecedents (prompts, tasks) and consequences following both the challenging and alternative behavior. Our instructions to teachers are based on the antecedents and consequences observed during the descriptive assessments, but their delivery may not have been consistent or may have been paired with other stimuli, and we were unable to isolate their effects. In the analog conditions, the delivery of antecedents and consequences is made as consistent as possible. The resultant analog assessment closely resembles those conducted in the clinic setting; however, the tasks, materials, setting, and people involved are those that are routinely present in the child's classroom.

By systematically observing the impact that naturally occurring antecedents and consequences have on the occurrence of challenging behavior, we are frequently able to employ very brief versions of the experimental analysis. In some cases, the results of the descriptive analysis are sufficiently clear that we need only an abbreviated series of analog conditions to verify this function. Using the procedures described by Northup et al. (1991) we can, for example, develop two separate analog conditions for the functional analysis: one analog condition to confirm the role of the hypothesized variable and a second to serve as a contrast condition. The case of Helga illustrates this.

Case Study: Helga

Helga, an 11-year-old girl with mental retardation, was referred to the project for aggressive behavior, which included pulling her teacher's hair and clothing. A brief series of naturalistic observations was conducted across a variety of structured and unstructured classroom activities. Some activities were conducted in a group. Others occurred during one-to-one learning sessions, while others occurred when Helga was alone. During observations, Helga engaged in aggression only during activities that were conducted with one-to-one supervision and that required frequent verbal and physical prompting to ensure task completion. Furthermore, engagement in aggressive behavior resulted in brief breaks from these tasks as the classroom teacher readjusted her clothing and hair.

Based on these results, it was hypothesized that Helga engaged in aggression to escape demanding tasks. To further test this hypothesis, a brief series of analog sessions was conducted to observe the effects of escape from demanding tasks for aggressive behavior versus gaining teacher attention for aggressive behavior.

The results of the analog sessions indicated that during sessions in which Helga was allowed to escape from tasks for aggressive behavior, she aggressed 20%–30% of the time. This was in contrast to the low frequencies (less than 5%) observed when aggression was followed by social attention. Thus, using the information obtained through a series of observations conducted within the normal classroom routine, hypotheses were formed that were confirmed through an abbreviated series of analog sessions, thereby minimizing disruption to ongoing classroom activities.

Conducting an assessment in the child's routine setting, using the antecedents and consequences typically experienced by the child, allows us to identify not only behavioral differences across clusters of stimuli, but also subtle variations in the ways that stimuli are presented (Berg, Wacker, & Northup, 1990).

Case Study: Clark

Clark, a 17-year-old male, was observed to engage in high frequencies of face-slapping, hand-biting, and screaming during "demanding activities" such as vocational training and eating. Although the self-injurious and disruptive behavior occurred most frequently during these activities, it did not occur consistently within these activities. That is, sometimes Clark engaged in the targeted behaviors as much as 38% of the time spent participating in one of the demanding tasks; other times, he participated in the same task throughout the entire observation period with no instances of challenging behavior.

A review of the videotaped data of sessions associated with both high and low rates of challenging behavior suggested that the task presented, the response requirements made of Clark, the amount of physical contact, and the activity and noise level of the immediate environment were relatively constant across all demand sessions. However, the amount of social attention (e.g., use of Clark's name, encouraging remarks, praise) provided to him was consistently higher during demand sessions that resulted in low frequencies of self-injurious behavior. The amount of social attention provided to Clark varied across personnel; it was high for his teacher and a staff assistant, but low for the teacher associate and other support personnel.

To confirm the role that social attention played in Clark's self-injurious behavior, additional analog sessions were conducted using two variations of the demand/escape condition. These analogs were identical to the original demand analogs, except that the amount of social attention provided to Clark varied across sessions. Task, teachers, demands on Clark, and the immediate environment were all held constant across the two conditions. These additional analogs verified the role of social attention as an important component of task demands for Clark.

By observing the differences across analog conditions, we were able to determine that the presence or absence of task demands was not as reliable a predictor of self-injury as was the way in which the task demands were presented to Clark. Had the functional assessment of Clark's behavior been limited to demand situations with low levels of social interactions, the results of the assessment (high frequencies of self-injurious behavior during demanding tasks) would have been contrary to his teacher's direct experience with Clark (little or no self-injurious behavior during demanding tasks), and the validity of the assessment may have been suspect. Through the use of on-site observations and assessments with the people, activities, and tasks inherent in Clark's routine setting, the substantial impact of subtle variations in task-presentation style was captured and incorporated into the subsequent assessment conditions. This change in assessment conditions, in turn, led to changes in our subsequent design of an intervention strategy.

In summary, the success of any functional analysis depends on the degree to which the antecedent and consequent stimuli presented in the analogs match those that the child experiences in his or her routine setting (Iwata, Vollmer, & Zarcone, 1990). A failure to produce the target behavior across analog conditions is most likely due to a failure to match the stimuli presented in the analog to the stimuli that are routinely available to the student. Displays of the targeted behavior may be limited to specific stimuli and, therefore, may not occur across all settings or assessment conditions.

In addition to identifying antecedents and consequent stimuli associated with the occurrence of challenging behavior, the results of an assessment should direct the intervention efforts with the student. The prescriptive nature of functional analysis is, perhaps, its greatest asset. When the conditions controlling the display of challenging behavior have been identified, intervention plans can be developed that modify the presence or presentation of antecedent stimuli associated with the behavior (as in the cases of Clark and Michael) or new, adaptive behaviors such as manding responses, which lead to the same outcome as the behavior, can be taught.

DEVELOPING ACCEPTABLE
INTERVENTION PROCEDURES FOR CLASSROOM USE

Given the validity of assessment, the effectiveness of the subsequent intervention will depend on the integrity with which the intervention is implemented. Integrity is especially critical to the success of those interventions based almost entirely on reinforcement, because these procedures often require a substantial amount of time for the successful long-term reduction of challenging behavior. Previous researchers have demonstrated that implementation of intervention plans is related to the acceptability of the procedures to the teachers or caregivers (Reimers, Wacker, & Koeppl, 1987; Walle, Hobbs, & Caldwell, 1984; Witt, Elliott, & Martens, 1984). Three factors listed as having a substantial impact on the implementers' perceptions of a proposed intervention appeared relevant to our project. These factors are: 1) the perceived understanding of the intervention (Berg & Wacker, 1988; Reimers & Wacker, 1988), 2) the time required for implementing the intervention (Reimers et al., 1987; Witt, Martens, & Elliott, 1984), and 3) the type of intervention approach recommended (Elliott, Witt, Galvin, & Peterson, 1984; Miltenberger, Lennox, & Erfanian, 1989; Reimers et al., 1987).

Perceived Understanding of the Intervention

Understanding refers to knowledge of both the rationale and specific applications of the intervention. Understanding appears to have a central role in the perceived acceptability of a treatment and, in fact, may transcend the impact of the remaining factors (Kazdin, 1980; Reimers & Wacker, 1988; Singh & Katz, 1985). The collaborative nature of the classroom-based analysis, with full inclusion of the teacher and support staff in the assessment and intervention process may promote greater intervention integrity by allowing all members of the learner's individualized education program (IEP) to gain a firm grasp of the rationale for the contingencies being implemented.

Typically, when a child is referred for an evaluation, the people directly involved in that child's care have a preconceived set of hypotheses regarding why the child demonstrates challenging behavior. In some cases, these hypotheses stem from a diagnostic label given to the child, but, in many cases, the hypotheses reflect the role of antecedent and consequent stimuli associated with the behavior. These latter hypotheses often match the variables addressed in a functional analysis.

In most cases, assessment can be modified as needed to directly test a proposed hypothesis in the natural setting. By directly observing the impact that different antecedent and consequent stimuli have on the occurrence of the target behavior, the teacher or caregiver is in a better position to interpret the results of assessment. Even for those individuals for whom the behavior is attributed to characteristics associated with a diagnostic label, direct observation of increases and decreases in the occurrence of challenging behavior across analog conditions may alter the teacher's or caregiver's perceptions of the role of environmental stimuli on the child's behavior. We have found that descriptive assessments often play a critical role in this regard by providing information demonstrating that the child does not engage in challenging behavior across all activities and settings, but, rather, the behavior occurs only within the context of specific antecedents and consequences.

As mentioned previously, the major advantage of functional analysis is that it leads to a class of intervention procedures. A classroom teacher who directly observes the impact that different consequences have on challenging behavior and the role of antecedent stimuli in triggering the occurrence of the behavior will understand the rationale for selecting a particular intervention. As a result, this teacher will be better prepared to assist in the development and implementation of the intervention in the classroom setting.

Time Required for Implementing the Intervention

The second factor affecting the acceptability of a proposed intervention is the time that is required to implement the procedure. Virtually all interventions for challenging behavior require a significant time commitment from the teacher or caregiver. However, the amount of time devoted to intervention is ultimately determined by those directly involved in its delivery. Two guidelines are suggested to address the question of how broad-based the application of an intervention should be across the child's day.

First, the extent to which an intervention is incorporated throughout the child's day depends on the confidence the teacher or caregiver has in the assessment process and the proposed recommendations. If the assessment clearly identifies a function for the challenging behavior, and the proposed intervention addresses that function, the teacher may wish to incorporate procedures across several activities within the child's daily routine. However, if the results of an assessment are not clear, and it is therefore likely that the intervention strategy will need to be modified, intervention might be limited to one or two brief activities to test its applicability and effectiveness. Once the intervention package has been tested and the necessary modifications made, it can be expanded across a broader range of activities and settings. Related to this, of course, is the degree of teacher involvement. If the teacher has been responsible for the assessment and has been involved actively in the identification of maintaining variables, then it is more likely that he or she will seek to carry out the intervention in as many settings as possible.

Second, in those cases in which the intervention package is very intensive in terms of time and response requirements from the student and educational staff, it is recommended that the intervention be limited in the number of sessions per day. The preliminary results of such an intervention could be reviewed to determine its applicability to that particular situation and the need for modifications before it is expanded across the child's school day.

Because the teacher is directly involved in the development of intervention strategies, the package can be developed to fit within the constraints of the school setting. Furthermore, because the assessment and intervention process is conducted on-site, additional support personnel can be included in the expansion of the intervention across school settings and activities.

Case Study: Rebecca

Rebecca participated in a preschool program for students with mild communication and learning disabilities during part of her school day and spent the remainder of her school day in a program for children with severe to profound disabilities. Rebecca engaged in hitting her head with her hand and in banging her head against any available hard surface. Following observations of Rebecca across a variety of activities at school, a brief experimental analysis was conducted in which the effects of providing attention contingent on the display of self-injurious behavior, providing a brief break from a task for self-injurious behavior, and leaving Rebecca alone except to block instances of self-injurious behavior were observed. The experimental analysis was conducted by the behavioral consultant, the local special education consultant, and Rebecca's classroom teachers. The assessment results indicated that she engaged in self-injurious behavior to escape nonpreferred tasks and to gain attention when left alone with an activity.

For Rebecca, intervention consisted of signing "Stop" to end an activity and "Help" to solicit assistance. The teachers from both programs, along with the educational consultant and speech-language pathologist, who served both programs, worked together to arrange times in both preschool programs in which the intervention could be conducted. Once the intervention was effectively implemented in the established times, both teachers expanded the program to include signing in the context of other activities. By the end of the first several months of intervention, the use of manual signs was incorporated throughout Rebecca's entire school day, across activities with other adults, and on the playground with her peers.

Type of Intervention Approach

Previous researchers have demonstrated that approaches focusing on increasing adaptive behaviors are judged more acceptable than approaches focusing solely on reducing problematic behaviors (Elliot et al., 1984; Reimers et al., 1987). As with the clinic-based assessments, the recommendations resulting from our school-based assessments have been consistently proactive. That is, treatment has focused on the development or increase of adaptive behaviors, with communication training as the primary intervention choice. Although the use of proactive procedures may increase the likelihood that the intervention plan will be acceptable, it is likely that specific components of the plan will need to be reconciled with the constraints of the classroom setting or the preferences of the classroom teacher.

FACTORS AFFECTING THE CONTINUED USE AND
EXPANSION OF ON-SITE FUNCTIONAL ASSESSMENT PROCEDURES

As previously described, assessments developed as part of the Proactive Treatment Project were conducted in two phases: a descriptive analysis of the normally occurring antecedents and consequent stimuli, and an experimental analysis in which the roles of specific stimuli were evaluated through the systematic manipulation of their presence or absence. Every effort was made to blend the assessment procedures into the routine activities of the classroom with as little disruption as possible. This was accomplished in two ways: through the manipulation of regularly scheduled activities to replace the analog conditions typically used in functional assessments, and through unobtrusive data collection procedures.

Simplification of Data Collection

For the purposes of data collection, each teacher was encouraged to check out videotape equipment and record the targeted activities once each week for later review and scoring. When videotaping was not feasible, teachers were encouraged to conduct simple frequency counts or duration measures over a specified time period during the targeted activities. Frequency counts were completed with hand-held golf counters or simple hatch marks on a piece of paper. Duration measures were used less frequently and consisted of depressing a stopwatch for the duration of each episode of the behavior.

Interpretation of Data

Although the teachers and educational support staff were capable data collectors, their ability to correctly interpret the data and determine the need for additional assessment sessions was not firmly established. To accommodate their perceived need for assistance in this area, an applied behavior analyst consulted with the teachers and support staff on a biweekly basis and viewed all videotaped sessions. As the project progressed, the school staff assumed greater levels of independence in this area, and two of the four school districts began conducting assessments and developing intervention plans independent of the behavior analyst's assistance by the end of the first year of the project. The amount and type of assistance needed by school personnel to implement functional assessment procedures has not yet been determined, but probably varies extensively across settings, depending on the familiarity of the staff with behavioral principles, their experience with functional assessment procedures, and their acceptance of a functional conceptualization of aberrant behavior.

Reduction of Problems Associated
with Displays of Challenging Behavior

The majority of functional assessments conducted within the classroom settings used occurrence of the challenging behavior as the dependent variable.

However, in a few cases, the display of the challenging behavior was extremely disruptive or dangerous to the child or others. For these children, the occurrence of adaptive behaviors was used as the dependent measure. Instead of determining the antecedents and consequences associated with high rates of challenging behavior, assessment consisted of determining the consequences that would lead to increased displays of new or rarely used adaptive skills, such as manual signs or vocalizations.

Case Study: Rick

Rick, an 18-year-old male with mental retardation, was completely dependent in all self-care routines. Rick was nonverbal and did not use any manual signs or recognizable gestures to communicate. Rick's episodes of self-injurious behavior (hitting his face and groin area with closed fists) were typically severe and extended over a long period of time. Removal from the immediate environment with one-to-one staff supervision was required to stop the self-injury.

Although Rick did not engage in any recognizable form of communication, he frequently made vocalizations during the descriptive analysis, which sounded like "Ayyy." To reduce the threat of tissue damage, the occurrence of the "Ayyy" vocalization was used as the dependent measure during the experimental analysis. That is, the delivery of consequences during the experimental analysis was made contingent on the "Ayyy" response rather than on self-injurious behavior. Three consequence conditions were conducted: 1) each occurrence of the vocalization resulted in staff attention, 2) each occurrence resulted in the removal of staff and materials associated with the current activity (e.g., plate and cup during eating), and 3) all occurrences were ignored. Within this assessment, differences in the frequency of the "Ayyy" vocalization were observed across the different consequence conditions to determine what stimuli served as a reinforcer for the "Ayyy" response. The results of this assessment demonstrated that the frequency of vocalizations was highest for those sessions resulting in staff attention. Intervention, then, consisted of training the staff to provide positive social attention to Rick whenever he engaged in the specified vocalization. The incidence of self-injurious behavior decreased to less than two instances per month; at 1 year following the implementation of treatment, self-injurious behavior was virtually nonexistent and Rick continued to use the "Ayyy" vocalization to gain attention.

CONCLUSION

Conducting functional assessment procedures in a child's classroom setting posed some challenges to us and the educational personnel involved. For example, conducting observations across the school day for a period of weeks and, in some cases, months, meeting to discuss assessment findings, and developing intervention plans was certainly more time-consuming for the school personnel than referring the child for an off-site assessment to receive a prepared set of intervention recommendations. However, regardless of the time demands, teachers and support staff repeatedly reported that they wanted to be involved in the assessment process. In fact, referral for a student's participation in the project was often contingent on the direct involvement of the classroom teacher.

Perhaps the most rewarding aspect of the school-based assessment procedure was that the teachers and support personnel involved in the project reported satisfaction with the procedures. Their acceptance of the assessment and intervention procedures was evidenced through the high ratings given to functional assessment and functional communication training procedures in an acceptability survey conducted during the last few months of the project. Both procedures were consistently rated as highly acceptable. The functional assessment and communication training procedures were rated as very effective in reducing inappropriate behaviors, increasing appropriate behaviors, and increasing the teachers' and caregivers' understanding of why certain behaviors occur.

Although the experimental analysis procedures received high marks on the survey, after the first 6 months of the project, the use of the procedures was typically reserved for very complex cases or for teachers new to the project. Rather than conducting the analog assessments to assess behaviors, the teachers incorporated a hypothesis-testing approach (Repp et al., 1988) into their classroom settings and across other students. Hypotheses were generated through observations of the conditions under which the challenging behavior occurred and tested through the implementation and evaluation of an intervention plan to address hypothesized variables. Several of the teachers reported that they viewed the occurrence of challenging behavior differently following their participation in the assessment process. Rather than viewing the behavior as being random or simply maladaptive, they now saw the challenging behavior as purposeful, communicative in nature, and as a response to be replaced rather than eliminated. The most common intervention, across all classrooms, was functional communication training. The popularity of this treatment approach was consistent across both years of the project.

In summary, the work completed over the last several years indicates that the functional assessment process is quite robust (Cooper et al., 1990; Mace & West, 1986; Northup et al., 1991), which suggests that the procedures can be applicable across diverse students and settings. In this chapter, we discuss issues surrounding the transfer of this methodology to field settings based on our 2-year experience conducting functional assessments in classroom settings. The success of this effort suggests that we have underestimated the social validity of classroom-based functional analyses. It has been suggested that functional assessments may be too complex, time-consuming, and burdensome for use by regular teachers and caregivers (Axelrod, 1987). However, there can be little argument concerning the potential benefit to students. The issue, then, appears to be one of continuing to identify ways to extend this technology to field settings.

REFERENCES

Axelrod, S. (1987). Functional and structural analyses of behavior: Approaches leading to reduced use of punishment procedures? *Research in Developmental Disabilities, 8,* 165–178.

Berg, W., Wacker, D., & Northup, J. (1990, May). *The role of antecedent stimuli in analogue assessments of self-injurious behavior.* Paper presented at the Association for Behavior Analysis annual meeting, Nashville.

Berg, W., & Wacker, D. (May, 1988). Promoting the use of single-case designs as measures of achievement in special education classrooms. In D. Test (Chair), *Measurement and analysis in the special education classroom: When and how?* Symposium presented at the Association for Behavior Analysis annual meeting, Philadelphia.

Bijou, S.W., Peterson, R.F., & Ault, M.F. (1968). A method to integrate descriptive and experimental field studies at the level of data and empirical concepts. *Journal of Applied Behavior Analysis, 1,* 175–191.

Carr, E., & Durand, V.M. (1985). Reducing behavior problems through functional communication training. *Journal of Applied Behavior Analysis, 18,* 111–126.

Carr, E.G., Newsom, C., & Binkoff, J. (1980). Escape as a factor in the aggressive behavior of two retarded children. *Journal of Applied Behavior Analysis, 13,* 101–117.

Cooper, L.J., Wacker, D.P., Sasso, G.M., Reimers, T.M., & Donn, L. (1990). Using parents as therapists to assess the appropriate behavior of their children: Application to a tertiary diagnostic clinic. *Journal of Applied Behavior Analysis, 23,* 285–296.

Derby, K.M., Wacker, D., Sasso, G., Steege, M., Northup, J., Cigrand, K., & Asmus, J. (1992). Brief functional assessment techniques to evaluate aberrant behavior in an outpatient setting: A summary of seventy-nine cases. *Journal of Applied Behavior Analysis, 25,* 713–721.

Durand, V.M., & Carr, E. (1985). Self-injurious behavior: Motivating conditions and guidelines for treatment. *School Psychology Review, 14,* 171–176.

Durand, V.M., & Carr, E. (1991). Functional communication training to reduce challenging behavior: Maintenance and application in new settings. *Journal of Applied Behavior Analysis, 24,* 251–264.

Elliot, S., Witt, J., Galvin, G., & Peterson, R. (1984). Acceptability of positive and reductive behavioral interventions: Factors that influence teachers' decisions. *Journal of School Psychology, 22,* 353–360.

Iwata, B., Dorsey, M., Slifer, K., Bauman, K., & Richman, G. (1982). Toward a functional analysis of self-injury. *Analysis and Intervention in Developmental Disabilities, 2,* 3–20.

Iwata, B., Pace, G., Kalsher, M., Cowdery, G., & Cataldo, M. (1990). Experimental analysis and extinction of self-injurious escape behavior. *Journal of Applied Behavior Analysis, 23,* 11–27.

Iwata, B.A., Vollmer, T.R., & Zarcone, J.R. (1990). The experimental (functional) analysis of behavior disorders: Methodology, applications, and limitations. In A.C. Repp & N.N. Singh (Eds.), *Perspectives on the use of non-aversive and aversive interventions for persons with developmental disabilities* (pp. 301–330). Sycamore, IL: Sycamore Publishing Co.

Kazdin, A.E. (1980). Acceptability of time out from reinforcement procedures for disruptive child behavior. *Behavior Therapy, 11,* 329–344.

Mace, F.C., & Lalli, J. (1991). Linking descriptive and experimental analyses in the treatment of bizarre speech. *Journal of Applied Behavior Analysis, 24,* 553–553–562.

Mace, F.C., & West, B. (1986). Analysis of demand conditions associated with reluctant speech. *Journal of Behavior Therapy and Experimental Psychiatry, 17,* 285–294.

Miltenberger, R., Lennox, D., & Erfanian, N. (1989). Acceptability of alternative treatments for persons with mental retardation: Ratings from institutional and community-based staff. *American Journal of Mental Retardation, 93,* 388–395.

Northup, J., Wacker, D., Sasso, G., Steege, M., Cigrand, K., Cook, J., & DeRaad, A. (1991). A brief functional analysis of aggressive and alternative behavior in an outclinic setting. *Journal of Applied Behavior Analysis, 24,* 509–522.

Reimers, T., Wacker, D., & Koeppl, G. (1987). Acceptability of behavioral interventions: A review of the literature. *School Psychology Review, 16,* 212–227.

Reimers, T., & Wacker, D. (1988). Parents' ratings of the acceptability of behavioral treatment recommendations made in an outpatient clinic: A preliminary analysis of the influence of treatment effectiveness. *Behavioral Disorders, 14,* 7–15.

Repp, A., Felce, D., & Barton, L. (1988). Basing the treatment of stereotypic and self-injurious behaviors on hypotheses of their causes. *Journal of Applied Behavioral Analysis, 21,* 281–289.

Sasso, G.M., Reimers, T.M., Cooper, L.J., Wacker, D., Berg, W., Steege, M., Kelly, L., & Allaire, A. (1992). Use of descriptive and experimental analyses to identify the functional properties of aberrant behavior in school settings. *Journal of Applied Behavior Analysis, 25,* 809–821.

Singh, N., & Katz, R. (1985). On the modification of acceptability ratings for alternative child treatments. *Behavior Modification, 9,* 375–386.

Steege, M., Wacker, D., Cigrand, K., Berg, W., Novak, C., Reimers, T., Sasso, G., & DeRaad, A. (1990). Use of negative reinforcement in the treatment of self-injurious behavior. *Journal of Applied Behavior Analysis, 23,* 459–467.

Wacker, D., & Berg, W. (1989). *Proactive treatment model for self-injurious behavior.* Unpublished manuscript.

Walle, D., Hobbs, S., & Caldwell, H. (1984). Sequencing of parents' training procedures: Effects on child noncompliance and treatment acceptability. *Behavior Modification, 8,* 540–552.

Witt, J., Elliott, S., & Martens, B. (1984). Acceptability of behavioral interventions used in classrooms: The influence of amount of teacher time, severity of behavior problem, and type of intervention. *Behavior Disorders, 9,* 95–104.

Witt, J., Martens, B., & Elliott, S. (1984). Factors affecting teachers' judgments of the acceptability of behavioral interventions: Time involvement, behavior problem severity, and type of intervention. *Behavior Therapy, 15,* 204–209.

15

Issues in Providing Training To Achieve Comprehensive Behavioral Support

Jacki L. Anderson,
Richard W. Albin, Richard A. Mesaros,
Glen Dunlap, and Marlene Morelli-Robbins

PERSONNEL PREPARATION IS AN IMPORTANT vehicle for promoting and facilitating change in education and support services for persons with developmental disabilities. Inservice training is a frequently used method for enhancing the knowledge and skills of professionals and paraprofessionals working in the fields of developmental disabilities and special education as well as for introducing and teaching new and innovative concepts and methods. Typically, inservice training is the primary means by which people in the field stay abreast of current developments in theory and practice. Because the conceptual approaches, practices, and procedures that define "best practice" in a dynamic field such as developmental disabilities/special education change and develop over time, effective inservice training approaches, capable of reaching a wide audience, are essential.

Unfortunately, inservice training by itself is not sufficient to ensure accomplishing all of the outcomes desired from effective education and support systems for people with developmental disabilities. However, an intensive and comprehensive approach to inservice can provide an excellent means for addressing not only specific skills and information but also the broader issues and necessary systems change perspective to facilitate those desired outcomes. This chapter describes an approach to inservice training in compre-

Preparation of this chapter was supported by Cooperative Agreement No. G0087C0234 from the U.S. Department of Education, National Institute on Disability and Rehabilitation Research. However, the opinions expressed do not necessarily reflect the position of the department, and no official endorsement should be inferred.

hensive, positive behavioral support for persons with developmental disabilities and severe challenging behaviors. This approach represents both a strategy for increasing the expertise and competence of local support personnel and for promoting systems development and systems change. A positive impact on broader service delivery and support systems is an anticipated outcome for inservice training. This expectation helped to shape its content and methods. Embedded within this inservice training approach are strong implications for the structure and operation of schools, community agencies, and local support systems. This chapter discusses the critical features of our inservice training project, Team Training for Positive Behavioral Support, and provides a brief description of outcomes and effects resulting from implementation of the training in 16 states.

RATIONALE FOR INSERVICE TRAINING IN POSITIVE BEHAVIORAL SUPPORT

Integration and full community participation are the predominant themes that motivate current developments in educational and support systems for people with developmental disabilities, including individuals who exhibit severe challenging behaviors. This emphasis on inclusion is informed by advocacy efforts and an increasing articulation of basic values, rights, and opportunities that apply to all people, regardless of physical, intellectual, or cultural characteristics; and is supported by a growing body of professional literature providing direction and documenting successes (Meyer, Peck, & Brown, 1991; Sailor, Anderson, Halvorsen, Doering, Filler, & Goetz, 1989; Taylor, Bogdan, & Racino, 1991). Progress toward inclusion for individuals with severe challenging behaviors is also sustained by a growing literature of empirically documented, community-referenced practices that have been successful in reducing problem behaviors and supporting people with challenging behaviors in typical community settings (e.g., Berkman & Meyer, 1988; Carr, Robinson, Taylor, & Carlson, 1990; Dunlap, Kern-Dunlap, Clarke, & Robbins, 1991; Durand, 1990; Horner et al., 1992; Janney & Meyer, 1990). For some people with disabilities, patterns of severe problem behavior continue to serve as a major barrier to full community integration. Disseminating and training of values-based practices for positive behavioral support for widespread implementation in typical community schools and programs is an ongoing challenge. Consequently, there remains a critical need to turn research and clinical demonstration findings into common practice. No current practices in community-referenced, positive behavioral support are based on a variety of factors, including values emphasizing a quality-of-life orientation and the necessary programmatic supports and interventions to help accomplish such lifestyle objectives (Horner et al., 1990; Meyer & Evans, 1989). One critical foundation of positive behavioral support is that behavior changes occur in the context of a rich lifestyle, *not* as a prerequisite to a rich lifestyle. A set of specific practices is available for providing comprehensive behavioral support (Carr, McConnachie, Levin, & Kemp, in press; Carr, Robinson, & Palumbo, 1990; Doss & Reichle, 1991; Durand, 1990; Helmstetter & Durand, 1991; Horner, O'Neill, & Flannery, 1993; LaVigna, Willis, & Donnellan, 1989; Meyer & Evans, 1989). However, positive behavioral support is much more than a specific set of procedures. Positive approaches reflect an important shift in the way support for persons with challenging behavior is approached. As such, dissemination and training for widespread implementation of positive support approaches must include a comprehensive transmission of values, information, skills, and processes. Support procedures designed to meet the needs of persons with disabilities and challenging behaviors must address not only the problem behaviors, but also an array of issues and variables related to broader life-style outcomes.

Effective implementation of this diverse, multicomponent technology requires training and dissemination that extends beyond traditional modes such as research and review articles, brief workshops, and lecture presentations. Comprehensive training must be delivered in a manner that promotes application across a variety of conditions over long periods of time (i.e., generalization and maintenance). Materials and content must be appropriate for use by a range of community members, including teachers and direct service staff, family members, specialized professional support staff, and others who are involved in the lives of people with severe disabilities. There must be a merging of the quality-of-life values that provide the impetus for full inclusion efforts with intervention and support strategies that will bring these efforts to fruition. Our inservice training approach is designed with these features as a guide.

DESIRED OUTCOMES OF THE INSERVICE TRAINING MODEL

The Team Training Model was developed to have three types of outcomes: 1) positive impact on the lives of persons with severe disabilities and challenging behaviors; 2) positive impact on the knowledge, skills, and behaviors of individuals providing support in school and community settings (e.g., residential staff, teachers, behavior specialists, family members); and 3) positive impact on the agencies and systems (both local and state) by which support is provided. These outcomes shaped the features of our training process, particularly the methods used to deliver training content, the logistical structure of the training process, the selection of trainees, and evaluation.

For persons with disabilities and challenging behaviors, staff training in positive behavioral support must result in outcomes that extend beyond reductions in problem behaviors. Reductions in problem behaviors are necessary and important, but improved lifestyles (as reflected by changes in social networks and interactions, activity patterns, independence and autonomy, and accommodation of personal preferences) must also be a major outcome of training in behavioral support. Inservice training in positive behavioral support must not only detail a set of outcome measures for evaluating the effectiveness of support plans and strategies, it must also show how to apply these outcome measures to evaluate its own success.

For support personnel involved in the training, the values-based strategies and technology that characterize positive support approaches are designed to result in outcomes consistent with best practices in the area of behavioral support to individuals who engage in challenging behaviors. Potential outcomes for support personnel include changes in values and perspectives regarding the delivery of support to these persons and changes in competence and skills in delivering that support.

Four major outcomes for participating personnel that could be expected from our inservice training are: 1) a focus on proactive strategies and hypothesis-driven interventions as the fundamental approach to behavioral support, 2) a shift from reliance on individual decelerative procedures to multi-component interventions and comprehensive support plans, 3) a broadened view of intervention success criteria that emphasizes behavior change in the context of good quality of life, and 4) recognition of the need to plan for long-term support and intervention rather than "quick-fix" strategies. Each of these is described briefly in Table 1.

Finally, along with outcomes for people with disabilities and the people who support them in community settings, training in positive behavioral support should affect the systems within which people live and work. Systems at all levels (e.g., agency, district, county, state, federal) influence the delivery of support. To have a broad impact, training must do more than affect individuals, it must affect systems. Desired systems-level outcomes from team training in positive behavioral support include adoption of policies and regulations that promote implementation of positive behavioral support approaches, administrative and financial commitment to staff training that is proactive rather than crisis-driven, the creation of flexible options for supporting people with severe challenging behaviors in the community, and the use of a support process that involves interagency as well as family collaboration and that empowers all of those involved in the life of a person with disabilities and severe challenging behaviors.

The remainder of this chapter describes an inservice training approach that develops individual expertise and local systems needed to ensure ongoing implementation of positive behavioral support approaches. The model is currently being implemented in 16 states as a training component of the Rehabilitation Research and Training Center on Community Referenced Non-Aversive Behavior Management (NIDRR, Cooperative Agreement No. G0087C0234).

Table 1. Desired outcomes for support personnel from training

Outcomes	Major features	Sources
1. A focus on proactive strategies and hypothesis-driven interventions as the fundamental approach to behavioral support	There is no more fundamental change in perspective and approach regarding behavioral support than the shift from reacting to challenging behaviors to adopting a proactive approach to addressing such behaviors. Best practice proactive strategies begin with a comprehensive functional assessment. The results of this assessment guide the development of an hypothesis-driven support plan that is based on a thorough understanding of challenging behaviors and their functions.	Carr, Robinson, and Palumbo (1990); Horner, O'Neill, and Flannery (1993); Pyles and Bailey (1990)
2. A shift from reliance on individual decelerative procedures to multicomponent interventions and comprehensive support plans	Another important change in perspective and approach that characterizes positive behavioral support is movement away from a narrow focus on single procedure behavior programs to the development and implementation of comprehensive, multicomponent support plans. The traditional single intervention approach to behavior management, particularly with its almost total reliance on consequence intervention procedures, is unlikely to meet the multiple behavioral support needs of persons with challenging behaviors. Comprehensive support plans are likely to incorporate intervention procedures that draw from: 1) ecological, environmental, and setting-event manipulation; 2) immediate antecedent event manipulations; 3) response and skill-training intervention; 4) consequence manipulations; and 5) reactive and emergency intervention procedures.	Dunlap, Ferro, and de Perzel (in press); Helmstetter and Durand (1991); Horner, Albin, and O'Neill (1991); LaVigna, Willis, and Donnellan (1989); Meyer and Evans (1989)
3. A broadened view of intervention success criteria that emphasizes behavior change in the context of good quality of life	Another important theme of positive behavioral support is that a broader set of variables must be looked at in evaluating the success of behavioral support efforts. Improvement in problem behavior(s) and acquisition of adaptive behaviors and skills are the two outcomes most emphasized in traditional evaluation of behavior interventions. While these evaluation criteria are important and necessary, they are not sufficient for support plan evaluation. Effective behavioral support should affect the lifestyles of persons with challenging behaviors, not just their challenging behaviors. Evaluation criteria for comprehensive behavioral support plans should include assessment of: 1) quality-of-life variables such as increases in community integration and inclusion, expanded social networks and improved social relationships, increased variety and accommodation of personal preferences in daily activity patterns, improvement in subjective quality-of-life indicators and positive	Horner et al. (1992); Horner et al. (1990); Kennedy, Horner, and Newton (1990); Kennedy, Horner, Newton, and Kanda (1990); Meyer and Evans (1989); Turnbull and Turnbull (1990)

(continued)

Table 1. (continued)

Outcomes	Major features	Sources
	perceptions of family members and significant others; 2) health and safety variables such as reduced need for nonroutine medical attention and reduced crisis intervention; and 3) expanded behavioral variables such as generalization and maintenance of reductions in problem behaviors and increases in adaptive behaviors, and side effects or collateral changes in behaviors.	
4. Recognition of the need to plan for long-term support and intervention rather than "quick-fix" strategies	Life-style outcomes are goals that involve durable, significant changes in a person's life. Such changes cannot be expected to occur quickly, so the concept of finding quick-fix solutions for challenging behaviors is not enough. Rapid decreases in challenging behaviors may occur with positive behavioral support, but long-term support plans are needed to achieve the durable, generalized behavioral and life-style outcomes desired from comprehensive behavioral support. Patterns of severe challenging behaviors do not simply "disappear." Long-term support plans must create and maintain settings and programmatic contexts in which these behaviors are made and continue to be ineffective, inefficient, or irrelevant. Only then will near-zero levels of challenging behaviors occur and be maintained in all settings relevant to a person's life.	Horner et al. (1992); Horner, O'Neill, and Flannery (1993); Meyer and Evans (1989)

CRITICAL FEATURES OF THE TEAM TRAINING MODEL

The Team Training Model involves the delivery of information over an extended period of time, integrated with repeated opportunities for application, feedback, clarification, and expansion of the material during the training process. Our inservice model incorporates the following features:

1. Following a trainer-of-trainers model
2. Targeting audiences from a variety of constituencies and agencies
3. Utilizing a case-study team format in training
4. Following a dynamic training process using inservice and modified coaching approaches
5. Providing a comprehensive, multitopic curriculum to address all aspects of positive behavioral support at the local level
6. Facilitating ongoing implementation and expansion of comprehensive behavioral support at the local level
7. Providing support for newly trained trainers during their initial training efforts

Each of these critical features is discussed briefly on the following pages.

Following a Trainer-of-Trainers Model

The use of a trainer-of-trainers model, which includes the element of targeting at least some participants to serve as future trainers, results in the greatest possible spread of effect from initial training efforts. This process, of training a small number of individuals who will in turn train others has proven to be an effective strategy in the efficient dissemination of information and skills to human services providers. For example, Demchak and Browder (1990) trained program supervisors in community group homes on instructional procedures for teaching daily living skills. These supervisors were then successful in training direct care staff to implement the procedures. This pyramid training strategy has also been used successfully in training elementary school teachers (Jones, Fremouw, & Carples, 1977) and institution staff (Page, Iwata, & Reid, 1982). Similarly, Peck, Killen, and Baumgart (1989) utilized an indirect training strategy to improve the ability of general education teachers to provide effective instruction related to specified individualized education program (IEP) objectives. These studies indicate that the desired spread of effect does occur following a trainer-of-trainers model.

Self-perpetuating training resources are critical to providing continued inservice training for positive behavioral support to the number and variety of individuals who need the information. Although some persons involved in the life of an individual with challenging behavior may remain constant (e.g., family, advocates, friends), most will change as the individual moves from one grade to the next, from school to work, from job to job, from residence to residence (or changing roommates), and from one interest to another. Individuals and agencies (generic and specialized) change and expand as the individual grows older, requiring ongoing personnel training in order to provide long-term support for a quality life.

Adding to the inservice training challenge are the shortage of personnel and high staff turnover plaguing the fields of education and human services (Buckley, Albin, & Mank, 1988; McLaughlin, Smith-Davis, & Burke, 1986; McLaughlin, Valdivieso, & Stettner-Eaton, 1990; Smith-Davis, 1985; Snell, 1990). The shortage of staff is exacerbated by high attrition rates (Mitchell & Braddock, 1991; Smith-Davis, Burke, & Noel, 1984; Zaharia & Baumaster, 1979). The development of local expertise and an established mechanism for providing ongoing training can proactively address the information and training needs of service providers.

In each state that participated in our project, an original state training team was trained by a cadre of trainers from the Rehabilitation Research and Training Center on Community Referenced Non-Aversive Behavioral Management, who are referred to as Project Trainers throughout the remainder of this chapter. During the first training, which is termed *level-one* training, the state training team members participated as trainees while Project Trainers provided training to a local community of service providers, family members, and consumers. Details and features of our training format and methods are described more thoroughly later in this chapter. After completion of their own level-one training, the members of the state team were ready to assume the responsibilities of trainers.

An important feature of our training approach (described more thoroughly below) is that newly trained state teams receive support from Project Trainers in delivering their first full inservice Team Training in Positive Behavioral Support. We view this first supported inservice by the state team members as an important part of their overall training, and use the term *level-two* training to identify it. The level-two training is a full-scale replication of our comprehensive inservice in positive behavioral support, conducted in a second local community, with technical assistance and feedback for the new state team members provided by Project Trainers. After completion of the two levels of training, the state team can then provide comprehensive training and technical assistance to communities throughout the state. Additionally, state trainers typically engage in a variety of other information-sharing activities (e.g., conference presentations, newsletter articles) to increase the awareness of agencies, service providers, and families regarding the viability of comprehensive positive behavioral support as an effective alternative to episodic, intrusive, or aversive behavioral intervention strategies. Ideally, the composition of the state training teams is interagency and interdisciplinary, and the teams include representatives from major state human services agencies (e.g., education, rehabilitation, developmental disabilities services, mental health). In some states, they also include parents and/or advocates. Careful attention to team composition facilitates interagency collaboration, resource sharing, and policy development. Additionally, it helps to ensure credibility and knowledge in the range of individuals who provide behavioral support in a local community. However, team composition does vary across states, reflecting different objectives and sponsoring agencies within individual states. Usually, individuals are selected to serve as state trainers on the basis of experience, expertise, and current job responsibilities.

Ideally, each team member: 1) has experience providing support for individuals with severe disabilities, including those with challenging behavior; 2) has familiarity with current best practices; and 3) is in a position that includes the provision of inservice training and/or technical assistance as a major part of his or her job responsibilities. A critical member is the team coordinator, who serves as the supervisor for all training activities for team members and who typically negotiates with community and state agencies for time commitments and other resources to implement the training. The coordinator may be one of the state trainers or a person who has only administrative responsibilities. Some states use representatives from more than one agency to serve as co-coordinators to facilitate training activities within and across agencies.

Targeting Audiences from a Variety of Constituencies and Agencies

At the local level, careful selection of state team trainees is critical for comprehensive training efforts to result in positive behavioral supports leading to an improved quality of life for individuals with significant behavioral needs. Inservice training efforts have typically been specific to a particular agency or program (e.g., residential program, vocational agency, school) with the training determined by policies specific to the local agency and/or the state or national agencies providing funding. Although there is a certain logic in program-specific staff development from an agency's perspective, there is less so from an individual consumer's perspective. A single agency or program rarely has an impact on all aspects of an individual's life. In fact, the more integrated an individual's life becomes, the greater the variety of persons and agencies that are included in it. Human services providers that support quality lives in integrated settings are shifting their focus from specific service categories or problem/deficit areas to the overall needs, strengths, and preferences of *individuals* with disabilities. Therefore, they require personnel training with a similar emphasis (Racino, 1990).

Although the use of teams to facilitate the delivery of services is a well-accepted practice, until recently teams themselves have not been targeted to receive training and technical assistance, unless the topic was the process of working as a team. Dunlap, Robbins, Morelli, and Dollman (1988), in their work with young children with autism, successfully utilized a team training process to improve service delivery in rural areas.

As knowledge of the positive effects of team efforts becomes more widespread, the need for training to support the teams becomes a major personnel issue. Snell (1990), and Racino (1990) advocated for cross-discipline training at the preservice level, in which university faculty would share responsibilities for a variety of types of personnel preparation. Baumgart and Ferguson (1991) recommend preservice training for teachers, which includes team collaboration to prepare them to establish communities of collegial support in order for them to share responsibility for providing best educational practices in inclusive settings. Meyer and Evans (1989) advocate providing training to *all* team members (including all direct service personnel, family members, or guardians) to facilitate effective nonaversive intervention for problem behavior.

Utilizing a Case-Study Format in Training

The Team Training Model utilizes a case-study team format for the supervised application of new skills and information as part of the training process. Individuals with challenging behavior are selected from the participating agencies to serve as "focus individuals" during the training. The case-study teams are then established to include the individual who needs behavioral support and the persons involved in various aspects of that individual's life who are likely to facilitate, monitor, or directly provide the support and intervention identified as helpful in the training process. An example of a case-study team for a school-age individual might include the focus individual, parent(s), teachers, teachers' aides, speech-language pathologist, psychologist, inclusion specialist, and peers. An adult's team might include parent(s), residential staff, job coach, recreational support person, case manager, co-workers, and friends. The members of the case-study teams then become the recipients of state team training for that community. Additional persons targeted to participate as trainees (e.g., administrators, agency staff development personnel) are assigned to a case study team. The teams function as a larger group unit and apply recommended techniques throughout their training, assisting one another in acquiring skills as they work together to provide positive behavioral support for the individuals with severe disabilities.

Following a Dynamic Training Process Using
Inservice and Modified Coaching Approaches

The Team Training model calls for using many methods of teaching and delivering content information. All trainees work in case-study teams throughout the training process to apply the content and skills they are learning. Therefore, this is a dynamic training process in which presentation of content information and opportunities for practical application and skill development are balanced. The strength of the training is the use of best practices from the models of inservice training and coaching. These practices, as used in the Team Training model, are briefly reviewed.

Inservice Training

Inservice training is defined as a program of systematic, structured presentations and activities designed to improve the professional performance, growth, and competence of staff through the acquisition of knowledge and skills and through reflecting on current professional attitudes and practices (Cline, 1984; Hasazi, Batsche, McKinney, Gill, & Cobb, 1982; Kirkpatrick, 1983; Schlicter, 1984; SETRC Program, 1985). Cline (1984) suggests that high-quality inservice training programs are: 1) designed via a collaborative decisionmaking and planning process, 2) conducted by inservice trainers who are competent in the targeted areas, 3) supported explicitly by the agency administration, 4) include continuing professional growth activities and collaborative local development of materials, and 5) have as the locus of training the community or school where skills will be utilized.

This training approach, like traditional inservice training, includes multiple methods of information delivery. Much of the specific content is initially presented in lecture-and-discussion format with supporting audiovisual materials and printed handouts. Copies of the training materials are provided along with lecture notes to the state and local trainers-in-training. A collection of current readings from journals and texts is provided for each area of training to help clarify and supplement the lectures. Large- and small-group discussions are another strategy for clarification of information. Exercises during training to promote understanding of the critical concepts include modeling, practicing of intervention and assessment techniques via role playing, and analyzing written and videotaped vignettes.

An additional element of inservice training, referred to as a "working session," occurs periodically throughout the training process. These "working sessions" provide the opportunity for case-study teams to work together to analyze data from the assessments and interventions conducted between each training session in order to develop specific activities to be implemented with the focus individual prior to the next training session. These working sessions also provide opportunities for the case-study teams to work informally with the state trainers regarding clarification of information or modification of interventions.

Although inservice activities continue to be a major vehicle for transmitting new information, knowledge, and skills to human services professionals, it has become clear that often they are not sufficient to improve professional performance and competence. Systematic and comprehensive coaching represents a particularly important component of the Team Training Model.

Coaching

It has been assumed that teachers and human services providers naturally transfer and apply what is learned in an inservice program to their own professional settings. Unfortunately, skills mastered in an inservice program are not necessarily integrated into a participant's "active repertoire" (Joyce & Showers, 1980; Smith, Parker, Taubman, & Lovass, 1992) without the assistance of what Joyce and Showers term *coaching* (i.e., an observation and feedback cycle *in an ongoing instructional or clinical setting*). Joyce and Showers note that the addition of coaching to high-quality inservice results in nearly all participants beginning to use new learning or a new model in their professional activities. Joyce and Showers (1980, 1982) discuss five major components of coaching:

1. *Provision of companionship through teams:* The primary purpose of coaching is to observe one another and comment, to reflect, to check perceptions, to share frustrations and successes, and to brainstorm mutual problems. This is typically done in coaching teams of two individuals.
2. *Provision of technical feedback:* Performance feedback is specific, non-judgmental, concise, and primarily directed at behavior that team members can change in themselves as they practice and perfect new skills and as they work through problem areas. (For a detailed discussion of performance feedback, see Cook & Cavallaro, 1985.)
3. *Analysis of application:* During training, teams learn to analyze content and their practice applications of the new skills.
4. *Adaptations to the individual:* A major role of the team members is to "read" the responses of the individual to evaluate the effectiveness of new strategies and techniques as they are implemented and to make adaptations to meet the individual's needs.
5. *Personal facilitation:* A critical role for teams is to help each member to feel positive about himself or herself and his or her efforts, particularly during early stages of skill transfer from the inservice training to their programs.

There are two types of coaches in this dynamic process. The first is the Project Trainer(s) who conduct(s) the initial training for state and community participants and who gives ongoing feedback and input. The second type of coach is the case-study team members who serve as coaches for one another, providing feedback, clarification, and support for application of the training content during and after the training process. In this way, inservice and coaching components of training are combined to maximize the transfer of the knowledge and skills for each participant at each training session.

Providing a Comprehensive Multitopic Training Curriculum To Address All Aspects of Positive Behavioral Support at the Local Level

A complex multitopic curriculum incorporates information and techniques from a variety of content areas. Curriculum components are addressed in the context of each individual's case-study team for their focus individual. Key issues and topics under each curriculum area are summarized briefly below. Topics should include, but are not necessarily limited to, the following:

Philosophy, Values, and Fundamental Themes Underlying Positive Approaches

Positive behavioral support approaches are values-based. Adoption and implementation begin with a commitment to the philosophy and values that underlie the approaches. Everyone in our society has a right to participate in a wide variety of typical, neighborhood, school, work, and community settings. In addition to being an active participant, each individual deserves friendships, choices, respect, variety, access to integrated activities and services, and support services that value each individual and meet community standards of acceptability. Another fundamental theme is that all behavior is meaningful and functional from the perspective of the individual engaging in the behavior and that the cornerstone of successful positive behavioral support is identifying the function of the challenging behaviors and assisting the individual in utilizing more socially acceptable strategies to serve the same purpose (Carr, Robinson, Taylor, & Carlson, 1990; Horner et al., 1993). Implications of this philosophy for services for persons with severe disabilities in general and specifically related to problem behavior are critical in determining curriculum content. A historical perspective of services for individuals with severe disabilities that concludes with current best practices should be part of the curriculum, along with a comparison of past and present behavioral intervention practices. Also included are a variety of strategies for assessing quality of life for case-study teams to use in the initial process of analyzing the individual's life-style and in developing a personal futures plan. Strategies are both formal and informal and include Resident Lifestyle Inventory (Kennedy, Horner, Newton, & Kanda, 1990), person-centered assessments (e.g., Mount & Zwernick, 1987; O'Brien & Lyle, 1987; Vandercook, York, & Forest, 1989), Social Network Analysis (Kennedy, Horner, & Newton, 1990), Program Quality Indicators checklist (Meyer, Eichinger, & Park Lee, 1987), Positive Environment Checklist (Albin, Horner, & O'Neill, 1993), and Curriculum Activity Profile (Foster-Johnson, Ferro, & Dunlap, 1991).

Assessment and Functional Analysis

Thorough, comprehensive functional assessment is the key to effective behavioral support. Although the analysis of immediate antecedent and consequent events remain important components of this process, the topic of assessment is greatly expanded to examine broader contextual variables. Extended analysis of the environment throughout an individual's life must be addressed to determine patterns of controlling variables (including setting events), as well as to examine the level of integration and control, and the opportunities an individual has for choice, interaction, and competent independent performance. General data collection strategies can be presented as well as specific instruments to assess the individual's social motivation for challenging other behavior aspects relevant to determining the communicative functions of the targeted behavior. Specific strategies include descriptive antecedent, behavior, and consequence data; Functional Analysis Interview Format (O'Neill, Horner, Albin, Storey, & Sprague, 1990); Communication Interview Format (Schuler, Peck, Tomlinson, & Theimer, 1984); Pragmatic Analysis Observation Format (Donnellan, Mirenda, Mesaros, & Fassbender, 1984); Scatterplots (Touchette, MacDonald, & Langer, 1985); Functional Analysis Observation Form (O'Neill, Horner, Storey, & Sprague, 1990); and Motivation Assessment Scale (Durand, 1988). Curriculum content regarding how to analyze assessment data to generate hypotheses regarding functions of behavior and strategies for hypothesis testing is essential (Dunlap, Kern-Dunlap, Clarke, & Robbins, 1991; Horner et al., 1992). In order to develop a comprehensive plan of behavioral support that emphasizes global positive programming, assessment activities that address the learner's overall behavioral and communicative repertoire must be included. Learning characteristics must be determined for effective and efficient teaching of competing behavior. Finally, ongoing assessment should be presented as a mode for continually evaluating the effectiveness of intervention, for the purpose of adjusting the support plans to meet the individual's needs toward long-term goals.

Comprehensive Behavioral Support Plans

In addition to serving as the blueprint for a comprehensive intervention program, the behavioral support plan also can serve as a framework for understanding and applying the curriculum content included as part of positive approaches to behavioral support. An overview of the process of building a positive behavioral support plan is provided in Table 2. A positive behavioral support plan should consider: ecological variables and setting events that may serve to increase the probability of the challenging behavior, antecedent manipulations and consequent interventions, response and instructional interventions appropriate to an individual's learning characteristics, a summary of overall positive programming or skill building, long-range plans for increasing quality of life, and (if needed) crisis and emergency procedures (cf. Horner, Albin, & O'Neill, 1991; Horner et al., 1993). The team learns to place emphasis on proactive and preventative intervention strategies. In addition to the components and structure of a comprehensive plan, discussion

Table 2. The process of building a positive behavioral support plan

1. Describe the learner and the contexts in which the learner spends his or her time.
   • Begin personal futures planning process.
2. Identify and operationally define the behavior(s) or behavior class(es) of concern.
   • Collect baseline data.
3. Implement behavioral supports as needed while conducting assessments.
   A. Lifestyle Enhancements I
      1. Integration: school, work, living, environment
      2. Enhanced interactions, participation, independence, choice, variety, predictability
   B. Positive Procedures I
      1. Stimulus change
      2. Differential reinforcement of alternative (desirable) behavior(s)
   C. Crisis Prevention and Intervention Procedures I (if necessary)
4. Conduct assessments.
   A. Quality of Life (e.g., Resident Life-style Inventory [Kennedy, Horner, Newton, & Kanda, 1990]), Person-centered assessments (Mount & Zwernick, 1987; O'Brien & Lyle, 1987; Vandercook, York, & Forest, 1989), Social Network Analysis (Kennedy, Horner, & Newton, 1990), Program Quality Indicators Checklist (Meyers, Eichinger, & Park-Lee, 1987), Quality of Life Cue Questions (Anderson, Mesaros, & Neary, 1991)
   B. Ecological Environmental Systems (e.g., Positive Environment Checklist [Albin, Horner, & O'Neill, 1993], Interaction Observation Form (Albin, Horner, & O'Neill, 1993), Curriculum Activity Profile [Foster-Johnson, Ferro, & Dunlap, 1991])
   C. Functional Assessment of Target Behavior(s) or Behavior Class(es)
      1. Interviews (e.g., Communication Interview Format [Schuler, Peck, Tomlinson, & Theimer, 1984], Functional Analysis Interview Format [O'Neill, Horner, Storey, & Sprague, 1990])
      2. Checklists/rating scales (e.g., Motivation Assessment Scale [Durand, 1988])
      3. Direct Observation (e.g., A-B-C [S-R-C] Analysis), Functional Analysis Observation Form (O'Neill, Horner, Storey, & Sprague, 1990), Scatterplots (Touchette, MacDonald, & Langer, 1985), Anecdotal Records, Behavior Maps (Ittelson, Rivlin, & Proschansky, 1976), Communicative Functions Analysis
   D. Communication Repertoire Assessment
   E. Learning Characteristics Assessment
5. Analyze results of assessments
   A. Generate hypotheses regarding function(s) of behavior(s) or behavior classes in reference to:
      1. Ecological variables
      2. Setting events
      3. Immediate antecedents and maintaining consequences
      4. Potential competing behavior(s)/functional equivalents
      5. Communication repertoire and communicative functions
      6. Quality of life
   B. Construct a competing behavior analysis
   C. Conduct functional analysis manipulations to test hypotheses (if necessary)
      1. Antecedent/consequence manipulations
6. Articulate new and ongoing questions and strategies for continued assessment
7. Design hypotheses-driven Comprehensive Behavioral Support Plan
   A. Lifestyle Enhancement II (same categories as I, but specific to assessment/hypotheses)
   B. Setting and immediate antecedent modifications (e.g., alter antecedents/triggers, remove environmental pollutants, alter grouping arrangements)

(continued)

Table 2. *(continued)*

    C. Changes in curriculum and instruction strategies (e.g., clarify expectations, meaningful tasks, task difficulty, variation, length, predictability, instructional strategies matched to learner characteristics)

    D. Functional equivalence training/instructional programs

    E. Communication, social skills instruction

    F. General skill-building across skill areas

    G. Positive Procedures II (e.g., DRO, DRL, stimulus control)

    H. Self-regulatory strategies

    I. Emergency management procedures

8. Outcomes of support plan implementation and evaluation criteria

    A. Improvements in quality of life

    B. Effectiveness of instruction

        1. Functional equivalents developed and/or increased

        2. General skills developed and/or increased

        3. Communication and social skills developed and/or increased

    C. Basic health and safety improved (e.g., decreases in visits to emergency room, decreases in SIB)

    D. Target behavior(s) reduced or eliminated (and replaced)

9. Establish process and schedule for ongoing positive behavioral support

    A. Team of friends, co-workers, family members, and service providers

    B. Long-term goals/personal future plans

    C. Evaluation of effects of intervention and subsequent adjustments

    D. Evaluation of life-style, social networks, personal preferences, and process for facilitating changes over time

    E. Mechanism for cycling back through the functional assessment intervention process as new behavior, needs, and/or situations arise

should be provided regarding issues in determining and monitoring support plans in accordance with positive intervention values. Examination of potential barriers to implementation of support plans, along with possible resources and creative solutions, should be a component of this content area.

Skill-Building

Effective individualized instructional strategies are critical to skill-building in a positive behavioral support plan. In training, an overview is provided of general instructional technology (e.g., prompts, correction procedures, discrete trial/errorless learning techniques, task analysis, natural cues and consequences, procedures for generalization and maintenance). Strategies to match instructional procedures to specific learning and communication characteristics of an individual are addressed. Specific instructional techniques such as time delay, incidental teaching, and shaping and chain interruption, which are used in teaching functional communication skills, are presented in more detail. Also, instructional strategies associated with reductions in problem behaviors (e.g., task variation and interspersal procedures, use of choice in instruction, procedures to enhance predictability in instruction) are described.

Accompanying information on how to teach effectively is information on what to teach within the context of positive behavioral support plans. Curriculum content most critical to address for individuals with challenging behavior are communication skills and augmentative communication strategies, social interaction and other social skills, self-regulatory and self-management skills (e.g., self-monitoring, self-reinforcement, relaxation, stress management, anger control, assertiveness training), and choice-making skills. However, emphasis is placed not only on what to teach to address existing problem behavior, but also on attending to modifying other curricular variables as part of a proactive approach to behavioral support (Dunlap et al., 1990). Finally, a framework for identifying specific alternative and competing behaviors to be taught is presented. This framework builds on a competing-behaviors model for addressing problem behaviors (Horner & Billingsley, 1988) and stresses the concept of functional equivalence (Carr, 1988). The basic strategy is to identify and teach an alternative behavior that serves the same function (i.e., a functional equivalent) as the problem behavior(s). An effective alternative behavior can compete successfully with, and therefore replace, problem behaviors. (See Horner, O'Neill, & Flannery, 1993, for more detail.)

Positive Consequence Procedures as a Component of a Positive Behavioral Support Plan

An overview of basic behavioral principles and traditional behavior modification strategies is presented as a framework for the positive reinforcement strategies typically associated with nonaversive behavior management. Specific strategies addressed include a variety of reinforcement schedules, including differential reinforcement of other behavior (DRO), differential reinforcement of low rates of behavior (DRL), and differential reinforcement of incompatible behavior (DRI), along with stimulus-control procedures, instructional-control strategies, stimulus satiation, and stimulus-change procedures. It is critical to emphasize that in a positive behavioral support model, these procedures are only one small element of the multicomponent intervention package. A discussion of the inappropriateness of the use of punishment and with the use of reinforcement in isolation is included to reinforce the necessity for comprehensive, multielement positive behavioral intervention packages. Broader discussion of problems and issues related to reliance exclusively on consequence-based procedures, including positive reinforcement procedures, to effect behavior change and provide support should also be included.

Crisis Intervention/Emergency Management

Predetermined crisis intervention strategies are an important component of a comprehensive behavioral support plan for any individual whose behavior results in injury to himself or herself or to others. While acknowledging this, information taught in this area emphasizes strategies for avoiding or diffusing a crisis before hands-on intervention is needed. Discussion regarding the difference between occasional crisis-intervention procedures to prevent injury and ongoing intervention programs to decrease crisis-provoking behavior is a critical aspect of this topic. The importance of critiquing staff performance during a crisis and of providing reinforcement to avoid crisis situations is emphasized. Discussion of the role of peer review committees and of policy in guiding and monitoring crisis intervention is a critical component in developing crisis intervention procedures.

Standards and Methods for Evaluating the Success of Comprehensive Support Plans

An important feature of positive behavioral support approaches is a broadened perspective regarding evaluation of intervention and overall plan success for the individual (Horner et al., 1990; Meyer & Evans, 1989). Although traditional measures of intervention effects, such as frequency, rate, duration, or intensity of problem behaviors and acquisition of new adaptive behaviors, remain important in evaluating effectiveness, these measures no longer can be viewed as sufficient to document support plan success. As noted earlier in this chapter, behavior change should occur in the context of a rich and meaningful lifestyle. Curriculum content in this area needs to include information on additional evaluation outcomes and procedures for their measurement. These outcomes include: generalization and maintenance of behavior changes; side-effects (both positive and negative) of intervention strategies; and changes in quality of life, such as measures of health and safety, physical and social integration, and activity patterns. This broadened perspective of evaluating intervention success also has important implications for the acceptability of specific intervention procedures (Sprague & Horner, 1993). Procedures deemed effective based on a very narrow evaluation criterion (e.g., reduction of problem behavior in a specific condition, such as the presence of a particular person) may not be viewed as acceptable when broader evaluation criteria are applied (e.g., generalization of behavioral effect, consideration of side effects, and measures of change in life-style).

Systems Issues and Implications for Positive Behavioral Support

Most individuals who have worked with education and developmental disabilities service systems recognize that "the system" can either facilitate or impede the delivery of effective support. Frustration can occur in our field when one knows what should be done and how to do it, but is thwarted by systems barriers. Systems change and development that facilitate implementation of best-practice procedures should be taught as important aspects of quality improvement. Training should cover local systems issues (e.g., organization and agency policy implications) and larger systems issues (e.g., advocacy for systems change, funding issues and implications, and state and federal policies such as prevention and early intervention). Trainees should be sufficiently knowledgeable regarding systems issues to be strong advocates for systems that facilitate best-practice approaches to behavioral support.

Training Issues and Strategies

Specific information must be provided to future trainers about strategies for conducting training. Topics should include presentation style, designing activities, coaching and feedback, using media, and discussion of training strategies and issues. Also, future trainers may find themselves providing technical assistance for a specific individual or for an agency as a whole. Strategies for providing technical assistance, including information on procedures to follow and on potential pitfalls to avoid, are additional areas of curriculum content.

Facilitate Ongoing Implementation and Expansion of Comprehensive Behavioral Support at the Local Level

Throughout training, issues related to support and systems changes needed for implementation are typically part of discussion about team field activities. Toward the end of the training process, specific activities occur to formalize the planning process for positive behavioral support efforts to continue in the community beyond the formal training. Each team develops long-term goals for the individual and identifies barriers to achieving those goals. These goals and barriers are compared across all teams participating in the training and a composite list is developed. Trainees then brainstorm possible solutions and action plans toward achieving these solutions. A part of this process is the identification of key individuals, in addition to those participating as trainees, who can facilitate change (e.g., administrators, politicians, community members). These individuals are invited to participate in a final training session where teams present a summary of the achievements and goals for each case-study focus individual, along with specific barriers and possible solutions. Input and support are then recruited from the invited community regarding the actualization of the long-term goals. The dynamic team training process, along with the documented successful application during training, typically results in initial community support and an action plan for future efforts. The nature of this support varies tremendously across communities, but often includes commitment to continued interagency efforts including sharing of resources and ongoing participation, implementation of positive behavioral support, and/or providing further training or technical assistance for the community. An example of such support with one focus individual is provided below.

Jose, a young man with challenging behavior, was a recipient of technical assistance through the case-study team training. He worked in a sheltered day program (9 A.M.–4 P.M.) and lived in a group home. It was determined that the primary function of his aggressive behavior (hitting and scratching) in the day program was to escape, and a community job was targeted as part of the intervention package. The position best suited to his needs required a split shift (8–11 A.M. and 2–5 P.M.), leaving him free in the middle of the day. Jose's need for supervision and the inability of either the day or residential program to provide this support across town in the middle of the day presented a serious barrier to his accepting the job. A second case-study team in training identified a need for assistance for an elementary-school student so that he could be included in more activities with his peers. Jose enjoyed interacting with children. It was determined that he could provide some support at the school from 11 A.M. to 2 P.M., with the teacher assuming responsibility for supervision and ensuring him a lunch and rest break before he went back to work for the second part of the shift. In this case, direct service staff and the directors of three agencies worked together to rearrange schedules and services, arrange transportation, and resolve issues of liability and interagency agreements to make this aspect of the intervention work.

Providing Support for Newly Trained Trainers During Their Initial Training Efforts

The final feature of the training promotes high-quality spread of effect via support for the newly trained trainers, known as the state training team. A critical component of effective training is the competence of the trainers in the content areas of training and in the ability to train others. The two-tiered training of trainers focuses on content during level 1 and on the process of conducting the training on positive behavioral support during level 2. From their experience as trainees and participants during level 1 training, state team members acquire basic competencies and enhance their skills by observing and participating in the training process with the types of individuals they themselves will be training. In level 1, state trainers meet with Project Trainers on a regular basis to discuss issues such as the rationale for the sequence and content of training for community teams, adjustments to meet the needs of individual participants, or political issues that need to be addressed to facilitate implementation of positive behavioral support. Level 2 consists of supported training with the developing state team conducting its first replication of the overall training process. Assistance is provided with logistical support (as discussed below) for the team's initial training efforts. Project Trainers provide support throughout the level 2 training process by attending each session and meeting with state trainers to debrief them on the day's training and to prepare for the next day's training.

INSERVICE TRAINING APPROACH:
IMPLEMENTATION OF THE TEAM TRAINING MODEL

The logistics of coordinating multilevel training are complex and critical to the success of the training. Primary logistical issues include the selection of participants and the structure and schedule of training. Each is addressed briefly, followed by a discussion of systems change and other considerations relevant to successful implementation of our Team Training Model.

Selection of State Teams

In our Team Training Model, the Research and Training Center on Non-Aversive Community Referenced Behavior Management distributed a request for proposals (RFP) to invite states to apply to participate in the Team Training Project. Request for proposals were sent to state human services agencies and advocacy organizations. Applications were to: 1) identify the agencies/ individuals targeted for participation in the project, along with evidence of prior collaborative efforts in providing innovative services for persons with severe disabilities; 2) describe the philosophy of human services in the state and how that philosophy was being realized; 3) delineate a training plan, including goals of the project, state team composition and expertise, and overview and timelines of projected training activities for 3 years (states were asked to commit to training a minimum of 3–6 communities). In addition, training plans had to outline commitment of training time for state team members and describe the first two communities for training to include the participants to be trained and characteristics and lifestyles of individuals with severe disabilities who would be focus individuals for case-study teams; 4) document support and commitment to the project; and 5) specify additional contributions or unique aspects of the proposed project, such as links with other systems change or training activities, support for release time for participants for training, and plans for follow-up technical assistance for the participating communities.

Applications were evaluated based on the comprehensiveness of the application in addressing each of the following areas.

1. The state's record and current efforts in providing quality innovative services to individuals with severe disabilities in integrated school, work, living, and community settings.
2. Composition of the state training team—desirable characteristics include: interagency representation, members with experience in providing direct services to persons with severe disabilities (including challenging behaviors) and in providing training and/or technical assistance, members currently providing inservice or technical assistance on a statewide level (or specific commitments from agencies for release time to conduct ongoing

training for this project), and familiarity with and support for the values and components of positive behavioral support.

3. Composition of the demonstration communities and commitment to the project—the variety in constituencies targeted for participation in case-study teams (e.g., educators, families, employers, residential and recreational agencies, co-workers, peers) is of critical importance along with commitments to serving individuals with significantly challenging behavior in integrated contexts. Full participation in the training project, including continued dissemination of information and supporting future state training efforts, are also important components of a comprehensive application.

4. Feasibility of and commitment to a long-term training plan—this includes demonstrated administrative and financial support for proposed training activities, including the percentage of time of each team member's position to be allocated to the training; the comprehensiveness of the long-term plan and timelines for training and dissemination activities; identification of a lead trainer or state team project coordinator to supervise training activities; evidence of collaboration across agencies, families, and advocacy groups; and commitment to systems changes to facilitate long-term positive behavioral support in school and community settings.

Selection of Demonstration Communities and Participants

The selection of communities and the individuals within those communities to receive training is a responsibility of the state training team. Community selection is based on the record of participating agencies in providing innovative services in integrated school and community contexts and the ability of the community to deliver the commitments described below. Successful training requires strong commitment by the agencies, programs, and individuals in the demonstration communities supporting the case-study participants. Most states, following the lead of the Colorado team, are requiring a formal proposal delineating how the community would meet all requirements and make future use of the training, along with letters of commitment from each participating agency or individual. Commitments to be addressed within the proposal include the number of training days, including a specified amount of time for case-study work outside of the actual inservice sessions and how these release days will be supported (e.g., substitutes, removal of certain job responsibilities during the training period, support for childcare for parents); ongoing support for interventions designed via the training process, which requires interagency collaboration and flexibility in resources and services; and the commitment of participants to ongoing training and technical assistance after their initial training.

The selection of individual trainees from the local community is also a key to success. There is a need to include both administrators (particularly supervisory or middle management) and direct service personnel from each participating agency. The interventions to improve quality of life and build skills that arise as part of the training process typically require structural changes in the way agencies provide services. These are, therefore, critical to include when training individuals who are directly responsible for providing services to individuals with severe disabilities and individuals who make decisions regarding how those services are provided. The individuals from a particular agency or program can support one another in implementation of assessment and intervention during and following the training.

Selecting individuals to serve as ongoing community trainers includes: targeting individuals whose jobs place them in positions to conduct training (e.g., supervisory or staff development personnel, program specialists, teachers, or related service staff), and recruiting individuals who demonstrate leadership qualities in the course of training and who are motivated to invest time and energy to help provide positive behavioral supports in their communities. Ideally, the selection strategies will result in a cadre of local trainers that is representative of the range of constituencies that will receive inservice training.

Selection of Individuals with Severe Disabilities as Participants

There are typically between 3 and 8 case-study teams included in training for a community. Selection of the persons with disabilities to participate as focus individuals for each team should be designed to include: 1) individuals with significantly challenging behavior; 2) individuals who are living, working, and/or going to school in integrated settings; 3) individuals for whom complete case-study teams can be formed; and 4) individuals representing a range of abilities, ages, and challenging behaviors. In order to train participants to successfully utilize Positive Behavioral Support Technology to support all individuals, even those with particularly challenging behaviors, in integrated contexts, it is important that the behavioral repertoire of at least some of the focus individuals includes serious behavior problems (e.g., self-injury, aggression, property destruction). Enhancements in quality of life, particularly in the areas of integration and social networks, is a crucial component of a positive behavioral support intervention package. Therefore, focus individuals must spend their time in settings where integration and interaction naturally occur or be supported by agencies committed to making whatever changes in placement, program, or the nature of support are necessary to accomplish this. Ideally, the individual is living, working, or going to school in integrated settings. In communities where this is not the case, agency commitment to move to more integrated settings must be established prior to participation in training. This commitment to the development of integrated settings is particularly important as experience suggests that achieving the targeted lifestyle or environmental changes in segregated settings is usually impossible. As the most effective case-study teams are those that include representatives from all aspects of the focus individual's life, priority should be given to selecting focus individuals for whom complete teams can be identified to participate in the training process. Finally, to facilitate generalized skills in applying the technology, focus individuals should be selected to represent a variety of ages, ability levels, and challenging behaviors.

Structure and Schedule of Training

Typically, inservice training involves 10–12 days (in 1- to 3-day blocks) of presentations, discussions, and work sessions during 4–6 months. From 2–4 days may be required for case-study activities that occur between inservice sessions. For some team members, training activities may be part of their existing job responsibilities. There is some flexibility in the curriculum sequence, although a general sequence of quality of life; assessment, intervention/evaluation; and community/systems issues has been used most often. State teams generally adopt the training sequence, materials, and activities to meet the needs of their constituencies. The length of each training session depends on the content and the time needed for activities and discussion by the case-study teams. One-day sessions occurring frequently may be as, or more, effective as 2- to 3-day inservice blocks. The time between sessions has ranged from 2 to 6 weeks and is determined by the fieldwork agenda to be completed by the team members prior to the next session. Generally, we have found that training proceeds when inservice sessions are close together at the beginning of the training sequence and farther apart as the training progresses. As the teams move from collecting assessment information to developing and implementing intervention plans, more time is needed between sessions in order to evaluate the effects of instruction and systems-change efforts. (A sample training sequence delineating training content, training activities, and case-study team field assignments has been provided in Appendix A.)

Issues of Systems Change and Other Considerations

Comprehensive training in positive approaches to behavioral support is an essential component in achieving full community inclusion of individuals with severe disabilities and very challenging behaviors. The knowledge and skills from inservice training produce no guarantees of success in dealing with any particular individual. Staff training represents only one component in the broader complex of variables and issues related to creating service support systems that work (Gilbert, 1978; Reid, Parsons, & Green, 1989). To effectively support people with disabilities and severe challenging behaviors in typical community settings, the individuals providing the support (e.g., professionals, paraprofessionals, and family) must receive adequate supports from the systems in which they operate (Gilbert, 1978).

Community support systems are enhanced by the comprehensive training approach delineated in this chapter in at least three ways. First, training increases the capacity of community systems to serve individuals with disabilities by increasing the competence of direct care, management, and administrative staff, who are responsible for providing support to individuals with challenging behaviors. Lack of trained personnel is a major barrier to the provision of support services in typical community environments. Inadequate training represents a major contributing factor to continued segregation and to removal of individuals with challenging behavior from the typical community. Second, a trainer-of-trainers approach provides an important, ongoing resource (i.e., a team of trainers) for increasing the competence of personnel. By training trainers who can teach both support personnel and additional trainers, a spread of effect is created that serves to increase the overall capacity of the support system. The team of trainers can be self-sustaining and, therefore, have a long-term impact on local systems. Third, by training the trainers in technical assistance skills, a resource of skilled experts who can work directly with agencies or communities who support individuals with challenging behaviors is created. Individuals with severe challenging behaviors may require expertise beyond that which is typically available in community agencies. Expert technical assistance may be essential to maintaining community placements for some people (Durand & Kishi, 1987; Janney & Meyer, 1990; O'Neill, Williams, Sprague, Horner, & Albin, in press).

Inservice training also affects support systems by including the curriculum content concerning systems issues and systems change. Issues of staff and organizational management (Reid et al., 1989), quality assurance (Bradley & Bersani, 1990), and methods and issues for quality improvement in human service organizations and systems (Albin, 1992) are among the systems-related topics included in the training curriculum. Topics such as the etiology of problem behaviors, prevention, and early intervention (Dunlap, Johnson, & Robbins, 1990; Guess & Carr, 1991) also have important systems implications. In the past, these content areas have rarely been included in training on behavior management.

SELECTED OUTCOMES AND EFFECTS OF THE TEAM TRAINING IN THE POSITIVE BEHAVIORAL SUPPORT PROJECT

The combined efforts of project trainers and state trainers have resulted in 59 communities receiving training, including 1,609 family members and service providers and 317 focus individuals with challenging behavior. The lives of these individuals have been positively changed by decreases in target behavior and increases in circles of support. Additionally, 13,871 individuals have participated in technical assistance and other dissemination activities conducted by state trainers. Participants are delineated by state in Table 3. It should be noted that the total number of 15,937 documented participants in

Table 3.   Team Training Project outcomes: Number of participants by state

State	Number of communities participating	Number of state team trainers	Number of local community participants	Number of individuals participating as focus individuals	Additional inservices, T.A. and dissemination participants
Arizona	3	10	63	15	130
California	5	4	161	54	2,547
Colorado	4	9	114	34	6,870
Connecticut	5	10	195	19	272
Delaware	2	8	20	8	105
Florida	3	10	77	15	(NA)
Indiana	4	8	102	25	1,277
Michigan	4	13	119	22	229
Minnesota	13	7	250	38	(NA)
New York	2	10	50	11	(NA)
Oklahoma	1	7	6	7	(NA)
Oregon	1	8	8	0	311
Tennessee	4	10	177	17	1,114
Virginia	3	12	128	29	320
West Virginia	4	6	122	17	367
Washington	1	8	17	6	329
Total	59	140	1,609	317	13,871

Total participants = 15,937.

NA = not available.

the Team Training Project training and dissemination efforts is very conservative. The individuals with challenging behaviors include only those who participated directly as case-study focus individuals. Most participants informally reported providing positive behavioral support for additional individuals during and after training. In addition, the number of individuals participating in state trainer technical assistance and dissemination efforts represents documentation by approximately 50% of the state trainers. Similarly, the number does not include informal efforts reported by community participants.

Follow-up questionnaires, sent at least 1 year after initial training, were sent to all team members in the first 10 states participating in the Team Training Inservice Project. The results of these questionnaires confirmed that training (state) team members have continued to provide training and technical assistance and to use the information and materials presented in the inservice. Of the team members responding (52% from the total surveys sent), 94% reported that they have been training other people since participating in the Team Training Inservice, and 86% reported that they have provided technical assistance or consulting on behavioral support or related issues. Of those team members who have provided training and/or technical assistance, more than 90% indicate that they have incorporated information and/or materials from the Team Training Inservice in their efforts. Most participants surveyed also responded positively to questions about whether participation in the Team Training Inservice had resulted in changes/modifications in their training efforts (92%) and in their technical assistance/consultation efforts (75%). A summary of the composition of several state teams, along with outcomes and current status, is provided in Appendix B.

The impact of the state training teams extends far beyond the actual participants in the training activities. In many cases, the interagency composition of the teams has been the first truly collaborative activity that has occurred across agencies of the state level. In many instances, this collaboration has set the stage for further collaboration and sharing of resources. In several states, the training teams are collaborating with statewide systems-change projects affecting school inclusion and/or supported employment. Training efforts have influenced policy at local and state school and agency levels as well as state legislation. For example, one school district now requires that every teacher be trained in positive behavioral support, and has revised its policies so that positive behavioral support is the acceptable mode of intervention for challenging behavior. Similarly, a county community mental health board revised its emergency management policies. Subsequently, they reported a 50%–60% decrease in the use of timeout and physical restraint procedures by staff who had positive behavioral support training. State teams have been extremely influential in increasing the awareness of agencies, service providers, and families of the value of positive behavioral support as a viable and effective alternative to more intrusive and aversive behavioral intervention strategies. In three states, teams organized statewide conferences on the topic. In most of the 16 states, team members have presented at major conferences for educators, adult service providers, advocacy groups, and families, and to legislators, school boards, and state agencies. Several teams have also made presentations at national conferences (e.g., Council for Exceptional Children, The Association for Persons with Severe Handicaps, American Association on Mental Disabilities, and Association for Behavior Analysis). Several have state teams are utilizing a regional training model and have split a team into groups of two or three to conduct replication training in their region. This makes more state trainers available for ongoing support and technical assistance.

Spread of effect efforts by participants are also noteworthy. Policy changes at one school district resulted in participants from the Team Training Project forming a team and training every elementary school in the district. Significant movement of students to integrated school settings occurred subsequent to training. In another community, four principals with teachers and students who had participated in the training banded together to write a proposal to the state education agency for funding to replicate the training throughout the district.

In spite of such success, the state teams continue to struggle with a variety of issues ranging from the need for: 1) modifications in content and training materials to include a wider range of educational and ethnic diversity across trainees to 2) strategies to effect long-term systems change at local and state levels. Although dissemination strategies such as those described above have had a positive impact on administrative support for systems-wide training, most state teams feel that statewide "ownership" of the training team and its activities needs to be improved. In addition to support for the state training team, state-level ownership can help provide direction and support for local communities in overcoming some of the typical barriers to successful participation in this training process. Such barriers often include problems in the areas of interagency collaboration, openness to systems change to support positive behavioral intervention, and commitment to the comprehensive, positive quality-of-life principles driving this intervention model.

In this era of recession and budget deficits, one of the primary issues facing the state teams is funding for future efforts. Thus far, funding in most states has come from human service agencies, but large budget cuts in many states have reduced (or eliminated) resources to support team training activities. Similar funding issues arise at the local community level where, although typically services of the state trainers are free of charge, funding is needed for release time for staff and for training materials. Support for local community participation in the Team Training Project has generally come from staff development funds of various local agencies. Several state (e.g., Michigan, California, Colorado) have made funds available to local communities on a competitive basis via a request-for-proposal process. Virtually all state teams are extremely committed to continuing their comprehensive training efforts and are enthusiastically and creatively pursuing funding to support ongoing implementation and evaluation of the team training model. We have no doubt that, as documentation and dissemination of the effectiveness of this type of comprehensive and dynamic training process increases, support for ongoing implementation will be made available.

In order to share issues and successful solutions across states, the state teams have formed a national state trainers network. To date, two annual meetings of the network have occurred, the first issue of a network newsletter has been distributed, and the second edition is being developed. Support and development of this network is vital to continuation of the Team Training Project.

CONCLUSION

Development of an effective technology of positive behavioral support is not enough. As stated previously, we must disseminate technology and train people in its use in ways that promote widespread adoption and implementation in the full range of community settings where people with challenging behaviors live, work, go to school, and recreate. This chapter has presented an intensive, comprehensive, multifaceted inservice training approach that is designed to meet these dissemination and training objectives. Key features of the training approach include: 1) use of a trainer-of-trainers model; 2) targeting of multiple constituency audiences; 3) utilization of a case-study team format; 4) provision of a comprehensive, multitopic curriculum; 5) a dynamic training process involving multiple methods of information delivery and application; 6) direct implementation of content during the training process; and 7) follow-up support for the trainers being trained. The outcomes of this training approach have positive effects on three levels: 1) on individuals with disabilities and challenging behaviors and their families; 2) on the trainers, program staff, administrators, and others who participate in the training; and 3) on the support systems in which all of these stakeholders operate.

REFERENCES

Albin, J.M. (1992). *Quality improvement in employment and other human services: Managing for quality through change.* Baltimore: Paul H. Brookes Publishing Co.

Albin, R.W., Horner, R.H., & O'Neill, R.E. (1993). *Proactive behavioral support: Structuring and assessment environments.* Unpublished manuscript, University of Oregon, Specialized Training Program, Eugene.

Anderson, J.L., Mesaros, R.A., & Neary, T. (1991). *Community referenced nonaversive behavior management trainers manual,* Vol. I. Washington, DC: National Institute on Disability and Rehabilitation Research.

Baumgart, D., & Ferguson, D. (1991). Personnel preparation: Directions for the next decade. In L.H. Meyer, C.A. Peck, & L. Brown (Eds.), *Critical issues in the lives of people with severe disabilities* (pp. 313–352). Baltimore: Paul H. Brookes Publishing Co.

Berkman, K.A., & Meyer, L.H. (1988). Alternative strategies and multiple outcomes in the remediation of severe self-injury: Going "all out" nonaversively. *Journal of The Association for Persons with Severe Handicaps, 13,* 76–86.

Bradley, V.J., & Bersani, H.A. (1990). *Quality assurance for individuals with developmental disabilities: It's everybody's business.* Baltimore: Paul H. Brookes Publishing Co.

Buckley, J., Albin, J.M., & Mank, D. (1988). Competency-based staff training for supported employment. In G.T. Bellamy, L.E. Rhodes, D.M. Mank, & J.M. Albin (Eds.), *Supported employment: A community implementation guide* (pp. 229–245). Baltimore: Paul H. Brookes Publishing Co.

Carr, E. G. (1988). Functional equivalence as a means of response generalization. In R.H. Horner, G. Dunlap, & R.L. Koegel (Eds.), *Generalization and maintenance: Lifestyle changes in applied settings* (pp. 194–219). Baltimore: Paul H. Brookes Publishing Co.

Carr, E.G., McConnachie, G., Levin, L., & Kemp, D.C. (in press). Communication-based treatment of severe behavior problems. In R. Van Houten & S. Axelrod (Eds.), *Effective behavioral treatment: Issues and implementation.* New York: Plenum.

Carr, E.G., Robinson, S., & Palumbo, L.W. (1990). The wrong issue: Aversive versus nonaversive treatment. The right issue: Functional versus nonfunctional treatment. In A. Repp & N. Singh (Eds.), *Perspectives on the use of nonaversive and aversive interventions for persons with developmental disabilities* (pp. 361–379). Sycamore, IL: Sycamore Publishing Co.

Carr, E.G., Robinson, S., Taylor, J.C., & Carlson, J.I. (1990). Positive approaches to the treatment of severe behavior problems in persons with developmental disabilities: A review and analysis of reinforcement and stimulus-based procedures. *Monographs of The Association for Persons with Severe Handicaps.*

Carr, E.G., Taylor, J.C., & Robinson, S. (1991). The effects of severe behavior problems in children on the teaching behavior of adults. *Journal of Applied Behavior Analysis, 24,* 523–535.

Cline, D. (1984). Achieving quality and relevance in inservice teacher education: Where are we? *Teacher Education and Special Education, 7,* 199–208.

Cook, L.H., & Cavallaro, C. (1985). *Materials development and field-based training for preservice resource specialist teachers: Final report.* Washington, DC: Office of Special Education, U.S. Department of Education.

Demchak, M.A., & Browder, D.M. (1990). An evaluation of the pyramid model of staff training in group homes for adults with severe handicaps. *Education and Training in Mental Retardation, 25,* 150–163.

Donnellan, A.M., Mirenda, P., Mesaros, R., & Fassbender, L. (1984). A strategy for analyzing the communicative functions of behavior. *Journal of The Association of Persons with Severe Handicaps, 11,* 201–212.

Doss, S., & Reichle, J. (1991). Replacing excess behavior with an initial communicative repertoire. In J. Reichle, J. York, & J. Sigafoos, *Implementing augmentative and alternative communication: Strategies for learners with severe disabilities.* Baltimore: Paul H. Brookes Publishing Co.

Dunlap, G., Ferro, J., & dePerczel, M. (in press). Nonaversive behavioral intervention in the community. In E. Cipani & F. Spooner (Eds.), *Curricular and instructional approaches for persons with severe handicaps.* New York: Allyn & Bacon.

Dunlap, G., Johnson, L.F., & Robbins, F.R. (1990). Preventing serious behavior problems through skill development and early intervention. In A.C. Repp & N.N. Singh (Eds.), *Perspectives on the use of nonaversive and aversive interventions for persons with developmental disabilities* (pp. 273–286). Sycamore, IL: Sycamore Publishing Co.

Dunlap, G., Kern-Dunlap, L., Clarke, S., & Robbins, F.R. (1991). Functional assessment, curricular revision, and severe behavior problems. *Journal of Applied Behavior Analysis, 24*(2), 387–397.

Dunlap, G., Robbins, F.R., Morelli, M.S., & Dollman, D. (1988). Team training for young children with autism: A regional model for service delivery. *Journal of the Division for Early Childhood, 12,* 147–160.

Durand, V.M. (1988). Motivation assessment scale. In M. Herson & A. Bellack (Eds.), *Dictionary of behavioral assessment techniques* (pp. 309–310). Elmsford, NY: Pergamon.

Durand, V.M. (1990). *Severe behavior problems: A functional communication training approach.* New York: Guilford Press.

Durand, V.M., & Kishi, F. (1987). Reducing severe behavior problems among persons with dual sensory impairments: An evaluation of a technical assistance model. *Journal of The Association for Persons with Severe Handicaps, 12,* 2–10.

Foster-Johnson, L., Ferro, J., & Dunlap, G. (Nov. 1991). *Do curricular activities contribute to problem behavior in the classroom?* Paper presented at the 36th Annual Meeting of the Florida Educational Research Association. Clearwater, FL.

Gilbert, T.F. (1978). *Human competence: Engineering worthy performance.* New York: McGraw-Hill.

Guess, D., & Carr, E. (1991). Emergence and maintenance of stereotypy and self-injury. *American Journal on Mental Retardation, 96,* 299–319.

Hasazi, S.B. (1985). Facilitating transition from high school: Policies and practices. *American Rehabilitation, 11,* 9–16.

Hasazi, S.E., Batsche, C., McKinney, I., Gill, D.H., & Cobb, K.B. (1982, May). *Vocational education for the handicapped: Perspectives on inservice personnel development.* Personnel Development Series: Document 6. Washington, DC: Office of Special Education and Rehabilitative Services.

Helmstetter, E., & Durand, V.M. (1991). Nonaversive interventions for severe behavior problems. In L.H. Meyer, C.A. Peck, & L. Brown (Eds.), *Critical issues in the lives of people with severe disabilities* (pp. 559–600). Baltimore: Paul H. Brookes Publishing Co.

Horner, R.H., Albin, R.W., & O'Neill, R.E. (1991). Supporting students with severe intellectual disabilities and severe challenging behaviors. In G. Stoner, M.R. Shinn, & H.M. Walker (Eds.), *Interventions for achievement and behavior problems* (pp. 269–287). Washington, DC: National Association of School Psychologists.

Horner, R.H., & Billingsley, F.F. (1988). The effect of competing behavior on the generalization and maintenance of adaptive behavior in applied settings. In R.H. Horner, G. Dunlap, & R.L. Koegel (Eds.), *Generalization and maintenance: Lifestyle changes in applied settings* (pp. 197–220). Baltimore: Paul H. Brookes Publishing Co.

Horner, R.H., Close, D.W., Fredericks, H.D., O'Neill, R.E., Albin, R.W., Sprague, J.R., Kennedy, C., Flannery, K.B., & Heathfield, L.T. (1992, May). *Oregon community support: Providing support for people with severe problem behaviors.* Paper presented at the Association for Behavior Analysis annual conference, San Francisco.

Horner, R.H., Dunlap, G., Koegel, R.L., Carr, E.G., Sailor, W., Anderson, J., Albin,

R.W., & O'Neill, R.E. (1990). Toward a technology of "nonaversive" behavioral support. *Journal of The Association for Persons with Severe Handicaps, 15,* 125–132.

Horner, R.H., O'Neill, R.E., & Flannery, K.B. (1993). Building effective behavior support plans from functional assessment information. In M.E. Snell (Ed.), *Systematic instruction of persons with severe handicaps* (4th ed.) (pp. 184–214). Columbus, OH: Charles E. Merrill.

Ittleson, W.H., Rivlin, L.G., & Proschansky, H.M. (1976). The use of behavioral maps in environmental psychology. In H.M. Proschansky, W.H. Ittelson, & L.G. Rivlin (Eds.), *Environmental psychology: People and their physical setting.* New York: Polk, Weinhart & Winston, Inc.

Janney, R., & Meyer, L.H. (1990). A consultation model to support integrated educational services for students with severe disabilities and challenging behaviors. *Journal of The Association for Persons with Severe Handicaps, 15*(3), 186–199.

Jones, F.H., Fremouw, W., & Carples, S. (1977). Pyramid training of elementary school teachers to use a classroom management package. *Journal of Applied Behavior Analysis, 10,* 239–253.

Joyce, B., & Showers, B. (1980). Improving inservice training: The age of research. *Educational Leadership, 37,* 379–385.

Joyce, B., & Showers, B. (1982, November). The coaching of teaching. *Educational Leadership,* 4–7.

Kennedy, C.H., Horner, R.H., & Newton, J.S. (1990). The social networks and activity patterns of adults with severe disabilities: A correlational analysis. *Journal of The Association for Persons with Severe Handicaps, 15,* 86–90.

Kennedy, C.H., Horner, R.H., Newton, J.S., & Kanda, E. (1990). Measuring the activity patterns of adults with severe disabilities using the Resident Lifestyle Inventory. *Journal of The Association for Persons with Severe Handicaps, 15,* 79–85.

Kirkpatrick, J.D. (1983). A three-step mode for more effective presentations. *The Personnel and Guidance Journal, 25,* 178–179.

LaVigna, G.W., & Donnellan, A.M. (1986). *Alternatives to punishment: Solving behavior problems with non-aversive strategies.* New York: Irvington Publishers.

LaVigna, G.W., Willis, T.J., & Donnellan, A.M. (1989). The role of positive programming in behavioral treatment. In E. Cipani (Ed.), *The treatment of severe behavior disorders: Behavior analysis approaches* [Monograph] (pp. 59–83). Washington, DC: American Association on Mental Retardation.

McLaughlin, M.J., Smith-Davis, J., & Burke, P.J. (1986). *Personnel to educate the handicapped: A status report.* College Park: University of Maryland, Institute for the Study of Exceptional Children and Youth, Department of Special Education.

McLaughlin, M.J., Valdivieso, C.H., & Stettner-Eaton, B. (1990). An analysis of the part D program and the relationship to preparation of personnel to educate individuals with severe handicaps. In A.P. Kaiser & C.M. McWhorter (Eds.), *Preparing personnel to work with persons with severe disabilities* (pp. 75–90). Baltimore: Paul H. Brookes Publishing Co.

Meyer, L.H., Eichinger, J., & Park-Lee, S. (1987). A validation of program quality indicators in educational services for students with severe disabilities. *Journal of The Association for Persons with Severe Handicaps, 12,* 251–263.

Meyer, L.H., & Evans, I.M. (1989). *Nonaversive intervention for behavior problems: A manual for home and community.* Baltimore: Paul H. Brookes Publishing Co.

Meyer, L.H., Peck, C.A., & Brown, L. (Eds.). (1991). *Critical issues in the lives of people with severe disabilities.* Baltimore: Paul H. Brookes Publishing Co.

Mitchell, D., & Braddock, D. (1991). Compensation and turnover of direct care staff in developmental disabilities: A summary of results. *Public Policy Monograph*

Series #54. Chicago: University Affiliated Program in Developmental Disabilities, University of Illinois at Chicago.

Mount, B., & Zwernick, K. (1987). *It's never too early, it's never too late.* St. Paul, MN: Metropolitan Council.

O'Brien, J., & Lyle, C. (1987). *Framework for accomplishment.* Decatur, GA: Responsive Systems Associates.

O'Neill, R.E., Horner, R.H., Albin, R.W., Storey, K., & Sprague, J.R. (1990). *Functional analysis of problem behavior: A practical assessment guide.* Sycamore, IL: Sycamore Publishing Co.

Page, T.J., Iwata, B.A., & Reid, D.H. (1982). Pyramidal training: A large-scale application with institution staff. *Journal of Applied Behavior Analysis, 15,* 335–351.

Peck, C.A., Killen, C.C., & Baumgart, D. (1989). Increasing implementation of special education instruction in mainstream preschools: Direct and generalized effects of nondirective consultation. *Journal of Applied Behavior Analysis, 22,* 197–210.

Pyles, D.A.M., & Bailey, J.S. (1990). Diagnosing severe behavior problems. In A.C. Repp & N.N. Singh (Eds.), *Perspectives on the use of nonaversive and aversive interventions for persons with developmental disabilities* (pp. 381–402). Sycamore, IL: Sycamore Press.

Racino, J.A. (1990). Preparing personnel to work in community support services. In A.P. Kaiser & C.M. McWhorter (Eds.), *Preparing personnel to work with persons with severe disabilities.* (pp. 203–226). Baltimore: Paul H. Brookes Publishing Co.

Reid, D.H., Parsons, M.B., & Green, C.W. (1989). Treating aberrant behavior through effective staff management: A developing technology. In E. Cipani (Ed.), *The treatment of severe behavior disorders: Behavior analysis approaches* (pp. 175–190). Washington, DC: American Association on Mental Retardation.

Sailor, W., Anderson, J.L., Halvorsen, A.T., Doering, K., Filler, J., & Goetz, L. (1989). *The comprehensive local school: Regular education for all students with disabilities.* Baltimore: Paul H. Brookes Publishing Co.

Schlicter, C.L. (1984). Talents unlimited: An inservice education model for teaching thinking skills. *Gifted Child Quarterly, 30*(3), 119–123.

Schofer, R.C., & Duncan, J.R. (1986). A study of certain personnel preparation factors in special education. *Journal of Special Education, 20,* 61–68.

Schuler, A.L., Peck, C.A., Tomlinson, C.D., & Theimer, R.K. (1984). Communication interview. In Peck, C.A., Schuler, A.L., Tomlinson, C., Theimer, R.K., Haring, T., & Semmel, M. (Eds.), *The social competence curriculum project: A guide to instructional programming for social and communicative interactions.* (pp. 43–52). Santa Barbara: University of California-Santa Barbara.

Smith-Davis, J. (1985, December). Issues in education: Personnel supply and demand in special education. *Counterpoint.*

Smith-Davis, J., Burke, P., & Noel, M. (1984). *Personnel to educate the handicapped in America: Supply and demand from a programmatic viewpoint.* College Park: University of Maryland, Institute for the Study of Exceptional Children and Youth, Department of Special Education.

Smith, T., Parker, T., Taubman, M., & Lovaas, O.I. (1992). Transfer of staff training from workshops to group homes: A failure to generalize across settings. *Research in Developmental Disabilities, 13,* 57–71.

Snell, M.E. (1990). Building our capacity to meet the needs of persons with severe disabilities: Problems and proposed solutions. In A.P. Kaiser & C.M. McWhorter (Eds.), *Preparing personnel to work with persons with severe disabilities* (pp. 9–23). Baltimore: Paul H. Brookes Publishing Co.

SETRC (1985). *Special Education and Training Resource Center Program: Final report.* New York: New York City Board of Education.

Sprague, J.R., & Horner, R.H. (1993). Determining the acceptability of behavior support plans. In M. Wang, H. Walberg, & M. Reynolds (Eds.), *Handbook of special education* (pp. 125–142). Elmsford, NY: Pergamon.

Taylor, S.J., Bogdan, R., & Racino, J.A. (Eds.). (1991). *Life in the community: Case studies of organizations supporting people with disabilities.* Baltimore: Paul H. Brookes Publishing Co.

Touchette, P.E., MacDonald, R.F., & Langer, S.N. (1985). A scatter plot for identifying stimulus control of problem behavior. *Journal of Applied Behavior Analysis, 18,* 343–351.

Turnbull, A.P., & Turnbull, H.R., III (1990). Reader response: A tale about lifestyle changes. *Journal of The Association for Persons with Severe Handicaps.*

Vandercook, T., & York, J. (1990). A team approach to program development and support. In W. Stainback & S. Stainback (Eds.), *Support networks for inclusive schooling: Interdependent integrated education* (pp. 95–122). Baltimore: Paul H. Brookes Publishing Co.

Vandercook, T., York, J., & Forest, M. (1989). The McGill Action Planning System (MAPS): A strategy for building the vision. *Journal of The Association for Persons with Severe Handicaps, 14,* 202–215.

Wehman, P., Kregel, J., & Barcus, J.M. (1985). From school to work: A vocational transition model for handicapped students. *Exceptional Children, 52,* 25–37.

Wehman, P. Kregel, J., & Schafer, M.S. (1989). *Emerging trends in the national supported employment initiative: A preliminary analysis of 27 states.* Richmond: Virginia Commonwealth University, Rehabilitation Research and Training Center.

Zaharia, E.S., & Baumaster, A.A. (1979). Technician losses in public residential facilities. *American Journal of Mental Deficiency, 84,* 36–39.

Appendix A.   Sample training process: Content, activities, and sequence

Day	Themes	Topics	Training activities	Team field assignments (all centered around focus individual)
1.	History of services and behavioral intervention for persons with severe disabilities	Overview of training process and expected outcomes	Finalize case-study team membership (including focus individual)	Evaluate quality of life of focus individual across contexts
		History of services for persons with severe disabilities	Identify behaviors of concern and issues in providing services	Generate initial strategies to improve quality of life
	Current best practices	Current/emerging services in integrated contexts and values driving them	Identify quality of life indicators for our lives and compare with lives of individuals with severe disabilities	
	Positive behavioral support	History of behavior modification	Teams to begin personal futures planning process	
		Current behavioral best practices/comprehensive behavioral support	Teams develop action plan for field assignments	
		Quality of life: definitions and strategies to assess		
		(Interim of 2–4 weeks)		
2.	Basic behavioral principles	Basic behavioral principles/operant paradigm	Team presentations/discussion, quality of life assignments	Collect descriptive antecedent behavior consequence (A-B-C) data across contexts and analyze patterns to generate initial hypotheses
		Rationale for analyses of variables controlling behavior	Group critique of acceptability of decelerative procedures	Continue quality of life evaluation, if needed
		Operational definition of target behavior	Practice defining behavior	Begin initial quality of life intervention
		Problems with the use of punishment	Analysis of S-R-C vignettes	
			Teams develop action plan for field assignments	
3.	Functional analysis	Ongoing assessment process	Teams present A-B-C data and analysis, group discussion regarding hypotheses and addi-	Conduct functional assessments using a variety of strategies and sources of information
	Dynamic assessment process	Assessing learning and performance characteristics		

(continued)

Appendix A. (continued)

Day	Themes	Topics	Training activities	Team field assignments (all centered around focus individual)
			tional information needed	Collect baseline data
		Desired outcomes of functional analysis	Teams generate initial hypotheses and questions regarding learning style and communication repertoire	
		Strategies to assess function(s) of behavior and communication repertoire	Demonstration interview (communication and/or functional analysis)	
		Data collection strategies/baseline	Teams complete motivation assessment scale and present results, questions, and additional information needed	
		Process components of a behavioral support plan	Teams develop action plan	
4.	Interpreting assessment results	Analyzing assessment data to develop hypotheses	Teams present functional assessment results, group discussion around hypotheses regarding maintaining consequences, conditions under which behavior will/will not occur, setting events, learning style, and communication repertoire	Continue assessments as needed
	Generating and testing hypotheses	Strategies for testing hypotheses		Test initial hypotheses
			Teams to design action plan to answer remaining questions and test hypotheses	Modify environment and curriculum on basis of assessment results
5.	Instructional technology	Characteristics of systematic instruction	Group to identify instructional strategies currently utilized and	Assess effectiveness of current instructional strategies
	Skill building			

	Competing behavior/functional equivalence	Discrete trial format Categories of instructional strategies Functional equivalence/competing behaviors	barriers to systematic application Group critique of instructional techniques: video or roleplay Group identifies pros and cons of strategies relative to activity, context, and learning style Teams to discuss implications of learning style for selection of instructional techniques	Continue to collect data on target behavior Continue to test hypotheses

(Interim of 2–4 weeks)

6.	Instructional strategies Choice-making Self-regulatory strategies	Issues in teaching competing behavior Instructional strategies: time delay, incidental teaching, shaping, interrupted behavior chains Strategies to facilitate and teach choice-making Self-regulatory strategies: relaxation/stress reduction, self-monitoring/management	Teams present results of hypotheses testing and initial environmental/curricular modifications Teams design instructional sequence using time delay, incidental teaching, shaping, or interrupted chain strategy and present to group Practice relaxation exercises and adaptations	Continue environmental and curricular interventions Implement instructional program(s)
7.	Communication Social skills Instructional program design	Issues in teaching communication Developing augmentative systems Facilitating and teaching social skills Assertiveness training Components of an instructional program	Teams discuss results of communication analyses and implications for instruction, systems, and vocabulary Teams design instructional sequence and action plan for implementation	Continue environmental and curricular interventions Implement instructional program(s)

(continued)

Day	Themes	Topics	Training activities	Team field assignments (all centered around focus individual)
			(Interim of 3–5 weeks)	
8.	Positive procedures	DRO, DRL, DRC, stimulus control, instructional control, stimulus change, satiation Issues of treatment acceptability Role of positive procedures in comprehensive positive behavioral support plan	Teams practice planning differential reinforcement program and report to group Teams develop positive procedure program and action plan for implementation	Implement positive procedural plan
9.	Comprehensive behavioral support plan Data-based adjustments to intervention	Review components of positive behavioral support plan and training Data-based adjustments to intervention	Teams report regarding instructional, life-style, curricular, and environmental interventions Group critique and brainstorm Teams adjust improvements to interventions and plan next steps	Finalize comprehensive behavioral support plan Implement adjustments and additions to multi-element intervention package
			(Interim of 4–6 weeks)	
10.	Long-range goals and strategies Community support/systems change Team-building	Facilitating teams supporting and serving as "experts" for each other Issues in systems change, team-building, community support, and ongoing training	Teams report on all components of positive behavioral support plans Group provides suggestions for improvements Teams identify long-term goals	Implement adjustments and additions to multi-element intervention package

		(focus on quality of life) and possible barriers and resources to achieving Group identifies common themes	
11.	Crisis management Behavioral intervention policies	Functional versus crisis intervention Crisis management guidelines Issues in behavior management and human rights/policies at state and local levels (presented by participants) Evaluation of positive behavioral support	Group identifies key individuals/organizations to support ongoing positive behavioral support and invite to final session Teams design crisis management plans (if needed) Develop agenda for final session	Finalize action plans for long-term positive behavioral support Prepare case studies and critical issues for presentations to community at final session
			(Interim of 4–6 weeks)	
12.	Community action plans Session with community	Overview of training project and positive behavioral support Case-study presentations including long-range goals and community support needed Issues facing community to facilitate ongoing support	Team update regarding intervention and action plans for long-term support Finalize presentations and desired outcomes of community session Teams and community brainstorm solutions/strategies for ongoing support and spread of effect Teams and community develop action plan	Continue comprehensive behavioral support Conduct ongoing training and technical assistance Revise policies Implement community action plan

Appendix B. State team composition, outcomes, and current status

State	Team composition	Outcomes	Current status
Arizona	Department of Education Department of Economic Security/Division of Developmental Disabilities Arizona School for the Deaf and Blind Phoenix Union High School District Parent/consumer/advocate	Training completed in two communities Ongoing technical assistance and dissemination by team members Team Training Model in Positive Behavioral Support added to statewide inclusion project	Training underway in third community Plans being finalized for third annual state team curriculum retreat Planning variations of training (e.g., week-long summer institutes, conferences)
California	University of San Diego Department of Education Jay Nolan community services Vantage Foundation	Training completed in five communities Trainer for Positive Behavioral Support—position created in State Department of Education State trainers assisting project trainers in other states Ongoing technical assistance and dissemination by team members	Full team replication efforts on hold awaiting funding Ongoing training by Department of Education Individual team members provide training and technical assistance
Colorado	Department of Education Rocky Mountain Statewide Training Institute Division of Developmental Disabilities Parent/advocate	Training completed in four communities Ongoing technical assistance and dissemination by team members Positive Behavioral Support Training added to statewide inclusion efforts	Developing user-friendly State Training manual Conducting replication training in fifth community
Connecticut	State Department of Mental Retardation Benhaven, Inc. Institute for Human Resource Development A.J. Pappanikou Center (University Affiliated Program)	Training completed in three communities Hosted statewide conference Ongoing technical assistance and dissemination by team members Developed "Learners Guide" for participants in training	Finalizing production of State Training Newsletter, Vol. 2 Plans in progress for communities to be trained

State	Agencies/Programs	Activities	Future Plans
Delaware	Department of Public Instruction; Ceasor Rodney School District; Kent/Sussex County Community Mental Retardation Program; Red Clay School District; New Castle County Comunity Mental Retardation Program; Delaware Autistic Program; Colonial School District	Edited and produced State Training Team Newsletter, Vols. 1 and 2; Training completed in one community; Team members helped coordinate regional behavior management conference; Regional behavior management policy and training in Kent/Sussex counties; Revamped behavior management policy and training in Kent/Sussex counties	Training underway in second community
Florida	Bureau of Education for Exceptional Students; Manatee County School District; Hillsborough County School District; Department of Health and Rehabilitative Services/Developmental Services Programs	Training completed in three communities; Ongoing technical assistance and dissemination by team members; Received grant award to develop training modules	Training modules to be developed and field-tested via training in two communities and replication to occur in three communities
Indiana	Institute for Study of Developmental Disabilities/Indiana Resource Center for Autism	Completed training in four communities; Ongoing technical assistance and dissemination by team members; Developed revised package of training materials; Team Training Model in Positive Behavioral Support incorporated into state-legislated training and technical assistance effort	Plans being developed for future training
Michigan	Wayne State University Developmental Disabilities Institute; Department of Mental Health	Training completed in four communities; Abbreviated training completed in one community	Reviewing applications for training; Developing protocol for team training on consultation basis

(continued)

Appendix B. (*continued*)

State	Team composition	Outcomes	Current status
	Macomb Oakland Regional Center	Policy changes in two communities	Revising training materials
	Department of Public Health	Local communities conducting replica-tion training	
	Washtinaw Intermediate School District		
	Lansing Community Mental Health Services	Team Training Model in Positive Behav-ioral Support added to statewide system inclusion project	
	The Arc	Hosted statewide conference on positive behavioral support	
	Copper County Community Mental Health Services	Ongoing technical assistance and dis-semination by team members	
	Ottawa Intermediate School District		
	Parent/advocate		
Minnesota	State Department of Human Services	Training completed in one community	State team training efforts on hold
	Human Service Support Network	Condensed training completed in 12 communities	Developing community support teams/state trainers to conduct regional training and technical assistance
	Institute for Disability Studies, Univer-sity of Minnesota	Training manual developed	Planning statewide conference
		Ongoing training, technical assistance, and dissemination by team members	
New York	State Office of Mental Retardation and Developmental Disabilities (OMRDD)	Training completed in two communities	Plans underway for future replication training efforts
	State Department of Education	Ongoing technical assistance and dis-semination by team members	
	Special Education Training Resource Center	Formal interagency agreement between State Department of Education and OMRDD	
	Family		
	Bronx Developmental Services		
	New York City School District #75		
	Institute for Basic Research		
	Mental Retardation Institute		

Oklahoma	State Department of Education Broken Arrow School Tulsa Public Schools State Department of Human Services/Developmental Disabilities Services Division Hisson Memorial Center University of Oklahoma Parent/advocate	Project training completed in one community Ongoing technical assistance and dissemination by team members	Replication training underway in second community
Oregon	State Developmental Disabilities Program Office Department of Education Douglas County Mental Health Marie Mills Center University of Oregon/STP Garten Foundation Multnomah County Mental Health	Training in one community Five regional 2-day workshops by team members Ongoing technical assistance and dissemination by team members	Team trainings on hold and original team inactive Ongoing dissemination and training by team members New training/consulting network being developed
Tennessee	State Department of Education University of Tennessee Knox County schools Fort Sanders Education Development Center LRE for Life Project CMRA Supported Employment Project	Training conducted in four communities Ongoing technical assistance and dissemination by team members	Revising training materials Planning trainings
Virginia	Department of Mental Health, Mental Retardation and Substance Abuse Virginia Institute of Developmental Disabilities	Training completed in two communities Awarded research and training grant to apply team training model to individuals with traumatic brain injury	Negotiation to finalize training plans for two additional communities Developing interdisciplinary preservice training in positive behavioral support

(continued)

Appendix B. *(continued)*

State	Team composition	Outcomes	Current status
	Virginia Commonwealth University Montgomery County schools Virginia Polytechnic Institute and State University George Mason University Center on Human Disability Department of Rehabilitation Services	Ongoing technical assistance and dissemination by team members	
Washington	Residential Technical Assistance Program/Catholic Social Services Department of Developmental Disabilities University of Washington O'Neill and Associates Northwest Center	Training completed in one community Ongoing technical assistance and dissemination by team members Some training content incorporated into statewide core training curriculum delivered by team members around the state Wrote chapter on behavioral support in state orientation manual for new adult direct service staff	Plan to incorporate training into State Department of Education technical assistance efforts Plan for first replication training, but implementation on hold until funding is available
West Virginia	Department of Education Coalition of parents/advocates West Virginia University/UACPD Autism Training Center Autism Services Center Department of Health and Human Resources State Developmental Disabilities Planning Council Cabell County Schools Parent/advocate	Training completed in four communities Incorporated team training project into state life quilters project Developed 16 training modules to assist in individualizing community training	Plans to train one or two communities every 4–6 months Planning to produce State Training Team Newsletter, Vols. 3 and 4

16

Meaningful Outcomes
in Behavioral Intervention

Evaluating Positive Approaches to the
Remediation of Challenging Behaviors

Luanna H. Meyer and Ian M. Evans

T HERE EXIST TO DATE HUNDREDS of published intervention reports of "successful" efforts to remediate problem behaviors in persons with developmental disabilities (see Schlosser & Goetze, in press). They illustrate the application of a variety of approaches and methods to decrease challenging behaviors and, in some instances, to replace those behaviors with alternative skills. The communication-based interventions described throughout this volume represent one of the most recent and perhaps most promising approaches to the skill replacement strategy in particular. Even in these early stages, the results are encouraging. Researchers working in this area have been primarily data-based and have documented both the specific methods and the results obtained according to the accepted conventions of scientific practice—thus allowing us to have confidence in the validity of the approach.

The publications that have emerged as part of this scientific validation process have been called upon to serve two purposes that are actually very different. First, of course, they provide the empirical basis for the practices we recommend. The extent to which a journal report clearly documents behavioral improvement as a function of an intervention establishes the treatment validity of our practices. But we also have had a second expectation of this literature—that published reports provide guidance to practice. Practitioners working with persons considered to be similar to the individuals described in research are typically expected to utilize this same empirical litera-

Portions of this chapter were completed while the first author was on sabbatical leave as a visiting scholar at the University of Washington in Seattle, and I would like to acknowledge the support of the Department of Special Education during this time period.

407

ture to design and evaluate their own interventions. Is it reasonable and realistic to expect the literature to serve this dual purpose?

Theoretically, the careful description of method has been emphasized to enable practitioners to replicate treatments when addressing the behavioral needs of persons known to them. The rationale for training practitioners in scientific method generally is based on preparing them to be good consumers of this research literature: They must be capable of recognizing whether the pattern of variables described in a particular research report is relevant to their situation. Practitioners might also be expected to make good judgments regarding the validity or effectiveness of an approach reported in the literature, although—if working as intended—the peer-review process presumably ensures that journal articles do meet certain scientific standards. Thus, training for practitioners would focus upon looking for enough information to judge whether the person, behavior, and situation in a given study is similar enough—in certain ways—to consider the intervention as potentially applicable to a specific clinical need. Then, the practitioner must find sufficient procedural detail to be able to replicate the intervention. Simultaneously, the practitioner needs evaluation strategies that will accurately monitor the behavior during the intervention—from the initial assessment through any necessary problem-solving as the intervention is implemented and, finally, to judge whether or not the intervention has been successful.

Historically, published research reports have been expected to perform all of these functions. In this chapter, we question the conventional wisdom of these expectations and suggest some alternative perspectives and strategies. We suspect that separating the two very different evaluation needs of science and practice is becoming inevitable. Therefore, our major theme is the development of alternative evaluation approaches that are more appropriate for the distinct agendas of research and practice. Developing alternative evaluation approaches could give the field a stronger database on the one hand and give practitioners more assistance with their day-to-day needs on the other. In addition, we discuss new directions for the mutual interdependence of science and practice that go beyond notions of identical training in the use of identical procedures. In the words of Hoshmand and Polkinghorne (1992):

> In our judgment, an alternative conception of the science-practice relationship is needed that emphasizes the mutuality of science and practice, in which psychological science as a human practice and psychological practice as a human science inform each other. . . . We propose a more radical effort of integration whereby the *processes* of knowledge in the two domains [science and practice] are considered under a new conception of psychology as a human science of practice. (pp. 55, 57)

These important issues are best discussed in the context of the goals of the research and practice endeavor—the achievement of meaningful outcomes. The definition of meaningful outcomes is implicitly addressed throughout this volume; the topic is inevitable when "management" of challenging behavior is conceptualized as anything beyond the deceleration of some negative target behavior. But having a clear picture of what is truly a meaningful outcome for a person with challenging behavior is so critical to any evaluation of the treatment—in research or practice—that a brief recap prior to moving on to our two major themes seems justified.

DEFINING AND MEASURING MEANINGFUL OUTCOMES

In the early days of applied behavior analysis, the focus in addressing behavior problems rested on strategies designed to decrease and eliminate target behaviors (e.g., Lovaas & Bucher, 1974). The word "specific" was not insignificant, as behavioral interventionists considered the need to carefully and objectively describe the behavior and changes in that behavior as primary and prerequisite to any effort to modify "behavior problems" (Sidman, 1960). This admirable focus on precision has, however, left us with an unfortunate legacy: Clear and objective descriptions of behavior in precisely measurable terms very often led to reports of what could be characterized as trivial outcomes. In order to specify behavior change in objective terms that could be reliably monitored by observers, researchers have often been reduced to reporting relatively minor motor topographies of behavior such as hand movements to head. Clearly, such motor behavior would have serious consequences if it involved self-injury, but the topographically reported outcome fails to communicate whether injury was or was not occurring *or* the nature of the person's affective state. What we have been least successful in doing is monitoring changes in the *reasons* we cared about the behavior in the first place.

What Are Meaningful Outcomes?

While risking subjectivism and circularity, we conceptualize meaningful outcomes as those things most of us seek for ourselves, know when we see them, and would generally regard as universally good. There are names for some personal and lifestyle constructs, and promising examples of attempts to define them (see, for example, McFall's 1982 review of social competence). There are still very few measures for operationalizing constructs such as competence, adjustment, friendship, and quality of life—outcomes that most would agree are very meaningful. Our data-based perspective on objective measurement of specific behaviors steered us away from trying to measure such complex phenomena. Thus, research reports on people with challenging behaviors would instead describe targeted change that could be reliably measured. This explains why the literature on self-injurious behavior is composed predominantly of monitoring discrete instances of head-hitting or self-biting, and tells us so very little about whether the person in the study learned to do anything else, became socially more proficient, developed new and more positive relationships (e.g., friendships), or was considered to be happier after a successful intervention. There were other sequelae of this narrow focus as well. Journal publication standards tolerated reports of such short-term and situation-specific changes in even the target behaviors so that most articles failed to tell the reader whether the results maintained over time or generalized to places and times outside the experimental situation (Evans & Weld, 1989). Thus, this literature could never be expected to guide practitioners or family members who *were* responsible for outcomes such as improved interpersonal relationships and a better life-style, in addition to decreases in behaviors such as head-hitting.

Increased advocacy for community life-styles for persons with disabilities has no doubt had an impact upon research practices (Meyer, Peck, & Brown, 1991). The movement of individuals from the highly restrictive settings of the past intensified the need to address behavior change in a variety of environments. Researchers have been obliged to take on the challenge of generalization, maintenance, and indirect target selection (Horner, Dunlap, & Koegel, 1988). But the need to improve success rates can be misunderstood as a technical demand, so that researchers slightly expand their scope of responsibility, yet still avoid addressing the larger issue of meaningful outcomes. Even in the communicative interventions described in this volume—surely communication is a meaningful outcome?—this pitfall exists unless we move beyond measuring the establishment, maintenance, and generalization of a communication response that occurs in the time and space previously occupied by a negative behavior. The real issue is whether or not the intervention process has resulted in a significant change in the person's lifestyle and human condition. Although conceptualizing individualized education program (IEP) goals such as "personal fulfillment" and "contributions to the social good" is difficult, these are the outcomes to be achieved by persons with disabilities if they are to become full participants in their family, community, and culture. Most importantly, such goals cannot be realized outside the context of a reasonable living standard and inclusion within the mainstream of our society, thus requiring researcher and practitioner alike to ensure that these are the contexts for our interventions (Meyer, 1991b).

Table 1 reproduces a "hierarchy" of goal outcomes that might be the focus of intervention, beginning at the top with the most molecular and traditional behavioral targets and moving to the more molar and difficult-to-measure constructs such as friendships and support networks. This table includes a listing of suggestions for measurement strategies that might be employed at each of these behavioral levels by *practitioners*. One of the challenges before us is to develop and validate measurement strategies that *researchers* can use to document the database for interventions associated with the kinds of outcomes listed at the bottom of the table. We return to this issue in more depth as we discuss our two themes.

Table 1. Behavioral intervention in children and youth: Meaningful outcomes

Outcome	Examples	How measured/documented
Improvement in target behavior (reduction of excess)	Decrease in frequency of head-banging to near zero levels	Frequency counts of hits recorded in *Daily Logs* *Incident Records*
	Decrease in tantrums	Same as above
	Decrease in operant vomiting behavior	Weight gain Quantity measures
Acquisition of replacement skills and behaviors	Asking for help rather than head-banging	Frequency counts of requests for help
	Asking for a break rather than tantrumming	Frequency of counts of requests for breaks
	Playing video games rather than engaging in hand-flapping	Time spent in arcade: game tokens used; time clocked on school microcomputer
Acquisition of general self-control strategies to support behavior change	Using an anger control technique in circumstances associated with aggression	Observed use of cassette player with headphones Observed movement to another room location or seat when "disliked" peer is close by
	Using a calendar and picture schedule to predict and better cope with changes in routine (transitions, cancelled preferred events, absence of preferred people)	Correct reply if asked, "What class is next?" Spontaneous interest in calendar and daily schedule (as recorded in *Daily Logs*)
	Learning zone discrimination behaviors for masturbation	Self-initiated and appropriate private times (family report)
Positive collateral effects and absence of negative side effects	Increased peer interactions as aggression declines	Participation in small group activities that were previously impossible
	Decrease in skin irritations as hand-mouthing decreases	Red and flaky skin becomes more normal in appearance
Reduced need for and use of medical services and crisis management for student and/or others	Decrease in cuts due to head-banging that requires sutures	Medical/hospital records
	Decrease in staff injuries due to aggression	Worker's compensation and health insurance records and claims; decrease in staff complaints to principal
	Decrease in medication prescribed to control behavior	Reduction and elimination of dosages
	Decrease in emergency hospitalizations and use of crisis management	Medical/hospital records *Incident Records*

(continued)

Table 1. (continued)

Outcome	Examples	How measured/documented
Less restrictive placements and greater participation in integrated school experiences	Attends regular school rather than special school	Student placement records
	Spends more time in regular classes rather than in self-contained special class	Changes in student schedule
	Participates in group experiences (social and academic) with typical peers	Changes in student schedule and staff "success" ratings
Subjective quality-of-life improvement: happiness, satisfaction, choices, and control	More smiling, less anxiety/sadness/crying/anger, and general positive affect	Observation and reports
	More student choice and control	Rating scale on choices/control and record of opportunities
	General motivation to participate in daily activities	Daily Log ratings
Perceptions of improvement by teachers/family/significant others	Family is pleased with behavior change	Communications from home to school
	Teachers are pleased with behavior change	Fewer complaints, end to requests for placements elsewhere, positive comments to home and school administration
	Child problems disappear as a school concern	School and district records involving child problems; nature of IEP; agenda of meetings; "reputation" of child at school
Expanded social relationships and informal support networks	Increased participation in school activities and play with peers	Activity records and informal observations at lunch, on the playground
	Fading of once-needed one-to-one staff assignment to student	Staffing changes; reduced need for staff presence and/or proximity Trusted to play alone with peers under typical general school supervision
	Friendships	Does child have friends? Observed friendship patterns and play
	Increased involvement of general school staff in support for child	Offers of assistance/involvement from general school staff and regular education personnel

From Meyer, L.H. and Janney, R.E. (1989). User-friendly measures of meaningful outcomes: Evaluating behavioral interventions. *Journal of The Association for Persons with Severe Handicaps, 14,* 266; reprinted by permission.

Shifting Paradigms

A final point regarding the need to shift to meaningful change relates to experimental method. We have critiqued the failure to document "meaningful outcomes" in behavior modification and suggested that the traditional sequence of clinical-behavioral practice and dominant research paradigms of how best to demonstrate experimental control share equal responsibility (Evans & Meyer, 1987; Evans, Meyer, Kurkjian, & Kishi, 1988; Evans & Scotti, 1989; Voeltz & Evans, 1983). Our concerns are founded on the results of two extensive traditional literature reviews (Voeltz & Evans, 1982; updated by Evans et al., 1988) and a comprehensive meta-analysis of 12 years of empirical research published in 18 major journals (Scotti, Evans, Meyer, & Walker, 1991). Despite widespread theoretical support for the emergence of unintended collateral (positive) and side (negative) effects, the typical intervention report continues to meticulously measure changes in the intended, single target behavior.

As currently conceived, the accepted single-subject research designs appear unable to accommodate more complex outcomes, thus our experiments will be restricted as long as we fail to develop more powerful research designs and methods. Test, Spooner, and Cooke (1987) disputed our assertions and suggested that certain designs, such as the multiple baseline, could indeed monitor durable behavior changes. They also argued that the very emergence of the universal concern over generalization and maintenance signified the attention paid to issues of meaningfulness. We remain unconvinced, however, and stressed in our reply to Test et al. (1987) that the paradigm required the impositions of restrictive circumstances that would inevitably limit the meaningfulness of possible findings (Evans & Meyer, 1987). For example, the need to limit outside sources of influence as potentially confounding variables in order to demonstrate treatment validity can be seen as contributing to restrictive environments for persons with disabilities. Major modifications in peer interactions and community experiences may be neglected or delayed in order to enable the experimenter to attribute changes in target behaviors to an intended intervention component. Literature reviews still bemoan the use of multifaceted treatments that do not pay sufficient attention to experimentally isolating what part makes what specific contribution to the results.

Obviously, it is important to know the contribution of an unintended independent variable—some outside influence that the experimenter did not plan or control—if it were otherwise not present for other potential intervention situations. But if such influences are readily available and the "target *person*" has a right to expect them (e.g., the presence of family and friends), the use of an experimental method that requires isolation from such social influences is unduly restrictive. We worry that this is continuing to happen in the experimental research with persons with disabilities. Our existing single-subject designs require compelling evidence of the effects of a specific intervention upon a single referral target behavior, so that multiplicity of variables present in typical environments may be viewed as a threat to the internal validity of an experiment. Attempts to address this issue by establishing behavior change in a controlled situation and *then* moving the person to more typical environments for demonstrations of "generalization and maintenance" could justifiably be regarded as a discriminatory intrusion of the demands of science upon the real life experience of people with disabilities.

A formal construct that has been proposed to incorporate these concerns into the scientific process is *ecological validity* or *educational validity* (Voeltz & Evans, 1983). The *Journal of The Association for Persons with Severe Handicaps* (*JASH*) included these criteria in its editorial guidelines for publication decisions beginning in 1986:

> Educational Validity: *JASH* emphasizes ecological and educational validity in the content of the journal. Applied research conducted in actual service delivery and community environments is likely to be more relevant to our readers than research conducted in highly artificial and controlled settings. Reports of validated interventions should also strive to meet three criteria for educational validity: (1) a demonstration of behavior change associated with the intervention or independent variable/s; (2) why and how the behavior change is meaningful; and (3) a description of the program strategies used which is replicable, along with documentation that implementation of those strategies was reliable. (*Editorial Policy and Author Guidelines*)

Ford and Gaylord-Ross (1991) reviewed intervention research in both *JASH* and the *American Journal on Mental Retardation* to determine the extent to which these issues were being addressed. *JASH* did reflect far greater attention to the context of the intervention than did *AJMR*, but it would be difficult to know whether this reflected enforcement of the new editorial guidelines or simply a difference in perspective between authors likely to publish in the two journals during the time period reviewed (1976–1988).

There are some additional practical considerations that might keep attention focused on educational validity. Practitioners are expected to see the relevance of published intervention studies to their own situation and needs. Yet, innovative practices validated and reported in the literature by researchers are not readily adopted in typical settings by practitioners (Anderson, 1973; Conner, 1976; Decker & Decker, 1977; Fullan, 1985; Wang, 1984). In their analysis of educational innovations, Wang and Zollers (1990) attribute this failure to the absence of important supports, missing in the nonresearch world of real schools, that would otherwise enable practitioners to implement innovations. These include, they argue, the need for staff development, changes in organizational structure at the building level, collaboration from related service personnel (e.g., therapists, psychologists), and family involvement (Wang & Zollers, 1990). But assertions that implementation of innovations is dependent upon fairly major changes in the service delivery system may beg the question (Ayres, Meyer, Erevelles, & Park-Lee, 1992). Whose fault is it if validated practices require the presence of "ingredients" that have consistently been unavailable in the real world? How valuable are programs that work only in laboratories and university-affiliated schools and agencies with unique resources?

Similarly, in their discussion of social validity assessment, Schwartz and Baer (1991) stress the importance of investigating *social invalidity,* defined as:

> The behaviors of consumers who not only disapprove of some component in the ongoing program but are going to do something about their disapproval. That something may include withdrawing from the program, encouraging others to do the same, complaining to community officials and the media, or, more subtly, not implementing some or all of the program's procedures after the program consultant leaves, despite positive responses on questionnaires. (p. 190; see also Baer, 1987, and Leduc, Dumais, & Evans, 1990)

Thus, research on the process of implementation, or what practitioners see as the obstacles to implementing an innovation, may be a critical component in validating interventions likely to be used in practice in addition to being featured in journals. Examples of such research, which remain rare, include Ayres et al. (1992) and Schwartz, Anderson, and Halle (1989).

An alternative perspective is to first formulate values about meaningful outcomes and then strive toward the development and validation of research and practices that will do the job without compromising the lives of individuals. Methodology should not dictate the opportunities made available to people. Furthermore, we urgently need expanded scientific paradigms that will work in typical, complex, integrated environments and that will incorporate both the possibility of multiple "treatments" (sources of influence over the person's behavior) and the expectation of multiple positive outcomes (upon the person and his or her caregivers) (Jacob, 1987; Meyer, 1991a). Finally, the dilemma of division between science and practice should be addressed through alternative perspectives and paradigms if our research findings are to become more than archives of something that happened once under rare circumstances that remain largely uninterpretable and clearly unreplicable in typical homes, schools, social situations, and communities.

STANDARDS FOR RESEARCH
AND CONSTRUCTING OUR KNOWLEDGE BASE

The knowledge base for intervening with challenging behaviors is constructed through empirical and clinical practice. As a field, we place confidence in the validity of a particular approach in solving behavior problems according to the existence of a research literature demonstrating a functional relationship between the application of that approach and positive change. This process also involves the application of implicit and explicit understandings of the value of various types of literature, with consensual judgments regarding which publications do indeed make a valid contribution to the empirical database. Some of these understandings are so ingrained in our own professional training and biases that it may even seem unnecessary to explain the components of an empirical database to anyone, such as what a "peer-reviewed" journal is and why the "peer-review process" is regarded as essential. The uncritical endorsement of these standards has negative professional and clinical consequences. For example, the traditional schism in science between "basic" and "applied" fields of study and the lesser status accorded to applied science in academic professional communities lead to copycat and defensive behaviors by applied scientists. Basically, applied scientists seem to accept the low status of their fields of study and strive to overcome it by emulating the exact forms of basic science. Thus, educators and clinical psychologists are entrenched in research paradigms that restrict their work to imitations of laboratory-type structures and settings, and preclude the development of alternative research paradigms better suited to investigating the needs of ordinary people engaged in complex social, educational, and other organizational structures. As a consequence, intervention studies in high-status journals such as the *Journal of Applied Behavior Analysis* and the *American Journal on Mental Retardation* often seem absorbed with issues of experimental control.

One example of this is the focus upon experimentally isolating the variable that must be responsible for the desired change (as discussed in the previous section, we believe this to be a futile quest in the real world of systems and behavioral interrelationships). Evidence for this preoccupation are discussion sections that most often note experimental limitations—such as the possibility of confounding variables and unknown influences—rather than address problems of implementation of the intervention strategy in either the original situation of the experiment or in other settings that might care to replicate the results.

There are parallel negative practical consequences to the failure to address the different needs of an applied science. The first author of this chapter recently served as an independent consultant in a dispute between a school district and a parent. Both parties agreed to review my recommendations in a prehearing negotiation of the parent's request that the district pay for one or more of three programs that she had personally investigated and believed would "cure" her child with autism and mental retardation. Indeed, the parent maintained that a key professional staff member at one of these programs had promised her that her daughter would be "normal" and functioning at grade level after only three more visits and treatments. The parent was obviously keen to have this cure for her daughter, and her advocacy and interpersonal skills, combined with her longstanding credibility as a member of her community, put her in a position of influence on behalf of her own child. As I had no knowledge of this particular program, I confidently asked her to share her information with me, certain that together we would then reach consensus and agree with my professional judgment of the value of the program. She produced a thick folder of self-produced mimeographed descriptions and an article from a supermarket-type popular magazine. *I* knew this was not a "peer-refereed journal" and that anyone can print copies of whatever one wants to write. I suddenly realized how internalized my own standards were and how seldom I had been challenged to explain to others what these standards mean regarding the kinds of practices we can support and recommend.

How do we respond to the growing trend of asking and answering "scientific" questions in the media—on popular network programs such as "60 Minutes" and in the numerous weekly and monthly publications seen and read by so many of the people we interact with in professional services? Because neither consumers nor most practitioners such as teachers and caregivers seem to have high regard for the relevance or readability of research journals, the gap between our "database" and typical practices threatens to widen. In the remainder of this section, we first summarize the critical issues to address in articulating clearer standards for contributions to our database, and then we consider the need for new approaches to communicating the "research integration" of the empirical evidence to those who need it.

The Status of Our Empirical Database

The empirical literature on intervening with challenging behavior in persons with developmental disabilities is substantial and varied. At least 18 major professional journals exist that regularly publish validation studies in this area, and the more recent interest in communicative alternatives to behavior problems has expanded this list even further. Professionals in the field generally believe, therefore, that a solid database exists, providing strong, empirical support for recommended practices. As one example, the proponents of both aversive and alternative nonaversive approaches to addressing a severe behavioral need, such as self-injury, argue that their perspective is scientifically grounded in the demonstrated efficacy of the techniques themselves. Scotti et al. (1991) summarize these beliefs in the introduction of their meta-analysis of 403 studies appearing in key journals across a 12-year period (1976–1987). Is this confidence in the published literature justified by the evidence?

The Scotti et al. (1991) report evaluates the data using two statistical measures of intervention effectiveness. Their evaluation includes measuring the impact of the various behavioral intervention strategies, along with the potential influence of other (possible independent) variables such as characteristics of the individual, the environment, and the manner in which the intervention itself was carried out. The findings largely fail to support several widespread assumptions regarding the standards of practice followed by researchers in the conduct of an intervention research study. If, for example, the published intervention report indicates that an intervention was designed without benefit of performing a functional analysis, to what extent is this an appropriate validation of the approach used? If there is no attempt to "program for generalization" despite the almost universal acceptance of the importance of doing so—and indeed, this was one of the intervention characteristics that related strongly to effectiveness—how legitimate is the scientific exemplar? It is improbable that the accumulation of dozens and even hundreds of studies, each of which violates different components of longstanding precepts of research standards, can move us along in building knowledge to support various interventions, which, incidentally, often yield highly variable outcomes. Indeed, Scotti et al. (1991) judged only 44 of the 403 studies as "highly effective" based on both effectiveness statistics. Results were not generally impressive across the remaining studies. We cannot assert that we are constructing a database if: 1) accepted conventions are widely violated in our research literature, thus calling into question the rigor and responsibility of scientific inquiry; and 2) the resultant outcomes for even the chosen target behaviors are minimally effective as well.

Constructing a Knowledge Base that Reflects Best Practices

Unless standards of practice become explicit requirements for research funding and the scrutiny of human subjects committees *and* are supported further as conditions of editorial review, our "database" will continue to be so equivocal that it could not provide enlightenment about the treatment validity of various procedures. Scotti et al. (1991) found that an unacceptably high percentage of published intervention studies failed to report having assessed the function of the dependent target behavior; gave no prior treatment history; included only anecdotal information on collateral behavior change; told the reader little about the person's life-style or even treatment setting; and did not include generalization, maintenance, or follow-up findings.

The absence of these and other recommended features of applied behavior analysis interventions in journal reports is disturbing. If researchers fail to model standards of practice in their reports, it is difficult to know how to evaluate the results of this literature. Perhaps some of the contradictory findings and limited outcomes now evident in this published literature would be quickly resolved if adherence to certain standards were required as a prerequisite condition for editorial review and publication consideration. Table 2 includes a listing of recommended features that should serve as minimal standards of practice for submission of a behavioral intervention report to any journal that purports to disseminate authoritative empirical information.

Reflective Research To Inform Investigation and Practice

In a provocative discussion of the link between psychological science and professional practice, Hoshmand and Polkinghorne (1992) advocate a better framework for this relationship, one that would reflect the integration of research and practice in a mutually interdependent exchange of information:

> We propose that the scholarly work of the academy should function differently in psychology, as a human practicing discipline, from the way it functions in highly theoretical disciplines, by encompassing the study of practicing knowledge. One of its roles would be to clarify the patterns of understanding developed in practice

Table 2. Essential information for published intervention research

I. Participant characteristics
   A. Age
   B. Gender
   C. Level of functioning
   D. Diagnostic characteristics
   E. Adaptive behavior measure
   F. Verbal/communication skills

II. Intervention setting characteristics
   A. Degree of integration/segregation
   B. Age-appropriateness of daily life-style and placement features
   C. Evidence of active educational/habilitative program
   D. Information on significant social relationships for participant

III. Intervention history of participant
   A. Results of previous interventions
   B. History of functional analysis of behavior
   C. Medication history
   D. Level of intrusiveness in prior interventions
   E. Standards of practice procedures/human rights review

IV. Assessment of behavior changes
   A. Functional analysis of behavior
   B. Baseline description and observable definition of behavior
   C. Delineation of desired (meaningful) outcomes and their measurement
   D. Anticipated collateral/side effects and their measurement

V. Intervention design and follow-up
   A. Replicable description of intervention
   B. Replicable description of needed resources and staff development
   C. Written intervention plan
   D. Documentation of integrity of intervention
   E. Sufficient baseline/intervention phase data reported to allow calculation of effectiveness statistics
   F. Evidence of generalization and maintenance
   G. Follow-up of 1 year or more

Adapted from suggestions made in Scotti, Evans, Meyer, and Walker (1991).

and to examine the process of skilled reflection. . . . Another would be to help sharpen the conceptual maps evolved by practice-based inquiry and to link them to the formal knowledge base. A third function would be to enhance our understanding of the differences between technical competence and professional wisdom. (p. 63)

In contrast, the traditional perspective views the practitioner as the consumer of research, and a paradox exists whenever the research conditions are so different from service-delivery circumstances that they would appear to have questionable relevance to the practitioner's needs. What Hoshmand and Polkinghorne (1992) recommend instead is an ongoing dialogue between academic researchers and what they refer to as practitioner-researchers:

In this sort of inquiry, the role of scholarship will extend from theory testing to (a) the discovery and description of knowledge processes used in practice and field research or practice-based inquiry and (b) the clarification of practicing knowledge generated by skilled practitioners and field researchers. Such scholarly work will be directly useful for practice. The methods associated with human science paradigms will be especially appropriate for the first type of inquiry. Their syncretic use along with experimental methods will likewise contribute to inquiry for the second purpose. (p. 63)

This new viewpoint would require multiple methodologies, each one of which might be best suited to a particular question or stage of research-into-practice, and combinations of which allow for progress in what is neither a basic nor an "applied," but is instead a human, science. It would be difficult to imagine that any single research paradigm is best suited to the many different questions or stages of the science-practice model proposed by Hoshmand and Polkinghorne (1992) and others (Kuhn, Amsel, & O'Loughlin, 1988; Schon, 1983; Tharp, 1981; Tharp & Gallimore, 1982). What needs to occur is the judicious selection of research strategies—some of which will be new to us— in a postmodern human science for the different research stages of theory-building, generating hypotheses, formally testing patterns that emerged from previous findings, investigating reflection-in-action to solve complex and new problems, and determining/addressing the barriers (including social invalidity) to implementation of proposed innovations in typical environments and service delivery settings.

For example, qualitative research models might be applied to monitor the design and implementation of integrated therapy goals by the educational team intending to replace a challenging behavior with a new communication skill. We could conjecture that one team member (perhaps the speech therapist or a behavior management consultant) initially generates ideas for a communication-based intervention to remediate a behavior problem. This planned instructional objective might be based upon a detailed functional analysis and clear evidence from observations of the student that the behavior problem has communicative purpose. Successful implementation of a communication-based intervention will require consistent interpersonal responses from all other team members, including family and peers/classmates, who interact with the student. Suppose that not all team members agree with the proposed intervention. What if someone on the team believes that the plan does not include enough guidance regarding what to do if the (serious) behavior problem *does* occur? Participant-observation research methods could be fashioned in such a way to allow for monitoring of all team activities, beginning with the original discussion of the intervention proposal. Over time, such a study might include interviews with all relevant participants by an interviewer who knows what questions to ask because he or she has seen staff, peers, and family members doing or not doing the planned procedures. Respondents would share their reflective processes to enable the researcher to identify the critical real and perceived variables of importance to these significant "interventionists." We know of no such research investigation of implementation obstacles, which is an example of what Schwartz and Baer (1991) would refer to as social invalidity. We think that events depicted in our hypothetical scenario are common occurrences and resolving such problems is critical to ensuring the integrity of an intervention.

STANDARDS OF EVALUATION FOR CLINICAL PRACTICE

There are at least two valid reasons for delineating evaluation standards for clinical practice, which are different from those that researchers are expected to meet: 1) different evaluation standards are appropriate because the purposes of the two endeavors are different and 2) different standards are necessary because the contingencies of the two endeavors are different. In the following section, we provide a rationale for the design of an evaluation system for use by practitioners that should be uniquely suited to the task at hand, and we suggest some procedures to accomplish that task.

The Demands of Service Delivery

Recommended data-collection procedures for professionals responsible for behavioral programs in an agency setting or a school historically have not differed from those originally designed for use in research reports (Browder, 1991). In particular, behavior modification programs typically involve baseline- and treatment-phase measures of a target behavior, including at least probe and, in some cases, continuous data collection such as frequency counts of the number of occurrences within specified time periods. Such data-collection systems are labor-intensive as they generally require either the presence of an observer who is not expected to provide services during data collection, or considerable interruption of the flow of instruction by a teacher who must stop to take data. The "program manager" must also provide training for staff in data-collection procedures and implement a system for monitoring the reliability of the data that are collected (thus requiring the presence of two observers for at least some of the data-collection intervals). The paperwork involved in this process can be considerable, because raw data must be converted into meaningful summaries and narrative descriptions for relevant constituencies.

Generally, the resultant data summary display is regarded as being readily interpretable by professional staff, who are expected to visually inspect the "trend" of behavior change and make judgments regarding progress (or lack of progress) and/or determine whether program changes are needed based upon the observed patterns. In some systems, however, the decision process can be quite complex. For example, precision teaching requires additional skills in use of log paper and mastery of certain basic mathematical formulae (Haring, Liberty, & White, 1980); these monitoring systems are applied to both measurement of planned decreases in challenging behavior and increases in skills being taught to the child. Indeed, one could argue persuasively that special education in particular has developed a technology of individualized instruction and program accountability for mastery that is unprecedented in the regular education system.

Yet, all is not necessarily as it appears. Apparently, even teachers who are well trained in data collection and the analysis of those data cease to use those skills shortly after they become teachers (Burney & Shores, 1979; Haring et al., 1980). In their national survey, Fisher and Lindsey-Walters (1987) reported that teachers described the kinds of data-collection strategies they had once been taught as "unreliable" as well as "demanding and difficult to manage." But teachers must make instructional decisions about their students' performance and progress. If they have ceased to use formal data-collection systems in the classroom, how *do* they make those decisions? Grigg, Snell, and Lloyd (1989) found that teachers reported using their "intuition" to make instructional decisions. Indeed, they openly disputed the validity of the kinds of objective and graphic representation of student performance recommended to them in their teacher preparation programs. This rejection of the kinds of formal data-collection systems they learned in college is not justified based upon the available evidence that teachers do make better decisions when those decisions are based upon data (see Farlow & Snell, 1989, for an excellent discussion of these issues). Nevertheless, objective evidence that they make better decisions with data than they do using intuition and clinical guesswork is clearly not sufficiently motivating to result in maintenance of these skills by this group of experienced practitioners.

We are reminded once again of the discussion of social invalidity by Schwartz and Baer (1991). Despite having been thoroughly trained in a procedure and being exposed to a professional tradition that supports the efficacy of these formal measurement strategies, teachers do not and apparently will not use them. Perhaps, then, it is time to ask the teachers why not—and to listen sincerely to their reasons, with a plan to address their concerns with a revised measurement system. This should be more productive than continuing to attempt to better indoctrinate the next generation of clinicians so they will live up to our scientific expectations. It must be possible to design measurement systems that are neither so arduous nor so difficult to manage in typical intervention settings that clinicians can and will use them. As Meyer and Janney (1989) noted:

> Although it is perhaps axiomatic that data collection can be demanding, we would also maintain that it is appropriate to consider the demands of the environment in addition to the demands of science in the design of alternative techniques that might better meet the needs of both schools and children. (p. 265)

In addition, they argued that more practical measures designed for use in the real world do not necessarily imply any compromise to the quality of information. Rather, careful planning of alternative measurement systems could in fact result in strategies that would not only be used, but might even be "more reflective of multiple outcome possibilities than the more traditional measures focused upon isolated targets" (p. 265).

Practical Measures of Desired Outcomes

In the previous section, we introduced a pragmatic reason for abandoning the expectation that practitioners mirror the evaluation procedures used by researchers: They simply won't use them, so we may as well try something else. In addition to this pragmatic perspective, however, we believe that the use of alternative practical measures of desired outcomes would be better suited to the evaluation needs of service delivery settings than would be clones of traditional research measures. First of all, a well-designed user-friendly (practical) measurement strategy would be one that does not interrupt the flow of instruction or intervention in the intervention environment—it would not, therefore, detract from the level of direct services experienced by the participant. Secondly, it may be that the juxtaposition of "objective data collection" and "intuition" is an artificial forced choice. Where, within this categorical framework, would we place the kind of experienced clinician judgments and problem-solving processes described by Hoshmand and Polkinghorne (1992)? What would seem to be desirable is a practitioner measurement system that allows for the collection of objective observations as well as "subjective" and divergent hypotheses about why certain behaviors are occurring. In such a system, what to do next would be the outcome of using all the available information through a reflective process that acknowledges a role for practitioner judgments variously supported by objective data and informed intuitions.

There are examples of promising developments of measurement strategies designed to work in just this fashion. O'Neill, Horner, Albin, Storey, and Sprague (1990) describe a model for carrying out a functional analysis based upon practical procedures for *describing, predicting,* and *determining the functions* of challenging behavior. Although their system includes the more traditional observation data collection forms, their formal Functional Analysis Observation Summary Form places such data in context and emphasizes the hypotheses that staff might have about the behavior and its possible functions. However, this system is still relatively complex, and no information has been provided to date about its actual use. In contrast, Durand's Motivation Assessment Scale (MAS) has undergone psychometric validation and been widely used in clinical practice precisely because of its high utility (see Durand, 1990; and Durand, Berotti, & Weiner, chap. 13, this volume).

Earlier in this chapter, in Table 1, we included a set of desired (meaningful) outcomes, examples of those outcomes, and how each might be measured or documented. Several of the measures are relatively painless to use and yet might be far more revealing of the extent to which behavior has changed than a traditional frequency count. For example, a student schedule used in the evaluation of a consultation model to address serious challenging behaviors in students with severe disabilities was completed only three times each year for each student. At baseline, this schedule typically revealed that the student was spending virtually the entire school day isolated from peers, needing one-to-one supervision, and engaged in restrictive activities in a highly controlled environment. By mid-year, changes in this situation began to appear and by the year's end, the student could be found working successfully in a variety of instructional groupings, spending a majority of his or her time with peers, and engaged in many school and community activities in settings typical for age peers. It would be difficult to imagine how such improvements in the student's daily lifestyle and need for supervision could have occurred unless there had been equally dramatic improvements in the student's behavior. In such instances, the indirect measure of the individual's schedule of activities may be a far more powerful indicator of a meaningful outcome than frequency data on a problem target behavior.

The student schedule is, of course, primarily a summative measure of behavior change and might not be helpful for ongoing problem-solving. Yet, the schedule includes "success" ratings across the different time periods, activities, staffing ratios, and other identifiable environmental variations in the student's day at baseline. Patterns in such ratings can then be used to generate intervention hypotheses. In addition, however, Meyer and Janney (1989) describe the use of simple techniques such as a daily log and incident records as strategies to both monitor behavior and provide information for team problem-solving. Their follow-up report of the 33 students with challenging behaviors who received services from this consultation effort seems to support the efficacy and utility of data collection measures such as these (Janney & Meyer, 1990).

CONCLUSION

We have examined the adequacy of the empirical database for guiding clinical judgment in the intervention of challenging behavior, and we have found it wanting. The common research designs, largely drawn from the methodologies that became popular in applied behavior analysis, have significant limitations. These designs tend to promote a focus on a narrow range of intervention outcomes—typically changes in the frequency of the original negative behavior targeted. In addition, meta-analyses of the literature reveal that widely accepted criteria for judging interventions to be effective, such as maintenance, generalization, follow-up, and the emergence of side-effects or collateral benefits, are very often not included in published research reports.

More adequate criteria for success could and should be developed, such as multiple outcome measurements and the examination of treatment effects in expanded contexts. However, there are other drawbacks to the accepted research methodologies that are more difficult to remedy. One of these is the perceived primary importance of establishing experimental control in order to isolate specific intervention variables. This results in interventions being evaluated under conditions that fail to resemble the realities of typical educational and community settings. Thus, expecting practitioners to apply this "new knowledge" to the clinical needs of the individuals in those typical educational and community settings is fraught with problems. Our conclusion is that in order to encourage greater scientific rigor and relevant clinical application, it is necessary to expand our empirical strategies and to be explicit about the different demands of research versus practice.

In this chapter we have considered one possible direction for this expansion. It is based on a reconsideration of the relationship between science and practice, or, more accurately, the relationship between basic (hypothesis-testing) and applied research. The published research literature obviously cannot inform the field if it contains flaws in empirical standards explained above. Neither can it do so if the presumption is that empirical studies determine the effectiveness of fixed treatments, which can then be implemented confidently by practitioners (Eifert, Evans, & McKendrick, 1990). The realities of current service systems are clearly too complex, and too far in advance of the "laboratory" demonstration contexts, to be usefully informed by artificial research paradigms. If the published research does not and cannot inform practitioners, what purpose does it serve?

One solution to the dilemma is to afford greater respect for the active interplay between science and practice—between greater and lesser controlled empirical analyses. Special education, like behavioral clinical psychology, has actually had a long tradition of attempting this interaction. It has been approached by scientist–practitioner models of training and the teaching of empirical designs as a method for guiding decision-making in practice. Until recently, however, the empirical designs taught as examples of data-guided clinical practice have been restricted to the very single-subject designs that are proving inadequate for establishing even the more basic database. We suggest alternative measures and concepts for allowing practitioners to evaluate their own activities. The objective is to ensure that practitioners are neither constrained by unworkable "scientific" criteria, nor totally undisciplined by reliance on intuition and subjective opinion.

Because there are fewer accepted rules in this approach and less well-developed guidelines for avoiding erroneous conclusions, traditional behavioral researchers may perceive these suggestions as a weakening of scientific standards. What we have tried to show is that the conceptual model is arguing for much more rigorous empirical criteria than we have had in the past. Knowledge about interventions, how they really work, what short-term and long-term effects they have, and whether they *really* help individuals achieve the lifestyles that may be possible and may be desired, is what we all seek. The emergence of such knowledge, it is argued, will be aided by careful reevaluation of the logic of applied research. Many of these dilemmas cannot be resolved until the implementation process itself becomes a major context for evaluating the validity of new knowledge through research on practice.

REFERENCES

Anderson, R. (1973). Mainstreaming is the name for a new idea. *School Management, 17*(7), 28–30.

Ayres, B.J., Meyer, L.H., Erevelles, N., & Park-Lee, S. (1992). *Easy for you to say: Teacher perspectives on implementing most promising practices.* Report submitted for publication consideration.

Baer, D.M. (1987, March). *A behavior-analytic query into early intervention.* Paper presented at the Banff International Conference on Behavioral Science, Banff.

Browder, D.M. (1991). *Assessment of individuals with severe disabilities: An applied behavior approach to life skills assessment* (2nd ed.). Baltimore: Paul H. Brookes Publishing Co.

Burney, J.P., & Shores, R.E. (1979). A study of relationships between instructional planning and pupil behavior. *Journal of Special Education Technology, 2*(3), 16–25.

Conner, L.E. (1976). Mainstreaming a special school. *Teaching Exceptional Children, 8,* 76–80.

Decker, R.J., & Decker, L.A. (1977). Mainstreaming the LD child: A cautionary note. *Academic Therapy, 12,* 353–356.

Durand, V.M. (1990). *Severe behavior problems: A functional communication training approach.* New York: Guilford Press.

Eifert, G.H., Evans, I.M., & McKendrick, V. (1990). Matching treatments to client problems not diagnostic labels: A case for paradigmatic behavior therapy. *Journal of Behavior Therapy and Experimental Psychiatry, 21,* 163–172.

Evans, I.M., & Meyer, L.H. (1987). Moving to educational validity: A reply to Test, Spooner, and Cooke. *Journal of The Association for Persons with Severe Handicaps, 12,* 103–106.

Evans, I.M., Meyer, L.H., Kurkjian, J.A., & Kishi, G.S. (1988). An evaluation of behavioral interrelationships in child behavior therapy. In J.C. Witt, S.N. Elliott, & F.M. Gresham (Eds.), *Handbook of behavior therapy in education* (pp. 189–215). New York: Plenum.

Evans, I.M., & Scotti, J.R. (1989). Defining meaningful outcomes for persons with profound disabilities. In F. Brown & D.H. Lehr (Eds.), *Persons with profound disabilities: Issues and practices* (pp. 83–107). Baltimore: Paul H. Brookes Publishing Co.

Evans, I.M., & Weld, E.M. (1989). Evaluating special education programs: Process and outcome. In D. Biklen, D. Ferguson, & A. Ford (Eds.), *Schooling and disability* (pp. 232–255). Chicago: The University of Chicago Press.

Farlow, L.J., & Snell, M.E. (1989). Teacher use of student performance data to make instructional decisions: Practices in programs for students with moderate to profound disabilities. *Journal of The Association for Persons with Severe Handicaps, 14,* 13–22.

Fisher, M., & Lindsey-Walters, S. (1987, October). *A survey report of various types of data collection procedures used by teachers and their strengths and weaknesses.*

Paper presented at The Association for Persons with Severe Handicaps annual conference, Chicago.

Ford, J., & Gaylord-Ross, R. (1991). Ecological validity revisited: A 10-year comparison of two journals. *American Journal on Mental Retardation, 96,* 95–98.

Fullan, M. (1985). Change processes and strategies at the local level. *Elementary School Journal, 85,* 391–422.

Grigg, N.C., Snell, M.E., & Lloyd, B.H. (1989). Visual analysis of student evaluation data: A qualitative analysis of teacher decision-making. *Journal of The Association for Persons with Severe Handicaps, 14,* 23–32.

Haring, N.G., Liberty, K.A., & White, O.R. (1980). Rules for data-based strategy decisions in instructional programs. In W. Sailor, B. Wilcox, & L. Brown (Eds.), *Methods of instruction for severely handicapped children* (pp. 159–192). Baltimore: Paul H. Brookes Publishing Co.

Horner, R.H., Dunlap, G.,& Koegel, R.L. (Eds.). (1988). *Generalization and maintenance: Lifestyle changes in applied settings.* Baltimore: Paul H. Brookes Publishing Co.

Hoshmand, L. T., & Polkinghorne, D.E. (1992). Redefining the science-practice relationship and professional training. *American Psychologist, 47,* 55–66.

Jacob, E. (1987). Qualitative research traditions: A review. *Review of Educational Research, 57,* 1–50.

Janney, R.E., & Meyer, L.H. (1990). A consultation model to support integrated educational services for students with severe disabilities and challenging behaviors. *Journal of The Association for Persons with Severe Handicaps, 15,* 186–199.

Kuhn, D., Amsel, E., & O'Loughlin, M. (1988). *The development of scientific thinking skills.* San Diego: Academic Press.

Leduc, A., Dumais, A., & Evans, I.M. (1990). Social behaviorism, rehabilitation, and ethics: Applications for people with severe disabilities. In G.H. Eifert & I.M. Evans (Eds.), *Unifying behavior therapy: Contributions of paradigmatic behaviorism* (pp. 268–289). New York: Springer.

Lovaas, O.I., & Bucher, B.D. (1974). *Perspectives in behavior modification with deviant children.* Englewood Cliffs, NJ: Prentice Hall.

McFall, R.M. (1982). A review and reformulation of the concept of social skills. *Behavioral Assessment, 4,* 1–33.

Meyer, L.H. (1991a). Advocacy, research, and typical practices: A call for the reduction of discrepancies between what is and what ought to be and how to get there. In L.H. Meyer, C.A. Peck, & L. Brown (Eds.), *Critical issues in the lives of people with severe disabilities* (pp. 629–649). Baltimore: Paul H. Brookes Publishing Co.

Meyer, L.H. (1991b). Why meaningful outcomes? *The Journal of Special Education, 25,* 287–290.

Meyer, L.H., & Janney, R.E. (1989). User-friendly measures of meaningful outcomes: Evaluating behavioral interventions. *Journal of The Association for Persons with Severe Handicaps, 14,* 263–270.

Meyer, L.H., Peck, C.A., & Brown, L. (Eds.). (1991). *Critical issues in the lives of people with severe disabilities.* Baltimore: Paul H. Brookes Publishing Co.

O'Neill, R.E., Horner, R.H., Albin, R.W., Storey, K., & Sprague, J.R. (1990). *Functional analysis of problem behavior: A practical assessment guide.* Sycamore, IL: Sycamore Publishing Co.

Schlosser, R.W., & Goetze, H. (in press). Effectiveness and treatment validity of interventions addressing self-injurious behavior: From narrative reviews to meta-analyses. In K. Gadow (Ed.), *Advances in learning and behavioral disabilities: A research annual.* Greenwich, CT: JAI Press.

Schon, D. (1983). *The reflective practitioner: How professionals think in action.* New York: Basic Books.

Schwartz, I.S., Anderson, S.R., & Halle, J.W. (1989). Training teachers to use naturalistic time delay: Effects on teacher behavior and on the language use of students. *Journal of The Association for Persons with Severe Handicaps, 14,* 48–57.

Schwartz, I.S., & Baer, D.M. (1991). Social validity assessments: Is current practice state of the art? *Journal of Applied Behavior Analysis, 24,* 189–204.

Scotti, J.R., Evans, I.M., Meyer, L.H., & Walker, P. (1991). A meta-analysis of intervention research with problem behavior: Treatment validity and standards of practice. *American Journal on Mental Retardation, 96,* 233–256.

Sidman, M. (1960). *Tactics of scientific research.* New York: Basic Books.

Test, D.W., Spooner, F., & Cooke, N.L. (1987). Educational validity revisited. *Journal of The Association for Persons with Severe Handicaps, 12,* 96–102.

Tharp, R.G. (1981). The metamethodology of research and development. *Educational Perspectives, 20,* 42–48.

Tharp, R.G., & Gallimore, R.L. (1982). Inquiry process in program development. *Journal of Community Psychology, 10,* 103–118.

Voeltz, L.M., & Evans, I.M. (1982). The assessment of behavioral interrelationships in child behavior therapy. *Behavioral Assessment, 4,* 131–165.

Voeltz, L.M., & Evans, I.M. (1983). Educational validity: Procedures to evaluate outcomes in programs for severely handicapped learners. *Journal of The Association for Persons with Severe Handicaps, 8,* 3–15.

Wang, M.C. (1984). Time use and the provision of adaptive instruction. In L.W. Anderson (Ed.), *Time and school learning* (pp. 167–203). London: Croon-Helm.

Wang, M.C., & Zollers, N.J. (1990). Adaptive instruction: An alternative service delivery approach. *Remedial and Special Education, 11,* 7–21.

Author Index

Datillo, J., 332
Davenport, R.K., 126
DaVerne, K.C., 7, 215, 304, 305
Davidson, D.P., 86, 87, 89, 95, 103
Davis, L., 271, 291
Davison, M., 114, 115, 116
Day, H.M., 20, 21, 30, 116, 141, 144,
    164, 165, 206, 261, 319, 325
Day, R.M., 103, 122, 124, 126
Deacon, J., 311
Decker, L.A., 414
Decker, R.J., 414
Deitz, S.M., 116
Deluty, M.Z., 73
Demchak, M.A., 369
DePaepe, P., 7, 219, 230, 243
dePerczel, M., 201, 367
DeRaad, A., 44, 45, 49, 124, 319, 320,
    343, 348, 349, 350, 352, 360
Derby, K.M., 45, 48, 49, 50, 51, 52,
    53, 55, 58, 213, 343, 345, 347, 349
Detrich, R., 308, 311
Devany, J., 27, 101
de Villiers, P.A., 114
Dixon, M.H., 101
Dodson, S., 96
Doering, K., 364
Doleys, D.M., 142
Dollman, D., 372
Donn, J., 113
Donn, L., 42, 48, 49, 136, 141, 148,
    161, 163, 164, 318, 320, 330, 336,
    343, 360
Donnellan, A.M., 161, 187, 275, 278,
    281, 283, 286, 291, 334, 365,
    367, 376
Dores, P.A., 318, 319
Dorsey, M.F., 6, 11, 29, 41, 43, 44, 45,
    58, 63, 68, 74, 85, 88, 90, 103,
    113, 125, 126, 160, 343
Doss, L.S., 275, 281
Doss, S., 99, 206, 212, 216, 318, 365
Duchan, J., 265, 270, 272, 273, 274,
    275
Dumais, A., 415
Dunham, P.J., 166
Dunlap, G., 7, 8, 13, 29, 47, 136, 137,
    139, 145, 152, 153, 179, 180, 181,
    184, 186, 189, 193, 196, 199, 201,
    288, 364, 367, 372, 375, 376, 379,
    380, 387, 410
Dunlap, L.K., 47

Durand, V.M., 4, 5, 7, 43, 44, 46, 63,
    65, 67, 68, 70, 74, 77, 85, 87, 88,
    103, 116, 121, 122, 124, 139, 140,
    142, 160, 161, 162, 163, 164, 165,
    166, 178, 180, 184, 187, 206, 218,
    225, 227, 239, 253, 271, 278, 281,
    282, 286, 288, 291, 318, 319, 320,
    322, 324, 327, 329, 330, 331, 332,
    334, 335, 336, 343, 364, 365, 367,
    376, 377, 387, 423
Dyer, C., 279
Dyer, K., 25, 181
Dykens, E., 265, 268

Egel, A.L., 145, 146, 155, 156, 166
Egel, S., 122
Eichinger, J., 375, 377
Eifert, G.H., 425
Elliott, S., 355, 357
Emery, R.E., 74
Engelmann, S., 222, 223
Ensrud, S., 265, 268, 269
Epling, W.F., 114
Epstein, L.H., 13
Erevelles, N., 414, 415
Erfanian, N., 355
Etzel, B., 303
Evans, D.W., 64
Evans, I.M., 137, 139, 161, 281, 286,
    288, 291, 322, 333, 364, 365, 367,
    368, 372, 380, 410, 413, 414, 415,
    417, 418, 419, 425

Falk, G.D., 199
Farber, J.M., 125, 127, 128
Farman, R., 223
Fassbender, L., 161, 187, 281, 283, 286,
    291, 376
Favell, J.E., 126
Faw, G., 143, 271, 291
Fay, W., 269, 270, 271, 272, 291
Fedorchak, G., 223
Felce, D., 26, 27, 29, 47, 74, 77, 123,
    124, 127, 160, 349, 360
Ferguson, C., 276
Ferguson, D., 372
Ferro, J., 201, 367, 375
Filler, J., 364
Finney, J., 123
Firestone, P.B., 137, 144, 152, 153

Subject Index

A-B-C (antecedent-behavior-consequence) assessment, 46–48, 188
  modified, in classroom evaluations, 55–57
  see also Functional assessment(s)
Academic demand, in systematic manipulations, stimulus control identification and, 88
ACCESS, *see* Assessment Code/Checklist for the Evaluation of Survival Skills
Accountability, treatment, child effects and, 78–79
Actions, correspondence with utterances, *see* Communicative correspondence
Activities, student interest in
  influence on problem behaviors, 180
  see also Preferences
Adaptability, to "real world," individualized curricula and, 197
Adolescent–staff interactions, reciprocal influences in, 67–68
  see also Reciprocal social influences
Adult—child interactions, reciprocal influences in, *see* Reciprocal social influences
Agencies, audiences from variety of, targeted by Team Training Model, 371–372
Aggression
  extended functional analysis of, 43–44
  see also Challenging behavior
AJMR, see American Journal on Mental Retardation
Alternative behavior, differential reinforcement of, *see* Differential reinforcement of alternative behavior (DRA)
Alternative stimulation, sensory, noncontingent, 126
American Association on Mental Retar-

dation Adaptive Behavior Scale, 332
American Journal on Mental Retardation (AJMR), research in, 416
  educational validity and, 414
Analog conditions, for functional analysis
  descriptive analysis data in design of, 14–17
  future of, 91–94
  limitations of, 88–90
  Proactive Treatment Teams Project and, 352–354
  reinforcement contingencies and, 118
  systematic manipulations and, 87–88
  see also Functional analysis
Analysis
  assessment versus, 85
  see also Assessment
  see also Data analysis; Descriptive analysis; Functional analysis
Antecedents
  consequences and, 84
  see also A-B-C assessment
  of unconventional verbal behavior, 282
  see also Stimulus(i)
Antecedent strategies, in unconventional verbal behavior intervention, 288–290
Appropriate behavior
  individual styles of, identification of, 19–20
  reinforcement schedule available for, identification of, 18
Archival records, in hypothesis development, 188–189
Assessment
  A-B-C, 46–48
  analysis versus, 85
  descriptive
    combined with functional analysis in classroom settings, 45–48, 52–58
    combined with functional analysis

439

the Complex Assessment of Preschool Environments
Escape-motivated behavior
child effects in maintenance of, 65, 68–70
see also Reciprocal social influences
negative reinforcement by, intervention selection for, 123–125
replacement of, with rejecting and leavetaking responses, 252–261
stimulus and response variation and, range of, 225–226
see also Avoidance-motivated behavior
Establishing conditions, 216
for attention as positive reinforcer, 120
see also Setting events
Ethics, of functional analysis, 321–322
Evaluation standards, for clinical practice, 421–424
Examples, teaching, *see* Teaching examples
Exceptions, inclusion of, in teaching examples, *see* Negative teaching examples
Experimental functional analysis, *see* Analog conditions, for functional analysis
Experimental method, meaningful outcomes and, 412–415
Explicit vocabulary
in requesting repertoire, 241–242
specificity of symbols and, 210–212
Extended functional analysis, 43–44
Extinction, 120–121
sensory, 126
Eye gaze, proximity of listener and, 208

Facilitation of program application, 7–8
functional assessment procedure transfer to natural settings, 343–361
see also Proactive Treatment Teams Project
meaningful outcomes and, 407–426
see also Meaningful outcomes
training for comprehensive behavioral support and, 363–391
see also Inservice training
Facilitative interaction, directive interac-

tion versus, unconventional verbal behavior and, 275–276
FAI, *see* Functional Analysis Interview
"False negative" error, in analog analysis, 88–89
"False positive" error, in analog analysis, 89
Familiarity
of environment, unconventional verbal behavior and, 274
with listener, propensity for communicative behavior and, 208–209
Family functioning, child effects on, 64–65
see also Reciprocal social influences
FAOF, *see* Functional Analysis Observation Form
FCI, *see* Functional communication intervention
FCT, *see* Functional communication training
Feedback
provision of, in correspondence intervention, 307–308
see also Reinforcement
"Focus individuals," in Team Training Model, 372
Forcing stimuli, averse, routines involving, 99
Functional analysis, 84
analog conditions for, *see* Analog conditions, for functional analysis
contingency management and, 178
covariation and, 160–161
ethics of, 321–322
extended, 43–44
functional assessment versus, 85
information-gathering strategies for, 85–88, 89
in outpatient and classroom settings, 41–60
descriptive assessment combined with, 45–48
mild disabilities and, 48–58
previous research on, 43–45
positive behavioral support and, 375–376
reciprocal social influences in, 63–79
see also Reciprocal social influences
stimulus control of behavior and,

reinforcement and
  automatic, 125–126
  immediacy of, 117
  negative, 123–125
  positive, 120–123
  quality of, 115–116
  rate of, 115
  response effort and, 116–117
  undifferentiated data series in func-
    tional analysis and, interpretation
    of, 127–129
  see also Intervention(s)
Interview(s), functional analysis, 29–30,
    85, 187
  see also Functional analysis
Iowa Department of Education, Bureau
    of Special Education, Proactive
    Treatment Teams Project of, see
    Proactive Treatment Teams
    Project

JASH, see Journal of The Association for
    Persons with Severe Handicaps
Journal of Applied Behavior Analysis,
    416
Journal of The Association for Persons
    with Severe Handicaps (JASH),
    editorial guidelines of, educa-
    tional validity and, 414

"Keystone" behavior, response covaria-
    tion and, 137–138
Knowledge base, construction of, re-
    search standards and, 415–421

Language
  conventional, unconventional verbal
    behavior replacement with,
    291–292
  relevant, provision of, 290
Language input, simplification of,
    unconventional verbal behavior
    and, 289–290
"Least-to-most-restrictive" assessment, 51
Leavetake program, 252, 253, 257–261
Listener variables
  establishment of initial requesting
    response and, 239–240
  influencing propensity for communica-
    tive utterance, 208

familiarity and prior relationship
    with speaker, 209
  number of prospective listeners, 209
  proximity and attention, 208–209
Lithium carbonate, 128
Low-constraint utterances, high-
    constraint versus, 276–277

Maintaining contingency, procedures for
    weakening
  automatic reinforcement and, 126
  negative reinforcement by escape/
    avoidance of tasks and, 123–124
  positive reinforcement by attention
    and, 120–121
Maintenance, of correspondence training
    effects, 308–309
Maintenance failure, child effects con-
    tributing to, 78
  see also Reciprocal social influences
Maladaptive behavior, see Challenging
    behavior; specific behavior
Mands, differential reinforcement of, 119
  escape behavior and, 124–125
Manipulations
  accessibility to, functional assessment
    and, 321
  systematic, for functional analysis,
    87–88, 89, 91–94
MAS, see Motivation Assessment Scale
Matching theory, intervention selection
    and, 114–119
  reinforcement immediacy and, 117
  reinforcement quality and, 115–116
  reinforcement rate and, 115
  response effort and, 116–117
Meaningful outcomes, 407–426
  definition and measurement of,
    409–415
  evaluation standards for clinical prac-
    tice and, 421–424
  hierarchy of, 410, 411–412
  research standards and, knowledge
    base construction and, 415–421
  shifting paradigms and, 412–415
Medication, intervention using, 127–128
Mild disabilities, functional analysis in
    outpatient and classroom settings
    with, 41–60
  descriptive assessment and, 48–58
  see also Functional analysis